More I...

ESCAPE F...

"Insightful . . . an outstanding modern summation of a strand of research which goes back at least as far as Montesquieu and David Hume."
—MARK KOYAMA, *Journal of Economic Literature*

"A sweeping academic survey comparing empires and eras. . . . *Escape from Rome* makes bold claims about the nature of empire and the roots of the modern world and backs them up with thoughtful analysis."
—DOMINIC LYNCH, *America*

"*Escape from Rome* is a well-written survey of an enormous literature on the history of the world . . . . It is fun and interesting to read. . . . An admirable book."
—PETER TEMIN, EH.Net

ESCAPE FROM ROME

THE PRINCETON ECONOMIC HISTORY
OF THE WESTERN WORLD

Joel Mokyr, Series Editor

A list of titles in this series appears in the back of the book.

ESCAPE FROM ROME

The Failure of Empire and the Road to Prosperity

WALTER SCHEIDEL

PRINCETON UNIVERSITY PRESS

PRINCETON & OXFORD

Copyright © 2019 by Princeton University Press

Published by Princeton University Press

41 William Street, Princeton, New Jersey 08540

6 Oxford Street, Woodstock, Oxfordshire OX20 1TR

press.princeton.edu

LCCN 2019943431

First paperback printing, 2021

Paperback ISBN 9780691216737

Cloth ISBN 9780691172187

British Library Cataloging-in-Publication Data is available

Editorial: Rob Tempio and Matt Rohal

Production Editorial: Natalie Baan

Jacket/Cover Design: Sandra Friesen

Production: Merli Guerra

Publicity: James Schneider and Amy Stewart

Jacket/Cover image: Marble head of the emperor Hadrian.
© The Trustees of the British Museum.

This book has been composed in Arno

Printed in the United States of America

for Joy

The days of empire are finished.

—UTOPIA IN JOHN CARPENTER'S
ESCAPE FROM L.A. (PARAMOUNT PICTURES, 1996)

CONTENTS

List of Figures and Tables   xi

Acknowledgments   xvii

Introduction: The Great Escape   1

PART I. THE EUROPEAN ANOMALY

1   Patterns of Empire   31

PART II. WHY ROME?

2   Core   51

3   Periphery   89

4   Counterfactuals   110

PART III. WHY ONLY ROME?

5   From Justinian to Frederick   127

6   From Genghis Khan to Napoleon   174

PART IV. THE FIRST GREAT DIVERGENCE

7   From Convergence to Divergence   219

8   Nature   259

9   Culture   307

PART V. FROM THE FIRST TO THE SECOND GREAT
        DIVERGENCE

10 Institutions   337

11 New Worlds   420

12 Understanding   472

    Epilogue: What Have the Romans Ever Done for Us?   503

    Glossary   529
    Technical Note to Chapter 1   533
    Notes   537
    References   603
    Index   647

FIGURES AND TABLES

FIGURES

I.1 Per capita GDP in the United Kingdom, China, and India, 1000–2000 CE   2

I.2 Distribution of global GDP adjusted for purchasing power parity in 1 CE   3

I.3 Distribution of global GDP adjusted for purchasing power parity in 1960   3

I.4 Distribution of people worldwide living on more than $200 per day in 2002   4

I.5 Social development scores in the most developed parts of western Eurasia, 5000 BCE–2000 CE   5

I.6 Social development scores in western and eastern Eurasia, 500 BCE–1500 CE   5

I.7 Social development scores in western and eastern Eurasia, 1500–1900 CE   7

I.8 The population of the single largest empire and the three largest empires in the world as a proportion of world population, 700 BCE–2000 CE   16

1.1 Macro-regions of state formation   34

1.2 The population of South Asia, Europe, the Middle East and North Africa, and the "Roman empire region" as a proportion of the population of East Asia, 200 BCE–2000 CE, at centennial intervals   35

1.3 The proportion of the population residing in the area covered by the Roman empire at its peak that was claimed by the largest polity in that area, 450 BCE–2000 CE   36

1.4 The proportion of the population of Europe claimed by the largest polity in that area, 250 BCE–2000 CE   37

1.5 The population of the area claimed by the Roman empire at its peak as a proportion of the population of Europe, 200 BCE–2000 CE   38

1.6 The proportion of the population of the MENA region claimed by the largest polity in that area, 700 BCE–2000 CE   39

1.7 The proportion of the population of South Asia claimed by the largest polity in that area, 500 BCE–2000 CE   40

1.8 The proportion of the population of East Asia claimed by the largest polity in that area, 250 BCE–2000 CE   41

1.9 Comparison between the proportion of the population of East Asia controlled by the largest polity in East Asia and the proportion of the population of China controlled by the largest polity in China, 250 BCE–2000 CE   42

1.10 Actual population and census population of the largest polity in China as a proportion of the total population of that region, 250 BCE–2000 CE   44

1.11 Proportion of the population of Europe and East Asia claimed by the largest polity in each region, 250 BCE–2000 CE   48

2.1 Italy in the early fourth century BCE   53

2.2 Political statuses in Italy in the third century BCE   60

2.3 Approximate military mobilization rates of the Roman citizenry, 346–31 BCE   62

2.4 Roman and Italian military deployments by region, 200–168 BCE   81

2.5 Expansion of the Roman empire to its peak size   83

2.6 (a) General form of the social structure of agrarian
     societies according to Ernest Gellner   87

2.6 (b) Adaptations of the Gellner model   87

3.1 The Middle Eastern political-military network,
     c. 1500–500 BCE   90

3.2 Political-military networks in the ancient Mediterranean
     during the third quarter of the first millennium BCE   92

3.3 Roman troop deployments by region as a share of
     all deployments, 200–168 BCE   98

3.4 Stylized typology of peripheries in the Roman-era
     Mediterranean   102

3.5 Time cost of transfers from Rome   107

3.6 Financial cost of transfers to Rome   108

3.7 The Mediterranean core of the Roman empire   108

4.1 The Akkadian, Neo-Assyrian, and Achaemenid
     empires   112

4.2 The Athenian empire (late fifth century BCE)
     and the empire of Alexander the Great (323 BCE)   115

5.1 The Mediterranean, c. 500 CE   132

5.2 The Roman empire, c. 555 CE   134

5.3 The Umayyad caliphate, c. 750 CE, and later
     successor states   140

5.4 The Carolingian empire, c. 800 CE   155

5.5 Carolingian partitions, 843–888 CE   157

5.6 The German ("Roman") Empire, c. 1200 CE   167

6.1 The Mongol empire in the late thirteenth century CE   184

6.2 The Holy Roman empire and the European possessions
     of Charles V, c. 1550 CE   194

6.3 The possessions of Philip II, 1590s CE   202

6.4 The Ottoman empire, c. 1683 CE   205

6.5 Europe in 1812 CE   211

7.1 Empires of the Old World, c. 200 CE   223

7.2 The Han, Tang, Northern Song, Yuan, Ming, and Qing empires   229

8.1 Altitude profile of Europe   262

8.2 Altitude profile of East Asia   262

8.3 The Eurasian steppe   271

8.4 Spatial distribution of the core areas of empires of at least 1 million square kilometers in Afroeurasia   273

8.5 Probability of being part of large polities (>1 million km²) at 100-year intervals, 500–1500 CE   274

8.6 Effective distance from the Eurasian steppe (by land)   276

8.7 Potential vegetation cover of Asia   277

9.1 Modern distribution of Chinese dialect groups   310

10.1. An ideal-typical model of the developmental dynamics of different types of state formation   339

10.2 Real wages of urban unskilled workers in different parts of Europe, 1500–1780 CE   372

10.3 Per capita GDP in different parts of Europe, 1500–1800 CE   372

10.4 Urbanization rates in England and Europe and the English share in the increase of the European urbanization rate, 1600–1800 CE   373

10.5 The share of the urban and nonagricultural rural population in different parts of Europe, 1500 and 1800 CE   374

10.6 Adult literacy rates in different parts of Europe, late fifteenth to eighteenth century CE   375

11.1 The world with Greater Afroeurasia rotated around its axis at 75°E   460

11.2 The world with Afroeurasia rotated around its axis at 63°E   461

E.1 Actual and counterfactual concentration of state power
     in Europe, 250 BCE–1800 CE   525

TABLES

1.1 Cumulative proportion of the population of different
     regions controlled by the largest polities in these regions   45

2.1 Expansion of the Roman state and alliance system
     in peninsular Italy, c. 500–225 BCE   76

3.1 Matrix of critical preconditions for military success,
     mid-third to mid-second century BCE   103

9.1 Determinants and outcomes of state formation in
     (Latin) Europe and China, c. 500–1000 CE   331

11.1 Minimum distances and differences between actual
      and counterfactual distances   463

ACKNOWLEDGMENTS

THIS BOOK has been long in the making. The "Stanford Ancient Chinese and Mediterranean Empires Comparative History Project," which I launched in 2005 to promote the comparative study of early empires in western and eastern Eurasia, steered me toward the distant roots of modernity. In 2007–2008, the Andrew W. Mellon Foundation sponsored a Mellon-Sawyer seminar on "The First Great Divergence: Europe and China, 300–800 CE" that I ran jointly with my Stanford colleagues Ian Morris and Mark Lewis. But this was only a beginning: my engagement with more recent economic and institutional history, which expanded over the years as my research interests increasingly outgrew the confines of the ancient world, encouraged me to explore the full length of the meandering path toward contemporary levels of prosperity, knowledge, and human flourishing.

After all, there is no bigger question for the historian than that of why the world has turned out the way it has done so far, transformed beyond the wildest imagination of our ancestors just a few generations ago. In offering my answer to this question, I hope to advance what I have found to be an unfailingly exhilarating debate. My book's main title is not just a nod to my own personal transition to global comparative history but above all seeks to capture the essence of our collective progress—our escape from traditional strictures and structures that once weighed down so heavily on humankind that they proved almost impossible to overcome. Traditional forms of imperial rule had failed to make the world a better place and needed to fail altogether in order to set us free. There was no way of "getting to Denmark" without "escaping from Rome" first.

It is a joyous duty to acknowledge the support I have received along the way. Between 2007 and 2019, I spoke about various aspects of my project and received valuable feedback at Arizona State University, the Austrian Academy of Sciences, Brooklyn College, Brown University, Claremont McKenna College, Columbia University, Cornell University, the Danish Academy in Rome, Dickinson College, McGill University, the Istituto Italiano per la Storia Antica, the National University of Singapore, New York University, Northwestern University, the Open Society Forum in Ulaanbaatar, Radboud University, Renmin University of China, the Santa Fe Institute, Stanford University, Texas Tech University, the University of California at Berkeley and Santa Barbara, the Universities of Cambridge, Cape Town, Copenhagen, Georgia, Leiden, Melbourne, Oxford, Texas, Tulsa, Utrecht, Warsaw and Zurich, and Yale University.

I wrote up most of this book during a sabbatical year in 2017–2018 when I was a visitor at New York University's Institute for Public Knowledge. I am grateful to Eric Klinenberg for his kind invitation, and much indebted to the John Simon Guggenheim Memorial Foundation and Stanford University for the financial support that allowed me to focus on the completion of my project.

I owe thanks of gratitude to John Hall and Philip Hoffman for reviewing an earlier version of my manuscript for the publisher; to Joy Connolly and Peer Vries for their detailed comments; and to Anna Grzymala-Busse, John Haldon, Kyle Harper, Reviel Netz, Sheilagh Ogilvie, and Richard Saller for further helpful observations. Daron Acemoglu, James Bennett, Victoria Tin-bor Hui, Reviel Netz, Şevket Pamuk, James Robinson, David Stasavage, Michael Taylor, Paolo Tedesco, Peer Vries, Kaveh Yazdani, and Dingxin Zhao shared unpublished or otherwise inaccessible work with me.

In 2015, when I finally resigned myself to the fact that my argument could not readily be accommodated within a single (long) article as I had originally intended, I proposed a (short) book to Rob Tempio at Princeton University Press. I am glad that he did not blink when the final product came in at twice the agreed length. My thanks go to Rob for his customary support and light touch, to Joel Mokyr, to Jonathan Weiland for expertly preparing the maps, and to Natalie Baan, Bob Bettendorf, John Donohue, Sandra Friesen, Therese Malhame, Matt Rohal, and Stephanie Rojas for ensuring a smooth production process.

ESCAPE FROM ROME

Introduction

The Great Escape

WHAT?

WHAT WAS the Great Escape? It made it possible for me to write this book, and for you to read it—which we could not do if we were busy farming the land, or were illiterate, or had died in childhood. It transformed the human condition by making so many of us so much richer, healthier, and better educated than our ancestors used to be.[1]

This escape from sickness, ignorance, oppression, and want, which remains very much a work in progress in large parts of the world, was not made up of slow, gradual, and linear improvements. For the most part, it represented a radical break from the practices and life experiences of the past, a break that changed the world in the course of just a few generations.

Before the nineteenth century, a certain amount of intensive—per capita—growth in economic output had taken place over the long run, but on a scale so modest that this cumulative increase becomes almost invisible when it is set against the breakthroughs of the past two centuries. Much the same is true of growth in the stock of knowledge and our ability to fight disease. This discontinuity accounts for the fact that any graph that tracks economic performance, or human welfare in general, in those parts of the world where modern economic development took off first—in Britain and then in other parts of Europe and their various

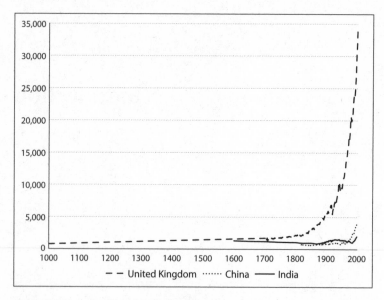

FIGURE I.I Per capita GDP in the United Kingdom, China, and India, 1000–2000 CE (in 2011 US$). *Source*: Maddison Project Database 2018.

global spinoffs—is shaped like a hockey stick. This upward turn opened up a growing gap with most of the rest of the world that has only recently begun to close (figure I.1).[2]

Thanks to this divergence, population number ceased to be the principal determinant of aggregate regional output. Global production and consumption shifted from what had long been the most populous parts of the world—East and South Asia—and came to be heavily concentrated where this novel type of transformative development occurred: in Europe and North America, and later also in Japan (figures I.2–I.3).[3]

Even though many Asian countries in particular have been catching up, narrowing the extreme imbalance that existed a couple of generations ago, the impact of the original divergence has been very slow to fade. Thus, most of the world's recipients of elevated incomes continue to be found in those regions that were the first to develop, with the United States and Western Europe maintaining a forbidding lead. While inequality also contributes to this pattern by boosting the standing of

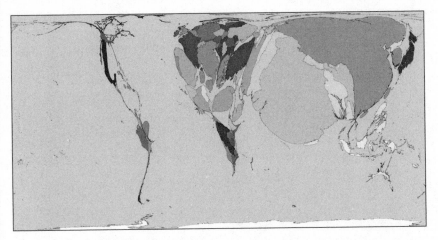

FIGURE I.2 Distribution of global GDP adjusted for purchasing power parity in 1 CE. *Sources*: http://archive.worldmapper.org/display.php?selected=159 and http://archive.worldmapper.org/display.php?selected=162 (© Copyright Worldmapper.org / Sasi Group [University of Sheffield] and Mark Newman [University of Michigan]).

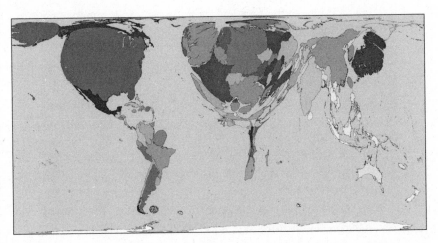

FIGURE I.3 Distribution of global GDP adjusted for purchasing power parity in 1960. *Sources*: http://archive.worldmapper.org/display.php?selected=159 and http://archive.worldmapper.org/display.php?selected=162 (© Copyright Worldmapper.org / Sasi Group [University of Sheffield] and Mark Newman [University of Michigan]).

FIGURE I.4 Distribution of people worldwide living on more than $200 per day in 2002 (adjusted for purchasing power parity, by country). *Source*: http://archive.worldmapper.org /display.php?selected=158 (© Copyright Worldmapper.org / Sasi Group [University of Sheffield] and Mark Newman [University of Michigan]).

the United States, South Africa, and South America, the timing of modernization remains the principal determinant of these imbalances (figure I.4).[4]

Ian Morris's social development index is perhaps the most ambitious attempt to quantify this massive transformation. It seeks to (very roughly) quantify and compare overall levels of material development by tracking four key components—energy capture, social organization, war-making capacity, and information technology—over the very long term in the most developed parts of western and eastern Eurasia. For the former, this exercise produces the same hockey stick as before (figure I.5).[5]

For a long time, variation between East and West was mere oscillation, reflecting in the first instance the moderately beneficial effect of empire on social development. Large imperial formations were associated with somewhat higher development scores, and their collapse (or plagues) with lower ones: the Roman empire helped Europe, the Tang and Song empires China. In the late Middle Ages, China was hit by the Mongols and Europe by the Black Death (figure I.6).

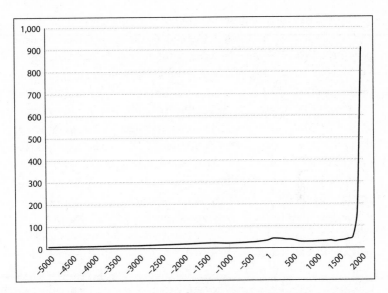

FIGURE I.5 Social development scores in the most developed parts of western Eurasia, 5000 BCE–2000 CE. *Source*: Derived from Morris 2013b: 240–41, table 7.1.

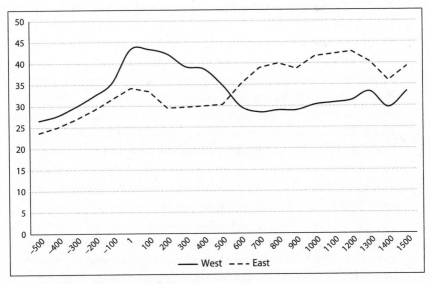

FIGURE I.6 Social development scores in western and eastern Eurasia, 500 BCE–1500 CE. *Sources*: Morris 2013b: 240–43, tables 7.1–7.2.

Very different mechanisms were required to generate more dramatic and self-sustaining progress. In the nineteenth century, development swiftly reached an unprecedented order of magnitude that made earlier fluctuations appear insignificant and defined the inflection point for the mature hockey stick.

The resultant divergence—from the past, and between different parts of the Old World—was so great that we no longer have to worry about the problem of (gu)es(s)timating historical GDP or other poorly documented metrics: it far exceeded any plausible margin of error. This was when the world truly did change: in David Landes's memorable turn of phrase, "The Englishman of 1750 was closer in material things to Caesar's legionnaires than to his own great-grandchildren."[6]

Energy capture per person accounts for most of Morris's social development scores, from 100 percent back in 14,000 BCE—when there would have been no meaningful differences in social organization or military capacity, let alone information technology, across the globe—to around 80 percent in 1800 and between 60 and 70 percent in 1900. Thus, changes in energy capture drove the divergence shown in figure I.7. In Morris's account, estimated per capita energy consumption rose from 38,000 kilocalories per day in 1800 to 92,000 in 1900 in northwestern Europe and on to 230,000 (in the United States) today.[7]

An alternative reconstruction envisions an even more rapid increase during the nineteenth century, from 33,000 to 99,000 daily kilocalories in England, all of which was sustained by coal. The transition from organic to fossil fuel economies was crucial. The former faced an iron constraint in their dependence on plant photosynthesis that converted a steady flow of solar energy into food, feed, and firewood that sustained human and animal labor and the processing of raw materials. The latter, by contrast, could draw on much larger accumulated stocks of fuel that had been built up over geological time, first coal and later oil and gas.[8]

Only in the twentieth century did war-making capacity and information technology, each of which grew by two orders of magnitude by Morris's reckoning (thanks to nuclear weapons and computers), take over as the most important drivers of development. Both are the fruits

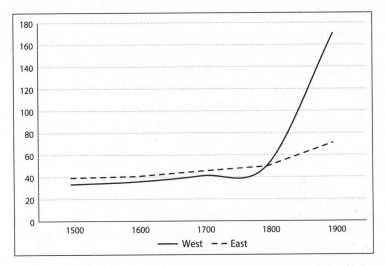

FIGURE I.7 Social development scores in western and eastern Eurasia, 1500–1900 CE. *Sources:* Morris 2013b: 241, table 7.1; 243, table 7.2.

of ever more sophisticated science and engineering that have kept deepening our break from the past.

What has all this economic growth and social development done for us? Most fundamentally, we live much longer. Life span is positively associated with economic performance, and as global average per capita output has risen about fifteenfold between the late eighteenth century and today, global mean life expectancy at birth has more than doubled from around thirty to seventy years. And we do not just live longer but also better. Poverty is down worldwide: the share of people subsisting on the real equivalent of about two dollars a day has declined from well over nine-tenths two hundred years ago to about one-tenth now. Its closest corollary, malnourishment, haunted half of the world's population in 1945 but affects only about one in ten people today.[9]

In the Western world, the original trailblazer, mature male stature rose by five inches between the late eighteenth and the late twentieth centuries. Overall, Westerners "are taller, heavier, healthier, and longer lived than our ancestors; our bodies are sturdier, less susceptible to disease in early life and slower to wear out." And once again, this trend has gone global.[10]

The world's literacy rate is up from one in eight adults 200 years ago to six out of every seven today. Freedom reigns: the proportion of humankind that lives in countries that count as more democratic than autocratic has exploded from maybe 1 percent in 1800 to two-thirds today—and had China's civil war in the late 1940s ended differently, the total could now easily be closer to five-sixths. On a scale from −10 (all autocratic) to +10 (all democratic), the average global score for major polities has risen from −7 in 1800 to +4 today. All this has made us measurably happier: GDP is linked to happiness and life evaluation more generally. Overall, even as economic inequality has been sustained within societies, and divergent development opened up a wide gap between rich and poor nations that is now only slowly narrowing, modern development has improved our life experience on many fronts, and has increasingly done so on a global scale.[11]

It goes without saying that we are hardly in a position to claim that the Great Escape has fully succeeded. Yet the painful truth that this same development has the potential to cause serious harm to us and our planet—through climate change, environmental degradation, weaponized pathogens, or nuclear war—merely reflects the sheer scale of this transformation: nothing like this had previously been within our reach. In both good and bad, we have far outpaced the past.[12]

WHY?

Why has the world changed so much? All this development was rooted in initial breakthroughs that took place in northwestern Europe: hence the inflection points in figures I.1 and I.7. But what made it possible for that corner of the globe to launch a process that unleashed previously unimaginable productivity and human welfare by harnessing an ever-broadening range of natural resources from coal and the vaccinia virus to silicon and uranium?

By now, answers to this question not only fill shelf-loads of learned books and binders—or rather electronic folders—of academic papers, entire books have been written to take stock of all those books and papers that propose answers. Scholarly opinion is divided. Some take a long-term view, searching for causes and trends that go back many centuries. Others stress the role of more recent contingencies that enabled some pioneering—or, depending on whom you ask, particularly rapacious or just plain lucky—societies to pull ahead. Some accounts privilege politics and institutions; others overseas trade and colonization; others still culture, education, and values.[13]

I argue that a single condition was essential in making the initial breakthroughs possible: competitive fragmentation of power. The nursery of modernity was riven by numerous fractures, not only by those between the warring states of medieval and early modern Europe but also by others within society: between state and church, rulers and lords, cities and magnates, knights and merchants, and, most recently, Catholics and Protestants. This often violent history of conflict and compromise was long but had a clear beginning: the fall of the Roman empire that had lorded it over most of Europe, much as successive Chinese dynasties lorded it over most of East Asia. Yet in contrast to China, nothing like the Roman empire ever returned to Europe.

The enduring absence of hegemonic empire on a subcontinental scale represented a dramatic break not only with ancient history. It also set Europe on a trajectory away from the default pattern of serial imperial state formation—from the boom and bust of hegemonic powers—we can observe elsewhere. By laying the foundations for persistent polycentrism and the transformative developmental dynamics it generated over the long run, this rupture was the single most important precondition for modern economic growth, industrialization, and global Western dominance much later on.

I develop my argument in several stages. In the opening chapter, I establish the fact that as far as imperial state formation is concerned, Europe differed profoundly from other parts of the world that supported major complex civilizations. After the demise of the unified

Roman empire in the fifth century CE, the greatest powers in Europe never laid claim to more than about one-fifth of its total population, a far cry from the four-fifths or more that had submitted to Roman rule. Likewise, the greatest powers that subsequently existed in the geographical space once held by the Romans never controlled more than a similarly modest proportion of its later population.[14]

This pattern is striking for two reasons: it reveals a sharp discontinuity between the ancient and post-ancient history of Europe, and it differs dramatically from outcomes in other parts of the world that used to be home to large traditional empires, such as East Asia, the Indian subcontinent, and the Middle East and North Africa region. The historically unique phenomenon of "one-off empire" in Europe is remarkable because regions that supported very large polities early on can reasonably be expected to have done the same later, and did in fact consistently do so elsewhere. In this respect, imperial state formation in South Asia and the Middle East—as well as in Southeast Asia, Central America, and the Andes region—had more in common with East Asia, the classic example of imperial persistence over time, than with Europe, which represents a genuine outlier.[15]

This raises four closely interrelated questions, which I address in Parts II through V of the book. How did the Roman empire come into existence—did its rise and success depend on rare or unique conditions that were never replicated later on? Why was nothing approximating the Roman empire in terms of scale ever rebuilt in the same part of the world? Can comparison with other parts of the world help us understand the absence of very large empire from post-Roman Europe? And finally, and most importantly, did the latter open a path to (much) later developments that eventually reshaped the entire world?

In Part II, I explain the creation of a very large empire that came to encompass the entire Mediterranean basin with reference to two principal factors. First, the Roman Republic managed to combine a culture of military mass mobilization of an intensity unknown among ancient state-level polities outside the Greek city-state culture and Warring States China with integrative capacities that enabled it to scale up military mass mobilization to levels unparalleled and arguably unattainable elsewhere in western Eurasia at the time (chapter 2). Second, in its formative phase, Rome benefited from its position at the margins of a larger civilizational zone that had expanded outward from the Fertile Crescent region for several thousand years but had been exceptionally slow in drawing the central and western Mediterranean into the growing network of sustained political and military interaction at that zone's core (chapter 3). In addition, prolonged domestic political stability and a fortuitous concatenation of circumstances that allowed Rome to establish effective naval hegemony across the Mediterranean at a relatively early stage of its expansion further contributed to its success.

None of the preconditions were—or in the case of the second principal factor even could be—repeated in later historical periods. Rome's rule had greatly extended the boundaries of the original Middle Eastern political-military system all the way to the North Sea. Large-scale military mass mobilization did not return to Europe until the French Revolution. Never again—or at least not until Trafalgar or World War II— was any one power or alliance able to claim naval supremacy across the entire Mediterranean basin.

After identifying the key factors that underpinned Rome's unique success, I assess the degree of contingency inherent in this process by considering counterfactuals (chapter 4). I ask at which junctures Roman expansion could have been derailed by plausible, "minimal rewrites" of actual history. This exercise suggests that the window for substantially alternative outcomes was fairly narrow, concentrated in the time of Alexander the Great near the end of the fourth century BCE. From the third century BCE onward, Roman capabilities—relative to those of its macro-regional competitors—made failure increasingly unlikely. Roman state formation thus turns out to have been both highly contingent (in terms of its foundational preconditions) and highly robust (once these preconditions were in place).

In Part III, I make short work of the extremely popular question of why the Roman empire fell: after all, most imperial entities in history that did not eventually morph into nation-states disintegrated at some point. Instead, I focus on a much more salient problem that has received much less attention: Why did it—or rather something like it—never return?

Chapters 2 and 3 already highlighted the peculiarities and sometimes irreproducible context of the Roman experience. I now expand my analysis to trajectories of state formation in post-Roman Europe. I identify and discuss eight junctures between the sixth and the early nineteenth centuries at which similarly dominant imperial states might conceivably have been created: the East Roman attempt in the sixth century to regain large parts of what used to be the western half of the Roman empire; Arab expansion in the seventh and eighth centuries; the growth of Frankish power around 800; the development of the German empire from the tenth to the thirteenth century; the Mongol advance in Eastern and Central Europe in the mid-thirteenth century; Habsburg policies in the sixteenth century; Ottoman power in the sixteenth and seventeenth centuries; and French policies from Louis XIV to Napoleon, with World War II added as a brief coda.

I argue that on all these occasions, a wide range of well-documented factors decisively militated against the reemergence of anything truly resembling hegemonic empire in Europe. No plausible minimal rewrite of history was likely to lead to that particular outcome. I conclude that post-Roman polycentrism in Europe was a perennially robust phenomenon.

In Part IV, I address a question that arises directly from this last observation: Why did large-scale empire building in post-Roman Europe *consistently* fail even as it continued *serially* elsewhere in the world? I approach this problem by comparing trends in state formation in different parts of the Old World, with particular emphasis on Europe and East Asia. I focus on this pairing because the Chinese imperial tradition was unusually resilient by world historical standards and therefore constitutes an ideal-typical counterpoint to the abiding polycentrism of post-Roman Europe.

This comparative perspective allows me to identify several factors that favored serial imperiogenesis in East Asia and obstructed it in Europe. At the proximate level of causation, fiscal arrangements and the characteristics of the post-Roman and post-Han conquest regimes played a major role (chapter 7). At the ultimate level, geographical and ecological conditions influenced macro-sociopolitical development (chapter 8). Among these environmental features, the degree of exposure to large steppe zones appears to have been a crucial determinant of the likelihood of imperial state formation, not merely in Europe and East Asia but also in other parts of Afroeurasia. In addition, though not necessarily fully autonomously, the nature of religious and secular belief systems as well as more general cultural properties reinforced divergent trends at the opposite end of the Eurasian land mass (chapter 9).

In all these respects, conditions in post-Han China differed profoundly from those in post-Roman Europe and help account for persistent long-term differences in the scaling-up and centralization of political and other forms of social power. I call this post-ancient divergence in macro-social evolution—centered on the sixth century CE—the "First Great Divergence."[16]

I conclude by proposing a taxonomy of features that were conducive or antithetical to empire-building on a large scale, which suggests that Europe—and Western or Latin Europe in particular—was a priori less likely to be brought under the control of such entities than were other regions. While East Asia experienced conditions that were favorable to iterative universal empire, South Asia and the Middle East and North Africa region occupied an intermediate position. This comparative analysis reinforces my findings in chapters 2 and 3 that the rise of the Roman empire depended on highly unusual circumstances. From this perspective, Rome's success was a greater anomaly than were later failures of imperial projects in Europe.

In Part V, I argue that what is now commonly referred to as the "Great Divergence," broadly understood as a uniquely (Northwest-)European and eventually "Western" breakthrough in economic and cognate capacities, was intimately connected with and indeed deeply rooted in the political "First Great Divergence" between Roman and post-Roman Europe (Parts II and III) and between Europe on the one hand and East Asia and intermediate regions on the other (Part IV)—a divergence between the enduring disappearance and the cyclical re-creation of hegemonic empire.

This is the case regardless of which of the competing explanations of the modern "Great Divergence" and the Industrial Revolution(s) we accept. Leading contenders include institutional developments from feudalism, church power, and religious schism to the creation of communes, corporate bodies, and parliamentarianism; social responses to perennial warfare, and more generally the overall configuration of the main sources of social power; the contribution of New World resources and global trade, and of mercantilist colonialism and protectionism; the emergence of a culture of sustained scientific and technological innovation; and a shift of values in favor of a commercially acquisitive bourgeoisie.

Drawing on these different types of explanations in turn (chapters 10 through 12), I show that all of them critically depend on the absence of Roman-scale empire from much of Europe throughout its post-ancient history. Recurrent empire on European soil would have interfered with the creation and flourishing of a stable state system that sustained productive competition and diversity in design and outcome. This made the fall and lasting disappearance of hegemonic empire an indispensable precondition for later European exceptionalism and thus, ultimately, for the making of the modern world we now inhabit.[17]

The transition to modernity was therefore a product of trends that played out over the long term: even if it only "took off" in the nineteenth century, it had very deep roots indeed, far beyond earlier signs of modernizing development that had appeared in the previous two centuries (and which I discuss in chapter 10). When it comes to the underlying dynamics, the long road to prosperity reached back to late antiquity. Europe's breakthrough was not a highly contingent process that might just as readily have taken place elsewhere: a protracted buildup was necessary—or at least sufficient—to make it possible, though by no means inevitable.[18]

From this developmental perspective, the death of the Roman empire had a much greater impact than its prior existence and the legacy it bequeathed to later European civilization. This may seem a bold claim, and I devote an epilogue to Monty Python's famous question, "What have the Romans ever done for us?" The afterlife of Roman cultural traditions, from language and (Christian) religion to law and elite culture, undeniably mediated the long-term consequences of the collapse of Roman imperial power. Specific elements of this legacy may indeed have provided a vital counterweight to the traumatic fractures of intensifying international and domestic competition, allowing productive exchange of people, goods, and ideas across a thicket of political and ideological boundaries.

This raises a final question: Was the actual historical scenario in which a monopolistic empire first created a degree of shared culture but subsequently went away for good more conducive to an eventual European breakthrough than a counterfactual scenario in which no such empire had ever appeared in the first place? Engagement with this problem pushes us well beyond the confines of defensible counterfactual reasoning and toward runaway conjecture but is nevertheless worth considering: Are there reasons to believe that the complete lack of Roman foundations would have derailed our tortuous journey toward the modern world?

• • •

My book stands in a long tradition of scholarship that has invoked fragmentation and competition as an important precondition or source of European development. It differs from existing work in that for the first time, it develops a much more comprehensive line of reasoning to establish once and for all a fundamental axiom: without polycentrism, no modernity.[19]

Empire was an effective and successful way of organizing large numbers of people in agrarian societies. Large, composite, and diverse, comprising multiple peripheries loosely held together by an often distant center whose dependence on local elites belied grandiose claims to universal rule, traditional empires were kept afloat by their ability to concentrate resources as needed without intruding too much upon their far-flung subject populations. Empire's adaptiveness is made strikingly clear in the fact that for more than 2,000 years, with primitive technology and under enormous logistical constraints, a very large share of our species has been controlled by just a handful of imperial powers (figure I.8).[20]

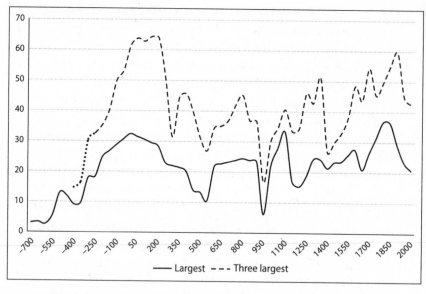

FIGURE I.8 The population of the single largest empire and the three largest empires in the world as a proportion of world population, 700 BCE–2000 CE (in percent). *Source:* Scheidel in press-b.

Yet from a developmental perspective, traditional empire failed in three ways, all of which mattered greatly for the making of the modern world:

- in the specific sense that the Roman empire released its grip on Europe and gave way to a very long period of polycentrism of powers both international and domestic;
- in the broader sense that near-monopolistic empire failed to be reestablished in Europe; and
- in the most general sense that empire, as a way of organizing people and resources, consistently failed to create conditions that enabled transformative development.

My focus is not on empire per se, a phenomenon increasingly studied from a global comparative perspective, most recently in the seventy-odd chapters of the *Oxford World History of Empire* that I have had the pleasure to edit jointly with Peter Bang and the late Chris Bayly. Even as

I repeatedly refer to specific characteristics of traditional empires—most notably in China—in the following chapters, I use them primarily as a foil to conditions in the post-Roman European state system to help cast the latter into sharper relief. For me, it is the escape that matters: not only what it was from, but how it came about.[21]

The productive dynamics of a stable state system were key: fragmentation generated diversity, competition, and innovation, and stability preserved gains from what worked best, rewarding winners and punishing losers. Empire contributes to this story insofar as it prevented both: monopolistic rule stifled competition, and the waxing and waning of imperial power rendered polycentrism intermittent and curtailed its cumulative benefits. Thus, traditional empires did not need to maintain hegemonic status all or even most of the time in order to derail modernizing development: sporadic "imperiogenesis" on a large scale was enough. Only the persistent absence of empire allowed polycentrism and its corollaries to flourish.

I do not track our entire journey from fracture to fracking. This is resolutely an analysis of origins. My emphasis is on foundational features, from the Middle Ages up to what is known as the First Industrial Revolution in England around 1800. I do not progress beyond that point because the First Industrial Revolution cannot be judged on its own, but only in terms of what it led to, far beyond cotton-spinning, iron-making, and the stationary steam engine. It was the Second Industrial Revolution, a great acceleration in macro-inventions and their widespread application from the last third of the nineteenth century onward that was driven by systematic scientific study and engineering, and concurrent progress in medicine and public health, the fertility transition, and political and institutional reform that accounted for most of the Great Escape: but once the door had been opened, a path of promise had been set. To quote Landes one more time, "The Industrial Revolution has been like in effect to Eve's tasting of the fruit of the tree of knowledge: the world has never been the same."[22]

Instead of taking the narrative forward in time, my book extends in the opposite direction, in order to gauge the true depth of the underpinnings of these much later developments. I do so not only because of my own professional interest in deep roots but also and indeed primarily because I am concerned with the robustness of historical outcomes. How likely was it that Europe would shift far enough toward a viable escape route? If post-Roman polycentrism was the norm, the very existence of the Roman empire was anomalous; otherwise it would have been the other way around.[23]

In the end, outcomes appear to have been overdetermined: just as the "First Great Divergence" can be traced to multiple factors, so scholars have linked the "(Second) Great Divergence" to a variety of features that have only one thing in common, namely, that they are predicated upon productive competitive polycentrism—or, in other words, the fact that in Europe, Roman power had remained unique.

In this respect, the story of modernity is also a story about Rome: Johann Wolfgang von Goethe was right to exclaim in 1786 that "an diesen Ort knüpft sich die ganze Geschichte der Welt an"—"the whole history of the world attaches itself to this spot." It does indeed, if only thanks to what Edward Gibbon two years later famously called the "the decline and fall of the Roman empire; the greatest, perhaps, and most awful scene, in the history of mankind." Yet when viewed from a great distance, it was not that awful after all: quite the opposite, in fact, as it ushered in an age of open-ended experimentation. It is for that reason alone that it deserves to be thought of as "the greatest scene in the history of mankind."[24]

The making of the modern world had a clearly demarcated beginning, forbiddingly remote as it may seem to us today. Europe had not always been fragmented and polycentric. It was not for nothing that its erstwhile rulers bequeathed to us the word "empire." They owned Britain, a belated afterthought of an acquisition, for about as many years as have now passed since Charles I lost his head. The last self-styled Roman emperor, the Habsburg Francis II, did not abdicate until August 6, 1806, twenty months after Napoleon Bonaparte had crowned himself emperor of the French and only about a year after the latter had shelved his plans to invade Britain, where the first steam locomotive had recently been displayed and steady improvements to the power loom kept the patent office busy.

But that would-be master of Europe, however revolutionary in appearance, was merely the last hurrah of ancient designs. The Roman empire remained unique, and the long shadow it had cast was just that. Europe had well and truly escaped, ensuring our collective release into an unexpected future.

In the heyday of Roman power, a certain Lauricius, otherwise unknown but probably a Roman soldier, carved a graffito on a rock in a desolate corner of what is now southern Jordan: "The Romans always win." This sentiment, which curtly echoed Virgil's famous and more eloquent vision that Jupiter had given the Romans "empire without end," held true for a very long time, well beyond actual Roman history. Empires in general did tend to win, at least for a while, before they fell apart only to be succeeded by others: in that sense, they were indeed without end. For untold generations, they imposed tributary rule and prevented stable state systems from forming and building a different world. Our lives today are different only because in the end, "the Romans"—the empire builders—did not, as it happened, *always* win, even if they came close.[25]

Their failure to do so may well have been our biggest lucky break since an errant asteroid cleared away the dinosaurs 66 million years earlier: there was no way to "get to Denmark"—to build societies that enjoy freedom, prosperity, and general welfare—without "escaping from Rome" first.[26]

HOW?

How can we substantiate this argument? The search for the causes of the (modern, economic) "Great Divergence" is of immense importance for our understanding of how the world came to be the way it is, yet it has largely been abandoned by professional historians. In an informal but hardly unrepresentative sample drawn from my own bibliography, only one in five of some forty-odd scholars who have made significant contributions to this grand debate have earned an advanced degree in history. Social scientists have been at the forefront of this line of research: economists led the pack and sociologists come in second. By contrast, political scientists have hardly been involved at all.[27]

It is true that quite a few of these economists effectively operate as historians, either by holding academic positions in economic history or, more commonly, in terms of their primary interests. Nevertheless, the limited commitment of—for want of a better term—"professional," that is, credentialed, historians is striking: judging from the age distribution in my sample, it cannot simply be waved off as a function of a turn away from economic or macro-history to cultural or micro-history, even if those trends may well play a role.

Then again, the glass is not only half empty but also half full: the relative lack of interest among historians has been more than offset by economists and sociologists' eagerness to tackle a big historical problem. Their engagement accounts for much of the continuing vigor of the debate, which cannot fail to benefit from genuine transdisciplinarity.

I approach this topic in the same spirit of openness. I am, by training and employment, a historian of the ancient Roman world whose interests have increasingly branched out into wider reaches of history, from the comparative study of ancient empires, slavery, and human welfare to the applicability of Darwinian theory to the past and the long-term evolution of economic inequality. I have long been following the literature about the origins of the British/European/"Western" takeoff, and especially the controversy between proponents of long- and short-term perspectives.

As a historian primarily of the more distant past, affinity for the long run might well seem a professional hazard. Not so: my initial intuition was that ancient legacies need not have mattered nearly as much as my immediate colleagues often like to assume, an issue that I take up at the very end of this book. Over time, however, it became clear to me that the many competing and complementary explanations of this takeoff did in fact have something in common that anchored them in developments that commenced a very long time ago—developments that were not limited to positive contributions that shaped later opportunities and constraints, but also included a massive absence. Yet even that absence—of hegemonic empire, from post-Roman Europe—needed to be explored, given that it was not a constant but had been preceded by an equally massive earlier presence. These entanglements made me a "long-termist" almost against my will.

Made in a rather different context, Garth Fowden's astute observation captures the scale of the challenge inherent in this project: "The ultimate goal of the Eurocentric historian ('modernity') is remote from, yet conceived of as standing in a relationship of dependence toward, the First Millennium. To depict such a relationship convincingly is a very difficult enterprise in itself." My own approach is therefore eclectic, by necessity (even) more than by inclination.[28]

In trying to explain why the Roman empire rose to such preeminence, I have to wear my Roman historian's hat. In trying to explain why it never came back, I need to survey different periods in a brutally reductive way, shunting aside infinite nuance in the search for those factors that mattered most for particular outcomes. The resultant account is both parsimonious—perhaps to a fault, as fellow historians would say—and, despite its considerable length, tightly focused on my key theme.

In chapter 1, I look at the Old World as a whole to establish how different Europe really was, and in chapters 7 through 9, I need to do the same as I seek to identify the underlying causes of that difference. In chapters 10 through 12, I address a large body of scholarship, much of it produced by social scientists whose work has driven the debate, and with whom I engage on their own terms. And at the end, I return once more to antiquity, to see which if any of its legacies can be salvaged to play a role in an explanation of the transition to modern development.

Throughout my discussion, I employ two specific approaches to build my argument: a comparative perspective, and explicit recourse to counterfactuals—"what-ifs." Both of these are means to the same end: to improve our sense of causation, of why different societies turned out the way they did.

Historical comparison promises various benefits, only the most important of which merit mention here. Comparative description helps "clarify the specific profile of individual cases by contrasting them with others." I pursue this goal in the opening chapter by establishing contrasting patterns of state formation.[29]

Comparison has an "alienating . . . effect": it defamiliarizes the deceptively familiar—deceptively familiar, that is, to the expert of a particular time and place: "The chief prize is a way out of parochialism."[30] Thinking about the Roman empire without considering what happened later on in the same geographical space, or how other empires developed elsewhere, blurs our vision for what may have mattered most for the rise and fall of Rome: comparanda help explain the specific.

Comparison also helps us transcend peculiarities of evidence for a particular case or the dominant academic tradition thereon. "Analyses that are confined to single cases . . . cannot deal effectively with factors that are largely or completely held constant within the boundaries of the case (or are simply less visible in that structural or cultural context). This is the reason why going beyond the boundaries of a single case can put into question seemingly well-established causal accounts and generate new problems and insights."[31]

A closely related benefit is the fact that "analytically comparison can help to refute pseudo-explanations and to check (or test) causal hypotheses." Parochial familiarity will favor factors that are prominent in the source tradition and/or the research tradition of a particular subfield. How can we tell how much weight to put on taxes, or religion, or geography, if we do not consider alternative cases? Such single-case explanations need not be pseudo, but they are at the very least local and thus run the risk of failing to capture significant relationships. The post-ancient "First Great Divergence" in particular is impossible to understand without comparing configurations of circumstances in different environments.[32]

I am primarily interested in explaining one particular phenomenon, the path to modernity in parts of Europe, and not in offering a comprehensive survey of different societies and outcomes. This renders my comparative perspective, in Jürgen Kocka's term, "a-symmetric": "a form of comparison which is centrally interested in describing, explaining and interpreting one case . . . by contrasting it with others, while . . . the other cases are not brought in for their own sake, and . . . not fully researched but only sketched as a kind of background."[33]

In the present case, I draw on the experience of China and—in less detail—other parts of Asia and North Africa in order to account for European development. This approach has a long pedigree, going back most famously to Max Weber's attempt to understand the emergence of capitalism and modern science in the West by probing Asian societies for contrast. I also apply this technique more superficially in contrasting the rise of Rome with the failure of later European states to follow suit. In Part V, I compare the effects of imperial persistence in China (and to a lesser degree in India and the Middle East) with those of Europe's post-Roman fragmentation.[34]

Chapters 7 through 9 offer a more symmetric treatment: in trying to account for the "First Great Divergence," I give equal weight to post-ancient developments in Europe and China up to the end of the first millennium CE, which represent the most divergent outcomes within Afroeurasia in that period. This approach is known as "analytical comparison" between equivalent units. It helps us identify variables that can explain shared or contrasting outcomes—in this case, the characteristics of conquest regimes and fiscal arrangements, ideation, and ecological conditions.[35]

In the same context, specifically in chapter 8, I move farther toward a more ambitious goal, that of "variable-oriented" "parallel demonstration of theory": I argue that proximity to the steppe was such a persistent precondition for empire formation that it allows us to subordinate individual outcomes to a broader normative prediction. This makes it possible to identify cases that are outliers, most notably the rise of Rome, which in turn helps us assess the relative robustness of historical processes and outcomes over time, in this case the failure of hegemonic empire to return to post-Roman Europe.[36]

My interest in robustness and contingency accounts for the relative prominence in this book of another tactic, overt consideration of counterfactuals. In a very basic sense, counterfactual reasoning is a necessary ingredient of any historical account that seeks to rise above the level of bare description: there is, after all, "absolutely no logical way to make causal inferences without simultaneously making assumptions about how events would have unfolded if the causal factors we consider cru-cial had taken on different form." Thus "we are all counterfactual historians"—and that "we" covers pretty much every person, not just professional historians.[37]

Even so, historians all too rarely highlight counterfactual reasoning in their research. This is a great loss. Explicit counterfactuals force us to confront the weaknesses of deterministic as well as revisionist assump-tions, however implicit they might be: the notion that deviations from what happened might have proven short-lived and some approximation of actual outcomes would have happened anyway, or, conversely, that minor contingencies could have produced massive divergences from observed history. Merely to think about this makes us more careful about causal inferences. Just like comparative history—of which coun-terfactual history is a more exotic variant—"what-ifs" are a valuable means of assessing the relative weight of particular variables.[38]

The key question must be this: How little change would have been enough for history to have taken an alternative path—in the nontrivial sense of altering outcomes enough to be visible and to make a difference in developmental terms? Procedurally, this question calls for adherence to what has been called the "minimal-rewrite rule": the least amount of tweaking of actual history and avoidance of arbitrary intervention.

Ideally, the direction of a counterfactual change should preserve "consistency with well-established historical facts and regularities, con-sistency with well-established generalizations that transcend what is true at a particular time and place, and consistency with well-established laws of cause and effect." This does not rule out recourse merely to space aliens and asteroid impacts but also to historical actors that display anachronistic or contextually implausible behavior. The closer the change hews to what could well have happened at the time—the more informed the counterfactual scenario is by what actually did happen— the more reasonable it is.[39]

In devising counterfactuals, it is essential to be clear about putative connections—to specify antecedents and consequents—and to ensure that connecting lines are logically consistent. One problem in particular is difficult to avoid in practice: counterfactuals inevitably generate second-order effects that complicate the prediction. The more they add to the complexity of counterfactual scenarios, the lower the overall probability these scenarios will be compared to that of any given link within them: the whole exercise becomes more tenuous and frail. Although the problem of complexity can be a function of design—if, for instance, we introduce multiple changes at once—more commonly it is simply a function of time: the farther we project ahead of actual history, the less we are able to control the thought experiment. Counterfactuals work best in the short term.[40]

I follow best practice in identifying critical junctures at which things either might well have gone differently or would have needed to have gone differently in order to generate significantly different long-term outcomes (that is, before a particular trend had become firmly locked in). Unlike much of the existing literature, however, I do not start with some ostensibly plausible change to explore its likely ramifications. Instead, I ask, as I must, how much would have had to go differently at a certain point to bring about change on a large scale—in this case, either the abortion of Roman expansion (chapter 4) or the restoration of Roman-style empire in post-Roman Europe (chapters 5 and 6).[41]

That these are very substantial divergences from actual history makes it easier to judge their plausibility because they often tend to be incompatible with the dictates of the minimal-rewrite rule: if it is not feasible to obtain dramatically different outcomes without straying far from what might plausibly have happened at the time when the counterfactual change is made, historically observed developments are revealed as having been fairly robust. This robustness helps contain the ever-present risk that we design counterfactuals that support our own preconceived notions of what was likely to have happened.[42]

The odds of Rome's failing to build a mighty empire steadily declined as time went by: whereas early changes could have derailed it from this trajectory, at later junctures it becomes more challenging to devise plausible pathways to a significantly alternative reality. The same is true for post-Roman Europe and the ascent of modern development in terms of economic growth and scientific and technological progress: trends that up to 1500 might quite readily have been aborted became more difficult to change during the following two centuries. In the eighteenth century, this exercise would require even more dramatic rewrites, and it becomes well-nigh impossible in the nineteenth. The real question is just how much this trend owed to compound and reinforcing effects, and how far these effects reached back in time: my own answer, of course, is that their roots were very deep indeed.[43]

Comparison is essential for establishing the European anomaly (chapter 1) and for explaining it (chapters 7 through 9) and its developmental consequences (chapters 10 through 12). Counterfactuals are essential in testing the robustness of what happened (chapter 4) and what did not happen (chapters 5 and 6) in Roman and post-Roman Europe, respectively. The epilogue takes the counterfactual approach even further, sharpening our appreciation concerning what exactly it is the modern world owes to the ancient past.

• • •

The final result is a book that is quite varied in content and perspective, moving as it does back and forth between ancient history, modern history, comparative historical sociology, and history that did not even happen. For this and other reasons it is bound to irritate: classicists and humanists of all stripes for giving short shrift to the (positive) legacy of the classical world; culturally and microscopically inclined historians by focusing on the big picture of state formation and economic development; even more historians by foregrounding the influence of ecology and geography; and most historians by being irremediably "reductive." I might even be taken to task for eschewing conventional indictments of the "West," or indeed of the very concept—a label for which I have little use. For balance, I also expect to annoy social scientists by dredging up proverbial ancient history and by relying on a great deal of qualitative reasoning.[44]

This is exactly as it should be. While it may be rare for such diverse elements to be brought together between two covers, that is the whole point of the exercise—to forgo business as usual and to experiment. Those challenging my argument will have to do so by drawing on a similarly broad canvas—or better still on an even broader one, or by showing why the canvas is too broad, or the wrong one. Any such critique will inevitably have to wrestle with a familiar conundrum: how to go about addressing the Very Big Question of why the world has turned out the way it has (so far). The more productive disagreement my book arouses, the better it will have done its job.

Yet needless to say, disagreement is not what I am after. I wrote this book to establish, as firmly and comprehensively as I could, two simple points: that interlocking forms of productive fragmentation were of paramount importance and indeed indispensable in creating the specific set of conditions that gave birth to modernity, and that the divergences that precipitated this outcome in only one part of the world but not in others were highly robust. In the end, only Western Europe and its offshoots fit the bill: had our "Great Escape" not begun there, it would most likely not have happened at all.

PART I
The European Anomaly

CHAPTER 1

Patterns of Empire

MEASURING IMPERIAL DOMINANCE

HOW COMMON was it for empires to dominate large parts of entire continents? How rare was it for imperial hegemony to end in persistent fragmentation? Just how unusual was the European experience of state formation? All these questions call for comparative evaluation. They can only be answered by examining how often empires swept all before them—or at least came close.

This is harder than it might seem. The boundaries of empire are notoriously difficult to define. Imperial rule was sometimes highly indirect in nature, relying on vassal regimes to manage subordinate populations. On occasion, imperial centers lost effective control over areas that nominally remained under their authority to local elites or warlords. We need to simplify: my survey is predicated on the assumption that an empire was formally unified for as long as no overtly independent polities had emerged in its territory.[1]

But even if we accept this fairly generous definition of imperial rule, we still the face the problem of how to measure the degree of imperial dominance in a particular region in a way that allows for systematic comparison across several continents and millennia. Existing scholarship on the scale of empire focuses on the territorial size of polities, on the amount of land they controlled and how this changed over time.[2]

And not without reason: space is undoubtedly a critical variable. Fernand Braudel famously labeled distance the "number one enemy" of civilization. Far-flung empires continuously struggled to maintain communication and to exercise power over diverse terrains: their very survival depended on this.[3]

Even so, territorial reach may not be the single most important factor in assessing the relative weight of particular imperial formations. If we want to understand the role of hegemonic empire in shaping social, economic, and intellectual development, it is people who matter most. Geographical reach was not always matched by demographic heft: whereas very populous empires generally tended to be fairly large, not all large empires were necessarily endowed with sizable populations.

Steppe empires in particular sometimes extended over thousands of kilometers and multiple modern time zones without holding sway over more than a small fraction of the subjects of smaller agrarian polities, and acquired demographic weight only if they expanded into more densely settled areas of sedentary civilization. This phenomenon was not limited to nomads: in 1815 the Russian empire ruled half of the terrestrial surface of Europe but only a quarter of all Europeans; and a hundred years later it claimed more than a third of Asia's landmass but fewer than 3 percent of its people.[4]

I thus focus on population as the most meaningful measure of imperial success. The most basic approach is to measure (or rather estimate) the proportion of the total population of a particular macro-region that was ruled by the most populous polity in that region. The larger its share in the overall regional population, the closer the leading polity came to enjoying effectively monopolistic power, and the more often or the longer this was the case, the more dominant was the role of hegemonic empire in the history of that region.[5]

Anyone who is even vaguely familiar with historical demography will appreciate that this seemingly straightforward exercise is something much easier said than done. The population size of early societies is not normally reliably recorded or otherwise empirically known. Census counts such as those that have survived from early China are rare and not without problems. For the most part, all we have are estimates—which are often little more than guesses—by modern scholars who have not followed consistent standards. I explain my own method and the steps I have taken in order to ensure a measure of consistency across space and time in the technical note at the end of this volume.[6]

I must stress that the following calculations are to be understood as a very rough guide to demographic conditions in the past—and the farther we move back in time, the rougher. Values that differ by a few percentage points are just as plausible as the ones in my charts. Even so, they are useful as long as it would seem impossible to envision significantly different levels of imperial dominance (of, say, over half instead of a third of a given regional population): my estimates are generally unlikely to be wrong to an extent that would affect the overall shape of the pattern. It is in this narrowly circumscribed manner that they provide a reasonably solid foundation for global comparison.

I have identified four macro-regions: Europe, the Middle East and North Africa (MENA), South Asia, and East Asia. A fifth one is a hybrid that overlaps with the first two, namely the area once claimed by the Roman empire at its peak, which I refer to as the "Roman empire region" (figure 1.1).[7]

Taken together, these areas had long been the core zone of human macro-social evolution. They cover more than a quarter of the earth's land surface but house a much larger share of global population, around 60 percent today. Their demographic predominance was even more pronounced in the past: 2,000 years ago, these four regions housed at least nine out of every ten human beings alive at the time, and about four in five both 1,000 and 500 years ago.[8]

They differ in size, albeit only to a moderate degree. At 10.18 million and 11.84 million square kilometers, Europe and East Asia form spatially equivalent units. Due to the presence of substantial arid areas that did not play a major role in historical state formation, the MENA region is more difficult to define: its nominal size of 12.59 million square kilometers could easily be reduced by about one-third by bracketing out the Algerian, Libyan, and Egyptian deserts and the Arabian Rub' al Khali. (While other regions also feature marginal terrain, such as the Gobi

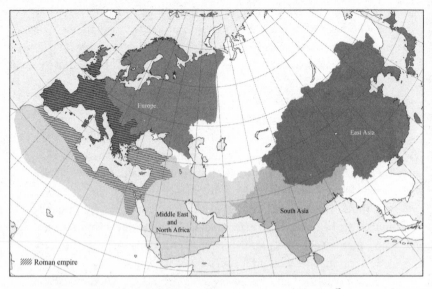

FIGURE 1.1 Macro-regions of state formation.

Desert or subarctic Europe, they do so on a comparatively smaller scale.) South Asia covers 4.53 million square kilometers, similar to the Roman empire that claimed between 4 million and well over 5 million square kilometers depending on how much desert area is taken into account. In terms of size, the five regions under review thus vary by a factor of between two and three.[9]

Much the same used to be true with respect to population: figure 1.2 shows that although East Asia was generally more populous than any of the other four regions, it was only rarely more than twice as populous. The MENA region of the past 1,000 years has been the only exception.[10]

This broad similarity in orders of magnitude ensures that we do not end up comparing apples and oranges by lumping together regions of greatly different size or population. For this reason, substantially smaller regions such as Southeast Asia, Mesoamerica, and western South America have not been included here; I briefly consider them later on.

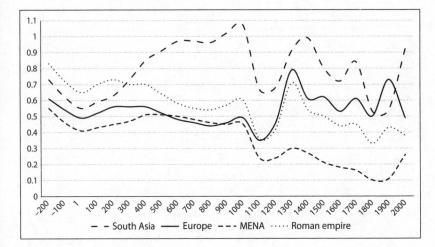

FIGURE 1.2 The population of South Asia, Europe, the Middle East and North Africa, and the "Roman empire region" as a proportion of the population of East Asia, 200 BCE–2000 CE, at centennial intervals (East Asia = 1). *Source*: Based on McEvedy and Jones 1978.

PATTERNS OF EMPIRE

The Mediterranean and Europe

Over the long run of history, the position of the Roman empire within the area it had come to claim at the height of its power in the first few centuries CE remained unique. It had been without precedent: in the fifth century BCE, the Achaemenid Persian empire had ruled no more than 30 percent of the population of the same region. Having thoroughly dominated the scene from the first century BCE to the end of the fourth century CE, Roman preeminence ceased only after an abortive attempt at restoration in the sixth century.

Subsequent efforts to rebuild a "Roman" empire proved unsuccessful: Charlemagne managed a modest resurgence around 800 while Ottonian rule produced merely a minute uptick two centuries later. Ottoman expansion in the early modern period likewise failed to improve on the Achaemenid population share of 2,000 years earlier, and later

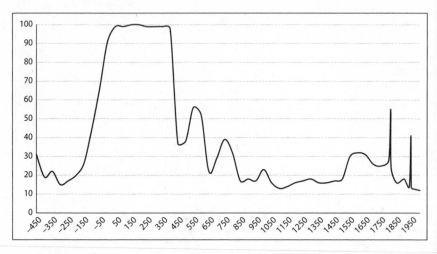

FIGURE 1.3 The proportion of the population residing in the area covered by the Roman empire at its peak that was claimed by the largest polity in that area, 450 BCE–2000 CE (in percent).

KEY: Achaemenid empire: 450, 400, 350 BCE; Ptolemaic empire: 300, 250 BCE; Roman empire (Seleucid empire): 200 BCE; Roman empire: 150, 100, 50 BCE, 1, 50, 100, 150, 200, 250, 300, 350, 400 CE; Byzantine empire (Western Roman empire): 450; Byzantine empire: 500, 550, 600, 650; Umayyad empire: 700, 750; Frankish empire: 800, 850, 900, 950; Fatimid empire: 1000, 1050; Holy Roman Empire (France): 1100, 1150, 1200, 1250; France: 1300, 1350, 1400, 1450, 1500; Ottoman empire: 1550, 1600, 1650, 1700, 1750; France: 1800, 1812, 1815, 1850, 1900, 1933; Germany: 1943; United Kingdom: 1945, 1950; Egypt: 2000.

blips under Napoleon and Hitler remained both relatively modest and utterly ephemeral (figure 1.3).[11]

Roughly 40 percent of the subjects of the mature Roman empire resided outside Europe. Even so, it is clear that the observed pattern was in the first instance the result of developments in Europe rather than in the Levant or northern Africa. The level of Roman imperial dominance in Europe was unparalleled. At the peak of their power, the Romans controlled between three-quarters and four-fifths of the European population, even though they claimed no more than a quarter of the continent's land surface.[12]

After the disintegration of the western half of the empire in the fifth century CE, the corresponding share of the eastern Roman empire plummeted to 20 percent or 30 percent. Ephemeral consolidation under Charlemagne was followed by an entire millennium of persistent

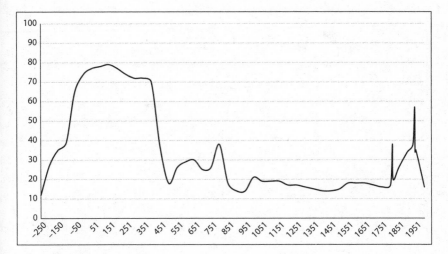

FIGURE 1.4 The proportion of the population of Europe claimed by the largest polity in that area, 250 BCE–2000 CE (in percent).

KEY: Roman empire: 250, 200, 150, 100, 50 BCE, 1, 50, 100, 150, 200, 250, 300, 350, 400 CE; Western Roman empire: 450; Ostrogothic kingdom/Visigothic kingdom: 500; Byzantine empire (Frankish empire): 550; Frankish empire: 600, 650, 700, 750, 800, 850; Frankish empire: 900, 950; Holy Roman Empire: 1000, 1050, 1100, 1150, 1200, 1250; France: 1300, 1350, 1400, 1450, 1500; Spanish Habsburg empire: 1550, 1600; France: 1650, 1700, 1750, 1800, 1812; Russia: 1815, 1850, 1900, 1933; Germany: 1943; Russia: 1945, 1950, 2000. In 1933, 1945, 1950: Russia = Soviet Union.

polycentrism as the most populous power did not normally rule even a fifth of all Europeans. Neither Napoleon nor Hitler managed to match the reach of the Romans even for a few years, and Russia's ascent up to the mid-twentieth century was eventually checked by the collapse of the Soviet Union in 1991 (figure 1.4).

Demographic change was insufficiently dramatic to call this very long-term perspective into question. Even though the three-quarters of Europe outside the former Roman borders gradually filled up, they never quite caught up with the original core and even today account for only a little more than half of the European population. For most of the post-Roman period, up to the sixteenth century, the proportion of all Europeans who lived in the territories once held by Rome did not differ greatly from that back in antiquity (figure 1.5). Thus, the distribution of population in medieval and early modern Europe was not somehow

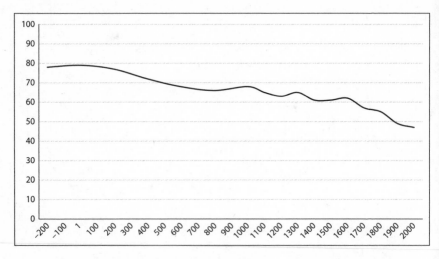

FIGURE 1.5 The population of the area claimed by the Roman empire at its peak as a proportion of the population of Europe, 200 BCE–2000 CE (in percent).

profoundly different from that in Roman Europe: continuities out-weighed shifts over time.

The Middle East, South Asia, and East Asia

The pattern of one-off near-monopolistic empire followed by endur-ing polycentrism that can be observed in the area once held by the Roman empire and more specifically in Europe is completely different from conditions in the other three macro-regions. Over the course of the past 2,500 years, the MENA region went through four distinct phases of imperial consolidation, most notably under the Achaemenids and the Umayyad and early Abbasid caliphates. Roman and Ottoman rule resulted in a slightly lower degree of demographic concentration, made similar by the fact that it extended over more or less the same territories.

Two further imperial projects failed, that of the Sasanians in the early seventh century (after defeat by the Romans) and of the Seljuqs in the late eleventh century (due to political fission). Although levels of

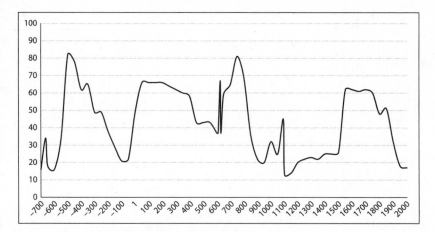

FIGURE 1.6 The proportion of the population of the MENA region claimed by the largest polity in that area, 700 BCE–2000 CE (in percent).

KEY: Assyrian empire: 700, 665, 650 BCE; Egypt: 600 BCE; Median empire: 550 BCE; Achaemenid empire: 500, 450, 400, 350 BCE; Seleucid empire: 300, 250, 200, 150 BCE; Parthian empire: 100 BCE; Roman empire: 50 BCE, 1, 50, 100, 150, 200, 250, 300, 350, 400, 450, 500, 550, 600, 610 CE; Sasanian empire: 626; Roman empire: 630; Umayyad empire: 650, 700, 750, 800, 850; Tulunid empire: 900; Roman empire: 950; Fatimid empire: 1000, 1050; Seljuq empire: 1092; Fatimid empire: 1100; Fatimid empire (Rum Seljuq empire): 1150; Ayyubid empire: 1200; Mamluk empire (Mongol empire): 1250; Mamluk empire (Ilkhanid empire): 1300; Mamluk empire: 1350; Mamluk empire (Timurid empire): 1400; Mamluk empire: 1450, 1500; Ottoman empire: 1550, 1600, 1650, 1700, 1750, 1800, 1850, 1900; Egypt: 1950, 2000.

imperial preeminence did at times drop to post-Roman European levels, most notably in the period between 1100 and 1500, renewed concentration took place until the dismantling of the Ottoman empire ushered in a new state system that is already showing signs of strain (figure 1.6).

A similar pattern can be found on the Indian subcontinent. Once again we are able to identify four episodes of hegemonic empire, under the Maurya, the Sultanate of Delhi, the Mughals, and the British empire that eventually gave birth to the modern Indian state (figure 1.7). Compared to the MENA region, dominant empires were less durable and for much of history alternated with formations that claimed approximately half of the overall population of South Asia, alongside intermittent periods of more intense fragmentation.

It is worth emphasizing that the population estimates for this region are fraught with margins of error that are particularly large even by the

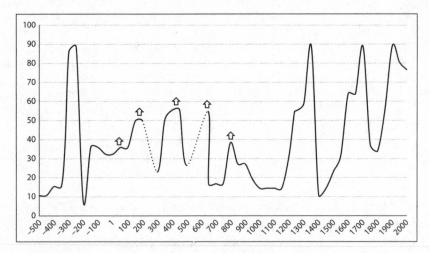

FIGURE 1.7 The proportion of the population of South Asia claimed by the largest polity in that area, 500 BCE–2000 CE (in percent).

KEY: Maghada: 500, 450, 400, 350 BCE; Nanda empire: 325 BCE; Maurya empire: 300, 250 BCE; Satavahara: 200 BCE; Shunga empire: 150, 100 BCE; Saka empire: 50 BCE, 1 CE; Kushan empire: 50, 100, 150, 200; Gupta empire: 300, 350, 400, 450; Gupta empire/Hephthalites 500; Harsha empire: 647; Chalukya of Badami empire: 650, 700, 750; Pala empire: 800; Pratihara empire: 850, 900; Rashtrakuta empire: 950; Chola empire: 1000, 1050; Chola empire (Western Chalukya empire): 1100; Chola empire: 1150; Ghurid Sultanate: 1200; Sultanate of Delhi: 1236, 1250, 1300, 1350; Vijayanagara empire (Bahmani Sultanate): 1400; Vijayanagara: 1450; Sultanate of Delhi: 1500; Mughal empire: 1550, 1600, 1650, 1700; Maratha empire: 1750; British empire: 1800, 1850, 1900; India: 1950, 2000. Dashed line: no entries for 250, 550, 600.

modest standards of this exercise. For the earlier stages of South Asian history, my reconstruction is bound to underestimate the relative demographic weight of the northern cores of the region that were located in the Indus and Ganges basins.[13]

Because of this, polities that were based in the northern reaches of South Asia such as the Saka, Kushan, and Gupta empires as well as the more ephemeral Harsha and Pala empires probably accounted for a somewhat larger share of the total population than shown in the graph (an adjustment indicated by the upward arrows in figure 1.7).

The easternmost macro-region, East Asia, has been characterized by much stronger dominance of hegemonic empire than any of the others (figure 1.8). Its leading polities attained population shares of 80 percent or 90 percent for much of the past 2,200 years. Polycentrism in the wake

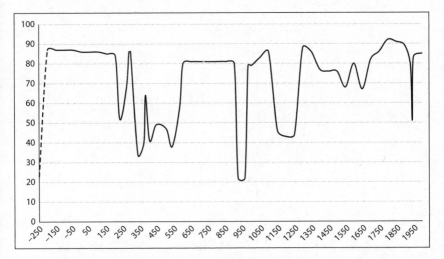

FIGURE 1.8 The proportion of the population of East Asia claimed by the largest polity in that area, 250 BCE–2000 CE (in percent).

KEY: Qin: 250 BCE; Western Han: 200, 150, 100, 50 BCE, 1 CE; Eastern Han: 50, 100, 150, 200; Northern Wei: 225; Jin: 265, 280, 290; Liu Han: 330; Former Yan: 366; Former Qin: 376; Eastern Jin: 400; Liu Song: 440; Northern Wei: 500; Liang: 535; Northern Zhou: 580; Sui: 590, 600; Tang: 650, 700, 750, 800, 850, 900; Later Liang: 920; Northern Song: 960, 980, 1000, 1050, 1100; Southern Song: 1150, 1200, 1250; Yuan: 1300, 1350; Ming: 1400, 1450, 1500, 1550, 1600; Qing: 1650, 1700, 1750, 1800, 1850, 1900; China: 1933; Japan: 1943; China: 1950, 2000.

of the Han/Jin collapse—the period of the "Sixteen Kingdoms" and the "Northern and Southern Dynasties"—was quite prolonged but never as intense as comparable interludes in other regions.[14]

Moreover, subsequent intervals between monopolistic super-states proved much more short-lived. The longest of them, in the twelfth and thirteenth centuries, was more apparent than real: most of East Asia's people were controlled by just two great powers—the Jurchen Jin in the north and the Southern Song—that divided China proper between them. Much the same was true for parts of the fourth and fifth centuries, and also much later during World War II, when the Republic of China and the empire of Japan claimed almost the entire population of the region.

Owing to China's enormous demographic weight, this East Asian profile was single-handedly generated by Chinese state formation (figure 1.9).

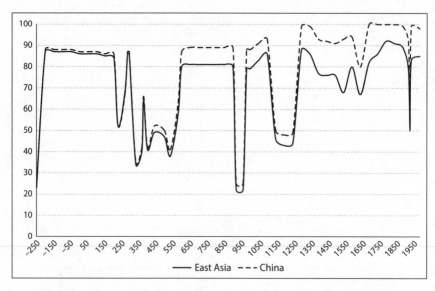

FIGURE 1.9 Comparison between the proportion of the population of East Asia controlled by the largest polity in East Asia and the proportion of the population of China controlled by the largest polity in China, 250 BCE–2000 CE (in percent).

KEY: See Figures 1.8 and 1.10.

Comparisons

All of these findings are based on a formalistic definition of imperial rule. Throughout this survey, population has been assigned to polities wherever those polities claimed to hold sway. Such claims need to be taken with more than just a grain of salt: premodern empires did not normally govern people the way modern states do. Rulers and central authorities were often remote, and effective power was dispersed across multiple layers of intermediaries and local elites.[15]

Yet in the end, this does not greatly matter here. Various forms of delegational and indirect rule were the norm for most of the period under review, a situation that only really changed in the past few centuries (in Europe) or even more recently (in the other macro-regions). For this reason, broadly comparable conditions applied throughout the roughly 2,000 to 2,500 years of premodern history that form the core of my survey, at least if viewed in ideal-typical contradistinction to more inclusive modern state formation.

To be sure, not all premodern polities were alike. Periods of relatively—that is, by the standards of the time—successful centralized control alternated with those of effective segmentation as the power of the central authorities dwindled away. It can be difficult to draw clear lines: the Abbasid caliphate or the Holy Roman Empire persisted for centuries after they ceased functioning as anything like unified polities, if indeed (in the latter case) they had ever done so.

This affects the overall profiles in subtle but not insignificant ways. In Europe, my emphasis on formal state claims serves to underestimate the effective extent of polycentrism that obtained in certain periods: treating medieval France or Germany as single imperial entities is generous at the best of times. A more hard-nosed assessment of political realities would push the population share of dominant polities far below the 20 percent mark indicated in figure 1.4. In the MENA region, even though I have classified breakaway kingdoms from the Abbasid caliphate as separate states, a similar problem emerges in the later stages of Ottoman rule when the sultan's suzerainty had often become purely nominal, most notably in the Maghreb prior to European colonization and in Egypt under the rule of the Muhammad Ali dynasty. In South Asia, the actual reach of the Maurya empire in particular remains very much an open question.

In East Asia, central government control repeatedly frayed long before alternative states were openly established on the territory of existing empires: the late Eastern Han and late Tang periods are classic examples. In the case of China, it is possible to illustrate the mismatch between mere claims and the actual exercise of imperial control by comparing the estimated share of the actual population that was formally claimed by the largest polity with the share of the actual population that was captured by census counts (figure 1.10).

This comparison shows that the Period of Disunion of the fourth through sixth centuries CE resulted in a more sweeping loss of state power than simple population estimates would suggest. It also suggests

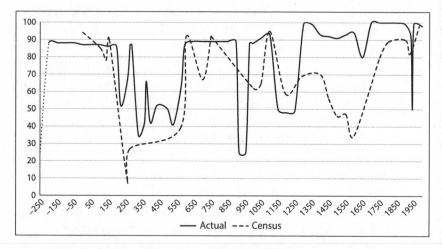

FIGURE 1.10 Actual population and census population of the largest polity in China as a proportion of the total population of that region, 250 BCE–2000 CE (in percent).

KEY: Actual population: Qin: 250 BCE; Western Han: 200, 150, 100, 50 BCE; 1 CE; Eastern Han: 50, 100, 150, 200; Northern Wei: 225; Jin: 265, 280, 290; Liu Han: 330; Former Yan: 366; Former Qin: 376; Eastern Jin: 400; Liu Song: 440; Northern Wei: 500; Liang: 535; Northern Zhou: 580; Sui: 590, 600; Tang: 650, 700, 750, 800, 850, 900; Later Liang: 920; Northern Song: 960, 980, 1000, 1050, 1100; Southern Song: 1150, 1200, 1250; Yuan: 1300, 1350; Ming: 1400, 1450, 1500, 1550, 1600; Qing: 1650, 1700, 1750, 1800, 1850, 1900; China: 1933, 1943, 1950, 2000. Census population (Bielenstein 1987: 11–140): Western Han empire: 2 CE; Eastern Han empire: 105, 140, 157; Wei 264; Jin: 280; Northern Zhou: 579/580; Sui: 609; Tang: 705, 754/755; Northern Song: 1006, 1050, 1100; Southern Song: 1193; Yuan empire: 1291; Ming empire: 1402, 1450, 1500, 1552, 1602; Qing empire: 1750, 1800, 1850, 1901.

that Chinese authorities under the late Tang and the early Northern Song found it difficult to register their subjects, and highlights the dramatic erosion of state control under the Mongol and Ming dynasties.[16]

While graphs such as these are the most suitable means of visualizing long-term patterns of imperial state formation, overall scores of political concentration are better capable of capturing the scale of difference between various macro-regions. In table 1.1 I calculate the average proportion of the population of a given region that was under the control of the most populous polity in that region, both over the full chronological range of my surveys and for major subsets.

These cumulative scores reveal very substantial variation among these macro-regions. Europe has the lowest score overall, even if the

TABLE 1.1 Cumulative proportion of the population of different regions controlled by the largest polities in these regions (in percent; averaged over fifty-year intervals)

	Europe	MENA	South Asia	East Asia
Overall	33	43	39	73
Roman	53	53	—	—
Post-Roman	**20**	38	—	—
Pre-Islamic	—	48	32	—
Islamic to 2000	—	38	55	—
Pre-Song	—	—	—	69
Song to 2000	—	—	—	77

Source: Based on the data sets underlying figures 1.4, 1.6, 1.7, and 1.8.

massive break between Roman and post-Roman conditions might make it seem a rather meaningless statistical artifact. East Asia's overall score is more than twice that for Europe and shows only moderate fluctuation over time: the secular trend toward greater concentration reflects the absence of prolonged disunion from the second millennium. The other macro-regions occupy an intermediate position. Roman state formation had a moderate effect on the MENA region, as did Islamic state formation in South Asia from the thirteenth century onward.[17]

European history has produced the most imbalanced profile overall, with a score that was almost three times as high in the Roman period as it has been since then. Similarly striking discontinuities are absent from the other macro-regions. As the graphs show, a 20 percent ceiling became the norm in post-Roman Europe whereas demographic dominance of the top polity only rarely dipped to such a low level elsewhere.

If we look at the twenty-six regular fifty-year intervals in the post-ancient period (from 650 to 2000), the most populous powers in Europe fell short of this 20 percent threshold no fewer than 19 times (or 73 percent), compared to not even once in East Asia, 4 times (15 percent) in the MENA region, and (probably) 10 times (38 percent) in South Asia. Conversely, in the same period the most populous empires in both the MENA region and South Asia cleared a 50 percent threshold 10 times each (38 percent), compared to zero times in Europe and 24 times (92 percent) in East Asia.

Very broadly speaking, the profiles for MENA, South Asia, and East Asia are all variants of the same underlying pattern, one of dominant empires interspersed with periods of deconcentration. They differ only with respect to the relative durability of the leading empires and the length of the intervals between them. South Asia occupies one end of this spectrum: relatively short-lived imperial formations alternated with sometimes substantial phases of abatement. East Asia is located at the opposite end, characterized for the most part by highly dominant and fairly durable (multicentennial) empires that were separated by increasingly brief periods of reconfiguration. The MENA region lies in between, with empires not as pervasively dominant as in East Asia yet more resilient than in South Asia.

Smaller regions in other parts of the world add little of substance to this picture. Polities in the Pre-Columbian New World operated on a much smaller demographic scale. In Mesoamerica, uncertainties surround the political reach of Teotihuacan and the nature of the Toltec polity. In the end, the eventual ascent of the Aztec empire and subsequent universal Spanish colonial rule across Central America snuffed out any semblance of polycentrism for hundreds of years. In the Andean region, the extent of Tiwanaku and Wari rule in the second half of the first millennium remains unclear. A period of fragmentation in the early second millennium preceded the rise of the Inka empire that captured what must have been a very large share of the total population of western South America until it too was absorbed into the global Spanish colonial empire.

Pre-Columbian cultures generally had not had enough time to reach the point at which they were capable of sustaining large empires: increasingly dominant polities had only just emerged when the Europeans arrived, an event that arguably preempted what might well have been the beginning of a pattern of concentration and fission similar to that found in several of the Old World macro-regions.

Southeast Asia is also a much smaller region: up to the nineteenth century it was roughly an order of magnitude less populous than Europe, South Asia, and East Asia. Since the later stages of the first millennium CE, episodes of imperial expansion alternated with times of more widespread polycentrism. On the continent, the Angkorian Khmer empire occupied a dominant position from the ninth through the fourteenth centuries, followed by several coexisting major powers (Ayutthaya, Khmer and Lan Xang), short-lived Taungoo Burmese expansion in the late sixteenth century, more intense fragmentation in the eighteenth century, and dominance by the Rattanakosin kingdom of Siam around 1800.

In Malaya and Indonesia, the Srivijaya empire exercised hegemony from the seventh through the thirteenth centuries, succeeded on the islands by the Singhasari empire of the thirteenth century and the Majapahit empire of the fourteenth and fifteenth centuries. Dutch colonial rule eventually took over in the eighteenth and nineteenth centuries.

Yet anything resembling hegemonic empire was always conspicuously absent from this region. Even during the most noteworthy peaks, demographic imperial dominance remained rather limited: perhaps one-third of the region's population under Angkor and Rattanakosin, and less for other imperial ventures. State formation never quite bridged the divide between continental Southeast Asia north of the Malayan peninsula and the Malay archipelago. In this respect, this region represents an outlier, different from MENA, South Asia, and East Asia as well as Mesoamerica and the Andes thanks to the absence of hegemonic empire, but also different from Europe in that this type of empire did not arise even once. In chapter 8, I consider whether the sheltered peripheral position of this region contributed to this outcome.

For ecological reasons, other parts of the world never supported large imperial states. Only a few substantial regions have thus produced sufficient relevant information to warrant systematic investigation. Because of this, our sample is just barely large enough to allow some basic generalization. What does emerge from the record is a widespread pattern of highly dominant universal empire alternating with periods of deconcentration. This back and forth is well documented in the Middle East and North Africa and in South Asia, and to a lesser degree in the more developed parts of the Americas. East Asia likewise belongs in this category, even as near-monopolistic empire increasingly crowded out other arrangements.

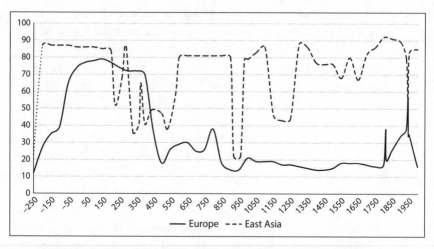

FIGURE 1.11 Proportion of the population of Europe and East Asia claimed by the largest polity in each region, 250 BCE–2000 CE (in percent).

KEY: See Figures 1.4 and 1.8.

Apart from Southeast Asia—a smaller and historically far less populous region—Europe has been the only genuine exception to this norm. European state formation followed a uniquely truncated trajectory marked by a one-time transition from hegemonic empire to intense and persistent polycentrism. There is a systematic difference between Europe and the other three macro-regions, and most strikingly so between Europe and East Asia (figure 1.11).

On one stylized count, the number of effectively independent polities in Latin Europe grew from about three dozen at the end of late antiquity to more than a hundred by 1300, compared to between just one and a handful in China proper, and this gap would be even larger if we included vassal states. It is this contrast that we need to explain.[18]

PART II
Why Rome?

CHAPTER 2

Core

EXPLAINING EMPIRE

IF POLITICAL unification on a very large scale proved to be so rare in Europe, why did the Roman empire exist at all? Were the circumstances of its creation so exceptional that no later state in this part of the world could hope to replicate Rome's success?

Imperial state formation results from the interplay of two components: a core or metropole with the capability to expand, and a periphery that is susceptible to domination. In this chapter and in chapters 3 and 4, I argue that Rome owed its ascent to a fortuitously favorable concatenation of conditions in both core and periphery that were either unique or remained very rare in European and Mediterranean history overall.[1]

In developing this argument, I focus first on the properties of the core—on how it was constituted and how it managed to scale up from very modest beginnings (chapter 2). I then turn to the highly diverse regions in western Afroeurasia that gradually succumbed to Roman power: here the key question is why this became an almost universal outcome (chapter 3). Finally, I also consider counterfactuals: How much would have had to be different for Roman imperialism to be checked by any of its neighbors (chapter 4)? Each of these three approaches addresses the same questions: to what extent the rise of Rome was rooted in the structural characteristics of both core and periphery, and what role more contingent developments played in shaping this process.[2]

NOT BUILT IN A DAY

Getting off the Ground

Just how far back in time do we need to go to identify the roots of Rome's eventual success? This question is in no small measure a purely theoretical one: the more we move into the early stages of Roman history, the less there is to see. The genesis of the Roman state is poorly documented. The surviving tradition was produced centuries later by writers who need not have known much more than we do now (and, as far as the archaeological record is concerned, indeed knew much less), and any modern reconstruction critically depends on how much weight we are prepared to accord to particular elements of that questionable tradition. Short of complete agnosticism—by no means an unreasonable position—the most defensible approach is one that relies as little as possible on reported specifics and seeks to produce nothing more than a bare outline of the likely trajectory of state formation, spruced up with a hearty dose of conjecture.

One thing we do know for sure is that the Roman polity emerged in an environment that was completely bereft of the type of sizable imperial tributary states that had sprung up in the Near East in the third millennium BCE. Despite long-standing economic and cultural contacts with the outside world, in terms of state formation the Italian peninsula in the first half of the first millennium BCE remained a world apart, characterized by city-states and similarly small-scale communities. Even Greek state-building along its southern fringe had not yet produced larger multicity states of the kind that first formed in the Aegean and in Sicily in the fifth century BCE (figure 2.1).

Rome was located on the river Tiber, the largest Italian river south of the Po, at the interstices of two emergent city-state cultures, the Latins to the south and the Etruscans to the north. Albeit part of a contact zone

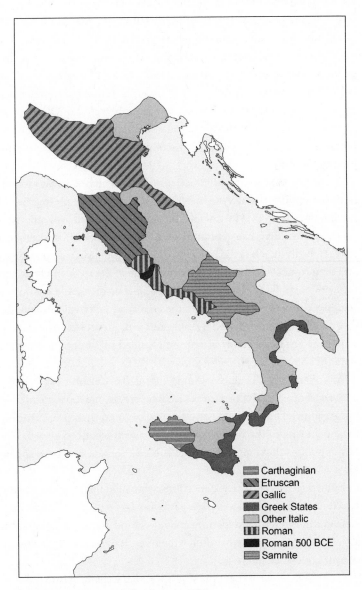

FIGURE 2.1 Italy in the early fourth century BCE.

between two different language spheres, the settlement that became the city of Rome primarily belonged to the Latin side, part of a culture of politically independent communities with shared ethnic affiliation, language, material culture, and joint cultic activities and sanctuaries. The product of a process of nucleation and absorption of smaller rivals that commenced in the eighth century BCE, around twenty city-states that are known to us by name came to form the core region of Old Latium. Their boundaries were initially porous: later rights of trans-polity intermarriage, movement, and contracts may well reflect this earlier fluidity.[3]

According to a recent and attractive model—which is the best we can hope for—military enterprises had originally been the prerogative of mobile clans (visible in aristocratic burials accompanied by weaponry), a hybrid Latin-Etruscan gentilicial warrior aristocracy whose members only gradually attached themselves to the emergent urban communities and their respective hinterlands in the course of the sixth and fifth centuries BCE. As these clans settled and became incorporated into urban centers, control over land became more important, and traditional raiding for plunder was augmented by conquest and protection of territory. This slow process of consolidation produced the independent city-states of Latium in their mature form.[4]

A similar process of state-building unfolded in neighboring Tuscany in the seventh and sixth centuries BCE where the most powerful polities swallowed and often destroyed smaller ones, thereby expanding their own reach. The final outcome was a well-balanced system of a dozen polities that ranged from 500 square kilometers to 1,500 square kilometers in size.[5]

Embeddedness in a city-state culture was a defining feature of early Rome and of Roman state-building later on. More than two dozen city-state cultures have been identified across world history, ranging from some comprising a mere handful of members to the sprawling network of over 1,000 ancient Greek *poleis*.[6]

A city-state environment presents formidable challenges to political scaling-up: closely attuned to one another, individual parties are well positioned to balance against any of their peers that seek to expand at their expense or threaten their independence. Outright absorption of mature city-states by others thus remained a relatively rare outcome, even if it sometimes worked, most notably for late medieval Florence, Milan, and Venice.

More often than not, however, scaling-up occurred in a more subtle fashion through the formation of alliances and leagues that facilitated cooperation without formal domination. Such arrangements mitigated structural tensions between often tightly knit civic communities and the benefits of pooling resources, especially for military purposes. The Athenian empire of the fifth century BCE, initially established as an alliance against the Persian Achaemenid empire, is a classic example (and fortuitously contemporaneous with early Roman alliance-building in central Italy); the Triple Alliance of Tenochtitlan, Texcoco, and Tlacopan in 1428 CE that gave rise to the Aztec empire is another. If such leagues managed to survive long enough, they might turn into more unitary states, such as Switzerland or the Netherlands.[7]

Capitalizing on an early size advantage, Rome's expansion followed the alliance template. For reasons that are lost in the mists of time, by 500 BCE Rome had already grown into one of the largest cities in central Italy and the largest city-state in Latium. Later rituals connected to borders may suggest that the nascent Roman community claimed a modest 150 to 200 square kilometers in the seventh century BCE. Yet by the late sixth century BCE, its territory appears to have grown to some 820 square kilometers, fully a third of the 2,350 square kilometers controlled by the fifteen Latin city-states that had not been taken over by outsiders. This made it more than twice as large as that of the runner-up at the time. By local standards, Rome's putative population, estimated at around 30,000, was substantial.

The much later Roman tradition ascribes this early advantage to aggressive expansion under the "kings," and more specifically to the presence of Etruscan rulers in the sixth century BCE. In the absence of reliable evidence, this version of events is impossible to substantiate but does not seem implausible a priori: after all, Rome was not only located right at the margins of the Etruscan city-state cluster but also resembled Etruscan city-states in terms of the size of their urban centers and their territories. Moreover, foreign rule would seem a rather odd thing to invent later on, at a time when Rome was already firmly in charge.

Regardless of whether early Rome outgrew its Latin peers thanks to Etruscan leadership—reflecting the power of the ethnically hybrid central Italian warrior aristocracy of the period—or because exposure to productive tensions along a cultural frontier had boosted its capacity for collective action, its close proximity to Etruria appears to have accelerated Roman state-building. Its unique riverine location that allowed it to benefit from trade and access to coastal salt deposits may well have been another contributing factor.[8]

Around 500 BCE, Rome found itself in a tantalizing position—more powerful than any other Latin city-state but contained by them if they made common cause, and roughly comparable to any one of its Etruscan neighbors but greatly outmatched by them in the aggregate. In the context of this double containment, breakout could best be achieved by means of alliance-building in response to some shared threat. This incentive presented itself in the form of groups from the Apennine highlands that pushed into the fertile plains to the west. Similar developments, driven by population growth and improved cooperation, are attested for other parts of Italy as local powers put growing pressure on coastal Greek cities.

By 500 BCE, five of the twenty Latin city-states had already been taken over by the Volscians. The remaining Latin polities spent the first half of the fifth century BCE engaged in warfare against them and similar opponents. As the leading Latin polity, Rome occupied a leadership position in this coalition. We cannot tell for sure whether this had been achieved by force of arms (as later Roman sources would have it) or in a more consensual fashion, but it ultimately does not really matter.[9]

What does matter is the overall outcome: cooperation among independent micro-states and Roman leadership that was likely limited to the military domain. This coordination of manpower successfully checked non-Latin challengers. Although these conflicts might best be described as a raiding and counterraiding for the purpose of acquiring booty, they also resulted in shifts in the control over arable land: about a dozen joint settlements were created in areas taken over by the Latin alliance. Both movable plunder and real estate were shared out under Roman supervision.

This process is discernible only in the barest of outlines, but unless we are willing to assume that the entire tradition was merely an anachronistic back-projection of later events (which is by no means impossible but does not seem particularly plausible), it provided an early blueprint for later Roman expansion. It established a mode of moderately asymmetric cooperation in which Rome exercised a degree of military hegemony without abrogating local self-rule, and whose raison d'être was joint war-making that yielded resources that could be shared, and benefited farming commoners as well as aristocratic leaders who were competing for status by displaying martial prowess and rewarding their retinues.[10]

Alongside coalition warfare, from the second half of the fifth century BCE, Rome also increasingly engaged in expansionary moves on its own account. This process commenced at a time when military participation was opened up to the agricultural population and what had been a confederation of warring lords merged into a single state and army that pursued community-based objectives of territorial expansion. There is no sign, in Rome or elsewhere in Latium, of one-man rule: political and military affairs were run by groups of aristocrats who led their followers and bargained among themselves.

In the Roman case, conflict with Veii, the closest Etruscan city-state, appears to have provided a powerful incentive to further state consolidation. This prolonged struggle culminated in Veii's defeat and the annexation of its entire territory in the 390s BCE. The surviving population was absorbed into Roman society, most likely through a variety of means from enslavement to enfranchisement.[11]

This episode was an important step forward because it provided Rome with resources from outside its own city-state cluster where it was locked into cooperative agreements. By then Rome controlled over 1,500 square kilometers, slightly more than all the other Latin polities combined, and whatever its earlier position had been, it was from then on effectively assured of hegemonic status. Any remaining constraints were removed sixty years later when a revolt of the Latins was suppressed in the early 330s BCE.

Rome's advances beyond Latium were only briefly interrupted by a raid of Gallic warriors from the Po Valley who sacked Rome before moving on. Even though this setback does not seem to have caused any major damage, it arguably served as a further catalyst, had one been needed, for scaled-up military commitments: heightened Athenian militarism in the wake of the Persian sackings of Athens in the early fifth century BCE represents a plausible analogy. More generally, repeated Gallic incursions into the Italian peninsula in the fourth century BCE likely created interest in military alliance-building, especially among the Etruscans and Umbrians who were more exposed to the Celts than Rome itself.[12]

Overall, in the first third of the fourth century BCE, several factors converged in furnishing Rome with enhanced resources and capabilities that helped it embark on ever-widening expansion in central Italy: access to additional land and manpower, strengthened hegemony over its fellow Latins, the shock of the Celtic assault, and the successful resolution of domestic political and social conflicts.

At the same time, the incorporation of Veii pushed Rome closer to the limit of the strategy of directly absorbing defeated neighbors. City-states with participatory institutions such as popular assemblies that are focused on a single center cannot easily continue to function as such once their territories exceed a few thousand square kilometers. Historically, further growth was sometimes made possible by the shift to a more unitary territorial state that turned former rival centers into subordinate units. Alternatively, the creation of peripheral layers of control and cooperation helped preserve existing and often highly inclusive institutions at the core. Late medieval Milan, Florence, and Venice are examples of the former approach; classical Athens and Carthage of the latter. Rome adopted a formally particularly parsimonious version of the layered model that allowed it to coordinate military activity on an increasingly large scale without having to invest in extensive governmental structures.

Co-optation and Mobilization

As Rome's expansion gathered momentum over the course of the fourth century BCE, some of the freshly subordinated communities were enfranchised—with or without the right to vote in Roman assemblies—but retained local management as self-governing *municipia*, while others became allies bound by bilateral treaties. Citizenship came to be concentrated in central Italy whereas allied status was more common to the north and south. By 264 BCE, Rome had concluded more than 150 treaties with individual polities across the peninsula. Their bilateral character helped preserve Roman leadership, placing it in the center of a rimless wheel from which spokes reached out to individual peripheral entities without connecting them into a coherent whole: after 338 BCE, Latin city-states that retained allied status were even forbidden from maintaining official relations with one another (figure 2.2).[13]

Regardless of their formal standing within this system, the one thing all involved parties had in common was the obligation to contribute military manpower under Roman leadership and to fund military operations: citizens paid a direct tax (*tributum*) specifically for this purpose while allied communities were expected to support their own levies.[14]

Scale and mobilization intensity were the two critical variables. Scaling-up was achieved by aggressive co-optation. Unlike in Greek city-states, where citizenship was often viewed as a prized privilege, Rome readily bestowed citizen status on outsiders, many of whom were defeated former enemies. Also unlike among the Greeks, citizenship thus became "divorced from ethnicity or geographical location." The effectively oligarchic nature of Roman government appears to have sufficiently devalued citizen status to ensure this unusual openness. The fact that Romans who resettled in most colonies forfeited citizenship also reflects the relatively low value of formal membership in the Roman state. Allied polities retained their existing governmental arrangements and merely contributed military resources without being incorporated into the republic.[15]

Ongoing advances were thus rooted in Rome's two-pronged strategy of accessing manpower on a large scale with only minimal intervention

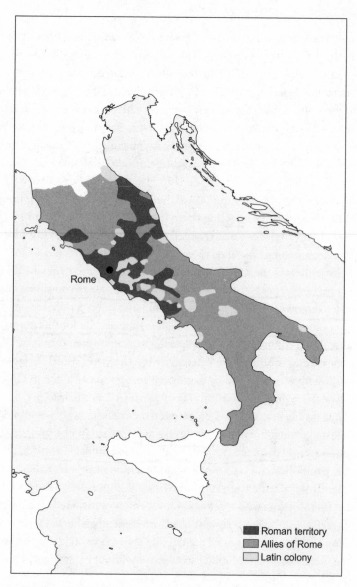

Rome

Roman territory
Allies of Rome
Latin colony

FIGURE 2.2 Political statuses in Italy in the third century BCE.

in local affairs. But scale was only half of the story: the other was a high military participation rate that made the most of Italy's demographic assets. The latter was achieved by a combination of low levels of taxation of material resources and intense exploitation of cheap military labor.[16]

Financial taxation of the Roman citizenry was light and intimately tied to warfare. Annual tax rates are very poorly known but undoubtedly very low, perhaps not more than 0.1 percent of the assessed value of personal assets, functionally equivalent to an annual income tax of not more than a few percent. The modest income tax of 3 percent the U.S. Revenue Act of 1862 imposed on middle-class citizens of the Union to help fund the Civil War may serve as a suitable if distant analogy.[17]

On occasion, these taxes were even refunded out of the proceeds of war booty, thus turning them into something more akin to loans. Allies owed no direct taxes to Rome, presumably relying on their own—undocumented—domestic revenues to sustain their military contingents. Low or no taxation generally benefited the local upper classes, boosting their willingness to follow Rome's lead. Conscription also lacked any progressive dimension, and was in fact regressive insofar as it favored older and thus more affluent men who were less likely to be called up.[18]

Apart from tolls and rents on public land, a large share of state revenue was obtained through plunder, later supplemented by indemnities extorted from defeated opponents. Direct taxes in money and kind only began to flow more freely once Rome acquired provinces outside Italy, a process that did not commence until the second half of the third century BCE. For quite a few generations before then, the use of military labor could steadily increase simply because it was relatively cheap: conscripts regularly supplied their own equipment and received very modest compensation for their service.[19]

Given high military participation rates, conscription was by far the largest share of the tax burden placed on Romans and their Italian allies. Men of property—often mere smallholders—were expected to serve for six or seven years, and even more in periods of military exigency. This estimate comes with a generous margin of error: while Roman army strength is fairly well documented, the size of the underlying

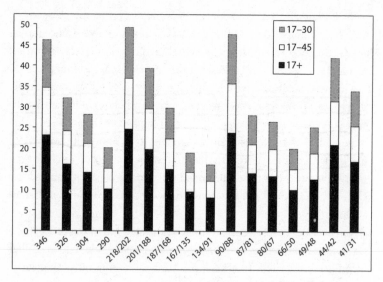

FIGURE 2.3 Approximate military mobilization rates of the Roman citizenry, 346–31 BCE (in percentage of men in a particular age group). *Source*: Scheidel 2006: 222, fig. 8.

population remains the subject of debate. Even so, relatively conservative assumptions about Italian population numbers convey a powerful sense of the extent to which Rome committed young and sometimes even middle-aged men to military endeavors (figure 2.3).[20]

The resultant figures are certainly very high but not impossible: Rome's suggested peak mobilization rate during the life-and-death struggle with Carthage in the late third century BCE matched that of the Confederate States during the American Civil War, in both cases excluding slaves from the calculation. Had the population of ancient Italy been somewhat larger than has traditionally been believed, military mobilization levels would be somewhat lower without altering the overall pattern. Even far less plausible, much higher population estimates would merely lower these levels from extravagant to extremely high. And in all this it is worth emphasizing that such mobilization rates were sustained for hundreds of years, and not merely during specific wars that lasted only years or decades.[21]

Why did Rome pursue this course? Several factors came into play. One is that taxing labor via conscription was a practice well suited to the economically underdeveloped environment of central Italy, especially in its mountainous interior. This favored what Charles Tilly calls a "coercion-intensive" mode of revenue extraction, in which "rulers squeezed the means of war from their own populations and others they conquered." What makes the Roman case noteworthy is that the single-minded focus on military labor (most of it self-sustaining infantry) obviated the need for (again in Tilly's words) concomitantly "building massive structures of extraction in the process"—an important qualification to a model designed to explain much later European state formation. Moreover, because the extent of military technology did not vary greatly across much of the Italian peninsula, there was no strong competitive demand to develop forces that were much more sophisticated than militias of peasant infantry, such as armored horsemen or large navies.[22]

Wealthier societies existed at the margins, in coastal Etruria and especially in the Hellenic south. From the 260s BCE onward, these polities were to provide critical support in establishing an ambitious naval program that ensured Rome's precocious Mediterranean supremacy, which I discuss below. However, by the time Rome came to engage more seriously with most of these polities in the preceding decades of the third century BCE, its coercion-intensive expansion elsewhere in the peninsula ensured that it did not need to engage in the generous bargaining that characterizes Tilly's "capital-intensive" mode of state-building. Instead, Rome was able to shift toward the hybrid "capitalized coercion mode" that 2,000 years later worked so well in early modern England and France, marrying coercive features with the smooth integration of rich sources of capital.

In addition to environmental conditions, Roman strategies of expansion were shaped by the existence of a tried and proven mechanism for scaling-up: the fifth-century-BCE model of military cooperation with Rome's Latin allies. Versions of this template were subsequently applied all over Italy. From this perspective, the formal incorporation of effectively autonomous communities into the Roman citizen body was the only novel addition to an old recipe.

It has been suggested that the open-ended Roman conscription system served to drain potentially dangerous manpower away from subordinated communities, and that other forms of tribute might have been perceived as too onerous and alienating even where they were feasible in economic terms. Expanding this line of reasoning, it is worth asking whether Rome's approach might not have been at least in part conditioned by its relative weakness vis-à-vis its competitors.[23]

This perspective requires some detachment from the vision of an assertive Rome that we owe to much later sources composed with the benefit of hindsight. The least invasive way of scaling up was to leave local structures intact and thereby reduce friction. Emphasis on taxing military labor maximized the honor of co-opted groups, which we may assume to have been of considerable importance in the martial environment of Iron Age Italy. It was bound to be more honorable for young men to fight (in the case of allies even under their own local commanders) and for the wealthy to pay (or lend) funds explicitly to support these young men on their campaigns than for everyone to be asked to hand over a tithe or poll tax to Roman tax collectors. The sharing out of spoils among combatants, discussed below, likewise cast them in the role of respected partners.

Finally, the Roman mode of co-optation succeeded because it enhanced capacity for collective action at the local level. Instead of disarming former enemies, Rome not only actively encouraged them to maintain their previous warlike disposition but institutionalized this quality even more solidly by routinizing it as a key obligation to a larger network of communities. It is true that this strategy was not without risk, as it augmented Rome's military capabilities even as it preserved the option of organized armed resistance. It speaks to the system's remarkable success that the latter did not occur on a grand scale until a number of the Italian allies revolted in 91 BCE. However, this episode also demonstrates that the option of armed resistance had remained viable even after many generations of cooperative expansionism, which in turn suggests that it must have been at least as viable before.

In mobilizing the linguistically diverse population of peninsular Italy for seemingly never-ending war-making, the Roman ruling class did in fact have the wolf by the ears. This introduced a latent risk of fission that needed to be managed in a way that turned it into a strength: the structural instability of the multilayered system of Roman control sustained dynamics that go a long way in accounting for the persistent drive for military commitments that I discuss in the following sections.[24]

Integration and the Nature of the Roman Commonwealth

The Roman literary tradition and much of modern scholarship that builds on it tends to view the metropolitan participatory political, social, and cultural institutions of the Roman Republic as a source of civic cohesion. In reality, war-making was by far the most potent force of integration in a very parsimoniously structured system. Among Roman citizens, military service was of vastly greater significance in fostering a shared identity and collective action than participation in the political process or public rituals and spectacles. Military participation rates greatly exceeded levels of involvement in metropolitan activities.

Popular political input, nominally critical because citizen assemblies had the last word on electing officials, passing laws, entering treaties, and declaring war, was strikingly limited in scope. From very early on, only a few percent of all eligible citizens would have fit into the space used for legislative assemblies, and the share of those who would have been physically capable of attending electoral gatherings in a much larger area (even assuming that it was in fact used instead of smaller ones) declined from less than half of the eligible citizenry in 338 BCE to maybe one-sixth in 225 BCE. Moreover, the fact that capacity constraints were never mentioned as a cause for concern even on particularly high-profile occasions suggests that actual participation rates regularly fell well short of these theoretical maxima.[25]

Socialization into the (male) Roman citizenry occurred in the first instance through exposure to years of military service from muster to campaign. The muster, held in Rome, was an elaborate ritual designed to bring together men from different parts of Italy. The more the Roman domain expanded, the more Romans would never have set foot in the capital city—but those who did most commonly did so as recruits. The selection process for military units sought to intermingle men from different backgrounds by breaking up local community ties. Prolonged service inculcated a shared sense of "Roman" as opposed to local identity, as well as solidarity and social discipline.[26]

For the Italian allies, excluded as they were from metropolitan politics until their eventual enfranchisement in the 80s BCE, military mobilization was of even greater importance in forging ties to the Roman state. As allied polities took care of their own levies and their soldiers served in local units separate from those of the Romans, opportunities for effective integration were much more limited. Cultural assimilation would primarily have taken place among the officer corps, whose members had to learn Latin and routinely interact with Roman commanders. However, in view of the oligarchic character of these societies, this was not a negligible matter.

More generally, formal subordination to Roman command drove home the message of Roman supremacy. The practice of Roman and allied units serving side by side on joint campaigns engendered productive rivalries as they vied for success and glory. By managing Roman and allied troops as unequal but similarly important partners, this system both cemented Roman leadership and promoted cooperation against common opponents that created a sense of mutual dependence and translated to shared material benefits from plunder and land assignments.[27]

In fact, inasmuch as any significant amount of integration occurred outside military campaigns, it was in the closely related context of colonial foundations and land distributions, which were a direct outgrowth of continued belligerence and not only served to reward faithful service, as described below, but also created hybrid communities of Romans and Italian allies. This process had already begun in the fifth century BCE and peaked during the wars of Italian unification from the 300s to the 260s BCE. Further schemes were undertaken in the early second century BCE and once again and on a much more massive scale between the 80s and the 20s BCE when over half a million people were resettled within and beyond Italy. All of these movements unfolded as the result of major military conflicts.[28]

Outside central Italy, military-induced integration preceded any broader social or cultural convergence by a wide margin: the latter commenced mostly in the first century BCE. And even within central Italy itself, military participation ruled supreme. There, the enfranchisement of local populations and the establishment of numerous colonial settlements created a more homogeneous bloc that more readily adopted the Latin language and came to coalesce into the more homogeneous heart of the Roman war machine, powerful enough to keep more peripheral allies attached to the system and ultimately capable of overcoming any open resistance.[29]

The Roman state that arose from these arrangements was one narrowly focused on warfare and little else. It serves as an almost ideal-typical manifestation of Tilly's four essential state activities: state-making (checking competitors within the area claimed by the state), war-making (attacking rivals outside it), protection (checking rivals of principal allies), and extraction (obtaining the means required to undertake the other three).[30]

In the Roman case, these activities were exercised in ways to sustain ongoing aggression directed against external targets. Low-friction co-optation of local communities reduced the need for the violent checking of internal competitors: only the southern Italian periphery of allies frayed on multiple occasions. Protection did not take much effort since local elites by and large took care of their own business: Roman interventions on their behalf are only very rarely documented.

As already noted, extraction respected local traditions and honor. In this environment, auxiliary state functions such as adjudication, distribution, and production were even less prominent: local arbitration and contracting for public services were paramount, and distribution (of land and other resources) was for a long time closely tied to war-making. Moreover, although Rome did indeed act as a "protection-selling enterprise" for its client states in Italy, it did not create anything like a monopoly on violence in Italy: the autonomy and massive military contribution of its allies alone made that goal illusory.[31]

The evolution of the Roman Republic exemplifies with exceptional clarity the adage that war made states and states made war. Roman political institutions arose as spin-offs of military activity, most notably the senior state offices that were principally concerned with military command and logistical support functions. The tremendous nominal powers of the most senior officials could only be reconciled with collective aristocratic control and citizen rights because these magistrates spent little time in Rome itself and so much in the field. Civilian governance was largely confined to the metropolitan core. Elsewhere, local boards took care of a growing share of the citizen population.[32]

Two factors rendered a larger ambitious apparatus both redundant and undesirable. One was the aforementioned concentration on the provision of violence at the expense of other governmental objectives. Oligarchic reluctance to strengthen centralized state capacity was the other. Eager to fill their own pockets and to prevent the ascent of leaders who might use state resources to seize power, aristocratic officials heavily leaned on patrimonial and clientelistic resources to fulfill their appointed tasks.[33]

As a result, public good provision in the form of civilian infrastructure other than temples (which had been sponsored by individual leaders) largely had to wait until provincial tribute began to flow in the second century BCE, and reached a large scale only in the first century BCE and mostly in the capital as political competition intensified and the aristocratic consensus collapsed. During the formative period and peak of the Roman war system from the fourth century BCE into the early second century BCE, by contrast, the parsimonious nature of the state was successfully maintained.

Adaptations in the Core

As far as we can tell, aristocratic families had always played a major role in running the Roman state, and were firmly in charge from the fifth century BCE onward. As Rome extended its influence into the Italian peninsula, a homogeneous ruling class of a few dozen noble houses emerged. Elected or at least confirmed by the citizenry, their members took turns holding public office. Most senior leadership positions were limited to a one-year term and were often collegial in nature in order to constrain individual ambition and ensure a degree of consensual decision-making.

For much of the Republican period, the four sources of social power—ideological, economic, military, and political—were unusually tightly bundled together: members of the same narrow elite acted as political leaders, military commanders, and priests, and controlled the largest private fortunes. The presence of a powerful deliberative body of peers, the senate, held individual aristocrats in check, and popular assemblies of adult male citizens (graduated for wealth) served as a carefully managed arbitration and legitimation device for intra-aristocratic competition and the state's military ventures. This well-balanced system remained stable into the late second century BCE, throughout the period of primary expansion across the Mediterranean basin.[34]

Expansion of military activity coincided with and was arguably sustained by the abolition of debt bondage for Roman citizens in the late fourth century BCE. This is best understood as a bargaining outcome designed to mobilize more men for war. Changes in equipment also allowed poorer strata to serve. The concurrent loss of labor was offset by the growing number of slaves obtained in war. Later sources suggest that chattel slavery already played an important role as early as the fourth century BCE, and records for mass enslavement during campaigns are available from the 290s BCE onward. This put Rome on a path to becoming what was by some measures the largest slave society in world history.[35]

In these various ways, Rome managed to combine a shared sense of identity with strong stratification: each class contributed to the war effort according to their means and standing. The influence of belief systems likewise merits notice. War-making and religion were closely conjoined. The leadership generously invested in the religious sphere: a massive boom in temple building in the city of Rome took place precisely during those decades when the Roman state gradually established control over the Italian peninsula.[36]

The Wages of War: Compliance and Rewards

What were the incentives for unceasing war? We need to look at this from different angles, considering the interests of leaders and commoners. The Roman aristocracy was highly militarized. While its likely origins in roving warrior clans may have been a contributing factor, the institutional setup of the mature Republican system was crucial in maintaining and reinforcing this martial disposition. In the absence of regular tribute-taking, the principal source of public elite income was leadership in war, and annual rotation of office restricted opportunities to benefit materially from these positions and to gain glory that could be instrumentalized in subsequent electioneering and the enhancement of one's family's status.

Over time, this gave rise to a pervasive culture of prowess in war. By the second century BCE, ten years of military service—probably in actual campaigns or in camps rather than merely pro forma—were considered a precondition for running for public office: thus, hopeful aristocrats would have spent their entire late teens and much of their twenties in the field. A strong warrior ethos permeated the ruling elite, inculcated through prolonged apprenticing, kept alive by family tradition and religious sanction, and avidly invoked in public displays: success in war was "their central criterion of achievement." The triumphal procession granted to victorious commanders consequently represented a pinnacle of personal accomplishment.[37]

Elite enrichment and the quest for prestige were thus critically predicated on the pursuit of military success, and were only gradually complemented by involvement in (at least at times) more peaceful provincial administration that opened up novel revenue streams. This shift occurred only once Rome had already eclipsed its most serious competitors: as a result, by the time martial norms and expectations began to be relaxed, the traditional war machine had already been in place long enough to achieve hegemony in western Eurasia.[38]

It is less clear why the leaders of the allied Italian polities complied with Roman demands for military support as fully as they appear to have done. After all, they found themselves excluded from the lucrative state offices in Rome itself. We can only guess that martial prowess played an important role in the allies' domestic affairs as well, providing impetus for active engagement. Moreover, the Roman state both directly and indirectly supported these local ruling classes. As already noted, constraints on taxation other than conscription inherently favored the well-off, making them more willing to follow Rome's lead even as their fellow countrymen bled on the battlefield.[39]

Yet in a system of aggressive popular mobilization, the masses also had to be kept motivated. Quasi-voluntary compliance was essential as the Roman authorities lacked autonomous means of coercing their own citizens into military service: despite formal compulsion, resistance to serve could not easily be overcome.[40]

During the formative stages of Roman hegemony in peninsular Italy, the distribution of spoils went a long way in ensuring widespread popular support for war. Large tracts of land were seized from defeated enemies and assigned to Roman settlers. Tens of thousands of adult Roman men were resettled with their families. By 218 BCE, some 9,000 square kilometers of land had changed hands that way, and probably as much again had been turned into state-owned land (*ager publicus*) and leased out or sold—overall a considerable portion of a peninsula of 125,000 square kilometers, not more than half of which could have been used for agriculture.[41]

In addition, colonization schemes in which both Romans and allies participated fostered cohesion by spreading benefits more widely. Between 338 and 264 BCE, twenty joint (or "Latin") colonies were set up, mostly in central Italy. In total, these self-governing entities covered a further 7,000 square kilometers and 70,000 adult men with their families. Located on conquered land, they came to form bastions of Roman control.[42]

But not all previous residents were routinely killed or enslaved: since the extent of *ager publicus* exceeded recorded assignments, we may assume that part of the original owners retained access to their land, albeit without title. It is hardly a coincidence that concerns about debt, which feature prominently in later sources for the period from the 380s to the 340s BCE, mostly faded once this colonization movement got under way. Some scholars have drawn attention to analogies between these

Roman schemes and land distributions to loyal soldiers organized by the kingdom of Qin in the Warring States period: in both cases, large numbers of smallholders were successfully induced to bear an extraordinarily heavy military burden.[43]

Alongside conquered land, allied soldiers also received a share of movable plunder and expected to be granted the share of campaign bonuses as Roman citizen troops. Beyond tangible economic rewards that were assigned to individuals, allied polities obtained valuable protection—not necessarily so much from credible outside enemies that soon disappeared from view but from neighboring communities. The Roman alliance system brought about lasting security at home, or at the very least suppressed old rivalries.[44]

The Logic of Continuous War

Reduced to essentials, the Roman-Italian cooperation system had not only been set up for the purpose of war-making but also required war to be successfully maintained and to yield benefits to different constituents. In this environment, in which conscription was the most important element of state revenue, forgoing war was tantamount to granting a tax rebate. Moreover, inasmuch as the Roman state depended on booty and war-related taxes as its main sources of nonlabor revenue, cessation of hostilities would have deprived it of vital resources.[45]

And although a shift to routine taxation of economic output—the default mode of tributary states—might in theory have reduced this structural need for continuous warfare, it would not have been easy to implement change on this grand scale. The high degree of effective local autonomy of heavily armed subordinates and allies alone would have posed a massive obstacle to the introduction of generalized harvest or poll taxes. In fact, the more successful the Roman model turned out to be, the more the path of least resistance was to rely increasingly on external material resources by expanding beyond Italy proper, resources that in turn drove further expansion.

From an institutional perspective, the Roman state was so poorly integrated beyond its urban center that in the absence of war, citizenship would not have meant much for most Romans. This was even truer of the allied polities, whose sole obligation lay in contributing military manpower to Roman campaigns. The entire system thus stood and fell with war: without ongoing war, key relationships would erode. Various seemingly undesirable consequences might have followed.

In the short term, spoils and opportunities to gain glory would have dried up. Over the longer run, existing ties based on military cooperation might have atrophied or, worse, alienated allies and even rural Roman citizens who lacked a shared experience of military service under metropolitan Roman command. Not only would alliances by treaty have been robbed of their most powerful activating impulse, peripheral Roman citizenship might likewise have been hollowed out. It is therefore hardly an exaggeration to say, as John North once did, that "war-making was the life-blood of the Roman confederation in Italy."[46]

Roman-style expansionism evinces attributes of a pyramid scheme: "The Roman system has been compared to a criminal operation which compensates its victims by enrolling them in the gang and inviting them to share the proceeds of future robberies." Success in turning former enemies into fellow citizens or allies depended in no small measure on Rome's ability to access new resources to reward those who had just been robbed—a dynamic that made it rather difficult to abandon robbing altogether without incurring serious political costs.[47]

This in turn makes it seem rather redundant to worry too much about the putative causes of individual conflicts: the underlying structural incentives were always present, skewing political decision-making in a predetermined direction. And as we will see below, this belligerent modus operandi survived for a while, even as it no longer produced any benefits other than reproducing established practices.[48]

The Sustainability of Continuous War

It was not enough for relentless warmongering to be structurally desirable—it also needed to be sustainable in the long run. Years of military service could readily be accommodated within the life cycle of farm households that were able to tolerate the absence of a son, at least in the aggregate if not in every single case. Later epigraphic evidence suggests that Roman men did not normally marry until their late twenties. To the extent that this was true across Republican Italy, Roman generals could avail themselves of a large pool of underemployed and unmarried young men. Only in extreme cases would older family men have to be drafted as well.[49]

Taking the demographic argument one step further, it has been argued that steady casualties may have helped contain population pressure. The culling of young men and the concomitant inflow of resources won in war increased per capita income, whereas an end of war would have put an end to both. In the later stages of the Republican period, even as the novel opportunities offered by accelerating urbanization and the growth of the slave economy changed many Romans' calculus of choice, military mass mobilization was successfully sustained for another century by relying on recruits from low-income backgrounds and by extending service duration through creeping professionalization.[50]

Slave labor did not merely enrich the elite, it also supported basic output functions while free commoners were tied up in military operations. This makes it easier to understand the extremely high mobilization rates shown above. In turn, militarism spurred on the expansion of slavery. Widespread popular military participation and large-scale migration to cities, colonies, and overseas militated against stable long-term employment (by self and others) in the civilian sector. In conjunction with rapid predatory capital accumulation among the elite and easy access to enslavable workers, these dynamics were highly conducive to investment in slave labor.[51]

By the first century BCE, there were probably more than a million slaves in Italy, perhaps a fifth of the total population. Unlike other large slave societies in history such as ancient Greece or the colonial Americas, Roman slavery, much like that in the nineteenth-century Sokoto caliphate, was to a substantial degree based on violent capture by domestic military forces, or at least until the sheer size of the servile population turned natural reproduction into the leading source.[52]

GROWTH AND TRIUMPH

Takeoff

What was the payoff of these expansion-bearing structures? Following the absorption of Veii and the shift to the incorporation of former enemies into the citizen body, wars against disunited opponents in central Italy pushed Roman power more deeply into Etruria. By 338 BCE, Rome had tightened its grip on its fellow Latins, most of whom were converted into Roman citizens.[53]

The stakes rose when the Romans engaged with a rival alliance system that had been built up by the Samnites in the south-central Apennines. Akin to the Romans and their martial orientation, their confederation was made up of upland villages tied to hill forts: politically fragmented, they submitted to unified leadership in war. The Samnites disposed of fewer economic resources than the Romans and their allies: urbanism was relatively underdeveloped, and they were unable to tap into capital-rich coastal areas, most notably Campania south of Latium. That region, controlled by rival Oscan conquest groups, instead joined the Roman side.[54]

This move in particular helped negate an initial advantage enjoyed by the Samnite federation, which had covered a much larger area with a larger population than the Romans and their allies. Even so, the incorporation of Campania and expansion elsewhere allowed the latter to catch up in terms of manpower (if not territory) by the time conflict commenced in earnest in the 320s BCE.

Rome's knack for successful co-optation reflects a major and arguably decisive difference between the two powers. Unlike the Romans, who aggressively invaded Samnite territory at great cost and gradually managed to encircle it with newfound allies and colonial settlements, the Samnitic league proved unable to project power, seize territory, or form lasting alliances beyond its home region. For all we can tell, its forces did not advance beyond raids and plunder even when they had the upper hand. By contrast, even though Rome struggled to operate in hostile upland terrain, it slowly added to its manpower both from within

TABLE 2.1 Expansion of the Roman state and alliance system in peninsular Italy, c. 500–225 BCE

Year (BCE)	Romans		Allies	
	Area (km²)	People	Area (km²)	People
490s	950	30,000?	1,400	?
390	1,580	> 50,000	1,400	?
346	2,000	125,000	4,000	190,000
338	5,500	350,000	3,000	140,000
326	5,900	365,000	3,600	165,000
304	6,300	400,000	17,700	520,000
290	15,300	570,000	38,600	970,000
264	26,800	900,000	99,000	2,200,000

Source: Mostly based on Afzelius 1942: 140–41, 153, 157, 169–71, 181, 190–92.

and without the Samnite domain until it eclipsed the latter by a wide margin.[55]

Dragging on from the 340s to the 280s BCE, this prolonged conflict was accompanied by Roman campaigns in central and northern peninsular Italy, as growing manpower facilitated simultaneous fighting on multiple fronts. By 295 BCE, the Romans were reportedly able to field 40,000 men, comparable to the largest armies ever mustered by Syracuse (the most powerful Greek city in the south) or the Macedonian kingdom.[56]

It is possible to track Rome's steady territorial and demographic expansion over time (table 2.1). While the geographical area under its control is reasonably well known, the corresponding population figures can be no more than rough estimates, and are perhaps somewhat on the low side.

Even allowing for substantial margins of error, this tabulation conveys a sense of the overall magnitude of change. Thus, Rome's power system grew from some 30,000 people at the beginning of the fifth century BCE to more than ten times as many by the mid-fourth century, 1.3 million by the end of the fourth century, and more than 3 million by the 260s BCE, when the entire peninsula had fallen under its sway. This adds to up to a hundredfold increase over the course of some 230 years. Accounting for 30 percent of the peninsula's population on a fifth of its land, by 264 BCE, the Roman citizenry formed a solid block across central Italy that separated the northern and southern allies, and thereby ensured Roman control from the inner line. Although some net population growth likely occurred during this period, most of this growth was caused by expansion. In demographic terms, this process was the equivalent of Iowa taking over the entire United States.

Standing on Ancient Customs—and Men: Manpower

And Rome did not stop there: the conquest of the Italian peninsula seamlessly merged into more wide-ranging campaigns. Encroachment on Greek cities in southern Italy prompted intervention by the kingdom of Epirus across the Strait of Otranto, which Rome thwarted by drawing on its huge reserves of recruits. The same pattern defined its wars against Carthage, the leading power of the south-central Mediterranean. By combining the resources of capital-rich naval societies—coastal Etruscans and Greeks—with sufficient manpower to staff large navies (and replace them when lost), Rome managed to prevail against an established naval power without having to introduce a much more sophisticated fiscal system that might have required a higher degree of state centralization. In the second war with Carthage, featuring Hannibal's invasion of Italy that led to devastating defeats and tested the alliance to the breaking point, intensive mobilization of Rome's demographic assets was once again decisive in mastering this serious and potentially fatal challenge.[57]

The depth of Rome's manpower is best documented by a breakdown of Roman and allied forces on the occasion of a muster in 225 BCE to repel a Gallic invasion. At that point, some 160,000 men were said to be under arms, out of a total of 700,000 infantry and 70,000 cavalry who were liable to military service. According to the latest scholarship, the overall total may have been closer to 900,000. Even though only part of these men could actually be called up, Roman commanders benefited from an extremely deep bench—and just how deep it was in practice (and not just on paper) became clear only a few years later when Hannibal entered Italy with the apparent objective of dismantling Rome's Italian alliance system.[58]

The ensuing conflict, known as the Second Punic War, demonstrated the strengths of the Roman war machine under maximum duress. Roman forces campaigned simultaneously in Italy as well as in Sicily, the Iberian peninsula, and across the Adriatic. Initial defeats were disastrous: from 218 to 213 BCE, fatalities net of natural causes amounted to 50,000 men or 15–20 percent of the entire adult male Roman citizenry, and to more than twice that number for Italy overall. Rome responded by raising mobilization levels to unprecedented heights. In a population of some 4 million people, approximately 225,000 to 240,000 men were called up between 214 and 212 BCE alone. The levies of the following decade were less extreme but still very substantial: 160,000 to 185,000 men served between 211 and 209 BCE, and 125,000 to 150,000 from 208 to 203 BCE. What is more, mass mobilization continued even once that war had been decisively won. From 200 to 168 BCE, annual enlistment averaged 120,000, ranging from 75,000 in years when only peripheral wars of choice were conducted to a peak of 180,000.[59]

In later generations, domestic wars produced even bigger armies. Some 300,000 Italians are thought to have fought each other in the Social War of 91–89 BCE between Rome and some of its Italian allies, and more than a quarter of a million in the civil war of 83–81 BCE. Even in the somewhat less belligerent 70s–60s BCE, annual army strength averaged 140,000. Renewed civil war prompted a final all-out effort. In 42 BCE, very roughly a quarter of a million Italians were under arms, and two-thirds of them fought a huge battle in the northern Aegean, far away from home. Between 49 and 32 BCE, more than 400,000 Italian men were recruited into the military.[60]

These numbers are best put in perspective by comparing them to later European levies. In the sixteenth century and the first half of the seventeenth, the Habsburgs and France never mustered more than 150,000 men each, a number the Roman Republic quite easily surpassed on several occasions. French military strength reached 200,000 only in the 1670s, and 400,000 by the end of the seventeenth century when Louis XIV pulled out all the stops. All these efforts, however, were founded upon a much larger base population. While it was certainly extraordinary for 650,000 Frenchmen to sign up between 1701 and 1713, it had been even more extraordinary for 420,000 Italians to enter the Roman army between 49 and 32 BCE.

France, after all, boasted 20 million people, whereas Italy was home to not more than 4 million citizens or, at best, about 2 million more. Moreover, French armies did not operate overseas the way Roman forces did in 42 BCE, more than 1,200 kilometers from their capital city by the most economical route. The Roman-on-Roman battle of Philippi that year and the battle of Actium eleven years later were the biggest engagements fought on European soil prior to Napoleon's biggest battles near the end of his career—more than 1,800 years later, when Europe was maybe six times as populous as it had been in the first century BCE.[61]

The exceptional scale of Roman war-making critically relied on very high military participation rates. We cannot really tell if Romans fought more fiercely than others, or whether high military participation rates generally increase ferocity. At the end of the day, it does not really matter: over the long run, sheer numbers were decisive. Rome's superior manpower reserves compensated for the weakness of its oligarchic system that prized rotation of office-holding over pertinent expertise: a premise that not only strengthened the elite's martial spirit but also welcomed amateurs to positions of command. Yet while this may have made warfare even costlier than it needed to be, in the end Rome's massed infantry could always be counted on to hold the line: for centuries Rome lost many battles but never a war.[62]

Schumpeter in Rome? The War Machine Grinds On

Back in 1919, in an indictment of the bloody follies of the Great Powers, Joseph Schumpeter sought to identify traits that turned a society into a "war machine," an arrangement in which war was the only means for the prevailing form of political and social organization to "find an outlet and maintain its domestic position." In this case, even when rational reasons for war-making were lacking, "War became the normal condition. . . . To take the field was a matter of course, the reasons for doing so were of subordinate importance. *Created by wars that required it, the machine now created the wars it required.*" This generated what Schumpeter regarded as an "objectless disposition on the part of the state to unlimited forcible expansion."[63]

In Rome—with the minor adjustment that it often placed even greater emphasis on war-making as such rather than on actual expansion—the logic of the war machine model became particularly visible once serious external challenges had abated after 200 BCE. If warfare had been driven primarily by material profit, greater energy would have been expended on subduing the wealthy polities of the eastern Mediterranean. Our best estimates leave no doubt that Roman warfare was not profitable during the first half of the second century BCE, as income from plunder and indemnities had to be topped up by taxes and other revenues to cover the cost of ceaseless mobilization and campaigning.[64]

Alternatively, if domestic security had been the guiding concern, further campaigning ought to have been confined to Northern Italy but spared the Iberian peninsula, which posed no imaginable risk at all and could easily have been shielded from a weakened Carthage. In reality, vast military resources were committed to operations in underdeveloped peripheries. During the early second century BCE, on average some 114,000 men were sent to the Iberian peninsula and Northern Italy year after year to grind down local tribes and chiefdoms (figure 2.4).

This persistent pattern (which in the case of the Iberian peninsula continued into the following decades) illuminates the underlying dynamics. Unless we believe in decades of inadvertent mission creep, the aristocratic quest for glory coupled with a pragmatic desire to keep Italian mobilization structures fully operational is the most economical explanation for this outcome. And although individual anecdotes cannot bear the same weight as systematic patterns, one is nonetheless worth mentioning. When in 157 BCE, after no fewer than sixty-eight consecutive years of active warfare, Rome had temporarily run out of targets, the senate immediately resolved to launch a new campaign in the Balkans to ensure that the people would not be softened by a "lengthy peace."[65]

The long-term record speaks volumes. Only 19 of the 310 years between 410 and 101 BCE were free from recorded wars, and even this

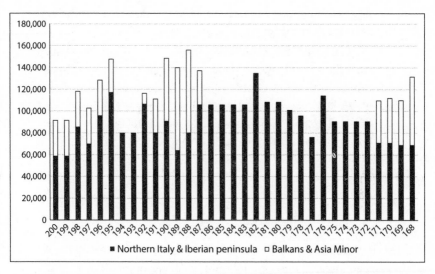

FIGURE 2.4 Roman and Italian military deployments by region, 200–168 BCE. *Source*: Data from Afzelius 1944: 47, 78–79, 89.

modest tally might be slightly inflated by gaps in the historiographical tradition. This profile ultimately extended into the second decade of the first century CE when Rome, now ruled by monarchs, finally gave up on the idea of controlling Germany east of the Rhine. Thus, for no fewer than 425 years, Rome was engaged in war well over 90 percent of the time. The sixteen years devoid of major conflict between the end of the Tacfarinas war in North Africa in 24 CE and risings in Morocco in 40 CE followed by Claudius's invasion of Britain in 43 CE were without precedent in known Roman history. At that point, more than half a millennium had passed since the conventional start date of the Roman Republic (and more than three-quarters of a millennium since the mythical founding date of the city itself).

This track record seems unique even by the dire standards of premodern polities operating in anarchic environments. The aptly named Warring States of early China are a good example. Over the course of 502 years, the state of Qin was involved in wars in which it was either the principal aggressor or target in "only" 186 years, or a little over one in three. Even if we pool the experiences of all major states, China registered 127 years of peace in the same period, or one in four.[66]

Historical societies were routinely bellicose, but not quite as much as Rome. The extent to which states acted on their natural predisposition to increase their power and security in environments of militarized anarchy was critically mediated by their institutions. In the Roman case, as I have tried to show, the structural characteristics of the core go a long way in accounting for the persistence and scale of war-making and expansion.[67]

Empire without End? The Final Phase of Expansion and the End of Conquest

By the second century BCE, the Roman sphere of control and influence had matured into a multilayered system composed of a rapidly growing capital city and its hinterland, which formed an inner or metropolitan core; an intermediate core of citizens in central Italy; an outer core of Italian allies in the north and south of the peninsula; and a continuously expanding periphery that was itself graduated into provinces run by Roman governors, client states, allies, and "friendly" polities.[68]

Notwithstanding Rome's military superiority, annexation was often delayed because outright conquest had never been the principal goal of the war machine: moreover, it was not in the interest of the ruling families to strengthen the hand of the state as an autonomous organization by augmenting its reach and revenue. In general, the mode of domination varied depending on the characteristics of specific peripheral regions (figure 2.5).[69]

Following a period of conflicts precipitated by external parties or internal upheaval—against roving Germans, the Italian allies, and the Anatolian kingdom of Pontus, and for the first time even among the Roman citizenry—from the 110s to the 80s BCE, the unraveling of the old aristocratic order gave rise to warlords who, unfettered by traditional constraints on the pursuit of individual glory and preeminence, availed themselves more liberally of Rome's military edge. Their ventures

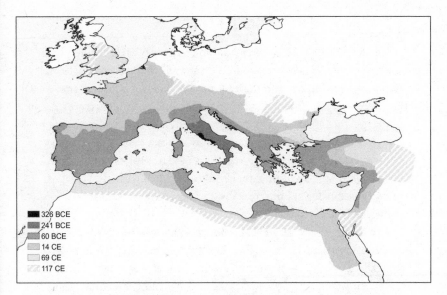

FIGURE 2.5 Expansion of the Roman empire to its peak size.

resulted in the conquest of the Levant (60s BCE), Gaul (50s BCE), Egypt (30 BCE), and, under the warlord turned first emperor (Augustus), of the Danubian basin (20s–10s BCE) and, temporarily, the western reaches of Germany (10s BCE–9 CE).[70]

The priorities of internal political competition drove aggressive expansionism throughout the period of regime change. From the 60s to the 30s BCE, Pompey had campaigned in the Levant and the Caucasus, Caesar attacked Gaul and Britain, Crassus attempted an invasion of Mesopotamia, and Antony campaigned there and in western Iran. Augustus followed in their footsteps, only on an even grander scale. Not all of his conquests made sense in terms of profit or even security: the first emperor not only took over well-taxed Egypt and mineral-rich northern Spain but pushed into the Alps, Germany, the northern Balkans, and the entire length of the Danube basin, alongside abortive moves into Bohemia, Sudan, and Yemen. Whatever the official justification or strategic benefits of these operations, they were undertaken above all to cement the position of the new ruler in the long term, reflected in the employment of family members to run several of these campaigns.[71]

The transition from oligarchy to monarchy was accompanied by a shift from popular military mobilization to a professional standing army. (Rome never adopted the historically most common model of augmenting moderately sized permanent forces with periodic levies as required.) In a sense, the inflationary militarism of the Republican order survived this change. Augustus's professional army appears to have been almost twice as large as it needed to be to protect the territories he controlled in 30 BCE. Large additional capabilities were maintained at great expense, possibly for political reasons, and these troops were at least initially kept busy by ongoing campaigning.[72]

Not entirely unlike his Republican ancestors, the first emperor had created an army in search of a war. Because of this, military service continued to weigh heavily on the Italian core: by 14 CE, one in seven male citizens aged twenty to forty was a soldier, at a time when most of them still hailed from the heartland. Militarism thus remained the defining feature of Roman citizen society well beyond the most intense phase of territorial expansion, with far-reaching consequences too complex to consider here.[73]

Even so, expansion did greatly slow down once the new regime had become firmly ensconced and survived its first orderly succession in 14 CE. From that point onward, a number of factors militated against further expansion on a grand scale. On its western and southern periphery, Roman power had reached natural boundaries—the Atlantic Ocean and the northern fringe of the Sahara. North of the Danube lay sparsely populated and heavily forested areas that were lacking in material resources. The only remaining state-level competitor was centered on southern Mesopotamia and Iran, at great remove from the Roman heartland and separated from the Roman Levant by what is now the ar-Rutbah district, a wide stretch of barren land wedged in between the cultivated zones of northern and southern Mesopotamia.

From an economic perspective, continuing expansion no longer made sense. With the exception of the highly developed client kingdom of Egypt, by 60 BCE the Roman state already controlled the most profitable parts of western Eurasia and North Africa. With few exceptions—notably rich mineral deposits in northern Spain, Dalmatia, and

Transylvania—none of the territories that were conquered during the following 170 years added to revenue net of the military deployments required to secure them. In fact, some of these acquisitions were bound to reduce average tax yield in per capita terms.[74]

This is not to say that we should expect Roman decision-making to have been rational in financial terms: the fact that wars could be costly did not necessarily deter. Even so, we cannot reject explanations that question the feasibility and profitability of further conquest out of hand. The status of Britain, most of it annexed in stages from 43 CE onward, is a particularly striking case. Although the geographer Strabo may simply have toed the previous official line when he claimed a generation earlier that the island was not worth occupying because "the expense of the army would offset the tribute-money," this did not make his observation any less correct. Much the same applies to the historian Appian's assertion more than a century later that the Romans "took possession of the better and larger part [of the world], not caring for the remainder— indeed, the part they do hold is not of much use to them": flattery, for sure, but not far from the truth. In peripheral regions, there were limits to the extent Roman provincial administration could develop and mobilize local resources in order to offset the costs of garrisoning.[75]

Under the monarchy, noneconomic factors acted as a brake on warmaking more generally. Unlike the aristocratic commanders of the Republic, emperors lacked peers with whom they needed to compete for glory. They could only try to outdo their deceased predecessors, a tempting but far less pressing concern. Delegation to surrogates also carried risks: putting others—whether relatives or not—in charge of major military operations might elevate them to the status of potential rivals. Monarchy severely restricted traditional elite autonomy in waging war: in turn, members of the ruling class stood to gain less from military service (and more from lucrative administrative assignments and from jockeying for influence at the court). As army recruitment very slowly shifted away from the Italian heartland and toward the (lower-wage) periphery, the Roman core finally became more pacified, and its elite with it.[76]

In this environment, war became optional, unless it was triggered by rebellions (which remained very rare) or external challenges (which did not gather steam until the late second century CE). The sole remaining motivation for wars of choice was the legitimation of emperors who had come to power under questionable circumstances, most notably Claudius (who initiated the conquest of Britain), Trajan (who conquered Transylvania, seized what is now Jordan, and invaded Armenia and Mesopotamia), and Septimius Severus (who likewise invaded Mesopotamia and later campaigned in Britain).

For all these reasons, expansion slowed and eventually ceased altogether. The abatement of expansion completed a prolonged transition from violent appropriation to managed exploitation: from campaigns of plunder to rule over taxpaying provinces.[77]

• • •

Long-term strategies of co-optation and mobilization were the two key ingredients of the successful creation of a highly capable and aggressive imperial core. In the opening phase of expansion, from the fifth through the early third centuries BCE, competition between Rome and other polities of the Italian peninsula was largely symmetric in character and resulted in a moderate degree of centralized state formation that was largely confined to the military domain and attendant institutions of registration and taxation. The resultant arrangements of governance and cooperation created and sustained dynamics that were conducive to open-ended warfare.

During the next phase, over the following two centuries or so, Rome carefully preserved the special status of the peninsula as an intensely militarized assemblage of largely self-governing communities and allies. Even as Rome established provincial rule outside this core region, it did not for a considerable amount of time follow the "Gellnerian" model in which peripheral elites joined the Roman aristocracy to form a single ruling class. Instead, the participatory Republican institutions of the Roman citizen state helped maintain stronger ties between elites and commoners and more rigid barriers between elites in the core and periphery (figure 2.6).[78]

Roman-style oligarchy served both as a brake on state formation in the core, by impeding centralization and bureaucratization, and as a

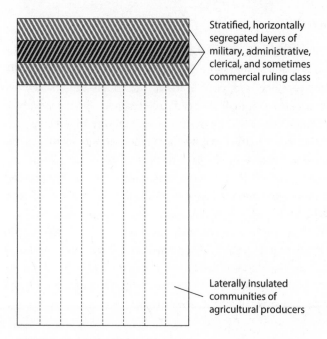

FIGURE 2.6 (A) General form of the social structure of agrarian societies according to Ernest Gellner.

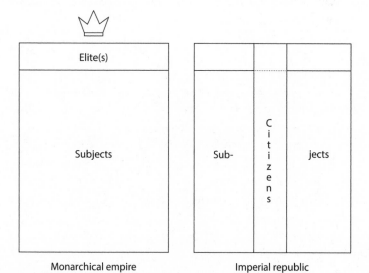

FIGURE 2.6 (B) Adaptations of the Gellner model.

catalyst of extensive imperial expansion, by incentivizing the leadership to pursue aggrandizement through war. By the time the privileged position of the core began to erode in the second half of the first century BCE, most of the empire had already been gained, either formally or de facto. And even at that point, its peculiar culture of military mass mobilization faded only gradually. In later centuries, Roman rule merely preserved and rounded off the existing domain as standing armies, increasingly drawn from the provinces (and much later also from frontier populations), supplanted popular mobilization in the original core. Because Rome had eliminated most state-level competitors and faced an initially intensely fragmented and underdeveloped periphery, its empire endured even under the constraints of strong local elite autonomy and a moderately ambitious fiscal system. For centuries, the lack of serious challengers simultaneously retarded centralized state formation and ensured the longevity of the imperial system.

CHAPTER 3

Periphery

THE MEDITERRANEAN DIVIDE

ROMAN EXPANSION within Italy took place in an environment charac-terized by a small degree of variation in polity size: individual states significantly larger than early fourth-century-BCE Rome were absent. Wars were fought among city-states and leagues of city-states or other small-scale entities. This changed once Rome advanced beyond the Italian peninsula, into a world of established empires. In this chapter and in chapter 4, I address two key questions in turn: What made (what were to become) Rome's peripheries susceptible to domination, and were there other powers that could have thwarted its seemingly unstop-pable ascent?

Rome greatly benefited from its semiperipheral position relative to the older civilizations of the Middle East and the Levant. Sufficiently far removed from powerful empires that might have interrupted its de-velopment or even absorbed it early on, Rome was also sufficiently close to capital-rich areas—Greek and Punic cities to the south, and the Ae-gean to the east—it could tap into as it laid the foundations for an impe-rial formation that could eventually afford to exercise power over less affluent societies all the way to Scotland.

In terms of international political and military relations, Italy as a whole long remained relatively isolated from the political-military

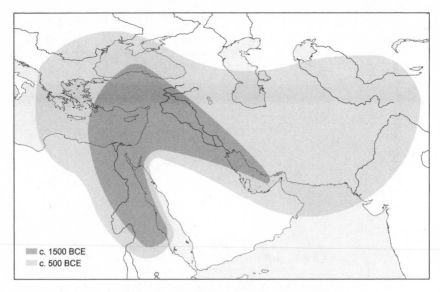

FIGURE 3.1 The Middle Eastern political-military network, c. 1500–500 BCE.

network that had developed in and around the Fertile Crescent. If we consider interconnectedness by means of routinized military conflict and political-diplomatic interaction among state-level societies as the defining characteristic of a political-military network (PMN), what may well have been the first such system worldwide arose in the middle of the second millennium BCE. At that time, New Kingdom Egypt and the empires of the Hittites, Hurrians, and Kassites in Anatolia, Syria, and Mesopotamia coalesced into a sizable competitive state system. A thousand years later, in large part thanks to the advances of the Persian Achaemenid empire, this PMN had expanded into Iran and the Indus Valley in the east and the southern and eastern Balkans in the west (figure 3.1).[1]

Throughout this period and even the following three centuries, the Mediterranean west of the Balkans was not yet drawn into any meaningful degree of political-military engagement with members of this massive network. There were two main reasons for this: one early and structural and the other later and more contingent. The first state-level societies of the eastern Mediterranean to advance into the western half of that inner sea were organized as city-states, located in Lebanon (Phoenicians) and the Aegean (Greeks). The traders and settlers who set out from these city-states faithfully replicated the political model of their home regions. Far from extending the sway of eastern city-states across the Mediterranean, these movements spawned independent polities that retained economic and cultural ties with their originators without submitting to their political authority. The resultant intensification of the pan-Mediterranean prestige good and information networks was not accompanied by the creation of a single PMN.[2]

Later, incursions—invariably from east to west—remained both rare and sporadic, failing to kindle any sustained engagement. Athens's Sicilian expedition (415–412 BCE) proved a disaster. Interventions by rulers of Sparta (342–338 BCE) and Epirus (334–331 BCE) in southern Italy on behalf of local Greek communities likewise ended in failure, and a more scattershot Spartan mercenary venture (303–302 BCE) was similarly unsuccessful. Pyrrhus of Epirus was unable to score more than Pyrrhic victories in Italy and Sicily (280–275 BCE). Farther south, the Macedonian general Ophellas's ill-fated march into Carthaginian territory to support a Greek Sicilian assault failed to expand the eastern PMN into the Maghreb. None of these failures were preordained: nor was the death of Alexander the Great at the tender age of thirty-three just as he had begun to turn his gaze toward the western Mediterranean, a highly contingent event I consider in chapter 4.

Effectively unencumbered by the ancient network that had grown out of the Fertile Crescent region, a smaller and separate western Mediterranean PMN eventually emerged along a north-south axis of conflict from Italy through Sicily to Tunisia (figure 3.2). It was rooted in intensifying hostility between Carthage and Syracuse (off and on from 410 BCE following an early clash in 480 BCE) and then between Rome and Carthage (264–241 and 218–201 BCE) and between Rome and Syracuse (264–263 and 215–212 BCE).

Roman military operations on the Adriatic east coast (229–228 and 220–219 BCE) were the first to cross the divide from the other direction, a harbinger of the storm to come. After inconclusive conflict with

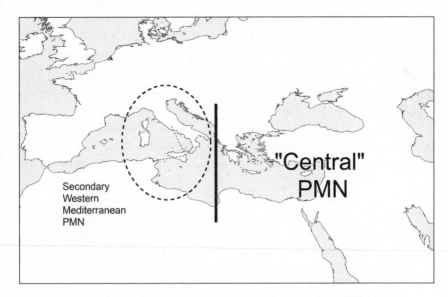

FIGURE 3.2 Political-military networks in the ancient Mediterranean during the third quarter of the first millennium BCE.

Macedon (214–205 BCE) as a sideshow of the Hannibalic War, it was Rome's subsequent invasion of Macedon (200–197 BCE) and its response to the Seleucid advance into Greece (192–190 BCE) that fully merged the western and eastern PMNs.

Rome did not enter what had initially been a very limited Carthaginian-Sicilian network until its control over peninsular had been consolidated, and crossed over into the much larger eastern PMN only after its principal rivals in the western Mediterranean—Syracuse and Carthage—had been neutralized. Rome consequently remained shielded from serious challenges by more complex polities while it was still in the process of scaling up its co-optation and mobilization strategy to maturity. I explore the contingent nature of this outcome in chapter 4 by asking how much would have to have been different for this process to be derailed.

THE SOUTHERN PERIPHERY

Once Rome had established hegemony over the entire Italian peninsula by the 260s BCE, further advances were to bring it in close contact with societies that were rather differently organized, and in many cases the more differently, the more distant they were.

Both the Greek polities in Sicily and the Carthaginian empire in North Africa shared certain characteristics with the Roman-Italian state and alliance system. The Greek or Hellenized populations were organized in city-states and had a long tradition of popular military participation. Compared to Rome, Syracuse, the principal Sicilian power, had followed a more capital-intensive path of state formation, most notably through its aggressive employment of mercenaries. However, a significant coercive dimension was also present.[3]

Much the same was true of Carthage, which had erected a multilayer power structure not unlike Rome's, made up of a privileged metropolitan center, closely connected allied cities of shared Punic ethnicity, indigenous subjects in the interior, and more peripheral allies and partners. Carthage relied on a combination of capital- and coercion-intensive strategies, the former embodied by its strong navy and recourse to mercenaries, the latter by exploitation of its rural hinterland.[4]

The greatest differences lay in the sphere of military capabilities. Sicily supported a much smaller population than peninsular Italy, and it appears that the island's military forces never exceeded 30,000–40,000 men. Attempts to build a Greater Syracusan state beyond Sicily by reaching into south Italy and North Africa had foundered on Carthaginian resistance coupled with recurrent internal instability.[5]

Thanks to its extensive continental hinterland and access to the coastal regions of the westernmost Mediterranean, Carthage was better positioned to pursue open-ended expansion. At the time of its major conflicts with Rome, its overall population base may have been roughly comparable to that of its opponent, and it was also able to recruit widely outside the Maghreb. The Carthaginian elite was imbued with a strong militaristic ethos, and military participation in the metropolitan core was high. Mobilization rates could reach Roman levels at least in emergencies, as citizens alternately staffed a fleet of up to 200 warships or fielded armies of anywhere from 20,000 to 40,000.[6]

Scale was a major constraint: because this strong mobilization capacity did not extend in equal measure to its subjects and allies, the surrounding layers of subordinates produced either levies at lower per capita rates or tribute to fund relatively expensive mercenaries. Indigenous military forces played an important role but were not very large relative to the source population. As a result, Carthage could either raise a large army or launch a powerful fleet, but not both at the same time. When faced with Rome's superior manpower, it increasingly drew on external mercenaries. Constrained by the size of its metropole, it lacked Rome's ability to replace lost citizen troops on a large scale.[7]

Moreover, Carthaginian control even of its immediate hinterland in northern Tunisia was fragile: based on military and tributary obligations without obvious rewards, it was vulnerable to defection whenever the occupying power's military fortunes waned. Carthage consequently lagged behind Rome in both demographic depth and organizational resilience. Its ventures in Sicily had been checked by the Sicilian Greeks, and systematic exploitation of the resources of the Iberian peninsula appears to have been a fairly late development.[8]

Even so, within these constraints, Carthage enjoyed considerable success in scaling up its efforts in wartime. We may question whether it could actually deploy more than 200 warships with some 60,000 crew, even if our main source for its first war with Rome credits Carthage with 350 ships for almost 150,000 men. But there is little doubt that in the second war, Carthage maintained up to 100,000 soldiers spread out across several different theaters.[9]

These commitments help explain why Carthage managed to challenge Rome for a prolonged period of time. Pushed by the latter to expand its military resources on an unprecedented scale, Carthage was ultimately unable to match or dismantle the mass mobilization system of the Italian peninsula. Once again, albeit delayed by Carthage's—most famously Hannibal's—intermittent tactical battlefield superiority, Rome's structural advantages proved too strong to overcome.

THE EASTERN PERIPHERY

To the east, the southeastern tip of Italy was not far away from Greek city-states and other groups that had merged into larger federal entities (*koina*). Endowed with considerable military resources—the ancient tradition of citizen levies and military training of young men continued in many Greek polities, even as recourse to mercenaries had become common—compared to Roman Italy, even the largest federations were severely constrained in manpower. The Aetolian league in northwestern Greece that initially sided with and then opposed Rome never fielded more than 15,000 soldiers and probably not even that many in any one place. Other major players in Greece were unlikely to marshal much larger forces.[10]

Most of the eastern Mediterranean was dominated by three Hellenistic kingdoms, successor states to the ephemeral empire of Alexander the Great. Their field armies were built around fixed formations of heavy infantry coupled with cavalry and, on occasion, war elephants. Core forces of professional soldiers and mercenaries could be supplemented by ethnic levies.[11]

Fortuitously, the kingdom closest to Italy, Macedon, was only the smallest. The principal source of manpower for Alexander's far-reaching campaigns, it had been drained of fighting men at exactly the same time as Rome was establishing its hegemony over peninsular Italy. Although Macedon rebuilt its military system in the third century BCE by combining local levies with hired mercenaries, it was never able to field more than 30,000–40,000 soldiers, and its naval assets remained fairly modest. Moreover, Macedon was enmeshed in and constrained by a competitive state system in the southern Balkans and Aegean that was fertile ground for opportunistic alliances and balancing as Rome advanced into this region.[12]

The two larger and more capable kingdoms were located farther away from Italy: the Seleucid empire stretched from Asia Minor to eastern Iran, and that of the Ptolemies covered Egypt, the Cyrenaica, and parts of the eastern Mediterranean and south Anatolian coastlands. Each of them could put together an army of 70,000 to 80,000, on a par with the largest Roman levies, yet without a comparable depth in reserves. Shaped by their origin as foreign conquest regimes, these two powers heavily relied on a limited number of professional soldiers but generally sought to avoid large-scale conscription among the diverse subject populations they ruled and taxed.

And while the Ptolemaic navy of 300 ships with up to 80,000 men in part of the third century BCE compares well with Roman naval forces at the peak of the First Punic War, the Ptolemaic state, separated from Italy by shared enemies real and potential, was never a hostile power. It is also unclear whether it could have replaced losses on the same enormous scale as the Romans did when they fought Carthage. The Seleucids neglected to build up significant naval resources until the beginning of the second century BCE, and even then never mustered more than 100 major warships, small fry compared to Roman sea power since the First Punic War.[13]

While all these specifics favored Rome, they are only part of a larger story of even more lopsided Roman political and military superiority. First of all, the Hellenistic world was thoroughly divided. By the time Rome entered the eastern Mediterranean, the major powers had been locked into unceasing conflict and shifting alliances for more than a century. Between 274 and 101 BCE, the Seleucid and Ptolemaic kingdoms were to fight no fewer than nine wars for control of their Levantine borderlands, known as the Syrian Wars. Although these conflicts spurred on state formation and honed military capabilities on both sides, it was a zero-sum game, interspersed with a periodic near-collapse of one party or the other.[14]

More specifically, when Rome first attacked Macedon in earnest from 200 to 197 BCE, the Seleucid and Ptolemaic states were embroiled in their fifth war. Although there is no good reason to believe that greater coordination among these kingdoms would have sufficed to block Rome's advance, this illustrates the pernicious consequences of their mutual antagonism: I discuss in chapter 4 the deliberately far-fetched scenario of a unified Macedonian empire on the scale of Alexander's and the odds of its withstanding Roman imperialism.[15]

Second, the well-trained Hellenistic field armies were precious in that they could not readily be replaced. The Seleucid and Ptolemaic empires each relied on core units of approximately 36,000 heavy infantry and cavalry augmented by some 15,000 mercenaries. Whereas the Seleucid state might have been able to replace half its core units within a reasonable amount of time, Ptolemaic reserves were even more constricted: in an emergency, Ptolemy IV had to train 20,000 of his Egyptian subjects to fight Macedonian style, a measure that risked undermining the ruler's own position as the head of a foreign conquest regime.[16]

The Seleucid and Ptolemaic "cleruchs" (military settlers) who formed the backbone of these core units were irreplaceable in the short term: their number, largely determined by the availability of crown land, imposed an effective limit on army strength. In the third century BCE, this manpower base stabilized just as Rome's kept expanding. The overall supply of suitably skilled external mercenaries was likewise inelastic. Additional forces would have had to be raised from subjects and allies of diverse background and reliability, an option that was both cumbersome and politically undesirable.[17]

All of this was a far cry from the high degree of homogeneity and coordination on the Roman side. As already noted, from 200 to 168 BCE, Rome fielded an average of 120,000 soldiers each year, ranging from a minimum of 75,000—equivalent to the largest armies ever amassed by Seleucids or Ptolemies—to a maximum of 180,000, well beyond its opponents' capacity. And even that was only the tip of the iceberg: whereas Rome could at least in theory fall back on 750,000 or more potential recruits, and had on an earlier occasion (in the 210s BCE) called up close to one in three of them after suffering over 100,000 fatalities, nothing even remotely similar would have been feasible for any of the Hellenistic states.[18]

The dramatic extent of this imbalance is thrown into sharp relief by the fact that Rome was able to prosecute several wars against major Hellenistic powers without having to put anything like the full weight of its military behind these efforts (figure 3.3). Thus, only about a

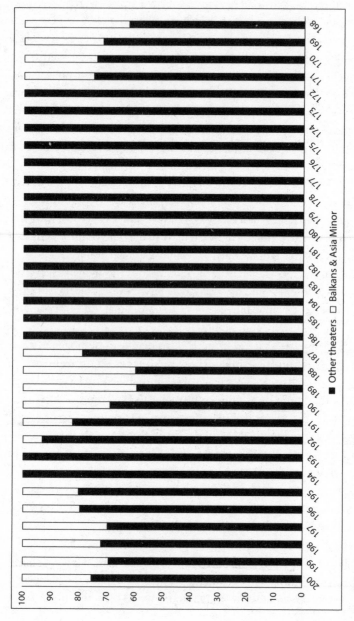

FIGURE 3.3 Roman troop deployments by region as a share of all deployments, 200–168 BCE.

quarter of the Roman and allied soldiers mobilized at the time were deployed in two wars with Macedon, and even the much larger Seleucid empire could be dealt with by a little less than half of Rome's overall levy. In the same vein, Rome never dispatched more than a little over 100 warships to these theaters, a small fraction of its commitment in its first war against Carthage. In a nutshell, the Romans were able to defeat Alexander's heirs with one arm tied behind their backs.[19]

Third, Hellenistic armies were much more expensive in per capita terms than the forces of the Romans and their Italian allies. Even allowing for wide margins of uncertainty, we may estimate that in nominal terms, a Seleucid or Ptolemaic infantryman cost anywhere from three to six times as much per day as the average soldier on the Roman side.[20]

There were two main reasons for this enormous gap: nominal prices and wages were higher in the economically more developed Hellenistic world than in Italy, and professional soldiers and mercenaries commanded wages that were much higher than those of Roman and allied soldiers not merely in nominal terms but also in real ones. Thus, while the Hellenistic powers struggled to channel vast financial resources into their voracious militaries, the more nimble Roman state relied on large numbers of low-cost conscripts and enjoyed the added advantage of recruitment below actual cost among its Italian allies, an arrangement sustained by allied self-funding and the promise of booty.[21]

None of this might have mattered much if the professional forces of the Hellenistic kings had offset their high price with superior performance on the battlefield. However, and this is the fourth and final point, after Roman intervention in the eastern Mediterranean gathered momentum in 200 BCE, the Hellenistic armies arrayed against them lost every single major engagement—the Macedonians at Cynoscephalae (197) and again at Pydna (168) and the Seleucids at Thermopylae (191) and Magnesia (190). The same was true of every pitched naval encounter. Even if actual casualty figures need not have been as lopsided as biased Roman sources made them out to be, this dismal record speaks for itself. Tactical superiority on the battlefield thus compounded Rome's strategic advantage in manpower and funding.[22]

In this context, the contingencies inherent in the outcome of battles are of little relevance: even if Rome had lost some or even all of these engagements, it could easily have deployed fresh military resources—just as it had done in its previous wars with Carthage—whereas its opponents were unable to do the same. When Seleucid and Ptolemaic commanders subsequently reorganized and equipped some of their infantry in the Roman style, these reforms failed to address the underlying structural causes of Roman military superiority: its ability to draw cheaply and deeply on a thoroughly militarized population numbering in the millions. We can now see that the later Roman historian Livy did not exaggerate when he wrote that the Romans had won these wars "not only without defeat but even without danger to themselves."[23]

This pattern continued during the first century BCE as Rome advanced farther east. In a series of conflicts from the 80s to the 40s BCE, the armies of the more distant Hellenistic powers of Pontus (in northeastern Anatolia) and Armenia were consistently defeated in every battle in which the Roman side fielded more than 10,000 men from Italy. It took the unfamiliar cavalry tactics of the Iranian Parthians (who had by then taken over much of the Seleucid empire) in 53 BCE to finally destroy a more substantial Roman army in difficult terrain—and even that episode did not detract from Rome's overall strategic advantage along its eastern frontier for the next 300 years.[24]

In the early second century BCE, the playing field could hardly have been more slanted in Rome's favor. The Hellenistic kingdoms were not only hamstrung by smaller effective forces, a lack of manpower reserves, and much higher costs, they also lost all the time. These factors make Roman success appear so overdetermined that it would be difficult to come up with any plausible counterfactuals to produce significantly different outcomes. From this perspective, the internal integrity of its opponents hardly counts as a decisive factor. But even in this sphere, the stable Roman commonwealth enjoyed a striking advantage. The Seleucid dynasty had only temporarily overcome a period of fission to fight the Romans and subsequently suffered from growing internal destabilization and growing pressure from the Iranian Parthians as they rolled up their empire from the rear. The Ptolemies likewise experienced

serious domestic conflicts and before long ended up under Roman protection to shield their Egyptian heartland from Seleucid encroachment
(168 BCE).

THE NORTHERN AND WESTERN PERIPHERY

I found it necessary to go into some detail to show why Rome had little
difficulty overcoming seemingly powerful imperial competitors in the
most developed part of western Eurasia. Most of its European periphery
can be dealt with much more briefly. To the north and west, Rome faced
a stateless periphery of chiefdoms and tribes. While the small-scale entities may well have boasted high military participation rates, they
were—with rare and fleeting exceptions—too fragmented to pool their
resources in an effective manner. This greatly reduced the risk of invasion or rival state formation.[25]

Yet they themselves were not easily conquered: due to the lack of
preexisting state structures, individual polities often had to be subdued
one by one and at increasing remove from naval supply routes, and
provincial administration needed to be established from scratch. This
helps account for the long duration of Roman campaigning in North
Italy and especially in the Iberian peninsula in the second century
BCE.[26]

Later, overwhelming concentrations of force produced faster results,
when Caesar took control of Gaul in less than a decade and Augustus's
forces secured the entire Danube basin. Even so, subsequent Roman
setbacks in Germany (9–16 CE) highlighted the limits of progress into
ecologically marginal tribal areas.[27]

From a Roman perspective, much of Europe, exposed to unilateral
imperial aggression and expansion, was a ready-made periphery—and
one whose formidable challenges were almost perversely well suited to
a military system that was not only capable but even desirous of sustained and not always profitable warfare over long periods of time.
Rome's advantage was thus just as deeply rooted in its oligarchic politics
and cooperative institutions as in its mobilization capabilities.

CORE AND PERIPHERIES COMPARED

The regions into which Rome came to expand varied considerably with respect to political organization and economic development. Figure 3.4 maps some key differences in ideal-typical terms, following Michael Doyle's taxonomy. Tribal peripheries lacked centralized state institutions and were characterized by low differentiation and high communal loyalty; patrimonial monarchies were large but lacking in political integration and the ability to mobilize their far-flung populations; fractionated republics were equipped with central state institutions but contained divided communities with factional loyalties.[28]

In this diverse environment, Rome enjoyed significant advantages relative to all its competitors. I focus on three key variables: intensity, scale, and integrity (table 3.1). Intensity is a measure of depth, expressed by the military participation rate. Scale measures breadth, in this case the size of the population to which a given level of mobilization intensity can be attributed. In the absence of major technological imbalances, military capacity can be defined as the product of intensity times scale. This

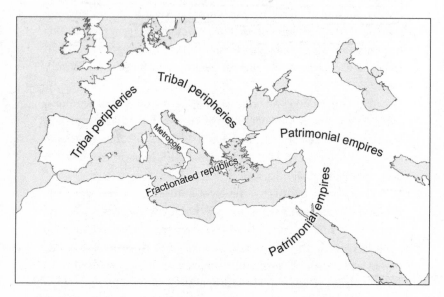

FIGURE 3.4 Stylized typology of peripheries in the Roman-era Mediterranean.

TABLE 3.1 Matrix of critical preconditions for military success, mid-third- to mid-second-century BCE

Factors	Rome	Carthage	Syracuse	Koina	Kingdoms	Tribes
Intensity	high (medium)	medium	high	medium	medium/low	high
Scale	high	high	medium	medium	high	low
Integrity	high	high	high/medium	high/medium	high/medium	(varied)

Key: Intensity = active military as proportion of total population: 1 percent = low, 2–3 percent = medium, 5 percent = high. Scale = polity population size: 10,000s = low, 100,000s = medium, millions = high.

capacity was critically mediated by integrity, in particular the degree of cohesiveness among the decision-making ruling class and more generally the stability of the polity.

Around 200 BCE, the Roman-Italian state and alliance system in peninsular Italy was the only entity anywhere in the world that scored high on all three metrics. Its military mobilization capacity was high and extended over several million people. Although territorial gains in Sicily and the Iberian peninsula reduced the average per capita military participation rate (hence the parenthetical "medium" ranking in table 3.1), conditions in the intensely militarized Italian core remained unaffected. Aside from some defections of allies during Hannibal's invasion, integrity was generally high and oligarchic consensus was (still) solid. Moreover, Rome's advantages in the other two categories were so large that it was able to score victories over external enemies even once its integrity was compromised later on (in the 80s and 40s BCE).[29]

By contrast, the continental tribal periphery was highly militarized but suffered from poor coordination: the latter was its key weakness. The Greek Syracusan state in Sicily depended on expensive mercenaries to raise its intensity to levels that were high relative to its midsize population but was constrained by demography and intermittent political volatility. In this case, population size was the decisive disadvantage. Mainland Greeks combined intermediate levels of intensity with intermediate scale: as a result, military manpower was insufficient to challenge Rome. Carthage, albeit endowed with a cohesive core and integrity, and roughly Rome's equal in terms of total population number, did not maintain high mobilization levels for as large a share of the people under its control as Rome did. The Hellenistic kingdoms score high on scale but medium (Macedon and the Ptolemies) or even low (Seleucids) on intensity, and from high (Macedon and, at least for a while, the Ptolemies) to medium (Seleucids and later Ptolemies).[30]

None of these societies were capable of adapting rapidly to meet the Roman challenge: Rome's rise to power in Italy in relative isolation from its future opponents had delayed the latter's response, and, more importantly, deep-seated structural differences militated against a shift toward Roman-style mobilization on a large scale: the fractiousness of Greek polities, Carthage's and the Macedonian conquest elites' alienation from their imperial subjects, and tribal units' inability to scale up stable cooperation.

On top of everything else, Rome's consistently high scores were reinforced by geopolitical constraints on its competitors: Carthage, the runner-up in scores and not coincidentally Rome's most tenacious adversary, operated for the most part on its own, geographically remote from potential allies in the eastern Mediterranean; and the Hellenistic kingdoms, trapped in long-standing mutual enmity, failed to balance against Roman pressure. Stronger ties between east and west or a more unified east—along the lines of the Ottoman empire much later—might well have made it more difficult for Rome to convert its structural advantages into successful expansion. Neither one of these constraints was particularly contingent, and no plausible conservative rewrite of history would produce a substantially different environment.[31]

ROME'S MEDITERRANEAN ADVANTAGE

Finally, one other factor merits attention. Rome attained naval security and then supremacy across the Mediterranean at a very early stage of its expansion beyond Italy. Rome's naval defeat of Carthage in 241 BCE, which concluded their first round of warfare, left much of the Carthaginian empire intact but effectively ended its sea power. Thanks to the lack of other major seafaring societies west of the Aegean and Egypt, this made Rome the undisputed hegemon over more than half of the waters of the Mediterranean Sea. By the same year, the Ptolemies had achieved naval supremacy in most of the remainder of this sea basin, from the Aegean (up to Thrace and the Dardanelles) and throughout the Levant all the way to the Cyrenaica.[32]

Their capitals separated by well more than 2,000 kilometers of sea travel as well as by shared enemies or sources of concern, these two powers had been on friendly terms ever since Rome had first consolidated control over the Italian peninsula. In the third century BCE, the Ptolemaic empire maintained a large navy that included some of the largest warships built in all of antiquity. Its interference in Rome's operations against Sicily and North Africa would not have been a trivial matter. As it was, cordial relations were maintained until the decline of Ptolemaic power in the second century BCE allowed Rome to extend its naval hegemony eastward simply by filling the vacuum this created while the second-tier navies of Macedon and the Seleucids were shunted aside without much difficulty.[33]

After 190 BCE, no Hellenistic state challenged Rome by sea. The true extent of its hegemonic status is reflected in the later spread of piracy: as the Roman state was able to neglect its naval capabilities because it had run out of state-level competitors, no other powers were able to step in to improve security. In the end, it was Rome that suppressed maritime raids by nonstate actors (or "pirates") with overwhelming force.[34]

Precocious naval supremacy was a boon to Roman expansionism. It made it possible to deliver supplies in support of troops in distant theaters: historical accounts underline the crucial importance of maritime logistics in the wars against Carthage and the Seleucids. In a more abstract manner, a highly schematic model of state formation suggests that secure coastal borders lowered the cost of expansion. According to a crude computer simulation that divides Europe into uniformly sized territorial cells that engage randomly in conflict and vary only in terms of the cost of defending their borders—with coastal borders and major mountain ranges (Alps and Pyrenees) enjoying lower costs than land borders—coastal borders that are only moderately cheaper to defend than land borders yield outcomes resembling the modern European state system. Conversely, substantially lower coastal defense costs favor larger-scale state formation.[35]

In this model, the lowering of coastal defense costs for only a single region—the Italian peninsula—in order to approximate Roman naval hegemony confers a considerable advantage. In this scenario, Italy, shielded by the Alps and long coastlines, tends to expand farther afield even if there is no variation at all in natural endowments, carrying capacity, and institutions. Several details merit particular attention. (1) Italy expands into Europe only if its coastal defense costs are massively lowered to less than one-third of those of other regions; otherwise there is no tangible effect at all. (2) Even under this specification, its coastal defense advantage works out reliably only if Italian expansion takes off early in the simulation, before less privileged rivals beyond the Alps have a chance to succeed. (3) Even in the most successful runs of the simulation does Rome fail to take over the Iberian peninsula.

All of this can readily be reconciled with actual historical developments. After 241 BCE, thanks to its naval hegemonic status, Rome's coastal defense costs were vastly lower than others'; Italy was a pioneer in ancient European state formation; and unlike in the model, which recognizes only terrestrial connections, maritime connections helped it operate in the Iberian peninsula early on. The model requires a combination of two factors—very low naval defense costs and a head start (especially with respect to the western periphery of Europe)—to precipitate Italian (i.e., Roman) expansion across large parts of Europe. Those conditions precisely match the ones encountered by Rome from the mid-third century BCE onward.[36]

Naval supremacy was the first step in establishing an empire that was centered on the Mediterranean basin. A different and less crude model that captures historical conditions in greater detail illustrates that Rome reaped significant benefits from its undisputed command of this maritime inner line. In the absence of hostile interventions, the Mediterranean Sea functioned as a core of connectivity that facilitated the movement of people, goods, and information at very low cost and risk.

A geospatial network model of the Roman world ("Orbis") that I developed together with Elijah Meeks visualizes the extent to which the coastal regions of the empire were much more interconnected—in terms of travel time and transportation cost—than their sprawling hinterland (figures 3.5 and 3.6): each unit of distance on the maps corresponds to a constant unit of cost.[37]

Not coincidentally, Roman expansion tracked this pattern quite closely: Romans first advanced into the most accessible regions (figure 3.7).[38]

More specifically, secure maritime connectivity afforded ready access to the capital-rich regions in the eastern Mediterranean that helped sustain costly expansion into non-Mediterranean Europe during the final stages of Roman conquest from the first century BCE to the second century CE.[39]

Roman mastery of the Mediterranean was unique: never again in history would one power exercise lasting control over its entire coastline, and its effective naval supremacy was not renewed until the days of Admiral Nelson, if not World War II. Moreover, the Roman dominions were unusual simply for being centered on the Mediterranean: among

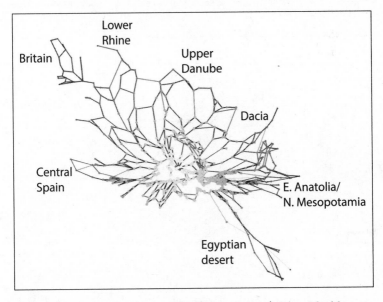

FIGURE 3.5 Time cost of transfers from Rome (military; summer). *Source*: Scheidel 2014: 15, fig. 3.

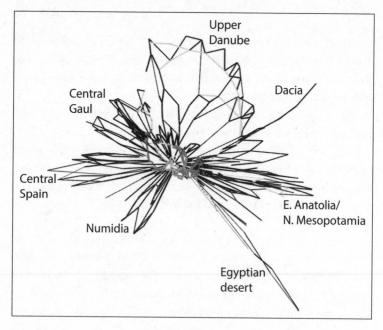

FIGURE 3.6 Financial cost of transfers to Rome (cargo; summer). *Source:* Scheidel 2014: 22, fig. 8.

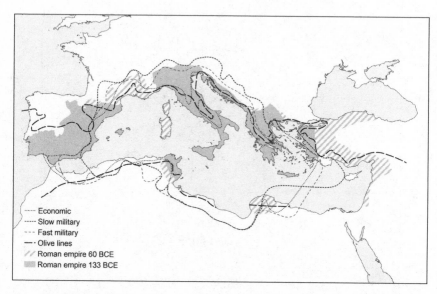

FIGURE 3.7 The Mediterranean core of the Roman empire. *Source:* Scheidel 2014: 23, fig. 10.

later sizable empires, only Habsburg Spain and the Ottomans shared this distinction, although on a smaller scale, especially the former. Neither one of them enjoyed anything like Roman hegemony.

This is easy to explain. Even though a unified Mediterranean may have been a highly suitable core for an empire that already dominated it, later history documents the difficulties of reaching the requisite position of preeminence. This happened only once, at a time when lack of competition made it less challenging to establish hegemony over the less developed western half of the Mediterranean. Considering how much Rome struggled against just a single opponent during its first war with Carthage, a more crowded naval environment might well have curbed its naval expansion. Due to the subsequent spread of naval technology, this favorable situation was impossible to replicate later: no medieval or modern state could hope to attain hegemonic status by overcoming so few contenders. Competition had become too widespread.

• • •

Once they stepped beyond the Italian peninsula, Rome and its allies encountered unusually favorable conditions for military success and ongoing expansion. Closest to home, they faced an inner periphery of polities such as Syracuse, Carthage, and the Greek federations that could not match Roman mobilization intensity on a comparable scale. Farther away, kingdoms with extensive coordination capacity suffered from relatively low mobilization levels rooted in military technology, socioethnic stratification, and high costs. Conversely, small-scale stateless societies boasted high military participation rates but suffered from lack of coordination. During the formative stages of its overseas empire, Rome consistently outscored all its competitors on the critical variables of intensity, scale, and integrity. Weak naval development in the western Mediterranean laid the foundations for Rome's precocious hegemony over the Mediterranean basin, allowing it to project power over great distances without having to worry about the security of its homeland. With the single exception of the initial resilience of the Carthaginian empire, it is hard to conceive of peripheries that would have been more vulnerable to Roman aggression.

CHAPTER 4

Counterfactuals

EMPIRE ABORTED?

I HAVE so far operated with the benefit of hindsight, defining core and periphery in keeping with actual historical outcomes. However, the world outside Italy was not merely a periphery-in-waiting ready to be conquered: it was also a potential source of threats to Roman state formation. Imperialism was not a one-way street. In studying what happened and trying to explain why it did, it is all too easy to err on the side of determinism—the notion that observed outcomes were the ones most likely to occur—or on the side of contingency—the notion that things might just as readily have turned out completely differently. Explicit consideration of counterfactual scenarios helps us chart a course between these extremes. The question is this: What were the odds that challenges from within or from outside could have derailed Roman expansion, preventing the creation of an empire that ruled 80 percent of Europe's population for almost half a millennium?[1]

ITALY

Domestic developments that could have had this result were most likely to occur at very early stages of Roman state formation, which are extremely poorly documented. This makes it virtually impossible to judge the probability of alternative outcomes. Nevertheless, if early fifth-century-BCE Rome had for some reason not been the largest city-state in Latium, it would not have been able to assume a hegemonic leadership position. If social conflicts, dimly attested for the fifth and early fourth centuries BCE, had severely compromised the integrity of the Roman state, successful expansion might well have proved impossible. Given the quality of our evidence, there is simply no way of telling whether any of this might plausibly have occurred. However, for all we can tell, once we reach the phase of open-ended Roman expansion into the Italian peninsula from the second third of the fourth century BCE onward, truly crippling internal mishaps were much less likely to strike. Serious domestic conflict—discussed below—did not flare up until the early first century BCE, when much of the empire had already been put in place.[2]

A counterfactual perspective can be more fruitfully applied to external challenges and their potential impact. Given that Rome did not suffer more than brief setbacks once it had broken out of Latium, opposition from within Italy does not seem to have been a particularly strong candidate for changing the trajectory of Roman state formation. Unable to project power over longer distances, the Samnitic federation was not a credible alternative to Roman hegemony. And while it may be true that had the Gauls who sacked Rome in the early fourth century BCE chosen to settle there, the Roman Republic would have ended there and then, such a decision would have been without parallel and is therefore not a plausible option either.

EASTERN CHALLENGES

In the most general terms, the most likely source of disruption lay to the east, in more developed parts of the Old World. Intervention or even absorption by a major power before Rome had fully extended its control over peninsular Italy would have posed the most serious obstacle to Roman imperialism. As I pointed out above, Italy was relatively

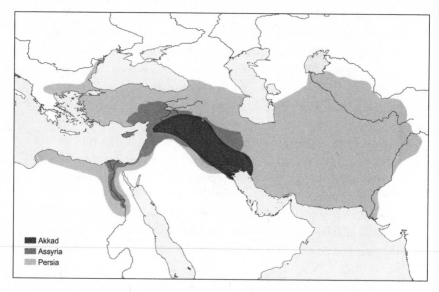

Akkad
Assyria
Persia

FIGURE 4.1 The Akkadian, Neo-Assyrian, and Achaemenid empires.

remote from earlier state formation in the Near East. Even so, the risk of hostile contact gradually increased over time as the eastern political-military network expanded.

The odds of any such contact increased only very slowly. When the earliest empires arose in the Fertile Crescent, starting with Old Kingdom Egypt and Akkad in the third millennium BCE, there was no realistic way of their ever interfering in Italy. A more recent iteration, the Neo-Assyrian empire of the seventh century BCE, briefly reached into western Anatolia and Egypt but likewise never had a good chance of developing far enough to threaten Italy (figure 4.1).[3]

The Persian Achaemenid empire of the fifth century BCE was the first even remotely plausible contender. As we saw in chapter 1, it represented a big step up the ladder of macro-social evolution, ushering in the era of empires that covered millions of square kilometers and tens of millions of people. Had the Persian king Xerxes conquered mainland Greece after 480 BCE, it would have become possible for him or a successor to advance into Sicily and peninsular Italy. Conflict with the western Greeks might have provided sufficient motivation: after all, the Persian invasions of mainland Greece had been triggered by its support for a revolt in western Asia Minor.[4]

Even so, actual history strongly suggests that any such advance would probably have been short-lived. The Achaemenid empire never managed fully to control Egypt, which broke away in the 450s BCE and more enduringly for the first half of the fourth century BCE. At the opposite end, the Indus Valley also appears to have slipped from its grasp. Unable to hold on to their eastern- and westernmost peripheries, the Persians were bound to run into similar problems had they attempted to extend their reach even farther across the complex and densely populated Greek city-state culture that comprised a thousand separate micro-states and at least 7 million people. Greek practices of citizenship, participatory politics, and popular military mobilization supported collective action that would have been difficult to suppress on a grand scale. Under these circumstances, an effective Persian presence in peninsular Italy, beyond the massive cluster of Greek city-states that stretched from Sicily and southern Italy to mainland Greece and western Asia Minor, was not a plausible outcome. Nor was fifth-century BCE Carthage sufficiently well developed to exercise power this far away on Persia's behalf.[5]

The Athenian empire was hardly a more promising spoiler. Had Athens and its allies succeeded in defeating Syracuse in the 410s BCE and established a permanent presence in Sicily, further expansion could certainly have taken place. The most plausible scenario would be Athenian involvement in conflict between the Italian Greeks and local populations that might have drawn it more deeply into the affairs of the peninsula, at a time when Rome had barely begun to reach beyond its Latin heartland. This counterfactual faces two serious obstacles. For one, Athens would have found it much more profitable to target Carthage or the vulnerable western periphery of the Achaemenid empire, thus directing its efforts away from an Italian peninsula that had little to offer to the cash-rich Athenians.[6]

Even more importantly, the requisite notion that Athens and its allies could in fact have evolved into a more unitary and stable state with the potential for sustained expansion—a counterfactual proposed by Ian Morris—neglects the countervailing forces produced by Athens's exclusivist model of citizenship and direct democracy and the intense fragmentation of its own imperial periphery of city-states. In the end, it may not have much to commend it.[7]

Athenian engagement with Carthage or Persia seems a more plausible counterfactual in the short term, followed by fission of the Athenian empire itself. But even in this scenario, some form of Athenian intervention in central Italian and thus Roman state formation in the fourth century BCE cannot be ruled out. In view of Athens's ability to project naval power over long distances, this outcome seems somewhat less far-fetched than that of Persian inference in Italy a century earlier. Before the Latin settlement of 338 BCE, Rome was only a fairly minor regional power that was exposed to outside intervention, especially by sea. Thus, even an Athenian empire that did not survive the fourth century BCE might, under the right concatenation of circumstances, have been able and inclined to do serious damage to Roman state-building (figure 4.2).

On balance, however, the likelihood of this counterfactual occurring was rather low. No comparably aggressive naval powers arose in the Aegean after the Athenian empire collapsed in 404 BCE. In the fourth century BCE, aside from one raid on a Roman ally, Syracuse either focused on its rivalry with Carthage or was hamstrung by domestic disturbances. For these reasons, outside intervention in Roman affairs remained highly unlikely until the final quarter of the fourth century BCE. Between 334 and 325 BCE, the Macedonian king Alexander the Great took over the Achaemenid empire. At the time of his death in Babylon, he was only thirty-three years old. Considerable military assets and vast financial resources were at his disposal. Had he lived, they would have supported further operations elsewhere. An expedition into Arabia that reportedly involved huge naval forces was already being prepared when he succumbed to fever.[8]

A much later account, arguably based on contemporary observations, credited Alexander with more sweeping plans for the future. They called for the construction of a fleet of 1,000 large warships to wage a

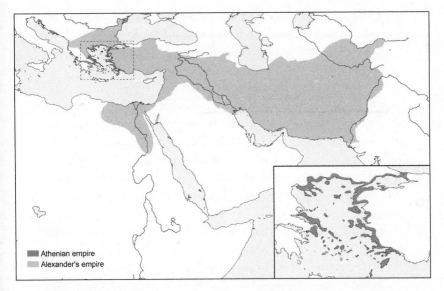

FIGURE 4.2 The Athenian empire (late fifth century BCE) and the empire of Alexander the Great (323 BCE).

campaign "against the Carthaginians and the other inhabitants of the coastal area of Africa, Iberia and the neighboring coasts as far as Sicily," an itinerary that appears to include the Italian peninsula as well. Whatever the reliability of this story—which has repeatedly been questioned—westward expansion was certainly not unfeasible.[9]

The proposed scheme meshes well with reports of contacts with Italian polities. In Babylon, Alexander is said to have received numerous embassies from the western Mediterranean: from Carthage and other parts of North Africa, from the Iberian peninsula and Sardinia, and also from the Lucanians and Bruttians in southern Italy and the Etruscans north of Rome. Whether a Roman delegation joined in continues to be debated.[10]

Even without such anecdotes, the geostrategic situation in 323 BCE could hardly have been clearer. Whereas the entire eastern Mediterranean and Near Eastern ecumene had fallen under Alexander's control, the western Mediterranean was highly fragmented. Counterpoised regional powers balanced each other: Lucanians and the Greek city-state of Tarentum in southern Italy, Rome and the Samnites in central Italy, Etruscans and Gauls farther north, and Syracuse and Carthage across the sea.

This environment not only facilitated but encouraged outside intervention, as Alexander would have been able to enter alliances to ease his advance. He might also have had a more specific reason to intervene in Italy. His uncle Alexander, the king of Epirus, had been killed there in battle in 331 BCE campaigning against south Italian tribes. All in all, had it not been for Alexander's untimely demise, the odds of Macedonian intervention in Italy in the late fourth century BCE would not have been negligible.[11]

Arnold Toynbee, in his counterfactual essay "If Alexander the Great had lived on," has the Macedonians conclude an alliance with Rome in 318 BCE that was directed against the Samnites, an arrangement that preserved Rome but severely curtailed its options for future expansion. In this scenario, no Roman empire would have emerged—and it is hard to see how Toynbee's own counterfactual in which Alexander conquered both India and China, and one of his successors added the Americas, thereby creating a perennial global super-state, could ever have come true.[12]

Toynbee was by no means the first to ponder the consequences of a Macedonian intervention in Italy. Writing more than 300 years after the death of Alexander, the Roman historian Livy preferred to think that the Romans could have defeated the Macedonians. He was right to emphasize Rome's superior manpower, a resource that might well have stymied Alexander's advance, especially as his own reservoir of seasoned Macedonian pikemen had already been depleted. At the same time, Livy neglects to consider how much later Roman troops struggled against the superior tactical skills of professional Hellenistic field armies. Nor was it a given that Rome would have formed an alliance with Carthage: the latter could easily have been overwhelmed first. Backed up by sophisticated siege equipment, a large navy, and full coffers, Alexander—or any ruler of a unified Macedonian-Persian empire—stood a better chance of checking Rome's progress (whether by defeat or co-optation) than Livy is prepared to accept.[13]

Even though Macedonian interference need not have stopped Roman expansion in its tracks, it certainly could have. The likelihood of this counterfactual is considerably higher than those of the previous (and, as we will see, subsequent) ones. This turns the last quarter of the fourth century BCE into a critical juncture of Roman state formation, a time when Rome and its partners faced off against formidable opponents in the Italian peninsula. Even short of outright conquest, outside intervention could have tipped the scales in a way that forestalled the emergence of anything like the later mature Roman-Italian state and alliance system that proved to be an irresistible juggernaut. It is not mere coincidence that both Livy and Toynbee gravitate toward this counterfactual: this was the one time when Rome's fate arguably did hang in the balance.

In actual history, this rare window of opportunity closed soon after Alexander's death. Once his general Antigonus had failed to prevent the rival warlord Seleucus from taking over Mesopotamia and Iran (311–309 BCE) or, at the latest, when the former was defeated and killed in 301 BCE, the chances of reuniting Alexander's domain—if that had indeed ever been any of his successors' goal—rapidly receded.[14]

Instead, Alexander's former lieutenants kept turning on each other, creating an inward-looking system of states that committed enormous resources to inconclusive internecine strife. Meanwhile, Rome was able to pursue its goals in Italy and wrest naval hegemony from Carthage without much outside interference. Focused on competition with other Hellenistic kingdoms and smaller Greek polities, Macedon and the Ptolemies, while logistically capable of intervention, had no compelling reason to become involved in these affairs.

By contrast, a lesser interstitial power such as Epirus (in northwestern Greece and Albania) that had an incentive to operate away from the superior militaries of the Hellenistic core region was too small to inflict any lasting damage once Rome had pressured most peninsular Italian polities into its alliance system. By 280 BCE, when the forces of the

Epirote king Pyrrhus landed in southern Italy, the cohesion and manpower reserves of this Roman-led system had already become too strong to overcome.

In the absence of credible challenges from the east, Carthage remained the only available contender. But right from the start, Rome acted more aggressively: in the First Punic War of 264–241 BCE, fought primarily for control of Sicily, Rome staged an ambitious landing in North Africa whereas Carthage never came close to threatening the Roman heartland. A generation later, a planned second attack on Carthage was narrowly prevented by Hannibal's daring gambit of invading the Italian peninsula. Yet despite major victories against the Roman and allied forces arrayed against him, he only partially succeeded in his objective of dismantling Rome's alliance system.

The debate about whether Hannibal could somehow have won began in antiquity. It is certainly true that his advance put the Roman system under tremendous strain, and we must not allow ourselves to assume that its perseverance and ultimate triumph had in fact been the most likely outcome. Even so, the most careful analysis to date persuasively concludes that Hannibal could not hope to turn enough allies away from Rome and hold on to them all at once: local rivalries that the Romans had worked for a long time to mitigate had only been suppressed but not eliminated, and once revived by defections and shifting allegiances they undermined the intended creation of a united front against Rome itself.[15]

Even in the darkest years of this war, Rome was more capable than it would have been a hundred years earlier if attacked by a longer-lived Alexander. Thus, short of the capital's outright destruction, which its massive fortifications rendered implausible, even Rome's reduction to a middling power would not have ruled out a later rebound. Continued Carthaginian meddling in Italy might well have prompted the emergence of a new Italian alliance system based on military mass mobilization, with or without Roman leadership. Moreover, it seems highly unlikely that success in Italy would have allowed the Carthaginians to build an empire on a Roman scale: their military manpower was inadequate to the task, and their peripheral geographical position would have been a major obstacle to any deep penetration of the European continent. In the long run, Carthage would have had a better chance of taking over Egypt than reaching Britain, the Rhine, and the Danube.[16]

Hannibal's throw of the dice turned out to be the final opportunity for an external opponent to derail Roman imperiogenesis, and an unpromising one at that. After Rome's victory in 201 BCE left Carthage a client state, none of the Hellenistic kingdoms had any realistic hope of intervening in Italy in an effective manner. This raises the hypothetical question of whether the might of a unified Hellenistic empire would have been sufficient to break the Roman war machine. What if, in an aggressively implausible counterfactual, the Macedonian-ruled successor states had somehow been reunited during the third century BCE, presenting a united front to Rome and its allies by the time of Carthage's defeat?[17]

If we simply add up the military forces the major Hellenistic powers could marshal in wartime, we arrive at an imposing tally of about a quarter of a million soldiers, most of whom could have been deployed against Rome, and at least 500 major warships. It is hardly a stretch to imagine that under unified leadership, these resources might well have sufficed to block any further Roman advance for good, and that they could also have been used to carry out attacks against Italy itself.[18]

It is, however, far from certain that a unified empire could have generated such massive military assets. The numbers for each kingdom and league that we are tempted to sum up were the result of several generations of intense conflict among the successor states, of wars making states and states making wars. From a comparative perspective, it is by no means a given that a single super-state would have had a sufficiently strong incentive to mobilize resources on this grand scale. Both the relative military weakness of the vast and supremely well-funded Achaemenid empire and the fact that the active military forces that were at Alexander's disposal at the time of his death were rather modest (relative to the size of the subject population) speak against this simplistic assumption. Sustained conflict with a similarly powerful opponent would have been required for a much larger military to be built up and maintained.

By the mid-third century BCE, the Roman war machine had reached maturity by complementing its huge reservoir of infantry with a powerful navy. From that point onward, war with a less mobilized eastern super-state would have found the latter relatively ill equipped to take on this challenge. The necessary military scaling-up would have taken some time, opening the door to Roman successes early on. Thus, even in the exceedingly unlikely event of a later restoration of Alexander's entire domain, Roman advances were a plausible outcome, even if they might have been bought at higher cost, including perhaps some form of rerun of the First Punic War in the maritime sphere.

DOMESTIC CONFLICT

This far-fetched scenario shows that by this time, even remotely credible external challenges to Roman imperialism had disappeared. Roman power had entered a phase of military superiority so pronounced that internal conflict became the only potential source for failure. The "integrity" variable radically deteriorated on two occasions in the first centuries BCE. The first of these was the Social War of 91–89 BCE between the Roman citizen state and some of its Italian allies. This was a serious rift that not only fractured a centuries-old alliance system but pitted two large and highly mobilized populations against each other. Even so, thanks to Rome's ability to draw on extensive resources from its provinces and its unified leadership, its survival and ultimate success were the most likely outcome.

In a less likely counterfactual, a resounding victory of the defectors might simply have led to their usurpation of Rome's overseas possessions and continuing empire under new management. Only a prolonged stalemate within the Italian core could have caused enough damage to upend the imperial project as such. The fact that political concessions were always an option for defusing this clash between long-term partners all but rules out that scenario: the exercise of imperial power over provincials could be reconfigured to benefit Roman and other Italian elites alike. This is a respectable reading of the solution to this war—the enfranchisement of the Italian allies into the Roman citizenry—unless we prefer to interpret it as a sign of the defectors' defeat.[19]

The second crisis arose from open warfare between rival parties within the Roman aristocracy. This precipitated intermittent separation of the eastern from the western parts of the empire in 49–48, 42, and 32–30 BCE. Yet looked at more closely, these short if bloody episodes do not support any plausible scenarios of lasting fragmentation or imperial decay. In all these instances, unification by the victorious party was a priori the most plausible outcome. The alternative, enduring stalemate between warlords in control of Italy and the western provinces on the one hand and of the Aegean and the Levant on the other, is somewhat irrelevant and also improbable: irrelevant because the "western" party would have controlled most of Roman Europe, which is the focus of this book; and improbable because the basic fact that military mass mobilization on a grand scale was confined to Italy helped ensure that the leaders of this region would eventually overcome resistance elsewhere.[20]

More specifically, the fundamental structural imbalance between the concentration of military power in Italy and of economic resources in the western Mediterranean effectively predetermined both the ultimate outcome—imperial unification—and the identity of the victors: namely, those in command of Italian manpower. From this perspective, merely the swift nature of "western" victories in 48, 42, and 31–30 BCE was historically contingent, but not imperial survival and restoration as such.[21]

Over the very long run, we perceive an arc of probability of failure of the Roman imperial project. Extremely unlikely to be preemptively forestalled by the intervention of early Near Eastern empires that lacked the means to reach, let alone rule, Italy, failure became somewhat less impossible with the appearance of the Achaemenid and Athenian empires. A rather sharp peak was reached with Alexander the Great, when the odds of a significantly different trajectory of state formation—while by no means overwhelming—were much better than before or after. After the Second Punic War had opened up less plausible prospects of alternatives, the likelihood of Roman failure rapidly diminished and indeed almost vanished.

Once the mature empire of the early monarchy had been consolidated, with its European portions extending from Britain to the eastern

Carpathians, the only remaining question was how long this edifice would remain intact. As the mass mobilization system of the core eroded, the Roman empire turned into a more traditional imperial formation burdened by the autonomy of local elites and fission within the professional army. Together with slow-moving secondary state formation at the frontiers and environmental change, these processes played an important role in determining the overall duration of hegemonic empire: but what matters in the present context is only that it was very large for a very long time.[22]

ONLY ROME

Rome's record in empire-building was unique in more ways than one. No other state would ever again rule four out of every five inhabitants of Europe. No other state would ever again control all of the Mediterranean basin as well as the entire population of its coastal regions. No other empire in world history that had arisen at considerable remove from the great Eurasian steppe belt was anywhere near as large or durable as *imperium Romanum*.[23]

This uniqueness was rooted in the similarly unique circumstances of Rome's rise to power. Military mass mobilization—and political republicanism—on the scale practiced by the ascendant Roman state and its principal allies did not return to Europe until the early modern age, at a time when competitive polycentrism had already hardened into an immovably stable state system. In no small part thanks to centuries of Roman campaigning, stateless peripheries had retreated to the northern and eastern margins of Europe. As a result, no later state in the temperate zone of Europe would ever again enjoy the privilege of being able to scale up its resources and military capabilities without having to worry about outside interference.

Never again were geopolitical conditions so favorable for the creation of naval hegemony, of the Roman *mare nostrum*—"our sea": by 241 BCE, two friendly powers, Rome and the Ptolemaic empire, had come to share effective control over most of the Mediterranean Sea, and the latter declined too fast, and soon became too dependent on the former for any serious rivalries to emerge between them. This unlikely sequence of events remained without parallel. Once the Vandals and then the Arabs had ended Rome's naval monopoly, the Mediterranean became and remained an arena for competing states and buccaneers. Not until the days of Admiral Nelson did any one power rival Rome's position of maritime supremacy. And never again would the surpluses of the well-taxed Levant be harnessed for state-building in Europe.

In short, Rome's manifold advantages, even insofar as it would have been possible to replicate them at all, were so unusual that they were unlikely to occur again later—and in fact they never did. This, in turn, helps us understand why nothing like the Roman empire ever returned.

PART III
Why Only Rome?

CHAPTER 5

From Justinian to Frederick

AFTER ROME

THAT NO LATER state ever again achieved a level of dominance within Europe comparable to that enjoyed by the Roman empire marks a double divergence: between Europe before and after the fall of Rome, and between post-Roman Europe and other parts of the Old World that had continued to produce huge empires. This part of my book deals with the first of these sharp discontinuities, and Part IV with the latter.

I trace the divergence *within* European history by identifying and analyzing, in chronological sequence, a number of junctures or sometimes more extended periods when renewed imperial state formation on a very large scale might have seemed possible: the restorationist campaigns of the eastern Roman empire in the mid-sixth century; the conquests of the Umayyad caliphate in the early eighth century; the ascent of the Frankish empire under Charlemagne; repeated efforts by rulers of the German empire from the tenth through the thirteenth centuries; the Mongol irruption into Central Europe in the mid-thirteenth century; the policies of the Habsburg monarchs Charles V and Philip II in the sixteenth century; the expansion of the Ottoman empire in the same period; and France's struggle for hegemony from Louis XIV to Napoleon Bonaparte.[1]

In keeping with my overall objective of relating Europe's eventual breakthrough to modernity to much earlier developments, I focus not so much on the totality of the areas once held by the Romans as on the prospect of hegemonic empire in Europe itself. My question is straightforward: Which polities, if any, might conceivably have had the potential to approach Rome's record of ruling four out of every five Europeans, and why did they fail to do so?

My discussion of these junctures revolves around key factors that militated against state formation beyond a certain scale: the weakening of centralized state authority and state capabilities that prevented scaling-up in the Middle Ages, and the ways in which growing state power and stability in the early modern period were contained by an increasingly extensive and resilient state system that balanced against potential hegemons. I thus move from an analysis of the roots of Rome's success in building a very large empire out of (southern) Europe to a discussion of later polities' inability to follow suit.

This approach deliberately gives short shrift to a much-debated event that occurred in between these two phases: the disintegration of the Roman empire in the fifth century. Somewhat paradoxically, the question of why Rome fell is both over- and underresearched. Overresearched, because when in 1984 the German ancient historian Alexander Demandt published a massive historiographical survey of all the various explanations for the demise of the Roman empire that had been put forward from late antiquity to the present, he was able to enumerate no fewer than 210 different causes that had by then been proposed. This figure alone leaves no doubt that our understanding of this event would surely benefit from a healthy dose of self-critical reflection and interpretive restraint.[2]

At the same time, this event nevertheless remains underresearched because it has never been properly contextualized. After all, most empires in history that did not eventually morph into stable nation-states "fell" at some point. Even the patron saint of modern students of Rome's decline and fall, Edward Gibbon, had already suggested that "instead of inquiring *why* the Roman empire was destroyed, we should rather be surprised that it had subsisted so long": after all, it was only a matter of time until "the stupendous fabric yielded to its own weight." From a global perspective, the fact that a particular empire crumbled when it did is not nearly as intriguing as it might seem if we focus only on that one case.[3]

A much more interesting question is whether there are patterns to be discovered and variables to be identified to help us establish a more general analytical taxonomy that can be used to frame our investigations of the end of any one empire. Yet the same academic industry that is responsible for many of the 210 putative reasons for the fall of Rome has so far neglected to invest even a tiny fraction of the energy that has been absorbed by this endless quest into a genuinely comparative assessment of how empires founder and fail. Thanks to this remarkable intellectual pathology, single-case studies continue to dominate the record, and even more broadly based cross-cultural studies tend to be fairly selective in their coverage.[4]

This is not the place to remedy that deficit, which would require a separate book—albeit one very much worth writing. For now, the deficit ought to deter us from accepting particular elements of an explanation without weighing them in the context of recurrent patterns. That said, the most basic outlines of the narrative of Rome's fall from power are not particularly controversial. The debate has traditionally revolved around the relative significance of internal versus external factors: flawed institutions, domestic power struggles over political position and surplus extraction, corruption, and economic weaknesses on the one hand, pressure from beyond the frontiers and shifting responses to it on the other. The latter category is now increasingly being augmented by the inclusion of detrimental environmental inputs from plagues to climate change.[5]

In the end, of course, the distinction between internal and external forces is rather artificial because they were so closely intertwined: "barbarian" challenges could boost military usurpations while the latter opened up space for the former; the costly expansion of administrative capacity in late antiquity did not merely seek to shore up imperial power against outsiders but was also a response to earlier centrifugal tendencies and fiscal constraints. Though ever-tempting, chicken-or-egg questions may well prove to be a dead end.[6]

Several long-term trends that undermined the integrity of the Roman empire are reasonably well discernible in the record. Local elites, on whose cooperation the central government critically relied, obstructed attempts to increase state revenue. Military capabilities as proxied by mobilization intensity declined. Geographical divisions deepened and became more formalized. Secondary state formation at the frontiers commenced wherever the Roman advance had finally run out of steam (or rather, incentives): what had once been a highly fragmented tribal periphery steadily accumulated organizational and technological knowledge. Scaling-up progressed far enough to challenge Rome's military supremacy but not enough to create suitable targets for counterattack, let alone sustainable conquest.

The spatial, social, and ethnic peripherization of military service—a feature common to many maturing empires—not only raised the profile of frontier forces but also drew in manpower from beyond. The resultant hybridization prolonged the life of the empire but became harder to manage once key revenue flows dried up. The system was highly vulnerable to the loss of regions that functioned as net exporters of the tax revenue required to secure poorer but more exposed areas: once the effective division of the empire into eastern and western halves had cut off westward transfers, protected zones such as North Africa and the Iberian peninsula assumed special importance, and their eventual loss to competitors was fiscally fatal.

Once the delicate balance between military powerholders, the semi-private wealth elite, and tax-exporting and -importing provinces began to unravel, as happened in the western half of the empire in the early fifth century, centralized control became ever harder to maintain. Burdened by revenue losses and infighting, rulers were compelled to make compromises with competing groups, a process that in turn encouraged local elites to reorient themselves toward new leaders as the traditional center receded from view. Ultimately, the empire was dismantled by nonstate actors that had formed at its margins, attracted by the resources the empire had to offer and sometimes also pushed by forces from farther away, most famously the Huns. By encroaching on the imperial tax base, they whittled away at the center's ability to confront or bribe them as needed. Their takeover of territory and population was gradual but inexorable.[7]

For the purposes of this study, it does not really matter which specific configuration of circumstances caused the western half of the empire to disintegrate as and when it did: the only thing that matters is that it fell apart. Whereas in the year 395, four in five Europeans had been ruled by a single imperial power, eighty years later they were not.

But how deep was Rome's fall? Across premodern history, many empires splintered only to be more or less swiftly restored under new management. Yet with the very partial exception of the East Roman restoration efforts of the sixth century, nothing like that ever happened in Europe. As we will see in this and in later chapters, the gradual but extremely thorough erosion of Roman-era institutions played a leading role in preventing imperial revival. It is almost as if Gibbon had it backward: in Europe, at least, the Roman empire fell when its long decline had barely begun.

I seek to capture this process of erosion in two complementary ways. In Part IV, I juxtapose developments in Europe with those in other parts of the Old World where empires continued to rise and fall well into the medieval and modern periods. This comparison shows that for a variety of reasons, empire-bearing structures were more potent and robust outside Europe (except for its eastern fringe).

An alternative path, taken in this and chapter 6, leads us to particular junctures in the history of post-Roman European state formation, and to the question of how conditions had evolved in ways that obstructed renewed imperiogenesis. This approach once again requires explicit consideration of counterfactuals: Can we identify any minimal or at least defensible rewrites of history that could have produced significantly different outcomes—in the form of renewed hegemonic empire—or were structural constraints so pervasive that this option never realistically presented itself? Assessing eight potential junctures from the sixth to the early nineteenth century, I argue that the latter was consistently the case. History would need to be rewritten on a grand scale to move European state formation back onto a Roman-style trajectory.[8]

THE SIXTH CENTURY: THE EAST ROMAN RESTORATION

At the end of the fifth century, a few successor states ruled by Germanic elites controlled most of what used to be the western half of the Roman empire: the Ostrogoths in Italy and Dalmatia, the Visigoths in the Iberian peninsula and Aquitaine, the Franks and Burgundians in Gaul, and the Vandals in North Africa and Sicily. Only peripheral areas such as Britain, Brittany, northwestern Spain, the Alps, and the western Maghreb had fissioned more intensely into smaller-scale polities (figure 5.1).

Thus, the overwhelming majority of the population of the former western provinces was claimed by no more than five powers. Because of this, and also because the new regimes heavily relied on Roman institutions to govern their territories, it is fair to say that beneath the current political divisions, much of the original empire still existed in some form. It was at this early stage of relatively modest fragmentation

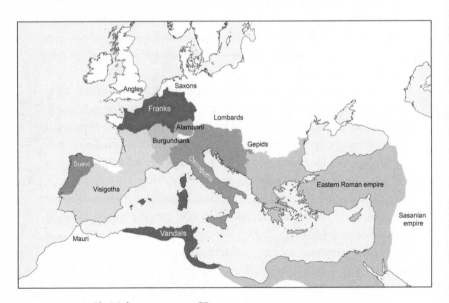

FIGURE 5.1 The Mediterranean, c. 500 CE.

and limited overall change that reunification might have been achieved without having to clear any forbiddingly high hurdles.

The fact that the eastern half of the empire, home to close to 40 percent of its original population, had survived the storms of the fifth century fully intact made this objective seem even more attainable. Even the Lower Danube basin, briefly overrun by Huns midcentury, had been reclaimed. Simply put, the eastern empire had thrived at the expense of its neighbors. As its western counterpart entered a death spiral of declining resources, internal rifts, and growing external challenges, mobile competitors were drawn into this area and thus by default away from the eastern empire, whose European borders were relatively short.

Moreover, its principal competitor, the Sasanian empire in Mesopotamia and Iran, had undergone a prolonged period of weakness. Between the 380s and the 520s, hostilities between the two empires remained rare—a striking departure from the previous one and a half centuries of repeated large-scale conflict. Alongside power struggles between rulers and the aristocracy, threats from the steppe were responsible for this hiatus. Over the course of the fifth century, steppe federations—the Red and especially the White Huns—put growing pressure on the northeastern frontier of the Sasanian empire. In 484, this conflict culminated in the defeat and battlefield death of a Sasanian king that was soon followed by the temporary overthrow of another one in response to anti-aristocratic reforms. The latter's subsequent restoration to the throne, courtesy of the White Huns, reflects the depth of Sasanian weakness at the time.[9]

This double meltdown beyond its borders made the eastern Roman empire look stronger than it was. In the fifth century, it had experienced episodes of political instability and armed conflict among rival elite and military groups. Doctrinal streamlining, exemplified by the assertion of orthodoxy at the Council of Chalcedon in 451, was bitterly resented and resisted by different Christian constituencies in Syria and Egypt. Ongoing expansion of elite landholdings curbed public revenue, especially after well-connected large landlords were put in charge of collecting taxes from tenants and employees on behalf of the state.

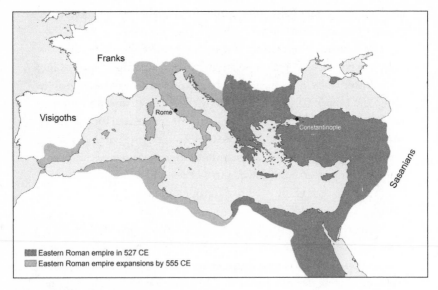

FIGURE 5.2 The Roman empire, c. 555 CE.

That favorable geopolitical conditions helped sustain this fragile imperial edifice makes the daunting scale of its later troubles less difficult to
understand.[10]

As it was, peace dividends allowed the eastern empire to accumulate
large reserves that could be applied to war-making. In a short campaign
in 533–534, its forces overthrew the Vandal regime that was centered on
what is now Tunisia. Between 535 and 540 much of Ostrogothic Italy was
conquered as well. At that point only two major Germanic powers remained, the Visigoths in the Iberian peninsula and the Franks (which had
by then absorbed the Burgundians) in Gaul. If the initial pace of this
advance was anything to go by, more comprehensive restoration might
have seemed within reach (figure 5.2).[11]

But this project quickly ran aground as several countervailing forces
converged against it. One was renewed Ostrogothic resistance in Italy
in the 540s and 550s, which absorbed troops and treasure. An intervention
against the Visigoths in the 550s did not proceed beyond narrow strips
of Iberian coastland. From the late 550s onward, a new front opened up

in the Balkans as Slavs and Avars stepped up incursions and autonomous settlement: within two generations, much of the region had been lost. Around 570, the Lombards overran much of Italy, canceling earlier hard-earned gains. And in the early seventh century, the Visigoths ejected the Roman garrisons from Spain.[12]

This pushback in the west and north coincided with a strong resurgence of the Sasanian empire in the east. Once Hunnic power had declined and the Iranian aristocracy had been tamed by reform, centralized tax collection and a more permanent army enhanced state capabilities. From the 530s onward, driven by the objective of extorting resources through plunder and unequal truces, a series of Sasanian rulers periodically waged war against the Roman empire.

After continuous conflict during the 570s and 580s, the Roman emperors found it increasingly difficult to pay their soldiers, a problem triggering unrest that was in turn exploited by the Iranians. In 602, they launched an open-ended offensive to seize as much Roman territory as possible, eventually annexing Syria, Palestine, and Egypt and advancing on the capital itself. In 626, a coordinated assault by Iranians and Avars on Constantinople was thwarted only by its massive fortifications and Roman sea power, and demonstrated just how vulnerable the empire had become.[13]

Not even the unlikely defeat of the Sasanians by last-ditch Roman campaigning and alliance-building was enough to hold off the empire's near-terminal contraction by more than a few years. In short order, bold Arab advances into areas that had been ravaged by war for a generation led to the loss of Syria, Palestine, and Egypt (636–642). Arab raids into Anatolia commenced without delay, followed by a massive naval buildup to challenge Roman command of the seas. In 655 a large Roman fleet was defeated: the first major naval setback since an isolated disaster involving the Vandals almost 200 years earlier, it heralded the end of what the Romans had long considered "our sea."

By then, Roman capabilities had been degraded to such an extent that Arab progress was curbed more by internal strife than by effective resistance. In the 660s, the Umayyad caliphate renewed operations with the goal of capturing Constantinople itself. The capital survived four years of seasonal naval blockades in the 670s only thanks to the deployment of a primitive version of napalm. In the meantime, the Arabs steadily advanced west of Egypt and took Roman Carthage near the end of the century. Annual raids into Anatolia were renewed in the 690s, coinciding with the rise of Bulgar power in the Balkans.

After an Arab land invasion in 717 had resulted in the loss of major cities in western Asia Minor, another failed blockade of the capital in the following year finally put an end to attempts to destroy the inner core of the empire, even if deep incursions continued into the 740s. At that point, all that was left of the Roman empire was Anatolia west of the Taurus and bits of the southern Balkans, Italy, and the surrounding islands. Sicily had only been saved by a Berber revolt against the Arabs in 740. Even after some recovery from the mid-ninth century onward, the Roman rump state—Byzantium—never again rose above the status of a midsize regional power.[14]

To make matters worse, Roman decline from the 540s into the eighth century coincided with the first appearance of pandemic bubonic plague in western Eurasia. In wave after wave for more than two centuries, this disease decimated populations that were expected to provide men and funds for the war effort.[15]

Given this near-apocalyptic onslaught from all directions, the failure of imperial restoration in Europe is not hard to explain—and certainly much easier to account for than the fact that the empire managed to survive at all, if only by a thread. Between the mid-sixth century, the high-water mark of reconquest, and the early eighth century, its territory shrank by about 60 percent, from 1.5 million to 600,000 square kilometers. Effective army strength halved from around 150,000 men in the 550s to 80,000 by the 770s. Fiscal attrition was even more severe: state revenue fell by four-fifths or more between the mid-sixth and the early eighth century. The reason that the latter exceeded the loss of territory and military strength by so much may be sought in the fact that the lost provinces had also been among the richest. A more generalized economic decline coupled with the demographic consequences of the plague also contributed: archaeological evidence points to de-urbanization and the contraction of surviving urban sites, as well as a dwindling of trade in bulk goods.[16]

In view of all this, there is no realistic scenario in which Roman campaigns could have continued after 540 in a way that would have resulted in durable imperial restoration. Too many obstacles arose in rapid succession. Even if the subjugation of the Ostrogoths had been handled more adroitly and the domestic problems of the Visigoths had been exploited more effectively, the Franks posed a formidable challenge, and new peripheral groups from Lombards to Slavs and Avars and later Bulgars were arrayed along an extended continental frontier, ready to probe the empire's defenses. The Sasanian revival ended what had been an anomalously long period of peace between two powers that had traditionally been locked into expensive conflict. Renewal of this conflict in turn opened the door to opportunistic competitors, enabling the freshly united Arabs to punch well above their weight. In addition, environmental forces from plague to climate change undermined the empire's ability to marshal the resources required to maintain its existing positions.

There is simply no moderate rewrite of history that would even remotely succeed in changing the overall trajectory of the Roman empire from near collapse to comprehensive restoration. To achieve this goal, the history of large parts of Europe and West Asia would need to be rewritten, and, moreover, so would natural history. As favorable as circumstances might have seemed when the eastern empire embarked on its ambitious westward expansion, with the benefit of hindsight we can see that this expansion occurred in the twilight of what had been an exceptionally fortuitous break from serious challenges.

It is true that some of the later setbacks were highly contingent: above all, the early Arab victories that set in motion their seemingly unstoppable advance across the Levant and North Africa might well have been averted. However, the Roman position in Europe was vulnerable to so many different competitors that longer-term outcomes could not simply be altered in favor of durable empire by modifying individual details. Between Franks, Lombards, Slavs, Avars, and Bulgars, there were simply too many moving parts and an overall redundancy in challengers to make this a defensible counterfactual strategy. At no time did the eastern empire dispose of the military manpower that had allowed late Republican and early monarchical Rome to penetrate and hold on to large parts of Western Europe. In sum, the chances of rebuilding anything resembling the mature Roman empire in Europe had been minimal.

This is important above all because the western Mediterranean campaigns represented the earliest determined attempt to restore a more hegemonic version of empire in Europe: close in time to the fall of the western Roman empire, it was therefore in some ways also the most promising. As already noted, political fragmentation had not yet progressed far. Swift victories over the Vandals—echoed by the Arabs' later success against the Visigoths—showed that at least some of these Germanic successor regimes, sustained by fairly small coalitions of conquerors, were shallow, brittle, and consequently vulnerable to decisive strikes by a more sophisticated imperial power that commanded the seas. With few exceptions, Roman institutions of governance had not yet eroded beyond salvaging.

That the persistent congruence of adverse forces over many generations made it impossible to exploit these otherwise favorable circumstances dramatically reduced the likelihood that the Roman empire would ever be more or less fully restored. And although a more benign environment might have made it much easier to capitalize on these advantages, such a counterfactual environment is hard to create in any plausible manner: too much real-life history would have to be abandoned in the process.

The most straightforward path to imperial unity—the restoration of a preexisting edifice of rule that had fissioned only a few generations earlier—was thus solidly blocked. Any later path would need to follow a more arduous route through the creation of new governmental structures, a more demanding exercise made even more daunting once we recall the exceptional and not always replicable starting advantages Rome had initially enjoyed. The setbacks of late antiquity raised the bar for Roman-style empire in post-Roman Europe very high indeed.

THE EIGHTH CENTURY: THE ARAB CONQUESTS

With little hope of a genuinely Roman restoration of the empire on anything close to its original scale, conquest by external powers that were able to build on existing Roman institutions was the second-best option. Had the Sasanian empire and its Avar allies succeeded in taking Constantinople, long-term control over the eastern half of the former Roman empire would have been a plausible outcome. At the same time, it is much more difficult to envision further advances into Europe. The Sasanian center of gravity was solidly set in Iran. Any attempts to penetrate Europe would have entailed considerable logistical challenges, comparable to the problems the similarly configured Achaemenid empire had encountered more than a millennium earlier.[17]

Operations might well have stalled in the Balkans in the face of Slav and especially Avar resistance, and campaigning in North Africa was unlikely to yield more than ephemeral gains akin to the subsequent Umayyad conquests in the Maghreb. The real-life serial defeats of the Sasanian military at the hands of Romans, Göktürks, and Arabs between 627 and 641 leave little doubt that the Sasanian forces lacked the wherewithal to establish control over the principal European territories once held by the Romans: Italy, the Iberian peninsula, and Gaul.

This leaves the Arabs as the only credible contenders. Far less tied to a developed core, they enjoyed great mobility that gave them an advantage in projecting power more widely beyond their region of origin. The explosive nature of their expansion was astounding. In 629 the great war between Rome and the Sasanians had finally ground to a halt, and the two powers had once again divided control of the eastern Mediterranean, Mesopotamia, and Iran between them. Within the next thirteen years, the Arabs seized the Roman territories in Palestine, Syria, northern Mesopotamia, and Egypt, overran Sasanian southern Mesopotamia, and crushed Sasanian resistance in western Iran.

Although their advance slowed down considerably afterward, it nonetheless continued for several generations. Eastern Iran and the Maghreb were subdued during the second half of the seventh century. As already mentioned, the caliphate also built up sufficient naval assets

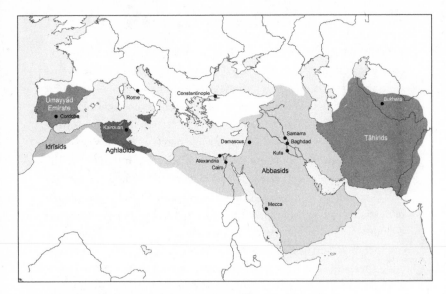

FIGURE 5.3 The Umayyad caliphate, c. 750 CE, and later successor states.

to challenge Roman supremacy at sea and attack Constantinople. In the 710s, Arab-led forces invaded the Iberian peninsula and destroyed the Visigothic kingdom, and took over the Indus Valley more than 6,000 kilometers to the east. In the following decades, they launched several raids into Gaul and pushed into Central Asia, where they defeated a Chinese-led army in 751—the first military encounter between East and West Asian states (figure 5.3).[18]

The resultant empire was very large: it covered as many as 11 million square kilometers, if arid zones are included, and up to 40 million people. Just as Rome had once controlled 80 percent of all Europeans, the Umayyad caliphate laid claim to 80 percent of the inhabitants of the Middle East and North Africa region, the same proportion as the Achaemenids had ruled in a less populous era and a considerably larger one than that controlled by the Ottomans later.[19]

Yet none of this had any palpable effect on European state formation: the caliphate failed to project power more deeply into Europe, and its unity ended shortly after its expansion had reached its limits. By 900, the caliphate had de facto fractured into nine major and several smaller polities that greatly differed in terms of their internal cohesion. The reasons for this outcome can be explored from two angles—by asking why the Arabs initially succeeded as they did, and why they were unable to advance further or at least maintain political integrity.

I already noted that when the eastern Roman empire embarked on its reconquest of the western Mediterranean in the 530s, unusual circumstances had made it seem more formidable than it would soon turn out to be. The same qualification applies in even greater measure to the new empire of the Arabs. Thus, the rapid pace of their initial gains owed more to exceptionally favorable geopolitical circumstances than to any intrinsic military or organizational superiority. With respect to both speed and stability, the Arab conquests were the exact opposite of Rome's halting expansion that had been solidly undergirded by cohesive might.[20]

In the late sixth century, the centralization of Roman and Sasanian military power led to the disbanding of client states at these empires' respective Arabian frontiers. This removed the previous cordon sanitaire and placed the full burden of defense on their professional armies. Once the Arabian peninsula pooled its manpower under the leadership of the Prophet and the first caliph, these empires were directly exposed to their attacks, which could hardly have occurred at a worse time. For close to three decades, the Roman and Sasanian empires had been locked into all-out war. In the Roman Levant, the Persian occupation had caused major disruptions, and although the Sasanians had formally made peace in 628, the Roman authorities had only just begun to reestablish control when the Arabs appeared on the scene a few years later. Conditions were even less settled across the border in the Sasanian domain: defeat by the Romans had triggered four years of civil war, which ended right before the Arabs first invaded.

The shocks of these preceding conflicts had created an enormous power vacuum that the Arabs eagerly exploited. Hugh Kennedy, a leading authority on their early conquests, offers a sobering counterfactual: "If Muhammad had been born a generation earlier and he and his successors had attempted to send armies against the great empires in, say, 600, it is hard to imagine that they would have made any progress at all." And even once the two empires had fought each other to mutual depletion, Arab success remained highly contingent. Early resounding victories against Roman and Persian forces may well have been of crucial importance in making subsequent expansion possible by boosting confidence and encouraging other Arabs to join in.[21]

Their good fortune continued at least in part. Roman North Africa, now only tenuously connected to the imperial center, was hard to defend and, burdened by heavy taxation, perhaps not too reluctant to change masters. The forces that ventured into the Iberian peninsula went up against a usurper who had just split the Visigothic kingdom, thus unwittingly paving the ground for Arab-Berber conquest. Wherever resistance was more determined, by contrast, the Arabs faltered: Constantinople in particular tenaciously held on.

Overall, their conquests had been greatly facilitated by serious dislocations among their opponents: what had long been the principal components of two large empires had been turned into a congeries of exposed peripheries. And on top of everything else, by the time the Arab expansion commenced, the plague had ravaged the densely populated regions of the Middle East and Europe for almost a century. Resistance had been weakened by depopulation and attendant fiscal attrition. The Arabs' avid slave-taking may well have been driven by labor shortages.[22]

The peculiar mode of organization of the conquering power helped it make the most of these rare opportunities. The Arab forces consisted of war-trained men, loyal to kin and tribe, and now also to their new religion. Often hardened Bedouin, they were highly mobile and able to cover large distances without slow supply trains. Their initial footprint was light, or at any rate less heavy than that of the centralizing high-maintenance empires they replaced. Their leaders demanded tribute but little else; destruction or terror remained rare.

The Arab forces settled in isolation from the local population in newly founded garrison cities, a strategy that helped them maintain cohesion and reduce friction with civilians. Thin on the ground—unlike Germans, Arabs did not resettle en masse—they did not push for religious conversion: their conquest societies were open, allowing allies to join. Islamization was slow and driven by benefits rather than compulsion. In the Christian Levant, the large Miaphysite and Nestorian communities were finally free to practice their creeds without high-handed interference from orthodox Constantinople.[23]

Moreover, the psychological impact of the Arab blitzkrieg must not be underrated. To them and to outsiders alike, the pace and scale of their triumphs reflected God's will: in the 680s, the Nestorian monk John Bar Penkaye marveled that

> only a short period of time passed before the entire world was handed over to the Arabs; they subdued all fortified cities, taking control from sea to sea, and from east to west—Egypt, and from Crete to Cappadocia, from Yemen to the [Caucasus], Armenians, Syrians, Persians, Byzantines and Egyptians, and all the areas in between: "their hand was upon everyone" as the prophet says.[24]

But why did nothing comparable to the Roman empire arise from this lightning expansion? In the end, the Arabs' zeal was no match for structural constraints that began to undermine their empire almost as soon as it was created. Two features played a critical role in this process: the organization of the Arab military and the allocation of state revenue. From the outset, the armies of conquest and occupation were rooted in tribal structures and allegiances and never cohered into a fully integrated whole. The forces that took over particular territories generally settled there and expected to be supported by revenue drawn from those regions.

As the empire grew, this resulted in the emergence of effectively separate domains controlled by different forces. The two principal parties were the army of Syria (in what used to be the eastern Roman provinces) and the armies of Basra and Kufa in Iraq (in what used to be the western part of the Sasanian empire). Additional regional entities formed in due course: the army of Egypt, which later supported operations in the Maghreb and the Iberian peninsula, the army of Khorasan in Iran, and forces on the northern frontier (or Yazira). Tax revenues were largely retained within these regions and expended in the first instance on their garrisons and, at least for a while, even on the descendants of the original invaders.

This constellation precipitated interregional rivalries that were further complicated by tribal divisions within the various armies. The Umayyad caliphs, based in Damascus, relied primarily on the army of Syria. The first civil war, fought not long after the initial conquests (656–661), was in large part a struggle over supremacy and privilege between different groups in Syria and Iraq. At the same time, both armies experienced frictions between northern Arab and Yemeni elements, as well as between those whose presence preceded the conquests and later arrivals.

The second round of civil war, in the 680s, witnessed renewed clashes between forces in Syria, Iraq, Iran, and the Arabian peninsula. The Syrian army, which was instrumental in pacification, subsequently supplanted the forces that had previously held Iraq. As the only remaining military entity west of Iran that was capable of supporting major campaigns (with the help of troops from the Caucasus frontier), it was responsible for the final push against Constantinople in 717–718, and in 741 sent reinforcements to the Maghreb to help suppress a Berber uprising. Meanwhile, the army of Khorasan in Iran gathered strength, assuming a balancing position similar to that previously held by the Iraqi units.

The third round of civil war in the 740s that brought down the Umayyad dynasty once again pitted northern Arab against Yemeni networks and several regional armies against one another. At first, the Syrian forces disintegrated in a conflict between contenders supported by north and south Arab elements. After an attempted defection of Egypt and risings in Iraq had been suppressed, Iran became a center of opposition, driven in part by Arab settlers in Merv and Yemeni elements hostile to the northern Arab-dominated caliphate farther west. Escalating war destroyed the Umayyads, who had had to fall back on northern frontier troops, and ushered in the rule of the Iran-based Abbasids, who immediately shifted the imperial capital to Mesopotamia (first Kufa, then alternately Baghdad and Samarra)—and hence farther away from Europe.[25]

This new arrangement, however, merely displaced tensions eastward, as Iraqi and Iranian interests collided. This eventually led to a fourth round of open warfare. Ostensibly a conflict over the Abbasid succession, it was fought in the 810s between Arab and Iranian forces but reverberated into the 830s, and encouraged the regime to employ Turkic mercenaries for its protection—a very belated acknowledgment that long-standing internal divisions and enmities could not be overcome and a novel strategy was called for.

By then, the Sunni-Shia rift had crystallized into separate political-military systems. The introduction of foreign mercenaries simply generated new tensions between what effectively represented a new conquest group and local elites who resisted taxation, especially when revenue was collected for the benefit of outsiders hired to keep these elites in check. Once the Turkic units enjoyed a monopoly on organized violence, they readily joined in lucrative partisan conflicts. During the Samarra crisis of the 860s, five different caliphs were raised up by competing Turkic factions.

This resulted in the most dramatic meltdown thus far: Iran was ceded to rebels, the authorities in Egypt stopped remitting tax to the center and pushed into Palestine and Syria, and southern Iraq was buffeted by a huge slave revolt. Brief and incomplete recovery was soon followed by renewed fragmentation from the 920s onward, as Egypt and Syria established de facto independence from the caliphate. In 945, the Buyids from Iran seized control over Baghdad and Iraq. At that point, the Abbasid caliphs, even if they formally hung on until 1258, had already lost any tangible political power.

By the late tenth century, the splintering of the formerly Arab empire had reached new heights: the Samanids controlled eastern Iran, two or three Buyid polities coexisted in western Iran and Iraq, two Hamdanid regimes shared Syria, and Ikhshidids and then Fatimids ruled Egypt. Kurdish dynasts and the Qaramita in the Arabian peninsula rounded off this mix. As described below, the Maghreb and Iberia had by then long gone their separate ways. For several centuries, the trend was unidirectional: fragmentation intensified over time.[26]

Regionalization and kin and tribal ties that persisted and were reproduced in occupied lands all converged in weakening the center's grip on its far-flung domain. Fiscal decentralization contributed significantly to the resultant process of segmentation. From early on, Arab soldiers received cash salaries, a practice that helped preserve the existing Roman and Sasanian tax systems.[27]

At the same time, fiscal redistribution was highly decentralized: the regional armies retained most of the taxes collected in their respective territories. From the outset, the system had been shaped by the expectation that the revenue collected from infidels belonged to their occupiers as a collective, and that the latter were entitled to it by right of conquest and not as a grant from the caliph. More strikingly, the male descendants of the men who set up the original garrisons fully expected to continue to receive emoluments as a hereditary right.

The question of whether receipt of public stipends should be contingent on actual military service or expand into a sinecure was hotly contested between the central authorities and the beneficiaries of the more generous interpretation of entitlements. The related question of whether what was left after these disbursements was to remain in the same region or to be remitted to the court of the caliph likewise proved controversial. In practice, only a small portion of all state revenue ever reached the imperial center. The Umayyad rulers in Damascus relied principally on Syrian taxes but received little from Iraq and Egypt, not to mention from more distant provinces: there is no sign that the Maghreb or Iberia ever contributed anything of substance.[28]

As a consequence, the caliphs were heavily restrained from accessing and channeling the abundant riches that their vast empire generated. Nominal military strength as derived from the tallies of those on the government payroll was highly deceptive: while some 250,000 to 300,000 men were entitled to stipends, only a small fraction of them could actually be mobilized, and even fewer were ready to be deployed outside their own regions. Caliphs' attempts to seize at least some of this surplus created tensions with regional interest groups. When arrangements were changed around 700 to limit pay to those on active military duty, this reform helped sustain effective forces in the various regions but did not address the more fundamental problem of effective decentralization.[29]

Instead, fiscal fragmentation facilitated political divisions. As revenues had always been largely retained in the regions where they had been levied, the establishment of new polities did not entail dramatic changes but simply formalized existing fiscal dispersion. The step from remitting a small fraction of total revenue to none at all was a small one, fraught with symbolic meaning but relatively easy to take in practice.[30]

Under these circumstances, it was not the eventual splintering of the political domain that was remarkable, but rather that unity endured for as long as it did. Military force was essential in maintaining a degree of cohesion: as long as the army of Syria was capable of suppressing dissent farther east (as it did in the 650s and 680s) or the army of Iran was strong enough to do the same in the west (as in the 740s), it was possible to maintain a single caliphate. When in the ninth century tensions became too difficult to manage, mercenaries were brought in to save the regime. These, however, merely reinforced the divisions between rulers and ruled without being invested in unity across different regions. In the end, their backing of rival factions accelerated political fission.

All this highlights the long-term costs of Arab-style "conquest-lite," which allowed a partially fragmented core to reproduce its divisions on a grander scale in newly acquired peripheries. Ceding control of much of the surplus to regional armies may well have helped ensure formal loyalty by reducing the benefits of outright independence, especially as long as the Syrian army was still in a position to punish defectors. Yet this also prepared the ground for fragmentation once a cash-deprived center had been weakened by internal divisions and attrition. In this unpromising context, an early Abbasid attempt to centralize the fiscal regime did not survive for long.

The empire had from the beginning been a congeries of franchises run by and for the benefit of discrete regional groups of armed rent-seekers. Tribal and geographical rivalries stoked latent centrifugal tendencies. The complex and interregional revenue flows of the mature Roman empire provide an ideal-typical counterpoint to arrangements in the caliphate, as does the former's much greater durability.

In the most general terms, conditions in the Umayyad caliphate were not favorable to what we might call the "Arab option"—the restoration of large-scale empire in Europe under Arab control. Conquests did not fill state coffers to support further conquests but primarily expanded the body of beneficiaries without boosting mobilization. This alone greatly reduced the likelihood that the resources of empire could be marshaled in sufficient concentration to break Constantinople or make major inroads into Europe.

More specifically, Umayyad advances west of Egypt, while successful in terms of handing Arab warriors new subjects and lands to exploit, proved fairly ephemeral in terms of extending the area ruled by the center. After the occupation of Egypt, it took the Arabs half a century to seize Carthage. They reached the Straits of Gibraltar shortly afterward, recruiting local Berbers along the way. In an invasion conceived perhaps as not more than a plundering expedition of fewer than 10,000 men, they took advantage of internal divisions within the Visigothic kingdom to overrun most of the Iberian peninsula with the exception of its mountainous northern rim (711–716).

Members of the Visigothic elite readily joined the new conquest class. Unlike farther east, no separate garrison cities were set up, and Arabs and Berbers lived interspersed with the local population. For the remainder of the eighth century, administrative structures remained minimal. Inasmuch as taxes were collected at all, this practice was limited to the more densely settled and developed south.[31]

Having secured this region with fairly modest effort, its new rulers directed their attention to raids across the Pyrenees, focusing on the sliver of coastland west of the Rhone that was still held by the Visigoths. A foray into the duchy of Aquitaine, formally part of the Merovingian kingdom of the Franks but de facto an autonomous polity, was checked by a major defeat at Toulouse in 721 that cost the governor of al-Andalus (the caliphate's new Iberian province) his life. Highlighting the fractured nature of the Arab front, the Berber leader in charge of annexing the Visigothic coastlands subsequently struck a deal with Aquitaine to secure independence from his Arab overlords back in Spain. He was in turn killed by the new governor of al-Andalus, who proceeded to attack Aquitaine and took Bordeaux. As he moved farther north to plunder Tours, he was defeated and killed by Frankish forces in 732.

The most important outcome of these operations was that Aquitaine was forced back under Frankish control, strengthening the Christian side in the process. A further Arab-Berber invasion in the late 730s brought new raids but no lasting gains; a third governor was soundly beaten in 737, even though he uncharacteristically survived. The Arabs managed to hold on to coastal Provence until the end of the 750s, when the Franks completed their takeover. In the 760s, the latter fully subdued Aquitaine, and at the end of the eighth century Charlemagne's forces crossed the Pyrenees to establish strongholds on the other side.

I relate these events in some detail to clarify the central trend, which was a shift in the balance of power against the Arabs over the course of the eighth century. Whereas they had overcome the Visigoths with relative ease, their actions against the more formidable Franks were largely limited to raiding for plunder, and repeatedly failed at great cost. Galvanized by these hostilities, the Franks soon took the initiative and made gradual but steady progress. There is little in this story to support Edward Gibbon's famously hyperbolic (if ironic) claim that the Arab incursions might have altered the path of European history:

> A victorious line of march had been prolonged above a thousand miles from the rock of Gibraltar to the banks of the Loire; the repetition of an equal space would have carried the Saracens to the confines of Poland and the Highlands of Scotland; the Rhine is not more impassable than the Nile or Euphrates, and the Arabian fleet might have sailed without a naval combat into the mouth of the Thames. Perhaps the interpretation of the Koran would now be taught in the schools of Oxford, and her pulpits might demonstrate to a circumcised people the sanctity and truth of the revelation of Mahomet.[32]

Yet even though the view that all the Franks did at the time was to curb pillaging operations has since gained ground, the potential for plausible counterfactuals is nonetheless worth considering. Frankish military capabilities were relatively modest and still in the process of being restored when the Arabs appeared on the scene. Thus, if a few of these battles had gone the other way—always a credible contingency—the Arabs and Berbers might well have been able to penetrate France more deeply and form alliances with local potentates, just as they had done in Spain and also attempted in the case of Aquitaine. Southern France could have become a launchpad for ongoing assaults to the north and also eastward into Italy. The counterfactual of a sustained Arab presence coupled with some degree of Islamization cannot therefore be dismissed out of hand. The key question, however, is whether any of this could somehow have led to the incorporation of large parts of Europe into a unified Arab empire.[33]

Based on real-life developments in the western periphery of the caliphate, the answer can only be negative. After the Umayyad dynasty had been wiped out after its defeat in civil war in 750, a lone survivor took over al-Andalus in 756, prompting the first enduring secession from the (now Abbasid-ruled) caliphate. The center's only attempt to restore control failed in 763 when an army of just a few thousand men was dispatched from North Africa. Local opposition had much greater impact: it took the new defector regime a couple of decades to suppress resistance within Spain itself, and even then the effective power of the emir of Cordoba was confined to the south of the peninsula while the other regions only nominally accepted his overlordship.

Around the middle of the ninth century, efforts at greater centralization on the early Abbasid model finally succeeded in imposing taxation more widely. However, this push for state-building soon alienated local elites and foundered in a prolonged period of internal conflict from the 880s to the 920s. Restoration of state power in the tenth and early eleventh centuries was followed by renewed collapse. By the 1030s the emirate had splintered into some thirty mini-kingdoms (taifs).[34]

Spain subsequently fell under the influence of Maghreb-based polities, first the Almoravids (around 1100) and then the Almohads (around 1200), until Christian states expanded from farther north. Not only was the only Arab-held region in Europe permanently severed from (and in fact hostile to) the caliphate, it experienced internal instability and fragmentation that worsened over time. Because of this, the Iberian peninsula was completely unsuitable as a staging area for further advances into Europe, even as Frankish power declined after Charlemagne: the Western European powers fractured but the westernmost Arab regimes were weaker still.

Moreover, the mid-eighth-century secession of Spain was part of a more generalized fraying of the caliphate's western periphery that faced Europe. In 740, a massive Berber revolt threatened the center's hold on the Maghreb. A substantial force dispatched from Syria to crush the rising failed: although the Tunisian and northeast Algerian core areas of Arab Ifriqiya could be saved, the central and western Maghreb were permanently lost to assorted Berber polities. The revolt also spread to the Berber units that made up the bulk of the occupation forces in Spain and had to be suppressed by the remaining Syrian forces, which then came to blows with the local Arab garrison. Armed conflict between the Syrian expeditionary force (dominated by North Arabian elements) and the regional army of Ifriqiya (dominated by men of Yemeni background) was only barely avoided and cooperation was poor. These tensions, together with the clashes in Spain, show the extent to which internal divisions obstructed coordinated military activity on a larger scale, even for defensive purposes.

Shortly afterward, the fall of the Umayyads prompted the defection of what was left of Ifriqiya in the 750s until it was regained for the Abbasids in 762. From 757, the Rustamids set up an independent theocratic imamate first in Tripolitania and then in Algeria: despite early attempts to suppress it, it survived for a century and a half. From 788, the Idrisids, originating in yet another refugee from a lost power struggle with the Abbasids, took over Morocco and lasted for two centuries. Meanwhile, Ifriqiya itself was run by the Aghlabid family throughout the ninth century, nominally under Abbasid suzerainty but in practice highly autonomous: governors were no longer appointed by the caliph as family members inherited the position, and there is no sign of tax remittances to the east.

Even that lip service came to an end when the Fatimid (rival) caliphate took over in 909. The Fatimids in turn were the first regional force to advance eastward, reversing three centuries of westward expansion of major Middle Eastern powers from the Sasanians to the Umayyads and Abbasids. Their capture of Egypt in 969 meant that Asian powers were shut out of Africa until the Ottomans appeared in the sixteenth century and established indirect and soon diminishing nominal control as far west as Algeria.

In Spain and North Africa, the power of Arab and Berber states waxed and waned throughout the Middle Ages, but hegemonic empire did not return. At no time after the mid-eighth century was the original caliphate in a position to launch attacks against Europe. Without such backing, none of the peripheral successor states had any hope of establishing larger imperial structures in Europe. I already mentioned the fitful weakening of Arab power in Spain. The Aghlabids of Ifriqiya, relying on their own limited resources, needed seventy-five years to conquer Sicily. Subsequent raids against southern Italy were suppressed in the early tenth century. There is no better illustration of the basic fact that none of these Arab-led polities were capable of sustained expansion into Europe.[35]

Overall, in no credible counterfactual scenario could Arabs (and their local allies) have established a larger empire on European soil by way of North Africa. Whether an Arab takeover of Constantinople—a less far-fetched alternative outcome—might have allowed substantial advances through the Balkans is more difficult to judge, although the Bulgar empire would have posed a significant obstacle. What matters most, however, is not whether any such advances could have occurred, but whether they might have drawn large parts of Europe into a very large caliphate. The insuperable structural divisions that steadily undermined the unity of the Arab conquest society that had emerged in the mid-seventh century all but rules this out. In the most optimistic scenarios, the best that might have been achieved was the creation of a few additional successor emirates alongside those that popped up in actual history—but not hegemonic empire on anything like the Roman scale.[36]

No even remotely economical rewrite could produce a credible counterfactual: we would need to do nothing less than to change the entire history of the late antique Arabian peninsula, and perhaps even its social structures, to obtain a different outcome. From this perspective, the "Arab option" of imperial restoration in Europe was never even on the table.

THE NINTH CENTURY: THE CAROLINGIAN EMPIRE

As neither the eastern half of the Roman state nor the most formidable foreign power of the period, the Umayyad caliphate, had succeeded in restoring hegemonic empire in Europe, the only remaining option was empire-building from within the formerly Roman regions of Europe that had been taken over by Germanic successor regimes. However, suitable candidates were in short supply: the Vandal and Ostrogothic kingdoms had fallen first to the East Romans and then to the Arabs and Lombards, respectively, while the Arabs and their Berber allies had supplanted Visigothic rule in the Iberian peninsula. The Lombard kings struggled to maintain a unified state in Italy. England, geographically peripheral and politically fragmented, was never a serious contender.

This leaves the Frankish kingdom in what used to be Roman Gaul. By the end of the fifth century, the Franks had seized northern Gaul, much of the Rhineland, and a slice of central Germany north of the Main. During the following generation, they also wrested Aquitaine from the Visigoths and subdued the Swabians in the Upper Rhine and Danube region and the Burgundians in southeastern Gaul.

Yet despite this rapid and ostensibly promising growth spurt, Frankish expansion subsequently largely stalled for about two centuries. Among the reasons for this were periodic divisions of the realm between the sons of deceased Merovingian kings, which commenced in 511 and reliably triggered internal conflict that took precedence over further conquests: the incorporation of Burgundy in the early 530s, the last major addition to the kingdom, was also the only one engineered by a fraternal royal coalition.[37]

Over the course of multiple partitions in the second half of the sixth and the first half of the seventh century, Francia came to be increasingly formally divided into three subkingdoms: Austrasia (in Germany and northeastern Gaul), Neustria (in central and eastern Gaul), and Aquitaine (in southwestern Gaul). Eventually, Aquitaine as well as the Duchies of Bavaria and Thuringia drifted out of the orbit of effective Merovingian power. In the two principal Frankish subkingdoms, meanwhile, royal authority was steadily eroded by aristocratic autonomy and the ascent of the kings' mayors as the actual political leaders.

Beginning in the late seventh century, centralizing measures finally began to reclaim some of the lost ground, albeit only haltingly and interrupted by renewed strife and division: even after the mayor of Austrasia had gained control over much of Francia in 687 and marginalized the Merovingian lineage, the mayoral succession in turn mimicked earlier royal practices by spawning civil war (in 714 to 718) and two further partitions (in 741 and 768). These setbacks obstructed state (re-)formation: internal consolidation and external conquest turned out to be feasible only under unified leadership.

This accounts for the four documented spurts of activity from 687 to 714 (under Pepin, who scored victories against Frisians and Alemanni), from 718 to 741 (under Charles Martel, who confronted invading Arabs and Berbers as well as Frisians, Saxons, and Bavarians), from 751 to 768 (under another Pepin, the Short, the first Carolingian to claim the kingship, who entered into an alliance with the papacy and intervened on its behalf against the Lombards in Italy), and most strikingly from 772 to 814, under Charlemagne.

This fourth and longest phase of unity produced the most ambitious advances: Frankish forces subjugated the Saxons between the lower Rhine and the Elbe, annexed the central and eastern Alps and the adjacent Danube basin, shattered the confederation of Pannonia's Avars, compelled various Slavic groups between the Elbe and the Oder and in Pannonia to accept tributary obligations, campaigned south of the Pyrenees, and, most important, overcame Lombard resistance in northern and central Italy. The last of these accomplishments enabled Charlemagne to share control over the Duchy of Rome and parts of the northern Italian peninsula with the papacy and offer it protection. In return, in 800 Pope Leo III crowned him emperor (*imperator*), the first ruler in what had been the western half of the Roman empire to bear this title after a 320-year hiatus (figure 5.4).

At that point, Charlemagne claimed suzerainty over up to one-third of the people who then lived in the territories that had once been held by Rome, and perhaps closer to 40 percent of the total population of

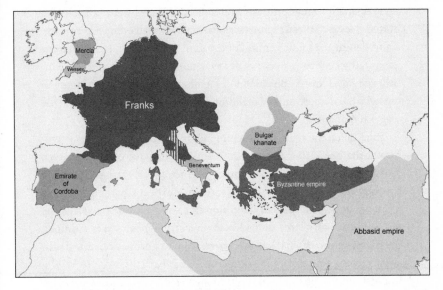

FIGURE 5.4 The Carolingian empire, c. 800 CE.

Europe. Serious state-level competitors were rare, limited in the first place to the Lombard principality of Beneventum in southern Italy and the emirate of Cordoba in Spain. At somewhat greater remove, the Roman possessions in Sicily and the southern and eastern Balkans, the Bulgars in the lower Danube basin, and assorted smallish kingdoms across the Channel in Britain rounded off this modest tableau. The Frankish empire exceeded all these polities in terms of people and territory. Only the eastern Roman empire approached it in manpower, and even though it was more cohesively organized, it was still struggling to recover from its near demise at the hands of the Arabs. Moreover, a cordon sanitaire from the Lombards to the Serbs separated it from the Frankish domains.

In theory, the geopolitical landscape favored Frankish expansion into other parts of Europe that had previously been ruled by Rome. The Umayyad emirate in Spain was brittle and internally fragmented, and in the mid-ninth century the Duchy of Beneventum split in two. England, while requiring a naval assault, was divided among seven major and

several smaller kingdoms and statelets, and Wales was similarly disunited. None of these regions was particularly well equipped to withstand determined intervention of the kind that had brought down the
Saxons, the Lombard kingdom of Pavia, or the Avar confederation. Further potential targets beckoned in Denmark, which was beginning to
coalesce into a more unified realm, and in Slavic Central Europe and the
western Balkans.

Thus, given the spatial and demographic heft of the Carolingian empire at the beginning of the ninth century, the pace of its expansion
during the preceding decades, and the serious shortcomings of its main
competitors in Europe, we might reasonably expect Charlemagne's immediate successors (the emperor himself passed away in 814 at the ripe
old age of seventy-two) to have been in a strong position to continue
the reunification of what had once been Roman Europe and to add substance to the title of Roman emperor—and, perhaps, even to lay the
foundations for more durable unity along the lines of the Roman model.

What happened was exactly the opposite. In keeping with Frankish
custom reaching back three centuries, Charlemagne had made arrangements for dividing his kingdom among three sons (for the Franks,
Lombards, and Aquitaine). After two of them predeceased him, the
remaining one, Louis the Pious, inherited an effectively unified kingdom.
Yet just three years into his reign he likewise arranged for another tripar-
tite division among his sons, one of whom also became his co-emperor.
Frontier wars in Germany, Pannonia, and Spain in the late 810s and the
820s accomplished little and were abandoned when Louis's attempt to
accommodate a fourth son in the allocation of territories triggered civil
war. Most of the 830s was taken up by open warfare between the emperor
and his various sons and nobles, accompanied by multiple short-lived
divisions of the realm; Louis himself was deposed for a year.[38]

His death in 840 unleashed even more intense fighting among his
three surviving sons. They soon carved up the empire into three effectively separate kingdoms—West Francia (the basis for what became
France), Middle Francia (or "Lotharingia," an elongated and diverse
domain that stretched from the Low Countries and Burgundy to Northern Italy), and East Francia (the core of future Germany). This step not

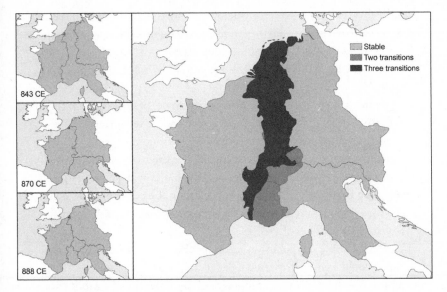

FIGURE 5.5 Carolingian partitions, 843–888 CE.

only fatally compromised the integrity of the empire but ushered in four decades of complex internal conflicts and renewed partitions, one of which briefly splintered Middle Francia into three separate kingdoms. A more durable settlement was reached in 870 and helped stabilize the geographical boundaries of West and East Francia and Italy. When abdications and inheritance put Charles the Fat in charge of all these kingdoms, this fortuitous restoration lasted only three years (884–887) and coincided with dramatic Viking incursions that delegitimated his position (figure 5.5).

Upon Charles's death, nobles in each of the three major kingdom elected their own rulers. The kingdom of Italy subsequently descended into more than seventy years of persistent instability and infighting until it was finally reclaimed by the rulers of East Francia. As we will see in the next section, the kings of East Francia had to contend with serious challenges to their authority. Even those, however, paled in comparison to the near-terminal decline of centralized power in West Francia, where the regions outside the old Frankish heartlands in the northeast came to be divided among powerful duchies. Viking conquests were formally acknowledged in 911 when they were granted rights to Normandy. Their now-vacant position as fearsome marauders was at once filled by the Magyars, who conducted raids throughout the first half of the tenth century.

By the end of that century, the effective power of the kings was confined to a sliver of land around Paris: nobles had carved up most of West Francia among themselves, marginalizing their nominal rulers. In the eleventh century, these duchies and counties themselves decomposed into smaller lordships. Any prospect of further expansion and empire-building that might have been had by then long evaporated: West Francia's—or France's—capacity for projecting power beyond its borders approached zero.[39]

This outcome was not in any meaningful way contingent in the sense that it could have been averted if particular events—successions, wars, and so on—had turned out differently. Rather, it was the product of deeply rooted structural conditions. One of them, specific to the Frankish experience, was the time-honored practice of dividing the realm among a king's sons. Because this tendency was particularly pronounced in times of relative strength, it effectively acted as a built-in—almost homeostatic—constraint on durable state formation.[40]

As noted, only periods of unity sustained expansion and consolidation. In this respect, one might consider Charlemagne's efflorescence the rare product of unusually good luck. His brother and rival king Carloman died after only three years of corule, opening up the path to an exceptionally long spell of one-man rule—Charlemagne's longevity was almost twice the average life span of the other eight Carolingian monarchs (all of whom appear to have died of natural causes), seventy-two compared to thirty-eight and a half years. The Frankish apogee under Charlemagne was the exception that proved the rule.

But even more powerful processes were steadily eroding state capabilities: the loss of centralized fiscal extraction and redistribution that made it harder for rulers to manage their senior followers, raise armies, and lay claim to the surplus produced by the working population, and the concurrent ascent of increasingly autonomous aristocrats who came to control material resources as well as military assets in ways that hollowed out royal power and ultimately the state itself. These developments took place not only among the Franks but in much of post-Roman Europe: they are crucial to our understanding of why large-scale empire proved so much more resilient in other parts of the Old World than in Europe, and will be discussed in more detail in chapter 7.[41]

For now, a brief outline is enough to assess the longer-term prospects of Frankish empire-building. The fall of Rome boosted the militarization of the elite. Rulership was legitimated by martial prowess, and the elimination of civilian career options beyond the church narrowed the composition of the ruling class: post-Roman Germanic and provincial elites primarily self-identified as warriors.[42]

Creeping defiscalization accompanied this shift. Although the Franks initially maintained elements of the Roman taxation system, land became the principal reward for service to the king. With few exceptions, direct taxes were phased out during the seventh century, and rulers relied on income from their royal land as well as tolls, fines, and booty. Over time, their estates, though still very extensive, were diminished by land grants to nobles, who likewise depended on land rents instead of delegated powers to tax.[43]

In the same period, the evolution of warriors into a landowning class that formally owed military service was completed. As land (rather than proceeds from land) was granted to nobles outright, they in turn made grants to their military followers and sought to obtain additional land from the king to compensate for these transfers, all of which were de facto regarded as permanent.

The formation of an entrenched military class, the allocation of quasi-hereditary land to its members, and the decline of centralized revenue collection and disbursement greatly narrowed the scope for the exercise of coercive power by the ruler and his patrimonial agents. The center no longer had direct control over the enforcement of service obligations: it fell to local estate owners to mobilize soldiers and present them to royal campaigns. Vertical ties of command and dependence developed, whereby nobles acted as intermediaries in raising and leading military forces. This simultaneously empowered the elite and served to downgrade the standing of less affluent free men, rendering military service more socially selective and detaching it ever further from direct royal control.[44]

In the eighth century, Frankish armies consisted of nobles and their retainers, who had grown in number as cumulative land grants and a more general economic recovery had boosted the fortunes of an increasingly assertive ruling class. This affected the scope of mobilization: nobles reluctant to commit their men to war could substitute fines for levies. As a result, additional incentives were required to ensure compliance with traditional service obligations. To an even greater extent than before, Frankish kings relied on military success to inspire loyalty. Expansionist wars that generated tangible rewards in the form of land and booty were the most reliable means of attracting aristocratic support.[45]

This opportunistic approach helps explain the successes of Charles Martel, Pepin the Short, and Charlemagne, who were able to marshal dedicated armies in exchange for material benefits: conquests produced "unmatched patronage opportunities for the Carolingian family, with a host of new counties, duchies, and royal lands to be given out" in Aquitaine, Catalonia, Saxony, Bavaria, and especially Italy. This kind of expansion also created a degree of social mobility that stabilized royal rule. However, as service became contingent on profit, war abated as soon as the Franks ran out of lucrative targets. This slowdown was already visible in Charlemagne's final years, when his campaigns against the Danes proved both unprofitable and unpopular. Falling income from plunder rapidly depleted the royal treasury.[46]

Meanwhile, the ample windfalls from the Carolingian expansion had empowered the nobility even further, turning them into a class of magnates who were able openly to resist royal orders and deploy their own resources to compete with their rulers or play off members of the royal lineage against one another. This kind of factional conflict was made particularly attractive by the fact that it allowed for "internal redistribution of wealth as an alternative to external expansion": war-making turned inward, as it were, undermining the state. Moreover, Charlemagne's reign witnessed efforts to demarcate Franks from other (often arbitrarily

defined) ethnic groups within the empire, which were placed in a subordinate position. This in turn obstructed the formation a unified ruling
class and precipitated resurgent regionalization.[47]

Taken together, these dynamics go a long way in accounting for the
persistent divisions and conflicts that rocked the Frankish empire after
Charlemagne's demise. Negotiation with powerbrokers replaced royal
command, and by the end of the ninth century, top magnates had assumed quasi-regal status.[48]

Although the Frankish emperors did not go down without a fight,
the system proved too resistant to change. In his later years, Charlemagne
showed growing concern over the service obligations of his vassals,
seeking to impel them by specifying their duties and imposing fines. He
may even have tried to raise an army drawn from the entire landowning
class and commanded by royal officers, but without success. Later
Charles the Bald also failed when he attempted to bypass lordly mediation by raising forces against the Viking threat and to assess noble and
clerical estates. Instead, during the ninth century, military service came
to be redefined as an aristocratic prerogative that replaced the previous
service obligations of free men. In the tenth century, military men of
lower status who had risen in the magnates' employ established their
own powers over an increasingly dependent peasantry, a process that
intensified the effective fragmentation of coercive capacity within the
realm.[49]

In the end, genuine reform was well beyond the reach of individual
rulers: power rested with dukes, counts, and bishops, and while substantial military operations remained feasible when all relevant parties
consented to them, the bar for ensuring this consent kept rising as growing revenue from larger and richer estates guaranteed a steady flow of
nonmilitary income that allowed elites to disengage from the royal
court.[50]

Internal fragmentation and attendant weaknesses were by no means
limited to the Frankish dominion, even if its relative longevity allowed
them to be taken to their logical extremes. Every single one of the Germanic successor polities was fairly brittle, buffeted by leadership struggles and elite autonomy: the Merovingians and Carolingians were merely

the most fortunate in that they—unlike Vandals, Ostrogoths, Burgundians, Thuringians, and Visigoths—did not succumb to determined external challengers. Government was fairly minimal and interpersonal relationships ruled supreme, which allowed for quick shifts in loyalty and
territorial configuration. Even Charlemagne's reach remained rather
limited: good intentions, however widely advertised, were hard to put
into practice, and his royal agents (*missi*), who were supposed to monitor
local powerholders, were not particularly effective.[51]

   Low levels of state power severely limited the scale of military ventures:
a few thousand armored cavalry formed the nucleus of the Frankish
forces, supported by a penumbra of more lightly equipped men. Growing emphasis on horses and armor reduced and devalued the contribution of the less affluent, thereby narrowing the social base of warfare—
the exact opposite of what had happened in the Roman Republic, when
a voracious conscription system ensnared an ever-larger share of the
citizenry. Logistical capabilities were likewise modest: armies of more
than a few thousand men were rare and had to be split up into detach-
ments in order to manage provisioning. Status priorities and logistical
constraints thus converged in favoring relatively small forces, sufficient
to overcome even weaker opponents but not enough to secure a larger
empire.[52]

   Fiscal atrophy, military weakness, aristocratic autonomy, and the exploitation of royal fraternal divisions by powerful factions were among
the key causes of the Carolingians' failure to re-create anything even
remotely resembling the Roman empire in Europe. Other constraints
of arguably lesser significance further reinforced this outcome. For
instance, environmental conditions may have contributed both to Charlemagne's successes and the misfortunes of his successors. Exceptionally
harsh winters that were frequently linked to volcanic activity became
more common after Charlemagne's reign, and associated famines appear to have been more severe.[53]

   In the ideological sphere, the vision of "Roma renascens," of a putative rebirth of the Roman empire, was primarily aimed at elites and was
of modest impact, however overrated it might have been by modern
scholarship: it worked best as long as it was accompanied by tangible

material benefits such as plunder and land grants. Rather than being driven by a desire to rebuild Roman power, Carolingian expansion sought to recover (and where possible augment) the Merovingian domain.[54]

In any case, Charlemagne's realm, with its poor infrastructure, primitive communications network, feeble urbanism, part-time military, ethnic divisions, and highly personalized rule bore little resemblance to the ancient empire that had once held sway over most of his lands. State formation under the Merovingian and Carolingian Franks is best viewed as a waxing and waning of state (and royal) power, marked by relative highs in the early sixth and the second half of the eighth centuries, which were separated and then followed by much longer stretches of infighting, aristocratic dominance, and disunity that weakened the center(s).

What is most remarkable in all of this is that the Merovingian kingdom avoided complete collapse in the seventh century, and that a trio of eighth-century rulers temporarily managed to reverse this decline and harness sufficient elite support to defeat and absorb (even) less well-organized external competitors, inflating Francia into the largest polity in Europe and advancing far enough into Italy to reclaim the mantle of emperorship. Any more than that—a rebuilding of state structures more akin to those of the Roman empire, or the creation of a differently organized (perhaps more confederated) but similarly durable entity on Latin European soil—remained well beyond the reach even of the most fortunate rulers and their shaky coalitions of supporters.[55]

That success itself added to the state's weakness—by empowering the nobility that benefited from royal campaigns—is a telling sign of deep-seated systemic flaws that could not readily be overcome by top-down reform or good luck. In order to prime the Frankish empire for more broadly-based and longer-lasting European unification, we would need to rewrite its history from the bottom up, starting with the land allocations that commenced at the end of the Roman period and continuing with the resultant erosion of direct taxation, the gradual reinforcement of divisive Frankish ethnic supremacy, and the development of the vassalage system that came to define to social order—and, for good measure, royal succession practices and perhaps even the climate. This is a brief that far transcends any meaningful counterfactual thought experiment.

FROM THE TENTH THROUGH THE THIRTEENTH CENTURIES: THE GERMAN EMPIRE

As centralized state power in West Francia (henceforth "France") unraveled, the eastern kingdom that emerged from the serial partitions of the Carolingian empire was the only one large enough to aim for a leadership role in Christian Europe. Yet the same problem that beset its western twin—growing aristocratic autonomy and resistance to royal rule—initially took it to the brink of disintegration. Conrad I, originally the duke of Franconia and the first non-Carolingian king of that eastern realm (henceforth, for simplicity's sake, "Germany") from 911 to 918, was locked in near-continuous conflict with his rebellious fellow dukes and was eventually killed in battle against one of them. At the same time, the Magyars, a confederation of steppe warriors that had recently taken over the Hungarian plains, stepped up their raiding into Germany and beyond. Conrad's successor Henry (r. 919–936) was more successful in containing open resistance among his nobles, heading a confederation of powerful dukes that was held together in no small measure by the Magyar threat.

Otto I (r. 936–973) further consolidated royal power by suppressing aristocratic dissent, decisively defeating the Magyars and recovering northern and central Italy, a feat for which the pope bestowed on him the title of "Roman" emperor in 962. For the first time, a German ruler claimed the same position as the earlier Carolingian rulers had. Yet he faced much stronger domestic constraints on his exercise of power and operated on a smaller geographical scale: successful military leadership had arguably been crucial in averting French-style partition.[56]

Yet this shift toward territorial expansion and (modest) centralization did not continue. In short order (977–983), Otto II had to put down yet another noble rebellion. He launched an intervention in

France that failed to take Paris, was defeated in his attempt to gain southern Italy, and was wrong-footed by a Slav uprising that cut into the eastern borderlands of the empire. His son Otto III likewise enjoyed little success against the Slavs and died shortly after having been igno-miniously evicted from Rome by a local popular rising. Upon coming to power, Henry II (r. 1002–1024) had to deal with renewed noble ris-ings and reverse the defection of his Italian possessions.

The Salian dynasty (r. 1027–1125) encountered more of the same problems, most notably repeated aristocratic rebellions and growing unrest and resistance south of the Alps. The peaceful incorporation by inheritance of Burgundy into the empire in 1034 merely added another highly autonomous entity to the mix. The German emperors proved unable to project power beyond the existing borders: sporadic cam-paigns to establish control over southern Italy and Sicily had already commenced in the 960s but consistently failed. By far the biggest chal-lenge to state formation emanated from power struggles within, between the emperor-kings and their dukes, margraves, and powerful cities. Up-risings by individual nobles or alliances among them occurred with some frequency, most notably in 1025–1027, 1077–1090, 1104–1115, 1114–1115, and 1138–1142.

Alternative strategies to tighten the rulers' grip on power also failed to bear fruit. The Ottonians had sought to counterbalance aristocratic dominance by handing over more land and authority to bishops and abbots, seeking to co-opt them by turning church leaders into enfeoffed vassals. However, by the 1070s, this approach opened up new tensions as a revived papacy asserted increasingly more prerogatives. When Pope Gregory VII barred secular rulers from appointing clergy, an escalating conflict between him and the emperor Henry IV resulted in the latter's excommunication and forced him to give in as his restless nobles ex-ploited this rift to their own advantage. Half a century later, Henry V renounced claims to the investiture of clergy.[57]

The ascent of the Hohenstaufen dynasty (r. 1138–1254) changed little of substance as princely, papal, and local urban power continued to ex-pand. Under Frederick I, Austria's status was raised to that of a duchy (1156), creating yet another autonomous entity at the margins of the empire. Later the same ruler was soundly defeated in northern Italy, had to acknowledge the pope as a sovereign ruler of the papal territories, and grant Italian cities the right to elect their own officials. His successor, Henry V, scored a rare success by conquering south Italy and Sicily in 1194—after more than 200 years of trying. Yet, although the crown benefited from the revenue generated by this more centralized domain, he was unable to have it formally incorporated into the empire proper.

At least Sicily provided a power base for his three-year-old son, Frederick II, when Henry V died in 1197 and two rival German kings were elected—the dukes of Aquitaine and Swabia—which ushered in an extended period of internal power struggle (1198–1215). And although Frederick II did eventually take over, he was forced to cede important royal privileges to his princes (1231–1232). Renewed conflict with the papacy during a period of intense campaigning in northern Italy saw him excommunicated in 1239, and he was unable to take Rome by force. In 1246, the church stepped up the pressure: the archbishops of Mainz and Cologne declared him deposed and crowned two consecutive anti-kings.

Frederick II survived a massive military defeat in Italy in 1248 by just two years, and his short-lived son Conrad II likewise failed to subdue this region. The latter's death in 1254 led to a prolonged interregnum without any emperor at all. During this period, a member of France's ruling family seized Sicily and southern Italy with papal support. When the Habsburg Rudolf I of Austria claimed the imperial mantle in 1273, he did so in return for renouncing any claims to the Papal States and Sicily (figure 5.6).

Even this bare-bones overview shows that the German empire did not succeed in expanding its reach or centralizing state control. Lasting additions were rare, limited to Burgundy in the eleventh century and parts of the Elbe-Oder region, most notably Brandenburg and Pomerania, in the thirteenth century. Control over southern Italy and Sicily proved short-lived (about two generations), and the full sovereignty of the Papal States in the mid-thirteenth century entailed the loss of territories that had been part of the empire for three centuries. Under these conditions, sustained imperial expansion was never a realistic option.

FIGURE 5.6 The German ("Roman") Empire, c. 1200 CE.

The most obvious target, France, was largely left alone after Otto II's intervention in the late 970s to install a friendly king on the French throne had failed. Military conflict remained highly regionalized for much of the Middle Ages, centering on two axes, England/France and Germany/Italy (plus Germany's Slavic periphery), with virtually no overlap between the two. The absence of challenges from major external powers—Byzantium was relatively distant, with conflicts confined to southern Italy, and France was long held back by internal weakness—may well have played a major role in impeding imperial state formation. Between the defeat of the Magyars in 955 and the appearance of the Mongols in 1241, the German empire did not face any serious threats that might have precipitated centralization.

Armed conflict was largely concentrated in two zones: in northern and central Italy, where a long line of emperors waged war against city-states and leagues that were nominally subordinate to them, and within Germany itself, pitting princes (and occasional anti-kings) against their overlords (as well as against each other). Both of these processes are emblematic of the profound structural weakness of the empire.

The fact that several centuries (from the 960s—and especially from the 1080s—into the 1250s) witnessed often inconclusive Italian campaigns speaks loudly to the failure of rulers to mobilize the ample manpower and resources of Germany against small-scale opponents that excelled at raising far more resources and commitments in per capita terms. This enabled these city-states and principalities to punch above their weight in military affairs, not least by investing in increasingly sophisticated fortifications that stymied aggressors. Greater German pressure simply generated stronger pushback, most notably in the form of the Lombard League of the 1160s–1240s, which, supported by the papacy, pooled the resources of most northern Italian cities against the emperor.[58]

In Germany itself, imperial governance was precariously founded on often hesitant elite consensus that was increasingly formalized over time. In the Ottonian period, the dukes enjoyed quasi-regal powers over castles and associated resources, and royals were usually of ducal origin. Under the Salians, the hereditary ducal elite expanded their estates, in part by converting crown lands. Attempts to impose a more command-oriented style of rulership failed: confiscations of aristocratic landholdings triggered resistance, and for a while, in the late eleventh century, the top nobility even took to holding meetings that excluded their emperor.

Cognizant of these risks, the Staufers abandoned earlier efforts to prevent fiefs from becoming fully hereditary. The aristocracy came to be formally stratified: as dukes were recognized as princes, they formed a top elite layer that intermediated between the emperor and lesser nobles. These lordly hierarchies created cascading power relationships that effectively detached rulers from the bulk of the aristocracy. No fewer than seventeen secular princes and forty-seven bishops or archbishops with de facto ducal powers emerged in the process.[59]

As greater numbers of princes took charge of local jurisdiction and the mobilization of resources, the imperial realm was increasingly segmented into territorialized quasi-polities. Discharging more and more functions without direct participation of their rulers, these dukes and cognate leaders enjoyed growing "political self-sufficiency." They set up their own chancelleries, building administrative structures that covered their increasingly stable territories.[60]

During the High Middle Ages, Western Europe filled up with castles. A disproportionate share of the growing wealth generated by the economic expansion of this period ended up in the hands of nobles who used it to shore up their defenses against the central authorities and their peers. While opposed to this trend, kings were often powerless to prevent it. In Germany, castle construction peaked in the late twelfth and the thirteenth centuries. More expensive but sturdier stone fortification replaced timber, and even cities were increasingly protected by stone walls.

Reflecting the elitist social order, warfare centered on knights and castles: military activity was the prerogative of the personal retinues of nobles who controlled strongholds and surrounding territory. For the same reason, progress in defensive capabilities coincided with stagnation in offensive capacities: as long as the "social exclusivity of the aristocracy dominated war," conservativism slowed technological and tactical innovation. The proliferation of strong defensive positions coupled with low levels of centralized state power that limited army size and quality heavily constrained royal intervention against unruly subordinates.[61]

Weak central power, in turn, was to no small degree a function of fiscal arrangements that reduced rulers' ability to exercise power against domestic challengers and external competitors. Most material resources were controlled by vassals, who were expected to answer claims to support by their overlords. De facto hereditary possession of fiefs had become the norm early on, and although forcible reassignments occurred in times of conflict, the overall distributional pattern proved quite durable.

Crown lands under direct ruler control were relatively small and shrank over time due to land grants to allies, especially church leaders, and remaining assets were increasingly pawned off. Sporadic attempts under the Salians to impose direct taxes remained unsuccessful. After Staufer expansion into southern Italy—a more fiscally productive environment—had promised some relief, the loss of these territories after the 1260s left later emperors bereft of funds. From that time onward, rulers increasingly relied on funding from their hereditary dynastic possessions, a practice that only added to the overall segmentation of the empire.[62]

Taken together, the growth of hereditary fiefs, territorial consolidation of princely domains, the spread and improvement of fortifications, and severe fiscal constraints on rulers ensured that consensual politics was the only viable option. Thus, rather than acting as a king of kings, the emperor was in many ways nothing more than a primus inter pares. Late medieval observers repeatedly likened regional princes to kings or emperors. The nominal emperor did not exercise outright hegemony—let alone direct rule—over his followers but relied heavily on negotiation and brokerage, resorting to military force only when elite relations broke down, and did so only with decidedly mixed success. These king-emperors fitted somewhat uneasily into a thoroughly fractured system of governance: their degree of detachment is reflected by the absence of an imperial capital and their itinerant lifestyle, which sustained large retinues but produced little by way of tangible governance. Only a trickle of documents are known to have emanated from the imperial court even as literacy recovered during the High Middle Ages.[63]

Power relations were further complicated by the influence of the church. The new "Roman" empire itself had arisen from an agreement between Charlemagne and the pope in which the latter initially had the weaker hand: the papacy relied on imperial protection, and renegade popes could be deposed. At first it also held little sway over senior church officials, allowing them to cooperate with secular rulers. Bishops in particular became important allies in government, enjoying privileges such as judicial authority and freedom from taxation. Ottonian and Salian emperors, eager to balance obstreperous princely power with that of bishops and abbots, stepped up the transfer of crown lands to the church.

From the mid-eleventh century, however, the papacy assumed an increasingly monarchical style and political persona, and imitated imperial symbols of authority. The creation of the College of Cardinals in 1059 freed papal elections from local secular intervention, which had been common. By 1076, as we have already seen, a pope could humble an emperor over the right to appoint senior clerics. In the early twelfth century, the papacy asserted superordinate authority over all secular monarchs, embodied in its right to confirm German kings as emperors. Subsequent Staufer pushback against this prerogative merely served to strengthen the standing of their princes, who were now charged with electing their ruler. This formalized a practice that had existed for centuries, even if kingship was in fact highly hereditary in nature.

At the same time, the Staufers continued the traditional strategy of empowering the ecclesiastical elite: they transferred even more secular jurisdiction to the church and enfeoffed bishops with ducal powers, creating ecclesiastical princes in the process. Even as the most senior church leaders in Germany—the archbishops of Cologne, Mainz, and Trier—managed to evade rulers' direct control, they retained their influence on legitimation in their role of electors. Finally, Frederick II's attempt to claim all of Italy for the empire precipitated open warfare with the papacy, which in turn backed his German princely rivals: the emperor found himself excommunicated several times and was declared deposed by a papal council. This clash ended without a clear winner—a stalemate that captures the spirit of centuries of never-ending balancing between rulers, princes, and popes that hollowed out centralized power.[64]

In Parts IV and V, I return to the processes that underpinned aristocratic and ecclesiastical autonomy and the fiscal and military muscle of city-states and their alliances. At this point, all we have to do is ask whether sustained imperial consolidation and expansion might have been at all feasible. The answer must be an unqualified no. Germany's rulers had nothing in common with Roman emperors beyond elements of their exalted title, and their realm could hardly have been more differently organized.[65]

In fact, the real question is not why the empire did not expand but why it did not collapse, turning its duchies into separate kingdoms. It appears that in this peculiar environment, the constraints on princely power were so modest that they were outweighed by the benefits of maintaining a formal framework for political and military cooperation and the performance of status. As sources of jurisdiction, territorial princes were genuine "co-constituents of monarchy" rather than mere counterweights to royal authority as in other medieval societies, and therefore had a vested interest in the empire's survival. Ecclesiastical princes, furthermore, did not have the option of becoming sovereigns in their own right, which increased their dependence on the existing system. Given a shared elite preference for weak rulers, there was always enough political will to preserve the empire in a format that did not encroach too much on elite interests.[66]

Once we add the aforementioned lack of serious external challenges—there were no big wars that made stronger states able to make more war, only small wars that helped a weak state stay alive—spatially stagnant persistence of an increasingly segmented realm was a viable long-term outcome. In this context, minimal rewrites could not possibly lead to significantly different counterfactual developments, such as reunification of the previous Carolingian empire, let alone expansion into Spain and Britain that might have added up to some form of stable imperial super-state.

Many of the defining features of this period would need to be changed even to create a capable imperial core: only a truly expansive counterfactual rewrite could tame lords, city-states, and the church, and establish a measure of centralized political, military, and fiscal control. The resultant German empire would be unrecognizably different from the one that existed in real life. Moreover, all of these modifications would run counter to more widespread trends of the eleventh, twelfth, and thirteenth centuries. If the Carolingians' chances of restoring hegemonic empire had been slim, those of the Ottonians and—especially—the Salians and Staufers were effectively zero.

CHAPTER 6

From Genghis Khan to Napoleon

THE THIRTEENTH CENTURY: THE MONGOL ADVANCE

DURING THE YEARS when Frederick II sought to expand his influence in Italy, much more momentous events were unfolding at the opposite end of the Eurasian land mass. In the opening years of the thirteenth century, the Mongol tribes united in a military confederation under Genghis Khan. Boosted perhaps by a spell of unusually favorable climatic conditions that brought a windfall in horses and livestock, the Mongols swiftly proceeded to attack and subjugate various neighbors. By 1221, the Uighurs, the Qidan north of China, and the Khwarezmian empire in Iran and southwestern Central Asia had submitted. The Western Xia state in northwestern China fell in 1227, followed seven years later by the Jurchen empire that covered the ancestral Chinese heartlands. By then, within a single generation, the Mongol empire had already outperformed a long line of previous steppe federations going back almost a millennium and a half to the time of the Xiongnu.[1]

The very next year, in 1235, Genghis's son and successor, Ögödei, and his council ordered a massive push into Eastern Europe. An earlier raid into the Volga basin and Ukraine in 1222–1223 had exposed the military weakness of the local polities, which now bore the brunt of a more determined assault. The operation was led by Batu, a grandson of Genghis via his son Jochi, Ögödei's half brother. His senior associates were a veritable "Who's Who" of the Genghisid inner circle: other Jochids took part alongside Batu, as well as Subutai, the most experienced Mongol general, and the sons of Genghis's sons Ögödei, Chagatai, and Tolui, including the next two future great khans Guyuk and Mongke. Large military forces including tens of thousands of Mongol cavalry were placed under their command. The prominence of its leadership suggests that this operation enjoyed priority over assaults on Song China, which also commenced in 1235 but failed to produce major advances for more than a decade. The same was true of much more modest operations south of the Himalayas.[2]

Batu's forces consequently advanced with great speed, sweeping all before them. The Bulgar state on the lower Volga was destroyed in 1236–1237. By 1239, the nomadic Turkic Cumans and Kipchaks had also been defeated and their warriors absorbed into the Mongol forces, where they added to the ranks of the light cavalry. A large troop of Cumans who fled west was subsequently granted asylum in Hungary.

The Slavic polities to the west and north were next in line. By then, Kievan Rus' had long devolved into a congeries of effectively independent principalities that stretched from Novgorod on the Baltic Sea to Kiev in northern Ukraine. The Mongols overran the most powerful of these states, the Grand Duchy of Vladimir, early in the winter of 1237–1238, destroyed its capital, and wiped out its army. Split up into smaller units, the Mongol forces ranged widely across Eastern Europe, sacking most of the principal cities, including Moscow, and killing their ruling families. Only Novgorod in the far northwest escaped devastation. The campaign culminated in the annihilation of Kiev at the end of 1240. Meanwhile, an independent Mongol force had completed the conquest of the Caucasus region.[3]

Central Europe lay wide open. The adjacent Latin Christian states were particularly weak even by the low standards of political centralization and military capacity of high medieval Europe. Poland was divided into no fewer than nine principalities run by four different dukes. The Teutonic Order held coastal territories to the northeast along the Baltic Sea. Farther south, Hungary, though formally a single kingdom, was saddled with a singularly powerful and stridently autonomous aristocracy: just twenty years earlier, a "Golden Bull"—a Magna Carta on steroids—had guaranteed the nobility and the church freedom from taxation alongside a series of other protections and privileges.

Farther west, the German emperor Frederick II, freshly excommunicated, was locked in a desperate power struggle with Pope Gregory IX: in 1241, the latter called for a crusade against the former when the emperor moved against Rome. England's king Henry III was preparing to invade western France. In the Iberian peninsula, Castile's attention was directed southward, to campaigns of wresting Andalusian cities from their retreating Muslim overlords.

Across Western and Central Europe, royal power, already heavily curbed by aristocratic autonomy and fiscal weakness, had recently been narrowed further by charters that explicitly limited its reach, and the conflict between the papacy and the imperial crown had reached a peak. Military capabilities were generally modest: armies centered on relatively small but expensive forces of lumbering knights who were supported by often low-quality infantry. Field armies were small compared to those in other parts of the Old World, including the Mongols: they did not normally exceed a few thousand men and only on special occasions reached 15,000 or 20,000. European forces that ventured beyond their native habitat were routinely beaten—during the Fifth and Seventh Crusades in Egypt (1218–1221 and 1250) and by the Ayyubids in Palestine (1244).[4]

Thanks to the absorption of numerous Turkic warriors from the steppe, Batu's forces may well have grown into the high tens of thousands. They advanced west in two directions. One division struck Poland, where the Mongols sacked major cities such as Kraków and Wrocław and, after scoring several battlefield victories, routed a joint force of Poles, Bavarians, and some Knights Templar at Legnica in April 1241, and killed the duke of Upper Silesia. A Bohemian army that had marched against them retreated. Larger Mongol forces simultaneously invaded Hungary where they crushed King Béla IV's army and then spent the rest of the year roaming the Great Hungarian Plains east of the Danube, harassing those who had not found refuge in fortified positions and drafting forced labor.[5]

At the end of the year they crossed the frozen Danube, sacked Buda, and attacked the capital city of Esztergom, which fell in January 1242, even though its stone citadel held out. Meanwhile, other forces were dispatched into Croatia and Dalmatia to apprehend Béla, who had escaped alive; they failed but caused substantial destruction in the process. The Danube crossing had removed the last natural obstacle between the Mongols and the easternmost reaches of the German empire. A small detachment advanced into Austria to Wiener Neustadt where it was beaten back. Scouting parties were sighted at Klosterneuburg north of Vienna and as far away as Udine in northeastern Italy. Contemporary accounts report panic across Western Europe all the way to Spain and the Low Countries, but no concerted preparations for defense. Calls for a crusade in Germany in mid-1241 had not borne fruit: instead, German nobles preferred to rise up against the emperor's son Conrad, drawing on crusade funds to fight the Hohenstaufens.[6]

At this ostensibly auspicious juncture, Batu ordered his troops to withdraw. In the spring of 1242, those of his men who had been hunting King Béla marched east through Bosnia and Serbia to join up with the main force in Bulgaria, which appears to have accepted tributary status. Then they all retreated back into the steppe. Mongol attacks on Central Europe did not resume for another seventeen years, and then only on a smaller scale and without causing comparable damage.

The reasons for Batu's retreat have been much discussed ever since. One position, rare in modern scholarship, is that if Mongol objectives had been limited to begin with, there would not be any need to explain their withdrawal. In this scenario, the principal goal was to establish control over the ecologically congenial steppe regions north of the Caspian and Black Seas and also over the adjacent Russian principalities, which could readily be dominated and compelled to pay tribute by cavalry forces operating from steppe bases. The assault on Poland was merely a raid for plunder—and indeed we do not know of any attempt to impose tributary relations—whereas the invasion of Hungary may have served the narrow purpose of punishing both the Cumans, who had evaded Mongol rule by escaping there, and King Béla, who had sheltered them and rejected Batu's demand for their return and his own submission.

This motive would be consistent with the Mongols' persistence in hunting down Béla across the Croatian coastlands. Once those efforts had failed and western Hungary proved resistant to raiding, this foray was brought to a preplanned if less than fully satisfactory conclusion. This reading of events also meshes well with the fact that by the time of his withdrawal, Batu had not positioned his main troops for further westward advances.[7]

The merits of this minimalist explanation are hard to evaluate: for instance, it is impossible to tell whether a planned conquest of Eastern Europe alone justified the extremely prominent status of the leadership team assigned to this operation. Mongols did not normally invade just to intimidate and plunder, whereas failed attempts at conquest could turn into large-scale raiding ventures. We are left wondering how seriously to take contemporary references to their plans to invade Germany or Rome, or their demand that Frederick II submit to them, or subsequent calls on other European monarchs to do so, such as on the king of France in 1260.[8]

Alternatively, we might argue that regardless of the Mongols' original plans, cumulative attrition between 1236 and 1242 had reached a level that persuaded them to abort operations. The winter of 1241–1242 appears to have been particularly harsh, thus adding to the logistical challenge. From this perspective, their retreat would have been a rational decision in response to unfavorable circumstances.[9]

By contrast, the most popular theory—which had already been proposed at the time—prioritizes domestic political concerns among the Mongol leadership. The Great Khan Ögödei died back in Mongolia in December 1241, and assemblies of Genghis's numerous descendants and their followers were expected to convene in order to work out the succession. During the Russian campaign, Ögödei's nephew Batu had fallen out with Ögödei's son Guyuk, a rift that may well have made Batu even more anxious to involve himself in the succession process and protect his own interests. If this issue did indeed lie behind his decision to withdraw, what might conceivably have turned into a more ambitious Mongol advance into Europe was averted by chance events.[10]

This interpretation invites criticism on two fronts, both empirical and counterfactual. Not all contemporary sources agreed on this motivation, and while it might have been possible for news of Ögödei's demise to travel fast enough to reach Batu before he ordered the retreat, we cannot be sure whether this had actually been the case. In the end, Batu did not attend any succession councils in Mongolia. It is difficult to draw analogies from developments on other fronts: smaller Mongol forces did invade Anatolia in 1243 and Syria in 1244 but were not led by descendants of Genghis, and fighting against the Mughals ceased around the time of Ögödei's death. At the end of the day, speculation about personal motivation seems rather fruitless. A much more important question is what would have happened if Ögödei had lived, or if he had died but Batu had continued his campaign. The simple fact of Mongol retreat in 1242 is far less significant than the potential consequences of perseverance.[11]

This change in perspective shifts the discussion from relatively trivial factors—such as planning objectives (which could have changed), cumulative attrition (which could have been remedied by reinforcements), and the death of the Great Khan (which need not have happened, or otherwise might only have occasioned a temporary lull in operations)—toward the role of more persistent structural features. These features came in four flavors and, while only imperfectly interconnected, all strongly converged in militating against successful Mongol expansion and empire-building on European soil west of Russia: the nature of the European political landscape and more specifically one of its more prominent physical manifestations, heavy investment in stone fortifications; the ecology of the western half of Europe; the dynamics of Mongol politics; and the incentives for pursuing conquest in other, generally less remote, parts of the Old World.

Latin Europe's intense armed fragmentation posed a powerful disincentive to sustained Mongol engagement, and a serious obstacle to any such engagement that had it in fact occurred. As noted in the previous chapter, the proliferation of increasingly sturdy fortifications—for noble and ecclesiastical strongholds and urban settlements—went a long way in weakening rulers and undermining state formation. Much as this development limited monarchs' ability to exercise authority in coordinating resources for large-scale operations—say, defense against a Mongol threat—it also yielded an unintended benefit: it made this part of the world an unattractive target for invaders who sought to rule or at least collect rents across large areas.[12]

Stone fortifications were not merely a hypothetical barrier to counterfactual future Mongol invasion: their role in thwarting Mongol objectives during their campaign in Central Europe is well documented. Eastern European settlements, the first to be attacked, were poorly protected by earthen ramparts and wooden palisades. The farther west the Mongols advanced, however, the more sophisticated were the installations they encountered. They had little difficulty overrunning eastern Hungary, which, in the words of a German chronicler, "had almost no city protected by walls or strong fortresses." Defensive earthworks were easily breached.[13]

Hungary west of the Danube, by contrast, featured more stone castles in the advanced Western European style, in the first instance because of its proximity to the Austrian border. This made a huge difference: even in those parts of Hungary that were overrun, all five stone castles positioned on hilltops survived intact. The Mongols' failure to take the citadel of Esztergom, the only part of the city fully built of stone, is particularly revealing: although great efforts were undertaken to seize the royal treasure that was kept there, they proved futile. In Silesia and Moravia, the Mongols likewise had trouble breaking into stone castles. The forces sent down the Adriatic coast to apprehend King Béla did not take any properly fortified places (such as Klis, Split, and Trogir) but destroyed poorly protected Zagreb. Conversely, they were more successful on their withdrawal campaign through Serbia and Bulgaria, which featured only less-sophisticated fortifications.[14]

European leaders learned to appreciate the power of well-built walls: after repeatedly getting trounced in battle in early 1241, they were quick to switch to defensive positions. As soon as Batu had departed, a wave of castle construction swept across Hungary and Poland. The payoff was substantial: when the Mongols returned to Poland in 1259–1260, they took the major city of Sandomierz only through subterfuge, and failed to break into the citadel of Kraków. During a subsequent Mongol attack on Hungary and then Poland from 1285 to 1288, key cities and strongholds held out, and only those that could be tricked into surrendering were destroyed, as were rural settlements.[15]

In all this, it is very much worth noting that what the Mongols encountered in the early 1240s was merely the outer fringe of an extensive network of stone fortifications that covered Western and Southern Europe and had only recently begun to diffuse into Central Europe. Farther west, in the feudal heartlands of Germany and France, and in the wealthy cities of former "Lotharingia" from Italy to Flanders, much more numerous and sophisticated defenses shielded castles, monasteries, and entire towns, as well as a larger share of the total population and its assets. That Batu's forces struggled to penetrate even the eastern periphery of this massive system of bastions did not bode well for any deeper advance.[16]

Before we consider the odds of successful Mongol countermeasures, we need to appreciate another and altogether different obstacle to more sustained expansion in Europe, one that was natural rather than manmade. West of the Ural Gap, the Mongols and their newly subordinated allies moved through the same kind of grasslands that supported vast numbers of horses farther east. Ukraine served as a secure staging area for cavalry expeditions into the Russian agrarian and forest zones while farther south, newly won access to the Caucasus provided summer pasture. Ecological conditions became far less favorable as the Mongols advanced west. Wallachia and Hungary form the outermost extensions of the Great Eurasian steppe, and rather modest ones at that. The grasslands in present-day Mongolia alone cover some 1.25 million square kilometers and in 1918 supported over a million horses alongside more than 8 million heads of cattle, camels, and sheep. The Mongols came to control this as well as adjacent grasslands all the way to Ukraine, enough to support several hundred thousand mounted warriors even at a high ratio of five to ten horses for each man.[17]

The Hungarian grasslands were much smaller, equivalent to only a few percent of the Mongolian pastures, and even in theory could not support more than 300,000 to 400,000 horses and, inevitably, far fewer than that in real life, and thus not more than a few tens of thousands of horsemen—and even that would have excluded the entire existing population from the herding business, a rather radical scenario even by Mongol standards.[18]

It is unlikely that cavalry forces on that scale would have managed to subdue Europe. Indirect support for this view comes from evidence for the "de-horsing" of earlier steppe conquerors—Huns, Avars, and Magyars—who had seized the Hungarian plains: constrained by eco-logical realities, they downsized their mounted troops and put greater emphasis on infantry. This in turn helps explain the ephemeral character of their incursions into Europe. It would also have robbed the Mongols of their principal advantage, their superiority in light cavalry. In chapter 8, we will see that this constraint was part of a larger and arguably decisive force in European state formation: much of the continent's relative dis-tance and protection from the steppe. From a long-term perspective, the Mongol retreat was merely a single instantiation of historically per-vasive dynamics.[19]

I am well aware that my focus on stone fortifications and grasslands is bound to raise objections. After all, in China and elsewhere the Mon-gols took massively fortified cities and they struck Syria, India, southern China, and even Burma and Java, all of them at considerable remove from their native steppe. But these points are easy to address. Ventures into exotic locales ultimately all failed; the Mongols never made a seri-ous attempt on India (the Kashmiri pastures under their control, though useful, were relatively small); and their armies in Iran and Iraq could fall back on the Azeri and Caucasus pastures.

In China and the Levant, the Mongols had ready access to highly skilled craftsmen, engineers, and—in the former—basic gunpowder weaponry. In Eastern Europe, they did not: Russian craftsmanship had been devastated by the destruction of many cities. In order to take on European fortifications, the Mongols would have had to draft local labor or, less time-consumingly, introduce experts and resources from East Asia or the Levant. This was not unheard of: in the 1270s, Kublai had Middle Eastern artillery experts help his men finish off the largest Song fortifications in southern China. This approach, however, would have required a degree of unity and coordination among the Mongols that was about to diminish rapidly and never stood a realistic chance of being restored.[20]

The reason for this lies in the growing political instability and segmentation of the Mongol domain, the third of the four principal impediments to successful expansion in Europe. While Ögödei's succession to Genghis in 1229 had been managed in a peaceful manner, his own death was followed by a lengthy interregnum, and that ended with the accession of his son Guyuk, who lasted only two years (1246–1248). The election of the next Great Khan, Mongke, in 1251 was preceded by prolonged factional disagreements. Bolstered by an initial purge of rival houses, he was the last supreme leader to preserve unity. His death in 1259 triggered five years of armed conflict over the succession that left the empire effectively fragmented into four khanates, even as Kublai emerged as their nominal overlord.

While the Ilkhanate in Iran and Iraq remained on friendly terms with his court, the Chagatai khanate in Central Asia fiercely guarded its independence and was openly hostile to the Great Khan. The Golden Horde in Eastern Europe nominally accepted his suzerainty, but loyalties were divided and open conflict broke out in the early 1260s. In the absence of a unified imperial entity, any further operations in Europe had to be launched by the Golden Horde with the men and resources under its own control (figure 6.1).[21]

Weakening ties between the Golden Horde and the Mongolian heartland and its growing Chinese possessions, which could otherwise have served as a source of the manpower and especially military technology needed to overcome Europe's extensive network of stone fortifications, were only one impediment. More importantly, the Golden Horde leadership was preoccupied with its rivalry with the Mongol domain to the south, which from the 1250s onward was ruled by the Ilkhans. Lack of pasturage hampered Mongol campaigning in Iran and the Levant: consequently, the summer pastures of the Caucasus were contested between the two khanates, a conflict reinforced by religious differences between their rulers. Open warfare lasted from 1262 to 1267.

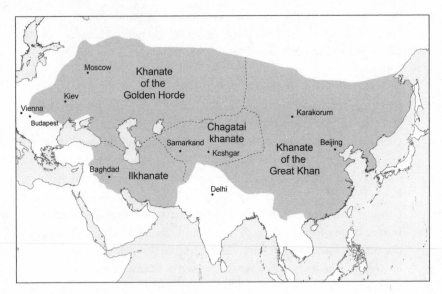

FIGURE 6.1 The Mongol empire in the late thirteenth century CE.

On this occasion, the Golden Horde, whose forces had come to be dominated by the Kipchaks, entered an alliance with the Mamluks of Syria and Egypt, who were of cognate ethnic descent, against the Ilkhanate, their common enemy. Further fighting took place in the late 1280s. In the 1280s and 1290s, power in the Golden Horde was de facto divided between a series of official khans and Nogai Khan, who had one khan killed in 1291 and fought a civil war against his successor in 1299–1300. It goes without saying that none of this was conducive to sustained aggression against European powers.

But divisions and infighting among the Mongols were not the only distraction from Europe. In 1242, the year Batu turned back, the richest part of China was ruled by the Song dynasty; northern India was ruled by the Sultanate of Delhi; and Iraq, Syria, and Egypt were under the control of various Kurdish and Turkic conquest regimes alongside what little was left of the Abbasid caliphate. All of these economically advanced regions supported tributary regimes that made them attractive targets for a Mongol takeover.[22]

It should therefore hardly occasion surprise that following the un-stable 1240s, in the following decade Mongke and his court decided to devote more resources to operations in East Asia and the Levant. Mongol forces soon flanked Song China to the west, taking Tibet and Yunnan and raiding Vietnam. Mongke spent the last years of his life campaign-ing in China, and his successor, Kublai, completed its conquest in the 1260s and 1270s with great effort and commitments of manpower. In the late 1250s, separate Mongol forces took over Iraq (killing the last Ab-basid caliph in Baghdad) and sought to conquer Syria but were repelled by the Egyptian Mamluks in 1260. Several later attempts on Syria be-tween 1271 and 1303 likewise failed.

The focus on East Asia and the Levant in the 1250s highlights the limits of Mongol power. Operations against Delhi were confined to the Indus basin and no all-out assault ever occurred. It was only in the early fourteenth century that the Chagatai khanate launched attacks against Delhi itself, and then without success. From the 1250s onward, the double push into East Asia and—on a lesser scale—the Levant left no resources on a scale large enough to make major headway into Europe. The great mobilization that had swept Batu's army across Russia and into Poland and Hungary was not to be repeated.[23]

In this context of competing priorities and progressive fragmenta-tion, the Golden Horde was on its own. Buffeted by conflict with the Ilkhanate and internal rivalries and cut off from advanced siege technol-ogy of Chinese or Middle Eastern origin, renewed incursions into Cen-tral Europe bore little fruit. As already noted, major fortifications were generally safe, and the invaders consequently looked for plunder rather than conquest: in Poland (1259–1260, 1287–1288), Hungary (1285–1286), Bulgaria (1270s–1280s), Serbia (1291), and Byzantine Thrace (1260s, 1320s–1330s). None of these ventures replicated even the limited successes of 1241–1242.[24]

Under the minimal-rewrite rule, the counterfactual of a Mongol inva-sion of Latin Europe therefore faces serious time constraints. Batu's existing forces might well have raided Austria, Bohemia, and the Po Valley, defeating armies bold enough to offer battle but unable to take major cities, let alone establish lasting control.[25]

More ambitious operations would have called for reinforcements and, arguably, large-scale mobilization of subject populations in Eastern Europe that would have been delayed by the weakness of existing administrative infrastructure. What would have been necessary to make this happen? The most parsimonious counterfactual is Ögödei's survival and doubling-down: he was fifty-five when he died, whereas Genghis lived about a decade longer and Kublai lived to be seventy-nine. Early khans who died younger did so under adverse circumstances: Guyuk, an alcoholic, died at forty-two, and Mongke passed away at fifty during a strenuous campaign. (Batu also lasted another thirteen years.) Just as Mongke prioritized East Asia and the Levant, Ögödei could have decided to do the same for Europe. Mongol operations in the Levant were supported by Chinese engineers, who could instead have deployed siege-engine and gunpowder weapons against European fortresses.

This seemingly attractive counterfactual scenario poses several problems. First, it is not at all clear that Ögödei ever wanted to conquer or even raid the western half of Europe: whereas the incorporation of the western reaches of the Eurasian steppe was an eminently sensible objective—and had already been foreshadowed by the successful incursion of 1222–1223—we simply cannot tell whether the lands west of Russia were ever in the crosshairs. Second, even if we build a more open-ended commitment to campaigning in Europe into our counterfactual, we must wonder how long this would have survived the Mongol elite's eyeing of other, more profitable targets much closer to home.

Political calculus aside, Europe is very far away from Mongolia. As the crow flies—admittedly a poor measure—Karakorum (as a proxy of the Mongolian center at the time) was 1,700 kilometers from Kaifeng, 2,800 kilometers from Guangzhou, and 3,000 kilometers from Samarkand. The most distant actual Mongol gains were even more remote: 5,100 kilometers in the cases of both Kiev and Baghdad. Yet potential European targets were still farther away, and in fact more so than other destinations that remained beyond the Mongols' reach (such as Java, at 4,600 kilometers, and Damascus, at 5,700 kilometers): Budapest was 6,000 kilometers away, Rome, Paris, and London close to 7,000 kilometers, and Toledo close to 8,000 kilometers. Distance from the rim of the Eurasian steppe, arguably a more meaningful metric, follows an analogous pattern, as shown in chapter 8, figure 8.6.[26]

Moreover, Europe west of Russia was large: including Britain but not Scandinavia north of Denmark, it covers some 3.75 million square kilometers, roughly twice as much as the Southern Song empire, which was much closer to Mongolia and took several decades to subdue. Even a more limited notional core target region from Poland to Hungary through Austria and Germany to the Low Countries, France, and Italy was about as large as the Southern Song domain. And while it is true that the former's population was much smaller, this crude comparison does not take into account Europe's intense fragmentation, which made conquest or merely tribute extraction more demanding in per capita terms than it was in larger and more centralized polities. It also neglects the fact that the sheer number of fortified positions would have taxed the capacity even of sizable teams of imported engineers.

There was no central government to offer surrender: these positions would have had to be reduced one by one. In this environment, the most plausible outcome was widespread raiding of smaller towns and rural areas and the opportunistic imposition of fleeting tributary obligations. Such actions would not have fundamentally altered the political landscape, and would most likely have encouraged a return to something close to the status quo ante once they abated.

The most meaningful historical analogies may be the operations of the fifth-century Huns and, more dramatically, the Magyars in the ninth and especially tenth centuries. Whereas the former made only very limited inroads into state-level polities, the Magyars proved more disruptive. After taking over the Hungarian plains, they conducted almost annual raids into Germany, France, and Italy, either as allies of parties in local conflicts or on their own, and scored major victories over all three parts of the Frankish domain between 899 and 910. At various points, the German kingdom, several of its princes, and the Byzantine empire acceded to tributary demands. In 942 the Magyars even briefly entered the Iberian peninsula.

Only decisive defeat in 955 ended their incursions. Although Otto I's victory boosted his standing and that of the German kingdom-empire, as we saw in chapter 5, it did not have any enduring effect on European polycentrism. Given political conditions three centuries later, there is no obvious reason to assign a greater potential impact to sustained Mongol attacks. Moreover, the fortifications of the High Middle Ages would have presented the Mongols with a greater challenge than those of the tenth century had.[27]

In view of all this, a more expansive rewrite is needed to produce a substantively different outcome in terms of subsequent European state formation: one in which Ögödei lived as long as Kublai (that is, for another quarter of a century), remained, or perhaps rather became, steadfastly committed to European conquest even in the face of determined resistance, as well as persevered—and convinced his senior associates to persevere—in grinding down German, French, Italian, Flemish, English, and Spanish defenses just as Kublai had ground down the Southern Song, albeit much closer to home and with more tangible rewards.

A counterfactual along these lines may or may not seem plausible: it is certainly not economical. In addition, we must assume that serious internal divisions, as they surfaced from the 1250s onward, could have been held in check long enough for European conquest to be completed; that the second-order counterfactual of the emergence of autonomous Mongol leadership in Europe through the transfer of resources over such a large distance could likewise have been avoided (say, a separate khanate under Batu and his successors—in real life, frictions appeared between Batu and Ögödei's son and successor, Guyuk, and Batu subsequently supported a rival lineage); and that even such an all-out effort would have been enough to bring Europe to its knees, which is by no means a given.

Under these maximalist assumptions, which are far removed from anything like a parsimonious—or, to my mind, plausible—counterfactual, two outcomes were possible: the erection of some form of empire, or ongoing devastation without stable control. Real-life developments in Russia provide us with the closest available approximation of the first option. Initial destruction was concentrated in the south, where it caused serious damage to economic activity and resulted in mass enslavement. The Golden Horde subsequently preferred indirect domination as the conquerors and their allies remained in the steppe, unlike in China or Iran where they moved into settled areas. It took a decade and a half for the first census to be held (1257–1259), which enabled conscription among the local population.

The Golden Horde played off Russian principalities against each other: after unpopular Mongol tax collectors had been removed and local princes charged with revenue collection, the grand-prince of Moscow was eventually granted the right to coordinate tribute-taking, which in turn boosted the standing of this principality. Moscow and other Russian polities adopted Mongol/Turkic-style institutions from tax systems and war levies to mounted courier services: cultural borrowing peaked in the fourteenth century. The conquerors' dominance fluctuated over time, from defeat by Moscow in 1380, which was followed by a quick reversal, and a renewed and more durable ascent of Russian power under Ivan III in the late fifteenth century. Even so, Crimean Tatars were still able to raid Moscow as late as 1571. It was only from that time onward, as the power of the Golden Horde gradually faded, that the nativist ideology of the "Tatar yoke" was crafted by the Muscovite church.[28]

In the event of a comprehensive Mongol victory, we might envision a similar scenario in Latin Europe: some polities would have served as the Mongols' proxies—Venice already had good relations with them—strengthening their own position in the process. Taxation and conscription could well have developed much faster and further than they did in real-life Europe. At the same time, given the greater distance from the steppe, it is doubtful that Mongol—or by then mostly Turkic—power would have lasted nearly as long as it did in Russia. The invaders could either have stuck to Hungary to preserve their cohesion and cavalry skills—a decision that would have made it harder for them to exercise effective control over Western Europe—or they could have decided to settle across Europe, thereby running the risk of becoming submerged in the local population. The same forces would have had to contain both Russians and Latin Europeans, a constellation that would have greatly improved the odds for successful resistance by either of them.

The fact that in actual history, the Ilkhanate rapidly disintegrated after 1335 and Mongol rule in China collapsed between the 1350s and

1380s makes it seem very likely that similar developments would have occurred in an occupied Europe, had it indeed been chosen over China and the Levant as the Mongols' main target. The dislocations of the Black Death from 1347 onward would have heightened existing tensions. Overall, even if we twist history enough to allow successful conquest, a long-term Mongol-Turkic empire in Europe was hardly a realistic outcome.

A different question may be more relevant: Would Mongol pressure or domination have been capable of steering European state formation toward a trajectory of centralization and the formation of large imperial structures in response to this pressure or domination? Russian—Muscovite—history offers a model of such a process. However, given how deeply entrenched polycentrism was in the political, social, and ideological structures of high medieval Europe, it is debatable whether Mongol influence on a halfway plausible time scale—say, for a century—would have been sufficient to remake the political landscape in later Russia's image, or that of ancient Rome.

The most likely outcome might have been a strengthening of regional rulers—whether in cooperation with or in opposition to Mongol power—through institutional adaptations and a dismantling of the castle network. This could have accelerated the emergence of the competitive state system of the early modern period to a considerable degree. Paradoxically, a stronger Mongol presence might in the end have reinforced polycentrism, if perhaps with fewer players: Germany and Italy in particular might well have emerged from this process in a more consolidated format. Whether the political, economic, and mental infrastructure that underpinned the eventual advent of modernity would still have been in place is, however, a question that, crucial as it may be, is too encumbered by complex second-order counterfactuals to be even worth considering here.

This question is also present in the second scenario, that of massive devastation. In this case, Europe's development is dealt a more direct blow—not by altering trajectories of state formation but by destroying the underpinnings of later advances. Cecilia Holland's counterfactual account presents a stark version of this outcome. In her telling, instead of retreating in 1242, the Mongols first strike the Low Countries, a center of prosperity, destroying Antwerp, Ghent, and Bruges. Then they swing south into France and move against Paris, using the meadows of Middle France as their temporary base. Another force, sustained by the grasslands of the Po Valley, devastates northern Italy.

Wiping out the Flemish cities would "erase the nascent financial center of Europe," and depopulation from slaughter would allow sea and swamps to return: "There would be no rise of capitalism or the middle class. No printing press, no humanism. No Dutch Revolt, the seedbed of the great democratic revolutions from England to America to France. No Industrial Revolution." The loss of Paris, on the other hand, would remove the university that provided foundations for Galileo, Kepler, and Newton. And if the pope had been killed just as the caliph had been when the Mongols sacked Baghdad, central religious authority might have collapsed altogether, and the Reformation would have been avoided: Christianity might have devolved into discrete sects.[29]

The historical experience of the Middle East might seem to provide a measure of support for this apocalyptic vision, considering that stalled development there is sometimes blamed on Mongol depredations. However, the Holland scenario does not even begin to consider the role of European fortifications, a serious shortcoming that disqualifies it at least as far as the early 1240s are concerned. This degree of devastation would have required not only more Mongols but above all the mobilization of the sedentary population of Eastern and Central Europe in support of sieges: in other words, a more sustained presence and gradual advance that takes us back to the first option of Mongol-induced empire-building. Europe's wreckage could not have been achieved without it.[30]

I must stress that both the empire-building and the devastation counterfactuals—which are so closely related as to be effectively indistinguishable—are logically predicated on a massive rewrite of history that suppresses not only highly contingent events (such as the life span or motivations of a Great Khan) but also more robust features such as geographical distance (both from Mongolia and the steppe), the Mongolian polity's built-in propensity to fracture, and the intrinsic appeal of alternative targets, foremost southern China. It also needs to posit that the extent of fortified resistance in Europe would not have derailed Mongol operations. Some of these notions run counter to real-life experiences elsewhere. Thus, the Mongols never staged a full-scale invasion of India, which was likewise remote and well defended. Setbacks in Japan and Indonesia were accepted rather than followed by renewed efforts. Unsuccessful invasions of Vietnam resulted in no more than nominal submission.

Although the counterfactual of significantly different developmental outcomes in Europe as a result of sustained Mongol pressure cannot be ruled out, it certainly requires aggressive rewrites of historical conditions and therefore does not seem plausible overall. The most one could argue is that at this juncture, the potential for a meaningful divergence from Europe's real-life trajectory of state formation was somewhat higher than it had been before (taking account of the Arab, Carolingian, and German empires) and after (taking account of Habsburg, Ottoman, and French policies).

This alone justifies devoting as much space to this counterfactual as I have done here. Nevertheless, "somewhat higher" was nowhere near enough. East Asia and the Middle East had long been exposed to pressures from the steppe, whereas the western half of Europe was not. Ecological constraints were so powerful that even the Mongols, for all their historically unique reach, were ill equipped to overcome them. In chapter 8, I explore this issue in greater detail and from a comparative perspective.[31]

THE SIXTEENTH CENTURY: THE HABSBURG STRUGGLE FOR HEGEMONY

After the Mongol threat had abated and German emperors had given up trying to tighten their grip on their heterogeneous domain, about a quarter of a millennium passed without producing any potential junctures that would merit counterfactual assessment. During this period, state power was slowly but surely rebuilt: rulers bargained more successfully for tax revenue, and armies grew in size. State consolidation strengthened the polycentric state system of Latin Europe: the remaining parties were fewer in number but more capable and resilient than before.[32]

By 1500, the Christians of Spain had subdued the last Muslim redoubts, and the English and their Burgundian allies had been expelled from France. Denmark, Hungary, Poland, Lithuania, and Muscovy had developed into often spatially extensive states along the periphery, and the Ottoman empire had taken over most of the Balkans. Only in Germany and to a lesser degree in the northern half of Italy did intense fragmentation prevail. Overall, the European political environment was even less conducive to the emergence of a single very large empire than it had ever been since the fall of Rome.

There were only two ways to disturb this increasingly stable equilibrium of balancing states: a massive exogenous shock or a sudden and dramatic increase in one party's power. The explosive growth of the Ottoman empire to the east falls into the former category: reaching westward from the Aegean into the Balkans and Carpathian region and advancing along the North African coast, it recalled the initial successes of the first caliphate 900 years earlier. I consider this option in the next section.

In the early sixteenth century, a sudden shift in the balance of power within Latin Europe created another possible juncture: in short order, the Habsburg prince Charles V acquired (by way of inheritance) Burgundy and the Low Countries (1506), Spain (Aragon and Castile) and the southern half of Italy (the kingdoms of Naples, Sicily, and Sardinia and the Duchy of Milan) (1516), and Austria (1519), and was elected emperor.

On the other side of the Atlantic Ocean, Christopher Columbus, in Castile's employ, had reached the Caribbean in 1492, opening the doors to expansion on the American mainland. In 1521, after the conquest of the Aztec empire, the colony of New Spain was established in Mexico (and upgraded to a viceroyalty in 1535), and the viceroyalty of Peru followed in 1542 a few years after the fall of the Inca empire in the Andes. Three years later, the mining town of Potosí was set up in what is now

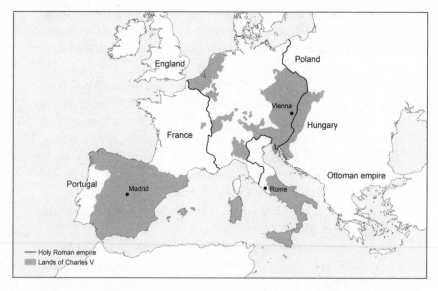

FIGURE 6.2 The Holy Roman empire and the European possessions of Charles V, c. 1550 CE.

Bolivia to exploit the richest silver mines thus far discovered: together with other Andean and Mexican mines, they proceeded to generate vast amounts of bullion for the Spanish crown (figure 6.2).

This fortuitous congruence of events not only elevated Charles V to a dominant position in the western Mediterranean that also encircled France and reached up toward England, it put at his disposal a growing revenue windfall that could be spent on war. Within a single generation, power had come to be concentrated on a scale unheard of since the days of the Roman empire, the last time Spain, much of Italy, the eastern Alpine region, and much of the Rhineland had reported to the same ruler, and the last time rich precious metal deposits had subsidized military activity—the Middle Ages had been a period of bullion shortage. At least nominally, Charles V could claim about 40 percent of the population of Western and central Europe.[33]

Yet notwithstanding the pronouncements of eulogists who cast the Habsburgs as descendants of Aeneas via Augustus, Constantine, and Charlemagne, Charles's position was dramatically different from that of a Roman emperor. His domain was characterized, and effectively riven, by intense particularism, resembling, in Anthony Pagden's apt turn of phrase, "a multinational corporation more than a state."[34]

Even in the ideational sphere, notions of universal empire, while promoted by some contemporaries, elicited resistance not only outside his realm—most notably by France—but also in his two Spanish kingdoms. The "empire" was conceived of as being territorially confined to the traditional German empire, where Charles's influence was generally much weaker than in his direct possessions. Only the New World, where he lacked serious challengers, was susceptible to the idea of truly imperial rule. In 1535, Charles felt compelled to publicly announce before the pope that he had no interest in universal empire at all. An alternative aspiration, leadership of a unified Christendom (leaving aside the Orthodox community, which was well beyond his reach), likewise proved elusive even as it absorbed growing resources that might have been committed to more promising strategies of state-building.[35]

Germany occupied an awkward position within the Habsburg system. As politically segmented and opposed to centralized authority as ever, the German principalities acted as a brake on Charles's ambitions and drained his treasury in internecine conflicts. Charles V and his son Philip II did not formally expand the German empire. Instead, their power increasingly rested on territories outside the empire's traditional boundaries: only Austria, Milan, Burgundy, and the Low Countries lay within them.

This structural dualism created tensions between the empire's consensus-driven constitution and the location of the resources its ruler drew on: incorporation of the other Habsburg domains—favored by the princes—would have given them a say in how these funds were spent. Instead, their emperor could now fall back on monies that were completely outside their control, and could even be used against them. Conversely, the emperor was not entitled to ask for German funds against Christian opponents, and even when an exception was made to move against France because of its alliance with the Muslim Turks, only a minute fraction of the costs of that war were borne by the empire's principalities.[36]

The imposition of direct rule by force held little promise: experiments with placing fortified garrisons in cities (such as Florence and Ghent) were not feasible in Germany. As a result, the emperor's suppression of princely resistance did not much outlast his army's presence, and opportunistic extortion of funds was often the best Charles could hope for.[37]

The unwieldy sprawl of his composite realm precipitated warfare on multiple fronts. The principal challengers were France, which sought to balance his rising power; the German princes, who sought to preserve their autonomy and politicized the Protestant Reformation; and, to a lesser degree, the Ottoman empire, freshly allied with France to offset Habsburg prominence. Broadly speaking, Charles's military ventures were not particularly successful, and generally failed to add to the domains he had acquired through inheritance. While he managed to retrieve the Duchy of Milan after several changes in ownership, his demand for the Duchy of Burgundy and Provence in return for the release of the captured French king failed in 1535, as did an invasion of Provence the following year. Further wars in Italy in the 1530s, 1540s, and 1550s accomplished little of substance.

The Ottomans' ascent added to the pressure: Austria's claim to Hungary was short-lived and Vienna itself was attacked in 1529, forcing Charles to assemble a large army to counter another attempt in 1532. His conquest of Tunis in 1535 was quickly followed by a major naval defeat in 1538 and a disastrous assault on Algiers in 1541 that cost him more than 150 ships. An invasion of France conducted jointly with England became bogged down in prolonged sieges and had to be aborted to deal with German Protestants: it did not alter the status quo. Finally, a massive and hugely expensive operation against the French city of Metz failed in the winter of 1552–1553.[38]

Only the Spanish advance in the Americas was a success story: indigenous societies that lacked steel, guns, cash, an advanced form of literacy, and sometimes even wheeled transport, and that were laid low by catastrophic epidemics that had been introduced by the invaders, were no match for Charles's conquistadores. It seemed as if his forces could only overpower opponents at a much lower level of social development but failed to make much headway against their Old World peers. But problems arose even in the New World, as quasi-autonomous colonial leaders, operating on the premise that their victories entitled them to hefty rewards, claimed enormous estates and masses of forced laborers for themselves. In the 1540s, reform attempts in Peru prompted them to rise against the crown.[39]

Lack of military success in Europe was compounded by domestic resistance rooted in German particularism and doctrinal schism. Religious unity, with or without Habsburg leadership, remained an illusion. In 1526–1527, in a distant echo of the papacy quarrel with Frederick II three centuries earlier, Pope Clement VII formed a league against Charles, whose mercenaries in turn sacked the city of Rome. More importantly, Charles's ascent to power in Spain and Germany coincided with Luther's dissident teachings in the Electorate of Saxony in the empire's northeast. Although the emperor had Luther banned at the Diet of Worms in 1521, this reformative movement, soon reinforced by the work of others such as Zwingli (from the 1520s) and Calvin (from the 1530s) and accompanied by Henry VIII's split from the Catholic Church (likewise in the 1530s), rapidly spread across northern and central Germany, Scandinavia, Britain, and Switzerland, forever dividing Latin Christendom.

With respect to imperial state formation, this process could not have occurred at a worse time, as it served to offset the concatenation of territorial amalgamation and resource windfalls on the Habsburg side. Among German princes wary of an overlord who could draw on growing external funds but denied them a voice in how they were spent, religious reform immediately became entangled with political priorities, coalescing into resistance to Catholic dogma and its imperial champion alike. As early as 1531, the Lutheran princes of Saxony and Hesse formed a defensive alliance against the eventuality of aggression by their own emperor. Its membership tied to Lutheran confession, this coalition, known as the Schmalkaldic League, soon attracted other principalities from different parts of Germany: by the 1540s, it covered most of the northern half of the empire's German-speaking lands and also extended into its west and southwest. In a less formalized way, princely solidarity extended across confessional boundaries: even arch-Catholic Bavaria was wary of Habsburg ambition.[40]

Having bought a break from war with France and its Ottoman allies, Charles turned against his dissident princes by employing both divisive diplomacy and military force. However, military victory in 1547 proved ephemeral. His efforts to compel a return to Catholic practices provoked renewed resistance not only in Protestant principalities but also in others that feared a more centralized imperial monarchy. In a telling reflection of just how deep divisions ran, even the pope himself initially disapproved of Charles's pro-Catholic ordinances because they encroached on the pope's own jurisdiction.

In 1552, another round of armed conflict with German opponents who had allied themselves with France caught Charles flatfooted: in a scene that captures the profound weakness behind the imperial splendor, Charles and his entourage had to flee Innsbruck, deep in the Catholic Alps, to avoid capture by Saxony's forces. After a failed campaign against France, Charles was forced to accept religious freedoms in Germany, and he abdicated soon thereafter.[41]

Both his military ambitions and his designs for religious unity had thus come to nothing. Upon Charles's death in 1558, the Habsburg domains were more fragmented than they had been before. Protestantism had swiftly become firmly entrenched and politicized in ways that reinforced existing divisions within the German empire and beyond. As the emperorship devolved upon the Habsburg line that ruled Austria, there was no longer a single figurehead for their entire domain. Only in the autobiographical account that Charles had dictated in the early 1550s did he eclipse that paragon of Roman imperialism, Julius Caesar: after all, Charles noted, Caesar had invaded Gaul only once, whereas he had done so no fewer than five times—a tally that neglects the inconvenient detail of how these invasions turned out.[42]

Yet this comparison between Caesar and Charles is instructive in a different way. It is worth remembering that the real cost of war had gone up considerably since the Roman Republican period. Charles's abortive attempt to take the French border city of Metz had cost him more than 3 million ducats. Converted into grain equivalent, this much gold would have paid for a year's deployment of well over 100,000 soldiers at the time of Caesar, or a joint force of close to a quarter million Romans and allies a century earlier—enough to succeed where Caesar did and Charles could not hope to.[43]

Throughout his reign, and in fact increasingly, Charles V was hamstrung by fiscal constraints. In economic terms, waging war was a losing proposition, as his European campaigns consumed growing amounts of money without generating new revenue flows or even helping to protect existing sources of income, such as Spain, the Low Countries, and the Americas, which were not under any significant threat. Instead, fiscal demands only served to alienate taxpayers in some of these areas, most notably the Low Countries, with fatal consequences later. Armies steadily grew in size and cost, from 15,000 men for an aborted invasion of Italy in 1529 to 80,000 by 1552. Meanwhile, the rising importance of mercenaries drove up per capita cost as well, as did expanding reliance on credit.[44]

Loans became increasingly important: 46 percent of the funds for Charles's wars from 1529 to 1541 was generated by loans from Castile, but 72 percent (of a total that was more than one and a half times as large) from 1543 to 1552. The growing inflow of silver from the Americas was the only thing that kept credit going without triggering violent unrest along the lines of the massive tax revolt that had rocked Castile in 1520–1521.[45]

Charles's ballooning debt eventually constricted his policy choices: thus, he was unable to capitalize on military successes by establishing garrisons he simply could not afford. In his conflict with the Schmalkaldic League, fiscal exhaustion prompted a five-year hiatus in hostilities, and renewed fighting pushed Charles to the brink of bankruptcy. In the absence of an effective fiscal bureaucracy, warfare on this scale was simply unsustainable—and a harbinger of worse crises to come under his equally warlike son and successor, Philip II.[46]

In sum, Habsburg ambitions faced an array of seemingly irresistible forces. One was the sheer diversity of Charles's dominions, which lacked both a capital and a unified administration: as a result, he was always on the move, much as Charlemagne, the first of many post-Roman "Roman" emperors, had been 750 years earlier. Another was the soaring cost of war, driven by mercenaries, gunpowder, and intricate fortifications. A third was growing ideological disunity that amplified existing political divisions in ways that eventually led to the cataclysmic struggle of the Thirty Years' War. Whatever it was Charles actually aspired to—universal empire, a hegemonic position in Europe, leadership of Christendom— none of these appeared to be within his reach.[47]

Consideration of these conditions makes it all the more striking to encounter a counterfactual that extrapolates very different outcomes from a perfectly plausible minimal rewrite of history. In this scenario, developed by Carlos Eire, Henry VIII either does not break with Rome or he dies early—either of which could easily have happened. England consequently remains in the Catholic camp: allied to Spain, it helps Charles defeat France and the Schmalkaldic League. Northern Germany and Switzerland are purged of Protestants; Luther and Calvin are cap- tured and burned in Rome. Later the offspring of Philip II and Anne rule England. A more unified Europe pushes back the Ottomans and is able to commit more of its resources to learning and science, thereby ushering in European global dominance sooner than it had happened in real life.[48]

However, Eire also considers radically different developments based on the same rewrite. Protestantism might well have survived in England, triggering civil war instead of a stable alliance with Spain. This could have fueled religious wars in Europe and the New World: England rather than the Netherlands would have become a money pit for the Spanish military, and the seventeenth century might have turned out even more violent than it actually did. Much hinges on how we assess the role of religion, as more or less pliable in the face of political and military pressure. Our position on this question to a large extent deter- mines overall outcomes—a valuable reminder of the pitfalls of counter- factual reasoning.[49]

The main merit of this exercise lies in its highlighting the importance of the (early) sixteenth century as a "key choice point," when some de- velopmental pathways opened at the lasting expense of others: this was when Europe's rise to global power commenced (and the question arose whether its reach could be monopolized by any one power or coalition); when its state system was consolidated (further); and when massive religious transitions took place. Because England came to play an outsized role in all of these processes—just as it would in the later breakthrough to modernity—it makes sense to position it at the center of a counterfactual.[50]

Even so, Eire's scenario is vulnerable on too many fronts. England, then a country of just 4 million (a quarter of the French population), was in fact allied with Spain against France but to little avail, and its support alone was unlikely to have been sufficient to allow Charles to crush both France and the German princes. Second-order effects also come into play: greater Habsburg dominance might well have encouraged more balancing even among Catholic powers, making the vision of a semidependent England less likely. France was so populous that it would have been hard to cow into submission under almost any circumstances. As important as England was going to be, it can hardly be instrumentalized as a pivot around which a substantially different history of Europe can be constructed, least of all one that yields durable hegemony under the Habsburgs—which, in any case, might well have been much more detrimental to European science than Eire allows for. Europe's potential for unleashing countervailing forces to any would-be hegemon was already very high.

In real life, Charles's son Philip II inherited most of the Habsburg domains: the spun-off Austrian territories were comparatively small and poor and beset by the Ottomans; and all overseas colonies belonged to Spain. This division within the Habsburg realm reflected the consolidation of a Spain-centered global empire, and a concurrent shift away from fantasies of universal rule under the aegis of the German empire. The prospect of imperial unification of Europe thus retreated even further (figure 6.3).

Failure in key military endeavors contributed to this trend. Philip's overall record was decidedly mixed. Spain gained respite from French pressure as France descended into religious wars between Catholic and Protestant factions (1562–1598): Philip supported the former and became

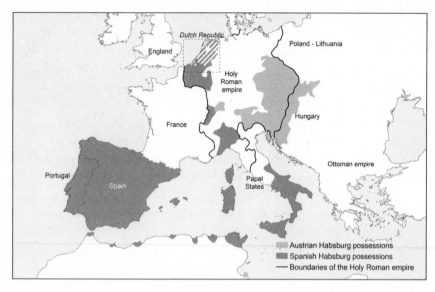

FIGURE 6.3 The possessions of Philip II, 1590s CE.

actively involved in this conflict during its final decade. Relations with the Ottomans were marked by naval defeat in 1560 and victory in 1571, effectively a stalemate. In 1580 Philip acquired Portugal and its overseas possessions, a move that—if only very briefly—cemented his global hegemony over European trade and colonization. The American territories and their silver production expanded, and Spain established a presence in the Philippines.

However, all these gains were more than counteracted by setbacks in the North Sea region that came to be the cradle of modernity. In the northern Low Countries, the tax burden, encroachment on administrative autonomy, and repression against Protestants triggered a revolt against Philip's rule in 1568. Despite early successes, his armies ultimately proved incapable of suppressing this defection. Relations with nearby England deteriorated after Philip's brief tenure as its king (by way of marriage) in 1554–1558. England's later support for the Dutch rebels and the execution of the Catholic Mary Stuart provoked a Spanish invasion attempt that failed in 1588. At that point, almost two-thirds of the Spanish military were set against England or garrisoned in the Low Countries.

Both of these theaters produced costly setbacks: renewed naval buildup in the 1590s did not deliver victories and the army of Flanders's direct engagement in France drained its resources, precipitating mutinies. In the end, enormous expenditures had been incurred without producing tangible benefits. England and the Netherlands retained their independence and stepped up their pressure on Spanish and Portuguese possessions overseas, and France remained hostile. Meanwhile, Philip defaulted on his debts no fewer than five times.[51]

It is hard to see how one might salvage from all this any even remotely plausible counterfactual of Spanish hegemony over Europe. The main options would have been to avert the Dutch revolt, to kill Elizabeth I and tie England under Mary Stuart closer to Spain, or to successfully invade England in 1588. The first of these objectives had been achieved under Charles V but became increasingly elusive as taxation, centralization, and the Reformation intensified. The second option was certainly feasible—the Dutch leader William of Orange was assassinated—but merely takes us back to Eire's counterfactual of a (mainly) Catholic England being allied to Charles V: the question remains whether Protestantism could have been fully contained, or whether a Catholic England would have placed religious affinity over national interests. After all, France was also primarily Catholic but reliably hostile to the Habsburgs.

The third scenario looks superficially more appealing at least in the short term: England's military and walls were no match for the Spanish troops and their equipment, and the country was very low on cash and credit. Spanish occupation or some sort of settlement with England would have cut off support for the Netherlands and stifled Atlantic raiding, helping Spain maintain its hold on its global assets and freeing up resources to crack down on the Dutch and on Protestants elsewhere. But once again, we must not ignore the possibility of second-order counterfactuals: Spanish heavy-handedness in England might well have galvanized resistance elsewhere, discouraging Dutch proponents of peace and emboldening Germany's Protestant princes.[52]

In the longer term, it seems unlikely that Spain would have been able to detach England from the Protestant zone in northern Europe and control its foreign policy tightly enough to avoid future conflict. Just as Spanish intervention in France in the 1590s weakened its flagging efforts against the Dutch, operations in England could have had similar consequences. The sheer number of theaters competing for attention—France, England, and the Low Countries—made it difficult to succeed in all of them, and offered Spain's opponents ample opportunities for balancing.

Thus, Spanish hegemony was improbable even in the short term, and even less plausible over a longer time frame. Not for the first time, too much history would need to be rewritten to allow parsimonious modifications to contingent events—such as the fate of Elizabeth I or the Armada—to generate substantially divergent geopolitical outcomes. Moreover, what is at stake here is some measure of Spanish hegemony in Latin Europe: a unified empire that covered much of Europe was far beyond Philip's reach, just as it had been beyond Charles's. In this sense, polycentrism as the defining characteristic of Europe's political order was never under any serious threat.

THE SIXTEENTH AND SEVENTEENTH CENTURIES: THE OTTOMAN ADVANCE

If European powers were unable to create a monopolistic super-state, was there any hope for outside contenders to succeed? The Ottoman empire was the only conceivable candidate. Rooted in a coalition of Turkic warriors and their allies formed in the early fourteenth century in northwestern Anatolia, this polity swiftly expanded across Asia Minor and into the Balkans and on to Romania. In 1453, the Ottomans took Constantinople, and in 1516–1517 replaced the Mamluks as rulers of Syria and Egypt. Hungary was overrun in 1526, and most of the Black Sea littoral fell under Ottoman control. Vassal regimes were established in the eastern and central Maghreb, which served as a base for naval operations against Christian states. The sultanate built a large navy that dislodged Europeans from their eastern Mediterranean strongholds and pushed farther west. In 1527, the sultan's standing army of some 20,000 was augmented by 90,000 land-grant soldiers, two-thirds of whom lived within reach of the European frontier, even if only part of them could actually be mobilized.

This was the first time since the Umayyad period that an empire of this size had emerged in such close proximity to Latin Europe. The Ottomans ruled territories that very roughly coincided with those held by the East Roman empire at its peak 1,000 years earlier—minus Italy but plus Mesopotamia, Romania, and the northern Black Sea basin— and even shared the same capital city. And unlike the first caliphate, the Ottoman empire turned out to be much more durable: it maintained its territorial possessions at close to their maximum extent until the end of the eighteenth century and at least nominally even beyond that (figure 6.4).[53]

Yet just like the Umayyad caliphate, the Ottomans did not make major headway into Latin Europe. Assaults on Vienna failed in 1529,

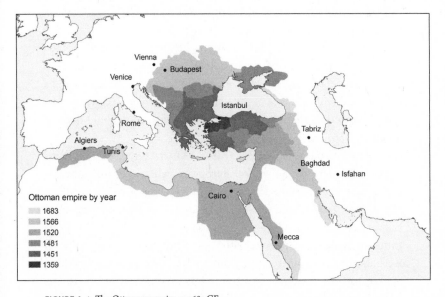

FIGURE 6.4 The Ottoman empire, c. 1683 CE.

1532, and again in 1664 and 1683, as did a landing in southern Italy in 1480–1481 and the siege of Malta in 1565. Naval operations in alliance with France in the mid-sixteenth century accomplished little of substance. Venice's loss of Crete in 1668 was the Ottoman's final gain, a trivial one.

By the early seventeenth century, Spanish fleets were already able to score victories in the eastern Mediterranean. From the 1590s into the 1650s, the Anatolian heartland of the empire was shaken by a series of revolts of military elements and provincial officials. The central authorities struggled to retain full control of its military resources. State capacity did not keep up with ongoing improvements in Europe. By 1600, Ottoman tax revenue in per capita terms lagged behind that of Spain, Venice, the Netherlands, France, and England. In absolute terms, Spain's annual revenues were three times as large as those of the Ottomans. From the sixteenth through the eighteenth centuries, Ottoman tax income measured in silver remained flat in both per capita and absolute terms, while it increased steadily and in some cases dramatically almost everywhere in Europe.

In 1600, the population of Europe west of the Ottoman realm—excluding anything east of Poland—was about two and a half times that of the Ottoman empire. This demographic imbalance was reflected by military manpower: in the mid-sixteenth century, the combined military forces of England, France, Spain, and Austria were two and a half times as large as those of the Ottomans, and by 1700 this ratio had risen to 4 to 1. Latin Europe was more than any sultan could hope to swallow.[54]

One might object that Europe's forces were fractured, and employed in the first instance to fight other Europeans, whereas those of the Ottomans reported to a single government. However, two factors offset this advantage. We need to control for second-order counterfactuals arising from a more determined Ottoman push into Europe: it was one thing for France to cooperate with them when their nearest outposts were almost 800 kilometers away, but it would have been another thing entirely had they penetrated Austria and Bavaria and reached the Rhine. More importantly, the Ottoman empire was locked into long-term conflict, alternately active and latent, with another formidable power in its Asian rear: Safavid Iran.

From 1514 to 1639, the two regimes—Sunni Ottomans and Shia Safavids—competed for control of Iraq, which the Ottomans had seized from the Safavids in 1514, and of the southern Caucasus. On eight separate occasions, they were at war with each other during 55 of these 126 years. While the Ottomans initially had the upper hand, in the sixteenth century Iranian reforms and Ottoman internal instability raised the pressure: Baghdad was lost for 14 years, and it took the Ottomans until 1639 to restore their positions. The European and Iraqi theaters continuously competed for attention: in the 1550s, Ottoman operations in the east curbed engagement in the west, whereas in the early 1600s it was the other way around.

All this leaves little room for credible counterfactuals of a larger Ottoman European empire. It is telling that the Ottomans were unable to make major inroads at a time when conflict among European states intensified. This does not bode well for a scenario in which more successful advances might have checked some of these conflicts enough to coordinate resistance. In terms of fiscal and military capabilities, the Ottoman state already lagged behind the major European powers when it appeared on the scene and then continued to fall behind as competitive European state formation accelerated.

Religious affiliation might also have served as an obstacle to further Ottoman expansion: while it is true that the Arabs had conquered and ruled many millions of Christians in the Levant, the Maghreb, and the Iberian peninsula (as well as Zoroastrians in Iran), these populations had not yet been organized in the type of more cohesive and capable state that had begun to emerge in early modern Europe. This makes the Ottoman conquests in the Christian Balkans a poor analogy for what might have happened farther west, where the time for the successful absorption of tens of millions of Christians and their lasting acquiescence to a Muslim regime might well have passed.

Plausible rewrites such as a fall of Vienna or an invasion of Italy cannot alter these structural features. Very major modifications of history would be required to allow the Ottomans to unite much of Latin Europe under their rule: we would have to boost their internal stability and fiscal capabilities, and write the Safavid empire (and any alternative Middle Eastern competitor) out of the story.[55]

The resultant environment would be dramatically different from that which actually existed at the time, a construct that cannot serve as a basis for credible counterfactual considerations. Despite its striking early successes and long-term resilience, the Ottoman state lacked the mobilization skills, the military edge, and the ability to concentrate all its assets in one theater that would have been necessary to carry its arms into Latin Europe.

FROM THE LATE SEVENTEENTH TO THE EARLY NINETEENTH CENTURY: THE FRENCH QUEST FOR HEGEMONY

By the end of the seventeenth century, France had become the leading power in Christian Europe: its state revenues exceeded that of any of its competitors, and it managed to field some 340,000 troops, compared to 580,000 for England, the Netherlands, Spain, Austria, Prussia, and Russia combined. Thus, although pan-European empire was beyond the reach even of the Sun King Louis XIV, France was the only credible contender for a hegemonic position. However, its aggressive foreign policy primarily had the effect of encouraging balancing coalitions among its opponents, most notably in the Nine Years' War (1688–1697) and the War of the Spanish Succession (1702–1714).[56]

Given England's ascendance in the same period—it had won two wars against the Dutch and was well on its way to becoming Europe's economic powerhouse—the most effective way to disrupt balancing against France's ambitions would have been to remove England from these coalitions and bring it over to the French side. The only time this might conceivably have been possible was under the Catholic English monarch James II in the late seventeenth century.

Jack Goldstone has developed a counterfactual scenario to this end. A minimal rewrite prevents William of Orange from bringing about the

Glorious Revolution, either in 1688 or in 1690. As a result, England continues to be ruled by James II and enters an alliance with France. This move would have reduced competition in Europe: there would not have been any Anglo-French conflicts in Europe or the New World; France would easily have contained the Netherlands and won the War of the Spanish Succession with less effort. In the end, Europe might have ended up divided along the Rhine between a French-led bloc that covered the Iberian peninsula, France, England (and the cowed Netherlands), and German-Austrian (and Russian) spheres farther east.

While it is hard even to guess whether this would have produced more peace or instead more massive wars across this divide, powerful consequences can be posited for the colonial world: Canada would have been dominated by the French, and the United States might have been stillborn. This suggests that the French Revolution might have been avoided as well, and thus also the secession of Spain's American colonies.[57]

This counterfactual extrapolation has been criticized as being too optimistic: we must wonder whether England would have allowed itself to be tethered to a dominant continental power, or whether its Protestants could have been cowed into submission, especially with their peers in the Netherlands, northern Germany, and Scandinavia not far away. But what matters most for our present purposes is that even Goldstone's sweeping counterfactual does not envision anything like unified empire in Europe, not even within the French-led bloc. The most France could hope for was some version of hegemonic primacy among allied states, forever latently under pressure from England's (and the Netherlands') maritime position and Protestant leanings.[58]

Even so, in view of England's critical importance in jump-starting the Industrial Revolution, the mere possibility that its independent development might have been curbed ought to give us pause. In Goldstone's scenario, political or economic modernity might very well not have arisen in more or less the same way it did in actual history. The answer to the question of whether this would merely have delayed, or geographically displaced, essential breakthroughs greatly depends on how much weight we put on the contingent nature of these processes. Only under extreme circumstances—if industrialization is deemed impossible without British coal deposits and protectionism, or "bourgeois values" could not have thrived outside the sheltered environments of real-life Holland, Britain, and North America—might Goldstone's environment have stifled Europe's progress.[59]

Yet even in that case, the most likely outcome was not enduring French hegemony and insufficient incentives for very specific forms of innovation but, before long, the completion of yet another Malthusian cycle and attendant pressures that would have upended the geopolitical order. More generally, any kind of domestic instability at the French core could have caused the periphery to fray, competitive polycentrism to be revived, and processes of disruptive social, economic, ideological, and technological innovation to resume.

If we allow actual history to proceed undisturbed and England to cement its economic and military power over the course of the eighteenth century, the dislocations of the Napoleonic period present us with the very last juncture at which the British breakthroughs and all that followed might still have been derailed. The most obvious way in which this could have been accomplished, a French invasion of Britain, was likely blocked by the considerable superiority of the British navy. An alternative route to European hegemony would have led through peaceful coexistence with Russia.[60]

Napoleon's zeal in engaging opponents across Europe stirred up countervailing forces that, in the aggregate, were always too powerful to overcome. By the early nineteenth century, the European state system—forged of centuries of inconclusive warfare and self-strengthening reforms—had become too deeply entrenched, too large (thanks to Russia), and too capable of drawing on external resources (thanks to Britain) for any one party in Latin Europe to overpower and control all the others. From this perspective, the balance of power was never in France's favor (figure 6.5).[61]

In fact, it is worth remembering that the most plausible counterfactual was not French victory and empire but failure well before it finally occurred. In confronting a variety of competitors. Napoleon repeatedly took great risks that could have resulted in decisive setbacks: for example, he could have been defeated by superior enemy forces in the

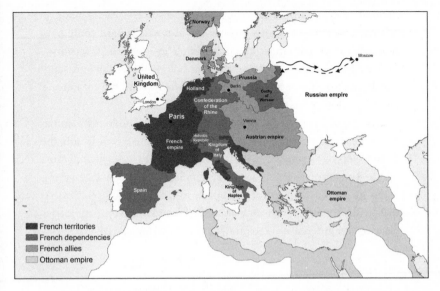

FIGURE 6.5 Europe in 1812 CE.

Austerlitz campaign in the fall of 1805, or been wiped out at Krasnoi in November 1812 during the retreat from Russia. A string of highly contingent victories between 1805 and 1807 was needed to turn him into Europe's momentary hegemon.

Yet Austria, Prussia, and Russia's humiliation only served to galvanize their resistance. Thus, once Napoleon's interventions in the Iberian peninsula and Russia to isolate Britain had drained his resources, hegemony could no longer be maintained. Moreover, French casualty rates kept rising as the war progressed, in part because the deployment of larger armies generated longer battles but especially because of heavier use of artillery. In this brutal environment, numbers did matter. Even victory at Waterloo would not have changed this basic fact.[62]

Napoleon faced a paradox. Had he been more restrained in his objectives, it might have been possible for France to make and preserve gains over the longer run, most plausibly by establishing hegemony or even direct rule over continental Europe west of Prussia and Austria. Yet that would not have created an empire of ancient Rome's demographic preeminence, and would have kept Britain's position (largely) intact. In this case, modern economic growth and industrialization could have proceeded unabated. A more ambitious Napoleon—the real-life version—by contrast, was bound to undermine his successes through unsustainable overreach. Either way, the ascent of Britain—and thus of Europe, and the "West"—was not in danger.

One might add as a coda that Hitler's efforts were undone by similar constraints, most notably the fact that thanks to the Soviet Union, the British empire, and the United States—Roosevelt's "arsenal of democracy"—the Europe-centered state system had by then became far too extensive to allow any European power to erect a durable empire. At that point, however, even such an unlikely outcome would no longer have made a difference—the modern world had long arrived.

FIFTEEN CENTURIES OF FRAGMENTATION

None of the states we might suspect of having had the potential to impose imperial rule on a large part of the population of Europe ever had a realistic chance to succeed. Individual events that are sometimes held up as turning points—in 732, 1242, or 1588—were hardly genuine junctures at which the political future of Europe hung in the balance. This should not occasion surprise: after all, as I tried to show in chapter 4, Rome's rise to power was also largely free of moments when minimal rewrites could have derailed its expansion once it had begun in earnest. Structural properties and systematic disparities between core and periphery were the principal driving forces. Much the same was true of the post-Roman period, as general conditions and broad trends proved more influential than specific events.

Different factors played a decisive role at different times. (East) Roman restoration was thwarted by geopolitical dynamics: it faced too many challengers to succeed, a situation similar to that experienced by the Habsburgs a millennium later. In both cases, aspirants lacked Rome's organizational superiority over its competitors that would have allowed them to engage multiple enemies at once and emerge victorious. Others were held back by internal fragmentation: Frankish and German rulers were tightly constrained by aristocratic autonomy, fiscal debility, and balancing among different sources of social power. Arab and Mongol instability was rooted in their social structure and the way it had shaped their conquest regimes. Europe was protected by the early fraying of their western peripheries, as Berbers and Cordoba defected and the Golden Horde turned on the Ilkhanate.

The variety and scale of the European state system likewise acted as a powerful brake on empire-building. Coalitions of city-states were able to block much larger powers: the Italian city-states and leagues that confronted the German emperors, and the Dutch United Provinces that defected from Philip II. In other cases, it was the sheer demographic heft and geographical spread of Europe that blocked contenders such as the Ottoman empire and early modern France.

Let us return for a moment to the key variables that I introduced in Part II and that played a decisive role in the rise of the Roman empire: the relative power of core and periphery, as well as scale, intensity, and integrity. Not all of the major post-Roman powers were endowed with a reasonably coherent and cohesive core: it was missing from the German empire and poorly developed in the Carolingian and Habsburg realms. The Umayyad core of Syria and the Arabian homeland was riven by ancestral divisions, and the confederated Mongol tribes increasingly dispersed across an enormous area. Only the eastern Roman empire and, much later, France shared the requisite attributes, as did, albeit less reliably, the Ottoman empire.

The only variable that was not an issue was scale: at their peak, all the polities surveyed here were very large, with populations in the deca-million range: the eastern Roman empire, the caliphate, the Franks (though perhaps just barely), the German empire, the Mongols, Habsburgs, and Ottomans, and France.

Their scale advantage was however frequently offset by poor performance regarding the other two metrics. Military mobilization intensity was low overall—1 percent of the general population or less. While the same had been true of the mature Roman empire, what is missing from the post-Roman cases is the presence of a core in the multimillion-member range that out-mobilizes larger but less committed rival states. The Mongols, who achieved very high rates of mobilization in their core, were the only exception. It was not until the French Revolution and the Napoleonic period that a country as large as France achieved mobilization levels of several percent, but at that point its competitors were rapidly catching up—which Rome's rivals had failed to do.

Integrity within the ruling class often varied over time. It oscillated between good and mediocre in the eastern Roman empire. It was poor in the caliphate almost from the beginning and increasingly poor among the Franks, and persistently so in the German empire. Cohesion swiftly declined among the Mongols, and to some extent also in the Ottoman empire in the first half of the seventeenth century. The Habsburgs faced defection of Dutch elites and resistance in Germany, alongside more sporadic challenges from the Spanish cortes and even their own conquistadores in the New World. The French Revolution aside, early modern France was generally in better shape, but so were its main opponents.

While scale was no longer a constraint—plenty of large states entered the fray over a millennium and a half—intensity (in some meaningfully defined core) and integrity undoubtedly were. Post-Roman Europe did not produce a single example of a sizable core with high levels of mobilization intensity and political integrity that was in a position to project overwhelming power against less well-organized competitors. Furthermore, as the states of early modern Europe gradually improved their capabilities in these categories, they did so in concert with their peers. As a result, no one state enjoyed the unique advantages of ancient Rome: never again would a powerful core face off against brittle patrimonial empires and fragmented ecologies of micro-states, chiefdoms, and tribes.

European polycentrism hardened over time. Some of the early post-Roman "Great Powers" were checked by a less developed political-military network (as happened to the eastern Roman empire) or were internally weak members of a poorly integrated and competitive state system (in the case of Franks and the German empire). As states rebuilt their capabilities, the entire state system became more resilient in the process—to the detriment of Habsburg, Ottoman, and French ambitions. Challengers from outside Europe—Arabs, Mongols, and

Turks—would have needed either a decisive military edge or other advantages to offset the obstacles of distance and logistics, but generally lacked such qualities. Thus, while the ongoing evolution of its competitive state system obstructed empire-building from within Europe, the absence of truly formidable external aspirants prevented conquest and unification from without. Both pathways to a return to Roman-style empire remained blocked.

The counterfactual modifications required to unblock these pathways are so extravagant that they would render the whole exercise meaningless: East Roman emperors who either co-opted or conquered Sasanian Iran; caliphs who erased old tribal loyalties and novel religious divisions at will; Germanic leaders who restored tax systems to their former imperial glory and kept their dukes and bishops on a tight leash; Mongol khans unaccountably determined to burn through their reserves of men and treasure as far away from Mongolia as possible; Habsburgs who not only inherited both England and France but held on to them for good and forged a single empire out of unwieldy complexity; French rulers who assembled a proto-European Union "plus" (with Russia and without Brexit) that was eager to submit to their command.

In a counterfactual universe far, far away from an even moderately defensible rewrite of history, any or all of this might somehow have happened. On planet Earth, by contrast, Roman-scale empire stood next to no chance of returning to Europe. But what made the barriers to this outcome so hard to scale—and so much harder than elsewhere? This is a question that calls for comparative analysis, to which we now turn.

PART IV

The First Great Divergence

CHAPTER 7

From Convergence to Divergence

UNDERSTANDING DIVERGENCE

THE "FIRST GREAT DIVERGENCE" was not merely a *break* between Roman and post-Roman modes of state formation in Europe. It was also a genuine *divergence*, as trajectories of state formation began to separate between post-Roman Europe and other parts of the Old World. As we saw in the opening chapter, it was the persistent absence of large-scale empire from the past millennium and a half of Europe's history that made it stand out. The proportion of Europeans ruled by Rome, some 80 percent or more, was similar to the share of population claimed by the largest empires of several other macro-regions, such as those of the Achaemenids and Umayyads (~80 percent) and the Ottomans (~60 percent) in the Middle East and North Africa region; the Maurya, Delhi, and Mughal empires (~90 percent) and the Gupta and Harsha empires (~60 percent) in South Asia; and various Chinese dynasties in East Asia (~80–90 percent). The recurrent creation of such entities outside Europe prevented the emergence of stable state systems.[1]

This divergence places the failure of hegemonic empire in post-Roman Europe in a much broader context. Identifying specific circumstances that accounted for this outcome, as I tried to do in chapters 5 and 6, can just be a first step. Only comparison between Europe and other parts of the Old World can tell us whether these outcomes were rooted in more fundamental differences. This, in turn, gives us a better sense of whether European polycentrism and competitive fragmentation were highly contingent or sustained by powerful structural conditions. In this chapter and in chapters 8 and 9, I argue that the latter is true.

Ideally, we would like to observe particular features that were most pronounced in East Asia—the most "empire-friendly" part of the Old World—weakest in, or even absent from, post-Roman Europe, and of intermediate strength in other subcontinental regions, including relevant portions of the New World. In practice, the comprehensive survey that is needed to systematically define, document, and assess a wide set of criteria could easily fill an entire book. In the following, I therefore focus in the first instance on a more straightforward juxtaposition of Europe and East Asia, employing the Chinese imperial tradition as a counterpoint to medieval and European state formation.

However, this contrast appeared only after the fall of Rome, and that is what made it a divergence. Up till then, Europe and East Asia had shared convergent trends that appeared to put them on similar tracks. This, of course, makes their subsequent and rather sudden divergence all the more remarkable and worth investigating. It also helps us pinpoint the most significant variables that drove this process, and to do so at different levels of causation.[2]

I develop my argument in two stages. In this chapter, I cover the ancient convergence and subsequent divergence between Europe and China, and the specific historical circumstances—or proximate causes—associated with the post-ancient disjuncture. I then explore more fundamental features that acted upon these historical processes: geography and ecology (chapter 8) and cultural traits (chapter 9). I expand my comparison by introducing material from South and Southeast Asia and the Middle East whenever it is expedient, but in less detail, in order to test the broader relevance of putative key variables such as fiscal arrangements, proximity to the steppe, and cultural homogeneity.

In the summary of my findings at the end of chapter 9, I argue that the most important outcomes—enduring fragmentation in post-Roman Europe and serial empire formation elsewhere—were substantially overdetermined. Notwithstanding Rome's early success, Europe was always less likely to be ruled by very large empires than other parts of the Old World, most notably East Asia. This holds true regardless of whether we privilege geographic, ecological, or cultural factors.

STATE FORMATION IN EUROPE AND EAST ASIA: ANCIENT PARALLELS, CONVERGENCES, AND DIFFERENCES

Parallels

The eastern and western ends of Eurasia had not always developed in such strikingly different ways. For more than a millennium, state formation proceeded in parallel or even convergent ways. In the early first millennium BCE, political power in Europe and the Mediterranean on the one hand and in East Asia on the other was spatially highly fragmented. Europe was a vast expanse of small and stateless groups lined by Mediterranean city-states. In the Levant, which had long been home to larger and more complex polities, widespread collapse at the end of the Bronze Age had shattered empires from Anatolia to Mesopotamia and Egypt, leaving mostly smaller kingdoms in its wake. In what are now the central-eastern reaches of the People's Republic of China, the Western Zhou regime gradually lost its grip on its numerous local vassals. The erosion of central authority created a web of more than a hundred smaller polities that were interspersed with ethnically different but similarly modestly sized groups.

Over time, diversity very gradually diminished as larger political entities emerged and absorbed competitors. This process commenced a little sooner in the West but in both cases yielded comparable results. In the Middle East, the Neo-Assyrian empire expanded from the ninth and especially the eighth centuries BCE onward, as did Kushite and Saite Egypt from the eighth and seventh centuries. Stretching from the Balkans to the Indus valley, the vast Iranian-centered empire of the Achaemenids that arose in the second half of the sixth century BCE eclipsed everything that had come before. After Alexander the Great's conquest caused it to unravel in the late fourth century BCE, several substantial imperial states took its place. Meanwhile Rome, Carthage, and Syracuse established growing domains in the western Mediterranean. In China, by the fifth century BCE seven major warring states had swallowed the many small polities that had emerged from the wreckage of the traditional Zhou order.[3]

In both cases, these processes of consolidation gave rise to increasingly powerful polities at the western margins of each ecumenical zone, Rome and its Italian alliance system in the West and the kingdom of Qin in the East. In building up their military capabilities, they benefited from their respective "marcher" positions that enabled them to expand without being heavily constrained by similarly developed neighbors. Thus, as noted in chapter 3, Rome was protected by Italy's location outside Western Eurasia's central "political-military network," while Qin was shielded by mountains that separated it from the more economically advanced states in the Central Plain and ensured its control over the "land within the passes" (Guanzhong), a peripheral region centered on the Wei River valley.

These positional advantages facilitated initial expansion away from major established powers: into the western Mediterranean for Rome (in the third century BCE) and southward into Sichuan for Qin (in the late fourth century BCE). Low protection costs boosted the value of these gains. These added resources as well as a particularly strong focus on martial capabilities allowed Rome and Qin to engage and overpower great powers to the east. In both cases, de facto hegemony morphed into direct rule, albeit much more rapidly in China (in the 220s BCE) than in the Mediterranean basin, where Rome drew out this process across the last two centuries BCE and in a few places even beyond that.[4]

Quasi-monopolistic authority on a subcontinental scale affected the political structure of both conquest empires. This included a shift from military mass mobilization to more professional and socially as well as geographically peripheral forces. The mature Roman empire sustained a standing army deployed in and increasingly replenished from frontier regions and augmented by provincial auxiliaries, whereas the Han empire (the much longer-lived successor to the Qin regime) gradually came to rely on a mixture of convicts, colonists, mercenaries, and

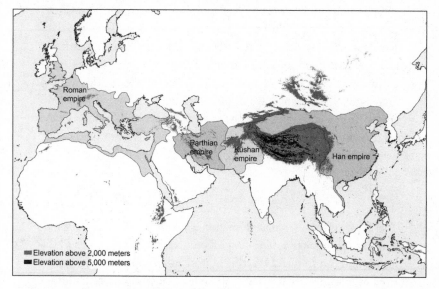

FIGURE 7.1 Empires of the Old World, c. 200 CE.

"barbarian" contingents. In both cases, territorial expansion slowed and then ceased altogether. At the same time, rent-seeking local elites increasingly constrained central authority and state control (figure 7.1).[5]

The two empires even failed in a similar fashion. The third century CE witnessed temporary splits into three subimperial states: however, Rome experienced a more robust recovery (from the 270s to the 390s CE) than Jin China (where unity was chiefly limited to a quarter century after 265 CE). Yet in the end, these differences in detail mattered little. In both cases, the more exposed halves of each empire were taken over by outside (or rather preinfiltrated) conquest regimes: groups from the steppe frontier region in northern China (in the fourth century CE) and Germanic confederations in the western Roman empire (mostly in the fifth century CE). Traditional rump states survived in the more sheltered southern half of China (from 317 to 589 CE) and in the eastern Mediterranean (from 395 CE), which unlike southern China was less well protected by geography but up to the early sixth century benefited from the temporary weakness of Constantinople's Iranian competitors.

In both the former western Roman Europe and in northern China, conquerors and local elites assimilated into new ruling classes, and transcendent religions that claimed autonomy from the state—Christianity and Buddhism—advanced. Determined attempts to reestablish empire on the previous scale were made in the sixth century CE. This was the final parallel experience: from then on, state formation lastingly diverged as imperial reconstruction succeeded in late sixth-century China (and would do so repeatedly on later occasions) but not (and in fact never again) in Europe.

Differences and Convergences

These parallel trends in state formation up to the middle of the first millennium CE masked underlying differences. Chinese polities of the Spring and Autumn and Warring States periods operated in a framework of elite interaction based on the at least loosely unifying traditions of Shang and Zhou (around the sixteenth through the eighth centuries BCE). Rome, by contrast, in most of its European territories created political unity where it had never existed before. It was only in the central and eastern Mediterranean that it could draw on antecedent networks and governmental infrastructure. This slowed but did not lastingly obstruct Roman expansion to the west and north.[6]

In terms of political and administrative structures, a sizable gap separated the monarchical systems and (by ancient standards) strongly centralized regimes of the Warring States period from the oligarchic system of the Roman Republic and the decentralized mode of Rome's governance of its provinces. This gap was widest during the last few centuries of the first millennium BCE but narrowed over time, even if it never completely disappeared. This reflects convergent trends over the long run.

During their expansion phases, both Rome and Qin (alongside the other Warring States) relied on mass mobilization of peasant infantry, and created conscription districts and conducted censuses for this purpose. From the fifth through the third centuries BCE, the Warring States were locked into prolonged inconclusive warfare whose competitive pressures prompted intrusive centralizing and homogenizing reforms.

The state of Qin may have gone the farthest in this regard: its rulers strove to break aristocratic power, subjected the entire population to a ranking system, divided it into small groups for mutual surveillance and collective liability, and instituted formalized rewards for military prowess. Taxes—in money, kind, and military as well as civilian labor—were relatively high. Qin's overarching ambition, to the extent that it could be realized, was the creation of a centralized territorial state that was fully controlled by employees of the ruler and left no political space for rival groups such as nobles or the wealthy.[7]

As we saw in chapter 2, Republican Rome achieved intense mass mobilization with the help of a much slimmer governmental apparatus and overt streamlining of local arrangements. Its state was highly spatially centralized in that the entire top tier of its leadership was concentrated in the city of Rome. Autocracy had long been blocked by an assertive anti-regal aristocratic oligarchy. In the absence of a monarch, competition within the aristocracy was constrained by tightly regimented popular political participation. This system was structurally opposed to formal bureaucracy and onerous taxes on insiders. A modest number of aristocratic houses relied on patrimonial resources to fulfill their public functions and on patronage relations and ritual performances to exercise power. Fiscal operations were largely farmed out to private contractors, and taxes were relatively low, especially in the Italian core, where military service represented the principal civic contribution for elite and commoners alike.

Overall, the Roman domain came to be hierarchically stratified into an Italian core and a growing provincial periphery, a feature that was largely missing from imperial China. Urban autonomy and effective self-governance were preserved, and no salaried state agents were imposed on or created in the numerous constituent communities. The main reason that this more loosely structured system managed to prevail lies in the fact that unlike the Warring States, the maturing Roman Republic engaged mostly in asymmetric competition with differently organized challengers: somewhat lopsided in Rome's favor, this competition did not spur invasive restructuring. It was only early on, as Rome struggled for supremacy over the Italian peninsula, that conflict with more opponents that were more similar encouraged—rather limited—organizational adjustments.[8]

Yet once the Roman and Qin-Han empires had grown into behemoths that between them claimed close to two-thirds of the world's population at the time, their institutions changed in ways that made them look more alike. Undermined by logistical challenges and growing stratification and erosion of consensus among the elite, oligarchy failed in Rome and was replaced by monarchy: although different in style from the Han version—in granting greater autonomy to elite groups and leaning more heavily on a bloated military sector—this was a big step toward the global historical default model of kingship. In China, the imperial center, while maintaining a numerically large bureaucracy of around 150,000 salaried state employees, gradually lost ground as local elites expanded their influence at the expense of these agents. A period of dynastic instability in the early first century CE in particular bolstered the power of magnates who supported the ruling dynasty. The concurrent abolition of conscription surrendered greater control over people and resources to wealthy landlords and patrons.

In the Roman empire, meanwhile, a patrimonial bureaucracy that had grown only very slowly received a major boost from serious dislocations in the third century CE that encouraged more determined centralizing reforms. As a result, the mature imperial state of the fourth century CE resembled that of the Han more closely than before, featuring a sizable bureaucracy of 20,000-plus men, an overhaul of the fragmented tax system, the separation of military and civilian commands, and half-hearted encroachment on urban autonomy. Ministries, powerful court eunuchs, and child emperors, long common in Han China, likewise appeared on the scene.[9]

It is true that this convergence went only so far: the Han administrative apparatus remained larger and Roman urban autonomy stronger. Reduced to essentials, these abiding differences reflect the resilience of the Greco-Roman city-state tradition and the more intense coercion-extraction cycle in China that had shored up centralized ambition and authority at the expense of local and especially urban self-governance.

Yet this contrast, while noteworthy, must not be overrated. Roman city officials and Han provincial agents hailed from comparable socio-economic backgrounds, and the formally bureaucratic features of Han administration barely masked rampant patronage and simony, which were similarly common in the Roman empire. Roman self-governing plutocrats and Han salaried state agents were equally adept at siphoning off resources claimed by the center, and landlords shielded their own assets and those of their clients, slowly but surely eroding the foundations of the imperial edifice. Whatever differences remained in terms of the relative weight of the military and civilian spheres, of center and periphery, and of bureaucracy and local self-rule, they were very much a matter of degree. Driven by the internal logic of traditional empire, the two systems had become about as similar as their discrepant starting conditions permitted them to be.[10]

MID-FIRST-MILLENNIUM EUROPE: THE FIRST GREAT DIVERGENCE

This gradual if imperfect convergence makes the following divergence in state formation seem even more striking. That process spanned roughly the second half of the first millennium of the Common Era. By about 500 CE, the Roman empire had split into an eastern half, ruled from Constantinople, and five major kingdoms under Germanic successor regimes in the west, a number that fell to only two within the next few decades. In China, the collapse of the Jin empire ushered in the period of the "Sixteen Kingdoms," a series of often ephemeral polities. Yet by the early fifth century, just two states controlled the northern and southern halves of China. This number fluctuated between two and three until the late sixth century when the north conquered the south. With only a brief interruption, China was then at least formally unified until around 900. The Song restoration ended another period of fragmentation in the first half of the tenth century.

By then, eleven major states, alongside a number of smaller entities, occupied the area once held by the Roman empire. Moreover, the larger polities that were located in the western and southern European parts of the former empire suffered from intense internal fragmentation, most notably the Frankish and German kingdoms and, before long, Islamic Spain. Geographically peripheral England was perhaps the single reasonably coherent polity in this zone, albeit modest in size and beset by aggressive Scandinavian neighbors.

The growing divergence between eastern and western Eurasia manifested in three different ways. First, during the second half of the first millennium CE, China had been either politically unified or split two or three ways for more than four-fifths of the time. (These latter years include about a century and a half of effective if informal interprovincial fragmentation under the later Tang dynasty.) The area once ruled by Rome, in contrast, was never unified and just barely met the criteria for a (short-lived) three-way split: its shift toward greater diversity was persistent, from only three major states in the mid-sixth century to close to a dozen by the year 1000.

Second, as we will see below, eleventh-century China was ruled by the most formidable empire in the world: it contained at least 100 million people and employed over a million soldiers. Nothing even remotely like that existed anywhere in what had been the Roman empire, and most decidedly not in its former European provinces.

Third, and most important, both the overall trajectories from 500 to 1000 and conditions around 1000 set the tone for the following millennium. Leaving aside short periods of regime change and allowing for intermittent spells of internal decentralization, China never again divided into more than two or three major states. Europe moved in the opposite direction, experiencing intense fragmentation in the High and Late Middle Ages (figure 7.2).

Thus, the number of independent polities in Latin Europe grew from late antiquity onward, at a moderate pace at first but faster after the fracturing of the Carolingian empire in the ninth century, which had imposed a short-lived semblance—or rather mirage—of Roman-scale unity on substantial parts of Western Europe. By the end of the Middle Ages, Latin Europe was contested among at least a hundred effectively independent polities, and the number of largely autonomous ones was even much greater than that. Consolidation only slowly gathered steam

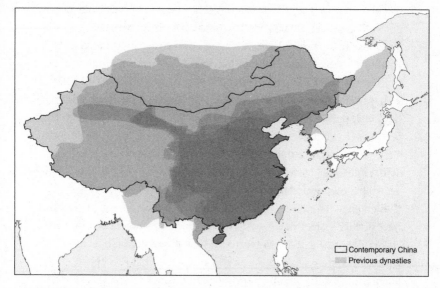

FIGURE 7.2 The Han, Tang, Northern Song, Yuan, Ming, and Qing empires.

in the early modern period but remained incomplete. In 1900, what had once been the Roman empire was—in a conservative count—divided among twenty-three states, all but two of them located on European soil. The current tally is at least forty, depending on how we define Roman rule and what qualifies as a state.[11]

The First Great Divergence brought about an enduring contrast between serial reconstitution of empire and the resultant absence of a stable state system in China and the lack of any comparable scaling-up and the resultant formation of a highly resilient ecology of political polycentrism in Europe. This does not mean that China was always unified: the figures in chapter 1 graph the extent to which this was not the case. Metrics vary, depending on how we define "China" or "unity." By one count, "core China"—defined as the territory held by the Qin state at its peak in 214 BCE—was unified under one ruler for 947 of the past 2,231 years, or 42 percent of the time (figure 7.2).[12]

Imperial persistence in China was thus relative—that is, compared to conditions in other parts of the world—not absolute. A different calculation shows that East Asia was characterized by a unipolar or hegemonic political system for 68 percent of the years between 220 BCE and 1875. This pattern presents a stark contrast to the prevalence of a balanced system in Europe for 98 percent of the years from 1500 to 2000, or indeed at any time after the demise of the mature Roman empire.[13]

It is true that imperial persistence in China was at times more formal than real: periods of effective decentralization can be observed in the late Western Han, Western Jin, mid- to late Tang, and late Ming periods. Yet even weakened empire prevented the emergence of anything like an actual multistate system, which had been present in China only in the Warring States period up to the 220s BCE.

Elements of a state system subsequently reappeared only twice, and on a smaller scale: from the 530s to the 570s CE, when the eastern and western successor states of Northern Wei in northern China faced off with a separate regime in the south, and somewhat less ephemerally during the Southern Song period, when most of China was split between Jurchen and then Mongols in the north and the Chinese Song dynasty in the south. Other periods of temporary disunity witnessed less intensive and unstable competition, most notably the tenth century CE, when a rapid succession of northern regimes coexisted with a number of southern kingdoms for about seventy years.[14]

None of these configurations amounted to a stable multistate system comparable to what we find in post-Roman Europe. This basic point is worth making given the tendency in recent scholarship to conflate the existence of multiple polities in East Asia with the presence of effective political polycentrism. For example, when in the Tang period, secondary state formation among Turks and Tibetans as well as in Korea, Japan, and Vietnam created a penumbra of polities that ringed imperial China, it did so in a highly asymmetric fashion. China claimed universal rulership—or hegemonic status, in modern parlance—and others often sought recognition as constituents of this Sinocentric world order. It is telling that serious attempts at expansion were unliteral: it was the Tang who first destroyed the Eastern Turk khaganate in the Tarim basin and then the Western one between the 620s and 650s CE, or prevailed in Korea in the 660s, or dominated Vietnam. With the brief and partial exception of Charlemagne's reign, no such hegemon ever existed in post-Roman (and pre-Napoleonic) Europe.[15]

Similar qualifications apply to a fashionable modern academic scenario that places "China among equals" from the tenth through the fourteenth centuries, beginning with the trifecta of the Northern Song in China and the Liao and Tangut states in the northern periphery, and continuing with the Southern Song and the Mongols in northern China. Inasmuch as this concept makes sense, it does so primarily with respect to military power and—consequently—diplomatic relations, but does not adequately describe the balance of material resources or population.

A significant degree of demographic division can only be observed in the period of the north-south split from 1127 to the 1270s. Yet even that century and a half was dominated by two powerful imperial states: each of them ruled tens of millions of people, and in so doing each of them approximated the heft of the unified Han and Tang empires. If this were to count as fragmentation or polycentrism, these very notions would be drained of meaning: if the concept of the multistate system were applied to post-Roman Europe and to post-221 BCE China alike, it could no longer serve as an analytical category.[16]

I call the widening chasm between post-ancient European and Chinese (as well as other Old World) trajectories of state formation the "*First* Great Divergence" because it prepared the ground for the much later political, economic, and scientific development and increase in human welfare associated with what is commonly referred to as *the* "Great Divergence"—the process of the economies of (parts of) Europe and some of its colonial spin-offs pulling away from those elsewhere in the world. My terminology adds to an increasingly crowded field. Thus, the latter "Great Divergence" of the eighteenth and nineteenth centuries—between (northwestern) Europe or the "West" more generally and the rest of the world—has already been joined by the earlier "Little Divergence" (on occasion also and confusingly called the "First Great Divergence") between northwestern Europe and the remainder of Europe from the early modern period onward.

To complicate matters further, Robert Ian Moore has proposed a different "First Great Divergence" that commenced in the High Middle

Ages when long-term developmental paths for Europe and China were set by the reinforcement of kin-oriented local hegemony in Song China and by growing efforts to subordinate such hegemonies to larger political and ideological structures away from kinship in Latin Europe: these trends, in turn, underpinned a divergence in institution-building capacity and thus political development and state formation.[17]

Yet even if we were to follow this argument, Moore's divergence would be firmly rooted in my own "First Great Divergence" as presented here: after all, it was the continuing preeminence of imperial power in China and its waning in Europe that made these particular shifts possible. Unlike the more established "Great Divergence" of the modern period, which is defined in the first instance by economic productivity, this "First Great Divergence" unfolded in the political sphere. In the end, it proved to be foundational: as I demonstrate in Part V of this book, post-Roman Europe's decisive departure from the standard consolidation-decentralization cycle of large-scale agrarian empire formation opened up space for the more famous—and now "Second"—"Great Divergence" to occur.

PROXIMATE CAUSATION: CONQUEST REGIMES AND FISCAL SYSTEMS

For Cicero, it already counted as a truism that (tax) revenue had "always been considered the sinews of the state," just as 2,000 years later, Charles Tilly deemed "extraction" to be essential for supporting the three key state functions of state-making, war-making, and protection. As the Austrian economist Joseph Schumpeter reminded us with reference to his fellow Austrian sociologist Rudolf Goldscheid, "The budget is the skeleton of the state stripped of all misleading ideologies." Whether as sinews or as bones, revenue sustained the state and its activities: "Follow the money, always follow the money"—Deep Throat's (apocryphal) Watergate movie quote—is as good a precept for analyzing power relations as we can hope for. It also provides a key to understanding the "First Great Divergence."[18]

Revenue collection has a long history. The modern fiscal state, with its centralized bureaucracy, budgeting mechanisms, and recourse to public debt, merely represents its latest stage. In the more distant past, rulers might rely on plunder or on income from their own estates. However, regularized revenue extraction—of material goods from food to money and of human labor from military conscription to corvée—from a broader base is necessary for sustaining any kind of state with more than minimal capacities. Empire, as the result of massive scaling-up of military reach and territorial consolidation, is impossible without it. Its characteristic articulation into center and peripheries all but requires resource flows between them. At the same time, the logistical challenges involved in controlling extensive possessions unfailingly turned local powerholders and distant agents into partners as well as competitors of the central authorities in extracting surplus. If those intermediaries became too autonomous, effective state power was bound to diminish as private rent crowded out public tax.[19]

An entire global history of empire could be written along these lines, tracking the rise and fall of revenue-collecting political organizations: rulers struggling to assert their prerogatives, local elites pushing back, and both compromising on an ever-changing modus vivendi while continuing to jockey for position. Outside pressures—war—either impelled a higher rate of extraction or precipitated state failure. Prolonged peace allowed fiscal systems to atrophy.[20]

Once in place, monopolistic empires might survive even if only modest revenue reached their centers: examples include the Umayyad empire, which accommodated pervasive regional retention of surplus, and the late Ming and Qing dynasties. By contrast, it would have been an incomparably greater challenge to establish an empire in the first place without being able to draw on considerable funds or draft soldiers. Actual practices varied depending on circumstances: Roman military mass mobilization, described in chapter 2, was one option; takeover of existing fiscal infrastructures, as practiced by the first caliphate, was another, as was Spain's import of bullion from the New World.[21]

When it comes to accounting for the "First Great Divergence," revenue extraction plays a key role as a predictor of rulers' ability to maintain state power and to build larger imperial polities. As we will see, fiscal capacity precipitously declined in post-Roman Europe but was more successfully maintained or restored in other parts of the Old World that subsequently hosted large empires. In Latin Europe, this erosion of fiscal capacity was not overcome until after a stable multistate system had formed and political power within polities had come to be critically constrained by domestic compromises born in no small measure of fiscal weakness.[22]

Europe

STATE DEFORMATION

The Roman empire operated a complex and regionally variegated tax system that focused on revenue from land alongside poll taxes, tolls on trade, and income from mining and imperial estates. An array of more specialized taxes and occasional absorption of elite wealth supplemented these revenue streams. During its first two centuries, a period of great stability, the Roman monarchy could afford to accept what appear to have been considerable discounts on nominal tax rates in peripheral areas and to rely largely on income from the most developed provinces and concentrated mining and commercial activities.

After the shocks of the third century CE—driven by foreign and civil wars and plagues—had disturbed this comfortable equilibrium, the restorationist military regime that took power launched a determined if ultimately insufficient effort to standardize and rationalize fiscal arrangements. As eastern provinces had long carried a disproportionate part of the burden, reform particularly affected the western parts of the empire: Italy was no longer exempt from most forms of taxation; heavy fiscal demands are reported for late Roman Gaul; and the considerable importance of revenue from the Iberian peninsula and North Africa is reflected in the fatal consequences of their eventual loss to outside challengers. In addition, frontier zones such as Britain and the Rhineland had long been developed for the purpose of supporting large military garrisons.

Thus, even if reliable measurement is beyond our reach, there can be little doubt that the Latin territories of the Roman empire were subject to considerable tax liabilities. The growth of countervailing forces such as patronage relations designed to shield assets likewise points to the weight of these claims. Taxation, even if increasingly contested, was very much a feature of Roman rule in late antique Europe.[23]

In all of this, local self-governance had always institutionalized effective decentralization of tax collection and ensured its structural dependence on rent-taking elites. Within these constraints, the system had been successfully maintained for centuries. It was only when central power weakened in the face of foreign intervention and renewed internal conflict in the early fifth century CE that local resistance to payments mounted and enforcement declined. Increasingly extravagant tax remissions are recorded from the 410s CE onward, and the fiscal capacity of the now separately managed western half of the empire shrank accordingly. This set in motion a death spiral of diminishing central authority and its intensifying contestation by rival constituencies from both within and beyond the empire.[24]

This was the environment that in the third quarter of the fifth century CE came to be dominated by Germanic successor regimes that dismantled the western empire—one in which centralized fiscal arrangements were under pressure but still in place. But from then on, these institutions were allowed to whither. In the principal kingdoms, a share of land was taken over by the new rulers, for their own benefit and that of their armed followers.

Due to the shortcomings of the evidence, the procedural circumstances of this shift remain debated. According to the most plausible reconstruction, Germans were given control of land allotments: they enjoyed access to that land and to its yield in exchange for loyalty and military service. At least initially, an alternative theory holds, they received only the revenue of that land—via disbursements of tax proceeds—but not the land itself. In this scenario, the allocation of benefits was mediated by existing fiscal structures: depending on the polity, followers received one-third or half of the revenue while the rest went to the king.

However, even this model is meant to be understood as a "provisional solution" that over time morphed into a more enduring arrangement of direct access to and control over the land. Thus, in the words of Walter Goffart, the leading proponent of this thesis, the beneficiaries eventually ended up "as full-fledged landowners enjoying the same rights over the land and its cultivators as the established owners of the countryside." In terms of overall outcomes, this is all that matters here.[25]

Land grants to subordinates removed the single most important function of taxation: ensuring control over organized violence. Applying Tilly's terminology, centralized extraction and distribution were no longer necessary to sustain state-making, war-making, and protection. Instead, the specialists in violence—Germanic warriors—who performed these elementary state functions could draw on prebendal (and gradually privatized) resources. The consequent erosion of fiscal institutions was gradual but inexorable.

The Ostrogothic regime that occupied Italy retained Roman forms of taxation but did not last long enough (from the 490s to the 530s CE) for abatement to set in. Following the East Roman reconquest from the 530s to the 560s CE, the Lombards who took over much of Italy initially may or may not have continued to collect taxes but by the seventh century are not known or no longer known to have done so. Income from domains became crucial: Lombard kings controlled much more land than the nobility, which served to shore up their standing. In North Africa, the Vandals (from the 430s CE) at first continued to tax but also settled their men on the land. As a result, by the time of the East Roman reconquest a century later, the regional tax system had already deteriorated.[26]

In the Iberian peninsula, the Visigoths (450s to 710s CE) made efforts to collect tax almost until the end of their period of control, but revenue was marginal. When the Arabs took over, they consequently found it hard to support their forces and settled them on the land to ensure their sustenance. This was a marked departure from standard practice: in other regions farther east, more developed fiscal systems had allowed them to maintain centrally funded military colonies.[27]

In Gaul, the Merovingians taxed the non-Frankish population in the sixth century but encountered growing resistance. As the tax-exempt Frankish-conquest elite and the ethnic identity associated with this immunity expanded, generalized taxation came to be considered an abuse of royal power. Over the course of the seventh century, with the possible exception of the Loire Valley, regular revenue collection disappeared from the record. The central authorities fell back on income from royal lands, tolls, and fines.[28]

By contrast, taxation survived not only in the eastern Roman empire but—as we shall see below—also in the formerly Roman and Sasanian territories that had fallen to the Umayyad caliphate. Fiscal retreat, even if of varying intensity and chronology, was limited to the Germanic successor states of the western Roman empire.

Numerous factors may have contributed to this outcome, but not all of them carry equal weight. Although the late Roman tax system was already under considerable duress at the time of the Germanic takeovers, it was still in place and is known to have continued to operate almost everywhere. This speaks against blaming its later demise on Roman legacy effects. Another potential reason is more abstract. The need for ongoing information flows makes fiscal systems costly to maintain: thus, the presence of an alternative means of supporting key state associates, such as land assignments, might render relaxation of collection efforts not only feasible but attractive. Even so, fiscal structures can survive even with minimal effort: the failure of the Ming and Qing to update tax records is the best-known example. But none of this can explain the wholesale collapse of land taxes among the Franks.[29]

Germanic regimes were cheaper in the sense that they incurred less overhead: they ran a much smaller administrative machine than the Romans had done and no longer had to support voracious capital cities with their corrupt officials and retainers. This made it more feasible for the central authorities to rely on patrimonial resources such as crown land and income from tolls (the latter much diminished by the concurrent decline in trade and money use). This, in turn, encouraged localization of taxation, which helps account for the uneven manner of its fading. But most importantly of all, Germanic rule had changed the status of the military: elevated above the erstwhile waged employees of the Roman era, self-sufficient soldiers now formed a new elite.[30]

In a process best attested in the longest-lived successor state, that of the Franks, the martial habitus of the conquest elite, the land assignments it received, and the devolution of the tax system produced a peculiar configuration of power in which rulers depended on the cooperation of select followers, yet increasingly lacked the means to coerce or bribe them. Neither of the two most powerful groups, warrior-landlords and clerics, was fully subject to state control.

Unlike the Roman empire, the Germanic successor regimes did not maintain substantial standing armies. Dukes and counts were responsible for raising troops, which were spatially dispersed and gathered only as required. By at least the late sixth century, soldiers settled on their land and took proper ownership, considering it de facto hereditary and tax exempt. They turned into a class of well-armed landowners.

By the seventh century, this conversion had been completed wherever Germanic regimes survived. Among the Visigoths, military power came to be concentrated in aristocratic retinues that were complemented (and balanced) by men drawn from royal estates and slave soldiers from private holdings. Over time, emphasis shifted from royal forces to magnate levies and growing reliance on private resources.

In Lombard Italy, land had been assigned to groups of soldiers, called up by dukes. This likewise gave rise to armed retinues of nobles. Frankish aristocrats subordinated men of lower status and raised troops from among them. Conditions in England were probably similar. Thus, across the Germanic zone we witness a gradual transition from paid armies under central control to levies managed by powerful landlords and characterized by increasing stratification and dependence, as rising inequality reinforced earlier differences in status and resources.

These trends continued and deepened in the eighth century. In Francia, the aristocracy's grip on their retinues tightened at the expense of royal command. And while Lombard rulers maintained a greater degree of control over levies and upheld the principle of a nobility of service

rather than of wealth, personal followings nevertheless gained in importance. In England, lordly retinues operated alongside royal bodyguards.

Developments diverged from the ninth century onward: whereas the
power of Frankish lords eclipsed that of their kings and eventually reduced them to a somewhat marginal position, England experienced a
trend reversal: a more compact territory, a weaker nobility, and the
strong Danish threat enabled King Alfred and his successors to establish
a permanent army. Sustained by men who rotated between their homes
and the field army, this created an instrument not just for defense but also
for domestic coercion.[31]

Yet for the time being, this remained the exception that proved the
general rule of aristocratic autonomy and declining state capacity.
Moreover, armies were small regardless of how they were raised. Alfred's
field army numbered in the low thousands. Entire kingdoms could
change hands in engagements of barely more than 10,000 men. Visigothic Spain and Anglo-Saxon England are the best examples. Logistical constraints—and the need for attendants—ruled out operations of
armies of more than 5,000 soldiers. Larger forces could only be concentrated for short-term defensive measures. Fast raids, the most common
format, involved hundreds rather than thousands of seasoned warriors.
Most campaigns focused on plunder, and cities were so unimportant
that siege warfare received little attention even though defenses were
poor.[32]

It should go without saying that none of this was conducive to expansion and state-building on a large scale. Sustainable empire was far beyond the reach of these rickety polities. The contrast to the Roman
period could hardly be starker. For much of the last two centuries BCE,
forces numbering in the tens of thousands had been deployed in the
Iberian peninsula to grind down local resistance. Caesar subdued Gaul
with ten legions—30,000–40,000 men even if seriously understrength,
and bolstered by considerable allied contingents—a display of military
might the region would not witness again until the early modern period.
In 43 CE, the emperor Claudius invaded Britain with some 40,000 men,
four or five times as many as William the Conqueror would marshal
in 1066.

THE DEATH OF EMPIRE

In chapter 5, I touched on the dynamics that enfeebled and splintered the Carolingian domain. The power of nobles, enhanced by a phase of lucrative expansion that culminated under Charlemagne, turned against the center once gains from conquest dried up. Dynastic feuding—fueled by the lack of primogeniture in the royal succession—not only weakened rulers but invited intervention by aristocratic factions. The resultant self-sustaining and self-reinforcing process of decentralization played out in different ways depending on local conditions, which favored rural lords in Francia and Germany and city-states and communes in Italy and Lotharingia. The overall outcome—intense fragmentation of power—was similar everywhere.[33]

As the aristocracy controlled a growing share of the land and the economy began to recover, lords set up their own castles, a practice emulated by lesser nobles and church leaders. Armed retinues turned into knights, whose presence simultaneously broadened the aristocracy and limited military service to a clearly defined in-group. This caused power to disperse more widely in elite circles and reduced any leader's ability to concentrate resources for the purposes of protection and state-building. The path of least resistance available to kings—further gifts of royal land to church and nobility—proved self-defeating in the longer term: it merely decreased what was left of what the ninth-century Frankish historian Nithard called their "wherewithal to reward followers."[34]

But rulers were not the only ones to lose ground. Aristocratic and church power expanded at the expense of the peasantry, which gradually lost its independence. This shift was exacerbated by the growing exclusivity of military service and the concurrent decline of assemblies—armies having served as political gatherings as well—except in England and in Italian communes. Rural dependence further debilitated rulers, who lacked autonomous means of coercion to counterbalance lordly control over the means of production.[35]

Following an early post-Roman hiatus, aristocratic hegemony had reached unprecedented heights. By the ninth century, hereditary land-ownership and office-holding by counts had become the norm in West

Francia and Germany, and super-magnates of regal or quasi-regal status emerged together with new duchies and kingdoms. In the tenth century, their knightly subordinates established control over the peasantry. By the eleventh century, power had become highly localized: lesser nobles relied more on their own resources than on the support of dukes and counts, and erected large numbers of castles that chopped up territory into autonomous blocks impeding state formation. Rulers had to forge alliances with ducal houses if they hoped to exercise any degree of control.[36]

By 1000, aristocracies were dominant everywhere in Latin Europe. Public power structures at the supralocal level failed with varying intensity, most notably in France and to some extent in Italy. Germany and Islamic Spain also moved in that direction. England, where governmental structures had collapsed more radically and had also been rebuilt earlier, was the only outlier, yet far too small and peripheral to embark on expansion beyond the Channel.[37]

In Joseph Strayer's judgment, these fragmentation processes had become so intense that—with the exception of what remained of the East Roman polity in the Balkans—"by the year 1000 it would have been difficult to find anything like a state anywhere on the continent in Europe." As far as the political order was concerned, at that point, in Chris Wickham's words, even the "shadow" of the "inheritance of Rome" had "faded away."[38]

China

DISUNION AND PERSISTENCE

The same year, many of the lands that once been governed by the Han lay united under the rule of the Zhenzong emperor. After severe disturbances that echoed the fall of the Roman empire, East Asian state formation had followed a very different path. The drawn-out demise of the empire of the Eastern Han dynasty in the late second and early third centuries CE led to a three-way split between the states of Wei, Shu, and Wu. Imperial restoration under the Jin dynasty in the late third century proved short-lived. Internal power struggles encouraged ethnic groups from the frontier zone that had been settled on imperial territory to take matters into their own hands. In the 310s, coalitions led by Xiongnu forces sacked the capital cities of Luoyang and Chang'an and forced the Jin court to retreat south.[39]

Several generations of instability and political disunity followed. In the fourth and early fifth centuries—labeled as the era of the "Sixteen Kingdoms"—northern China was dominated by a series of often brittle conquest regimes. Power kept shifting between military coalitions associated with several peripheral ethnic groups: Xiongnu, Xianbei, Tuoba, and Di. Although the Later Zhao and Former Qin states managed to seize most of northern China from the 320s to the 340s and in the 370s and early 380s, respectively, both of them failed in short order.[40]

A general pattern is visible behind the chaotic dislocations of this period. The principal northern regimes established dual systems of rule that distinguished between conquerors of steppe or frontier descent and Han Chinese. The former were known as *guoren*, "compatriots," whereas the latter were subordinated to them as taxpaying subjects, liable to provide grain and labor services. Ethnic cavalry, obliged to fight for their leaders, formed the backbone of the field armies, whereas Chinese could be drafted as needed to serve as foot soldiers or provide logistical support.[41]

Flight and other types of attrition had opened up land and made labor scarce. The conquest regimes consequently focused on capturing people rather than land. Forcible mass transfers of subjects to core areas of regime control were meant to secure manpower. Regime change could lead to resettlement to new centers. Rulers' grip on population outside these core zones was generally much weaker.

Much of the northern elite had fled to the south to join the Jin. Those who remained—local gentry clans—organized fortified settlements in defensible positions. As cities were ravaged or abandoned by competing military coalitions, these positions became focal points of local government and formed basic blocks of power. Soon numbering in the thousands, these self-defense communities could form leagues: the centralized conquest regimes were left with only two options—to confront or co-opt them—to assert preeminence.[42]

Northern rulers' reliance on unstable military coalitions rendered their polities fragile: these constructs were readily dismembered and reconfigured upon defeat by rival forces. The underlying power relations were more enduring, as effective control was balanced between the conquest cores with their reservoirs of ethnic cavalry and native forced labor on the one hand and numerous small-scale but capable local communities on the other.

This environment differed from post-Roman Europe in two crucial respects. One was the presence of strong centrally managed and highly mobile cavalry forces that, even if unable to sweep everything before them, were generally capable of checking local power blocks. This in turn prevented the evolution of feudal relations: military assets remained sufficiently centralized and local power bases were insufficiently autonomous for military and subsequently also economic and political power to disperse and devolve upon small-scale units. As Ray Huang points out, "Had this trend been allowed to continue, a new form of feudalism might have taken root in China. . . . But mobile warfare over a large region, which favored huge bodies of fighting men, settled the course in a different fashion." Ethnic cavalry, rooted in steppe traditions, proved vital in first containing local units and later pressuring them into cooperation.[43]

The second key factor was the persistence of fiscal structures to support these core military forces by taxing agricultural production and mobilizing civilian labor. Evidence for fiscal institutions is exiguous but intriguing. There can be no doubt that the collapse of the Han order drastically curtailed the ability of subsequent central authorities to count and tax their subjects. Han census totals for the second century CE averaged about 10 million households with 50 million residents. By contrast, the "Three Kingdoms" of the mid-third century counted merely 1.7 million households, while the Western Jin mustered 2.5 million after reunification. Notwithstanding potentially significant population losses, most of this decline reflects eroding state capacity rather than demographic change.[44]

Under the northern conquest regimes, registration quality began to recover from this nadir. In the 370s CE, the Murong state of Former Yan counted 2.5 million households with 10 million people in an area that was only a fraction of the size of that covered by the highly deficient third-century censuses. It thus achieved much better penetration, especially allowing for attrition and the sheltering and concealment of parts of the remaining population in walled villages. The fact that two centuries later, the better-organized state of Northern Qi was able to register 20 million residents in a roughly equivalent territory shows that fourth-century state power, however constrained by local obstruction, was by no means negligible and was capable of capturing a sizable share of the actual population, perhaps close to half.

This impression is consistent with accounts of mass mobilization during a campaign against the south in 383 CE: even though the reported totals of 270,000 cavalry and 600,000 infantry are hardly credible, even a reduction by an entire order of magnitude would leave forces much larger than any medieval European state could hope to muster. The first post-Roman polities in Europe to encompass 10 million people—leaving aside a brief blip under Charlemagne and Louis the Pious—were Germany and France in the High Middle Ages. But European rulers would have been ignorant of this fact and could not have hoped to impose regular taxes on most of their subjects.[45]

Manuscript evidence for civil service examinations dating from 408 CE has been unearthed from a tomb in Gansu, an area then ruled by the short-lived and peripheral state of Western Liang. This tantalizing tidbit speaks to the robustness of bureaucratic traditions in unexpected places. More generally, northern conquest regimes recruited Chinese literati to perform administrative services. The aforementioned Murong state was dominated by the Xianbei, a frontier group that had long enjoyed deep contacts with China. This provided a basis for sustained cooperation, and prompted rulers to rely more on taxation than on outright pillage, as earlier Xiongnu leaders had done.[46]

In sum, despite repeated regime change, the central state managed to hold its own in its struggle against local interests. Its administrative capacity was sufficient to maintain adequate registration and taxation systems, which in turn enabled it to field enough forces to curb local autonomy. Instead of accommodating a hybrid elite of tax-exempt landowner-soldiers, the state retained control over revenues and military compensation. As a result, the tributary state as a means of managing people and resources did not dwindle nearly as much as it did in post-Roman Europe.

The root causes of this divergence are a matter of conjecture. While it is true that the Han empire had fostered more ambitious traditions of bureaucracy and granted local communities less autonomy than the Roman empire ever had, the enormous deficiencies of Chinese censuses in the third century CE cast doubt on the notion that the continuous persistence of imperial institutions had ensured higher levels of state capacity under the northern conquest regimes than under the Germanic successor regimes, which had inherited an arguably somewhat less dysfunctional fiscal infrastructure.

Instead, the difference between individual and group land allotments to Germanic warriors that invited privatization on the one hand and greater emphasis on taxation and centralized provision among the conquest regimes of northern China on the other may well have been of critical importance. As a corollary of that emphasis, the latter were more invested in directly managing core areas and their residents, which provided them with the means required to prevent runaway decentralization.

Modes of subsistence and combat help account for these divergent priorities. The dominance of cavalry forces in the Chinese case was more conducive to the concentration of military power—as they could easily be gathered to project power across the Central Plain region— and to social separation between (foreign) horsemen and herders and (local) farmers. Both factors encouraged centralized provisioning by a sedentary subject population.

In the Germanic successor states, military forces came to be dispersed to make use of desirable farmland. Even as armored cavalry gained in importance from the eighth and ninth centuries onward, this shift unfolded in the context of intensifying localism. In northern China, by contrast, cavalry forces tended to be not only more concentrated but also larger. Ecology played a role: access to the steppe ensured a greater supply of horses, effectively "democratizing" their use.

Finally, this proximity added another factor to the mix that was mostly missing from post-Roman Europe. The steppe did not merely produce horses but also new challengers to those conquest groups that had already established themselves in northern China: the Tuoba and Rouran, discussed below, are the most prominent examples. This ongoing pressure placed a premium on the scaling-up of military capabilities. As we saw in chapter 5, the political fracturing of the Islamic world and the logistical limitations of Avars and Magyars saved the remaining Germanic states of the Early Middle Ages from comparably intense competition. In this sheltered environment, unlike in northern China, state deformation driven by localized self-interest was a viable option.

EMPIRE REDUX

During the fifth and sixth centuries, centralized state power in northern China continued to recover. The collapse of the Murong state in the 380s enabled the Xianbei Tuoba clan to regain independence and to take over much of the former's territory. By the late 430s, the Northern Wei dynasty of the Tuoba had expanded their rule across the whole of northern China. For most of the fifth century, they operated the traditional dual status system: military garrisons that were mostly made up of Tuoba—classified as *guoren*—maintained control over the local population. Over time, these units became more mixed, admitting Xiongnu as well as some Han Chinese. However, even though Chinese could be conscripted and served in support roles, they did not routinely participate in military activities: yet, unlike military commands, administrative positions were open to them. That many Tuoba continued to practice herding highlighted their detachment from the Chinese agricultural population.[47]

These farmers were subject to direct taxation that sustained the conquest regime. A variety of land taxes are attested, and from the 420s onward civilian officials were in charge of fiscal affairs. This strengthened the hand of the central state at the expense of local autonomy. Large numbers of clan leaders were pressured into surrendering their often sizable communities, which could comprise thousands of households. In return, the Tuoba court bestowed official titles on these fortress chiefs to incorporate them into formal state hierarchies. This process of co-optation arrested and reversed earlier trends toward localization that had counterbalanced central power.[48]

Tuoba military capabilities critically relied on access to horses from the northern grasslands, where a new steppe confederation, the Rouran, had arisen concurrently and in interaction with the Tuoba state. Ongoing conflict between these two powers provided strong impetus for centralization. Adopting a strategy common among earlier Chinese empires, the Tuoba set up garrisons along the steppe frontier.[49]

A series of integrative reforms accelerated Tuoba state-building. In the mid-480s, their Northern Wei state launched an "equal-fields" program in which plots of land were assigned to households in exchange for tax and service obligations. Different versions of this arrangement survived for the next three centuries. The land remained state property, keeping elites from taking over and subordinating the peasantry. This measure was accompanied by the appointment of prominent villagers to verify census registers and supervise tax collection. Improved registration density shored up the center's position by ensuring access to manpower and material resources, which allowed a uniform salary schedule for state officials to be introduced.[50]

In the 490s, the regime followed up with "Sinicizing" measures designed to close the gap between the conquest class and the Chinese majority population. These interventions targeted the elite: the capital city was moved to the old Han center of Luoyang; Xianbei and Han elites were encouraged to intermarry; and the use of Chinese language and costume at court became mandatory. This embrace of Chinese culture not only acknowledged existing trends but also reflected rulers' desire for greater unity. Chinese governors were appointed to govern provinces, Chinese served in militias, and in a shift away from the previous model of dispersed occupation, ethnic Tuoba garrisons were concentrated at the center and the northern frontier.[51]

Although these reforms were meant to boost internal cohesion, the move of many Tuoba military units to the steppe periphery proved to be both unpopular and destabilizing. Retaining their native language and customs, these forces were increasingly alienated from the central authorities. In the 520s this led to a rebellion that triggered internal wars, and in 534 split the state in two. These dislocations, however, proved conducive to further state formation as endemic and symmetric conflict between the two successor polities raised demand for institutions that bolstered capabilities.[52]

The western successor state (under the Western Wei and then the Northern Zhou dynasties) controlled fewer economic resources and a smaller population. Initially struggling to survive eastern attacks, state leaders co-opted Chinese militias to compensate for the relative dearth of Xianbei warriors. Censuses and land allocation programs were revived. The 550s witnessed the creation of the "24 Armies": composed of Xianbei and even more so of Chinese, they mobilized commoners through direct recruitment or the co-optation of local forces.

At the same time, under the *fubing* system, more adult men were granted land in exchange for regular military service obligations. This added farmer-soldiers to an expanding infantry even as horses obtained via the Gansu corridor helped maintain strong cavalry forces. These policies simultaneously mobilized a growing share of the population for military purposes and buttressed the rural smallholder class. Chinese elites became more widely involved in administration, and bureaucratic reforms created ministries. All of this raised state capacity and helped cement centralized authority. The overall result was a shift toward the kind of well-integrated high-mobilization state that had been characteristic of the Warring States and Western Han periods. The payoff was large: army strength grew from perhaps 50,000 in the 550s to well more than 100,000 by the 570s.[53]

By contrast, the eastern successor state continued to be run by Xianbei as officials and fighters. Co-optation of Chinese forces was constrained by the influence of magnate families. Society was riven by greater divisions between locals and Xianbei, and political conditions were less stable.[54]

This growing imbalance in state capacity enabled the western state to overcome and annex its eastern counterpart in 577. Soon thereafter it confronted southern China, where development had followed a rather different path. The fact that a single state had been maintained there for 270 years following the Jin retreat masks a considerable degree of state deformation. Initial efforts to retake the north between 349 and 369 failed and led to gradual demilitarization of the southern elite. Centralized state power waned for about a century until the takeover of the Liu Song dynasty in 420: low-born military men wrested power from the great landowning families, commerce and remonetization revived urbanism and checked the influence of landlords, and professional troops replaced magnate-led forces. However, although this arrangement contained rural elites, it also gave rise to intensifying civil wars.[55]

Before long, powerful families dominated the scene, whether magnates or military clans, and even the latter were unable to establish a more militarized culture comparable to that of northern China. Military colonies did not take root in the south. The court failed to raise large armies as it faced a two-way struggle against domestic rivals and the growing northern threat. Large landlords' shielding of the rural population from registration and thus taxation and service obligations was a persistent problem: as a result, military assets were always in short supply, prompting recourse to convicts, vagrants, and aboriginals of low combat effectiveness.[56]

Census numbers from northern and southern China highlight a growing disparity in state capacity. In 464, the southern Liu Song regime counted a little more than 900,000 households with some 5 million members, in an area that 300 years earlier had housed twice as many, even before migration and population growth had raised densities further. By 589, the final year of the southern state, the Chen regime registered 500,000 households and 2 million people in a significantly smaller territory, which in 140 had contained closer to 10 million people.

By comparison, the northeastern state of Northern Qi alone counted 3.3 million households with some 20 million residents in 577, at a time when registration quality was not particularly high. An empire-wide census in 609 suggests an actual total in excess of 9 million households, more than one-sixth of which were bound to be located south of the Yangzi. All this unmistakably shows that the southern authorities were unable to capture more than a modest fraction of the households in their territory, most likely fewer than a third, and an even smaller proportion of its residents, quite possibly as few as one in five.[57]

This stark imbalance in state capacity goes a long way in explaining why imperial restoration emanated from northern China. The south had not failed for want of trying. However, none of the invasions attempted between the 340s and the 570s accomplished anything of substance. It is true that geography also contributed: without sufficient cavalry, southern armies lacked mobility and shock power, and heavily relied on a river network that did not support northward operations. Even so, political conditions were crucial. In the long run, southern unity was not only not an advantage but a distinct impediment: southern China experienced none of the bloody yet productive rivalries that drove northern state formation in the fourth and especially in the mid-sixth century.

Before the late sixth century, northern states had shown little interest in attacking the south, for two reasons. One was that endemic competition among similarly belligerent peers kept northern forces busy and spared the south. The other lay in operational difficulties: it was challenging for northern cavalry to operate against fortified southern positions and in riverine areas. The only major attack, in 383, had ended in defeat and triggered regime collapse.[58]

Stable unification of northern China changed all that as it removed internal divisions and generated the resources required to take on the south on its home turf. In the late 580s, the northern Sui state deployed a large fleet and is said to have mobilized 518,000 men to invade a south that was defended by much weaker forces. This massive assault swiftly succeeded, and a subsequent magnate-backed rising against registration and taxation was likewise crushed.[59]

As a result, by the 590s most of the lands that had belonged to the Han empire were once again ruled from the old Han capitals of Chang'an and Luoyang. Elite autonomy was safely contained, as the Sui regime abolished noble ranks and hereditary rights: the principal status distinction was between officials and commoners, with the former being rotated among positions to keep them on their toes. Mobilization of military and civilian manpower occurred on a scale not seen for half a millennium. Chang'an was rebuilt with outer walls that extended thirty-five kilometers, and vast numbers of workers—supposedly 2 million—were drafted for construction in Luoyang. A whole network of lavish palace complexes followed.[60]

The most ambitious infrastructure project was the construction of an interlinking system of canals that for the first time connected northern and southern China. From the Sanggan (later Beijing) area in the north it traversed the Central Plain and linked the Yellow River, the Huai, the Yangzi, and Hangzhou Bay: at least on occasion, more than a million workers toiled on 2,357 kilometers of canals. This grandiose scheme became a reality in the first decade of the seventh century, a time the later Song historian Sima Guang called the "height of the Sui": in many ways a reincarnation of the Han empire, their domain encompassed over 190 prefectures and 1,225 counties and registered almost 9 million households.[61]

In operations reminiscent of the terminal phase of the Warring States period or the Xiongnu wars of the Martial Emperor of the Western Han, enormous resources were committed to warfare in the northeast. In 612, the regime followed up on previous invasions of Korea by supposedly mobilizing 1,133,800 combat troops and twice as many support personnel. And although these numbers are undoubtedly hyperbolic, if the troops were divided into no fewer than thirty separate armies that could be supplied separately, a grand total in the hundreds of thousands was in fact perfectly feasible.[62]

Even for the freshly unified empire, this was a step too far. These megalomaniacal exertions unleashed popular resistance that brought down the Sui regime and ushered in a brief phase of renewed state weakness. Under the early Tang dynasty, compromises with local power-holders allowed only a small fraction of its subjects to be counted and taxed. Yet by the middle of the eighth century, the official census tally had returned to more than 9 million households with 53 million people, equivalent to Han and Sui levels. More than 600,000 *fubing* farmer-soldiers were on the government's rolls, and each year several hundred thousand civilians were drafted for auxiliary service. Fiscal administration was once again highly centralized.[63]

These capacities dwarfed anything that could have been achieved in Europe at that time, even in the headiest days of Charlemagne. Rulers could only guess at the number of their subjects, found it increasingly hard to draft them, and no longer had any hope of taxing land outside royal estates.

What accounted for this dramatic divergence? The evidence I have briefly laid out gives pride of place unequivocally to the coercive capacity of rulers to frame conditions in favor of elite cooperation and subordination. European-style aristocratic polycentrism did not appear in China because the principal dynasts always, and especially from the fifth century CE onward, disposed of sufficient military assets to check the local power of magnates and ensure centralized revenue collection that in turn sustained military resources. This encouraged elite families to commit to imperial rule as a source of wealth and status, and enabled central authorities to stem and reverse recurrent trends toward devolution of power.[64]

Cavalry forces that were either drawn from the margins of the steppe zone or supplied with horses imported from the great grasslands, recourse to hereditary soldiers who occupied state-owned land, and more generally the ability to mobilize complementary resources to support their operations proved critical both to the maintenance of centralized state authority and to state-building on an imperial scale. As I argue in chapter 8, thanks to its physical proximity to the steppe frontier, northern China was particularly likely to experience these conditions. Conversely, none of them were present in Latin Europe.

Intermittent abatements of state power did not fundamentally alter outcomes. Thus, after internal disorder in the 750s, the Tang domain came to be effectively divided among governors, generals, and warlords, only some of whom remitted taxes to the center. Registration levels once again plummeted to just a few million households. Eventually, the collapse of what was left of the Tang regime around 900 precipitated temporary fragmentation, which in its most basic outlines resembles that of the much longer Period of Disunion from the fourth through the sixth centuries.[65]

In northern China, early successor states (Later Liang and Later Tang) rested on core zones where an intact bureaucracy maintained population registers but struggled to control provincial governors while a steppe regime, Liao, consolidated its position along the northern frontier. Conflict of the Later Jin dynasty with Liao in the 940s visited defeat and devastation on the capital and the Central Plain region. Liao's subsequent retreat opened up space for a more centralized regime (Later Zhou, following Later Han): prolonged warfare had depleted the governors' resources and ability to resist the center, which was now able to rebuild a strong unified army and embark on a grand expansionist program that first unified the north and under the subsequent Song dynasty (from 960) took over the various smaller states of the south.

Those polities, meanwhile, had replicated earlier conditions, such as a shift from military to civilian rule, strong reliance on commerce, interference by powerful landlords who concealed taxable land, poor military capabilities, and rifts among rival elites. Just as they had done for the Liu Song and Chen of the fifth and sixth centuries, these weaknesses led to the loss of lands north of the Yangzi followed by conquest from the north.[66]

The Song empire exceeded the mature Han, Sui, and Tang empires in terms of population, military might, and fiscal capacity. In the late eleventh century, the central authorities counted some 20 million households. The state maintained more than 2,000 well-staffed tax stations to collect dues, overseen by a powerful central fiscal agency. The careers of high government officials often began in public finance. Total central tax revenue equaled at least 3,500 tons of silver, four-fifths of it in cash, roughly four or five times what the Roman empire took in at its peak and approaching a tenth of total output, a highly respectable rate by premodern standards. This bonanza not only supported a capital city of 750,000 but also an army in excess of a million soldiers, at least on paper.[67]

Even though the Song soon relinquished control over northern China, the tenth century remained the last time China formally fractured into a handful of states: up to the end of the monarchical era, there was usually just one empire, except in the Southern Song period when there were two. By the year 1000, when the vestiges of Roman imperial institutions had faded away in Latin Europe, the Chinese tradition of hegemonic empire had become more firmly entrenched than ever before.

"Follow the Money"

In the early sixth century CE, the cleric and future saint Eugippius, in his biography of Saint Severinus of Noricum, reported a much earlier encounter between himself and the German Odoacer, the future ruler of Italy. As a young man, the latter had stopped on his way across the Alps to pay his respects to the holy man, who duly foretold his coming greatness and bid him farewell with the words, "Go to Italy, go, now covered in mean hides; soon you will make rich gifts to many!" And so Odoacer did, seizing power with the support of Italy's restless Germanic mercenaries who demanded land assignments. His peers who led Goths, Vandals, Franks, and Lombards in carving up the western Roman empire bowed to the same calls for largesse. State resources became first localized and then privatized, tax collection fell into abeyance, and central authority withered. For centuries, "rich gifts" trumped state power. Imperial restoration became a distant dream.[68]

Northern China during the Period of Disunion moved in the opposite direction. In both East and West, conquest regimes had started out with dual-status systems that demarcated newcomers from locals. I already noted the *guoren*–native divide. The Ostrogoths in Italy did not assume Roman citizenship, were barred from holding civilian office, and may even have been subject to separate laws. In Gaul, the Franks were initially the only group exempt from taxation.[69]

In both cases, integration gradually blurred these boundaries. Yet, whereas in Western Europe tax immunity and its replacement by localized rent and service obligations spread across the general population, in China everybody became subjected to homogenized claims by the central state. This crucial difference determined whether it was landed lords or state rulers who captured most of the surplus. State capacity differed accordingly, with noble levies, small armies, and rudimentary administrative structures on the one hand and extensive censuses, huge militaries, and ministries full of literate bureaucrats on the other. The former sustained intense polycentrism, the latter hegemonic empire.

These outcomes merely represent two extremes on a wider spectrum. Developments in the Middle East, where much of the eastern Roman empire and the entire Sasanian empire succumbed to the caliphate, occupied an intermediate position. Just as the Germans in Europe and the Xiongnu and Xianbei in East Asia, the Arabs had long interacted with neighboring empires: they had accepted their patronage, fought proxy wars, and even settled in imperial lands. Outright takeover was simply the next step.[70]

Unlike Germans on Roman soil, Arabs often settled in garrison cities such as Basra and Kufa in Iraq, Fustat (Cairo) in Egypt, and Kairouan in Tunisia. Iraq was occupied by tribesmen from the northern and eastern Arabian peninsula who, tied to their garrisons, gave up pastoralism and became wholly dependent on tax revenue. There and elsewhere, Sasanian and Roman practices of taxation were generally maintained: the Iberian peninsula remained an exception. There the lack of an adequate fiscal infrastructure—which had once existed but failed to survive Visigothic rule—necessitated dispersed settlement. Because the occupying forces received mostly cash stipends, in-kind taxes declined and land grants did not play a significant role. These practices stood in marked contrast to those in Western Europe, where land assignments made land and poll taxes redundant, and in fourth-century CE northern China, where requisitions supported the conquerors until regularized tax systems were restored. As a result, the Arab military class depended directly on the state for its sustenance and status.[71]

The principal weakness of these arrangements, discussed in chapter 5, was that the state was focused more on individual provinces than on the caliphal center: regional armies controlled their respective tax bases. The Umayyad system was better at preserving administrative and extractive institutions beyond the local level than the Germanic regimes but less so than the regimes of northern China. It likewise occupied an intermediate position in terms of recognizing nonsoldiers' customary rights to receive revenue: in this regard, it bore greater resemblance to the increasingly hereditary Germanic land assignments than to Chinese practices, even though the *fubing* model also invited creeping privatization of state resources.

After the 680s, the Umayyad regime moved away from sinecures, tying receipt of tax income to actual service in a standing army. For a while, the Abbasids levied taxes even more vigorously to fund court and military, and Baghdad became the focal point of a more centralized fiscal network. Later Abbasid caliphs increasingly relied on outsiders—Turkic- and Persian-speaking cavalry—to hold down local elites and extract revenue. This gave rise to ethnic conquest regimes that carved up the empire along the fault lines generated by earlier fiscal regionalization. In the Iraqi core, taxation did not collapse until the tenth century, when the military elite began to obtain income directly from farmers.[72]

The original Arab conquests had established a pattern that continued over the long run: successive regimes of regional armies were superimposed on and parasitic upon more continuous civilian government. Under the first two caliphates, local elites of the Sasanian period retained their estates and performed fiscal functions for the center. And even when soldiers eventually gained the right to extract income (*iqta'*) from individual bits of land, the central authorities usually retained sufficient fiscal capacity to protect their power in the face of widespread attempts to privatize allocations and seek shelter from taxation by ceding land to influential patrons.

In no small measure, this was made possible by the fact that *iqta'* remained restricted to military beneficiaries, whereas civilian landowners, denied similar entitlements, continued to work with state agents. Unlike in medieval Europe, where landownership coincided with military power and central government was crowded out by localized interests, medieval Middle Eastern urban wealthy elites lacked military muscle and *iqta'* remained a gift of the state: together, these constraints kept public service an attractive option and limited the breakup of states to regionalization instead of wholesale devolution into smaller units. Moreover, recurrent conquest from the outside facilitated the reallocation of gradually privatized military grant holdings.[73]

Overall, starting conditions were logically consistent with different outcomes. In medieval Western Europe, tax erosion coupled with land assignments and localization of power resulted in intra- and interpolity polycentrism and low state capacity. In the Arabo-Turkosphere, maintenance of fiscal infrastructure and enforcement of service obligations sustained reasonably strong regional states run by detached conquest elites. In China, the rebuilding of the tax state and centralized control paved the way to large-scale empire and greater consolidation in elite circles.

Conditions in South Asia are less well known but likewise conformed to this template. The universalist aspirations of the ancient Maurya empire have to be taken with a lot of salt, and it is quite clear that the Gupta empire, at its peak in the fourth and fifth centuries CE, relied heavily on tributary kings it sought to contain with the help of resources drawn from the Gangetic core. Southern India remained politically fragmented. The resultant regionalization of fiscal structures meshed well with the dominance of multiple regional states in the second half of the first millennium and the early second millennium. It was only the later Sultanate of Delhi and the Mughal empire that pursued more centralizing objectives, albeit ultimately with limited success. State formation oscillated between Middle Eastern–style regional states and larger empires of the Roman, Chinese, or Ottoman mold.[74]

The fact that specific configurations of fiscal and military institutions correlate with polity scale—fragmentation in Europe, unification in China, and intermediate outcomes in the Middle East and North Africa region and South Asia—suggests that the fiscal "sinews of power" played a major role in shaping the geopolitical landscape. The causal linkages behind this correlation are straightforward: at the end of the day, it was simply not possible to build large empires without sufficient centralized bundling of energy inputs in the form of material resources (taxation) or military labor (conscription).[75]

In China, imperial restoration was invariably driven by military action: an effective, unified military organization came first. Even if some Chinese dynasties later relaxed demands, they always started out with strong centralized assets. In post-Roman Europe, by contrast, fiscal decay drained the state of its strength. It took many centuries for intensifying competition to revive broad-based taxation. But by then, as we saw in chapter 6, competitive fragmentation had already become too deeply entrenched to give way to hegemonic empire. Instead, state capacity had been divorced from, and indeed become antithetical to, that very concept: a new type of extractive dynamic, focused on interstate conflict, intrastate integration, and strategically developmental policies, had been born. Both traditional empire and taxation had to wither first to make this possible.[76]

. . .

So far, my account has tracked specific events and developmental sequences, focusing on what we might call proximate causes: the interplay of preexisting conditions and the preferences of particular conquest regimes, modes of military mobilization, and the resilience of fiscal extraction. These factors were critical in skewing outcomes in a particular direction, toward or away from large-scale empire. Yet it is one thing to identify such variables and assess their impact. It is another altogether to account for their relative prevalence. The persistence of certain trends in the long term, from 1,500 to more than 2,000 years—enduring fragmentation in post-Roman Europe, serial imperial reconstitution in China, and more hybrid outcomes elsewhere—raises the very real possibility that the institutional and organizational features that sustained these robust trends were themselves embedded in and molded by more fundamental preconditions. Chapters 8 and 9 explore the question of what these ultimate causes might have been.

CHAPTER 8

Nature

GEOGRAPHY

GEOGRAPHY IMPOSES basic constraints on the scope and scale of human social interaction. State formation is no exception. Going back at least to Charles-Louis de Secondat, Baron de La Brède et de Montesquieu, observers have sought to explain European fragmentation and Chinese unity with reference to the nature of the terrain. Back in the middle of the eighteenth century, the baron declared:

> In Asia they have always had great empires; in Europe these could never subsist. Asia has larger plains; it is cut out into much more extensive divisions by mountains and seas; and as it lies more to the south, its springs are more easily dried up; the mountains are less covered with snow; and the rivers being not so large, form smaller barriers.[1]

That much of this is dubious—what about the Himalayas, or the Yellow and Yangzi rivers; and don't rivers connect rather than divide?—ought not deter us from developing this line of inquiry. One does not have to be a geographical "determinist" to acknowledge that the physical environment matters—and by now we can do better than Montesquieu.

Articulation: Coastlines

In much of Europe—especially in its Latin western parts—land and sea are entangled in complex ways. Jared Diamond was not the first to consider its "highly indented coastline," coupled with multiple peninsulas, conducive to political fragmentation: these features are simply the inverse of Montesquieu's "much more extensive divisions" of Asia. East Asia's coastline is smooth, with Korea as its only significant regional peninsula. Islands in close proximity to the mainland—Hainan and Taiwan—are much smaller even than Ireland, and Japan and the Philippines, each of them larger than the British Isles, are farther away.[2]

Even though critics of geographical perspectives on history cannot deny that this is true, they doubt its relevance. Thus, in his account of "why Europe conquered the world," Philip Hoffman notes that Europe's islands were not immune to naval invasion, and its peninsulas did not develop into coherent states earlier than other regions. However, his reference to Italy as an example of intense fragmentation during much of the post-Roman period is qualified not only by the stability of the Kingdom of the Two Sicilies in the more isolated south but more importantly by the precocious unity of Roman Italy. Moreover, the key issue is not so much unity within peninsulas as their relationship to larger imperial formations: it is worth noting that with the partial exception of the Mongol period, Korea, the only major peninsula in East Asia, was never fully ruled from China. More generally, coastlines did have a discernible effect on state formation: Britain, Ireland, Denmark, Italy, Sweden, and even France (more on which below) are all well delimited by the sea.[3]

But these are just details. Cherry-picking is not helpful. Once we address this question in systematic quantitative fashion, Europe does indeed emerge as a serious outlier within the Old World. In this respect, David Cosandey's work has produced striking results. Almost half of the surface area of what he labels "Western Europe"—generously defined as Europe west of what used to be the Soviet Union—is located on peninsulas and another tenth on islands. Conversely, the aggregated peninsular and insular shares of China, India, and the Middle East and North Africa region range from 1 percent to 3.6 percent.[4]

Because of this, Europe's coastline is much longer than that of East and South Asia: 33,700 kilometers for "Western Europe" as opposed to 6,600 kilometers in China and 7,300 kilometers in India. This in turn means that Mandelbrot's fractal dimension—an index of complexity bounded at 1 (lowest) and 2 (highest)—is higher for "Western Europe" (1.24 and 1.42 without and with islands, respectively) than for China (1.13 and 1.26) and India (1.11 and 1.19). The latter two are overall more compact than Europe west of Eastern Europe—a landlocked region eventually subsumed within a single very large land empire, Russia. Even without factoring in other features, Western—Latin—Europe's relative physical complexity should have made it more likely for stable and smaller polities to emerge there than elsewhere.[5]

Integration: Mountains and Rivers

Mountain ranges likewise contribute to physical segmentation, and ruggedness more generally imposes additional cost on communication. Although it has been claimed that Europe is not overall more rugged than China, it is the relative intensity of compartmentalization that matters most. The Alps, Pyrenees, and Carpathians are relatively high compared to mountain ranges that can be found in China east of Tibet: the first two generally rise above 1,500 meters. Moreover, well less than half of Western Europe lies less than 300 meters above sea level, mostly England, Ireland, northwestern France, northern Germany, and Poland, as well as the Po Valley (figure 8.1).

By contrast, "core China" (excluding Tibet, Xinjiang, Inner Mongolia, and Manchuria) enjoys conditions that favor greater connectivity. Much of that area lies less than 300 meters above sea level, and elevations of 1,500 meters are rare, confined in the first instance to the northwest where the state of Qin developed sheltered "within the passes" (figure 8.2). Core China is an excellent illustration of Montesquieu's "much more extensive divisions by mountains."[6]

Mountains helped define the territorial features of European state formation, not only for the aforementioned islands and peninsulas but also for France, whose Pyrenees borders have been quite stable since

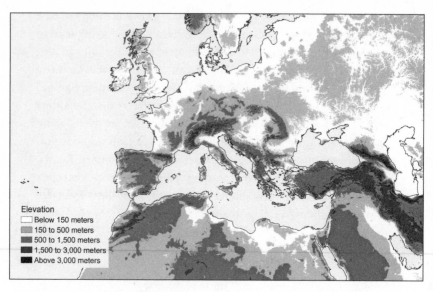

FIGURE 8.1 Altitude profile of Europe.

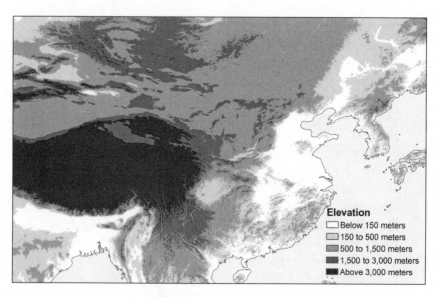

FIGURE 8.2 Altitude profile of East Asia.

the Frankish period but which throughout the Middle Ages and into the early modern period was unable to absorb its more mountainous southeast. Chinese development, by contrast, was framed above all by its largest rivers, which created two very extensive basins that are not separated by major natural barriers and could be connected even with sixth-century CE technology. As a result, to quote Diamond one more time, China "very early became dominated by two huge geographic core areas of high productivity, themselves only weakly separated from each other and eventually fused into a single core."[7]

This sanguine statement may seem to give short shrift to several rather important points. There already had to be a powerful empire before the task of fusing could be undertaken by building the Great Canal. In the long term, maintaining the canal system required even bigger efforts. The lack of tidal rivers other than the Yangzi hampered connectivity along the coast. And whenever China splintered—up to the twelfth century CE—it did so between these two core areas. Fusion took hard work and was not a given.

Nevertheless, the Chinese river basins forcefully support the notion that geography matters. Relatively modest physical obstacles between them had a palpable effect on state formation and could only be overcome by centuries of repeatedly enforced political unification. If that was the case in China, would we not expect more serious obstacles to have had an even greater impact on Europe?[8]

Moreover, China's riverine interconnectivity was only the beginning. The Yellow River was navigable for about 600–800 kilometers inland, similar to the Nile below the First Cataract, and the Yangzi for 1,100 kilometers east of the Gorges. Between and beyond them, the Great Canal, multiple smaller rivers, and feeder canals created, in the words of environmental historian John Robert McNeill, "a huge fertile crescent united by cheap and safe transport. . . . No inland waterway system in world history approaches this one as a device for integrating large and productive spaces."[9]

This was not a one-way street from geography to empire: it was a dialectical process in which the physical environment and state formation, both contingent and acting upon each other, fostered ever-stronger path dependence. Thus, again according to McNeill, "The durability and resilience of the state depended in large part on Chinese geography, but Chinese ecology in turn depended on the state to an unusual degree." The imperial state assumed responsibility for big waterworks and flood control. Canals, dam, and paddies required constant maintenance, and the more invested, the more at stake. In this precociously anthropogenic environment, decay would have been very costly and not readily reversible, unlike in rainfall-fed Western Europe. In consequence, Chinese society became "unusually dependent on demographic and political stability, and unusually vulnerable to disruption by neglect. . . . No other major society so locked itself into a situation demanding constant intensive maintenance to prevent sharp ecological degradation."[10]

Even as statements such as these might seem to propound an updated version of Karl Wittfogel's model of hydraulic despotism, they help us identify the features that contributed most to long-term development. Unlike in China, rivers played a less dominant role in Europe. The two longest ones, the Danube and the Rhine, are shorter than the Yellow and Yangzi Rivers and connect less of Europe. They also flow in different directions, thereby raising the logistical penalty on moving toward the central regions.[11]

Concentration

The cumulative effects of coastlines, ruggedness, and river basins support a simple observation: Europe consisted of multiple smaller core regions whereas China initially had just one—the Central Plain—and then two, with the Yangzi basin added into the mix. Increasingly interconnected, the northern basin consistently remained politically and militarily dominant.

As I argue in the next section, proximity to the steppe was part of the reason for the latter. But other natural endowments played a similarly important role. The Central Plain was not only flat but highly productive. Loess deposited by sandstorms up to 250 meters deep in the west—in Shaanxi, Western Shanxi, and Southern Gansu—was then carried by the aptly named Yellow River into the Central Plain where it boosted agricultural yields.[12]

Whoever was in charge of this core also controlled China: it is not by accident that virtually all imperial unifications proceeded from this area. Its demographic dominance was similarly pronounced: for a long time, it towered over other parts of China not only in population number but also thanks to the state's ability to count and burden its concentrated and accessible residents.[13]

No such "natural" core existed anywhere in Europe. It was divided into a number of smaller pockets of development, alluvial plains separated by mountains (the Alps and Pyrenees), marshes (in the northern Low Countries), forests, and the sea (around the British Isles and Scandinavia). Following in the footsteps of others, Eric Jones made much of this configuration: the Paris and London basins, Flanders, and the Po Valley jointly yet severally represented the High Middle Ages. Montesquieu's "larger plains" of Asia are conspicuous by their absence.[14]

It is easy to overestimate the impact of these differences. Rome, after all, had succeeded in uniting the aforementioned zones alongside others all the way to the Nile valley. And we cannot take it for granted that these conditions would predictably result in a particular type of state system: Jones's observation that "enough states were constructed each about its core and all of a similar enough strength to resist the logical conclusion of the process of conquest and amalgamation: a single unified European state" is mere description, not an explanation.[15]

Moreover, large plains as such were not a sufficient factor. Had they been, empire ought to have been more durable and hegemonic in India than it turned out to be in China. Huge northern river basins created a farm belt from Pakistan to Bihar as early as the first millennium BCE. As Victor Lieberman notes, by 1700 the North India plain contained some 60 percent of India's total population, compared to the 25 percent or 30 percent of the Central Plain's share of China. India was made up of fewer and smaller micro-regions than China. However, it lacked an integrating water-support system like China's that would have allowed the northern state to expand south. Connectivity mattered as much as plains did.[16]

Interspersion of arid and cultivated zones farther south added to South Asia's fragmentation, and although the western deserts of Sind and Rajastan and the arid central Deccan plateau were not obstacles as formidable as the major mountain ranges of Europe, they did foster separation. The more difficult terrain and the dispersion of agrarian zones in the south correlate well with the prevalence of smaller polities there. Empire-building invariably proceeded from the north to the south, and southern state formation was often secondary to that process. In addition, the arid Deccan areas supported warrior communities and armed pastoralists that were capable of challenging the northern basin empires, in ways unknown in China. In sum, these traits help account for intermediate outcomes in terms of political centralization: more than in Europe but less than in China.[17]

Shape, Isolation, and Scale

Its relatively square shape makes East Asia more compact than Europe. When Rome turned the elongated Mediterranean Sea into its imperial core—useful for low-cost transfers but bereft of people—outward power projection created very extended frontiers. If we discount the Atlantic and ignore the arid African frontier, the Roman empire still had to protect close to 6,000 kilometers of potentially contested borders. Even though the various strands of the Great Wall add up to much more than that, the effective length of the frontier from Korea to the far end of Gansu was only about half the Roman value. For most of the time, this was the only front that really mattered, whereas Rome faced serious challengers from different directions.[18]

Other features arguably mattered less. China was objectively more isolated than Europe. Joseph Needham characterized China as "an amphitheatre facing the Pacific Ocean"—and, he might have added, for a long time with little of note out there. Europe, by contrast, has always been closely connected to the Middle East and North Africa region. There is no clear physical boundary between the Atlantic in the west and the Hindu Kush and the east Iranian and Balochi deserts in the east, and even the latter cannot rival the Tibetan highlands and the Taklamakan desert.

In a very basic sense, this made hegemonic empire more feasible in East Asia: no one power could hope to control all of temperate Eurasia from the Atlantic to eastern Iran. When the Umayyads tried, the extreme east–west stretch of their realm invited fraying from the edges. Much of the time, fragmentation within this space put pressure on less expansive empires. Yet the inverse did not necessarily apply: had isolation been a decisive feature, South Asia, which is just as isolated as China, should have been similarly united.[19]

Finally, the spatial extent of state systems may also be relevant. Once again we need to be careful. Core China and Latin Europe are of comparable size. The geodesic distance from Seoul to Hanoi is the same as that from Lisbon to Warsaw (2,750 kilometers). The Chinese empire grew early on by expanding to the northwest: Kashgar, at the western end of Xinjiang, is 3,400 kilometers from Beijing and almost 4,400 kilometers from Seoul. Similar metrics apply to the early modern European state system once we include the Ottoman and Safavid empires: Lisbon lies more than 5,400 kilometers from Isfahan. Even if we stick to Christian societies, Moscow is 3,900 kilometers away.[20]

If we merely looked at these figures, we might conclude that European and Chinese state-building and competition played out on a similar scale. But there was one big difference: unlike in East Asia, the European state system kept growing over time. Korea and northern Vietnam had been part of the Chinese ecumene since the Western Han period, and with minute exceptions—Mongol incursions into Southeast Asia at the end of the thirteenth century and the Japanese invasions of Korea three centuries later—most of Southeast Asia as well as Japan effectively remained outside the China-centered political-military network even as more stable polities developed in its periphery.

To the north and west of Italy, ancient Rome had occupied a space that lacked prior state structures. Its success forever changed the political landscape by extending state-ness, for want of a better term, into continental Europe. At first, Rome's fall did little to change the scope of this process: the successor states barely extended beyond the old Rhine–Danube frontier, and only Charlemagne regained what Augustus might once have projected as Rome's Elbe frontier.[21]

What Peter Heather calls "the ancient world order in western Eurasia: a dominant Mediterranean circle lording it over an underdeveloped northern hinterland" was finally overcome in the Early Middle Ages. Alongside literacy, state-building spread eastward and northward, a grand move "towards greater homogeneity right across the European landmass." Slavic peoples played a central role. In the ninth and tenth centuries, they established large if fluid polities, driven in part by German eastward predation. The tenth century in particular witnessed a massive extension of political and social hierarchies beyond the old civilizational cores, into Poland, Bohemia, Hungary, Rus', and coastal Scandinavia. Much of Central and Eastern Europe filled up with increasingly ambitious regimes and incipient states or hegemonies. By 1000, recognizable polities stretched all the way to the Volga.[22]

External inputs contributed greatly to this process, which did not take the form of imperial conquest but was spurred on by decentralized initiatives backed by military, clerical, and mercantile elites—decentralization that reflected the fractures of their places of origin, most notably Germany. Where an aristocratic diaspora of castle-building knightly cavalry led, farmers and burghers followed. Thanks to the widespread replication of Western European structures—towns, churches, and noble estates—this expansion did not create core-periphery relations but simply enlarged the reach of a certain set of institutions eastward. As a result, as Heather puts it in not quite politically correct bluntness, "Barbarian Europe was barbarian no longer."[23]

What we are concerned with here is not "barbarousness" but statehood, and in that respect homogenization made major headway: in Europe, the spatial extent of state-level political organization grew from roughly three million kilometers in 800 to maybe three times as much in 1600. Aside from northern Scandinavia and northern Russia, most of this enlargement took place during the first half of that period. According to one estimate, Latin Europe alone doubled in size between 950 and 1350, and by then boasted the largest cluster of similarly organized polities anywhere in the world.[24]

It is true that it took some time for this expansion to have a major impact on interstate competition within Europe. Although Bohemia played a significant role in the affairs of the German empire from the thirteenth century onward, conflict among the Great Powers of the Iberian peninsula, France, England, Germany, and Italy unfolded without eastern or Nordic interference, a situation that changed only with Sweden's intervention in the Thirty Years' War. Before the Napoleonic Wars, Russia, facing Swedes and Poles alongside Ottomans and Tatars, exercised little tangible influence on Western Europe.

In that sense, the medieval expansion of the European state system did not directly contribute to the stabilization of polycentrism in its Latin core. The mere existence of Central and Eastern European states, however, made this fragmentation more robust in that it provided additional checks to any imperial ventures that might otherwise have been launched. When Russia finally intervened in the early nineteenth century, its military power proved all the more decisive in preserving Europe's balanced state system.[25]

For the most part, Europe's colonial empires overseas played a more indirect role. While Spain's access to American silver overtly threatened the balance of power, this threat also helped galvanize resistance that ultimately shored up political polycentrism. Overseas resources were not generally critical for maintaining the European state system, even if England was able to draw on global assets in its successful containment of France after 1800. In the end, it was the size of Europe's sphere of competitive integration that mattered most.

Expansions such as those into Central, Northern, and Eastern Europe (or overseas) did not occur in South, Southeast, or East Asia. Indian states were largely confined to the subcontinent. Their principal political-military interaction zone with the outside world was a relatively narrow frontier to the northwest, made permanent by formidable natural obstacles. Much the same was true of China with its steppe frontier, and Southeast Asia was even more tightly hemmed in by mountain ranges. There was generally little if any scope for substantial offshoots that could have contributed to political fragmentation.

• • •

What, then, does geography tell us about state formation? By a number of counts, the East Asian environment favored large-scale empire and hegemony: limited articulation, considerable compactness, weaker internal obstacles, and a rich, "natural" core that could be further integrated with the help of manageable human inputs. Europe, by contrast, was much more segmented by mountains and the sea, and lacked large concentrations of natural resources. South Asia scored somewhere in between, and the same applies to the Middle East and North Africa, with their mixture of fertile river basins, highland plateaus, and arid zones.

What is at stake here is emphatically not the old bugbear of "geographical determinism." Geography is not destiny, but it does tilt the field in favor of particular outcomes by making them more or less costly and therefore more or less likely to occur in some parts of the world than in others. It would be self-defeating to approach the problem of the First Great Divergence without taking account of the physical environment.[26]

In fact, it is imperative to expand our analysis beyond coastlines, rivers, mountains, and soils to consider a more specific and arguably even more powerful factor: proximity to the steppe. State formation was not merely shaped by spatial scale and the properties of the terrain upon which it unfolded. It was also strongly influenced by conditions *outside* those settled zones where agriculturalists produced the surplus that fed cities, armies, officials, and courts.

ECOLOGY

The Steppe Effect

The vast Eurasian Steppe, a belt of continuous grass- and shrublands, once stretched more than 7,000 kilometers from Manchuria to Wallachia (figure 8.3). Its vegetation cover and gentle relief afforded considerable ease of movement to riders and livestock. Northern China abuts this zone and was the locus of intense imperial persistence. Latin Europe, situated at greater remove, was not. The Middle East and North Africa region, bordering on the Eurasian steppe and several more arid frontiers, repeatedly gave rise to large empires. So did northern India, more detached from the Eurasian steppe but exposed to it through links on its northwestern flank. Conversely, state formation generally unfolded

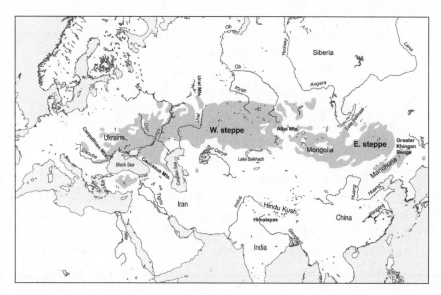

FIGURE 8.3 The Eurasian steppe.

on a smaller scale in more sheltered southern India and Southeast Asia. Were these correlations coincidental, masking diverse causes, or do they reflect a broader dynamic of causation in imperiogenesis?[27]

Recent scholarship supports the latter interpretation. In 2009, Peter Turchin observed that up to 1800, except for modern European overseas colonies, most empires that covered at least 1 million square kilometers (a convenient metric equivalent to three-quarters of a percent of the earth's land surface outside Antarctica) emerged in close proximity to a steppe frontier. My own revised and updated version of Turchin's survey shows that 62 out of 73 such polities more or less clearly belong in this category. No fewer than 54 of these 63 developed either in or very close to the Eurasian steppe. We must not put too much weight on precise numbers: some of these empires were effectively continuations of previous ones and need not be classified as discrete cases. Even so, the overall pattern is robust.[28]

The observed distribution cannot equally well be explained with reference to natural endowments. Latin Europe, southern India, and

Southeast Asia, large areas that were equipped with enough people and natural resources to support large-scale state formation but were distant from the steppe, rarely produced similarly substantial empires. Away from the steppe, empire-building on this scale remained limited to just a few cases: the Roman and Carolingian empires in Europe, the Angkorian empire in Southeast Asia, and the Inca empire in the Andes. Among these four, the Frankish and Khmer polities barely cleared the size threshold, and the former proved rather brittle. Only Rome could rival the largest agrarian empires of the Middle East and South and East Asia in terms of both heft and longevity.[29]

This geographic clustering is best captured by maps. Figure 8.4 pinpoints the source regions of traditional Old World empires in excess of 1 million square kilometers. The grid pattern in figure 8.5 visualizes the odds of being part of such a polity: the darker the color, the longer a particular area had been ruled in this way. Taken together, these two maps reveal a distinctive pattern. Large empires were concentrated in East and Central Asia, the Middle East, and Egypt but were rare in Europe, southern India, and Southeast Asia. Northern India occupies an intermediate position. I discuss these regional specifics later in this section.[30]

An alternative measure, focusing on population rather than territorial extent, controls for the proliferation of steppe empires that could be extensive but sparsely inhabited. This approach yields similar results. Up till 1800, thirty-two traditional land empires claimed at least 8 percent of the world population at the time, a threshold that empirically allows fairly clear demarcation from lesser cases. Twenty of these originated at or close to steppe frontiers, and another seven at somewhat greater remove. In this sample, the Roman empire was once again the principal outlier.[31]

Whichever way we look at this, the global distribution of mega-empires reflects a "strong statistical regularity" as their incidence declines rapidly with distance from the Afroeurasian steppe zones. This allows us to advance a parsimonious working hypothesis: the scale and intensity of imperiogenesis were profoundly shaped by ecological features that drove state formation via intermediating proximate mechanisms.[32]

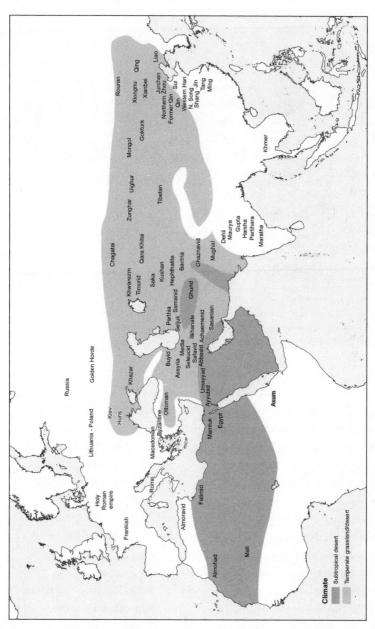

FIGURE 8.4 Spatial distribution of the core areas of empires of at least 1 million square kilometers in Afroeurasia. *Source:* Adapted and expanded from Turchin 2009: 204, figure 1.

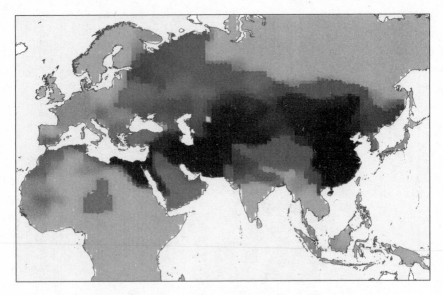

FIGURE 8.5 Probability of being part of large polities (>1 million km²) at 100-year intervals, 500–1500 CE (probability rising from medium gray = low, to black = high; light gray = zero). *Source*: Scheidel in press-b: figure 2.13(b). Data provided by James Bennett (University of Washington) on November 9, 2017, drawing on the data underlying Turchin et al. 2013: 16386.

This hypothesis proceeds from the premise that antagonistic relationships between steppe pastoralists and settled agriculturalists precipitated scaling-up of state power and size in response to competitive pressures. In keeping with a wide range of scholarship on the drivers of state formation, this perspective privileges the role of intergroup conflict in the creation and evolution of powerful political-military entities.[33]

It is also rooted in ecological fundamentals. Very broadly speaking—and this ideal-typical sketch accommodates a great deal of real-life diversity and hybridity—steppe peoples inhabited grasslands primarily as pastoralists who reared livestock, especially horses and sheep, even as they supplemented these activities with farming, foraging, and hunting. To varying degrees, this mode of subsistence favored a mobile lifestyle conditioned by seasonal movements and access to horses.

Such groups found it hard or were even unable to produce many of the goods found in sedentary societies. In order to obtain such goods, they had to trade with, serve in the military of, or raid sedentary societies. Access to and facility with horses supported all of these pursuits. Cavalry warfare enabled steppe warriors not only to compensate for agriculturalists' superior numbers but also to enjoy high mobility. Moreover, the nature of the steppe, lacking the numerous and vital fixed positions associated with settled life, made it easier to retreat from counterattacks. By combining flexible forward-striking power with great strategic depth, steppe forces were in a position to punch far above their demographic weight.[34]

On the other side of the ecological divide, the economies of sedentary populations generated resources that were not only attractive to steppe groups but also could be used to build up massive military capabilities. These complementary differences and capacities created "fundamental structural incompatibilities" that could be managed in a variety of ways: open conflict was by no means the only option. Even so, over the long run, the ecological pressures of steppe life and rulers' ambitions made periodic outbreaks of conflict more likely than not. For this reason alone, scaling-up held considerable appeal.[35]

This idea has a long pedigree, associated with Owen Lattimore and other students of the steppe rim. It also represents a variant of Turchin's "meta-ethnic frontier theory" that expects the strongest impulses for state formation to manifest along civilizational fault lines, such as diversity of religion, language, mode of subsistence, and intensity of warfare.[36]

In his massive comparative survey of Old World macro-social development, Victor Lieberman argues that the degree of proximity to the steppe split Eurasia into "exposed" and "protected" zones: "Insulation/vulnerability to Inner Asian occupation is the central criterion of protected zone/exposed zone status." His "protected" areas include Southeast Asia, most of Europe, Japan, and Korea, the Himalayan region and Tibet, and coastal South Asia and Sri Lanka. China, continental South Asia, and Southwest Asia were much more exposed. In general, "protected" regions remained more isolated and produced charter

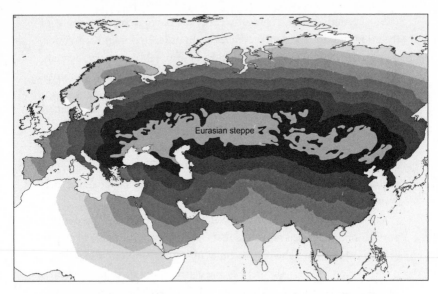

FIGURE 8.6 Effective distance from the Eurasian steppe (by land). *Source*: Adapted from Ko, Koyama, and Sng 2018: 290, fig. 4.

civilizations later and with smaller polities than "exposed ones." He identifies Inner Asian influences as the key coordinating agent behind this difference: for most of their history, and consistently so after 1400, the "protected" zones regions were sheltered from occupation by Central Asian nomads and generally led by indigenous elites.[37]

A region's level of protection was mediated by three principal factors: proximity to the steppe by distance, the presence of barriers such as mountains and the sea, and links to the steppe (figures 8.6 and 8.7). For instance, it mattered that South Asia, albeit quite far away from the Eurasian grasslands and protected by the Himalayas, connects to Central Asia via river basins and shrublands. Western Europe was better shielded by the interposition of woodlands but faced a detached steppe bridgehead, the Pannonian plain, even if only on a modest scale.[38]

Models of large-scale state formation fueled by antagonistic interaction between steppe and settled areas work best for empires that emerged in the steppe itself, in the form of entities that were secondary to and in

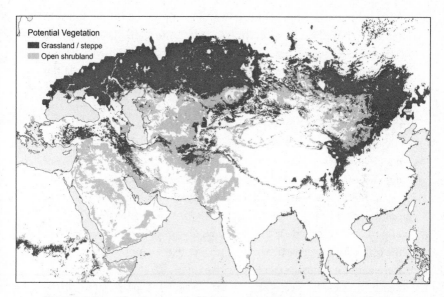

FIGURE 8.7 Potential vegetation cover of Asia. *Source*: https://nelson.wisc.edu/sage/data-and-models/atlas/maps/potentialveg/atl_potentialveg_asi.jpg, displaying "vegetation that would exist at a given location had human forms of land use never existed" (https://nelson.wisc.edu/sage/data-and-models/atlas/maps.php?datasetid=25&includerelatedlinks=1&dataset=25). Data used by permission of The Center for Sustainability and the Global Environment, Nelson Institute for Environmental Studies, University of Wisconsin–Madison.

some ways parasitical upon agrarian societies on the other side of the ecological divide. The underlying dynamic has most famously been captured by Thomas Barfield's concept of steppe-based "shadow empires." Steppe populations formed confederations out of a need to organize manpower in order to obtain material benefits from adjacent sedentary societies by a variety of means from trade to plunder from raiding and the extraction of tributary payments. Access to such goods buttressed and legitimated centralized authority among nomadic and seminomadic groups by enabling leaders to reward and thus control followers whose mobile lifestyle granted them considerable exit options.

In Barfield's view, steppe empires were locked into a symbiotic relationship with agrarian polities: "They could not exist except as part of an interaction with an imperial state because they lacked most of the essential characteristics of primary empires," most notably the ability to tax large populations directly. This warrants their designation as "shadow" or "mirror" empires. In creating spatially extensive empires, steppe groups did not merely borrow from the institutional toolkit of their sedentary neighbors but responded directly to the latter's development. Thus, the larger and more complex primary empires grew to be, the greater the number of steppe empires that followed suit.[39]

Simplifying as it is, this scenario is not inherently biased against nomads. Contrary to what is sometimes averred, this perspective does not depend on steppe peoples taking the initiative in aggression: scaling-up among herders could just as readily be triggered by expanding sedentary polities' encroachment on their pastures. Nor does it denigrate nomads as poor or "barbaric." Both sides generally sought out resources from the other: horses in particular were prized steppe exports. Yet even if we were to follow Christopher Beckwith in picturing steppe groups as primarily interested in peaceful trade and in casting agrarian empires in the role of aggressors that provoked hostilities by unilaterally restricting the flow of goods, the structural tensions identified by Barfield would remain unchanged: conflict and empire-building arose from a fundamentally unbalanced distribution of resources and capabilities.[40]

This imbalance was further exacerbated by climatic variation. From the third century BCE, the intensity of steppe pressure on China—proxied by the frequency of battles and southward incursions—was inversely correlated with precipitation levels: drought undermined the fragile ecology of the grasslands and provided an impetus to move on. The migration of the Seljuq Turks may have been similarly motivated. At other times, climatic conditions generated additional resources, as at the beginning of the Arab expansion and again for Genghis Khan's Mongols. All of this introduced a "natural" element into the relations between the settled and nomadic spheres that superseded specific cultural dispositions.[41]

No matter how much the literate elites of sedentary societies vilified steppe inhabitants as bloodthirsty savages—or how deeply modern observers have variously been taken in or appalled by such tropes—our task is not to assign or deflect blame but to acknowledge key elements on which all sides in the academic debate consistently agree: that even though inhabitants of the steppe were able to control or produce many vital resources directly, they generally strove to acquire outside goods, whether by trade, war, or military service for others; that agrarian polities either pushed them away or defended themselves, depending on who happened to have the upper hand; and that thanks to their lifestyle, nomadic and seminomadic groups tended to excel at horse-riding and mounted warfare in ways that helped offset their numerical inferiority. These few ingredients were sufficient for sustaining endemic conflict.[42]

Viable solutions were in short supply. Conquest of sedentary regions by steppe invaders was rare and invited either expulsion by the local population or renewed invasion by the next wave of steppe warriors. Pacification and settlement by overwhelming force or the transformation of the steppe into farmland—as in modern Ukraine—became technologically and logistically feasible only a few centuries ago. For a much longer period before that, competitive friction between agrarian and steppe was structural in nature and therefore highly persistent.[43]

A straightforward model of antagonistic scaling-up works less smoothly for agrarian empires. Barfield's model treats them as antecedent, which means that steppe power cannot be used to explain their existence. Moreover, traditional empires were not generally established in order to combat nomadic challengers. The earliest large states in particular appeared well before steppe inhabitants mastered cavalry warfare and turned into a force to be reckoned with. All this creates serious problems for overly abstract notions of agrarian responses to nomadic raiding, such as Turchin's competing options of alliance-building (vulnerable to free-riding) and conquest (to centralize command) within settled areas. It thus will not do to quip, with Kent Gang Deng, that "the irony of history decreed that the Chinese had to kill each other in civil wars to unify the land and cooperate with each other in order to fend off the nomads." Even if this idea contains a kernel of truth, it cuts too many corners to be of much use to historians.[44]

The presence of the steppe acted upon the formation of agrarian empires in a more indirect and mediated manner. Geographically and ecologically intermediate contact zones between the agrarian and nomadic spheres—Owen Lattimore's "marginal zone"—played a critical role. It was there that the most intense and consequential interactions—trading, raiding, co-optation, and acculturation—took place. In these areas, such as Manchuria, settled groups were exposed to and had ready access to steppe assets—to a "reservoir," in Lattimore's parlance, of horsemen and horses—that gave them disproportionate influence on state formation in the fully settled zone. The "marginal zone," rather than the steppe grasslands proper, was the principal source of conquest. This was as true of the Xianbei tribes of the Period of Disunion and the later Manchu takeover as it was of the late antique Arab formations that mediated between Bedouin and the Fertile Crescent.[45]

But outright conquest was merely the most dramatic manifestation of that influence. More generally, resources from the steppe shaped processes of state formation in the agrarian sphere, most notably access to horses (much sought after in South Asia, for example), cavalry, and military services provided by steppe groups. The history of Jin and Tang China and of the many Middle Eastern regimes that employed and then came to be ruled by Turkic forces would have unfolded very differently without them. The historical record thus favors a somewhat more complex model in which nomad/settled antagonism is supplemented by recourse to steppe-sourced assets to create large agrarian polities. In this scenario, cavalries' ability to project military power was a powerful driver of empire-building in the cultivated sphere.

Once more, Turchin and associates have taken the lead in generalizing this relationship with the help of a deliberately simple model of state formation in the Old World between 1500 BCE and 1500 CE. In their simulation, which takes account of only a few basic features such as land cultivability, elevation, rivers, and coasts, military technology is seeded at the steppe frontier in order to simulate the impact of chariots and then cavalry. Their presence in turn helps shape the evolution of ultrasocial traits that sustain political scaling-up.

A large number of simulation runs based on these parsimonious premises predicts patterns of state formation that fairly closely approximate historical outcomes. In projecting the probability that any particular cell on the model's grid was part of a state of at least 100,000 square kilometers at certain intervals during this three-millennium period, the simulation captures about two-thirds of the variance observed in actual history. This finding suggests that equine warfare was critical to processes of large-scale state-building. Given that the spatial distribution of states of 100,000 square kilometers or more closely resembles that of empires of a million square kilometers or more (as shown in figure 8.4), the same conclusion applies to the formation of many of the largest traditional empires in history.[46]

It thus appears that the steppe precipitated imperial state formation both directly—by encouraging cooperation among agriculturalists and among pastoralists and conflict between these two—and indirectly, in the first instance by supplying horses (and horsemen) for military purposes. One big caveat applies. Broadly generalizing statements derived from parsimonious premises are bound to be greeted with skepticism by most historians, who tend to focus on the trees at the expense of the forest.[47]

This is not unreasonable: on their own, statistical correlations and spatial patterns do not necessarily make a compelling case. We also need to consider in greater depth the proximate mechanisms that translated what we might call the "steppe effect" to specific outcomes in state formation. I do so by delving a little more deeply into the dynamics of regional political and military history as they unfolded over the long term. As we will see, this historical evidence from China, Europe, and other parts of the Old World provides ample support for a steppe-focused account of premodern imperiogenesis.

East Asia

In China, empire emanated almost exclusively from the northern frontier. Over the course of 3,600 years, all but one of a dozen unification events originated in the north. Seven of them were rooted in the northwest, especially the Wei River valley: Western Zhou (twelfth century BCE), Qin and Han (third century BCE), Sui (sixth century CE), Tang (seventh century CE), Yuan (thirteenth century CE), and the communist takeover out of Shaanxi (twentieth century CE). The Manchu Qing came from the northeast (seventeenth century CE), and the Shang (sixteenth [?] century BCE), Western Jin (third century CE), and Northern Song (tenth century CE) from the north-central area. Two further unifications merely of northern China—Northern Wei (fourth century CE) and Jin (twelfth century CE)—originated from the northwest and northeast, respectively. The Ming regime (fourteenth century CE), centered on the Yangzi basin, was the sole outlier.[48]

The origin of the leadership reflects the same long-term pattern. Victor Mair's survey of the ethnic and regional affiliation of ruling houses from the Shang dynasty to the People's Republic finds that most unifying dynasties were founded by individuals from the northwest: Shang, Western Zhou, Qin, Eastern Han, Sui, Tang, Northern Song, Yuan, and Qing, nine overall, compared to only three—Western Han, Western Jin, and Ming—that were not, alongside the Republic of 1911 and the current regime. Much the same is true of dynasties that controlled less than the whole of China but more than half of it. Moreover, dynasties from the northwest were on average more durable. Thus, in Mair's words, northwestern actors "were nearly always responsible for the recurrent creation of an Extended East Asian Heartland"—"for the building of vast empires" in that part of the world.[49]

This focus was not simply a function of ethnicity: both early Chinese dynasties (Western Zhou, Qin, Han, and Western Jin) and later regimes that were either of foreign origin (Yuan and Qing, alongside Wei and Jin) or of a more hybrid nature (Sui, Tang, and to some extent even the Northern Song) shared this characteristic. Geography was key.

Northern predominance went back a long time, well before the first steppe conquest regimes appeared in the fourth century CE. The emergence of the Shang coincided with the appearance of domesticated horses and war chariots. In a striking reflection of steppe influence, Shang and Western Zhou royal burials were replete with horses and chariots. More tantalizingly, accounts of the First Emperor of Qin and the founders of the Western and Eastern Han dynasties emphasize somatic features—long noses and facial hair—that were coded as markers of ethnic identity pointing to admixture from the steppe and only much later came to be associated with European foreigners.[50]

In the grasslands northwest of China, the transition to pastoral nomadism occurred during the Western Zhou period, and classic nomadic steppe culture appeared in the seventh and sixth centuries BCE, at a time when the states began to coalesce in the agrarian zone. It is true that this process was primarily driven by interstate warfare. But this does not mean that proximity to the steppe had no significant impact. The ultimate victor, the kingdom of Qin, was located in China's northwest and appears to have owed much of its strikingly martial disposition to its frontier position. It was there that state-strengthening reforms—which had been pioneered elsewhere—were taken the farthest and were implemented with the greatest success, even though Qin, centered on the Wei River valley, was less exposed to rival states than others.[51]

Yet Qin's belligerence exceeded that of its rivals: by one count, it launched several times as many offensives during the Warring States period as its principal competitors. The runner-up, Zhao, was even more exposed to the steppe frontier. Some version of the "steppe effect" may well have made itself felt. The Qin were later said to have started out as herders. They were locked into prolonged conflict with surrounding chiefdoms ("Rong," some of which may have been pastoralists) over control of the Wei River basin, alongside wars with the state of Jin and its successor Wei to the northeast. These efforts helped produce a precociously strong state with a relatively weak aristocracy, and muted cultural attainment.[52]

The expansion of the Sinosphere into Rong and Di areas in this period brought the Warring States into closer contact with pastoralists. Subjugation of Di tribes in the Ordos region from the eighth through the sixth centuries BCE removed earlier buffers and for the first time led to conflict between the northern states and actual nomads. The states of Yan, Zhao, and Qin abutted the grasslands of Inner Mongolia and southwestern Manchuria. From the late fourth century BCE, the first two of them set up long border walls to fence off land they had seized from pastoralists. Aggression was stepped up upon the Qin conquest of China: existing walls were connected and ambitious campaigns targeted herders. The displacement of the pastoralist Xiongnu from the

Ordos in 215 BCE encouraged them to pool their forces under centralized leadership.[53]

This consolidation process enabled them to put growing pressure on
the Han empire, which in the late second and early first centuries BCE
responded by adopting an aggressive policy of massive incursions into
the steppe. Even though these extremely costly operations could not be
sustained, they provided strong impetus for domestic state-building
measures from crackdowns on nobles and merchants to greater government intervention in economy, and also pushed Han power into Central
Asia all the way to Fergana, a rich source of horses.[54]

The "steppe effect" on Chinese state formation increased tremen-
dously during the following millennium and a half, when groups from
the frontier zone set up a series of conquest regimes. From the fourth
century CE, the proverbial "Five Barbarians," mostly herders—the
Xiongnu, Xianbei, and Jie from the steppe and Manchuria and the
Qiang from the western highlands, alongside the sedentary Di—
dominated the political landscape of northern China. More than half of
the "Sixteen Kingdoms" from 304 to 439 CE were established by these
groups: Former Zhao, Northern Liang, and Xia by the Xiongnu; Southern
Liang, Former, Later, and Southern Yan, and Western Qin by the Xianbei;
Later Qin by the Qiang; Later Zhao by Jie; and Later Liang by the Di.[55]

The Tuoba clan that restored unity in northern China as the Northern Wei was of Xianbei extraction, as were various successor regimes
from Eastern and Western Wei to Northern Zhou and Northern Qi.
Tuoba rule depended in no small measure on access to horses from the
steppe. Throughout the fifth century CE, they launched attacks on
the Rouran steppe federation to keep it at bay and ensure a steady flow
of equine imports: thirteen major conflicts are attested between 402 and
522 CE.[56]

Sui and Tang rulers were of mixed Han and Turkic-Xianbei descent
and relied on the state apparatus that had been built up by the previous
northern regimes. In the seventh century CE, the Tang's Turkic generals
commanded largely non-Chinese cavalry in far-flung campaigns across the
steppe. Just as under the Han empire, expansionary efforts were concentrated on the grasslands in the northwest of China. Between the 620s

and 650s, Tang forces destroyed both Turk khaganates and claimed authority over Xinjiang and areas to the west all the way to what are now Afghanistan and Uzbekistan. By the 660s, Tang cavalry were said to have owned 700,000 horses.[57]

In the 750s, Uighur forces helped the Tang dynasty survive a massive rebellion. After the Tang's eventual collapse, renewed fission opened up space for northern military regimes. In the tenth century CE, the Shatuo Turks set up the Later Tang and Later Jin dynasties, which were beholden to the Qidan state of Liao. The subsequent Later Zhou and Northern Song dynasties built on this Turkic governmental apparatus to unify first northern and then all of China. The Northern Song empire, unable to overcome the Liao Qidan in Manchuria and Inner Mongolia by force, invested massively in military capabilities, an effort that led to the creation of a powerful centralized fiscal-military state.[58]

In the early twelfth century, the Jurchen, Tungusic tribes from the woodlands of eastern Manchuria that had once been subordinate to the Liao, established the Jin dynasty that quickly took over northern China and put even greater pressure on what remained of the Song state until both succumbed to the Mongols. Combining his growing populous and wealthy Chinese territories with extensive steppe cavalry forces, in the late thirteenth century Kublai Khan claimed the largest empire the world had ever seen, even if much of it only nominally acknowledged his suzerainty.[59]

In China, Mongol rule soon gave way to the one dynasty that did not originate in the north: it was Han rebels based in the lower Yangzi valley who brought the Ming to power. While some Mongol groups were incorporated into the new empire's frontier defenses, others remained outside: from 1410 to 1424, the Ming launched five massive campaigns against them. In 1449, the Oirat Mongols invaded in turn, capturing the sitting emperor. The Ming subsequently adopted a defensive posture, symbolized by the most ambitious iteration in a long series of northern walls.

From the late sixteenth century onward, Manchurian tribes began to unite and encroach on the empire. In the middle of the following century, they took over and ruled the country under the Qing dynasty, reviving a version of the ancient dual system that segregated conquerors from indigenous subjects. Occupation forces known as the "Eight Banners," mostly mounted archers of Manchu and Mongol extraction, were kept apart from the Han population in separate garrisons.

Qing imperialism targeted the steppe: between the late seventeenth century and the 1750s, their troops battled the Oirat Mongol Zunghar khanate that sought to establish hegemony across Xinjiang and Kazakhstan. Breaking their resistance in a series of wars, the Ming took control of Outer Mongolia, Tibet, and Xinjiang. China had reached its greatest territorial extent in sustained conflict with a steppe federation.[60]

Even this highly superficial sketch leaves no doubt that engagement across the steppe frontier was of paramount importance in guiding Chinese state formation: developments in the contact zone from the Ordos to Manchuria as well as in the actual steppe—from conflict with the Xiongnu and Turks during the Han and Tang periods to the Mongol conquests and beyond—all made crucial contributions.

Moreover, the "steppe effect" served to put China back together whenever it fractured. Fractures almost invariably arose from within. Western Zhou hegemony dissolved in the early first millennium BCE as vassal rulers gained independence. The unified Qin empire was brought down by revolts in the final decade of the third century BCE. Massive popular rebellions undermined the Eastern Han in the late second and early third centuries CE and empowered warlords. The Western Jin regime of the third century CE was perennially fragmented and effectively destroyed by hostilities among rival princes: steppe militias from within the empire merely delivered the coup de grâce.

Centrifugal tendencies reasserted themselves with the An Lushan rebellion in the 750s that greatly weakened the central authorities of the Tang empire, and the Huang Chao uprising of the late ninth century proved fatal. A wave of popular unrest ended Mongol rule in the mid-fourteenth century and temporarily splintered the empire into multiple fiefdoms of competing movements and warlords. Renewed rebellions in the 1630s and 1640s preceded and enabled the Manchu takeover that restored political unity. From the late eighteenth century, the Qing themselves faced popular risings that culminated in the exceptionally bloody Taiping rebellion of the 1850s and 1860s. Since the 1910s the Nationalist government struggled to contain regional warlords alongside the communist insurgency.

For more than 2,000 years, mass rebellions were heavily concentrated near the end of individual dynasties: imperial rule carried within it the seeds of its demise, and was repeatedly undone by popular unrest and the countervailing forces it unleashed. From the middle of the first millennium CE onward, resources from and interaction with the steppe proved essential in repeatedly restoring political order on a large scale, most notably in the fifth, sixth, seventh, tenth, thirteenth, fourteenth, and seventeenth centuries.[61]

At the same time, the "steppe effect" of imperial consolidation extended well beyond China proper. Barfield developed his model of "shadow empires" based on parallel trends in state formation in the agricultural and pastoralist spheres that suggest close developmental linkages: bipolar cycles with centralization or collapse on both sides. Thus, when China united, so did the steppe: the creation of the Qin-Han empire coincided with the unified Xiongnu empire (third through first centuries BCE), the Tuoba consolidation with the rise of the Rouran (fifth and sixth century CE), the Sui-Tang consolidation with the two Turkish khaganates (sixth through eighth centuries CE), and the Uighur khaganate (eighth and ninth century CE) (as well as the Tibetan empire in the seventh through ninth centuries CE).

While steppe inhabitants' desire to obtain resources from the sedentary zone was a constant, the potential to do so grew with imperial unification, which increased, mobilized, and concentrated surplus. However, rising imperial power also necessitated broader coordination of military assets within the steppe, both to withstand encroachment and to extract goods via raids or tribute that sustained more centralized forms of leadership among the nomads.[62]

The capacities of steppe empires increased over time. Whereas the ancient Xiongnu had accommodated great tribal autonomy, the Turks and Qidan developed more robust polities, and the Genghisid Mongols even more so. The dominant mode of resource extraction likewise evolved. Nicola di Cosmo distinguishes between tribute empires that depended on payments from China and subordinates, from the Xiongnu at the end of the third century BCE to the Rouran up to the mid-sixth century CE; trade-tribute empires—exemplified by the Turks and Khazars during the following 350 years—that added control over long-distance trade routes to tribute-taking; dual-administration empires such as those of the Liao and Jurchen from the tenth through the mid-thirteenth centuries that increasingly relied on taxation; and the direct-taxation empires of the Mongols and Manchu that were made possible by the wholesale conquest of China.[63]

Throughout this period, as steppe powers shored up their capabilities, the interstitial phases between monopolistic (or duopolistic) empire in China itself kept contracting. Large-scale state formation thus became more deeply entrenched on both sides of the ecological divide. Intensifying interactions across the divide greatly contributed to this trend: just as exposure to the steppe increasingly shaped Chinese state formation, proximity to China prompted analogous developments in the steppe.[64]

Much of this hinged on two factors: the effective concentration of military power in the steppe and the persistence of the steppe frontier. Steppe polities performed way above their demographic weight. In one estimate, as late as the early twentieth century, all of Inner Asia from the Amur to the Pamir held maybe 12 million people, compared to half a billion in China proper. A thousand years earlier, the split had been closer to 5 million versus 80 million. The steppe coalitions that put serious pressure on the mighty Song empire were even more modestly sized: the Liao Qidan numbered less than a million people, and the Mongols under Genghis Khan not much more than that.[65]

Huge imbalances in military participation rates evened the odds. In nomadic societies, all able-bodied men could in principle be mobilized for combat. There were no native Turkic or Mongolian words for "soldier": the Turkic *er* equates any grown man with a warrior. Men (and also women) who grew up riding and hunting became inimitably well versed in horsemanship and mounted archery. Steppe armies enjoyed great mobility, as the vast grasslands allowed each fighter to draw on multiple horses for riding and carrying supplies.[66]

These advantages helped sustain endemic conflict. A broad survey counts more than 500 nomad incursions over the course of a little over two millennia (from 220 BCE to 1839), and almost 400 in the opposite direction. And even this underestimates the true scale of hostilities: according to just one standard reference work composed in the eleventh century, between 599 and 755 CE Turks in Mongolia accounted for 113 of 205 recorded attacks on Sui and Tang China, or 1.31 per year.[67]

It was thus for good reason that northern agriculturalists set up long border walls as early as the fourth century BCE, and that 2,000 years later, Ming and Qing cities along the Inner Asian frontier were equipped with walls that were significantly taller and thicker than those in other border regions. Finally, and most strikingly, statistical tests show a robust long-run association (from 220 BCE to 1839) between attacks from the steppe and the probability of China being a unified empire.[68]

Access to horses and exposure to nomadic combat styles enhanced military capabilities in the northern reaches of China, mainly though not only under the rule of conquest regimes from the contact zone. The success of northern Xianbei regimes that led to the Sui and Tang unifications and expansions, the role of steppe forces in preserving Tang rule, and the use of northern China as a launchpad for Jurchen and Mongols all reflect this long-term trend. It was not by coincidence that forces from the north generally captured southern China, rather than vice versa.

The underlying "steppe effect" was so powerful because it was perennial: for millennia, the presence of the steppe created a "persistent frontier" between China and Inner Asia. China's steppe frontier was determined by the limits of suitability for agricultural development regardless of political circumstances. This relative fixity set it apart from temporal frontiers elsewhere, such as the shifting frontier of colonized North America, or even the Pontic steppe—the grasslands north of the Black Sea—once it was gradually taken over by Russian settlers.[69]

This persistence was modulated by climatic variation that caused back-and-forth shifts in the extent of the cultivable zone: in the Middle Ages, for example, the grasslands appear to have been more extensive than they were later on. This volatility increased the likelihood of hostile encounters and generally added to the instability of steppe polities. The only constant was the principle that control of the (shifting) "marginal" border zone was a critical precondition for regional supremacy: if it was held by steppe groups, it facilitated southward attack; if held by China, it provided horses for its military and a buffer region for garrisons. Imperial regimes would alternately move in, as the Tang did, and retreat, as under the Ming.[70]

Students of premodern China are increasingly embracing an integrationist perspective, emphasizing international relations and especially the role of the northern frontier in macro-social development. This has greatly improved our understanding of the prominence of large-scale empire in East and Central Asia. But it is not enough to marshal evidence for the "steppe effect" in areas where it was particularly strong: we must also consider the inverse, its absence from large parts of Europe, and how it played out in other parts of the Old World.[71]

Europe

Interaction with steppe populations was of marginal significance for much of European state formation. Ecology was decisive: much of Latin Europe in particular was simply too far removed from the central Eurasian grasslands (see figure 8.6).

Only the eastern reaches of Europe were different. The westernmost segment of the Eurasian steppe, the Pontic steppe, had long hosted spatially extensive tribal confederations of horsemen. The Scythians and Sarmatians of antiquity were followed by the Hunnic federation of the fourth and fifth centuries CE, the khanate of the Bulgars and Onogurs in the seventh century, the Khazar khaganate from the late seventh through the tenth century, the Pechenegs in the tenth century, and the Cuman-Kipchak khanates from the eleventh through the thirteenth century. In addition, the Volga Bulgar polity persisted west of the Urals from the ninth or tenth century through the thirteenth century.

Eastern Europe was the only part of the continent where farming societies were consistently exposed to powerful steppe challengers, and consequently the only part of Europe that produced large empires after the fall of Rome and independently of the Roman heritage. A shadowy "khaganate" of Rus', established by Norse migrants in the eighth and ninth centuries, appears to have competed or otherwise closely interacted with the Khazar khaganate. Both set up incipient state structures that were sustained by slaving and taxing trade.[72]

Archaeological remains of ninth-century forts that protected Slavic agriculturalists point to political intensification in response to steppe predation. The arrival of the Pechenegs caused many of these positions to be abandoned by the early tenth century. The Turkic Khazar khaganate, centered on the Ciscaucasian plains, extended its reach up the Dnjepr, Don, and Volga basins in its quest for tribute. Yet at the same time, Kiev underwent significant development. It expanded at the expense of the seminomadic Khazars, pushing toward the Black Sea. Campaigning all the way to the Caspian Sea and drawing on elite cavalry forces, Rus' eventually succeeded in toppling the khaganate in the second half of the tenth century. Conflict with the Pechenegs likewise peaked at the turn of the millennium.[73]

Its ruler, Vladimir the Great, embarked on an ambitious fortification program to secure the center. Analogous to the long walls of the Chinese steppe frontier, massive ramparts designed to obstruct equestrian operations rose up to shield Kiev, precariously located "on an exposed outcrop of the Rus land" close to the nomadic zone. In a striking illustration of scaling-up impelled by competition with steppe challengers, its rulers strove to extend their power to the Slavic north and west to obtain resources for supporting a capital without much of an immediate hinterland. By the early twelfth century, campaigning in the steppe—often against the nomadic Cumans—had established greater stability. Turkic forces were employed to guard the borders.

It was in the wake of this triumph that the Rus' polity reached the zenith of its power. At that point, the decline of Byzantine influence and the lack of strong steppe opponents opened up space for centrifugal trends that effectively fragmented the realm well before the arrival of the Mongols in the following century. Cuman groups allied with Rus' factions were drawn into domestic power struggles. Both the rise and fall of Rus' were thus closely tied up with developments in the steppe.[74]

In the late Middle Ages, the Grand Duchy of Lithuania grew amid conflicts fanned by its prolonged retention of pagan customs and bitter rivalry with the Teutonic Order. Although in its formative stages it was sheltered from significant steppe influences, this changed as it expanded into the lands of former Rus': much of the fourteenth century came to be filled with conflict with the Golden Horde that culminated in campaigns all the way to Crimea.

In chapter 6, I briefly discussed the impact of nomadic invasion and rule on Russian state-building. Muscovy amassed power first in cooperation and then in conflict with its Tatar overlords. Muscovy benefited from Mongol-Tatar patronage when it was put in charge of collecting taxes on their behalf, and borrowed their military tactics and administrative practices. Tax revenue strengthened the hand of Muscovy's rulers and the central state. Well into the sixteenth century, nomad-style bow-armed light cavalry remained the backbone of their military. Anti-Tatar doctrines encouraged ideological integration. In 1571, almost an entire century after Muscovy had asserted full independence from the Golden Horde, Tatars were still able to torch the city of Moscow, and for another century or so Russian territory remained vulnerable to raids even as Tatar power steadily waned.

These interactions and pressures provided Russia with both the means and a strong motivation to expand, not only at the expense of the herders but also that of Poland-Lithuania to the west and rival Russian principalities. By 1820, Russia claimed control over 18 million square kilometers. Coupling this vast expanse of land with a relatively modest population of some 40 million, large parts of it had more in common with sparsely settled steppe empires than with other European states.[75]

Much of Europe, by contrast, was only lightly and intermittently touched by steppe influences. As noted in chapter 6, the Hungarian Plain supported only a limited number of mounted warriors. The Sarmatian Iazyges entered the Pannonian basin around the beginning of the Common Era, causing problems for the Roman military without ever rising to the status of a major challenger. The Huns were responsible for the first significant irruption of steppe forces into Latin Europe: yet after briefly challenging both halves of the Roman empire in the mid-fifth century CE—seeking tribute rather than conquest—their brittle hegemony quickly collapsed.

In the 560s, the Avars entered the Hungarian plain from the steppe. Their khaganate proved more resilient than Attila the Hun's but was also far less extensive: after expanding beyond the plains and threatening Constantinople in the early seventh century, they were unable to maintain control over Slavic populations south of the Danube and remained a regional power until they were shattered by Frankish assaults at the end of the eighth century.

As we already saw in Part III, the Magyars made a somewhat bigger splash. A century after the fall of the Avars, they took over the Pannonian basin and launched cavalry attacks on Latin Europe. In their raids of Germany, France, and Italy, they defeated all three parts of the Frankish domain and extracted tributary concessions until in 955, a German victory rather suddenly put an end to their predation.[76]

Their temporary successes owed much to the pervasive weakness of the European polities of the period, described in chapter 5. In the end, the Hungarian Plain's limited carrying capacity for horses and its relative isolation from the Eurasian steppe prevented Huns, Avars, and Magyars from exercising greater influence in European politics. This fundamental ecological constraint induced gradual shifts away from cavalry that in turn reduced the ability of these groups to project power. While the Hunnic domain was too expansive to be governable, the Avar polity could not withstand a determined challenger, and the kingdom of the Magyars was eventually incorporated into the European state system. And as noted in chapter 6, environmental conditions may also have played a role in the reluctance or failure of the Mongols to establish a stronger presence during the thirteenth century.[77]

Its geography and ecology protected Latin Europe even when its states were fragile and their defenses were feeble. With the exception of the Iberian peninsula, it was also shielded from incursions from the Maghreb. North African steppe tribes rarely achieved the level of organization required to enter the temperate zone, quite possibly because they lacked a sufficiently substantial settled hinterland against which to develop integrative capabilities.[78]

Most importantly, the core areas of later development—France, Italy, England, the Low Countries, western Germany—were particularly well sheltered from the steppe. This was also the zone in which post-Roman state deformation progressed the farthest. What little impetus clashes with organized herders gave to state-(re)building—the German victory over the Magyars in 955 temporarily strengthened the ruler's hand—soon fizzled in the absence of sustained challenges. Just as pressures from the steppe encouraged state-strengthening and empire-building in China and elsewhere in the Old World, their absence favored the opposite outcome in Latin Europe.[79]

From this perspective, it is telling that precocious state formation in early medieval England can be linked to meta-ethnic conflict with invaders from Scandinavia that prompted Wessex's expansion from the 860s to the 920s and concurrent domestic reforms. This process was but a pale shadow of what nomadic aggression might have accomplished, both in terms of conquest and in terms of the agriculturalists' response. No other European frontier generated similarly severe friction: conflict between Germans and Slavs could be managed on a more local scale, and other credible challenges were missing.

Remoteness from the bulk of the Eurasian steppe was a constant, invariant across European history. Just as it did not matter if Latin Europe's states were weak, it also did not matter if a large empire was in place. Unlike Chinese dynasties, the Roman empire did not bring forth a nomadic "shadow empire": there was no ecological potential for it. The Pontic steppe, where Sarmatian tribes might have coalesced in response to the inducements of Roman wealth, was too detached from the Roman heartlands that lay behind the Carpathians, the Alps, and the Adriatic. To the west of the plains of Eastern Europe, both components of the "steppe effect" were conspicuous by their absence: and so—at least after Rome—was empire-building on a large scale.[80]

Old World Parallels

Conditions in other parts of the Old World mirror the stark contrast between persistent imperiogenesis along the steppe frontier in East and eastern Central Asia and persistent political polycentrism in post-ancient Latin Europe: while those in South Asia and the Middle East bear some resemblance to those farther east, Southeast Asian outcomes were more similar to those in Europe. In all these cases, the relative strength of the "steppe effect" can be shown to have been of considerable importance.

SOUTH ASIA

India is situated at a considerable remove from the Eurasian steppe. However, the vegetated river plains of the Amur-Darja and Syr-Darja and zones of open shrubland form conduits for the southward movement of horses between them. In antiquity, the west of northern India used to be dominated by pastoralists. Over time, flows of invaders and the horse trade from or through that frontier region exerted growing influence on state formation on the subcontinent. Just as in early China, the first steps toward empire were not yet heavily affected by this factor: the Maurya military of the fourth through second centuries BCE mostly relied on infantry and elephants.[81]

For the next several centuries, conquerors from the Central Asian steppe took their place, first the Sakas and then the Kushanas, who boasted large numbers of mounted archers. Both the Kushanas and the homegrown Gupta empire in the fourth and fifth centuries CE faced challenges from Hunnic horse warriors. These conflicts led to the adoption of heavy cavalries of archers and swordsmen. Campaigns were waged across the Indus valley against Huns and Sasanian Iranians, and also in order to procure horses from beyond; the composite bow was introduced from the steppe. A massive Hun incursion in the late fifth century did not last long, hamstrung perhaps by the lack of sufficiently large pastures: in the longer term, sedentarization, as practiced by Kushanas and later Turks, was the only viable option, just as it was for steppe invaders of the Hungarian plain.

In keeping with Barfield's and Turchin's theoretical predictions, the end of the Gupta empire coincided with the cessation of nomad invasion and ushered in a period of prolonged polycentrism. Inasmuch as it did occur, sporadic empire-building relied on horses: in the first half of the seventh century, Harsha used a large cavalry force—established to defeat the Huns—to impose short-lived imperial rule. By contrast, in deference to ecological conditions, successive smaller regional states such as the Pala empire and south Indian polities deployed large herds of war elephants sourced from Bengal, Assam, and Orissa alongside infantry troops. At that time, in the late first millennium, only the Gurjara-Pratiharas of Kanauji marshaled a cavalry strike force to fight the Arabs in Sind.

Whereas the caliphate had been kept at bay, later Turkic conquest regimes made deeper inroads. In the tenth century, Ghaznavid cavalry proved superior to the Rajput armies of northwestern India. In the early eleventh century, the Ghaznavids conducted raids far into India to fund wars against Central Asian nomads who threatened their sultanate in Afghanistan, and recruited horse archers from Transoxania into their service. Once again, South Asia was drawn back into the orbit of belligerent steppe formations.[82]

The next frontier regime to take the Ghaznavids' place, the Ghurids, allegedly fielded a cavalry numbering 120,000—that is, "a lot" of cavalry—when they trounced the Rajputs in the northern Ganges basin in 1192, and came to rule not only Afghanistan but also the Indus basin and northern India. Their appearance marked a fateful shift from raiding to conquest, a project made possible by their access to horses from Central Asia and even Arabia and Iran.[83]

The next iteration, the Sultanate of Delhi, was credited with even vaster cavalry forces. Having subdued northern India, it managed to contain even the Mongols and briefly expanded into the Deccan. Horsemen were the backbone of their rule: in yet another example of the tax-and-empire nexus typical of steppe conquest regimes, much of the revenue from land taxes was used to remunerate them in cash, and the authorities maintained control over the supply of war horses. As their polity fractured, Timur invaded with a large cavalry army, sacking Delhi in 1398.[84]

The dramatic success of cavalry warfare and its crucial role in propping up large empires impelled imitation even in parts of the subcontinent

that lacked native sources of horses. In the Deccan plateau, the Vijayanagara empire arose in direct response to Muslim aggression spearheaded by a superior cavalry: in the fourteenth century, the ruler of the
Bahmani Sultanate in the northern Deccan plateau (a successor state to
the Sultanate of Delhi) was known as Ashavapati or "Lord of Horses."
Only once Vijayanagara began to recruit Muslim soldiers and built up
sizable cavalry forces by importing horses from the Middle East was it
finally able to compete, helped along by Bahmani's eventual fissioning.
Vijayanagara became the most militarized of the non-Muslim southern
polities: the semiarid environment of western India permitted the diffusion of high-quality horses—local breeds were inferior—and horse-
riding equipment from the northwest, such as the stirrup. This enabled
locals to catch up with established steppe-sourced cavalry regimes. As
a result, cavalry assumed a decisive role in combat even this far south.[85]

When Vijayanagara was defeated by Muslim sultanates in 1565, it was
cut off from the horse trade, retreated, and soon collapsed. A generation
earlier, Babur's invasion of northern India had succeeded thanks to the
deployment of a combination of horse archers and firearms. His Mughal
empire continued to privilege cavalry over local elephant forces. Once
again, an ambitious tax system supported a huge and expensive cavalry
of maybe 100,000 to 200,000 men that built the largest and most centralized empire India had seen thus far.[86]

Even though the influence of steppe groups on earlier Indian state
formation had already been considerable, the appearance from the
late twelfth century onward of conquest regimes that drew on steppe-
sourced horses and sometimes personnel was a major turning point. It
reversed a trend toward regionalization that had commenced after the
Gupta collapse and might have steered Indian state formation onto a
rather different trajectory.

Between the sixth and twelfth centuries, South Asia was divided
among regional states that were quite populous in absolute terms but
not relative to its total population. Their intermediate size and fairly
symmetric interstate competition fostered enhanced military and fiscal
capabilities and extended their longevity beyond that of the earlier hegemonic empires. In Lieberman's view, their "increasingly coherent

personalities suggest that South Asia may have been headed toward a permanent competitive multistate system not unlike that of Europe."[87]

Even so, exposure to Inner Asian pressures made this outcome less likely in the long run. Similar to the "marginal zone" between northern China and the great steppe, Afghanistan served as a conduit for exchanges with Central Asia and as a launchpad for invasions of northern India. In a further analogy, south Indian militaries were generally deficient in cavalries (but strong in naval assets), just as south Chinese ones were. South Asian ecology placed serious constraints on riders and herders: the lack of extensive grasslands limited their numbers, and high levels of humidity damaged their bows.

Yet these obstacles could be overcome by learning from local practices and, above all, by taxing large subordinate sedentary populations to sustain large cavalry forces that were replenished by ongoing imports of horses from farther north and west. High-endurance *turki*-horses were Central Asia's main export item to Mughal India: as many as 100,000 of them are said to have arrived there each year. Medieval Latin Europe, by contrast, lacked not only sufficient grasslands but also the fiscal infrastructure that might have made comparable forms of Magyar or Mongol rule viable.[88]

For close to 2,000 years, from the arrival of the Sakas in the first century BCE to the decline of the Mughal empire in the early eighteenth century, empire-building in South Asia was increasingly fueled by inputs from the steppe. As foreign conquest regimes relied on cavalry, indigenous polities sought to adapt and imitate accordingly. In this respect, the Indian and the Chinese experience had much in common.[89]

IRAN

Beginning in the early first millennium BCE, similar influences shaped Iranian state formation. Iran is connected to the Inner Asian steppe through rivers east of the Caspian Sea, which traversed terrain that was probably less arid than it is now. Farther west, the Caucasus, a formidable geological barrier yet endowed with meadows that nourished passing horsemen, could not prevent complementary infiltration.

While there is no solid evidence for nomadic pastoralism in prehistoric and Bronze Age Iran, the early Iron Age state of Urartu in the northwestern Iranian highlands was already associated with horse breeding and cavalry warfare. Cimmerian and Scythian raiders from the Pontic steppe assaulted Asia Minor and Mesopotamia. These advances coincided with the establishment of a culture of "equestrianism" in the high plains east of the Zagros Mountains that affected a whole range of traits from military tactics to costume, most notably the adoption of trousers that became a hallmark of Iranian culture.

The emerging hegemony of the Medes was the most visible political manifestation of these developments. Horse tributes from western Iran had greatly contributed to the apogee of Assyrian power from the mideighth century BCE onward. For all we can tell, the Medes' ascent was rooted in the fusion of cavalry forces into organized armies that managed to cut off the Assyrian empire from these vital supplies and subsequently wipe it out near the end of the seventh century BCE. It appears that the Persian Achaemenid dynasty that took over the Median domain likewise heavily relied on mounted troops when it assembled its enormous empire in the second half of the sixth century BCE. Horses and horsemanship played a prominent role in royal self-representation.[90]

Through co-optation and conflict alike, steppe power was crucial to Iranian empire-building. Various Iranian-speaking groups from the northeastern Iranian steppe frontier—Daians, Mardians, and Sagartians—served in the Achaemenid military. In the third century BCE, the Parthian empire of the Arsacid dynasty originated from a Daian confederation east of the Caspian Sea, in what is now Turkmenistan. Folkloric traditions that the Achaemenid and Arsacid dynastic founders Cyrus II and Arsaces I both originated from among these mobile herders reflect the latter's contribution to state formation.

At the same time, confrontation was endemic. In the sixth century BCE, Cyrus II died fighting the Massagetians, a grouping of nomads south of the Aral Sea, and Dareios I campaigned against the Scythians in the Pontic steppe. In the late second and early first centuries BCE, several Parthian kings battled Scythians, two of them losing their lives in the process. Not much later, a coalition of Daians and Sakas attacked the Parthian empire, and in 73 and 135 CE Alans from the Pontic steppe invaded by crossing the Caucasus.[91]

These conflicts continued under the Persian Sasanian dynasty. From the early fourth century CE onward, a succession of warlike steppe federations—Huns, Hephthalites, and Turks—posed a severe threat to the Sasanian empire, pushing back its garrisons across its northeastern frontier region. During a peak of hostilities in the late fifth century, King Peroz I was slain by the Hephthalites (or "White Huns") and his forces were annihilated. His successor, Kavadh I, deposed by his own nobles, fled to the Hephthalites and depended on their support to regain power later in exchange for accepting tributary obligations.[92]

These are not mere anecdotes. The largest Iranian empires of antiquity, those of the Achaemenids and Sasanians, were established and maintained in a symbiotic relationship with the equestrian societies of the Medes, Parthians, Huns, and Turks: both accommodation and conflict provided vital inputs. Interstate competition with Assyrians, Babylonians, and Romans, which is better documented in the surviving sources, tends to overshadow these dynamics, which were as foundational as they were persistent. Only the most dramatic incidents surface in the record: it is telling that whereas three Parthian and Sasanian kings died fighting steppe enemies, none of their peers succumbed to Macedonian or Roman opponents. Nor was the heartland of the Parthians ever threatened by Romans the way it was by challengers from the steppe. Cumulatively, these experiences were among the most potent drivers of state formation. It was not by accident that "Iran" came to be defined in contradistinction to "Turan," the term applied to the steppe regions beyond the northeastern reaches of settled Iran. Antagonism ran deep.[93]

Inputs from arid frontier zones further intensified beginning in the seventh century CE, as military groups first from the Arabian peninsula and then from Inner Asia took over Iran. Their cavalry forces played a central role in creating imperial polities and in reconfiguring domestic power relations in their own favor. Their regimes dominated the region for more than a millennium, from the early seventh through the late eighteenth century.

Arabs held on to power under the Umayyad, Abbasid, and Samanid dynasties, the last of these rooted in Khorasan and Transoxania right at the northeastern steppe frontier. The Umayyad caliphate inherited endemic conflict with the Central Asian Turks from its Sasanian predecessors. Not long after the ninth-century Abbasids had turned to Turkic mercenaries to maintain control, Turkic military regimes, sourced from the steppe, took over. They spawned a whole series of tribal-origin dynasties: Ghaznavids, Seljuqs, Khwarazm Shahs, Aq-qoyunlu, Qizilbash, and Qajars, while on occasion yielding to the Mongol Il-Khans and the Mongol-Turkic Timurids. Even in the northwest, Iranian Safavids mobilized nomadic Turkic tribes to establish their empire.[94]

THE LEVANT AND NORTH AFRICA

To the west of Iran, the Levant was similarly affected by the Arab conquests, the Turkic Seljuq takeover, the Mongol irruption, and the expansion of the Ottoman empire. By comparison, the contribution of pastoralists to regional state formation in the more distant past remains much less clear. The Amorites, who came to dominate the southern Mesopotamian core after the end of the third millennium BCE, cannot readily be identified as external herders. The same is true of the Hurrians who set up the Mitanni state in northern Mesopotamia and northern Syria soon after domesticated horses, war chariots, and composite bows had appeared in that region.[95]

Elsewhere, these new technologies as well as migrant groups associated with them, can nevertheless he shown to have been of some consequence. In Egypt, occupation by the Hyksos—most likely pastoralists from southwestern Asia—gave lasting impulses to later imperialism. They introduced horses as well as the composite bow and probably also chariots to the Nile valley. Their exclusive habit of burying horses in elite tombs called attention to their self-image as martial horsemen. Founded after the Hyksos' expulsion, the New Kingdom state accorded unprecedented prominence to military affairs: it oversaw the creation of a professional army that campaigned widely across the Levant, whose terrain offered improved access to horses and allowed chariot warfare to be massively scaled-up. The resultant empire was larger than anything Egypt had previously sustained.[96]

In other cases, the appearance of pastoralists did not turn out to be particularly conducive to polity growth: thus, the movement of the Aramaeans into the Syrian-Mesopotamian core, completed by the tenth century BCE, did not generate large empires. For most of the region, the explosive expansion of Iranian power in the seventh and sixth centuries BCE, outlined above, marked the true turning point. The most economical explanation for this transition might be that it took the more sustained engagement with the vast "reservoir" of the Eurasian steppe to make a real difference, whereas other, smaller marginal zones had, at least at the time, been too small or underdeveloped to exert a comparable influence.[97]

In this respect, the Maghreb occupied an intermediate position. Sizable empires appear to have been difficult to maintain. Both the lower organizational capacity of North African pastoralist tribes and the lack of a deep agricultural hinterland have been held responsible: however, we have to allow for the possibility that the former may have been influenced by the latter.[98]

Even so, some spatially extensive imperial polities did eventually appear under the Fatimids, Almoravids, and Almohads. The Fatimids depended on the military muscle of Berber tribes. The Almoravids received at least initial support from local nomads, and the Almohads were backed by Berber tribes from south of the Atlas. All of these nascent empires formed and matured in predatory interaction with more substantial agrarian hinterlands beyond their original heartlands. The Fatimid state's center of gravity first shifted to Tunisia and then on to Egypt. For the other two, the Iberian peninsula provided vital material resources and depth. Overall, outcomes were consistent with basic expectations related to the "steppe effect": while the often smaller scale of interactions between settled and steppe zones helps account for the relative paucity of indigenous imperial formations in North Africa, significant scaling-up of these interactions was essential for those few that did in fact come into existence.

SOUTHEAST ASIA

Were there any regions that were as well protected from the steppe as Latin Europe? Southeast Asia is the most promising test case: endowed with enough natural resources to support complex societies and large-scale state-building, yet far removed from the Inner Asian grasslands or any other steppe frontier, it was never dominated by hegemonic empires.

On the continent, a first phase of scaling-up commenced in the ninth century CE: Pagan expanded in Burma, Angkor in Cambodia and Thailand, and Dai Viet in Vietnam. Largely confined to the lowlands, these sizable but brittle polities were propped up by close cooperation with religious institutions—comparable perhaps to what had happened much earlier in ancient Egypt and Mesopotamia—and by favorable environmental conditions fostered by the Medieval Climate Anomaly that ensured strong monsoon rains. In the thirteenth and fourteenth centuries, all of them succumbed to escalating problems associated with population growth and climate change.

The period from the late thirteenth to the mid-fifteenth century was thus defined by political decentralization, followed by a phase of renewed concentration that lasted until the mid-sixteenth century. Even so, the latter did not result in hegemonic unification: in Lieberman's count, the number of polities merely fell from twenty-three in 1340 to nine or ten in 1540. In a region of a little more than 2 million square kilometers, this reflected a considerable degree of fragmentation.

Even this modest consolidation ended in a shorter and less dramatic phase of collapse in the second half of the sixteenth century, which was reversed by the expansion of Burma and Siam across western and central continental Southeast Asia while devolution continued farther east until Western colonial powers began to intervene. Over the long run, in terms of internal structure, the political landscape gradually transitioned from "solar polities" composed of quasi-sovereign satellite regimes that were loosely attached to small cores to more cohesive states with stronger centers—a shift not wholly dissimilar to what we observe in post-Roman Europe.[99]

Maritime Southeast Asia, split into many islands and even more distant from any steppe, was completely immune to steppe inputs: the Mongol attack on Java in 1293 remained a freakish outlier. Local horses were small and imports rare. In keeping with the "steppe effect" model, the entire region was characterized by enduring polycentrism. Segmented vassalage empires heavily relied on naval assets.[100]

I confine myself to the Old World. Prior to the reintroduction of the horse by European settlers, the New World likewise lacked steppe inputs, an absence that makes the imposing scale of the Inca empire even more remarkable than it would otherwise be: it joins the Roman empire as the only other genuine example of hegemonic imperiogenesis detached from the steppe.[101]

"Follow the Horses?"

Despite its brevity and inevitable simplifications, this survey has revealed a strong correlation between military inputs from the steppe and the scale of state formation across the premodern world. If taxes, highlighted in my discussion of fiscal institutions earlier in this chapter, were indispensable for empire-building, so were horses. The conspicuous scarcity of large empires in regions that were ecologically well equipped to support them but were sheltered from major grassland zones highlights the causal dimension of this association. My series of vignettes of the "steppe effect" from Western Europe to China focused on the mechanisms that rendered proximity to steppe frontier zones conducive to imperiogenesis on both sides of the ecological divide: the pooling of military assets for the purposes of predation, preemption, and defense; the dissemination of steppe-sourced military techniques; the infiltration and repeated takeover of exposed agricultural regions by steppe warriors, as well as responses to these intrusions.

The agrarian empires that were forged in these complex interactions were often large because they were close to the steppe, rather than close to the steppe because they were large. Hoffman, in his dismissal of geographic factors, reverses causation when he claims that large states like China were more likely to abut thinly populated regions where low rainfall would rule out sedentary agriculture and where herders, hunters, and armed raiders could thrive. . . . The large neighboring state would then face the risk of attacks by these nomadic groups, but the ultimate cause behind that threat would not be low rainfall in a nearby region but rather the size of the state itself, which was the result of politics.

Alongside an exceedingly rich historical record of which I have merely scratched the surface, statistical analysis of the correlation between the odds of China being unified and the frequency of nomadic attacks on it contradicts Hoffman's reading. Behind all this lies a more fundamental problem—his notion that political history created "different political geographies," and that "physical geography" can be juxtaposed with "political history" as if they were autonomous features. They were not. Political outcomes, such as patterns of state formation, were in no small measure contingent on geographic factors.[102]

Wherever it was ecologically feasible, Inner Asian interventions intensified over time. Although we ought not to underestimate their role even in some instances of ancient Near Eastern and ancient Chinese state formation, they did not generally make a decisive contribution to the emergence of the earliest empires. Inputs were mostly indirect, such as the diffusion of the chariot. As steppe cultures developed, their influence steadily grew. From the beginning of the fourth century CE, China's macro-political evolution was increasingly shaped by it, and from the seventh century CE onward, conquest regimes from marginal zones became the principal drivers of state formation in the Middle East. In South Asia, irruptions commenced near the end of the first millennium BCE and gave rise to the most dominant empires of the second millennium CE. In the High Middle Ages, Eastern Europe was likewise reshaped by interactions with the Inner Asian grasslands.

The impact of the steppe frontier peaked in the early modern period: whereas the Mughals ruled 5 million square kilometers and 175 million people in 1700 and the Qing 12 million square kilometers and more than 300 million people in 1800, the largest states of the "protected zone"—France, Burma, Siam, Vietnam, and Japan—in 1820 covered between 300,000 and 900,000 square kilometers and housed between 4 million and 32 million people.[103]

One final observation. Proximity to the steppe mattered not only because of the competitive dynamics it engendered among agriculturalists and pastoralists alike. It also skewed the deployment of resources in ways that could have a profound impact on polity size. Chiu Yu Ko, Mark Koyama, and Tuan-Hwee Sng have developed a simple model that tests for the effects of threat direction and strength on state formation. They compare a scenario in which a large region faces a severe threat but only from one side—the Chinese case of relative isolation combined with exposure to the steppe to the north—with one in which it faces two-sided but weaker threats, a stylized analogue of Europe with its robust linkages to Asia and North Africa but greater detachment from the steppe. In their model, political centralization—a single empire—turns out to be more resilient to a one-sided threat. On the other hand, fragmentation—a state system—is more resilient to a two-sided threat as long as military power projection by these external opponents is not efficient. The absence of strong steppe inputs satisfies this last condition.

These predictions mesh well with what we observe at opposite ends of Eurasia. In East Asia, the concentration of challengers to the north favored hegemonic empire among the agriculturalists, as well as the decentering of the capital cities toward the threat zone, a feature well documented for most Chinese dynasties. In Europe, the absence of a severe one-sided threat facilitated decentralization. Otherwise, overwhelming challenges might have destroyed members of a state system that were concurrently engaged in competition with their peers. The lack of such challenges thus both encouraged and enabled European polycentrism.[104]

CHAPTER 9

Culture

BUT WHAT ABOUT CULTURE? Didn't the First Great Divergence also grow out of beliefs and ideologies that influenced state formation? It is easy enough to enumerate contrasting ideational traits that distinguished Europe from China and may plausibly be linked to observed outcomes—and I will indeed do so in the course of this chapter, just as I already identified a series of putatively significant environmental features. Yet the chief question is that of priority. Within historical time frames, the physical environment was a given; culture was not.

Cultural evolution unfolded within the geographic and ecological constraints of that physical environment. As agriculturalists and pastoralists created niches that allowed them to elaborate their respective modes of subsistence, they were in many cases unable to overcome the most fundamental obstacles to transformative change, such as temperature and precipitation regimes. Dramatic interventions in the environment that were driven by political preference were rare, and with the exception of China's Great Canal were bound to remain rather limited in their overall impact on state formation.

It is not enough to show that culture and ideas mattered. That is banal. We also need to assess the extent to which they had been conditioned by the often intractable ground rules imposed by the physical environment. As we will see, while geography and ecology did not determine the cultural preconditions for macro-social scaling-up, they shaped and reinforced them through the outcomes they helped bring about. Over time, this caused different trajectories of state-building to become associated with different sets of cultural traits and ideological commitments, especially in elite circles.

LANGUAGE AND WRITING

China

Chinese logographic script can be traced back to the Oracle Bones of the Shang period in the late second millennium BCE, when it already appeared to be well developed. It underwent considerable evolution in the Western Zhou and Warring States periods. Two versions—now dubbed "seal" and "early clerical"—that had been systematized in the state of Qin spread across China proper upon conquest. Although cursive versions developed and were disseminated alongside them, different writing styles coexisted without resulting in meaningful regionalization. The writing system eventually became more fixed in late antiquity (as the so-called regular script).[1]

The Chinese language is likewise documented from the Shang period onward. Rime dictionaries reflect attempts to impose uniform pronunciation of characters. The creation of the most famous specimen, the *Qieyun* of 601 CE, coincided with the imperial restoration undertaken by the Sui and arguably sought to reconcile differences in usage between northern and southern China. Even so, regional deviations from Classical Chinese, which had crystallized during the Warring States and especially the Han periods, persisted.

At the same time, two factors contributed to linguistic unity. First, the fact that Classical Chinese dominated formal writing throughout the imperial period ensured a great degree of cultural homogeneity among the literate elite. From the twelfth century CE, vernacular Chinese came to be dominated by northern China dialects (Old Mandarin). "Official speech," rooted in this tradition, was employed as a uniform spoken language for late imperial—Ming and Qing—officials to guarantee mutual intelligibility. It was only in the twentieth century that this version was turned into modern Standard Chinese.[2]

Second, linguistic diversity within the core regions of Chinese had long been relatively moderate (figure 9.1). The long reach of Mandarin dialects was in no small part a function of the considerable ease of communication across the Central Plain—their original and much smaller core zone—as well as their more recent dissemination to the colonized frontier regions of Sichuan and Yunnan and later on Manchuria and Xinjiang. Conversely, much greater linguistic diversity survived in the southeast and south of China.

This pattern, not coincidentally, maps onto genetic variation, which is low in northern China and much higher not only between north and south but also among southern groups. The unusually high degree of homogeneity in the north was facilitated by gene flows across flat and politically united terrain.[3]

All this suggests that for all its diversity, China was relatively unified in ways that mattered to state formation. Elite communication was eased by a single writing system that allowed exchange across regional dialects, by an elite language that, unlike Latin, was never allowed to fade, and by uniform pronunciation among state agents, imposed from above. Moreover, the physical environment of northern China was conducive to demotic integration.[4]

Western Eurasia

No comparable unity existed at any time in western Eurasia. At the elite level, the Roman empire was resolutely bilingual and bi-alphabetic. Thanks to antecedent Greek migration and Macedonian imperialism, Greek was dominant in the empire's eastern half, whereas Latin became dominant in the west. While the two alphabets shared a common root and did not differ greatly, the languages were mutually unintelligible. The state class helped preserve this dualism: although Latin was obligatory in the military (and in Roman law), the elite of the politically dominant

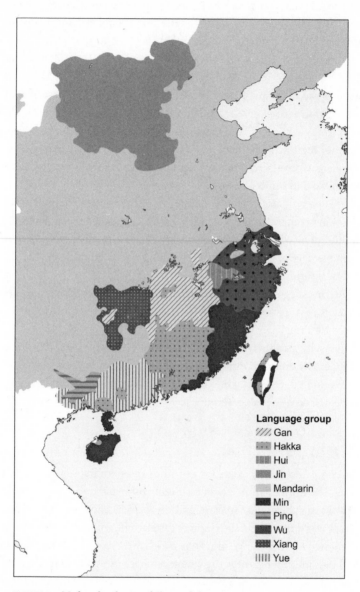

Language group
- /// Gan
- Hakka
- Hui
- Jin
- Mandarin
- Min
- Ping
- Wu
- Xiang
- ||||| Yue

FIGURE 9.1 Modern distribution of Chinese dialect groups.

west embraced bilingualism as a mark of high culture. Greek received an additional boost from the spread of Christianity, which was long dominated by Hellenophones from the east.

In addition, parochial languages continued to be spoken by large segments of the empire's population. Aramaic was common in the east, in Syria and Palestine, and a substantial corpus of literature was produced in Syriac. The Egyptian language flourished in its homeland and even acquired a new alphabet, Coptic, that was likewise employed in literature, even as Greek retained its leading position in this domain. Punic survived in North Africa until late antiquity, with Latin script being used to record it in inscriptions. In Gaul, spoken Celtic likewise persisted throughout the Roman period, quite possibly on a large scale. Asia Minor boasted a whole range of local languages: Phrygian even made a comeback in Christian inscriptions. Thracian languages are likewise known to have survived into late antiquity, and in Britain, Celtic endured and receded only after the end of Roman rule. By analogy, there is no compelling reason to assume that local languages disappeared from other regions such as (Iberian and Celtiberian) Spain, the (Celtic) Alps, and the (Illyrian) northern Balkans.[5]

In these regards, the sphere of Roman power was substantively more diverse than that of the contemporaneous Han dynasty: there was no single elite language and writing system, and parochial languages were much more prominent. The east–west split in elite circles was arguably the most consequential: while logistical constraints—foreshadowed by limited economic integration beyond often state-sponsored transfers and conduits of exchange—would have greatly contributed to the empire's eventual partition, it was hardly a coincidence that it fractured almost precisely along this linguistic fault line.[6]

Post-Roman developments further added to the mix. Arabic was introduced to the Levant and the Maghreb as well as, albeit less perduringly, to the Iberian peninsula. In Europe, the impact of the Germanic and Slavic diffusions varied a lot across regions. Gothic never became dominant in the Iberian peninsula, and Frankish (Old Franconian) made only limited inroads into Gaul, even though its northern and eastern reaches remained bilingual for centuries. Italy, where Latin was more deeply entrenched than elsewhere, was even less deeply touched by the presence of Goths and Lombards.

Other areas were more strongly affected. In England, Celtic (Common Brittonic) languages mingled with and were gradually pushed back by a complex array of Old English (introduced by Anglo-Saxon settlers), Old Norse (from Danes and Normans), and Old French (again via the Normans). On the continent, Germanic languages came to dominate Bavaria and Austria. Slavic infiltration took over much of the Balkans and the western Carpathian region.

Regional versions of Latin slowly but surely diverged into separate Romance languages. From the ninth century onward, in a process I briefly summarize in the Epilogue, literate residents first of France and then of Italy and the Iberian peninsula began to write down their own vernacular forms of Latin. As a result, even as the church maintained a single Latin standard, the language gradually lost its monopoly on literate and elite discourse. Instead of being blocked, linguistic regionalization was readily acknowledged and facilitated by political divisions. In the High Middle Ages, intensifying state formation actively promoted this process: at that point, most writing was no longer done in Latin at all.[7]

In all of this, it is important to distinguish cause and effect. China's single writing system existed because it had been sponsored by a single state. Mandarin was both imposed by the central state and spread under the umbrella of imperial unity and expanding settlement in the peripheries. Empire sustained and on occasion impelled cultural harmonization, and was in turn strengthened by it.

Despite this mutual reinforcement, basic counterfactuals suggest that the arrow of causation from state power to cultural unity was stronger than the one pointing in the opposite direction. Classical Chinese had been cemented by four centuries of Han rule, and its subsequent susceptibility to splintering leaves no doubt that political fragmentation mattered: had it run unchecked, linguistic divergences might well have continued, ending mutual intelligibility even in elite circles. Multiple writing systems might have emerged alongside these vernaculars. Nothing in the Chinese language or writing system per se favored unity and consolidation: it was the exercise of political power that provided the necessary impetus. As we will see shortly, the same principle applied to content, to the ideas that were being maintained and spread by means of a unified elite script and language.

In Europe, the degree of cultural heterogeneity was likewise heavily mediated by state formation. Ancient elite bilingualism and the persistence of parochial languages reflected the Roman laissez-faire style of provincial governance: while it would be unrealistic to assume that existing diversity could have been completely overcome, more deliberate policies of homogenization could presumably have made some headway over the course of half a millennium. Yet under the Roman template of local self-rule, this was not a plausible option.

Just as in China, the political order was a key determinant of the extent of cultural variety. On balance, the serially unified Chinese state was better able to foster some degree of homogeneity in elite circles and even beyond. Post-Roman Europe—or the post-Roman Mediterranean—faced much bigger obstacles. Arabic (and Islam, on which more below) spread because what was left of the Roman empire could not prevent it. Provincial versions of Latin morphed into Romance languages in part because they came to be associated with different (clusters of) polities. Latin became marginalized because the medieval sources of power were so strongly fragmented.

Once again, these developments mutually reinforced each other, as greater political fracture allowed greater cultural diversity, and vice versa. Yet also once again, at least in the early stages of this coevolutionary process, state (de)formation appears to have been the critical driving force. From this perspective, cultural features such as language and script are best seen as proximate and even secondary factors in accounting for the relative prevalence of large-scale empire.[8]

BELIEF SYSTEMS: RELIGION

How much did content matter in this regard? Maybe *what* was thought and said and written down—rather than *how* this was done—made a bigger difference. I begin my brief survey with religious beliefs before moving on to secular ones.

Western Eurasia

The ascendance of Christianity marks the biggest watershed in Europe's religious history. In substantive terms, this creed was undeniably imbued with considerable potential for constraining and challenging state power. Its most canonical texts drew a line between obligations to secular rulers and to God—"render to Caesar the things that are Caesar's, and to God the things that are God's." Its founding figure was thought to be the Son of God (and also part of God himself), not a mere prophet or some human pretending to be divine as Rome's emperors did.[9]

Most importantly, Christianity developed in latent conflict with the imperial state for the first 300 years of its existence: not only was it denied official recognition, let alone sponsorship, it appears to have been formally outlawed early on and was subject to sporadic local crackdowns. In the second half of the third century CE, as the empire narrowly survived an existential crisis, the central authorities adopted harsher policies of coercive suppression, even if they failed in the face of steadily growing Christian numbers, the state's poor infrastructural power, and divisions at the very top.

This backstory promised trouble for the state when the emperor Constantine in 312 CE performed a startling U-turn by embracing Christianity and his successors, with just one fleeting exception, followed suit, increasingly at the expense of established religions. The hopeful notion that rulers would be able to impose their will on the church and quell internal divisions proved largely illusory: the Christian movement preserved too much autonomy even as its elite cozied up to the imperial authorities for patronage, material and legal benefits, and support in the persecution of rivals within and beyond their own circles. Doctrinal disputes raged unabated despite repeated state intervention. Overall, the church's rapid accumulation of wealth and political influence at the central and local levels leaves little doubt that the Christian leadership in particular derived much greater benefits from its cooperation with the late Roman state than the latter obtained in return.

Bishops enjoyed tax immunity, managed growing largesse and estates, and assumed some delegated judicial functions. As the church was organizationally assimilated to the empire, a mirror hierarchy evolved, topped by leading bishops in the imperial centers, followed by metropolitan bishops with special prerogatives in provincial capitals and ordinary ones for individual urban settlements. This created a parallel career path to that in public service.

The most senior bishops displayed considerable assertiveness. In 390, Ambrose, bishop of Milan, excommunicated Theodosius I, the last to rule the unified empire, for ordering a massacre, and imposed a lengthy penance before readmitting him to communion. A century later, Rome's bishop Gelasius famously wrote a letter to the eastern Roman emperor Anastasius, reminding him in no uncertain terms that the world was primarily ruled by two powers, "the sacred authority of the priests and the royal power," of which the former "carried greater weight." Even though the meaning of this continues to be debated and Gelasius may not have intended more than affirming the principle that priests were in charge of spiritual affairs while subject to imperial regulation, the underlying dualism was normative. In practice, however, clergy were increasingly involved in the secular affairs from which this division of responsibilities was ostensibly meant to shield them. Even before the western empire unraveled, bishops came to perform civic functions and acted as community leaders.[10]

The subsequent fading of imperial governance weakened church leaders as they lost the backing of a vast imperial state but also increased their autonomy and allowed them to fill a growing secular power vacuum. In the end, the bishop of Rome, elected by the city's clergy and people— de facto local elite factions—benefited the most: detached from new centers of authority to the north and east, he never ran the risk of ending up as the appendage of an imperial court.

All over Latin Europe, bishops struck bargains with the rulers of the various Germanic successor states, who drew on them for subsidiary services and human capital. The weaker the central authorities were, the more they relied on such allies. In return, they granted the church greater judicial powers and freedom from obligations. Once again it was state formation that drove other developments: in the High Middle Ages, as social power became even more diffused and a reformed papacy rose to greater prominence, power-sharing between secular and religious leaders generated growing friction. Popes were now able to excommunicate emperors and foment risings against monarchs by backing their unruly nobles: as each side claimed supremacy, they undermined the other's position, as well as the cohesiveness and capacities of the polities involved.[11]

This form of conflict was not a given: Byzantine history demonstrates that notwithstanding its genesis and substantive claims, Christianity could be successfully "tamed" and subordinated to a centralized state, provided the latter lasted long enough. Just as the patriarch of Constantinople resided next to the emperor's palace, imperial and ecclesiastical power were closely enmeshed in an unequal relationship that privileged the former. The emperor appointed and invested the patriarch as a de facto state functionary, and could convene and preside over councils. Church property was liable to taxation. Earlier opposition by schismatic groups had waned following the loss of their core areas of support to foreign powers.[12]

The Byzantine experience, and subsequently that of Russia's Orthodox Church, amounts to a natural experiment that allows us to assess the determinants of Christian autonomy. Comparison of the Catholic and Orthodox churches strongly suggests that the extent to which Christianity's potential for divisiveness was expressed in practice was largely a function of state power. A political center's ability to control elite constituents, coerce rivals, and tax resources was the key variable: the lower this ability, the more the church was likely to interfere with state formation.

The larger polities of medieval Latin Europe generally scored poorly on all these metrics, and suffered the consequences. Conversely, had the entire Roman empire survived much longer or been restored on a comparable scale, a more acquiescent church might well have evolved. It is therefore misleading to identify "Western Christianity" as an ultimate cause of Europe's fragmentation: its path was secondary to outcomes in state formation. While Christianity undoubtedly contributed to post-Roman polycentrism, it was above all the antecedent weakening of centralized political authority that allowed and, indeed, encouraged it to do so.[13]

The rise of Islam probably had a much smaller influence than interference by the church on the scale of post-Roman state-building. In theory, the division of what had been the Roman Mediterranean between Christians and Muslims ought to have made it harder for a similarly large empire to be constructed in the same space even if this had been a viable project (which, as we saw in chapter 5, it was not). But it took a long time for this divide to harden. In Egypt, Iran, and later in Asia Minor, conversion to Islam appears to have taken several centuries following their conquest.[14]

Moreover, religious affiliation as such was not a serious obstacle to imperial expansion: in fact, diversity of customs and beliefs was a defining characteristic of many large empires. When in the seventh century Arabs took over the then largely Christian Levant, Egypt, and Maghreb as well as predominantly Zoroastrian Iran, they had no trouble ruling those territories. In the Iberian peninsula, Muslim rulers readily co-opted Christian Visigothic elites. The Seljuqs set up an empire that covered much of solidly Christian Anatolia, and the Ottomans later occupied the entire Christian Balkans and held on to them for centuries.

There is no good reason to believe that during the last third of the first millennium CE, the time of the First Great Divergence, the expansion of Islam was a significant obstacle to empire-building in Europe: while it may have added to the existing list of impediments, it was surely dwarfed by several of those. Most importantly, this issue is of no particular relevance for our understanding of polycentrism at its most durable, in Latin Europe. Inasmuch as religious beliefs interfered with the return of hegemonic empire, it was Christianity and not Islam that mattered.[15]

China

In China, the expansion of Buddhism represents the closest parallel to the rise of Christianity in late Roman and medieval Europe. Like

Christianity, Buddhism is a transcendent belief system, not tied to any particular polity, culture, or ethnic affiliation. Having originated in South Asia, it incorporated China into a larger ecumene that extended far beyond the confines of its imperial state, and offered an alternative to its traditional family- and state-centered rituals, the worship of ancestors, soil and grain deities, and Heaven (alongside its imperial intermediary). In short, Buddhism carried the potential for establishing significant autonomy from imperial institutions.

First referenced in China in 65 CE, merchants from Central and Southeast Asia helped spread this new creed. Just as Christianity had capitalized on the intermittent weakness of the Roman state in the third century CE, the Buddha's following soared during the Period of Disunion of the fourth through sixth centuries CE. Several of the northern conquest regimes provided support, in part because they regarded Buddhist communities as a counterweight to indigenous power networks. The rebuilding of state capacity in northern China consequently increased the scope for patronage.[16]

At the time, Buddhism might have seemed to have a chance to reshape power relations the way Christianity did in Europe. In southern China, under the Eastern Jin dynasty, it was agreed that Buddhist monks did not need to bow to the emperors, who in turn took vows to forgo Nirvana until they had redeemed all living things. Rulers posed as redeemers and saviors, and generously sponsored Buddhist temples and rituals.[17]

In the ascendant north, however, more autocratic regimes, while sympathetic to Buddhism, imposed more stringent regulation and formal hierarchies. In the late fourth century CE, the Northern Wei authorities appointed a chief monk to supervise religious activity. Emperors identified as incarnations of the Buddha and required gestures of subservience from monks. State sponsorships thus came with strings attached, and the supremacy of the secular ruler was not to be in doubt. Before long, an entire government department was put in charge of regulating the affairs of Buddhist monks and monasteries, and imposed restrictions on their proliferation.[18]

Even so, such interventions were widely disregarded. In the sixth century CE, the Northern Wei capital Chang'an alone supposedly boasted 1,367 Buddhist sanctuaries, and a similar number also existed in Luoyang, where only a single one was formally permitted. These figures need not deserve more credence than the reported existence of more than 700 such temples in southern Jiankiang, but they undoubtedly reflect a very strong presence. As illicit shrines and votive towers populated the countryside and itinerant monks spread the religion, 30,000 sanctuaries with 2 million monks were said to be found across the Northern Wei realm. The ranks of the monks were inflated by their exemption from taxation and labor services, which heightened the appeal of devotion just as similar privileges had done in the later Roman empire.[19]

Under the Sui, Buddhism became the primary state religion, and state support continued under the Tang. Over time, it was increasingly subsumed under the imperial order. The goal was to turn it into an extension of the state—its "spiritual arm," in Mark Lewis's words. Monks remained ubiquitous, most of them laymen claiming clerical status for personal gain.[20]

Unlike in late Roman or medieval Europe, however, patronage could easily give way to oppression. In a pro-Confucian backlash in 574, the Northern Zhou regime turned on Buddhists (as well as Daoists). Their monasteries, which hoarded money and grain, were targeted in order to raise funds for war. But only four years later, full restoration commenced.[21]

A similarly short-lived intervention occurred in the 840s when a new emperor favored Daoism. From 842, policy measures escalated, ranging from moves against unregistered monks and the confiscation of private property of clergy members to prohibitions of donations and pilgrimages and the purging of the court of Buddhist personnel and paraphernalia. In 845, the government outlawed temple estates and called for the surrender of institutional assets. Monks and nuns under the age of forty were to be laicized, and most foreign monks were expelled. Cult statues were melted down. The emperor boasted about the dismantling of more than 4,600 monasteries, the destruction of more than 40,000 chapels and hermitages, and the laicization of 260,000 clergy alongside extensive land confiscations. Only 49 monasteries and 800 monks were to remain in all of China. Once again, only a few years after the emperor's death, restoration was in full swing.[22]

These episodes are powerful testimony to the resilience and continuing appeal of Buddhism, but also demonstrate that the state retained the ability to intervene as it saw fit—even if it rarely did. The Roman emperor Julian's modest pushback against the Christian Church in the early 360s paled in comparison to these sweeping measures. Moreover, no Buddhist leader would have lectured an emperor on division of powers. Even though personal exemptions invited abuse and cut into tax revenue, institutional assets—of Buddhist monasteries and other bodies—were never sheltered from taxation. Thus, unlike in Europe, land and rents did not move beyond the state's reach. There were no clerical leaders to challenge or rival secular officials.

In the end, the imperial authorities succeeded in co-opting a potentially disruptive belief system at relatively modest cost. This accommodation had much more in common with the arrangements regarding the Orthodox Church than with the relationship between secular and religious leaders in Latin Europe. In all these cases, it bears repeating, state capacity was the decisive variable.

BELIEF SYSTEMS: IDEOLOGIES OF EMPIRE

Comparison highlights another, potentially highly significant difference between China and Europe: that China was endowed with a secular belief system that was arguably conducive to stabilizing and universalizing the state, whereas Europe was not, either in the Roman period or at any time thereafter.

A recent version of the argument runs like this. The Western Han period—the first phase of stable hegemonic empire—witnessed the rise of a dominant ideology that merged Confucian norms with elements of the Legalist doctrines that had flourished in the late Warring States. Both of them concentrated on human social relations and ethics: while Confucian teachings emphasized loyalty, respect for parents and ancestors, altruism, rules of propriety, social harmony, and a sense of being part of a network of mutual obligations, Legalist writers were more mundanely concerned with the practicalities of shoring up the power and resources of the state and strengthening the central government vis-à-vis the individual and especially elite groups by means of legal and administrative intervention.[23]

Once the swift collapse of the imperial Qin regime had discredited narrow applications of Legalism, a broader-based belief system that married Confucian ethical and social precepts with Legalist regulations and techniques proved much more resilient. In practical terms, the combination of the celebration of the state's dominance—focused on the image of an idealized yet constrained ruler—with the political and social dominance of officials who were inculcated with Confucian norms created an elite-centric ideological edifice that was "tailor-made for the support of the state."

Generally privileging it over competing beliefs, state sponsorship and elite collusion turned this powerful construct into "the dominant political ideology and the normative base of cooperation between emperors and their officials." Even though lineage, patronage, and wealth continued to matter a great deal, access to public office was at least ideally to be governed by considerations of canonical learning and social mores. This approach permitted an effective fusion of traditional and meritocratic principles. It also placed limits on rulers in the exercise of their power that in other cultures might have been imposed by religious prescriptions.[24]

Other doctrines played a lesser role in Chinese state formation. In the first century BCE, ancestor worship that revolved around the founder of the Han dynasty was replaced by the cult of Heaven, which placed the emperor at a pivotal position between Heaven and Earth. This cult grew in importance under the Eastern Han but remained limited in scope and largely confined to the capital region. Confucianism, by contrast, was more organically connected to the widespread and steadily growing custom of ancestor worship. It maintained its dominance among elite circles in competition with rival perspectives such as Daoism. Although the imperial collapse of the fourth century CE weakened political Confucianism and the early northern conquest regimes favored Buddhism, the subsequent restoration of centralized state power went hand in hand with a growing commitment to traditional elite Confucianism within the rebuilt administrative apparatus.

From the late Tang period onward, Confucianism underwent a more general revival and gained momentum under the Song, which presided over a massive expansion of the imperial examination system. At the expense of hereditary elites, officials came to be equated with scholars. The gentry class claimed status based on immersion in the canonical texts. As the number of learned graduates greatly exceeded that of available positions in the civil service, many of these individuals operated at the local level in unofficial capacities, where they disseminated Confucian thought among larger segments of the population. Its preeminence thus secured, this system of norms and beliefs remained of central importance until the end of the monarchy.[25]

Confucianism's impact on economic development will be considered in chapter 10. At this point, the question is how it was related to state formation and especially to the persistence of large-scale empire. Prima facie, the Chinese arrangement ought to have supported state stability and capacity: its principal tenets were "government-friendly," and the fusion of political and ideological power in the hands of the administrative class helped check both military and economic power bases.

Just like the imperial state itself, this dominant belief system became more deeply entrenched over time. Once again, much in the same way as in the cases discussed earlier in this chapter, the arrow of causation points primarily from state formation to beliefs. The Confucian-Legalist system was first set up under unified rule. It was revived when state power recovered in the north during the later stages of the Period of Disunion. And it greatly gathered strength under the Song dynasty, which had established the strongest state in China thus far.

This belief system did best when the state was strongest and the empire was intact—and thus able to provide sponsorship and material and status benefits to rent-seeking elites. It was at its most stable during the second millennium CE, when China was essentially either united or, at worst, split in two. All this speaks strongly in favor of explaining the success of this particular brand of elite Confucianism's success with reference to the fortunes of empire, rather than the other way around.

This, however, is not the whole story. In a series of fascinating studies, Yuri Pines has argued that the idea of imperial unity preceded actual political unity, and that it persevered also when China was more fragmented. This would complicate the proposed link between state formation and hegemonic beliefs. According to Pines, a paradigm of unity had already developed during the Warring States period, perhaps in response to the increasingly violent failure of its multistate order. Most of the surviving texts that engaged with these issues favored political unity and rejected the existing competitive state system.[26]

In this reading, thinkers promoted universal empire as it were *avant le fait*, as the best or only way to bring about peace. Their reasoning was often embedded in the past, harking back to conditions under the hegemonic Shang and Western Zhou dynasties. The main question was not whether but how to unify the various states. Pines notes that not a single surviving text openly endorsed a regional state's independence. Even though we have to allow for the possibility of later redactions or censorship under imperial rule that might have suppressed such unwelcome preferences, this overall preoccupation with imperial unity is certainly worthy of attention.[27]

At the time, rather limited geographic horizons may have made it possible to "consider the creation of a state unifying the whole known world to be a feasible goal," although China's actual geographic isolation would deserve some credit for this perspective. But even later, the concept of imperial unity enjoyed "political-cultural hegemonic status." It also endured under regional conquest regimes.[28]

The idea of a single emperor formed a natural corollary: early sources such as the *Mengzi* already attributed to Confucius himself the adage, "There are neither two suns in heaven nor two monarchs on earth." Pines notes that there could be many gods in China but only one legitimate ruler, as opposed to the One God and many rulers of Christian Europe—a telling contrast, even if this analogy misrepresents the Chinese emperor's standing, which was nothing like God's.[29]

Overall, these notions were reinforced by an ongoing project of streamlining elite thought that can be traced back to concerns about division as early as the late Warring States period and to the overt support of the Han authorities for Confucianism. This "drive toward ideological uniformity" greatly strengthened during the second millennium CE. Moreover, the longevity of the gentry class whose socialization was so heavily influenced by these beliefs helped preserve and spread them in the long run.[30]

All of this is well and good as long as we are interested in the history of ideas about political unity and the hegemonic role they played in elite thought. Pines is surely right to remind us that an exclusive focus on texts produced by and for the ruling class is not a problem as long as we seek to understand dominant notions specifically in those circles rather than among the population as a whole.[31]

The possibility that later revisions would have allowed the early literary tradition to be adjusted in the light of the later imperial unity represents a more serious concern. I must leave to the experts the question of the extent to which the impression of an ancient normative commitment to a single empire is a function of selective transmission, retrospective state-sponsored production of literature, and other constraints. What I am interested in here is what this tradition could tell us if we were to accept it as representative of actual elite preferences.[32]

In that case, how (much) did such beliefs influence state formation? On this point, Pines is coy. On the one hand, he makes it clear that he does not seek to give a comprehensive interpretation of "the empire's exceptional prowess"—which (he notes) would need to take account of geographic, economic, military, religious, and (other) cultural features—but elects to home in on ideas of unity. On the other, there is considerable slippage from merely foregrounding this feature to effectively privileging it in explaining overall outcomes: thus, the reasons for imperial persistence "and, most of all, for its regeneration after periods of division," "should be sought primarily in the realm of ideology."[33]

The problem with this approach is immediately apparent: a research design that concentrates only on ideas while ignoring other factors cannot, by definition, establish the relevance and relative weight of this or any other factor—and, strictly speaking, cannot even show that ideas mattered at all. For instance, when Pines curtly dismisses the notion that geographic properties might have been decisive by averring that "clearly, preserving the empire's unity was as challenging a task in the Chinese case as it was for other continental empires," nothing is in fact less "clear"—not because this observation is right or wrong, but because in order to tell whether it is right or wrong we would have to engage in systematic cross-cultural comparison well beyond what I have been attempting in this section of the chapter. Talking about ideas alone, as Pines does, provides absolutely no basis at all for such a sweeping judgment.[34]

Throughout his discussion, a particular relationship between ideology and actualization is assumed rather than argued, let alone demonstrated. Thus, while it is indeed remarkable that notions of imperial unity predate its existence, it in no way follows from this that "the Great Unity paradigm was not an outcome of, but rather a precondition for the imperial unification of 221 BCE"—which may or may not be the case.[35] Pines's claim that "insofar as everybody expected unification, it became a self-fulfilling prophecy" amounts to yet another non sequitur.[36]

The fact that the violent Qin unification unraveled almost immediately ought to discourage notions of self-fulfilling prophecies. No matter: according to Pines, even as the empire fractured a number of times, it was invariably saved by an "inherent understanding that political fragmentation must inevitably be reversed." This is a gloss on the famous saying from the *Romance of the Three Kingdoms*, that "they say that the great forces of All-under-Heaven after prolonged division must unify, and after prolonged unity must divide." It should hardly be necessary to point out this is merely an empirical observation of what happened in Chinese history and not a causal analysis.[37]

Nor is it a given that "this ideological paradigm deeply influenced political behavior in the ages of unity and division alike." Consideration of basic counterfactuals shows us why. If dynasties in charge of all of China had lacked this ideational input, would they have failed sooner? Or not arisen at all? If polities in times of division had lacked it, would they have refrained from trying to conquer each other, or been less successful at it? All of this is perfectly possible but would need to be argued rather than blithely assumed. It is objectively true that in times of disunity, Chinese states failed to develop a durable state system along European lines and were keen to launch mutual wars of extermination that left unity as the only viable solution. Yet this outcome might just as readily have been a function of factors other than normative elite beliefs, just as the European state system was itself an anomaly derived from very specific circumstances in a variety of different domains.[38]

It may well be true that thanks to the administrative class's deep immersion in canonical texts that endorsed imperial unity, "The empire . . . throughout its history had been primarily an intellectual rather than merely a sociopolitical construct." Yet Pines's plausible rejection of an exclusive role for the latter does not logically establish the former's primacy—and once again it does not tell us anything tangible about how empire came about.[39]

None of my observations detract from the likelihood that ideology contributed meaningfully to imperial longevity, actuated by the attitudes and behavior of elite members that sought to ally themselves to a powerful state and thereby increased its capacities. However, there is nothing to suggest that empire on this scale would not otherwise have existed, or that elite preferences were a critical driving force. The former notion entails extravagant counterfactuals, and the latter is better replaced by a dialectical dynamic of empire and ideology mutually reinforcing one another over time, alongside other features such as cultural learning—which taught the central authorities what worked best—and the elite's symbiotic dependence on state support and vice versa.[40]

I belabor the pitfalls of Pines's approach so as to clarify the risks inherent in prioritizing ideology. Scaled back to a more reasonable level, the idea that, all other things being equal, beliefs made China's political unity more likely than, say, Europe's is perfectly unobjectionable. But other things were not at all equal. Was Chinese-style ideology more likely to flourish in a physical environment that otherwise facilitated unity?[41]

Apart from geography and ecology, institutions also mattered. The Greco-Roman world, with its city-state ecosystem and precocious republicanism, was not only less likely to develop a belief system akin to China's Confucian-Legalist blend, but such a construct would also have been less likely to succeed. By contrast, once the Warring States period had centralized and homogenized territorial polities with an intensity unknown in ancient western Eurasia, beliefs that showed strong affinity to this political order had a better chance to prosper than the many other schools of thoughts that had once bloomed, not least because they were stronger candidates for sponsorship by the state.

Philip Hoffman provides a parallel in his speculative attempt to link post-Roman European polycentrism and belligerence to cultural evolution rooted in the absence of a strong state. This helped give rise to an unfettered warrior ethos that might otherwise have been stifled by more intrusive political institutions. Cultural norms that prized martial prowess and victory worked best for elites and their retainers that operated within rudimentary governance structures, which in turn reinforced fragmentation. This trend can be set against a different trajectory of cultural evolution in China that tended to pacify elites, a process that would presumably have been more difficult to sustain in a war-oriented competitive state system.[42]

The cumulative weight of history was bound to make itself felt. Whereas empire had been unheard of in most of Europe before the Romans came along, city-state culture had long been entrenched across the Mediterranean basin as an alternative—and thriving—mode of social organization. As part of its expansionist project, the Roman imperial state actively disseminated this tradition into Western Europe, encouraging local communities to organize themselves according to a quasi–city-state template.

Conversely, the early Chinese experiment of self-governing city-states was short-lived, and never produced a comparable ecology of inclusive micro-polities. Much the same was true of feudal relations as another alternative format of sociopolitical organization. They effectively disappeared from China during the Warring States period. Peter Lorge invokes their absence for more than a millennium when he notes that by the tenth century CE, when China entered another phase of fragmentation and renewed restoration, "the only higher-order political structure intellectually available was the imperial one"—and that had arguably been true for a long time.[43]

Trying to detach the formation of belief systems from the formation of states is a quixotic endeavor, an idealist game that privileges high-end thinking simply because it can. One does not need to be a hardened materialist to grasp this fallacy, and the critical response to Pines's work demonstrates that it is in fact widely understood, even in an academic field as traditionally text-centered as the study of early China: "What Pines is describing and explicating is the endurance not of an eternal empire, but rather the persistence of a common discourse of imperial authority."[44]

CULTURE, STATE POWER, AND STATE SCALE

So what about culture? As we have seen, it is not hard to identify a whole range of differences: between a single script and elite language in China and the multiple writing systems and languages in the Roman empire; and between the persistence of the elite Chinese tradition and the gradual marginalization of a shared elite language in Latin Europe as vernacular languages and literatures emerged. Latin Europe hosted an initially and then once again increasingly autonomous church that simultaneously partnered with and checked the state. In China, Buddhism, which had the potential to play a similar role, operated under tighter constraints imposed by a stronger state. In the secular ideological sphere, China boasted a unifying elite belief system that Europe utterly lacked, and that helped draw the gentry into sustained cooperation with the central state.

Setting aside the question the extent to which these features were secondary—a function of state formation—there can be little doubt that on balance, the Chinese traditions offered greater support to the integrity and capacity of the state than those that prevailed in Europe. Some of the Chinese traits, such as commitment to public service, favored the state as such. Others, from language and writing to the hegemonic emphasis on universal empire, lowered the cost of large-scale political unity.

In medieval Europe, ideological features limited state capacity while linguistic diversity impeded unity. Even so, empire generally accommodated variety: multilingualism may have raised the threshold for imperial unification and persistence but did not by itself prevent imperiogenesis. In that sense, cultural constraints on universal empire in Europe were weak, especially given that the most serious ruptures within Latin Christendom did not arise until the sixteenth century. By comparison, traits that restricted state capacity more generally were more potent, interacting with other sources of power dispersion that I discuss in chapter 10. In the end, it was low state capacity rather than an insufficient degree of cultural unity that impeded large-scale state formation.

This assessment is consistent with what we observe in other parts of the Old World. The Islamic world was divided by the use of Arabic, Persian, and later, Turkic languages but held together by the religiously dominant Arabic script. The religious establishment exercised considerable influence yet remained subordinate to militarized conquest regimes. Rifts within the *umma* appeared very early on, just as they had among Christians. Nothing like the medieval papacy ever evolved in Islamic societies, nor did a secular belief system of the Chinese variety. Overall, and putting it very crudely, key cultural features contributed more to state capacity than in Europe but less so than in China. Outcomes in empire-building likewise occupied an intermediate position.

Much the same was true of South Asia: characterized by considerable linguistic as well as alphabetic diversity, it featured a deeply entrenched religious establishment, lacked a secular ideology associated with the state, and experienced a rift between Hindus and Moslems just when Hinduism had supplanted Buddhism. Self-replicating castes and self-regulating temples did not rely on state authority, and unlike the Chinese gentry, Brahmins were assured high status without joining a civil service. In all these respects, as far as integrative cultural traits are concerned, India bore a greater resemblance to Europe than to China. And its largest empires often proved brittle.[45]

Notwithstanding the spread of an early Sanskrit ecumene into its elite circles, Southeast Asia was similarly diverse in language, writing systems, and religious beliefs, and home to powerful religious organizations. As part of the "protected zone," it was spared foreign conquest regimes. Instead, as Lieberman notes, its polities were run by elites who were ethnically and religiously the same as their subjects and thus "often sought to politicize ethnic loyalty as an aid to governance and wartime effort," a strategy that also played a role in modern European state formation and ultimately favored political regionalism over universal empire.[46]

Across the Old World, long-term patterns of state formation were associated with specific configurations of cultural traits that can be thought to promote or inhibit imperiogenesis. After the fall of Rome, the polities of Latin Europe were long exposed to, and in turn amplified, a colorful mix of cultural "spoilers." In China, the opposite was the case, as universal empire proved ever more resilient. Conditions in the Islamic world and South Asia fell in between, whereas Southeast Asia had more in common with Europe.

CONCLUSION: THE FIRST GREAT DIVERGENCE AS A ROBUST AND CAUSALLY OVERDETERMINED OUTCOME

Let us pull the various threads together. In this part of the book, my discussion has centered on a recurrent theme: that a wide variety of physical, institutional, and cultural properties were associated with and arguably conducive to empire-building on a large scale in East Asia but not in (Latin) Europe. Some of these features were constants, others more specific to the second half of the first millennium CE. In their complex interactions, they help us explain the phenomenon of the First Great Divergence (table 9.1).

The terseness of this matrix calls for explication. "Extractive capacity" covers both fiscal performance and—complementarily or alternatively—the intensity of military mobilization, and refers to the extent to which central state authorities managed to appropriate resources for their own purposes. This capacity was lower in the sub- or post-Roman polities of Latin Europe than in the principal Chinese states that were able to count and tax their populations in ways

TABLE 9.1 Determinants and outcomes of state formation in (Latin) Europe and China, c. 500–1000 CE

Region	Predominant features				Predominant outcomes			
	State extractive capacity	Geographic integration	Steppe effects	Cultural/ ideological integration	State power/ stability	Weak regional states	Strong regional states	Universal/ hegemonic empire
Europe	low (declining)	–	–	–	declining	yes (←)	?no	no
China	med. ↔ high	+	+	+	med. ↔ high	no	yes ↔	yes

Germanic regimes were not. During the period in question, it almost universally declined from a low base to even lower levels.

In China, by contrast, capacities varied between phases of strong centralization with good registration coverage and respectable fiscal extraction rates and phases of retrenchment, albeit—and crucially—not normally to levels as low as those in early medieval Europe, except perhaps in the most ephemeral of interstitial polities. These shifts were oscillations, as opposed to the generally downward trend observed in most of Latin Europe.

Geographic, ecological, and cultural factors have been discussed in some detail. While it is admittedly awkward to assign each of them a single value, my metrics are strictly *relative*: "plus" and "minus" simply denote conditions that were "more" or "less" conducive to large-scale state formation.

Among outcomes, state power and stability are correlated with the pattern produced by the previous columns: decline in Latin Europe and oscillation at higher levels in China. The shift back and forth between relatively capable regional states and more or less centralized hegemonic empire in China matches the other fluctuations: these shifts occurred on a spectrum between centralized empire and regional states that sometimes teetered on the brink of more serious devolution but never quite succumbed.

By comparison, the regional polities of Latin Europe of this period are best defined as weak. In a more charitable reading, one might think of their development in terms of a shift from stronger to weaker states:

yet even the early sub-Roman regimes, or the Carolingian empire, were not as capable as the northern Chinese kingdoms of the sixth and tenth centuries. At most we might concede the possibility of a lesser shift, marked as doubtful in table 9.1.

Two things matter most. One is the unidirectional character of European developments compared to the back and forth in China. The other is the level of state capacity and scale from and to which these shifts occurred. If we look at the notional endpoints of around 500 and 1000 CE, the dominant trends moved toward imperial restoration in China and toward inter- and intrastate fragmentation in Latin Europe.

My matrix is designed to show, at a glance, how consistently putatively significant factors pointed in one direction in one case and in the opposite case in the other. In post-Roman Europe, multiple circumstances obstructed large-scale state formation, whereas in post–"Sixteen Kingdoms" China, they favored it. Some—geography and ecology—did so by nature, as it were, although the Sui regime actively enhanced spatial integration. Others—most notably language and belief systems— operated over the long term. Others still—extraction and mobilization capacity—were more narrowly circumscribed and contingent.

This synopsis presents us with an analytical problem and a pragmatic insight. The problem is that the congruence of different factors makes it harder to identify the essential variables. The insight is that for present purposes, this does not matter all that much. Regardless of which variables we privilege, the finding is always the same: that prevailing circumstances favored a certain outcome in China and a different one in Europe. In this fundamental sense, these discrepant outcomes were robust, and they were robust because they were overdetermined.

This striking degree of congruence and thus overdetermination likely owes a lot to interaction effects between anthropogenic and environmental factors. Both this mutual reinforcement and the minimal sample size $(N = 2)$ makes grudging acceptance of overdetermination instead of a weighing of individual variables seem a justifiable rather than merely an intellectually lazy compromise.

Moreover, the congruence that is reflected in my matrix meshes well with the robustness of the counterfactual findings in Part III, which dispel the notion that post-Roman Europe was at any time gravitating toward hegemonic empire. The trifecta of consistent patterns in historical outcomes, in plausible counterfactual outcomes, and in the basic drivers and correlates of state capacity and empire formation highlights the overall solidity of the First Great Divergence—as well as, once again, the outlier status of the Roman empire. From this perspective, what is astonishing is not that the First Great Divergence happened, but that it needed to intervene at all, that the preceding convergence had occurred in the first place.

• • •

Table 9.1 could be expanded to include other parts of the Old World. I refrain from this exercise mainly because it would be a challenge to assign simplified values in a consistent fashion to a larger number of different cases. In the most general terms, South Asia and the Middle East and North Africa region would retain their by-now-familiar position between the extremes of China and post-Roman Europe.

In the Middle East and North Africa, frequently high levels of state capacity persisted under a long sequence of conquest regimes that were more or less adept at erecting larger imperial structures. The Nile valley and Mesopotamia permitted some concentration of resources but did not form huge natural cores such as China's Central Plain. The Middle East was heavily exposed to multiple steppe frontiers. Religious and political leaders found themselves locked into mutual interdependence, yet without developing the intimate accommodations of Confucianism. In South Asia, state power could be more brittle, yet without sinking to the lows of early medieval Europe. River basins formed natural cores but were (still) less subjected to inputs from the steppe. The dominant belief systems were not closely tied to the state.

In both cases, state formation oscillated between large-scale empire and capable regional polities, but differed in specifics, between a temporary shift away from hegemonic empire in the Middle East and North Africa region as regional conquest regimes formalized the effective decentralization of fiscal structures, and the generally stronger resilience of regional states in South Asia. These broadly intermediate outcomes between China's imperial revival and Latin Europe's deepening polycentrism correlate well with the lack of consistent trends among key features ranging from extraction rates and cultural traits to geographic and ecological conditions. Across the Old World, the scope and resilience of large-scale empire in the age of the First Great Divergence was intimately bound up with a mere handful of crucial variables.

PART V

From the First to the
Second Great Divergence

CHAPTER 10

Institutions

WHAT MADE THE SECOND GREAT DIVERGENCE POSSIBLE?

WHY DOES it matter that Europe was so fragmented? My answer is straightforward. This polycentrism is key to explaining the (Second) Great Divergence, the Industrial Revolution(s), and thus the Great Escape. Almost all of the many competing interpretations that seek to account for these radical transformations are predicated on this one feature of European sociopolitical evolution. This is true irrespective of whether these reconstructions privilege institutions, global connectivity, or cultural characteristics—and whether or not their proponents are aware of this shared underlying premise. By all accounts, the transition to the modern world was deeply rooted in the First Great Divergence.[1]

This perspective has a long pedigree. Montesquieu thought that Europe's fragmentation "formed a genius for liberty" by favoring the "government of the laws" over despotism. He was on the right track: as we will see, smaller polities enjoyed greater capacity for more inclusive forms of rule than large empires, and interstate rivalries were a crucial driver of institutional development. Immanuel Kant likewise objected to the idea that all the states should be merged into one under a power which has gained the ascendancy over its neighbours and gradually become a universal monarchy. For the wider the sphere of their jurisdiction, the more laws lose in force: and soulless despotism, when it has choked the seeds of good, at last sinks into anarchy.[2]

One and a half centuries later, Chairman Mao opined:

One good thing about Europe is that all its countries are independent. Each of them does its own thing, which makes it possible for the economy of Europe to develop at a fast pace. Ever since China became an empire after the Qin dynasty, our country has been for the most part unified. One of its defects has been bureaucratism, and excessively tight control. The localities could not develop independently.

This is in some ways even closer to the mark, even if it greatly exaggerates the reach of centralized power: as it turns out, empires' relative lack of infrastructural capacity was an even greater retardant of modernizing growth.[3]

Modern scholarship has addressed the relationship between state-building and human welfare in incomparably greater depth. The insights it has generated help us identify significant variables and connectivities. I begin with a deliberately overly simple model of two starkly different ideal types of state formation and their respective developmental corollaries (figure 10.1).

The "polycentristic" variant provides a rough approximation of conditions in post-Roman Europe. The fall of Rome ultimately gave rise to multiple states that did not dramatically differ in terms of capabilities (smaller but more cohesive polities balanced less-well-organized larger ones), mobilization intensity (Roman-style levels of conscription did not return until the French Revolution), mode of production (most Europeans were farmers and lived far from the steppe frontier), and religion (Christianity steadily spread into the northern and eastern reaches of the continent while Islam failed to make much headway). All this ensured that interstate competition was fairly symmetric in style:

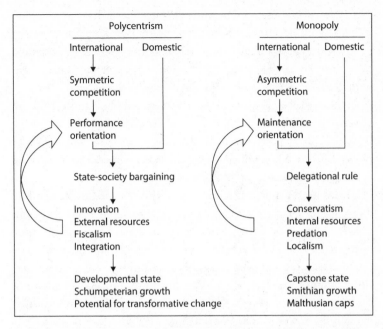

FIGURE 10.1. An ideal-typical model of the developmental dynamics of different types of state formation.

with like fighting like. Not least because of this, it also remained inconclusive, as no one party ever managed to overpower all the others.

In the long run, this environment rewarded political, military, and economic performance, which was largely a function of state capacity. In principle, this impetus might have fashioned European states into ever-more-tightly centralized and autocratic entities akin to the ancient Warring States of China. That this did not generally happen in Europe—and that individual states greatly differed in terms of how far they shifted in that direction—was due to a second, complementary kind of polycentrism, which manifested itself within individual states and societies.

After Rome's collapse, the four principal sources of social power became increasingly unbundled. Political power was claimed by monarchs who gradually lost their grip on material resources and thence on their subordinates. Military power devolved upon lords and knights.

Ideological power resided in the Catholic Church, which fiercely guarded its long-standing autonomy even as its leadership was deeply immersed in secular governance and the management of capital and labor. Economic power was contested between feudal lords and urban merchants and entrepreneurs, with the latter slowly gaining the upper hand.

In the heyday of these fractures, in the High Middle Ages, weak kings, powerful lords, belligerent knights, the pope and his bishops and abbots, and autonomous capitalists all controlled different levers of social power. Locked in unceasing struggle, they were compelled to cooperate and compromise to make collective action possible.

As Europe remained sheltered from major outside threats, many of its conflicts took place *within* sometimes large but increasingly brittle polities. Over time, the growth of population and economic output both enabled and encouraged more sustained competition *between* states. These pressures provided growing incentives for the reconsolidation of domestic power. The long and tortuous process of rebuilding state capacity involved both top-down coercion and extensive bargaining to bring powerful constituencies into the fold.

In the early modern period, rulers for the most part managed to regain control over the concentrated means of violence, co-opt economic powerholders, and incorporate the church(es) into emergent national structures. Yet the scale of Europe's political fragmentation—the sheer number of its sovereign states—ensured considerable variety of outcomes as differences in initial conditions and subsequent opportunities and constraints sent individual states along their own specific pathways of institutional elaboration. The durability of the multipolar state system—the fact that the major states were not periodically swallowed up by larger empires—allowed incremental changes along those pathways to accumulate over time.

Intensifying interstate competition and concurrent intrastate bargaining favored certain performance-enhancing strategies. Innovation, whether institutional or technological, helped increase and mobilize domestic resources to prevail in interstate conflict. This environment also generated powerful demand for the acquisition of external resources: where appropriation of domestic elite wealth or the conquest of neighboring polities were not viable options, overseas colonies represented an attractive alternative. Back home, meanwhile, integration had the potential to boost state capacity, most crucially in the conjoined spheres of fiscal extraction and military mobilization.

These moves toward state-strengthening in turn raised performance expectations: the more some states embraced these strategies, the greater the pressure on others to follow suit or fall behind. This feedback mechanism rendered these developmental dynamics self-sustaining as well as self-reinforcing, promoting a circle that was vicious in its relentless violence and (eventually) virtuous in terms of economic outcomes. It also prepared the ground for transformative breakthroughs, for Schumpeterian growth through creative destruction of established orders and techniques. Britain's peculiar mix of parliamentary bargaining, mercantilist protectionism, overseas expansion, naval power, and technological progress was merely the proverbial tip of a much bigger iceberg of European experimentation and adaptation.

Contrast this massively simplified outline of the dynamics of productive competitiveness with a different but equally ideal-typical scenario, in which a region of subcontinental proportions is dominated by a single ("monopolistic") super-state. Under these conditions, any remaining external competition will be asymmetric in nature, between the imperial hegemon and groups in peripheral and often ecologically marginal areas beyond the former's logistical reach: the persistent conflict between China and steppe formations is a classic example; ancient Rome's containment of Germanic tribes is another.

Hegemonic empires were likely to prioritize maintenance. Once they controlled most people and assets in a given geomorphologically circumscribed macro-region, the potential for further gains was bound to be trivial compared to what had already been obtained. Holding on to far-flung possessions by checking elite autonomy and regionalism became the principal challenge.

This environment generated weaker demand for state capacity and performance than a competitive state system, especially if power projection was impeded by structural asymmetries: for instance, a larger infantry army was not necessarily effective against nimble steppe opponents. These constraints favored the persistence of a traditional "capstone" state in which a ruling elite and its institutions "capped" and held together a congeries of areas and constituencies they were unable or unwilling to penetrate, mobilize, and integrate. "Keeping its various components in place, but incapable of stimulating further development," this type of government sought to perpetuate itself by limiting centralized extraction and accommodating the prerogatives of established localized power bases.[4]

The absence of strong internal polycentrism served to amplify these tendencies. In imperial China, the closest historical approximation of this scenario throughout much of its history, political and ideological power were closely allied, military power was for the most part safely contained, and economic power was relatively marginalized.

This combination of international and domestic hegemony reduced the need for explicit bargaining and favored a different set of dispositions. Conservatism, congruent with the emphasis on maintenance, was one of them. Reliance on domestic resources was another: as energies were devoted to the vast challenges of taxing those who were already subject to the empire's rule, rulers lacked strong incentives to develop external assets. In turn, prioritization of maintenance and conservatism supported delegational localism that limited the state's ability to penetrate society.

In the case of China, the overall result was a sociopolitical order that helped secure peace and basic welfare for a large population but did not lend itself to disruptive innovation. It generated Smithian growth by promoting division of labor, market integration, and intensification of established techniques but could not lastingly overcome Malthusian constraints.

The differences between these two schematic scenarios are relative, not absolute. Innovation did occur in China, and the societies of early modern Europe labored under the burden of inherited elite privilege and rampant corruption. This comparison is meant to show that certain traits were likely to be more strongly associated with enduring polycentrism than with imperial hegemony, and vice versa. As I argue in this chapter and in chapters 11 and 12, the empirical record broadly supports this impression of variance in developmental dynamics in the aggregate and over the long run.

Figure 10.1 deals in ideal types. Their closest real-life approximations were late medieval and early modern Europe on the one hand and long stretches of Han, Tang, Ming, and Qing history (as well as the mature Roman empire) on the other. These cases delimit extremes; most others fell in between. Not all very large empires achieved a quasi-monopolistic position: the less they did, the more they strove to enhance their capacities. The later Roman and the Mughal empires belong in this category. China itself underwent phases of increased competitive pressure, most notably under the Song: the self-strengthening measures taken at the time are fully consistent with the predictions of my model. Nor were all state systems effectively competitive: for a long time, many of medieval Europe's states were so feeble that their wars remained fairly modest affairs, and most conflict took place within their brittle shells.

Even so, ideal types and extreme cases are useful in offering a template for organizing historical accounts. Most importantly, they encourage us to assess the causal connections between clearly specified base conditions—polycentrism within and without versus imperial hegemony and consolidated social power—and long-term outcomes. Therefore, this part of my book focuses above all on imperial China and post-Roman Latin Europe.[5]

I pursue this comparison across three chapters that cover political and cognate institutions, the quest for and exploitation of external resources, and scientific, technological, and valuatory innovation. My approach is at once selective and eclectic. I proceed selectively in that I do not wish to burden my discussion with comprehensive overviews of competing explanations but ask instead how features that other scholars deem to have made a meaningful contribution to the (Second) Great Divergence are linked to Europe's signature inter- and intrastate fragmentation of power. I do so by focusing on those parts of Europe that were most intimately associated with this process—Latin Europe in general, northwestern Europe more specifically, and, most of all, England—and by moving in time from foundational developments in the Middle Ages to more concrete and recent features such as early modern mercantilism. Throughout, I rely on traditional Old World empires as a foil, most notably imperial China, to put the specific dynamics of European polycentrism in context.[6]

But I am also eclectic in my deliberate agnosticism: this is not yet another attempt to critique the many conflicting accounts of the underpinnings of the (Second) Great Divergence and to judge their relative merits. Taking sides in any way would undermine my approach by opening it up to charges of cherry-picking only those theories that can meaningfully be connected to the First Great Divergence. I must cast my net as widely as possible: accordingly, reference to any particular theory should not be construed as an endorsement. The more that existing explanations can be shown critically to depend on Europe's enduring polycentrism, the more firmly this nexus will be substantiated.

THE LONG MARCH OF THE INSTITUTIONS

Eric Jones famously claimed that the European state system "is as crucial to understanding long-run economic development as it is to explaining the pattern of the industrial world that emerged in the nineteenth century." Yet the precise linkages can prove elusive. Peer Vries, to whom we owe the most detailed critiques of scholarship on the (Second) Great Divergence, defines the problem well: "Those who think there was something like a Western state or a Western state-system that caused the Western economic *démarrage* must take up the challenge of how exactly to connect political power and steam power." If we regard steam power as emblematic of modernity, this does indeed take us to the heart of the matter. But this is not merely about the state: polycentrism more generally and the fragmentation of social power are the core issues, as is the need to connect developmental outcomes to institutional evolution.[7]

If the onset of the industrial age is our destination, this chapter cannot stop before we reach the early 1800s. But where to start? How far back in time do we need to go? The fall of the Roman empire in the west and the subsequent erosion of its institutions under Germanic rule did not create a blank slate. Cities had long enjoyed considerable autonomy, an ancient tradition that arguably prepared the ground for even stronger localism later on. The church, which had embraced imperial models of hierarchy and administration after its accommodation with the central state, was and remained a supraregional organization, even if it initially lacked the centralizing focus on Rome it would eventually acquire in the High Middle Ages.

In a more mundane way, even the physical remains of empire produced persistence effects over the very long run. Cities located at Roman road hubs later housed larger populations than did others. More generally, modern road density, medieval and modern urbanism, and even economic activity in the present are measurably correlated with the density of the Roman road network in what used to be Roman Europe.

Yet these legacies tend to be weak. In some ways, the demise of the empire's infrastructural inputs mattered more than their endurance. In England, the collapse of Roman urbanism allowed later cities to develop closer to waterways, a proximity that was conducive to commercial development. In France, by contrast, greater urban resilience preserved less favorably located sites, which negatively impacted long-term growth.[8]

Overall, however, material residue did not count for much. Institutions were decisive, in terms of both their survival and, especially, their disappearance. In the wake of the empire's disintegration, centralized state structures faded while the church persisted and became more centralized over time. Eroding state capacity did not merely prevent the return of hegemonic empire, as discussed in Part III. It also laid the foundations for institutional arrangements that subsequently promoted economic activity and helped create political conditions that were conducive to sustainable growth. Let us review some of the most influential features and developments that contributed to this outcome.

Church and Papacy

The Christian church was the most powerful and enduring legacy of the Roman empire. As we saw in chapter 5, church leaders supported Germanic rulers by acting as their vassals, councilors, and legitimators.

Their services added to state capacity, and rulers' investiture rights and feudal claims sustained rulers' authority over these enfeoffed clerics, even as the latter's abiding loyalty to a separate organization was a potential source of friction. These conflicting commitments were not normally a serious concern as long as the church itself remained regionally decentralized, mirroring therein the growing fracturing of secular power across early medieval Latin Europe.

This changed once the introduction of the pontiff's election by cardinals in the eleventh century had put the papacy on a more secure footing. In the twelfth century, centralization enabled popes to arrogate to themselves hugely increased powers, including supreme doctrinal authority, control over canon law as sovereign lawgivers and judges, and the right to confirm archbishops. By 1300, the Roman curia had grown to a thousand mostly celibate clergymen, a body without equal among the secular courts of the period. Papal legates acted as roving agents who overrode the decisions of local bishops.

The harmonization of canon law—which among many other topics also covered wills and contracts—had repercussions far beyond the clerical sphere: by shaping wide-ranging socioeconomic interactions, it bolstered the church's influence in secular affairs. Investiture agreements with the kings of France and England and the German emperor in the early twelfth century not only affirmed the existence of separate spheres of authority but effectively positioned the pope as an equal partner of the major rulers of Latin Europe.[9]

Roman emperors had been able to summon several hundred bishops to their councils: around 300 for the very first one, at Nicaea in 325, and more than 500 at Chalcedon in 451. While Byzantine emperors continued this practice, in Latin Europe, synods and councils gathered much smaller numbers of church leaders in regional circuits. Only with the First Lateran Council of 1123, convened by Pope Callistus II in Rome, did the Catholic Church match earlier imperial traditions: several hundred bishops and an even larger number of abbots from all over Latin Europe followed the pontifical call. The Fourth Lateran of 1215, a particularly grand affair, attracted some 1,400 clerical leaders alongside representatives of several kings and Italian cities. Not only did the pope ensure attendance: the resultant canons, which covered a wide range of issues, were disseminated all over Europe.[10]

The church thus became Europe's only functioning international organization. Its reach benefited from its vast infrastructure and regularized communications system, rooted in the ubiquity of local churches and steadily expanding, thanks to the conversion of Europe's northern and central-eastern peripheries. Monastic establishments recorded explosive growth: by 1200, some 2,000 monasteries existed in France, the Low Countries, Germany, and Northern Italy, three times as many as there had been just two centuries earlier.[11]

Drawing on this immense network of followers, popes targeted foreign and domestic opponents in concert with secular rulers. At the Council of Clermont in 1095, Pope Urban II called for the First Crusade, and half a century later Eugene II convinced the French king and the German emperor to launch the Second. Innocent III secured Venetian support for the Fourth Crusade and also got the Fifth off the ground. In 1209, the same pope, in concert with the French king, helped instigate a crusade against reformist Cathars, and in 1420 Martin V authorized a crusade against the dissident Hussites of Bohemia. Announcing crusades was not merely a formal papal prerogative: secular rulers generally lacked the capacity to coordinate resources and operations on this scale. Much the same was true of the inquisition, another innovation of the medieval papacy.

By the same token, papal authority could just as readily be employed against the secular establishment, most famously when Pope Gregory VII capitalized on aristocratic resistance to the German emperor Henry IV to humble him at Canossa in 1077, and again when in 1245 Innocent IV convened some 250 bishops and other principals in Lyon to declare the Roman/German emperor Frederick II excommunicated and deposed.[12]

Such spectacles were without parallel elsewhere in the world. Papal might amplified the dispersion of social power in medieval Latin Europe. Intersecting with royal claims to authority, it forced secular rulers into compromises not only with the church itself but also with other constituencies from nobles to cities and other communal bodies that might otherwise enter into alliances with the religious leadership. However much the church contributed to cultural integration within Europe—and I return to this in the epilogue—this was outweighed by its role as a driver of the multifarious polycentric fragmentation that shaped institutional development.[13]

In the end, of course, church power itself proved vulnerable to the same trend. The papacy was never in a position to construct an imperial polity: it influenced, checked, and balanced but did not rule, at least not beyond Rome's own hinterland. Increasingly, it became a victim of its own success, as growing benefits from administrative and financial opportunities, centered on Italy, invited criticism and dissent.

The Great Schism of the thirteenth century temporarily brought the papacy under French domination and reduced its revenue and control over appointments. In the following centuries, the growth of the vernacular revived regional divisions within the church that posed challenges to the increasing centralization and intrusiveness of the papal network. Its eventual fracturing by reformation movements was in no small measure made possible by the political fragmentation of Latin Europe that the church had effectively helped sustain.[14]

Councils and Estates

The huge papal councils that commenced in the High Middle Ages were merely the most dramatic instantiation of a deeply entrenched tradition of collaborative and consultative decision-making within the church. Any synod required consensus to pass resolutions. Bishops had traditionally been elected by the local clergy of their dioceses. Growing royal influence in this process was stemmed by charging the canons of the episcopal cathedrals with selecting their bishops. It was not until the fifteenth and sixteenth centuries that papal control was imposed and shared with secular rulers.

Even as the fortunes of collective choice among the clergy waxed and waned, secular deliberative traditions that were not rooted in Roman precedent proved highly resilient and gathered strength. Perpetuating customs that were typical of the small-scale face-to-face societies of northern Europe, the Germanic successor regimes generally featured political and judicial assemblies. These bodies operated on different scales. On specific occasions, rulers convened mixed councils of bishops, counts, and assorted noblemen to debate and make decisions regarding war and political disputes as well as legal affairs. In less-rarified settings, local assemblies, variously composed of notables or even all free men, tended to focus on conflict resolution. These gatherings did not reflect continuity of earlier Roman practice, which had not survived urban collapse: "an importation from the North," they "represented in almost all respects a break with the Roman past."[15]

As a matter of fact, assemblies were at their strongest where Roman traditions were weak or nonexistent. Under the Visigoths, royal councils played only a minor role, and Lombard rulers in Italy found it easy to control them. The Frankish *placitum generale* convened powerful aristocrats who needed to be carefully managed by their kings to broker consent.

In Anglo-Saxon England, both rulers and elites keenly participated in deliberative gatherings. Emphasis was put on collective decision-making: resolutions were passed by the "king and his witan," the "wise men" who upon England's political unification in the tenth century came to be understood as representatives of the entire realm. Second-tier assemblies that drew in participants from well beyond elite circles were held at the level of the individual shires, and lesser ones in their subdivisions. I return to this tradition below. Norwegian and Swedish kings faced unrulier assemblies, and at the extreme end of the spectrum, in Iceland, an island-wide supreme deliberative and legislative assembly—the Althing—made kings altogether redundant.[16]

In continental Europe, as post-Carolingian rulers found themselves progressively constrained by the effective autonomy of formally subordinate secular and clerical powerholders, the consent of their principal vassals eclipsed mere consultation. Nobles increasingly entered sworn agreements to monitor their rulers' conduct and to withhold support if they failed to honor their obligations. Wherever royal power declined, these arrangements not only imposed significant controls on rulership but also laid the foundations for the later formalized dualism of kings and estates.[17]

Thus, the grand councils convened by kings evolved into more broadly based meetings of the "estates." Rulers of the High Middle Ages, faced with growing fiscal pressures to fund war, expanded the scope of these gatherings beyond clergy and nobles by admitting representatives of cities and other types of communities. Members of the gentry were included in England and France, and agents of castles and certain village communities in Spain. In Flanders, cities came to dominate meetings and eventually even displaced lesser nobles.

Meetings became structured into chambers and curias that represented differed orders, bringing together personally entitled participants such as lords and representatives of larger groups, such as the English Commons. On these occasions, rulers and the estates came to jointly represent the state and exercise power. Within the humongous German empire, the multiplicity of hierarchies eventually gave rise to two types of estate gatherings, one for individual principalities and one for the empire as a whole.[18]

This marked the beginnings of the parliamentary tradition: no longer mere royal councils, these more inclusive and independent bodies exercised greater power by negotiating and authorizing taxation. Gatherings of magnates, bishops, and elected representatives of cities commenced in Leon in the late twelfth century. This practice soon spread across the Iberian peninsula and to Sicily. France convened the first kingdom-wide assembly in 1302, after regional conventions had already begun a century earlier. The English parliament, established in the thirteenth century, came to meet with considerable regularity. On the continent, the autonomy of cities was of critical importance in widening the base of powerholders who needed to be heard. In England, the boroughs played that role.[19]

Yet even as participation broadened, aristocratic assertion of liberty remained a crucial driving force. Thirteenth- and fourteenth-century charters such as the English Magna Carta, the Hungarian Golden Bull, the Unions of Aragon and Valencia in Spain, and the Pact of Koszyce in Poland compelled rulers to recognize rights and to formally seek consent for royal initiatives.[20]

Overall, the parliamentary tradition gathered strength during the High and Late Middle Ages up to the fifteenth century, when trends began to diverge among different countries. This medieval growth phase was sustained by elite confidence and communal self-organization and owed much to the fact that negotiation improved rulers' access to the means of war: the recognition of estates was thus not merely a function of internal relations but was driven by interstate competition.[21]

Whether rooted primarily in cities or among the nobility, the resultant "society of estates ... was unique to Europe." Its most important legacies were twofold. For one, it created a template for later separation of powers: while rulers and their court staffs acted as the executive, the estates, even if not yet elevated to legislative bodies, already performed basic functions of later parliaments. For another, this setup facilitated integration by establishing denser social ties between local units: rooted in quasi-familial feudal relations as well as urban (and sometimes also rural) communalism, it prepared the ground for the subsequent assimilation of the many building blocks of society into more cohesive fiscal-military and then national states—a feature that was lacking from conventional tributary empires.[22]

In many cases, these integrative processes favored federated structures that reflected and preserved the post-Roman shift toward intense decentralization. Rulers who bargained under conditions of fragmented sovereignty needed to recognize urban communes. Regional estates helped create distinct identities and considerable autonomy that likewise limited central power. The incorporation of bishoprics and monasteries acknowledged them as parties to secular power dynamics but also invited conflict with a centralizing papacy.

Overall outcomes were marked by structural tensions and ubiquitous compromise: a combination of increasingly formalized dispersion of political power and social integration prevented open-ended fissioning while constraining authoritarian centralization. This uneasy balance gave rise to polities that were highly fragmented yet adequately functional. Representation and consensus played a greater role in sustaining this balance than they did in other political systems, most notably in traditional empires.[23]

Communes and Corporations

The erosion of state capacity that plagued the Germanic successor regimes encouraged communalism. Urban communes were personal, oath-based associations of all or many of the local (male) citizens. They convened in assemblies that collectively chose or validated the appointment of magistrates and generally sought to protect property rights and govern local affairs.

In Italy, the commune movement took off during the power vacuum of the late eleventh century. Conflict between popes and emperors further weakened distant imperial overlordship and boosted urban ambitions. By the mid-twelfth century, most of the cities of northern Italy were organized as communes that were de facto autonomous in the prosecution of war, the administration of justice, and increasingly also in fiscal matters. A second major cluster developed in northern France and Flanders, linked to Italy by the Rhineland. In a complementary process of defining community rights and obligations, huge numbers of cities across Latin Europe were incorporated by charter, alongside thousands of monasteries and, increasingly, universities.[24]

On a smaller scale, merchants and professional groups likewise associated in communal bodies known as guilds. Precedence varied: in Italy, urban communes came first whereas in northwestern Europe, guilds were the first to appear on the scene. The underlying principle was the same: groups of (unrelated) individuals formed corporations that remained in existence even as membership changed over time. Such corporate bodies generally proved adept at developing and adjusting institutions: they combined the flexibility needed to respond to change and to negotiate with other parties—most notably rulers—with a high degree of permanence that fostered economic stability and development. In the aggregate, they helped protect commoners against the powerful. The dissemination of this organizational mode across Latin Europe reduced the unpredictability inherent in doing business abroad, a vital benefit in an environment that was so intensely fragmented.[25]

The rise of estates and the communal movement shared one crucial characteristic: they produced bodies such as citizen communes, scholarly establishments, merchant guilds, and councils of nobles and commoners that were, by necessity, relatively democratic in the sense that they involved formalized deliberative and consensus-building interactions. Over the long run, these bodies gave Latin Europe an edge in the development of institutions for impersonal exchange that operated under the rule of law and could be scaled up in response to technological change.[26]

Urban Autonomy

As social power dissipated beyond the ranks of the dukes, counts, bishops, and abbots who had carved up the remaining successor states, numerous urban communes gained effective autonomy. This process was concentrated in the twelfth and thirteenth centuries, and even though it was largely reversed between the Late Middle Ages and the early modern periods—except in Germany, where consolidation was often delayed into the eighteenth century—it was by no means ephemeral: in a sample of 81 cities, autonomous status was on average maintained for 341 years.[27]

David Stasavage observes that spatial proximity to the principal fault line of successive Carolingian partitions in the ninth century was a crucial determinant of the incidence of urban autonomy. These divisions first created a narrow strip of territory between France and Germany (dubbed "Lotharingia") that stretched from the North Sea to the Alps and (as shown in chapter 5, figure 5.5) was subsequently partitioned twice. The Treaty of Meersen in 870 permanently split it between the Frankish and German kingdoms. The closer cities were to that final line of partition, the more likely they were to turn into self-governing city-states and the longer that status endured.

This zone was thus characterized by precocious political fragmentation. It centered on the Rhine axis that sustained interregional trade. Polycentrism, commercial development, and existing urban infrastructure converged in supporting a rich ecosystem of mercantile cities that fiercely guarded their local institutions and prerogatives. In northern Italy, the subsequent near-collapse of the Frankish imperial order produced similar outcomes.[28]

Urban self-governance entailed considerable economic benefits. For a while, politically autonomous cities grew faster than others. The local dominance of commercial interests was advantageous: merchant guilds exercised considerable political power, on occasion even to the extent that only their members were entitled to hold municipal office. Among well-documented autonomous cities before 1300, merchants occupied on average almost three-quarters of the seats on governing councils. For all intents and purposes, in this environment mercantile guilds were in charge.

From the fourteenth century onward, power frequently came to be shared with craft guilds, an arrangement that broadened the base of governance without altering its character. This fusion of political and economic power protected property rights, upheld commitments within the elite and to the community, and encouraged human capital formation through established training procedures. These inducements in turn attracted trade and fostered innovation.

It is true that in the long run, both unfettered guild power and scale constraints inherent in urban self-governance became uncompetitive. Within cities, oligarchic structures raised barriers to entry and eventually stifled adaptive change: by the early modern period, the initial growth advantage of politically autonomous cities had been lost.[29]

Moreover, as territorial states began to overcome their internal divisions, the medieval balance between princely states, city-states, and city leagues was upended in favor of the largest polities. Yet even as city-states were gradually incorporated into territorial states, their merchant elites were well positioned to participate in administration and obtain state support for colonial and capitalist ventures. Absorption into larger polities did not destroy accumulated capital and established social and political structures, and merchants continued to occupy powerful positions in commercial cities. They generally proved adept at using the expanding infrastructure generated by territorial state formation to their advantage.[30]

Political consolidation did not merely grant mercantile elements a seat at a larger table. Rich merchants were the main driving force behind Latin Europe's "systematic policy of capital accumulation derived from an ongoing process of colonization, exploitation, and domination of a subjugated periphery by a core area." As we will see in chapter 11, it was independent Italian city-states such as Venice and Genoa that pioneered this strategy in the Mediterranean, from where it gradually expanded into and then across the Atlantic to create the vast complex of slavery and plantations that helped fuel Britain's industrial takeoff.[31]

Assemblies and Development

As we have seen, assemblies had multiple roots: in local gatherings for dispute arbitration, in the much grander meetings of the estates that had grown out of (top-down) royal councils, and in the (bottom-up) communal movement. In practical terms, their operations and thus their influence were constrained by logistics and therefore by geographical scale. The presence and the power of such bodies consequently tended to be inversely correlated with polity size or whatever else determined their catchment area.[32]

According to a study of twenty-four countries from 1250 to 1800, statewide assemblies that exercised control over public funding were more likely to exist and met more frequently in more compact polities. The same principle even applied within states: in France, provincial estates that bargained with rulers over taxation convened more often in the kingdom's smaller provinces. Scale thus appears to have been critical in sustaining representative bodies that exercised tangible power. For example, France, unlike England, might simply have been too large for an active national assembly. When it came to the intensity of political participation, less (territory) was more.[33]

Owing to this constraint, city-states were best positioned to develop and maintain powerful representative institutions. During the Late Middle Ages and the early modern period, assemblies that exercised fiscal authority—in terms of approving and collecting taxes and administering spending—were therefore more likely to be found in city-states than in territorial states. Moreover, and again in contrast to most territorial states, merchants were much more strongly represented in the governance of city-states.[34]

This favored economic development. Local political autonomy and the presence of an assembly raised a city's growth rates. In several Western European countries, assembly control over taxation increased growth correlations between cities, which suggests that assemblies favored freer trade.[35]

Most important, the combination of representative institutions and commercial bias provided city-states with significant advantages in developing public credit arrangements. When elite groups were small, cohesive, and dominated by the mercantile element, the decisions of assemblies were likely to be aligned with those of creditors. This rendered commitments to repay debt more credible. In territorial states, where assemblies did not meet often enough and included fewer members of the commercial elite, credit formation lagged behind. As a result, autonomous city-states introduced long-term loans much earlier than territorial states did, and up to the seventeenth century enjoyed lower interest rates.[36]

This yielded two major benefits for Western Europe. For one, it helped city-states survive longer alongside more populous and gradually centralizing territorial states than would otherwise have been possible. This persistence significantly contributed to European polycentrism in terms of interstate fragmentation and institutional diversity. More specifically, the Dutch United Provinces, a product of the vibrant city-state ecology of the Low Countries, relied on the sale of annuities backed by local revenues to resist their much larger and bullion-rich Habsburg enemy. In so doing, the Dutch not only helped stymie the latter's aspirations to imperial hegemony but also pioneered a new form of developmental state that fostered higher economic growth.[37]

As a second benefit, public debt appeared on the scene earlier than it might otherwise have, if indeed it would have done so at all. It is hardly a coincidence that in all of documented history, only city-states invented public credit, first in the ancient Greek world and then once again in the Middle Ages.

Given that the credit financing of public expenditures and the financial instruments it spawned played an important role in later economic development, it must count among the key contributions that Europe's intense political fragmentation (which produced and sustained city-states) and domestic fracturing of power (which allowed merchants to dominate such polities) made to economic modernization. For all we can tell, these innovations were highly unlikely to arise in traditional empires that could cover shortfalls by coercive means and lacked substantive constraints in dealing with creditors' claims.[38]

War and Development

Several of the features highlighted here—assemblies, bargaining over tax collection, public debt—were intimately bound up with war. War—both within and (increasingly) between states—compelled rulers and other constituencies to cooperate and compromise in multiply fractured environments. Funding was key: intensifying interstate competition coupled with technological change generated demand for larger armies and more and better armaments that required ever-larger expenditures. While the economic recovery of the High Middle Ages provided the necessary means, bargaining mechanisms regulated access to them. As states rebuilt their capacities, they did so in order to meet this challenge. Warfare made England precociously united; it limited fragmentation in Castile, a frontier society facing Muslim polities; and the Hundred Years' War helped restore royal wealth and power in France.[39]

Sustained by the security threats and promise of rewards for aggression that a polycentric state system offered, European belligerence was exacerbated by the pervasive dominance of Germanic-inflected warrior elites that influenced elite preferences over the long run. Thanks to the way society had come to be organized during the post-Roman and post-Carolingian dispersions of power, military culture proved extremely persistent.

Internal fragmentation of social power was another vital factor: warfare furnished otherwise weakened rulers with an opportunity to mobilize and coordinate the resources of the nobility and the commercial class. The effective fusion of military control and local civilian governance in the knight-and-castle system of the High Middle Ages had turned military institutions into the principal integrative force, which shaped norms, values, and expectations. Religious motivation also boosted belligerence, first in the struggle against heathens within and outside Europe and later between Catholics and Protestants.[40]

Endemic warfare, enduring international fragmentation, and the polycentric configuration of social power that sustained a balance among political, military, ideological, and economic forces were thus the main ingredients of early European state formation. Notwithstanding its very considerable costs, warfare is widely regarded as a driver of economic advancement.

John Hall telescopes centuries of European history into his assertion that "only when long-lasting states were forced by military competition to interact strongly with their civil societies was economic progress possible." What this means is that states had to be durable in order to permit and benefit from the evolution and accumulation of institutional adaptations and their economic consequences; that they had to be locked into open-ended and inconclusive competition and conflict in order to maintain a focus on performance; and that they had to be constituted in a certain way for rulers to be compelled to engage with civil society through negotiation and compromise in order to obtain the material means for interstate conflict. Only under those conditions did transformative economic development arise.[41]

In the next section, as we move on to the early modern period, I review these connections in more depth. For now, one argument that reaches farther back in time shall suffice. Jean-Laurent Rosenthal and Bin Wong argue that warfare played a role in the rise of urban manufacturing in Europe. Unlike agriculture, manufacture was mobile and could shift behind protective walls. War-rich regions such as Italy and the Low Countries thus experienced a concentration of manufacture in urban settings.

Mark Dincecco and Massimiliano Onorato develop this "safe harbor" argument more broadly by documenting a positive correlation between exposure to conflict and urban growth between 1000 and 1800. Artisans and entrepreneurs moved to cities, bringing financial and human capital with them. They benefited from fortifications and scale effects, and even though the concentration of resources turned cities into more attractive targets, the relative rarity of sackings, the mobility of urban capital, and common regeneration after wars compensated for this risk. Moreover, cities were not merely physically safer. They also offered personal freedoms and protection from predation by the powerful. Urban residents benefited from local governance and the privileges rulers granted as they bargained for funds for war.

Urban density lowered exchange costs and fostered division of labor and thick labor markets, while higher real wages provided incentives for technological innovation and human capital formation and, more specifically, for the substitution of capital for labor. For all these reasons, endemic warfare made Europe not only more urban but also more developed than it might otherwise have been.[42]

England, by contrast, followed a different path: for the most part—and unlike Scotland—spared similarly intense conflict, rural manufacture thrived and most cities long remained relatively small. As we shall see, England relied on other drivers of industrial development that were however equally firmly grounded in violent competition.[43]

Fragmentation and Development

The beneficial effects of political multipolarity took many forms. In the High and Late Middle Ages, more strongly fragmented regions—the Low Countries, Germany, and northern Italy—experienced higher rates of urban growth and greater book production than others. More generally, Latin Europe's competitive state system offered exit options to minorities, dissidents, and material and human capital.[44]

These options are often considered crucial. David Landes calls fragmentation "the strongest brake on willful, oppressive behavior," and Eric Jones notes that even in the absence of political "voice," exit options ensured a measure of leverage over rulers: "Latent competition between states remained a minimal guarantee that the difference between an empire and the European states system would not slide into merely that between one big despotism and a lot of little despotisms." Formal models, meanwhile, focus on the economic consequences, showing that high mobility of capital within a state system can be expected to lower the rate of expropriation and increase economic growth.[45]

From this perspective, states competed to attract and retain the most attractive constituents and were incentivized to do so by providing public goods such as order and adjudication. That in practice, historical regimes frequently failed to behave in this manner—consider repeated expulsions of Jews and measures against Protestants—does not detract from the principle: after all, the states that most consistently met these standards eventually reaped the greatest benefits.[46]

Fragmentation of powers also protected property rights. Lords secured them by privatizing their assets and guarding them by force. Later, urban communes and corporate bodies were able to protect property rights through commerce-friendly local governance and their ability to resist predation by rulers.

This security encouraged investment in immobile labor-saving capital goods such as water mills, windmills, and cranes. From the Early Middle Ages to the early modern period, the use of such installations expanded in Western Europe but not in the Middle East. In the latter region, prebendal assets were never similarly well privatized or protected, and the advent of Turkic and Mamluk conquest regimes increased the odds of arbitrary confiscation.[47]

The impact of political fragmentation on trade varied. Even though one might reasonably suspect more intense polycentrism to have raised transaction costs, the opposite could also be the case. The presence of multiple autonomous polities along the same trade route did in fact harm exchange by prompting serial predation. At the same time, inter-route fragmentation that enabled traders to choose among "multiple politically independent routes" lowered tariffs. In the end, whatever the costs of fragmentation in terms of lives and treasure, it reliably opened up room for choice and bargaining.[48]

Medieval Foundations of Modern Development

By 1000, Latin Europe had, in Michael Mann's words, turned into "a multiple acephalous federation" that lacked a dominant center and was composed of complex interaction networks. None of the four principal sources of social power was unitary, and most social relationships were highly localized.[49]

Political power, formally vested in rulers, had de facto largely devolved upon regional and local nobles and bodies. Military power was widely dispersed among knights in their castles. Ideological power resided with a church whose growing centralization and political appetites faced ever-stronger counterpressure from dissidents. Economic power had first been captured by rural lords and then become increasingly concentrated among commercial elites, most notably in autonomous cities and city-states.[50]

Different legal traditions existed side by side: canon, urban, feudal, and manorial law, complemented by the rediscovery of Roman law. This variety showed rules to be the product of evolution rather than of an immutable order: consequently, conflicts and inconsistencies were to be resolved through debate rather than fiat. In this, the fragmented legal system reflected the fragmented power system overall. Power became constitutionalized and thereby subject to negotiation between different types of powerholders: at the very top—between emperor and pope—as well as at less exalted levels, those of nobles, bishops, cities, and guilds. Outcomes trended toward compromise: between state and church regarding investiture, between rulers and taxed regarding procedure and objectives, and between rulers and communes regarding their respective rights and obligations.

In practice, of course, even the most solidly hegemonic imperial regimes had always had to accept limitations on the centralized exercise of power and to delegate much of it to local elites. The principal difference between this acquiescence and developments in medieval Latin Europe lay in the fact that the latter cumulatively rendered power *constitutionalized*, *openly* negotiable, and *formally* partible all at once. These attributes stand in stark contrast to the lack of constitutionality, ubiquity of implicit bargaining, and informal partitioning of power that was typical of conventional empires where limited infrastructural capacity rather than institutional checks acted as the principal constraint on the spasmodic exercise of despotic power.[51]

As state power recoalesced in Latin Europe, it did so restrained by the peculiar institutional evolution and attendant entitlements and liberties that this acutely fractured environment had engendered and that—not for want of rulers' trying—could not be fully undone. These powerful medieval legacies nurtured the growth of a more "organic" version of the state—as opposed to the traditional imperial "capstone" state—in close engagement with organized representatives of civil society.[52]

The small-scale nature of politics that revolved around lordship and cities that had become widely dominant by the eleventh century required processes of rebuilding state capacity to be based on the same cellular units: for a while, as local collective power, concentrated in assemblies, emerged in response to reassertions of royal power, both grew in tandem.

Integration that arose from negotiation between interest groups needed to be supported from below, an approach uncommon among the imperial conquest regimes that continued to rise and fall in other parts of the Old World.[53]

By the end of the Middle Ages, this mode of integration had brought about increased public discussion of the political, marked by greater intensity of critiques and analysis that focused on the public good and the costs of policies. The need to obtain consent for taxation (and legislation) helped create a public sphere with more capacity for organized dissent. Assemblies, church councils, and more elaborate legal systems at once contributed to and were a manifestation of this trend. As Chris Wickham concludes, the combination of local cellular politics, rising literacy, economic growth, and a newly intrusive state (which in turn was made possible by taxation, literacy, and the economy) supported political systems "which allowed engagement."[54]

Pathways differed: political coherence could be forged by autocratic and rich kings (such as in France) or arise from well-organized internal decision-making and legal structure (as, in different ways, in Italy and England). This variation was crucial: even as medieval institutional adaptations came under pressure and frequently eroded in favor of more centralized and authoritarian forms of government, persistent interstate polycentrism preserved them better in some places than in others. This diversity was of critical importance for economic and human development over the long run. Hegemonic empire was the antithesis that never came to pass.[55]

"In Almost the Furthest Limit of the World"

The formation of political institutions in Britain illustrates the range of variation of outcomes in medieval Europe: traits that were widely shared across much of the continent, such as assembly politics and aristocratic power, were significantly mediated by regionally specific conditions that prevented state deformation on the scale observed in France, Germany, and Italy. Given that Britain was to play a leading role in triggering the "Great Escape," its particular trajectory merits special attention—as does the question of whether this trajectory's arc bent toward these later breakthroughs.

In the fifth century CE, the Roman order collapsed more spectacularly in Britain than it did anywhere else in the former western provinces: Roman-style urbanism and hierarchies effectively disappeared. The resultant absence of large post-Roman kingdoms paved the ground for more cooperative forms of government.[56]

Germanic infiltration contributed to a mix of small-scale conquest regimes and indigenous communities. It took England's Anglo-Saxon warlords several centuries to rebuild state structures from the bottom up. In the sixth century, the region was divided among dozens of small polities. Consolidation gathered pace in the eighth and ninth centuries driven by the growth of the kingdoms of Mercia and Wessex and above all by conflict with Danish settlers.

The rising Anglo-Saxon polities came to be organized around burhs (boroughs), fortified positions that grew into centers of royal power and nodes of extraction. Shires, which already existed in embryonic form in eighth-century Wessex, spread as that kingdom expanded. By the turn of the millennium, they had become the normal form of territorial organization: as administrative units for managing conscription and taxation, they built up communities of landowners who convened to settle disputes, witness sales, publish wills, distribute tax liabilities, and raise levies. Smaller subdivisions (the hundreds or wapentakes) hosted more frequent judicial meetings that brought locals in contact with state authority.[57]

These gatherings revolved around the witan, the "wise men." At the local level, they directed the proceedings, which could attract large numbers well beyond elite circles. Kings convened grander meetings of witan for the entire realm. These witenagemots generated diplomas, charters, and laws; settled disputes; and conducted various other kinds of business ranging from royal "elections" and coronations to senior ecclesiastical appointments, treaties, and decisions about war and peace.

No mere councils tasked with advising rulers, they were essential to the performance of government, providing a forum for producing consent via two-way interactions. If the witan could not meet, much of the business of government was put on hold. This as well as the regularity of elite attendance demonstrates that king and notables relied on each other. The strong emphasis on decisions made by the "king and his witan" reflects the collective nature of their decision-making. This interdependence did not simply serve as a check on royal power but also enhanced royal authority by being constitutive of it: "Kingship was not so much limited as enabled by assemblies."[58]

By the tenth century, levels of attendance were already comparable to those for thirteenth-century Parliament. Legislation remained part of the witenagemot's writ even as analogous prerogatives were dying out in France and Germany. The conciliar tradition likewise survived the Norman takeover. Initially, as the new conquest elite found itself detached from its subjects by language and culture, assemblies were reduced to gatherings of magnates who could no longer claim to represent the local commons. Before long, however, this ruling class became better integrated once it was forced to assume obligations for taxpayers: this created new connections that brought nobles and other stakeholders together, and a shared English identity gradually emerged.

By the early thirteenth century, the previous notion that the royal assemblies were meant to represent the entire free population had been reestablished. Newly confrontational politics were the main driving force. Rulers' ambitions to exercise power freely clashed with their need for military funding. The link between taxation and conciliar consent proved to be crucial: after 1215 taxes could not be gathered without the latter. Legislative powers were restored to Parliament at the end of the thirteenth century. Participation in assembly politics once again broadened as knights of the shire—the lowest rung of nobility—joined in, paving the way for the politicized gentry of later centuries. The growing volume of petitions and claims for redress afforded kings a larger audience and made certain the lower orders were heard.

To be sure, the shift toward formalized fiscal bargaining negotiation and the social widening of assembly politics were part of broader European trends. Yet England stood out in a number of ways. Its size made it less difficult than in larger states to convene comprehensive councils on a regular basis. There were no entrenched regional power blocs. Counties (the erstwhile shires) rather than cities served as the primary constituent units, ensuring that the rural gentry were strongly represented in the political process. More generally, sustained involvement of local elite members in their double capacity of community leaders and royal agents forged closer ties between different social strata and the central state.

Unlike in France, nobles did not enjoy personal exemptions from public obligations. This increased the value of corporate consent, which favored rules that provided for the sharing of benefits and burdens. Insofar as power was derived from conciliar politics rather than personal access to the ruler, the nobility had a strong incentive to be actively involved in policymaking. The lack of noble privileges that were common on the continent—from tax exemptions to claims to private warfare and high justice—prevented ruptures within the elite and fostered commonalities of interest among nobles, bishops, barons, and knights that were expressed and negotiated in the shared forum of Parliament. As magnates entered alliances with lesser landowners, England precociously became a community of taxpayers whose national assembly reflected "so close an enmeshment of central authority and local action."

Resting as it did on a broader base than that of the privileged estates that typically made up the assemblies of continental Europe's territorial states, the strength of allied representatives not only compelled monarchs to share power in the key domains of taxation and legislation but also contrived to curb both royal power and aristocratic patrimonialism at the same time. This was a distinctive outcome rooted in the severity of the post-Roman collapse and the precocious rebuilding of political unity.

By contrast, the successor states of the Roman empire in continental Europe had started out as relatively powerful kingdoms. Once central authority declined, takeover by powerful aristocracies cemented the dominance of patrimonial practices. Later, when state rulers strove to reassert and centralize power, they often drew on Roman political and legal traditions in order to reduce their dependence on compromises with their estates. In the English case, neither of these processes played out in quite the same way.[59]

The timing of the onset of sustained interstate competition also mattered. In polities where it commenced on a significant scale before the fifteenth century, rulers were routinely compelled to make concessions to key constituents so as to obtain administrative and financial resources and human capital at a time when these were still in relatively short supply. England, long exposed to Danish and Norman aggressors and later engaged in a grandiose military venture in France (the Hundred Years' War), squarely fell into that category. This exposure to military pressures promoted communal involvement in the pursuit of shared interests. Elsewhere, delays in the intensification of serious conflict allowed rulers to benefit from greater affluence and literacy, making it less challenging for them to set up administrative apparatuses and apply greater bureaucratic control.[60]

Two features were thus critical: strong local government and its routinized integration into polity-wide institutions, which constrained both despotic power and aristocratic autonomy, and sustained interstate conflict. Both were direct consequences of the fading of late Roman institutions and the competitive polycentrism born of the failure of hegemonic empire. And both were particularly prominent in medieval England: the least Roman of Western Europe's former Roman provinces, it experienced what with the benefit of hindsight turned out to be the most propitious initial conditions for future transformative development.

But in all of this we are dealing with differences in degree, not in kind: medieval England was merely one among a family of cases that shared historically unusual characteristics. Inclusive and participatory institutions had evolved all over Latin Europe. By shaping state formation across a large area, they helped forestall the reemergence of hegemonic empire that might have absorbed England or any of its peers. Radically transformative processes in later centuries owed as much to transnational characteristics as they did to any particular outlier: outliers could only survive in a sufficiently sympathetic environment.

TOWARD TAKEOFF

War

Throughout the early modern period, Europe was riven by war. The major powers were involved in warfare in more than 90 percent of the years of the sixteenth and seventeenth centuries and in 80 percent of the years in the eighteenth century. One survey counts 443 wars in Europe between 1500 and 1800, or one and a half per year, compared to an annual mean of 0.2 in China from 1350 to 1800. Another database of 856 conflict events in Western Europe from 1000 to 1800, mostly battles and sieges, shows a rising trend in the early modern period that peaked in the eighteenth century.[61]

Why was war so common? Philip Hoffman has developed a "tournament model" of warfare in which great efforts were made to capture a prize but hostilities were not overly destructive for belligerents, especially for their leadership. Enduring polycentrism was an essential precondition, as was the persistence of martial tastes that I already mentioned.

More importantly, Hoffman's model seeks to explain the progressive character of European warfare: that by channeling ever more resources into warfare, this competition sustained innovation in weapons technology and public organization. For war to have that effect, it had to be common and desirable (by promising glory, territorial gain, and commercial advantage); fixed costs had to be low (military infrastructure was already in place, beginning with medieval castles and knights, which represented a huge sunk cost); variable costs had to be similar (allowing efficient smaller parties to balance larger ones that found it harder to raise revenue); conditions had to be conducive to investment in modern technologies such as firearms and in navies (which was ensured by sufficient distance from the steppe and the coastal articulation of much of Europe); and obstacles to innovation had to be low (which was all but guaranteed by the relative openness of European polities and ease of transnational diffusion).

The convergence of all these conditions, which was arguably unique to Western Europe from the fifteenth century onward, fueled enduring competition and continual upgrades that boosted military productivity and commitment of resources, which in turn prompted and enabled European expansion overseas, the topic of chapter 11. In Europe itself, these massive exertions left an even deeper mark: the painful transition from weak and fragmented medieval polities to more centralized and increasingly capable early modern states was in large part driven by warfare.[62]

Military affairs grew to an immense scale as mobilization rates eventually rose to heights not seen since the days of the Roman Republic. Campaigns that involved ever-larger numbers of soldiers and navies absorbed huge financial resources: by the end of the eighteenth century, several hundred thousand trained sailors were employed by the Atlantic states alone. At the same time, balancing maintained the state system even as warfare kept expanding. Competition thus ensured the persistence of international fragmentation while sustaining the momentum of performance enhancement: it rewarded innovation as a means to survive an ongoing arms race.[63]

Taxes and Credit

Escalating warfare consumed unprecedented amounts of money. Overcoming prolonged fiscal weakness, the reconstitution of centralized governmental power created fiscal-military states. Military demand for funding was systemic: unlike hegemonic empires that might relax their efforts with impunity (as we will see below), Europe's states were locked into relentless competition. As the Great Elector memorably put it in the middle of the seventeenth century, "The military preparations of all our neighbors compel us to follow their example." His neighbors, needless to say, would have seen it exactly the same way.[64]

Tax yield per capita rose dramatically in response to these pressures: between 1500 and the 1780s, it went up to almost five times the previous level in Spain, to fifteen times in France, and to thirty times in England in silver terms, and to three times in Spain, five times in France, and ten times in England in real terms (relative to certain urban wages). As troop numbers soared and technological change—the spread of firearms, warships, and more elaborate fortifications—kept pushing up cost, some 70–90 percent of state budgets was committed to the military.[65]

Smaller polities had to raise more revenue per capita or succumb to larger territorial states. Venice and especially the Netherlands and England rose to the challenge. As naval powers, their funding requirements were particularly heavy but met by effective collection programs. Measured in gold and silver, by 1700, the Netherlands and England boasted the highest per capita tax rates in Europe—and as far as we can tell anywhere in the world.[66]

State size continued to be correlated with regime type: smaller states with functioning representative institutions were able to impose higher tax rates than larger absolutist states. The former were more enterprising in terms of what and how to tax, and pioneered long-term debt and debt markets. More generally, the need for higher revenue and credit helped keep medieval arrangements alive, as rulers needed to consult and compromise with elites to achieve their funding goals. Thus, while fragmentation among sovereign states sustained military conflict, residual fragmented sovereignty within states to varying degrees protected "voice" and facilitated coordination in favor of taxation of commerce, which boosted state support for the latter.[67]

The price was high. Warfare was certainly capable of hurting economic development by prompting overspending, unsustainable debt loads, and excessive taxation that led to stagnation: Spain and later even the Netherlands are among the best-known examples. Yet at the same time, it influenced the evolution of financial institutions in ways that benefited the private sector. The expansion of warfare raised both the scale and sophistication of credit markets, which came to feature unsecured loans between individuals, commercial debt, and collaterized debt as well as public-sector debt that was taken on by cities, the church, and sovereigns.

The large scale of public borrowing provided the strongest impetus for innovation: credit needed for war gave rise to central banks, long-term bonds, bond markets, and debt-for-equity swaps. Intermediaries who covered the short-term needs of rulers were backed by markets for trading long-term bonds. Such financiers then expanded their activities into the private sector where they helped fund new ventures up to industrialization.[68]

More capable fiscal systems did not merely pay for external security, internal stability, and the legal and institutional frameworks that undergirded market expansion and integration. They also helped secure public credit that allowed government to operate smoothly by covering shortfalls without having to resort to predation. At the time, these arrangements were unique to Europe.[69]

The North Sea Economy and the Little Divergence

In the seventeenth and eighteenth centuries, European states became less diverse as state power grew at the expense of local elites. In many cases, fiscally fragmented regimes gave way to more absolutist styles of government. Relying on a mixture of repression and indoctrination, state-centered imperatives built what Thomas Hobbes called the "Leviathan." This in turn intensified international disunity as states grew more homogeneous and Europe as a whole less so.[70]

Religious ruptures contributed to this process. The Reformation ended the hegemonic status of the Catholic Church and fostered closer linkages between religious establishments and states. Henry VIII's separation from the church in 1534 as well as the Peace of Augsburg in 1555 and the Peace of Westphalia in 1648, both of which acknowledged rulers' rights to determine their state religion, were symbolic milestones.

In this more sharply fractured environment, state formation, institutional development, and economic growth proceeded in tandem. According to a variety of metrics, the economies of the North Sea region performed best.[71]

Urban real wages offer some of the most robust evidence. In the Late Middle Ages, the purchasing power and living standards of workers had markedly improved as a result of the shift in the ratio of capital to labor brought about by the Black Death: mass mortality raised the price of labor relative to that of fixed assets. Yet once the plague had abated, renewed demographic growth put downward pressure on real wages. From the sixteenth through the eighteenth centuries, the consumption levels of workers in much of Europe gradually slid back down to what had been very low pre-plague standards. By contrast, real incomes soon recovered and broadly stabilized in the principal urban centers of the Low Countries and England (figure 10.2).[72]

Overall economic output is much more difficult to estimate, and any reconstruction must be handled with caution. Only occasionally do we encounter trends that are so clear as to exceed any reasonable margins of error. This is the case here. There can be no doubt that Dutch per capita GDP took off in the sixteenth and seventeenth centuries. England followed suit, catching up in the eighteenth century, while continental Europe stagnated (figure 10.3).[73]

This impression of divergent development meshes well with information concerning urbanization and sectoral distribution. The proportion of the urban population, a rough indicator of economic development, rapidly expanded in seventeenth- and eighteenth-century England to rise far above the European average. In fact, thanks to secular stagnation on the continent, a large and growing share of the net increase in overall European urbanization during this period took place in England (figure 10.4).[74]

Likewise, between 1500 and 1800, the share of the population not engaged in agriculture rose much faster in the Low Countries and especially in England than it did in other parts of Europe (figure 10.5).[75]

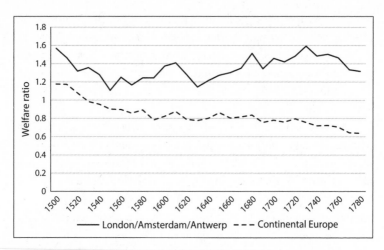

FIGURE 10.2 Real wages of urban unskilled workers in different parts of Europe, 1500–1780 CE. *Source*: Based on the dataset underlying Pamuk 2007: 297, fig. 2 (data not weighted for population size).

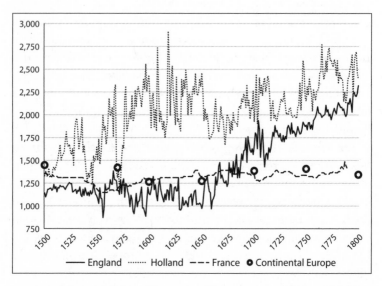

FIGURE 10.3 Per capita GDP in different parts of Europe, 1500–1800 CE. *Source*: Maddison Project Database 2018 (data not weighted for population size).

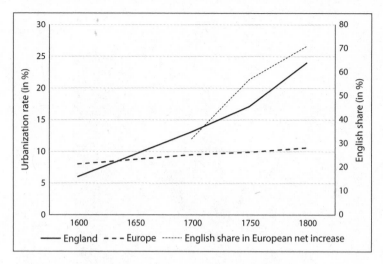

FIGURE 10.4 Urbanization rates in England and Europe and the English share in the increase of the European urbanization rate, 1600–1800 CE. *Source*: Wrigley 2016: 47, table 4.1.

Literacy improved in a similarly uneven manner: by the seventeenth century, the Netherlands and Britain were greatly advancing (figure 10.6).[76]

Taken together, their weaknesses being offset by their consistency, these guesstimates unambiguously point to a regional divergence in economic growth and human welfare that favored the North Sea region. Known as the "Little Divergence," this parting of trends allowed certain northwestern European economies that faced the North Sea to pull ahead of others long before the Industrial Revolution began.[77]

A number of factors contributed to this process. Access to world markets—an issue discussed in chapter 11—disproportionately benefited small countries such as the Netherlands and England that managed to capture large shares of international services in trade, transport, and finance and established growing export industries. These societies were large and wealthy enough to hold their own against larger military competitors but also small enough for growth in specific sectors such as trade and finance to make a palpable difference overall.

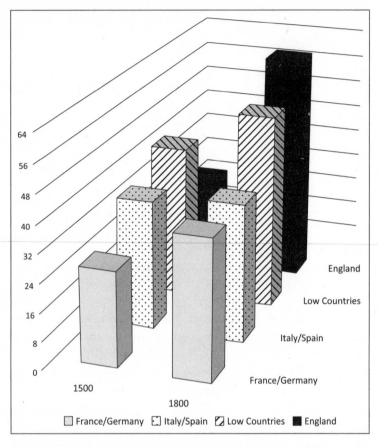

FIGURE 10.5 The share of the urban and nonagricultural rural population in different parts of Europe, 1500 and 1800 CE. *Source*: R. Allen 2003: 408, table 1.

Moderate size was a direct function of interstate competition: England had failed to take over France during the Hundred Years' War of the Late Middle Ages, and the United Provinces were the only portion of the Low Countries to escape from Spanish rule. Their ability to provide protection rested on fiscal resources that in turn depended on the state's ability to mobilize them for collective action.

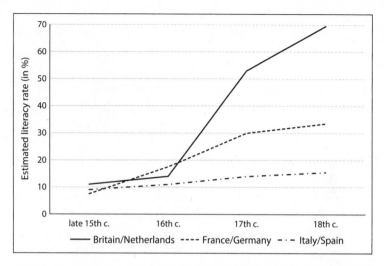

FIGURE 10.6 Adult literacy rates in different parts of Europe, late fifteenth to eighteenth century CE. *Source*: Van Zanden 2009: 193, table 8 (data not weighted for population size).

In this respect, it made a difference that the North Sea region was alone in preserving medieval decentralized political structures and communitarian legacies and building on them during the Reformation while more authoritarian monarchies rose across much of the continent—what Jan Luiten van Zanden deems "an unbroken democratic tradition" from the communal movement of the High Middle Ages to the Dutch Revolt and England's Glorious Revolution. Both geographical advantages—the marshy terrain of the Netherlands and Britain's island position—and access to foreign and commercial resources favored the survival and elaboration of constitutionalism and representative institutions that elsewhere proved vulnerable to the centralizing pressures of war.[78]

As a result, developmental states arose that openly favored merchants and commerce. Literacy and the low cost of capital and skills sustained not only urban and economic growth but also the fiscal and military assets that protected it and helped expand trade, shipping, and attendant services. Structural transformation away from farming both depended on and promoted productivity in the latter. All these features were inextricably intertwined. Absolutist government, by contrast, was associated with lower economic growth. Alongside the quality of geographic access to Atlantic trade, the rise of absolutism in Italy, Spain, France, and Austria and its failure in the Netherlands and England have been viewed as decisive factors in economic development.[79]

This difference was reflected in the evolution of parliaments. After they had generally become more prominent up to the fifteenth century, trajectories diverged. The frequency of meetings went up (mostly) in northwestern Europe (in England, Scotland, the Netherlands, and Sweden, as well as in Switzerland) but declined in southern and central Europe. These trends were correlated with economic progress proxied by urban growth. Moreover, domestic conflict over rights was often driven by parliaments: in the Netherlands in the 1570s, Bohemia in 1618, Spain in 1640, England in the 1640s and 1688, America in the 1770s, and France in 1789. Outcomes differed depending on whether parliaments failed or carried the day.[80]

The Netherlands was the trailblazer of the North Sea economy. By scaling up institutions first developed in Italian city-states, it created a flourishing credit market that soon shifted from Habsburg Bruges and Antwerp to free Amsterdam. Innovations such as letters obligatory (IOUs) and deposit banking coupled with falling interest rates made it easier to obtain and apply capital. Deeply entrenched traditions of urban citizenship that had grown out of medieval communalism provided a template for national citizenship and engendered trust, ensured tax compliance, and supported high levels of public debt.[81]

Thus able to raise loans at lower rates than less trustworthy monarchs, the Dutch spent lavishly on the military for the sake of securing the interests of a commercial elite that dominated politics. They introduced mercantilist protections that were later emulated by England. From the late sixteenth century, economic growth was high by premodern standards, recurrent warfare notwithstanding. In fact, the frequency of conflict was strongly and positively associated with the urbanization rate and per capita GDP. At least for a while, the Netherlands was able to fight and get rich at the same time.[82]

Yet in the end, smallness had its drawbacks. Early pioneers of economic development such as Venice and Genoa had boasted textile export industries, novel financial institutions, and integration into international markets, but in the long run proved incapable of competing with more powerful neighbors. In due course, Flanders lost out to the Netherlands, which was in turn eclipsed by England. Having held the latter at bay in a series of wars from the 1650s to the 1670s, the Dutch began to fall behind just as they had drawn England into their orbit in 1688.

In the following years, they struggled—at punishing cost—to contain an increasingly domineering France. The abiding power of their cities, which prevented the formation of a unified ruling class, ultimately made it hard to adapt to changing circumstances. Meanwhile Britain, endowed with a more secure geographic position and a larger population than the Netherlands and united in a relatively homogeneous territorial state (de facto from 1603 and formally from 1707), took over as the North Sea region's engine of growth.[83]

"A Nation That Is Governed by Shopkeepers"

POLITICS

Many different factors conspired to turn England into the cradle of the Industrial Revolution. In chapters 11 and 12, I consider the significance of overseas trade and resources and the formation and application of human capital. Here, in keeping with the institutional focus of this chapter, I want to highlight three crucial and closely interrelated elements of the English and then British experience in the early modern period: law and politics, war, and mercantilist protectionism. Together, they created an environment that was singularly conducive to productive experimentation and sustainable economic development.[84]

Independence—embodied in formal sovereignty as well as institutional autonomy—was paramount: without it, none of these three elements would have been present in a comparable manner. England successfully avoided absorption into larger imperial projects within Europe: the Carolingians never reached across the Channel, French intervention in

1216–1217 failed, and thanks to the Armada's later defeat Philip II's short-lived tenure as king of England (by virtue of his marriage to Queen Mary I from 1554 to 1558) remained inconsequential. The one time an invasion did succeed—by the Dutch in 1688—it ushered in more enlightened and business-friendly governance.

England managed to escape Rome in three different ways. As we have seen, the fact that England had escaped most thoroughly from Roman imperial traditions helped it establish durable local units of government and political representation. Later, the break with papal Rome under Henry VIII made England a pioneer in creating a national church.

In addition, England largely escaped from the renewal of the Roman legal tradition. In the Middle Ages it had shared in the spread of canon law. Yet from the sixteenth century onward, the monarch was the head of the church, and the standing of common law, as a collection of wisdom derived from earlier arbitration, was strengthened. In this context, the contrast between common law traditions, in which judges refereed among competing lawyers and layman juries, and continental courts, dominated by expert judges and prone to enhance top-down control by the central state, is worth noting.[85]

As a safe haven, England benefited from receiving persecuted and often particularly skilled groups that exited rival polities on the continent. Financial innovation was boosted by successive waves of émigrés: starting with the expulsion of Sephardic Jews from Granada in 1492, this inflow peaked in the 1680s with the Huguenot exodus from France that was closely followed by the emigration of Dutch Jews and Protestant dissidents. Members of these communities had long been key players in international finance.[86]

Sovereignty also helped England protect other features that arguably contributed to economic development, such as the superior physical and cognitive condition of workers that owed much to improvements in nutrition sustained by rising agricultural productivity, to job training, and to Poor Laws that helped feed the labor force. Independence ensured that all these benefits accrued to the English population: there were no countervailing modes of coercive redistribution—such as transfers to a distant imperial center—that could have interfered.[87]

Thanks to its long history of post-Roman political integration, England was relatively cohesive and its elite, centered on a national representative assembly, was likewise fairly unified. For a long time, this cohesion and political focus restrained rulers and facilitated collective action. England was an outlier in that its elected assembly did not merely survive the Middle Ages but grew stronger over time and more adept at balancing royal power. So did its corporate institutions.[88]

The representation of merchant interest in the English Parliament played a crucial role in limiting royal power and expanding the protection of property rights. In the High Middle Ages, agency and information problems that beset royal revenue collection led to mutually beneficial agreements ("farm grants") whereby merchant towns obtained the right of self-administered tax collection and enforcement. Such grants became stepping-stones toward representation once Parliament had been set up at the end of the thirteenth century.

Boroughs in locations that were conducive to trade and had obtained farm grants ended up being overrepresented in Parliament. In the long term, this produced more inclusive local elections and, by the seventeenth century, greater support for parliamentarians during the Civil War. Thus, medieval compromises about tax collection, rooted in the weakness of the central authorities, strengthened the mercantile element in the national assembly and policy outcomes.[89]

Most important, the critical period of recurrent civil war and reconstruction from the 1640s to the 1680s created elite consensus in favor of a stronger and more centralized state that protected commercial interests at home and overseas. The "Glorious Revolution" of 1688 has long been considered a breakthrough in this process. Rooted in the struggle between absolutism and its opponents, it marked the success of a broad (if elite) coalition against absolutism that was sustained in no small measure by the rise of merchants and businessmen that the state could not fully contain.[90]

This success fostered more pluralistic political institutions that were more open to economic and social aspirations. In the economic sphere, it has been credited with shoring up property rights, improving financial markets, undermining monopolies on foreign trade, and removing barriers to the expansion of industry.[91]

This picture applies in broad outlines even as details remain debated. In their classic exposition, Douglass North and Barry Weingast maintain that reforms associated with the Glorious Revolution secured property rights in ways that allowed capital markets to prosper, an effect reflected in the huge growth of public debt alongside falling interest rates, a startling combination made possible by credible commitments to creditors. This in turn boosted private capital markets: the stock market and the number of banks expanded.[92]

Much of this might better be viewed as the result of longer-term trends. Yet even in a more restrained reading, political reform removed concerns about constitutional rights, establishing parliamentary primacy over absolutist tendencies. Most significantly, Parliament's power over taxation and its control of the executive increased. In the process, in North and Robert Thomas's words, "The supremacy of parliament and the embedding of property rights in the common law put political power in the hands of men anxious to exploit the new economic opportunities and provided the essential framework for a judicial system to protect and encourage productive economic activity."[93]

After 1688, Parliament met more frequently and generated more legislation in response to a growing number of petitions, compared not just to previous years but to any other European assemblies. Unlike the latter, it enjoyed an unusual degree of authority over public finances and freedom of interference by local power bases. Because it was not organized into estates, it was also more open and permeable.

Unlike in the past, party politicians rather than monarchs set policy. This mattered because as the balance of power changed in favor of the commercial class, represented by the Whig faction, policymakers embarked on a costly war with France that prompted the expansion of fiscal and military capabilities as well as the creation of a central bank. This shift also focused policy more expressly on growth of the manufacturing sector.[94]

As a further result of this trend, Parliament showed itself increasingly responsive to demands for acts that reorganized property rights. By modifying less-flexible archaic rights regimes and loosening constraints on investment by eroding customary rights in favor of those that responded to changing economic opportunities, legislation removed obstacles to economic development. Acts frequently aimed to lower transaction costs within society and displayed particular interest in transportation issues. Enclosure acts benefited capitalist farming. And as we will see in chapter 12, Parliament's willingness to side with innovators against incumbents accelerated industrial development.[95]

All of this, to be sure, was very much a work in progress. The large volume of legislation betrays its incremental and piecemeal character, often enacted to grant special favors to proponents. By current standards, Parliament was corrupt, often favoring legislation that targeted specific constituencies in exchange for inducements. Even so, over the course of the eighteenth century, rent-seeking gave way to considerations of national interest: instead of pleasing the highest bidder, Parliament sought to arbitrate among competing interest groups. Moreover, the sheer volume of acts underlined their relevance and Parliament's responsiveness to interest groups from across the country. These interactions strengthened the ties between center and regions, promoting integration.[96]

In Julian Hoppit's words, parliamentary intervention in the aggregate represented "a commercialization of political power leading to an intensification of market relations within society." Landholding elites acquiesced to this ongoing shift of political power in favor of the mercantile class because they themselves benefited greatly from early industrialization well into the nineteenth century, when this process had already advanced too far to be reversed.[97]

As Parliament acted as a mechanism for balancing the interests of different elite groups from aristocrats to merchants, it ensured that legislation relating to property rights and related economic issues enjoyed fairly broad support and was therefore durable. This created a predictable framework for economic activity. Without an assembly that could routinely and expeditiously deal with competing interests and was able to tackle a substantial workload with the help of fixed procedures and an expanding bureaucratic apparatus, such broad-based support, durability, and predictability might well not have materialized.[98]

The seventeenth century was thus a period of decisive change. The first patent laws encouraged innovation, joint-stock companies flourished, coffeehouses served as precursors of organized insurance, commodity and securities markets and deposit banking appeared, and a central bank, the privately held Bank of England, extended loans not only to the government to support war but also and at low interest to manufacturers.

By the end of the century, a favorable institutional framework was firmly in place. Industrial regulation and the power of guilds declined while a variety of organizations encouraged mobility of capital. These changes had become "irreversible and cumulative," directed against the old regime of status, stasis, and royal control. Inasmuch as modern state structures were a prerequisite of capitalist markets and secure property rights, England had cleared this hurdle.[99]

WAR

England's precocious political and economic development unfolded behind the shield of sovereignty and naval power. Rising taxes were the foundation: per capita income tax grew fourfold in real terms between the 1680s and the 1830s. In a powerful reflection of the expansion of trade and commerce, customs and excise duties accounted for 60–80 percent of this revenue, much of it derived from duties on alcohol, salt, sugar, tea, and tobacco—consumer goods that were neither necessities nor extravagant luxuries and were increasingly abundant across society.[100]

At times during the eighteenth century, up to 90 percent of public revenue was spent on war. Between 1688 and 1815, loans covered a third of wartime expenditure. By the end of the Napoleonic Wars, British debt had grown to more than two times annual GDP: only Dutch levels of public debt were higher.[101]

That the country was able to take on this burden was the result of the financial revolution of the seventeenth century. It equipped England with the most sophisticated financial system in Europe and indeed the world. The costly wars against France after 1688 were a major driving force: they could only be funded by long-term public debt. Holding these bonds turned citizens into stakeholders whose trust in their government was crucial—and trust it they did. By the time of the Napoleonic Wars, the number of debt holders had expanded to about 300,000, well beyond the elite circles of a dramatically unequal society. Interest rates halved while debt soared.[102]

This was not so much a payoff of inclusion—Britain was not a democracy—as a powerful demonstration of trust in the law and the state's willingness to honor its commitments to the public. This trust had to be earned. Parliament and the Bank of England monitored the way revenue was spent, enabling a "virtuous circle" of spending on debt service and naval expenses that protected more and safer trade. Public debt thus fostered transparency and helped build trust between state and society.[103]

This confidence in state commitments enabled Britain to keep up with growing challenges. The French Revolution pushed up mobilization levels to unprecedented heights: Napoleon drafted 2 million men from among 44 million subjects and allies. Yet Britain outdid him in per capita terms: about 1 million men out of 11 or 12 million people in Britain and another 5 or 6 million in Ireland became involved in the army, the navy, or the forces of the East India Company. In addition, Britain paid for half a million allied troops and built more than 500 warships in the early years of the nineteenth century. At that point, no country anywhere could rival its relative mobilization capacity.[104]

Given the scale of these efforts, it is scarcely surprising that the business of war dwarfed any other businesses. Around 1800, the fixed capital of the British navy was worth more than five times that of the 243 textile mills in the West Riding woolen industry, one of the largest sectors of the country's export economy. Military rather than civilian enterprise took the lead in changing the organization of management and production.[105]

How was economic development related to military capabilities? In continental Europe, the buildup of military resources continued steadily during the eighteenth century even as wars became somewhat less common than they had been. However, British-style economic growth was absent.[106]

It appears that competing was not enough: winning was crucial. In this respect, Britain also stood out. It was spared war on its own soil: there had been no serious combat in England since the end of the Civil War in 1651, which was followed by only minor engagements during the Dutch invasion of 1688 and a foray from Scotland during the Second Jacobite Rising of 1745. Scotland was pacified the following year. The British navy was exceptionally successful. In the end, Britain won or at least did not lose most of its wars after the 1670s, except for one against the nascent United States, which inflicted no lasting damage on trade relations.[107]

Recurrent success in the wars of the late seventeenth and eighteenth centuries stimulated the British economy by securing a large share of international trade, which sustained urbanization, higher wages, and agricultural productivity, the latter as farmers responded to rising demand. This created an environment in which the presence of coal, capital, high wages, and protectionism favored the substitution of capital for labor and thus industrialization. I return to this at the end of chapter 12.[108]

PROTECTIONISM

In Britain's case, one of the most potent effects of interstate conflict on economic progress was indirect: it encouraged protectionist strictures that prompted creative experimentation and technological break-throughs. Across early modern Western Europe, mercantilist policies benchmarked countries' economies against each other in an endless search for competitive advantage. A manifestation of economic nationalism, these policies were driven by concerns about state strength and its financial foundations. Designed to skew trade balances in one's own country's favor and to increase domestic bullion stocks, the protectionist systems promoted manufacturing in order to add value and substitute for imports, as well as trade—ideally conducted by one's own countrymen—to sell goods abroad.

External barriers to exchange went up just as internal ones were dismantled in order to raise productivity. Improvement was the explicit goal, to be achieved by intervention in markets and even in production itself. In the eighteenth century, this mind-set was dominant among European elites who prized war and state interests over citizen welfare.[109]

Yet early modern European states had not yet developed coherent national political economies and thus struggled to implement economic policies and exercise effective control. England was the principal if partial exception, in the sense that it pursued relatively consistent policies of protecting its industries and traders. Even as it remains doubtful just how well bans worked in practice—smuggling was common—at least they worked better than elsewhere.[110]

England's institutions empowered rent-seeking members of the elite and its legal system favored the wealthy and stood ready to deploy coercive powers against the poor. In no small measure, it was thanks to this bias that coalitions in favor of British goods were usually sufficiently powerful to sway Parliament: "Mercantilist policies, to the extent that they benefited anyone, protected a narrow range of merchants, manufacturers, financiers, ship-owners, and planters and thus constituted redistribution from the tax-paying public to a small special interest group."[111]

These interests also extended to international trade. In the seventeenth century, shares in overseas ventures had become available to members of the elite, including Members of Parliament. This helped unify elite interests by opening up access to investment opportunities and aligning the interests of politicians with those of traders.[112]

Legislation supported national trade through a variety of measures. A series of Navigation Acts, passed in the third quarter of the eighteenth century and directed mainly against the Dutch, provided for coastal shipping by British-owned ships, limited imports of certain goods to British ships or those of their country of origin, reserved long-distance imports for British merchantmen, and stipulated that a variety of colonial products had to be brought to England first before they could be reexported to Europe. All these measures sought to cut out middlemen and boost the volume of British shipping and related services.

Chartered companies such as the East India and Hudson Bay Companies blurred the boundaries between war and commerce: their modus operandi was to weaken their foreign competitors by all means necessary, including military force. Since the same was true of their continental peers, protection—both legal and in the form of a strong navy—was a necessity to sustain commerce: under these circumstances, free and fair trade was simply not an option.[113]

Customs duties, initially imposed for fiscal reasons, grew into instruments of protectionism to shield fledgling domestic industries from foreign competition. Tariffs protected special interest groups such as colonial planters or specific industries, most notably cotton processing and iron manufacturing.[114]

As we will see in chapter 12, the British textile industry owed much of its prosperity to duties on the export of raw wool that had first been imposed in the Middle Ages. Later, manipulation of the trade in cotton played a key role. Import restrictions on Indian cotton cloth, introduced in 1685 and increased five years later, failed to stem the flow. Thus, in 1700 the legislature decided to ban the import of certain types of Indian cloth (printed and painted calicoes) altogether, unless they were earmarked for reexport rather than domestic consumption. This created a de facto monopoly for local cloth printers, followed by a huge expansion in production. In 1721, a comprehensive ban on cotton textile imports for sale in Britain closed remaining loopholes. Only white cloth continued to be imported to be printed or dyed for export.

These aggressive interventions limited the supply of cotton in Britain in the face of strong demand, not only at home but also in West Africa, where slaves were traded for cotton cloth. This prompted a search among domestic manufacturers for ways of producing more and cheaper cotton cloth that was suitable for printing. In response, a series of innovations greatly increased productivity in spinning and weaving, first by raising output per worker and then, crucially, by introducing water-powered machinery. Between the 1730s and the 1770s, the flying shuttle and the spinning jenny were followed by the water frame and the spinning mule, which was perfected into a fully automated device in the 1820s. But it was earlier with Samuel Crompton's invention of the mule that the Lancashire muslin industry took off from the 1780s onward.[115]

Interstate competition and interventionism also affected the British coal industry. Export duties on coal rose in the seventeenth and eighteenth centuries to keep down prices for domestic users. Crackdowns on collusion between mine operators and dealers also lowered prices. As a result, the real price of coal held steady despite growing demand.

The more London and the arms industry came to rely on energy from coal, the more the government took an interest in its procurement. The Royal Navy protected coastal traffic, using the main coal route as a training ground. At a critical juncture of industrial takeoff, the great French Wars favored autarky and accelerated import substitution of British coal for Baltic timber and wood fuel, causing mining output to double.[116]

The picture was similar for iron: rising tariffs on Russian and Swedish imports shielded the domestic iron industry during the seventeenth and eighteenth centuries until the switch from charcoal to coal fuel greatly reduced costs. Even as the imposition of such dues was motivated in the first instance by strategic considerations and concern about dependence on foreign sources, in practical terms it encouraged innovation that improved productivity.[117]

Mercantilist protectionism served as the crutch on which the modern machine-based and fossil fuel economy learned to walk. The earliest stages of the Industrial Revolution cannot be properly understood without reference to state intervention and a dirigiste political economy that were rooted in war, taxation, and public debt.[118]

These conflict-driven features also mediated the way in which other factors contributed to economic growth. Thus, when high real wages and growing work inputs in response to consumption incentives—the so-called Industrious Revolution—among a large segment of society created a growing consumer market, this process provided impetus for industrialization only in the very specific context of import substitution impelled by protectionist import restrictions.[119]

THE FISCAL-NAVAL-MERCANTILIST STATE AND ECONOMIC DEVELOPMENT

In the end, the visible and often heavy hand of the fiscal-naval-mercantilist state that had emerged in Britain mattered as much as the invisible hand of the market. The economy benefited from mobilization effects: war required intensive use of resources. British cotton production tripled between the 1790s and 1813, while iron and steel output quadrupled. Massive demand for arms and uniforms lay behind this, coupled with a determined push for rationalization.[120]

During those years, capital fled war-torn Europe. Policies that favored autarky promoted coal and iron at the expense of imports, and domestic diffusion of relevant technologies accelerated. The rate of high-value patenting increased. Meanwhile, other countries' mercantile sectors suffered, thereby widening Britain's lead.[121]

More immediate connections between war-making and technological innovation merit particular attention. The precision demands of firearms manufacturing guided the development of instrumentation and machinery including steam engines. It was cannon precision boring applied to cylinders that first made steam power viable.

Even before then, in the early eighteenth century, war with France had stimulated coke-smelting techniques that made it possible to use domestic iron to produce bar and pig iron. Within just a few years of Henry Cort's patent of 1784, the Royal Navy embraced the puddling process, which allowed the manufacture of higher-quality bar iron without charcoal. The French Wars then enabled the state to raise both tariffs and domestic production, protecting the profits of manufacturers whose investments funded the proliferation of furnaces and foundries. At the same time, steam engines sustained the huge expansion in coal mining that was required to keep the iron industry growing.[122]

Economic nationalism boosted nation-building and made mass warfare a reality: economic and military mobilization went hand in hand. In this context, "interstate competition often provided the *stimulus* if not the sheer *necessity* to develop." But did the resultant economic growth and technological change owe more to the promotion of "benign" forces than to the removal of impediments?[123]

In Britain, and increasingly elsewhere, some impediments were in fact being removed—Eric Jones invokes the "withering away of arbitrariness, violence, custom, and old social controls." "Benign" institutions arose from competitive political adaptations. Yet some of the most potent policies did not promote overtly "benign" features but the exact opposite: war and protectionism, as well as colonial slavery.[124]

War was lethal, expensive, and on the face of it produced little tangible gain. Much the same was true of overseas empire, although in terms of economic payoff Britain may have been a rare exception. Bargaining with elites burdened consumers with protectionist tariffs and trade barriers. As Rosenthal and Wong point out, growth was thus associated with policies that were not deliberately benign or growth-enhancing but mere by-products of competition and conflict between states and bargains that favored capitalists within states. If political competition did in the end stimulate economic development, it did so indirectly and often unintentionally.[125]

Yet even as a comprehensive balance sheet remains beyond our reach, there is a case to be made that the British economy expanded and modernized in part *because of* rather than *in spite of* the tremendous burdens of war, taxation, and protectionism. By focusing on trade and manufacture as a means of strengthening the state, Britain's elites came to pursue developmental policies geared toward the production of "goods with high(er) added value, that were (more) knowledge and capital intensive and that were better than those of foreign competitors so they could be sold abroad for a good price."[126]

In this, the advantage lay with producers and traders, not domestic consumers, however much the latter's purchasing power sustained domestic demand. In chasing these goals, the political elite spurred development by boosting imports and exports in sectors that proved critical for the eventual industrial takeoff and that in the absence of such targeted intervention might well not have flourished in the same way. In this specific sense, the fiscal-naval-mercantilist state may be considered a necessary—if far from sufficient—condition for the creation of a modern economy.[127]

This version of the state was the product of multiplicities—of a multiplicity of polities that generated the competitive pressures that shaped state formation; of a multiplicity of forces that were arrayed within these polities in a multiplicity of configurations; but also of the multiplicity of trajectories and outcomes that these multiplicities of polities allowed to appear. The greater these multiplicities, the better the odds of truly transformative divergence.

Thanks to a combination of historical legacies and geography, England and then Britain happened to make the most of their pricey membership in the European state system. Economic growth had set in early; medieval integrative institutions and bargaining mechanisms were preserved and adapted to govern a more cohesive state; elite commitments facilitated high levels of taxation and public debt; and the wars that mattered most were won.[128]

In chapters 11 and 12 I will highlight other contributing factors, such as steadily improving access to overseas trade and resources, an emerging culture of toleration and improvement, and synergistic collaboration between entrepreneurs and engineers that promoted practical application of technological innovation. Even so, it cannot be our primary objective to compile the most comprehensive list of features that distinguished British development from that of its continental European peers. The main point is much more basic: regardless of how much of an outlier we judge early modern Britain to have been, its success and subsequent influence would have been unthinkable without the diversity, pressure, and opportunity generated by a polycentric state system. Far from acting as an increasingly remote background condition, fragmentation shaped Britain's path every step of the way.[129]

The Institutionalization of Progress

British development was embedded in broader processes that unfolded across Latin Europe. To varying degrees and at greatly differing speeds, they sustained momentum toward "well-defined, medium-sized states, burgeoning commerce, and a culture of vigorous critique." Even if in practice only a few European societies met all these requirements, this particular blend of features was at the time unique in the world.[130]

The state was the ultimate bundle of institutions. The more developmental it was in nature, the more innovative were the outcomes that followed. The early modern style of state intervention—which, as already noted, was generally more strongly motivated by strategic concerns than by economic rationales—offset and undid some of the earlier medieval openness that had resulted from the decline of centralized state power. Perhaps paradoxically, it was this tightening that allowed capitalism to flourish, shielded by the exclusions and privileges imposed and conferred by the warfare state.[131]

Reduced to its essentials, the story of institutional development followed a clear arc. In the Middle Ages, the dispersion of power within polities constrained the intensity of interstate competition by depriving rulers of the means to engage in sustained conflict. In the early modern period, these conditions were reversed. Interstate conflict escalated as diversity within states diminished and state capacity increased. Enduring differences between rival polities shaped and were in turn shaped by the ways in which elements of earlier domestic heterogeneity, bargaining and balancing survived and influenced centralization to varying degrees.

The key to success was to capitalize on these medieval legacies in maximizing internal cohesion and state capacity later. This alone made it possible to prevail in interstate conflict without adopting authoritarian governance that stifled innovation. The closest approximations of this "Goldilocks scenario" could be found in the North Sea region, first in the Netherlands and then in England. Given that these societies pioneered vital elements of the transformative development that eventually changed the world, it is with good reason that Peer Vries identifies the "non-monopolization but at the same time close interaction of the sources of social power, between and within states" as "the fundamental cause of the rise of the West in all its varieties."[132]

Societies were made modern by institutions that rendered continuous change possible. This required the presence of institutionalized mechanisms—what Erik Ringmar calls "enabling conditions"—for discovering potentialities, acting on them, and accommodating them. Diversity was conducive to the discovery of potentialities because it created natural experiments: thus, discrete but interconnected polities addressed shared challenges in different ways and learned from outcomes. Domestic pluralism likewise contributed by weakening orthodoxies.[133]

The proper enabling conditions arose from the institutionalization of spaces and activities that fostered debate and innovation: parliaments, learned societies, patent offices, and economic organizations from public banks and joint-stock and chartered corporations to stock and bond markets. More generally, capitalism could flourish only in a capitalist society in which elite support was assured: sustained modernizing development was fueled by synergies between the economic and the political orders.[134]

Joseph Bryant succinctly captures this relationship in his defense of the view that "the nascent European fusion of mercantilist imperialism with a technologically driven capitalistic transformation of production and exchange was the decisive development." Even if Western Europe's political economy as such did not create industrialization, it "created a set of institutions able to promote industrialization once it appeared."[135]

This assessment, however, may well be too conservative. Had it not been for the competitive pressures of Europe's state system, would industrialization and the fossil fuel economy have taken off at all? Or, at the very least, might they not have been delayed?

But there is no need to delve into such counterfactuals: for present purposes, the question is moot. Institutions played a crucial role regardless of whether they made transformative breakthroughs possible in the first place by providing the required set of incentives or whether they "merely" allowed such breakthroughs to succeed.[136]

"ALL UNDER HEAVEN UNDER ONE LINEAGE"

The Logic of Imperial Institutions

How do conditions in traditional empires compare to the European experience? In addressing this question, I focus on China before I more briefly turn to other cases. The Chinese example illustrates several key points: how imperial continuity preserved inefficient arrangements and blocked change; the drawbacks of monopolistic policymaking; the impact of sustained competition as revealed through its absence; and the weight of persistent imperial traditions in general.[137]

We must be careful not to perpetuate outdated narratives. Imperial rule outside Europe used to be portrayed as despotic and oppressive. Modern accounts were mired in Orientalizing tropes that ultimately go back to the ancient Greeks almost two and a half thousand years ago. More often than not, this biased perspective generated long lists of what was "wrong" with China and other Asian societies. Eric Jones's blithe assertion that "despotic Asian institutions suppressed creativity" is representative in this regard.[138]

Revisionist scholarship has criticized this school of thought, reminding us that "it is time to bury the despot." Subtler assessments have taken over, emphasizing features that were intrinsic to the logic of imperial rule and may even have contributed to public welfare but did not support the dynamics that pushed European societies into uncharted territory.[139]

In one of the most ambitious interpretations to date, Dingxin Zhao seeks to explain China's macro-social evolution with reference to the configuration of the principal sources of social power over the long run. In his telling, the pressures of intensifying military competition during the Warring States period gave rise to an instrumental culture in which bureaucracy, varied intellectual traditions, and economic activity expanded side by side but state power came to outweigh all its rivals: aristocratic autonomy was suppressed, Legalist principles carried the day, and merchants remained politically disempowered.[140]

As already noted in chapter 9, the rigid Legalist template proved unsustainable once interstate competition subsided and was replaced by a hybrid of Confucian and Legalist norms under the Han dynasty. The resultant "highly stable crystallization" merged political and ideological power, ensured its control of military power, and marginalized economic power. The symbiotic relationship between rulers and Confucian scholar-officials created a powerful and highly resilient political system. While imperial unity curtailed the autonomy of the scholarly elite, the latter's cultural hegemony and access to state rents offered ample compensation. With some exceptions, discussed below, the state neither inhibited nor promoted private commercial ventures. Denied a power base from which to defend their own interests, merchants were compelled to defer to the Confucian scholar elite.[141]

Zhao takes pains to stress that deviations from this pattern—such as periods of warlordism and political disunity or the late Tang/Song transition to more commercially oriented cities—do not undermine the fact that this template remained in place in the long term and, crucially, matters most for "*comparing* China as a whole with other civilizations, especially the West."[142]

The twin hegemonies of the dominant belief and value system and of universal empire were closely intertwined. Confucianism was revived under the Northern Song, which greatly expanded the civil service examination system by setting up more than 400 schools for candidates, helping to establish a gentry class based on canonical education rather than inherited wealth. Firmly attached to the state, this elite supported it whether from within or outside the civil service and remained loyal regardless of which regime was in power.[143]

At the same time, in the absence of an arms race that might have generated demand for new forms of finance, China's "capitalists remained a subordinate social group with no capacity to subject the general interest to their own class interest"—or, more modestly, even to counterbalance state power.[144]

China's cities generally enjoyed less autonomy than their European counterparts. Their fortunes were tied up with dynastic changes and centralized political and administrative decisions. Lacking political standing, merchants were strongly motivated to join the official class via kinsmen, to ally themselves to gentry families, and to participate in government at the local level: whatever formal standing they could hope to gain would accrue from public service and proximity to traditional power brokers. The contrast to medieval and early modern Europe, where financiers and associations of merchants and craftsmen could dominate local politics and overseas trading companies were equipped with their own military arms, could hardly have been more dramatic.[145]

Low fiscal capacity stifled state formation and developmental policies. A simple model developed by Loren Brandt, Debin Ma, and Thomas Rawski envisions revolts and invasion as the biggest threats to imperial authority and unity. A tax system centered on privately owned land triggered conflicts between rent-seeking officials and landowning households that were allied to local gentry. Moreover, due to monitoring problems that were inevitable in a centralized hierarchy that operated across such a large territory, state agents could not be sufficiently deterred by internal checks. The results were informal taxation, bureaucratic predation, and tax avoidance by the privileged, all of which undermined the standing of the central authorities.[146]

For the most part, formal tax rates were low and the bureaucracy was relatively small. In fact, public revenue declined from the Song to the Qing periods just as it rose in Europe. This limited spending to basic welfare programs and defense and encouraged emphasis on maintenance rather than performance. Dependence on informal or de facto property rights meant that legal processes were primarily determined by social hierarchy and status. Commercial and civil law codes were absent. Thus, property rights remained secondary to the political standing of property holders: "The foundation of property rights in imperial China, especially in the sphere of commerce, rested on politics rather than law."[147]

This in turn compelled entrepreneurs to seek accommodation with officials: the wealthy obtained titles, the poor relied on patronage networks, and merchants pursued state-approved monopolies. Heads of merchant associations were expected to control members and deliver tax revenues, and acted as officials' surrogates to block unwelcome initiatives. Instead of charters, patronage relations played a central role in these bodies.[148]

Taken together, these factors favored a long-term equilibrium characterized by "mutual reinforcement between ideology and incentives." Investment in Confucian education was tied to the status, power, and income enjoyed by officials, a nexus that also attracted well-off merchants. The ensuing "cross-fertilization of economic resources, status, and political power represented both a bulwark of stability and a formidable obstacle to reform." As a consequence, institutional arrangements were stable, resilient, and path-dependent.

The repeated success of imperial restoration after intermittent shocks shows how much the interests of rulers and various elite groups from bureaucrats and scholars to commercial and landed property owners overlapped and coalesced into "a tight web of vested interests, that, once established, proved extremely difficult to dislodge." Overall, these structures impeded economic development due to lack of vision, fiscal capacity, and administrative support. Instead, they sustained a patronage economy governed by interlocking elite interests that made it resistant to change.[149]

Other scholars have painted a similar picture. To name just one more example, Bin Wong contrasts the multiple divisions of Europe that manifested themselves both in competition between states and, domestically, in centralizing governments' negotiating "with distinct and delimited social groups which developed their claims on the state as the state expanded its capacities to extract resources and make war" with conditions in China, where neither elites nor commoners "enjoyed institutionalized positions of autonomous power from which they could place claims on the state as a counterweight to its continued expansion." Instead, the Chinese merger of officials and elites "produced a continuum between state and society" with an enduring preference for "a vertically integrated unitary state."[150]

Fragmentation: Exceptions Proving the Rule

Before we take a closer look at some of these traits and their impact on development, it is worth starting by considering counterexamples— periods of fragmentation that tended to be associated with greater innovation. These phases reveal the conservative climate of universal empire through its temporary absence, and thus offer further support for the fragmentation thesis. More specifically, polycentrism and the pressures of war proved conducive to commercial development as competition opened polities to new influences and experimentation. As Jean Baechler put it, "Each time China was politically divided, capitalism flourished."[151]

The Warring States period was marked by seminal creativity, from the rebuilding of state structures to the Hundred Schools of Thought that advertised a wide variety of worldviews. The centralizing measures taken to standardize landholdings, mobilize the general population, and protect it from local elites were quite radical. They also fostered selection, as polities either succeeded in copying adaptive traits or risked failure. The competitive state system created a vibrant marketplace of ideas in which roving experts ("sages") changed patrons at will. Perhaps most important, given the much later European experience, the desirability of organizing and increasing resources for the purpose of competition was explicitly recognized.[152]

The imperial Qin and early Han regimes, by contrast, indulged physiocratic tendencies, privileging the agrarian sphere at the expense of commerce. The Qin conquered China in part by arresting the rise of the merchant class in the Central Plain, in economic terms the most advanced part of the region. Cities were turned into "bastions of bureaucratic rule." When the Western Han, most notably under the emperor Wu, felt the need to mobilize greater resources, they sought to do so by supplanting private enterprise with state-run institutions.[153]

Centuries later, the Han collapse exposed northern China to foreign rule but released the more sheltered south from some of these strictures. Under the Southern Dynasties of the fifth and sixth centuries CE, the southern capital Jiankang grew into a prominent hub of commerce. In a turn away from older traditions, the city boasted more markets and fewer internal walls than the more regimented Han capitals had. The southern port of Guangzhou traded with Southeast Asia, India, and even Europe, and served as a conduit for Buddhism's entry into China. Overall, the independent states of the south "stimulated robust economic growth." The Sui/Tang unification subsequently slowed commercial development, sidelining Jiankang as a rival power center.[154]

Yet innovative development returned on an even larger scale from the late Tang period onward. The upheavals of the mid-eighth century had hollowed out imperial unity and made the central state dependent on salaried soldiers, some of whom were drawn from beyond the empire. Commercialized warfare escalated demands for revenue, which in turn gave a big boost to monetization, indirect taxes, and the professionalization of tax collection. At the same time, waning state power lifted restrictions on merchants and private commerce.[155]

Maritime overseas trade took off in the first half of the tenth century, when the independent coastal kingdoms of Nan Han (in Guangdong) and Min (in Fujian) emerged from the wreckage of the Tang empire and developed "unparalleled dependence on trade." Urban poll taxes and tolls replaced revenue from land that was withheld by powerful landlords.[156]

Even though the Northern Song brought an end to political diversity in that part of China, the restored empire's need to maintain an army in excess of a million men (at least on paper) to protect the northern border zone against the Liao and Western Xia polities in Manchuria, northwestern China, and Inner Mongolia encouraged the government to promote trade. Similar to conditions in later European states, the military absorbed as much as four-fifths of total revenue. The security situation worsened when the Jurchen took over northern China in the late 1120s. Thus, even in the absence of a fully fledged state system, the empire for once experienced sufficient competitive pressures to embrace policies and institutions that were conducive to commercial development.[157]

The Song empire confronted these challenges by shoring up its fiscal system. The share of indirect taxes in government revenue rose from about a third at the end of the tenth century to two-thirds by the 1070s. Excise taxes focused on urban consumption and long-distance trade. Massive urban growth, unfettered marketplaces, a huge expansion of water transport and exchange, and the growing sophistication of financial intermediation led to an economic boom that filled the state's coffers: the silver value of revenue increased 140 percent between the end of the tenth and the late eleventh centuries.[158]

This boom also heightened demand for credit. From the late Tang period onward—a time of fading state capacity—merchants had developed novel financial instruments. Learning from these innovations, the Northern Song authorities introduced vouchers to pay suppliers, which then circulated and sustained a speculative securities market. The Southern Song, ever more pressed for income, expanded this market by issuing promissory notes. By the mid-thirteenth century, the notes in circulation equaled seven times annual state revenue: credit had become the principal means of funding war.

This did not create a viable bond market: notes were redeemable in the short term, were traded in voucher and pawnshops, and were devalued by hyperinflation once the wars against the Mongols gathered steam. Even so, they represented an innovative and disruptive deviation from the conservative imperial tradition of prioritizing bronze coinage that was unlikely to have occurred under different circumstances, and was not in fact repeated after the end of Mongol rule. Thus, as William Liu observes, military needs turned the Song period into "probably the most creative period in the financial history of China."[159]

Yet in the end, all of this remained atypical, for the simple reason that periods of persistent interstate competition along European lines were relatively rare in Chinese history. Apart from the chaotic dislocations of the Period of Disunion of the fourth through sixth centuries CE, the Song era was the only major exception. Traditionally, domestic revolts and frontier wars were the leading sources of conflict, far more so than symmetric interstate warfare was. Beginning under the Western Han, asymmetric competition with steppe opponents was the norm. In the fifth and sixth centuries CE, the Northern Wei state battled the Rouran. In the seventh century, the Tang campaigned from a position of strength; Ming clashes with Mongols led to a stalemate and upgraded border walls; and the Qing finally managed to pacify the steppe and ushered in a period of deceptive peace that ended once again in internal uprisings, whose ferocity dwarfed the impact of hostile European intervention.[160]

It might seem excessive to speak, as Giovanni Arrighi does, of "The Five Hundred Years' Peace" from about 1400 onward, which, aside from campaigns along the steppe frontier, was punctuated only by brief encounters with Japan and, later, Britain, and a few engagements in Southeast Asia. But this phrase captures an important truth: from the sixteenth to the eighteenth century, China was at war with parties other than steppe opponents for merely 3 percent of the time. The empire's huge size reliably deterred potential state-level challengers, insofar as there were any left in that part of the world.[161]

That said, campaigns and defensive measures against steppe enemies could also be expensive, and the need to fund them ended only after the 1760s. Nor was war completely marginalized: the Qing in particular cultivated a martial image. During the Mongol period, the sieges and combat on rivers and the sea that characterized warfare in southern China had been a boon for gunpowder weaponry and shipbuilding. Yet once these conflicts ended after 1368, the remaining wars against horsemen retarded Chinese firearms technology and reduced demand for naval assets. In Europe, by contrast, continuing and indeed steadily growing investment in precisely those two sectors provided a powerful stimulus for innovation in technology and financing. Thus, even as late imperial China engaged in warfare, the latter's asymmetric character greatly reduced its developmental benefits.[162]

Monopolistic Policymaking

Under conditions of substantively uncontested unitary imperial rule and macro-regional hegemony, competitive pressures subsided while the scope for idiosyncratic centralized decision-making increased. Empires were not as autocratic as they were formerly portrayed in Western scholarship not because they were not organized around centralizing autocracies, which they usually were, but because their nascent despotism was tempered by the aggregate power of local elites. This does not mean, however, that imperial centers had no bite and could not, if unconstrained by external exigencies, decree sweeping measures without regard to human welfare and consultation with civil society. China's history shows that rulers and their inner apparatus were perfectly capable of doing so, and sometimes in ways that inflicted serious damage on the economy.

Early Ming policies are an (in)famous example. In the late fourteenth century, the dynasty's founder, the Hongwu emperor, embarked on ambitious antimarket reforms that sought to restore autarkic village economies and eliminate the inequalities brought about by market exchange. This goal was to be accomplished by returning to payments in kind and labor services in lieu of monetary transfers, and by reestablishing the kind of self-sufficient military farms that had gone out of fashion under the Tang 600 years earlier.[163]

These measures stand in stark contrast to the numerous institutional innovations that had peaked under the Southern Song, such as "commercial brokers, credit financing, bills of exchange, advance sales contracts, commenda partnerships, and joint-capital enterprises." Past performance, as they say, does not guarantee future results, at least not as long as a monopolistic government could execute a U-turn without having to worry too much about the consequences.[164]

From the late fourteenth to the mid-fifteenth century, the shift from a market to a command economy resulted in widespread demonetization, as land taxes were rendered in-kind. Forced migrations and labor services curbed market interactions, and many farmers resorted to barter. The turn away from the market-oriented Song economy that had largely persisted under Mongol rule could hardly have been more radical.[165]

Multiple economic indicators expose the adverse effects of these policies. Per capita income was much lower under the early Ming than it had been in the eleventh century. Jiangnan, the most developed region, was no exception: land confiscations interfered with cultivation on more than half of its land, and rural household incomes fell. Elsewhere, the promotion of extensive farming likewise caused a major economic regression. Infrastructural investment focused on the Grand Canal: undertaken for the purpose of supplying the north with tax grain, these works bypassed many secondary cities, cutting them off from exchange. Coastal transport, which would have been cheaper, was neglected. Resources that were funneled to the north were unavailable for local investment, which created considerable opportunity costs. And in northern China itself, in order to strengthen military capabilities, the command economy expended great efforts on bolstering military farms and forcibly resettling farmers to reclaim land.[166]

Economic historian Richard von Glahn's verdict deserves quoting at some length not only because of his eminence but also because of his generally optimistic perspective on China's economic development:

> The anti-commercial policies of the early Ming state, coupled with its expropriation of the wealth of the Jiangnan elite, wreaked havoc on the flourishing market economy of the Jiangnan region and arrested the commercial and urban growth that had continued with little disruption throughout the era of Mongol rule. Commerce and industry foundered, hampered by mismanagement of the monetary system, a sharp decline in overseas trade, and a system of hereditary artisan households that impeded the rational allocation of labor. Urban population fell, and many market towns were abandoned. The economic malaise that resulted from the traumatic transition from Mongol to Ming rule persisted for more than a century.[167]

Even in the absence of plausible alternatives, despotism had its limits. None of these deleterious policies could be maintained for very long: communal organization of labor, hereditary occupational groups, and labor services all faded in the course of the fifteenth century. Market activity and prices recovered in the sixteenth century, yet without ever quite matching the levels of the Song era. What matters most, however, is that hegemonic empire made such sweeping interventions possible to begin with.[168]

Top-down decisions on how to engage with the outside world fall in the same category. In chapter 11, I consider in some detail the extravagant naval expeditions of the early fifteenth century and their sudden termination. They exemplify a textbook case of monopolistic decision-making: launched at enormous expense for no tangible material benefit, they were equally swiftly shut down once political preferences at the imperial court changed.[169]

Restrictions on trade and seafaring were imposed with greater frequency, invariably in the context of uncontested imperial hegemony: reduced competitive pressures not only weakened the state's need to profit from commercial exchange but also gave it more leeway in passing deleterious regulation. Thus, the Mongol regime first set up a state monopoly on overseas trade and then banned private merchants from dealing with foreign parties altogether. The Ming followed suit: in the late fourteenth century, coastal residents were forbidden to venture overseas. Only state-run "tribute missions" were allowed to do so. Further bans of private maritime commerce were issued in the fifteenth century and sometimes even extended to coastal shipping.[170]

At various points in the sixteenth century, the government prohibited the construction and operation of large oceangoing ships and authorized coastal authorities to destroy such vessels and arrest any merchants on them. In a back-and-forth that highlights the intrinsic capriciousness of monopolistic decision-making, the ban on private overseas trade was partially rescinded in 1567, then reintroduced in the early seventeenth century and again by the early Qing during their campaign against Taiwan until 1684. A short interlude of relaxation was followed by renewed bans from 1717 onward, until Guangzhou was designated as the only legitimate port for foreign trade in 1757. As Mark Elvin points out, it was precisely the huge size of the empire that made such policies possible in the first place: smaller states could not readily have shut themselves off like this, or would have paid dearly if they had done so.[171]

Bans did not stop trade but slowed it down, most notably from the fourteenth through the sixteenth centuries, when European overseas commerce embarked on its great expansion. Yet even if state fiat could not hope to put an end to private ventures, it did create antagonism between the authorities and merchants, deprive government of revenue, limit the scale of exchange, and promote corruption. The criminalization of commercial activities imposed additional costs, as merchants were forced to evade detection and bribe state agents to turn a blind eye. Instead of entering European-style partnerships with the state, "the energies of tough seafaring folk, which might have been turned outwards, were spent in running contraband and fighting with government troops."[172]

Land-based gentry who protected smugglers benefited from trade restrictions. Their involvement strengthened the nonmercantile element of Chinese society, keeping traders dependent on patronage. It was structural trends such as this that mattered most in the long run, more than whether particular forms of trade were permitted or constrained at any point in time. Thus, even when merchants and officials entered a symbiotic relationship under the later Qing, it was on the latter's terms.[173]

Much of what was achieved was accomplished despite the state rather than thanks to it. Even earlier, under the Song and Yuan, when the political climate had been more favorable, the development of commerce in coastal Fujian had been held back by the fact that maritime and property laws and contracts only stood a chance of being enforced "when local government was not particularly corrupt."[174]

In the late imperial period, Chinese traders did not generally receive active support from the state. At that critical juncture of emergent global integration, China's commerce was both laissez faire and constrained, rather than "state-pulled" and protected as it was under the European system of mercantilism and its reinforcement by naval power that boosted trade. In this respect, of course, China's experience was representative of that of traditional empires overall: regardless of whether their leaders were sympathetic, indifferent, or hostile to trade, such polities were invariably deficient in institutionalized bourgeois power and the commerce- and growth-oriented policies their influence might have inspired.[175]

Much the same was true of domestic exchange. In late imperial China, merchants' involvement in the grain trade was circumscribed by hoarding in state granaries and relief schemes that sought to limit their profits. Merchant groups associated with salt and iron monopolies were closely supervised and acted mainly as distributors, performing functions the state had outsourced to them. Monopolies were less common than in Europe, offering fewer opportunities and "privileged niches" for entrepreneurs. Moreover, even though domestic trade was only lightly taxed, the authorities remained concerned about high profits and merchant wealth and could arbitrarily decide to intervene. Unlike in Europe, merchants were thus subordinates rather than partners of the state, and their position was much more precarious.[176]

Monopolistic decision-making in other domains added to the burden. For instance, the repeated relocation of capital cities interfered with cumulative growth in metropolitan centers and the surrounding regions. Bans on ideas were also an option. The central authorities had little compunction about suppressing unwelcome thought by fiat and force. Ming censorship led to the punishment or maltreatment of outspoken memorialists. The Qing conquest regime was sensitive to anti-Manchu sentiments, a stance that encouraged a retreat into apolitical and conservative scholarship.[177]

Overt suppression had a long pedigree, ranging in time from the First Emperor's (perhaps doubtful) burning of numerous historical and didactic books to the safely attested great book proscription of the 1770s that caused the permanent loss of more than four-fifths of the 2,665 targeted texts. But it is striking that such measures were on the whole far less common and systematic than the countless doctrinal and intellectual persecutions that run like a red thread through European history. It appears that the overwhelming weight of imperial authority muted conflict: as Derk Bodde ingeniously observes, the relative weakness of Western oppressors—constrained in their actions by exit options and internal divisions of social power—made it easier for dissenters to resist, which led to more intense struggle. In China, by contrast, intellectuals' acceptance of imperial control was a deeply ingrained habit and it reduced the odds of open clashes.[178]

In the final analysis, whether particular policies promoted or impeded economic development and innovation may well be a secondary issue. Two features were crucial: the latent potential for doing harm, and the structural lack of diversity. Concerning the first point, the scale of malignant intervention mattered less than "the simple fact that government might interfere any time it saw fit."[179]

Such interventions went far back. When the regent Wang Mang usurped the throne from the Han in 9 CE, he reportedly instituted a series of ambitious economic reforms from land-distribution schemes, a ban on private land transactions, and the abolition of slavery to the confiscation of private bullion stocks and the distribution of a bewildering variety of fiduciary coins. It remains unclear just how much damage was done: the relevant sources date from after the restoration of the Han dynasty in 23 CE and are implacably hostile to the Wang Mang regime and thus prone to exaggerate its shortcomings. Even so, we get a sense of the unsteady nature of the usurper's decision-making: some of his measures were already repealed during his reign. The disruptive potential of radical decrees emanating from the imperial court was considerable.[180]

The "New Policies" that were adopted under the Northern Song are a more recent and much-better-documented example of this approach. Promoted by a faction led by the imperial chancellor Wang Anshi in the 1070s, they were designed to raise state capacity and boost commercial development by means of expansive intervention: the state increased the money supply, imposed price and wage controls, and offered state loans to farmers. Implementation was intermittent, governed by ongoing power struggles between reforming and opposing factions that persecuted one another to the best of their abilities. After several policy swings over the course of a few decades, the defeat and retreat of the

Song in the 1120s discredited the program and led to its demise. Once again, the key point is not the substantive content of these measures but the manner in which they were decided and reversed in response to highly volatile power dynamics at a monopolistic center.[181]

The second problem associated with monopoly was even more serious: over the long run, imperial persistence lowered diversity in policy approaches. This is well illustrated by China's traditional governmental emphasis on preserving the agrarian economy and especially the free peasantry, which was considered the foundation of the imperial edifice. Vries labels this prioritization "agrarian paternalism"—the premise that the state's chief responsibility was to stabilize the social order and ensure human welfare by protecting family farms.[182]

Given the recurrence of massive peasant revolts in Chinese history, this preoccupation made perfect sense if the overarching goal was maintenance of existing arrangements. Chinese policies reflect ancient concerns that appear as early as the Confucian *Analects*: "I hear that rulers of states and heads of families fear inequality, but not poverty; they fear instability, but not scarcity of people."[183]

Kent Gang Deng has elevated this conservative stance into *the* defining principle of Chinese economic history: a "trinary structure" composed of "interlinked counterpoises" between agricultural dominance, a free peasantry, and physiocratic government that evolved in the Warring States period and proved highly resilient over time. The Song embrace of commercialism remained the only significant exception to this norm. In Europe, by contrast, rural production systems and social relations varied greatly, from the enclosure movement and the proletarianization of the labor force that facilitated rationalization and capitalistic exploitation of the countryside in England at one end of the spectrum all the way to Russian serfdom at the other.[184]

Conducive to the survival of an imperial behemoth and its ruling bureaucracy, Chinese-style agrarianism was antithetical to the deliberate promotion of commercial development. Thus, China's merchants and entrepreneurs were not merely constrained by the aforementioned configuration of social power that has been traced back to antiquity: this constraint was also a direct function of imperial self-preservation and perpetuation. Transcending individual dynasties, the government's agrarian-paternalist bias reveals the true impact of monopolistically centralized policy choices: they shaped outcomes over the long run primarily because there was no institutionalized political space for alternatives—space that Europe's competitive state system provided in abundance.

Taxation and Corruption

Even so, policymaking, however persistent or capricious, was arguably a lesser impediment to modernizing development than the generically laissez-faire tendencies of the imperial monopolist. China's empire, just as many others, was a "capstone" state, perched atop local and regional societies. If anything, this detachment grew over time. Having absorbed the lessons of multiple more or less successful previous iterations of imperial rule, the Ming and Qing regimes had perfected this style of governance. Spared any serious outside competition, they contented themselves with fragmented fiscal operations, low centralized revenue, and modest state capacity.[185]

In this environment, free markets operated under benign neglect, dominated by groups with little faith in imperial institutions but ample trust in family and lineage. As a result, support for entrepreneurship was privatized and lacked public backing. Protection of property rights and contract enforcement were weak spots. Whereas in Europe, competing states offered formal enforcement because they sought out revenue from contract registration and conflict resolution, the Chinese government gave less weight to formal arrangements.[186]

Low state capacity adversely affected the financial sector. Whereas European credit markets benefited from the mountains of public debt incurred by warring governments, no such stimulus existed in China. The empire did not issue public debt until the mid-nineteenth century. There had generally been little demand: either taxes were sufficient to cover expenses, or potential lenders would have been reluctant to provide funds to a monopolist in times of crisis. During crises, the government would fall back on currency manipulation and predation on the wealthy. These options in turn exposed merchants to bullying and made them less inclined to trust the authorities.

Moreover, the sheer physical scale of the empire helped substitute movements of resources across regions (i.e., transfers in space) for credit (i.e., transfer in time). After all, the ability to concentrate extensively distributed means as needed had always been a hallmark and key benefit of large empire: yet it also represented a disincentive to more sophisticated solutions that might have spurred further innovation and growth. As a result, China's financial system remained underdeveloped.[187]

Limited demand for private credit also contributed to this outcome. Not only did the dominance of labor-intensive rice farming and household handicraft production fail to generate strong demand for financing: when needed, lineages and clans provided resources for their members. Empire played a role in this as well: as we will see below, the expansion of these bodies and their social significance was meaningfully linked to the persistence of imperial rule.[188]

Thanks to more restrained military spending, taxes were low compared to those levied in much of early modern Europe. For various reasons, regular per capita tax income actually declined under the Qing: dues were often not fully collected, levies relied on registers that dated from the Ming period and were only schematically updated, and newly cultivated land frequently went unregistered. Moreover, endemic corruption siphoned off revenue.[189]

These tendencies were part of a time-honored pattern. Whereas newly installed dynasties managed to override vested interests, in the later stages of their rule, elite groups had learned how to conceal assets, which in turn diminished the state's ability to respond to popular risings triggered by elite predation and demographic pressures. Only under the Song and after the mid-nineteenth century did serious external or internal threats impel fiscal intensification.[190]

In the late imperial period in particular, neo-Confucian agrarian paternalism and low fiscal intakes degraded the state's infrastructural capacity to lows that "limited potential for economic growth along Schumpeterian lines"—growth born of creative destruction of established practices—in favor of less sustainable Smithian growth driven by market expansion, intensification, and specialization of labor. Weak fiscal institutions also "left little scope for the state to promote economic development," not least because consumption-focused welfare schemes such as granaries absorbed civilian funds.[191]

Low state capacity and rampant corruption conspired to weaken de facto protection of industrial and commercial property rights. We owe to Chen Qiang an illuminating model of real tax rates as a measure of property rights protection. The "real" tax burden was composed of the central tax rate (revenues levied and received by the imperial authorities), which could be low; local tax rates, that is, rents taken by officials; and the public-security tax rate, defined as the cost of poor governance and banditry. Once all these complementary elements are taken into account, the real tax rate in late imperial China appears to have been both high and highly variable, sensitive as it was to frequent turnover among officials and changes in security conditions.[192]

While the considerable fiscal exertions and adequate officials' salaries of the Song period—driven by competitive pressures—helped contain rent-seeking and security risks, the Ming and Qing regimes, programmatically focused on frugality and simplicity, kept central taxes too low, which had the unwelcome effect of raising the real tax rate. Underpaid and understaffed local offices embraced institutionalized corruption, extracting fees from traders and manufacturers. Corruption incomes that amounted to a large multiple of official stipends highlight the scale of the problem, which was exacerbated by a weak judicial system.[193]

As a result, late imperial real tax rates need not have been lower than they had been under the fiscally aggressive Song, but were made more burdensome by their greater randomness. This might even have contributed to the deurbanization that occurred under the Ming and Qing: the concentration of officials in major cities negatively impacted commerce and encouraged manufacturers and bankers to decamp for more peripheral locations.[194]

In all of this, the degree to which the empire enjoyed hegemonic status was of critical importance. Song policymaking had been galvanized by severe and growing competitive pressure from the northern periphery. It was not ideological commitment to small central government and light taxation as such that accounted for the late imperial inclination to let things slide: the absence of serious challenges made this predisposition viable in the first place.[195]

It is one of the supreme ironies of history that ostensibly benign policies in China—low taxes, a largely hands-off approach to the economy, and basic food relief schemes for the general population—constrained development whereas the wasteful and blood-drenched nexus of ceaseless war, ever-rising taxes, and fierce protectionism in Western Europe boosted it in the end.[196]

Firms and Clans

Late imperial China's property rights regimes were not favorable to the creation of large and vertically and horizontally integrated industrial and commercial firms. Even though firms functioned better than earlier scholarship was prepared to accept, they were held back by a very limited regulatory framework that made codified law a poor means of enacting rules regarding business affairs.[197]

The rise of kinship networks from the Song period onward checked concentration of landownership—and thus agricultural productivity—and more generally promoted a kin-based and collectivist value system, kin morality, and personal modes of rule enforcement. During the same period, the Western European model of corporate organization favored a generalized and individualistic value system, generalized morality, and impersonal enforcement. These differences shaped institutional evolution in China, constraining civil and commercial law, credit, and the development of impersonal exchange, features that undergirded Western innovation and progress. Over time, lineage trusts adopted a rentier mentality that privileged broad portfolios over the efficiency of individual firms and helped keep unprofitable ventures afloat.[198]

The secular expansion of clan networks cannot be separated from imperial persistence. Direct promotion by the state was unlikely to have been decisive: although the Song permitted ancestor worship beyond aristocratic houses, the Ming extended this right to all commoners, and

the early Qing took a more active role in encouraging this mode of social organization, state measures tended to be reactive to existing private
activity rather than a driving force in their own right. On the whole, the
imperial state was simply too weak to launch or sustain this extremely
widespread process.

Its influence was more indirect. After the destruction of the Tang
aristocracy in the early tenth century, officials in the reconstituted empire of the Song were eager to establish their own networks as markers
of status and vehicles of advancement. Their preferences proved seminal
beyond their own circles, and were taken and emulated by aspirational
commoners. Repeated imperial restoration sustained this trend and facilitated the gradual spread of lineage networks.[199]

While Europe Took Off

Had China begun to move in a more promising direction when it was
overtaken by the European expansion? Revisionist scholarship has made
much of the easing of restraints and economic growth that took place
under the Qing. Markets performed similarly well in late eighteenth-
century China and Western Europe, although by some measures Britain
already claimed the top spot. And we must not forget that while China
was still enjoying the fruits of peace, the wars and trade barriers of Europe
did not merely promote but also burdened economic development.[200]

Even so, most indicators leave no doubt that economic divergence
was already well under way. Real wages in the most economically developed parts of China were lower than their European equivalents in Britain
and the Netherlands, and real incomes declined during the eighteenth
and into the nineteenth centuries. Capitalistic features remained underdeveloped: the share of wage workers in the English labor force was
much larger than in China. Commercial networks bypassed most of the
countryside because of high transportation costs and the lack of access
to waterways in the north. In the late eighteenth century, interregional
integration consequently began to wane.[201]

Even the economy of the Yangzi delta region, the most advanced in
China, continued to be shaped by Malthusian processes and an

agricultural sector dominated by peasant households and a ruling class that preyed on them. Living standards and agricultural labor productivity were in decline. In England, by contrast, workers who were relatively well protected from extra-economic coercion had become dependent on market relations for their subsistence and operated under intense competitive constraints.[202]

Although permanent partnership firms had by then come into existence, China still lacked a market for formally trading shares, and partnerships relied on equity investments rather than credit. Pawnbrokers remained the principal source of credit, and there were no genuine banks in the European sense. In part because of this, interest rates and the real cost of capital were much higher than in Western Europe.[203]

At best, therefore, conditions reflected what Zhao calls "mid-dynasty prosperity," an intermediate phase of pragmatic management of a large stable empire after the economy had recovered from the dislocations of the Ming–Qing transition but before population growth curbed Smithian growth—yet without any discernible potential for transformative change. From this perspective, there was no compelling reason that this mid-Qing flourishing should not have petered out just as previous efflorescences had done, even if European aggressors had not appeared on the scene. In fact, the White Lotus rebellion of the 1790s, fully half a century prior to the Opium Wars, was a typical sign of late dynastic decline.[204]

Review of two millennia of imperial history offers ample support for this reading. On average, two centuries passed between the founding of a new dynasty and the onset of serious popular rebellions that undermined it. Under the Qing, risings commenced about 150 years into their rule, followed by the cataclysmic Taiping rebellion another half century later. Comparatively speaking, these crises arrived right on time.[205]

More specifically, the growth of an unmarried male population and signs of Malthusian pressures in the eighteenth century cast the subsequent famines and risings as the culmination of a drawn-out process. And even if the strength of these demographic and resource constraints remains contested, there can be no doubt that—in von Glahn's words—the "lack of significant innovation in productive technologies" placed a growing burden on the agricultural base. At the same time, England benefited hugely from an agricultural revolution that supported both ongoing population growth and concurrent urbanization.[206]

In all of this, details matter little. A simple counterfactual shows why. Even if, on that occasion, imperial destabilization and breakdown could somehow have been avoided or, perhaps more plausibly, if an equivalent empire could swiftly have been put back together after such a break- down and resumed business as usual—featuring ostensibly benevolent and light-handed central policies such as low taxes, agrarianism, basic welfare provisions, and the preservation of peace—such outcomes were not likely to precipitate transformative innovation.[207]

It is telling that "despite China's integration into global trade net- works, movement toward an industrial revolution was almost wholly absent before the twentieth century." Elite groups to whom vital tasks had traditionally been delegated could not be expected to mobilize suf- ficient material and human resources for industrialization even when the Qing and later the Chinese Republic underwent generations of "na- tional humiliation." Effective responses to the growing pressures that arose in the nineteenth century would have required a systematic over- haul that was incompatible with existing elite entrenchment. Thus, be- lated state initiatives from the 1860s onward failed to harness adequate support from the private sector and were hobbled by predation by local powerholders.[208]

Powerful and opportunistically uncooperative elites were a defining characteristic of the capstone state, which had reached its most mature form in hegemonic tributary empires. Absent credible, symmetric com- petition, "China's rulers were not constantly benchmarking their em- pire." Nor were the rulers of similar empires.[209]

Beyond China

In modern scholarship, political economy has long been assigned a cen- tral role in accounting for developmental outcomes, not least with re- spect to economic innovation: when we compare early modern Europe and late imperial China, "the key reasons for economic divergence were political." As Bin Wong notes, even though it was ultimately macro-inventions that made European modern economic growth possible, they did not arise in a vacuum: rather, they needed to mesh well with capitalist institutions to transform the economy. Thus, "the Industrial Revolution fit within European economic institutions more effectively than Chinese ones," given that the former "sought competition and growth" whereas the latter "aimed for . . . static efficiency." As a result, as we just saw, the late imperial Chinese economy "lacked the range of financial markets, business organizations, and resource bases created by commercial capitalism supported by European states bent upon making themselves stronger and wealthier than their competitors."[210]

These outcomes were by no means limited to imperial China. While some features, such as the Confucian inflection of governance, were indeed specific to its elite culture, others were widely shared among mature traditional empires, most notably relatively low state capacity and emphasis on maintenance of the status quo.

Size as such may have acted as a significant constraint on development. Internal diversity and logistical obstacles put large empires under continual strain. This alone would have helped encourage conservative policies aimed at preservation. As John Hall explains, "Pre-industrial empires are too centralized for their logistical capacity, and thus have produced capstone government based on their accurate knowledge that secondary organizations are dangerous."[211]

Such polities might simply have been "too big and too diverse to be efficient" or to develop into developmental states. Comparative review suggests that the often huge empires that formed in the "exposed zone" bordering the great Eurasian steppe were less able to sustain progressive centralization than were states in the "protected zone." Population size rather than territory was the critical variable: unlike Chinese or Indian empires, Russia found it easier to manage its relatively modest population, which was strongly concentrated in the western and southwestern parts of its growing empire.[212]

Spatially extensive integration may also have been an impediment to intensive economic development. At first blush, it would seem to have been advantageous for imperial China to enjoy a free-trade zone the size of Western Europe, whereas war and protectionism imposed heavy costs on the latter. Yet historically, initial takeoff only occurred in modestly sized countries such as the Netherlands or Britain. The latter's export-driven expansion of its textile industry, for example, would have had a much lesser impact on a more populous country. In a polity as large as China, innovation was unlikely to be as concentrated, and thus as consequential, as in Europe.[213]

Moreover, at least in the Chinese case, that kind of transformative regional concentration was itself antithetical to the preservation of imperial stability. Whereas the parties to the European state system strove to amass resources at the expense of their rivals, an overarching policy goal of China's imperial government was to avoid stark imbalances. Systematic exploitation of peripheries was not an option.[214]

In theory, other imperial regimes might have been less concerned about such issues. Consideration of their properties at the same level of resolution as for China would require a much longer survey than is feasible here. But luckily for us, broad trends offer a convenient shortcut. After the end of antiquity, the largest Old World regions that hosted traditional empires, the Middle East and South Asia, came to share a characteristic that decisively interfered with developmental politics along European lines. They increasingly succumbed to foreign conquest regimes of steppe extraction: in the Middle East from the seventh century onward, and in India from the eleventh.[215]

These irruptions imposed two massive constraints. One was that iterative empire, however ephemeral it might sometimes have been, effectively prevented the formation of a stable competitive state system in which beneficial institutional adaptations could have been selected for and their cumulative gains preserved.[216]

In the Middle East, fragmentation, which was most pronounced in the eleventh and twelfth centuries, invariably gave way to reconsolidation under Turkic or Mongol rule. It is difficult to judge whether medieval Indian polities could have evolved toward more sustained polycentrism had they been given more time to do so. Their prospects were rather poor: indigenous regional empires of the post-Gupta period— Chalukya, Rashtrakuta, Pratihara, Pala, and Chola—although they could endure for centuries, were not particularly stable and fluctuated in size and power. In the end, of course, Islamic conquest regimes thwarted further political stabilization.[217]

The second constraint was that strong military rule, which became the norm across most of these regions, did not leave enough space for the kind of institution-building and state-society bargaining that occurred in medieval and early modern Europe. If anything, sultanistic tendencies grew over time: whereas the caliphate had sought accommodation with established civilian elites, Turkic and Mongol conquest regimes kept a greater distance. India's Muslim overlords remained (even) more detached from their subjects than earlier indigenous rulers had been. The Mughal regime in particular was principally run for the benefit of a tiny conquest elite that imposed heavy taxes on the peasantry.[218]

The dominance of Mamluk armies precluded the "productively adversarial relationship between rulers and local elites" that prevailed in Latin Europe, where feudalism, communalism, and other institutionalized forces restrained the executive and generated political stability. Even as the survival of earlier imperial fiscal and administrative structures (discussed in chapter 7) funded military services, the ensuing dominance of an often ethnically, culturally, and legally detached military caste diminished the bargaining power of gentry elites during the same period when the latter's peers became more powerful in Europe. The result was a perennial conquest society: in Patricia Crone's pithy conclusion, "Politics . . . remained the domain of the barbarians."[219]

Intellectual traditions reflected and reinforced this split between an alien militarized state and civil society. Contestation of despotism under the first caliphs had given way to its acceptance as fait accompli. Political power was regarded as indivisible—something to be delegated but not shared. Moreover, the canonical premise that social order and morality could only emanate from divine revelation militated against any notions that humans might be able to devise and opportunistically adjust their own codes. Political thought was more concerned with religion than with statecraft per se.[220]

Other attributes resembled those of late imperial China. Thus, although Mughal nominal tax rates were very high, it is unclear to what extent they translated to effective revenue for the central authorities, especially as collection always remained highly decentralized. The Ottomans encountered growing collection problems, and the share of income that reached the center declined: only in the nineteenth century did rising competitive pressures (caused by military defeats) induce effective reform. Mughal rule, by contrast, failed altogether.[221]

Compared to European polities, large Asian empires faced a disproportionate threat of internal rebellion. They traded off fiscal capacity for appeasement of local ruling groups, a compromise that left them with lower per capita revenue. Not only late imperial China but also the Ottoman and Mughal empires consequently lacked the European system of taxes and public debt that "promoted the development of institutions for financial intermediation and better-regulated supply of money for the economy at large."[222]

Likewise, Middle Eastern and South Asian merchants were just as institutionally marginalized as their Chinese counterparts. The Ottoman authorities prioritized the provisioning of the capital and the military, forcing merchants into an unequal relationship to ensure this objective, which overrode any desire to protect their own commercial constituents: "While European states focused on production and protection for local enterprises and workers, Ottoman officialdom was concerned with consumption and the adequacy of supplies of goods at the right price without regard to their place of origin." Following the same logic, the Mughals even granted trade privileges to (European) foreigners.[223]

The violent disruptions associated with building far-flung empires also dampened development. Northern China suffered from repeated invasions, even if the actual scale of demographic contractions may be impossible to ascertain. Except for the Black Death and, in Germany, the Thirty Years' War, Europe did not experience similarly massive downturns. Huge population losses have traditionally—if hyperbolically—been ascribed to Mongol campaigning, and serial Islamic invasions caused considerable damage to northern India.[224]

This mattered not least because technological knowledge could decline in the wake of demographic attrition: thus, societies in the "exposed zone" of the Old World were more susceptible to "interruptions in cumulative innovation." In South Asia, empire-builders' takeovers first sought plunder and then land revenue while neglecting the development of commercial resources. Moreover, the repeated relocation of political and commercial centers as a result of top-down decision-making or imperial transitions interfered with long-term cumulative growth.[225]

In addition to these relatively straightforward consequences of imperial rule, more indirect influences also inhibited economic progress. In Islamic societies, unincorporated trusts (*waqf*) were increasingly set up to ensure funding for services that was sheltered from state interference. Compared to European self-governing corporations, these endowments were less flexible in their objectives: their purpose, once established, could not easily be altered, not even by their founders. Their main appeal lay in their ability to shield assets from confiscation by serving as sacred wealth shelters. This made sense in the context of latent predatory threats but would have mattered less in societies in which state power was more effectively contained, as it often was in Latin Europe. The retardative economic impact of Islamic trusts was thus a function of state power: whereas medieval European rulers were too weak to block corporations, the early caliphates lacked serious challengers and later sultanates were generally capable of resorting to arbitrary coercion.[226]

It also made a difference that Islam had been closely tied up with early state formation whereas Christianity had emerged within a settled empire. This left rulers of early Islamic polities with less political influence in bargaining and in greater need of legitimation by a religious elite that favored restrictions detrimental to economic development, such as usury laws and, much later, bans on printing. While this accommodation dates back to the first caliphate, later conquest regimes became even more dependent on the religious establishment as they distanced themselves from civilian wealth and administrative elites. As we will see in chapter 12, this process also impeded intellectual innovation. Overall, it was a corollary of imperial rule and its relative detachment from civil society, which stood in growing contrast to European trends in state formation.[227]

Very broadly speaking, the Middle East and South and East Asia suffered from a dearth of productive polycentrism *within*—of bargaining processes and compromises that would have fostered innovation-sustaining institutions—and of enduring polycentrism *without*, which would have selected for competitiveness-enhancing adaptations. Thus, both serial imperiogenesis and key characteristics of imperial rule converged in producing long-term outcomes that were increasingly different from those we observe in Latin Europe. As I note in the Epilogue, much the same had already been true of the Roman empire itself: this was emphatically not a question of "East" versus "West," but of different modes of state formation.[228]

In term of outcomes, the association between multiple polycentrisms and modernizing development is clearly documented: historically, the latter only arose in the context of the former. In this chapter, I have gathered elements of an explanation as to why this was so. Yet institutions could only provide a framework and did not on their own generate transformative change. They may well have been necessary but were never sufficient. I now turn to two other vital ingredients: access to commercial opportunities and material resources, and the intellectual foundations and practical application of technological innovation. As we will see, state formation and the configuration of the sources of social power exerted just as much influence on these factors as on the institutional landscape.

CHAPTER 11

New Worlds

CONSUMING THE WORLD

A Globalist Perspective

LOOKING AT THE domestic attributes of European societies and their affinities to modernizing development, and at how these compare to other parts of the world, as I did in the previous chapter, is only one way of probing the origins of the (Second) Great Divergence and the Great Escape. Europe also stood out in other respects—most notably, for its ever-widening reach. After violently inserting themselves into Asian maritime trade flows and conquering the Americas, Europeans relentlessly turned their home region into a global hub of exchange and manufacturing. The most heavily involved part of Europe, centered on the North Sea, was also the first one to experience modern economic growth and transformative change. At first sight, at least, the correlation between globalization and modernity is strong.

European intervention gradually refashioned relationships of production, exchange, and power around the globe. This process has been most famously captured by Immanuel Wallerstein's model of the "world-system," with Europe at its center. From this perspective, a series of earlier "world empires" (such as Rome and China) that relied much more on tribute collection than on commercial revenue were succeeded or absorbed by a global capitalist "world-system" rooted in commercial relations and market exchange coupled with unfree labor and state centralization. Over time, the linkages created by European commerce drove economic integration as well as a growing hierarchical division of labor whereby northwestern European workers converted raw materials supplied by less developed parts of the world into manufactures. While this new core came to enjoy higher real wages, subordinate peripheral zones were reduced to contributing cheap (slave or forced) labor, food, and other plant and mineral resources.

Within the core itself, a sequence of competing states gained and lost the lead: Portugal, which spearheaded exploration and set up early strongholds; Spain, which took over the most developed parts of the New World; the Netherlands, which benefited from the Baltic grain trade and access to New World resources that boosted its financial and shipping sectors. England, whose entrepreneurs made the most efficient use of land, developed new industries, and built up an extensive re-export trade, eventually eclipsed its rivals, in no small measure thanks to military successes. In the following, the "world-system" expanded by mobilizing resources in the Americas—no longer just bullion but lumber, sugar, tobacco, and cotton produced by slave labor—and entered those Old World regions where existing empires or ecological conditions had checked earlier advances, above all in South Asia and Africa.[1]

The initial steps in this process most closely resembled traditional tributary imperialism: the capture of the Americas allowed the Spanish crown to mine and import large quantities of silver. This windfall was used not only to prop up Habsburg ambitions in the (failed) pursuit of European hegemony (as discussed in chapter 6), it also enabled European traders to raise their profile in richer regions such as South and Southeast Asia. In the early modern period, when Europeans had little else of value to offer, American bullion bought them a place at the table. The silverization of Ming China's monetary system contributed greatly to this development.[2]

Colonial silver was used to purchase goods from the Indian Ocean basin and China, where this precious metal was rare and in high demand. From the sixteenth through the eighteenth centuries, a sizable proportion of these silver transfers, although not nearly as much as is sometimes claimed, ended up in Asia. At the time, European exchange with Asia critically depended on New World bullion that paid for imports, many of which were destined for reexport. Silver was also needed for strategic food and lumber imports from the Baltic.[3]

Yet increasingly, North Atlantic trade as such gained in importance. It quickly eclipsed Mediterranean trade in volume and value terms. Access to Atlantic commerce helped shape institutions that empowered merchants in their relations with monarchs and protected property rights. This beneficial influence was reflected in stronger urban and gross domestic product (GDP) growth in countries that were exposed to Atlantic trade, although less so in France and especially Spain. It was thus primarily in states with nonabsolutist political conditions that involvement in the Atlantic economy strengthened commercial interests and investment. Whereas Italian city-states with similar political attributes lacked direct access to the Atlantic, the Netherlands and England enjoyed both advantages.[4]

Dynamic models suggest that international trade made a considerable contribution to European economic development after 1500, especially in Britain, Portugal, and the Netherlands. Gains from this activity helped offset the tendency for real incomes to decline in response to population growth. Britain arguably benefited the most: I return to this near the end of chapter 12.[5]

In the early modern period, most intercontinental trade was maritime and increasingly controlled by Europeans. By the eighteenth century, the total value of Dutch trade was broadly comparable to GDP, and equivalent to up to a quarter of GDP in Britain. Processing of raw materials and reexports caused more and more value to be added and retained in Europe. In a process dubbed the "Industrious Revolution," imports of tropical goods incentivized people to work harder to participate in a growing consumer culture.[6]

As transatlantic commerce increased massively between the early sixteenth and the late eighteenth centuries, Britain captured a large share of it both directly and indirectly: naval power secured colonies and shipments, and British exports to the Iberian peninsula, sustained by the latter's colonial bullion imports, added to the overall volume of Atlantic-driven exchange.[7]

Trade and colonial empire contributed significantly to British domestic income and investment. Trade profits were distinctive: even though the volume of overseas trade remained modest relative to the size of the domestic market, its impact was concentrated among innovative sectors of the economy and therefore disproportionately important. Thus, overseas sales accounted for more than half of the growth in British industrial output in the late eighteenth century. The growth of an entrepôt trade fueled by the reexport of foreign manufactures helped create a larger overseas market. This expansion in turn boosted the development of financial institutions, such as the insurance industry, banking, and stock-trading. Growth in the shipping industry was driven in the first instance by Atlantic trade with the Americas and West Africa.[8]

Technological and organizational innovation and the industrial application of inventions were sensitive to persistent demand stimuli. It is telling that the fastest growth occurred in the cotton textile and metal industries, which were the most exposed to Asian imports and American demand. Increases in overseas sales were concentrated in those sectors and in just a few regions, such as Lancashire and West Riding for textiles and the West Midlands for metal products—the crucible of the First Industrial Revolution that substituted machinery and steam power for human labor. By 1815, 60 percent of the British cotton textile industry produced for export. British innovators thus depended on overseas markets to expand their businesses. And in the eighteenth century, the principal market for British manufactures—first metal and then textiles—was the Atlantic complex consisting of the British Caribbean, North America, and West Africa, much more so than continental Europe or South Asia.[9]

As Joseph Inikori in particular has emphasized, Africans played a crucial role in these processes. From the sixteenth to the mid-nineteenth centuries, with the sole exception of Andean silver, African slaves produced the bulk of all export commodities in the Americas. Under conditions of land abundance, settlers and free labor could not have sustained the large-scale production of gold, sugar, coffee, and cotton in Brazil, the Caribbean, and North America. Economies of scale and low wages contained costs, helping to create mass markets in Europe.

Around 10 million Africans were shipped to the New World as slaves. Britain dominated this business in the eighteenth century, which generated both private wealth and demand for sophisticated credit institutions to deal with the unprecedented complexities of the international slave trade. West Africa provided not only slaves but also palm oil and dyes that were vital to the British textile and machine industry. In exchange, the region was the principal destination of British cotton and linen exports in the late eighteenth and early nineteenth centuries, when industrialization began to take off. All of this required massive transfers of people and goods across the Atlantic Ocean.[10]

Kenneth Pomeranz has drawn attention to the favorable characteristics of the New World as a new periphery for Atlantic Europe. Real resources were produced on its islands and coastal areas, which benefited from low transport coasts and access to the slave trade. In the Caribbean, the slave economy critically relied on imports. This made the periphery's dependence structural and permanent, turning it into a major source of land-intensive exports and a destination for imports of capital, slaves, and manufactures.[11]

For Pomeranz, the "ghost acreages" of the New World were key. This concept refers to land that a country would have had to commit from its domestic resources to obtain the goods that were actually produced elsewhere and imported. Such transfers increased effective carrying capacity and the amount of resources available per capita. In 1815, Britain's ghost acreage for imported cotton alone stood at 3.5 million hectares, defined as the surface area required to raise enough sheep to generate an equivalent amount of wool. At the time, British arable land may not have exceeded 4.5 million hectares. By 1830, the cotton ghost acreage had risen to 9 million hectares, far in excess of domestic capacity.

Timber imports from the New World translated to another million ghost acres, in addition to 650,000 from the Baltic. Caribbean sugar provided calories that would have required around 0.6 million extra hectares of British grain fields in 1815 to produce. By 1830, combined imports of cotton, timber, and sugar equaled 10 million–12 million ghost hectares, roughly comparable to the total amount of both arable land and pastureland in Britain. Coal provided additional ghost acreages from domestic sources, but on a smaller scale than New World crop-lands. The implication is that British economic takeoff critically relied on these contributions.[12]

Britain emerged as the chief beneficiary of this system of peripheral slave labor and land. To sustain the Lancashire textile industry, raw cotton imports rose fiftyfold between the 1780s and the 1850s, first from the Caribbean and then from the United States. From the 1820s until the American Civil War, the United States provided between 60 percent and more than 80 percent of British cotton imports. It was the combination of an abundance of land in America and an abundance of labor from Africa, developed and exploited by European actors, that made this growth possible.[13]

Limits of Globalism: Criticism and Response

There can be no doubt that the Atlantic world outside Europe provided ample supply and demand that boosted the most innovative sectors of the British economy. Yet this globalist approach, which seeks causally to tie the First Industrial Revolution and thus the maturation of the (Second) Great Divergence to external inputs, has increasingly faced criticism, not in terms of the facticity of the described developments, which are reliably documented, but more specifically with regard to their relevance in explaining precisely this takeoff.

The developmental contributions of coercive relationships, which form the basis of popular global history narratives, are contested. Primitive accumulation was not very large relative to the size of the European economies: even the 150,000 tons of silver extracted from the New World from the sixteenth through the eighteenth centuries remained a relatively modest windfall overall. Only some of this bullion was transferred to Asia, and in any case imports of Asian goods did not make Europeans substantively richer, let alone making their economies more developed. The fact that interest rates were lower in parts of Europe than elsewhere—a vital precondition for capitalist credit creation—had nothing to do with bullion inflows.[14]

Claims of supernormal and rent-like profits from coercion or colonialist interventions by Europeans are more difficult to address. The question of what exactly slavery contributed to the British economy may be too complex to be settled conclusively.[15]

Much the same can be said about the results of European overseas expansion more generally. The picture was mixed at best. Owing to the political allocation of resources and competition by free-riding challengers, imperialism did not redound to Portugal's or Spain's long-term benefit. In France it accounted only for a modest share of a larger economy, and while the opposite was true of the smaller and more mercantile Netherlands, even there it remains unclear whether or not it made a decisive contribution to growth over the long run.

Britain is an outlier: as we have seen, its industrialization was meaningfully linked to mercantilist protections and the economic incentives it created. Overseas trade encouraged the growth of manufacture and urban services. Britain exported perhaps a third of its increase in industrial output that occurred from the mid-seventeenth to the early nineteenth centuries. Profits from servicing global commerce—from transport and financial intermediation—helped London grow, and made merchants wealthier and more influential in politics. Whether empire paid overall is a moot point as long as it benefited the entrepreneurial class.[16]

Yet even such profits from trade were modest compared to British GDP—a few percent at best in the late eighteenth century—even if they made some monopolists very rich. These gains could surely have supplied enough capital to finance the First Industrial Revolution. But so did other sectors, given that the overall investments required were not that large.[17]

Finally, ghost acreages did not by themselves generate development: other European countries also had access to them, as did China, which imported huge quantities of cotton from India and could at least in theory have turned internal peripheries over to commodified staple crop production. Most important, ghost acreages did not just spring into existence: they emerged in response to technological change that created demand for their output. European investment in creating them was enormous, first by means of acquiring slaves and then by the transfer of free settlers and the buildup of extensive infrastructure on a continent that had been dominated by indigenous Stone- and Copper Age societies.[18]

It was European institutions that made these commitments possible. This alone suffices to reject Pomeranz's claim that ghost acreages—from New World resources to coal—"did more to differentiate western Europe from other Old World cores than any of the supposed advantages over these regions generated by the operation of markets, family systems, or other institutions within Europe." Yet it is also true that even the most powerful institutions could not simply cause these additional assets to appear: there had to be an ecological basis for them. British machinery may have made it profitable to import them, but these imports had to come from somewhere.[19]

Could they readily have been supplied from elsewhere? When the American Civil War interrupted cotton exports, India and Egypt could not fully fill the gap despite increases in production and exports. Up to that point, plentiful and predictable access to American cotton had ensured Britain's early lead in industrialization. American cotton had longer fibers and was easier to clean than Indian cotton. It would have been a challenge to replace American slave labor and the formidable output of New World ghost acreages, at least at comparable cost and with the technology available at the time. No part of the Old World offered similarly favorable endowments. Eastern Europe's failure to export more food and timber to the richer northwest is a case in point: the physical potential existed, but the same local institutions that did not mobilize it for domestic growth also constrained the volume of production.[20]

Even if substitution had been feasible, we need to recall that intercontinental shipping was run by European powers: without this infrastructure, how would substitution (for instance, in the form of imports from India, the most important alternative source of cotton) have worked in practice? We simply cannot change one part of the equation—the commercial development of the New World—without altering others.

Pomeranz is right to insist that ghost acreages sustained divergence as and when it occurred. Even though they cannot *explain* Europe's breakthrough, as he avers, they made it possible: another necessary though not a sufficient precondition of the (Second) Great Divergence.[21]

The question is not so much whether the First Industrial Revolution could have happened under different circumstances—whether New World resources were indispensable, which is by no means a given. It is whether this breakthrough, as and when and where it took place, was significantly indebted to these resources and linkages. Empirically, there is "no gainsaying the positive connexions between imperialism, trade and long term economic growth" up to the mid-nineteenth century. Continuous expansion of demand was a driver of rising productivity at the core, and much potential demand was located overseas. Imports supported Britain's specialization and exports, and the latter were only viable if they were competitive in terms of pricing. Without growing trade, the resultant incentives for and the payoff of innovation would have been lower.[22]

In view of all this, the claim that "the Industrial Revolution in England was a product of overseas trade" could be seriously contested only if it were taken to mean that trade and global commercial expansion *on their own* were responsible for this breakthrough—a position that nobody advocates. By itself, trade could not sustain transformative development unless it coincided with technological and organizational change.[23]

Industrialization occurred in a specific environment that mobilized resources and innovation by a number of means: protectionism, which compelled manufacturers to chase higher productivity; naval supremacy, which guarded imports and exports, effectively subsidizing trade profits by making taxpayers bear the social cost of protection; exploitation, which provided a horrifically violent shortcut for developing New World resources; and advances in financial institutions, which were driven by both war and trade. All of these elements arose from the combination of competition within Europe and access to overseas resources and markets.

GETTING THERE

Marginals

If external supplies and global connections are an integral part of any realistic account of divergence and modernization, we must ask how these assets became available to begin with. Societies that were much larger and wealthier than those of late medieval Europe had shown no interest in pursuing these opportunities. I argue that Europe's competitive fragmentation created powerful incentives for overseas exploration and development, whereas hegemonic empire did not. For this reason, the different paths taken by Latin Europe on the one hand and China and other imperialized regions on the other were not primarily a function of geography, except insofar as geography had helped shape the political landscape in the manner described in chapter 8. Even if Europe had faced the Pacific and China the Atlantic, outcomes would not greatly have differed: macro-political dynamics, not winds or maritime distances, were the key to global expansion.

For Europeans to benefit from overseas trade and colonies, they had to get out there first. In their eagerness to do just that, the coastal polities of Western Europe conformed to a much broader historical pattern. From a world-historical perspective, maritime exploration had long been a domain of peripheral and small-scale polities. Large agrarian empires, by contrast, barely became involved.[24]

This pattern dates back to the Phoenicians, who, setting sail from their city-states on the Lebanese coast, not only traversed the full length of the Mediterranean (about 3,700 kilometers as the crow flies) but also ventured out into the Atlantic Ocean. Around 600 BCE, an Egyptian pharaoh (or perhaps a Persian king of kings a century later) was said to have commissioned a Phoenician circumnavigation of the African continent proceeding clockwise from the Red Sea. After three years, this expedition was supposedly brought to a successful conclusion—a tale that already elicited suspicion at the time but receives some support from anecdotal detail that suggests penetration of the southern hemisphere.

Several subsequent expeditions or attempts are dimly reflected in confused ancient traditions. Sailors from Carthage, a Phoenician city-state colony in what is now Tunisia, followed the African coast in the other direction down the Bay of Biafra. Others visited the British Isles or ventured out into the mid-Atlantic, perhaps (though probably not) even as far the Azores and the Sargasso Sea, which begins about 3,000 kilometers east of the Straits of Gibraltar, halfway to the American East Coast.[25]

Greeks, hailing from city-states in the Aegean, followed suit. From their base in Marseille they established trade connections with Britain to obtain metal. By the fourth century BCE, Greek sailors had mapped routes to the Shetlands and into the Baltic. Pytheas sailed in the waters surrounding Britain and Ireland and advanced northward to (probably) the Faroes and finally "Thule," just possibly Iceland. Famous Greek scholars such as Aristotle and Eratosthenes raised—though did not endorse—the possibility of crossing the Atlantic in order to reach India.[26]

A similar degree of engagement can be observed in other parts of the Old World. Around the beginning of the Common Era, Madagascar was settled by people from Indonesia, more than 6,000 kilometers away. By then, Polynesian explorations of the Pacific out of Tonga and Samoa were already well under way. In the course of the first millennium CE, riding their outrigger canoes, these Polynesians reached and populated New Zealand, Easter Island (2,600 kilometers east of the closest staging post, Mangareva, and 6,700 kilometers from Samoa), and Hawai'i (3,500 kilometers north of the Marquesas). Their zone of transfers eventually spanned some 9,000 kilometers from Hawai'i in the north to the Auckland Islands south of New Zealand. East to west, dispersal extended across 25,000 kilometers from Madagascar to Easter Island.[27]

Back in Europe, meanwhile, the Norse of the ninth and tenth centuries advanced from Scandinavia to Iceland, Greenland, and Newfoundland in the New World. In late medieval Europe, it was once again city-states such as Venice and Genoa and the small island kingdom of Majorca that invested in naval assets, opening up routes to the Canaries and Madeira. The coastal kingdom of Portugal embarked on a similar course in the fourteenth century, when its people numbered not more than about a million. In the fifteenth century, intensifying efforts took its sailors to the Azores and along the African coast to equatorial Africa. The Cape of Good Hope was rounded in 1488.[28]

Larger states only gradually entered the fray, foremost the kingdom of Castile, which in the fifteenth century very slowly took over the Canary Islands. Critical advances were concentrated in the final decade of that century, when Christopher Columbus, in Spain's employ, reached the Caribbean in 1492 while Portuguese initiatives had Vasco da Gama sail around Africa to India and back to Lisbon between 1497 and 1499, and also led to the discovery of the Brazilian coast in 1500.

In the Indian Ocean, the Portuguese rapidly expanded their footprint by taking over Kannur in Kerala in 1505 and Socotra and Muscat in 1507, defeating the navies of the Egyptian Mamluks and local Indian forces at Diu in Gujarat in 1509, taking Goa in 1510, Malacca in 1511, and Makassar on Sulawesi in 1512. Backed by concurrent deployments along the African coast, these operations took place at enormous remove from the home country: Makassar lies 20,000 kilometers from Lisbon by the most direct sea route, and more in practice.

The most ambitious venture of all was managed by a seasoned Portuguese commander, Ferdinand Magellan, who in Spanish employ crossed the Atlantic, discovered straits at the southern tip of South America, and crossed the entire Pacific Ocean. The whole voyage took one week shy of three years from 1519 to 1522 and covered some 60,000 kilometers, including a stretch of 99 days without landfall between Chile and Guam. From 1525 to 1527, another mission proceeded from Spain to the Moluccas. The Spanish conquest of central Mexico led to another expedition from there to the Moluccas in 1527–1528, a mere eight years after Hernán Cortés had first set foot there.

Incumbents

Phoenicians, Greeks, Norse, and Polynesians had set a trend: the European pioneers in Italy and the Iberian peninsula were also predominantly modestly sized polities, as were their main rivals, the Netherlands and England. Conversely, France, by far the most populous unified state in Europe at the time, kept punching well below its demographic weight. But so did all large imperial entities, and the more so the more powerful they were. Even if it might not have been Necho II of Egypt who funded the Phoenician circumnavigation of Africa but Dareios I of Persia, and even if the latter's son Xerxes I really forced someone to attempt the same voyage counterclockwise, none of this led to any further ventures that we know of.[29]

The still more durable and powerful Roman empire, which disposed of resources that were orders of magnitude larger than those of Phoenician or Greek city-states, did not rouse itself even to such sporadic missions. Insofar as any expeditions took place at all, they were undertaken for military reconnaissance purposes and narrowly limited in scope. In the north, Roman vessels operating along the Danish coast may or may not have entered the Baltic Sea around the beginning of the Common Era when the empire sought to subdue parts of Germany. A circumnavigation of Britain in the 80s CE lacked follow-up. In the mid-Atlantic, it reportedly fell to a local client king, Iuba II of Mauretania, to claim the Canary Islands, which has not yielded evidence of Roman presence beyond some trade goods.

In the 60s CE, a one-off land/river expedition led by two imperial guard officers to find the sources of the Nile probably progressed as far as the Sudd marshes in what is now South Sudan but does not seem to have produced any tangible results. Rome's Indian Ocean trade operated by following established routes, south to Mozambique and east to the Gulf of Bengal. Whereas Greek scholars had pondered the challenges of an Atlantic crossing, Roman imperial rhetoric preferred to emphasize the supposed impermeability and evil nature of the high seas.[30]

Later large empires such as the Umayyad and Abbasid caliphates are not known to have been any more deeply engaged in exploratory projects, nor are the large South Asian empires. And while the general scarcity of information about the Maurya or Gupta, for instance, cannot be taken as evidence of absence, the lack of Mughal initiatives is not in doubt.[31]

In keeping with my overall approach, I move on to China, which represents a particularly striking case of imperial indifference to overseas exploration and the development of overseas assets. These attributes are cast into high relief by what might be considered an apparent exception, the Ming naval expeditions of the early fifteenth century.

Following rebellions that led to the overthrow of Mongol rule, by the 1360s the new Ming dynasty had restored the political unity of core China. The revived empire drew on enormous resources: a census in 1403 registered 9.7 million households with 66.6 million residents, and that was bound to be an undercount. The state owned one-seventh of the 57.1 million hectares of cultivated land assessed in 1393. According to a contemporary report, "The empire's grain taxes totaled more than thirty million piculs [c. 1.9 million tons], and taxed in silk and paper money exceeded twenty million. At that time, the empire within the four corners was rich and prosperous, and the government enjoyed abundant and surplus revenues." And on top of taxes and income from state-owned resources, the authorities were also able to mobilize labor the old-fashioned way: 300,000 workers were said to have been drafted to connect the Grand Canal to Beijing, and over 200,000 were put to work on a huge imperial palace complex centered on the Forbidden City in Beijing.[32]

Given this abundance, the Ming empire could well afford the seven massive naval expeditions that it launched between 1405 and 1433 under the command of the eunuch Zheng He. If the sources are to be believed, no fewer than 2,149 oceangoing ships were built between 1403 and 1419. Although the tradition envisions flat-bottomed, shallow-draft ships that were 450 feet long and displaced 20,000 tons, ships of 200–250 feet seem more in line with engineering constraints and documented crew numbers. According to the most realistic estimates, some 40–60 very large "treasure ships" and maybe 200 smaller vessels staffed by close to 30,000 men participated in each of these ventures.[33]

Without exception, these fleets followed well-established sea routes south to Indonesia and west into the Indian Ocean. The first one, from 1405 to 1407, intervened in civil strife on Java and Palembang and sailed as far as Sri Lanka. The second, from 1408 to 1411, focused on the Gulf of Bengal, and a much smaller concurrent third mission advanced a little farther, to the Persian Gulf and Aden, and on the way defeated and captured a potentate in Sri Lanka. The fourth, from 1412 to 1415, set up a temporary base in Malacca and visited Bengal, the Maldives, Aden, and Somalia, and engaged forces on Sumatra. The fifth, from 1417 to 1419, proceeded to Hormuz and the east coast of Africa, as did the next one, from 1421 to 1422, which also visited the Red Sea coast close to Mecca. A final outing, from 1431 to 1433, once again stuck to several of these familiar destinations.[34]

Although the total expenditure lavished on these ventures is impossible to specify, it was bound to be substantial. By one estimate, the cost of the total number of treasure ships built for these operations—about 150—would have equaled about 10–30 percent of a year's total public revenue, a figure to which we need to add outlays for smaller ships and operations. Yet even at, say, three times the upper end of this estimate averaged over the life of the initiative, annual expenses would not have exceeded a few percent of total state income: not trivial but affordable.[35]

What *was* trivial was the yield of these expeditions: a flood of exotica to delight the imperial court—pearls and ivory and rare animals such as okapi, zebras, rhinoceroses, elephants, giraffes, and lions—and the arrival of numerous diplomatic missions from foreign parts that these naval visits inspired. The fleets' few military interventions in Indonesia and Sri Lanka did not lead to a permanent Chinese presence or any substantive gains.[36]

These operations ended almost as suddenly as they had commenced. All but one of them were compressed into just eighteen years of the reign of the Yongle emperor, the third Ming ruler. The program was suspended in 1421 while the sixth mission was still under way, and formally terminated three years later by his short-lived successor. Even though this decision was reversed by the fifth Ming emperor, only one more expedition took place.

Implicit condemnation followed. In 1436, merely three years after the end of that final operation, the court turned down requests for more craftsmen to build ships and even banned the construction of oceangoing vessels. Not long after, the blueprints and sundry documentation relating to these voyages were ordered destroyed by a powerful official: rival traditions differ only on the date (either in the 1450s or the 1470s– 1480s) and the identity of the instigator of this event.[37]

Why were these missions, which were unique in China's history, undertaken at all, and why did they end the way they did? The answers to these questions are closely connected, rooted in the dynamics of hegemonic empire that handed ostensibly unfettered power to monopolistic rulers but at the same time militated against engagement overseas.

The Yongle emperor had come to power by waging three years of war against his own nephew, the grandson and chosen successor of the dynasty's founder. This younger rival met an unseemly end—or so the official version goes—as his palace was set on fire upon the fall of the capital city of Nanjing in 1402. These events stood out as a glaring exception to China's generally more orderly power transitions within dynastic lineages, and left the usurper with plenty to prove.[38]

The new ruler's strategy of choice to bolster his standing was to embark on an ambitious program of military aggression and diplomatic activity backed by force. One of these goals was to expand the foreign tribute system by corralling as many foreign powers as possible into its network of ceremonial interactions. From the beginning of his reign, agents were dispatched to acquire pearls, crystals, and incense as "tribute." Dozens of states sent trade missions to China. In 1405 the government set up three maritime trade superintendencies to promote state-controlled tribute trade, in which Chinese goods (or "gifts") such as porcelain, silk, and precious metals were exchanged for foreign materials or "tribute."

Some seventy-five known eunuch missions were tasked with increasing China's influence beyond its frontiers. Much of this outreach took place by land: Korea, Mongolia, and Champa in Southeast Asia were the principal destinations alongside Tibet, Nepal, and Turfan. Efforts were made to impress the Buddhist and Muslim polities of Central Asia: China initiated an annual exchange with Herat in Afghanistan, Samarkand was courted, and emissaries traveled as far as Isfahan in Iran. Occasional missions also targeted Cambodia and Siam, as well as Japan and the Ryukyu Islands.[39]

The treasure fleets were thus merely the flashiest and most extravagant element of a much broader initiative to establish diplomatic relations and advertise China's—and its ruler's—unmatched greatness. For what it is worth, the official history of the Ming dynasty considers this the principal purpose of these missions: the emperor's desire to "display his soldiers in strange lands in order to make manifest the wealth and power of the Middle Kingdom." While insights into his actual motivation are beyond our reach, it does matter that later historians accepted this as a plausible explanation—and indeed there is nothing in the record to suggest any substantive alternative or complementary reasons. For modern scholars, a usurper's quest for glory remains the most plausible rationale.[40]

This was decidedly not an attempt at exploration: the routes traveled were all well known, and had been for hundreds or even thousands of years. The fleets simply followed the established cycle of monsoon winds. The heft of the larger ships made them all but useless for exploration or naval combat. The creation of effective naval hegemony in the Indian Ocean basin would have been well within China's capacities at the time, but there is no indication that this was ever intended: there was no follow-up, and no permanent bases were established. The contrast with the Portuguese less than a century later could hardly be more striking: operating at a much larger distance from home and with vastly smaller resources, within just a few years they managed to traverse much of the same area with a handful of ships and set up strongholds from which they controlled trade, challenged rivals, and entered productive alliances with local rulers.[41]

Insofar as we can determine, the Ming ventures did not generate any material benefits at all. Chinese traders had already gained a dominant position by the time of the Mongol conquests, displacing Arab shipping. There is nothing to support the notion that the expeditions were designed to shore up their influence. If protection of trade had been an objective, it would be puzzling that China failed to take steps to secure its own coasts against pirates and instead spent lavishly on long-distance voyages. Inland waterways, restored and expanded after prior disruptions, rendered coastal traffic less important, at least from the state's perspective.[42]

The overall purpose was political. Just as the naval expeditions were part of a wider array of missions, these missions were themselves part of an activist program that appears to have been similarly unprofitable and poorly thought out. Thus, early in his reign, the Yongle emperor intervened in and formally annexed Annam (Vietnam). This unleashed determined local resistance that would drag on for the remainder of his reign, finally compelling withdrawal three years after his death.

More serious conflicts were initiated with the Mongols to the north. A strategy of containment was centered on Beijing, which remained the capital despite plans to return to Nanjing, and on a chain of major frontier fortresses plus 6,000 kilometers of Great Wall. In addition, the emperor embraced a more offensive approach. Between 1410 and 1424, he led in person five major campaigns into the steppe, and died during the last of these. Notwithstanding some successes, the Chinese forces suffered heavy casualties and expenditure, the mobile Mongols evaded defeat, and nothing of lasting significance emerged from these operations. Mongol pressure persisted: in 1449 they even managed to capture the sitting emperor and held him prisoner for years.[43]

These calamities highlight the fact that just as before and after, the true challenge to the empire lay at its northern frontier. Everything else was of secondary importance and hardly justified massive outlays on the scale required to launch the treasure fleets. Scholar-officials duly criticized these ventures as expensive and pointless. Their criticism reflected rivalries at the imperial court: eunuchs had promoted the maritime expeditions while Confucian officials opposed them. Implementation and the subsequent backlash were thus rooted not only in the ruler's desires and the limits of his power but also in political dynamics at the center. The two officials who are variously credited with destroying the documentation regarding the voyages, war ministers Yu Qian and Liu Daxia, both belonged to the anti-eunuch faction. A century later Congjian Yan's *Shuyu Zhouzilu* had the latter denounce the expeditions as having "wasted tens of myriads of money and grain . . . what benefit was it to the state? This was merely an action of bad government of which ministers should severely disapprove."[44]

The Yongle emperor's aggression against the Mongols and his commitment to the drawn-out and failing intervention in Annam raised similar concerns. The announcement of a third Mongolian campaign in 1421 had already triggered protests by the most senior officials. This prompted the ruler to imprison some of his outspoken ministers but also to suspend further overseas voyages: if one of his costly prestige projects had to be dropped, it was not going to be the fight against China's northern opponents.[45]

The swift policy reversal after his demise in 1424 was thus scarcely surprising. There were not going to be any more preemptive wars in the steppe, Annam was abandoned, and diplomatic engagement with Central Asian potentates was sharply curtailed. The fading-out of the naval expeditions was part of a larger process of retrenchment.[46]

In no small measure, this was a rational response to the empire's challenges: maintenance of domestic control and containment of the Mongols. Of all the ventures undertaken by the Yongle emperor, the naval missions were the ones least likely to contribute to these vital objectives, and consequently also the ones most resoundingly disavowed.

However, the retreat from overseas engagement went further than fiscal calculus alone dictated. By the end of the fifteenth century, it had become a capital offense to build ships with more than two masts. As already noted in chapter 10, in 1525 coastal authorities were charged with destroying all oceangoing ships, and by 1551 travel in multimasted ships was criminalized. These decrees emanated out of an ongoing struggle between court eunuchs and the officials who had pushed for the abolition of the treasure fleets. Eunuchs were involved in foreign trade and backed merchants whom the government, guided by a blend of factional rivalries and neo-Confucian doctrines, sought to suppress. Shutting down shipyards—and destroying pertinent records—was merely one facet of this age-old struggle, albeit one that caused critical nautical and engineering skills to be lost.[47]

As China's government became more inward- and northward-looking, its interest in maritime commerce faded. Malacca developed into a hub of trade for Muslim sailors who took over routes until they were in turn challenged and partly displaced by the Portuguese. The latter moved swiftly along the same network of connections that had been used by the treasure fleets. Vasco da Gama visited several of the same ports from Somalia to India where the Chinese navy had anchored ninety years earlier. In 1557 the Portuguese set up a post in Macao that they retained for the next 442 years.[48]

What accounts for this divergent experience? The Ming empire did not need to extend its reach to prosper, and while it was free to choose to do so, other concerns were more much pressing: I return to this aspect in the next section. Policymaking was monopolized by a single imperial court. If that court, under a particular ruler in cooperation with a particular faction, decided to launch huge fleets, enormous resources were mobilized to make this happen. But when the same court, under a different ruler and a different group of courtiers, decided to revise this decision, that was all it took to snuff out the entire program.

The treasure fleets were commanded by the Muslim court eunuch Zheng He. Had the missions ended during his lifetime—he seems to have died during the last mission—and had he wished to continue to lead naval missions, he would have had nowhere else to go. More significantly, the captains and navigators and shipwrights who were made redundant by the abolition of the program had nowhere else to go either, unless were prepared to defy the government by participating in increasingly curtailed and criminalized private trade. And that was as the authorities wanted it to be, for the same rationale applied to the suppression of the records of the voyages: as later critics put it, "Even if the old archives were still preserved they should be destroyed in order to suppress at the root."[49]

By contrast, when Christopher Columbus needed a few ships to cross the Atlantic to get to China, he petitioned Portugal, Venice, Genoa, England, Spain, and assorted nobles for support, only to be turned down by all of them. When the Spanish crown later granted him a retainer that kept him around for several years until the project was finally launched, it may have done so to prevent rival powers from cashing in if his venture turned out well, even if that seemed rather unlikely.[50]

We could hardly wish for a better illustration of the benefits of productive fragmentation: political polycentrism preserved a multiplicity of options, interstate competition encouraged support even for highly uncertain undertakings, and a degree of cultural cohesiveness—another "productive" dimension of Latin Europe's state system—made it easier for mavericks to find employment in a variety of locations.

Columbus was by no means alone. The Venetian Giovanni Caboto left his hometown to escape debt and tried his luck in Spain and Portugal before England commissioned the voyage that took him to Newfoundland in 1497. Magellan, whose ships were the first to circumnavigate the globe in the 1520s, had long served for the Portuguese until he fell from grace and was picked up by Spain. The cartographer Amerigo Vespucci worked for both Portugal and Spain. Unlike in China, there was no single ruler who could "turn off the tap for all of Europe."[51]

Monopolies of power expressed themselves in other ways as well, by promoting the coordination of resources across large areas at the expense of local preference and advantage. The opportunity costs could be huge: as Wallerstein memorably observes, "When the Turks advanced in Europe, there was no European emperor to recall the Portuguese expeditions." In a hegemonic empire, it was entirely up to the central authorities to promote, ignore, or suppress trade and overseas contacts.[52]

Chinese history illustrates this premise with exemplary clarity. When the Song and Mongol regimes supported maritime trade, merchant communities sprang up in continental Southeast Asia and Indonesia. The Ming volte-face that privileged state-controlled tribute missions and eventually banned private international trade pushed the latter into illegality and threatened to cut off the diaspora communities. Thus, just as the court could decide whether to sponsor treasure fleets or shut them down and burn the records, it could also more broadly decide whether to sponsor or obstruct maritime trade more generally. The lack of "independent bases of power and alternative states" with different preferences, a coupling of conditions that was emblematic of hegemonic empire, left no other options.[53]

GOING OUT THERE

Neither Needing nor Wanting to Go Out There: Agrarian Empires

Constraints on overseas ventures were not merely a function of monopolistic authoritarianism. Indifference or even hostility to such initiatives represented perfectly sensible responses to the incentive structure of hegemonic empire.

Relative economic development contributed to preferences. In the aggregate, imperial China's resources were so large that there was no strong pressure to seek out more elsewhere, as Europeans endeavored to do. From this perspective, as Ian Morris notes, "It was always likely that fifteenth-century China's administrators would eventually shut down the costly voyages into the Indian Ocean, and it was never likely that they would send fleets into the Pacific. Economic geography made exploration irrational." In that sense, withdrawal was far less arbitrary and contingent than the launching of the treasure fleets had been. The question of why China did not pursue opportunities overseas may well be a red herring: the European experience cannot be accepted as a normative default.[54]

There is simply no point in imagining a counterfactual continuation of the treasure fleets' operations by grafting European motivations onto Ming China. Notions that reconnaissance by smaller naval units around the Cape of Good Hope would eventually have led to encounters with the Portuguese and might have checked their advance into the Indian Ocean; that control of the Straits of Malacca would have benefited Chinese economic development; and that maritime advances would have allowed China to sell its products to European customers far closer to the latter's home are technically correct and at the same time completely antithetical to any actual initiatives at the time. Predicated on a dramatic break with existing preferences and practices, such counterfactuals would entail nothing less than a refashioning of Chinese empire in the European mold. The same applies to the suggestion that China might then also have crossed the Atlantic to the Americas.[55]

The political economy of hegemonic empire was the decisive factor in forestalling not just exploration but even the very idea of overseas development. If the principal challenge was to hold on to an existing base well in excess of a hundred million people and to access their labor and assets, the outside world was of limited interest and consequence. In late imperial China, only 2 percent of the population was engaged in maritime commerce, compared to the 80 percent who cultivated the land. Trade never escaped from the crushing dominance of the agrarian sector. And more generally, the economic cost of forgone trade was much lower for large empires than for small states.[56]

As we saw in chapter 10, the imperial center embraced an "agrarian paternalism" that regarded farming as the foundation of the economy and people's welfare, and—however unsuccessfully—strove for the stabilization of wealth. Cities lacked autonomy, depriving urban traders and financiers of the kind of influence that stimulated European engagement overseas. Confucian elites did not endorse going abroad: "All people in motion were potential sources of anxiety." Instead, their unwavering support for a social order that was considered intrinsic to China obviated the need to leave. The authorities sought domestic security and control: they had no interest in having particular constituencies gain too much wealth and influence from foreign trade, let alone in supporting mercantile colonies outside the empire's contiguous territory that had the potential to evolve into rival power bases. Overall, subordination to an inwardly directed public sector constrained mobility.[57]

It may well be that the smug condescension on display in the Qianlong Emperor's famous letter to Britain's King George II in 1792 was directed in part at a fractured domestic audience and tactically preferable to intimations of curiosity. Yet even if the Qing ruler's professed lack of enthusiasm in "the manufactures of foreign barbarians" need not have been quite sincere, his claim that "our Celestial Empire possesses all things in prolific abundance and lacks no product within its own borders" was demonstrably emblematic of the self-image of universal empires well beyond China itself.[58]

It was not by coincidence that the one—if partial—exception to this principle occurred at a time when imperial China faced sustained interstate competition. Not only did the independent southern kingdoms of the tenth century greatly expand foreign trade. Under the Southern Song in particular, the state actively promoted maritime commerce. After the loss of northern China in the early twelfth century, the first ruler of the southern rump state, the Gaozong Emperor, was credited with the observation that "the profit from overseas trade is the greatest," a sentiment informed by the increasingly desperate need for additional funds. Before long, foreign trade purportedly brought in one-fifth of total state revenue.[59]

The Southern Song state consequently sponsored innovation in ship design, fielded hundreds of warships, and sought out Arab and Indian navigational and geographical knowledge. The floating mariner's compass was developed at that time. As a result, Chinese vessels came to be the best in the Indian Ocean, and the Chinese share of maritime exchange kept growing. These advances later enabled the Mongols—foreign invaders not yet socialized to accept the ideal of stable and self-contained empire—to launch grandiose if generally unsuccessful naval expeditions against Japan, Annam, and Java. Overseas trade continued on a large scale under their rule of China until it was curbed by the Ming.[60]

Both the Ming and the Qing regimes derived most of their income from the land. No business communities lobbied for navies that could protect long-distance trade: "There was no political-economic imperative, unlike in the case of Western maritime powers of the early modern era, to establish and maintain the overseas empires." The Manchu conquest regime was much more concerned about internal rebellion: in their political calculus, security risks greatly outweighed potential gains from overseas connections. A ban on maritime trade in 1661 was meant to isolate the renegades who had taken over Taiwan. In 1717, the Kangxi emperor ordered all Chinese in South Asia to return within three years or they would never be allowed back at all. Severe restrictions on trade with Europeans followed in 1757.[61]

And regardless of the state's position on overseas trade as such, overseas Chinese were invariably on their own. The Chinese community in Malacca in the fifteenth century was strong in numbers but maintained, at best, minimal contact with officials back home. When a modest

Portuguese force seized Malacca in 1511, the Ming empire could not be expected to intervene. Upon establishing a foothold in the Philippines in 1565, the Spanish encouraged immigration from China to develop their new territories. Before long, the massive growth of the Chinese community in Manila soon raised security concerns that culminated in a series of massacres (in 1603, 1639, and 1662). The Chinese government was unimpressed. The same was true when the Dutch later massacred Chinese expats in Batavia on Java in 1740, even though on that occasion the possibility of retaliation was at least discussed at court.

Factors that ought to have worked to the Chinese communities' advantage—superior numbers and proximity to their mighty homeland—failed to do so: "Abandoned by Chinese officials," they were "helpless against Spanish imperial power and . . . many became instruments of Spanish expansion," playing a vital role in introducing New World silver and crops into China on behalf of the Spanish. In the Japanese port of Nagasaki, Chinese merchants struggled to compete with Dutch traders who enjoyed the benefits of a treaty that had been negotiated by their distant state: their Chinese peers lacked comparable backing. Wang Gungwu captures the essence of the contrast between Chinese indifference and European state sponsorship as "the difference between merchants barely tolerated by a centralized empire and those whose rulers and governments used them for their imperial cause."[62]

China's lack of interest and incentive was also reflected in its persistent rejection of military expansion across the sea. In keeping with the geostrategic conditions set out in chapter 8, engagement with the steppe was the principal focus of attention. At no time in its history had China made serious efforts to expand with the help of naval forces. (The Mongols' bold overseas raids, conducted at the one time when China and the grasslands shared the same overlords, could almost be taken as the exception that proves the rule.)

Overall, we observe a striking disparity between terrestrial and maritime operations. Chinese expansion into Central Asia, driven by the desire to check and preempt steppe opponents, dates back to the Western Han period, and it resumed under the Eastern Han and the Tang. Comparably ambitious naval ventures were missing: an early presence on the southern island of Hainan a mere thirty kilometers from the mainland hardly counts. Taiwan, located about 180 kilometers from China's east coast, was long left to its own devices. It fell to distant European powers to stage the first foreign intervention there. In the second quarter of the seventeenth century, the Dutch and Spanish competed for control of the island—and even that conflict, fought on China's doorstep, failed to draw in the late Ming state.

The imperial center finally took a reluctant interest only when Taiwan became a base for interference on the mainland. In the early 1660s, Zheng Chenggong, a Ming-friendly opponent to the newly installed Manchu regime, was ejected from China and ended up wresting Taiwan from the Dutch. The island became a launchpad for raids and invasions of the coastal mainland, prompting a Qing takeover in 1683.[63]

Manila lies about 1,300 kilometers from Guangzhou and not much more than 1,000 kilometers from Tainan in Taiwan, considerably farther away from the mainland but only a tiny fraction of the huge distances covered by the treasure fleets and well within the reach even of less ambitious Chinese navies. Three thousand kilometers of mostly inhospitable terrain separate Kashgar in westernmost Xinjiang from Chang'an, and yet the former was targeted multiple times. The Philippines never were, even though they could have been secured with very little effort. After all, the Spanish, within six years of invading with a paltry five ships that carried 150 sailors, 200 soldiers, and 5 friars, had defeated the local sultan and taken over Manila.

Had an Asian power suddenly seized the Canary Islands in, say, 1400, Portugal or later Spain would very likely have contested this takeover. Not only did China do nothing of the kind: it was the Spanish who for a while toyed with the idea of invading China. Various hopeful schemes were devised, permanently shelved only after the defeat of the Armada back in Europe.[64]

The Chinese state intervened in the Philippines just once and in much the same manner as it later would in Taiwan. In 1573–1574, a Chinese pirate who had been raiding China's coast departed for the Philippines where he sought to dislodge the Spanish, albeit without success. A Chinese fleet was dispatched to kill or apprehend him. It thus appears that offensive naval operations were undertaken only against fellow Chinese who challenged imperial authority. Conversely, the authorities remained unmoved by the aforementioned massacres at the hands of the Spanish and Dutch. If anyone deserved to be punished, it was those who had removed themselves from the clutches of monopolistic rule.

Even when in the eighteenth century Taiwan became a major and lucrative source of sugar, China made no attempt to add similarly sugar-rich Luzon to its portfolio. There was simply no need: 90 percent of the Chinese sugar supply came from domestic sources, along with all its silk and tobacco. At that stage, trade in foreign luxuries, not to mention overseas colonization, promised little tangible gain. China's politically unified domestic market generally obviated the need to develop overseas trade.[65]

This negative preference was not primarily a function of limited capabilities: rather, it was shaped by the logic of hegemonic empire. It was not necessary to venture out as long as foreign merchants went to great lengths to come to China. It was not expedient to develop overseas assets when the task of managing and preserving a huge empire absorbed a thinly spread bureaucracy's full attention. It was not desirable to support colonial communities that might slip out of the center's grasp. On the rare occasions that the empire projected power beyond its terrestrial core, it was either to advertise its hegemonic supremacy or to crack down on renegade Chinese who challenged its monopoly from the margins. All this makes it fruitless to wonder why the empire did not send out explorers or found colonies: the framing conditions could hardly have been more different from those that prevailed in Europe's competitive state system.

In this respect, the Chinese experience was merely a particularly intense manifestation of a much broader pattern. Other large empires faced similar constraints. South Asia did not usually generate major maritime initiatives in the European mold. Empire formation was based on plunder and revenue from land, and state investment in navies was often modest.[66]

Developments in Chola—far away from the northwestern frontier—in the late tenth and early eleventh centuries remained a rare outlier. Chola's naval ventures began with an invasion of Sri Lanka followed by

westward expansion to Nicobar, the Andamans, Laccadivs, and Maldives, and culminated in an expedition against Srivijaya in Malaya and
Sumatra in 1025. This undertaking involved capacious transport ships,
similar to those the Ming treasure fleets employed 400 years later. Just
as in the latter case, the Chola projects were driven by ambitious rulers,
the father–son pair of Rajaraja I and Rajendra I. In a further parallel, this
blue-water navy proved to be an unsustainable extravagance: more
pressing concerns in the form of rivalry with a more traditional land
empire—the Western Chalukyas—absorbed resources, just as war with
the Mongols would in Ming China.

Structural incentives to develop expansion by sea were transient,
weak, or absent. Occasional interest did not lead to transformative
change in ship design or armaments, let alone to cooperation between
the state and mercantile groups. Merchants, for all their sometimes very
considerable wealth, lacked institutionalized power. Even though merchant associations existed—most notably in Chola—that collected
taxes and maintained armed forces for protection and to assist rulers,
they were always subordinate to domineering centers.[67]

The same constraint applied to the Ottoman empire. In his somewhat
disingenuously titled study *The Ottoman Age of Exploration*, Giancarlo
Casale succeeds above all in demonstrating that there was in fact no
such thing. Just as in Ming China, politics at a monopolistic imperial
court played a decisive role. An elite faction in favor of expansion and
international trade in the Indian Ocean region competed with those
who were staunchly opposed to these goals: initiatives were launched
or aborted depending on which side held the upper hand. Thus, two
viziers in the 1560s and 1570s were the driving force behind a southward
push—with failed plans for a Suez canal and an expedition to Sumatra—
that fizzled once the leading proponent, Sokollu Mehmed Pasha, had
been outmaneuvered by those favoring the more traditional imperial
pursuit of war with Iran, and was finally assassinated. Support at the
center faded, and renewed initiatives in the periphery, notably Yemen,
were inadequate.[68]

By the 1570s, the threat of a Portuguese naval blockade had receded
and Ottoman traders no longer required state support. Reliance on their

own resources left them high and dry when the empire underwent a generalized crisis during the early seventeenth century, Yemen was lost and the appearance of new European rivals—Dutch and English— encouraged allies to defect. Under these circumstances, a strong presence in the Indian Ocean basin turned out to be no longer feasible. As it happened, initial state support had been prompted in the first instance by European intervention. In Casale's own words:

> Had it not been for the threat posed by the Portuguese to Muslim trade and pilgrimage routes, neither the original articulation of Ottoman claims in maritime Asia nor the subsequent dedication with which members of the Indian Ocean faction defended these claims would ever have been possible. And once this Portuguese threat was removed, the Ottomans' grand imperial project quickly became an unsustainable venture.[69]

Reactive in nature, such initiatives were easily undermined by power dynamics at the court and quite predictably eclipsed by conflict over Mesopotamia with a rival empire. Nothing in the Ottoman empire nourished structural incentives for naval exploration, mercantile aggression, and colonial development. The lack of pluralism ruled out alternative pathways; traditional concerns and constraints of imperial rule kept asserting themselves. The contrast to the European "age of exploration" could hardly have been more starkly defined.

Outcomes in China, India, and the Middle East were consistent with key characteristics of hegemonic empire: focus on domestic resources; monopolistic decision-making that was highly susceptible to power dynamics at the very top while shielded from inputs by other constituencies; and, above all, emphasis on loosely guarding and taxing large agrarian populations. What all these polities lacked were the twin spurs of competition within a durable state system and internal fragmentation of social power that created space for constituencies that pursued gain from overseas trade and development. The resultant ideological default—"An empire cannot be conceived of as entrepreneur as can a state in a world-economy. For an empire pretends to be whole"—was merely icing on the cake.[70]

Wanting to Go Out There, and Making the Most of It: Europe

In these respects, traditional empires differed hugely from Latin Europe on the cusp of the modern age: there, increasingly stable states were locked into intensifying competition that fueled their hunger for novel resources. Political fragmentation created a market for explorers and investors, and domestic balancing mechanisms protected their autonomy.[71]

Polycentrism was key. Interstate conflict did not merely foster technological innovation in areas such as ship design and weaponry that proved vital for global expansion, it also raised the stakes by amplifying both the benefits of overseas conquest and its inverse, the costs of opportunities forgone: successful ventures deprived rivals from rewards they might otherwise have reaped, and vice versa. States played a zero-sum game: their involvements overseas have been aptly described as "a competitive process driven as much by anxiety over loss as by hope of gain."

As if rulers' ambition had not been enough, fear of losing out lent even greater urgency to an open-ended arms race. Persistent and often violent competition called for the formal acquisition of distant strongholds and territories to preserve access to overseas resources: simply getting somewhere first was never enough, as Portugal and Spain were soon to discover. And even though challengers such as the Netherlands and England were initially more interested in markets than in land per se, they could not escape this logic either.[72]

Hemmed in by powerful competitors that readily entered and abandoned alliances, Western European states generally faced enormous costs in expanding their territories at the expense of their immediate neighbors. By reaching out to new shores, these states were able to project military force against sometimes less capable opponents and open up new fronts in the struggle against their peers. Conflict over colonial territories became an organic extension of endemic warfare within Europe itself. The urge to explore and colonize was thus deeply rooted in the routinized interstate competition that distinguished Western Europe from other parts of the Old World from the Islamic world to China. Its parties were ready to strike whenever opportunities arose.[73]

Sectoral institutions within states reinforced this impetus. Multiple institutional actors—rulers, capitalists, and the Church—promoted overseas initiatives as states centralized. Autonomous merchant bodies and the organizations they supported, from guilds to stock companies and trading houses, provided human and financial capital. The religious leadership backed mission and conversion. Rulers co-opted and cooperated with these two sectors to further their own political goals. This convergence of interests resulted in what David Abernathy calls a "triple sectoral assault" of soldiers, entrepreneurs, and clergymen on the outside world.[74]

As mentioned in chapter 10, mercantile city-states—the earliest beneficiaries of Europe's fragmentation—played a critical role in laying the foundations. Amalfi, Gaeta, Pisa, Naples, and then, above all, Genoa and Venice engaged in pioneering commercial ventures. After reaching out into the eastern Mediterranean to obtain raw materials for soap and glass production, they invested heavily in sugar plantations that came to stretch from Palestine and Cyprus to Valencia and the Algarve and out into the Atlantic, and served as the template for the plantation complex of the New World. Genoa had long-standing ties with Portugal: their sailors jointly or separately probed the African west coast from the twelfth century onward. Since 1385, Portugal was ruled by a dynasty that enjoyed the support of merchants and the bourgeoisie against its conservative nobility. A productive partnership between Genoese capital and Portuguese logistics ensued.[75]

Subsequent developments owed much to this nexus of private and public inputs. The timing of the breakthrough of the 1490s was by no means coincidental: the previous decade had been profitable for investors in Atlantic voyages. This encouraged them to take risks: Columbus's backers had all been involved in the exploitation of the Canary Islands. In the end, his first expedition was financed without direct royal support. Organized by a treasury official who drew on Genoese merchants in Seville, it nonetheless earned the interest of the Spanish crown, which was concerned about Portuguese advances in Africa and the possibility that the Canaries might turn out to be a dead end. Columbus's making a show of hawking his strange project to various potential patrons skillfully played on precisely these competitive anxieties.[76]

But those were merely humble beginnings. Over time, the interplay of international and domestic polycentrism gave rise to mercantilism as an alliance of capitalists and state rulers that regarded trade as a means of increasing national wealth and power in order to prevail within a competitive state system. Protected by political privileges and military intervention, a strong private sector developed chartered companies that captured oligopoly or monopoly rents.[77]

Trade and warfare, private and public, were tightly enmeshed. Chartered companies spent and earned huge amounts of money on and from war and privateering. They spearheaded expansion, seeking to secure strategic points before taking over more territory and conquering new markets. In so doing, they were close allies of the states that nurtured them: the Dutch East India Company, for instance, had been established expressly to harm Spain's and Portugal's interests.[78]

States that were relatively small or heavily coastal in nature—and more often than not, both—came to be disproportionately involved in overseas trade and colonization. For Portugal such ventures served as a means to raise its status from that of a lesser power. Spain capitalized on the military and organizational capabilities it had gained during the Reconquista. The Netherlands, locked into conflict with larger opponents, benefited from its efficient private sector institutions and a government that was controlled by urban interests, and pioneered chartered companies. England, then still a fairly thinly populated island, sought to balance threats from continental powers by staking claims to territories overseas. France, by contrast, Latin Europe's largest state, was more focused on terrestrial operations and less in need of colonies than its competitors: although it pursued the latter to live up to its reputation as a great power, it confined itself at first to the relatively neglected northern reaches of the Americas and, later, prioritized northwestern Africa, neither one of which delivered major economic benefits.[79]

Europe's conflictual dynamics not only provided powerful incentives for overseas expansion but also helped ensure its success. Endemic interstate warfare had given Europeans a competitive edge in the military arena. Growing investment in gunpowder technology and associated domains—"firearms, artillery, ships armed with guns, and fortifications that could resist bombardment"—paved the way for Europe's ascent to global hegemony. Thus, if colonies and the military force that had secured them were indeed an essential precondition for later economic breakthroughs, they were a direct outgrowth of Europe's competitive state system rather than just "happy accidents."[80]

European takeovers eventually reached a previously unimaginable scale: by 1914, between four-fifths and five-sixths of the earth's land surface were under European control, about half as colonies. Most of the early stages of this expansion had occurred in the New World: in 1760 almost all colonial territory and three-quarters of the colonial population were located in the Americas. It was only during the following seventy years that widespread American independence movements and concurrent expansion in Asia led to the latter accounting for half of the area and almost all of the population of Europe's colonies.[81]

Early on, the Americas had been a more vulnerable target due to the lower level of development of Pre-Columbian societies and the devastating impact of the various Old World diseases that the colonizers introduced. Meanwhile, much of Asia was still protected by huge traditional empires: Ottoman, Mughal, and Qing.[82]

Yet even these seemingly formidable opponents gradually fell behind. Philip Hoffman's intriguing explanation is that the specific bundle of conditions that sustained ongoing military innovation in Europe did not apply in like manner to any of those empires. Late imperial China's wars in the sixteenth through eighteenth centuries were almost exclusively waged against steppe powers, in conflicts that were not conducive to the use of firearms or the development of a navy. Episodes of greater interest in gunpowder weaponry—at the end of the Mongol period and around the time of the Manchu takeover—did not translate to steady improvements.

In Japan, gunpowder innovation ceased once internal conflict abated with the establishment of the Tokugawa Shogunate after 1600. Although late and post-Mughal India experienced incessant warfare, the high political costs of mobilization and constraints on tax collection limited sustained investment in better arms technology. The Ottoman empire relied more on cavalry (against nomads) and war galleys (in the Mediterranean) than Western European powers did, collected lower tax revenues, and encountered greater obstacles to mobilization. Only Russia gradually caught up as it imported know-how and built up the requisite infrastructure, which enabled it to join the ranks of the Great Powers.[83]

In this period, Europe was unique in that all the prerequisites for sustained expansion—most notably frequent, symmetric, and financially expensive but politically less costly warfare, strong incentives to focus on gunpowder technology, and low obstacles to innovation—applied simultaneously and persistently. As a result, the price of firearms relative to food was lower in Europe than in Asia, and Europe enjoyed higher productivity growth in the military sector. These advances helped Europeans overcome resistance either by force or by recruiting allies. It certainly also helped that potential competitors—China, the Ottomans—had withdrawn from the field: yet as I have tried to show there were no compelling structural incentives for them to compete to begin with.[84]

Europe's advantages were reinforced by sectoral fragmentation. Privateering was rampant in early modern European military affairs: contractors and mercenaries played major roles. Private engagement extended to overseas ventures. It made sense because states could not reliably monitor distant operations, a constraint that was acceptable to rulers who had long been used to contracting for services and delegating authority to autonomous constituents. Moreover, windfalls such as those accruing from the conquest of the Americas would have held less appeal in large empires that offered ample opportunities for domestic rent-taking than it did for small polities.[85]

None of this would have been possible had the Roman empire, or something like it, survived or returned. Abernathy captures this fundamental precondition well in his observation that "ironically, the invasions which destroyed western Eurasia's greatest empire laid the foundation for new rounds of empire building centuries later"—but this time overseas.[86]

COUNTERFACTUALS

Did geography also have a hand in this? In chapter 8, I argued that the physical environment significantly influenced the spatial scale of state formation. It is therefore reasonable to ask whether it might also have contributed to observed regional variation in overseas commitments.

I approach this question from two directions. First, when we look at European efforts from the late Middle Ages onward to establish more direct connections to South and East Asia—efforts that led to the take-over of the New World—we might conclude that the empires of the Middle East and South and East Asia simply did not need to launch comparable ventures not (only) because their incentive structure had been shaped by an alternative set of priorities but (also) because they were, in a very basic sense, already where the Europeans wanted to go: close to the (ecologically determined) sources of certain "exotic" goods from spices and perfumes to silk and ivory.[87]

Alternatively, we may choose to emphasize more fundamental geographical idiosyncrasies. The distribution of continents and oceans made it easier for the inhabitants of coastal Western Europe to accomplish certain goals than for those of East or South Asia: to circumnavigate Africa and, above all, to cross the seas to reach the New World. The Atlantic is not nearly as wide as the Pacific, which separates China from the Americas, and South Asia is extremely remote from the western hemisphere. More specifically, the relative ease and predictability of monsoon sailing left Asian societies poorly prepared for ambitious maritime expeditions. Did plate tectonics ensure that Europe succeeded simply by luck of the draw?[88]

Not quite. I hope to show that neither one of these interpretations can explain the observed outcomes. In so doing, I once again need to resort to counterfactual reasoning in order to assess the weight of geographical factors relative to the institutional ones I have already discussed at some length.

Shortcuts

Early exploration was indeed driven by the desire to access goods that were not produced in Europe and could be sold at profit there (such as the aforementioned exotica), or existed but were scarce and in high demand (most notably bullion). In a particularly crude counterfactual, one might relocate all these resources in great abundance to Europe itself or to neighboring regions such as North Africa or the Levant. Needless to say, this would flagrantly violate the "minimal-rewrite" rule: many of the plant products in question flourish only in tropical latitudes, and the rocks that contain gold and silver ore formed several billion years ago.

This far-fetched scenario allows us to imagine a lack of interest in overseas exploration, likely coupled with fierce conflict over which party would control the sources of these goods. This competition might well have intensified antecedent political fragmentation, especially given that physical proximity would have made it harder for any one power to monopolize access and to leverage this preeminence into a hegemonic political position.

A far less extreme counterfactual deserves more serious consideration: a scenario in which it was fairly easy for Europeans to access exotic resources even if they were physically remote, by relying on existing trade networks and by tweaking them to minimize intermediation costs. In this environment, the Ottoman empire would not block access to the Indian Ocean; Western European importers would not have to contend with rival Mediterranean networks such as Venice's; and access to these resources would not be obstructed by conflict among warring parties within Western Europe seeking that access.

This world, remote as it is from conditions in the fifteenth and sixteenth centuries, did in fact exist at one point in time. The mature Roman empire imported vast quantities of luxury goods from East Africa, southern Arabia, South Asia, and China, and did so to a large extent—though by no means wholly—by sea. Imperial unity had removed the problem of competition among interested parties. All imports were routed through a single conduit, that of the empire's border posts and internal toll stations. Private or state-directed trade swiftly distributed them throughout its entire domain.

The empire's reach ensured that no external challengers interfered with this process. The central authorities controlled all access points to the Mediterranean, from the Straits of Gibraltar to the Egyptian ports that linked to the Red Sea and the Indian Ocean. The Iranian polities that held Mesopotamia could levy tolls on overland trade from farther east—and the prosperity of the Syrian oasis city of Palmyra attests to the value of these flows—but could be circumvented by maritime exchange, as they indeed were on a massive scale.[89]

When Rome formally incorporated Egypt into its empire in 30 BCE, the region had already been an increasingly dependent client state for about a century and a half. The completion of its takeover permitted Rome to extend its influence toward the Indian Ocean. A Roman naval assault on Aden resulted in the city's sack and destabilized the Sabean kingdom, which had long ruled western Yemen and controlled access to the Red Sea. Trade was diverted to rival ports, and the Sabean regime was soon replaced by that of the Himyarites, whose rulers, styled friends of Rome, made sure to send envoys laden with gifts—possibly tribute—to its distant emperors, and liberally exported myrrh and white marble.[90]

At the beginning of the second century CE, Rome seized the Nabatean kingdom, a client state centered on what is now Jordan but extending far along the Arabian west coast. The reins were tightened: inscriptions document the presence of a Roman prefecture and a garrison on islands of the Farasan archipelago north of the Mandeb Strait that connects the Red Sea with the Gulf of Aden. Merchants from within the empire had long imported ivory, tortoise, and turtle shell from Axum (Ethiopia/Eretria) and myrrh, cassia, and cinnamon from Somalia. Before the second century CE, trade (especially in elephant tusks) with coastal Kenya and Tanzania had been checked by outposts of the Saba-Himyarite kings of Yemen, but now Roman ships would sail directly all the way to Tanzania and deal with local suppliers.[91]

Effective control over the Red Sea basin and its southern access point also guaranteed unencumbered relations with the Hadramawt kingdom in eastern Yemen and Dhofar, a major source of frankincense, and helped secure the route to India. Direct commercial and diplomatic relations with South Asian rulers date back to the reign of the first Roman emperor, Augustus, who had seized Egypt and was the first to receive embassies from the Indian Ocean region. Roman vessels came to sail both to Gujarat and to Tamil southern India often directly from Africa or Arabia by taking advantage of the seasonal monsoon winds. The city of Muziris in Kerala became the principal hub: it even featured a temple of the deified Augustus. Sizable merchant communities grew up there and at other ports. Black pepper was the top export item alongside indigo and precious stones. As early as 20 BCE, the kingdom of Pandia south of Muziris had dispatched envoys and gifts of pearls and gems to Rome and, later on, local sources point to the presence of Roman mercenaries in the service of local rulers.[92]

Trade with Sri Lanka had initially been in the hands of Tamil intermediaries, but once direct contact was established in the 50s CE, an embassy from the island arrived in Rome, and high seas crossings began to supplement the ones via Indian ports. Just as in East Africa, middlemen had fallen by the wayside as Rome reached out to more distant polities. Its merchants eventually extended their routes to the east coast of India and crossed the Gulf of Bengal to reach Burma. By the second century CE, they may have sailed around the Malay peninsula to Thailand, and perhaps even all the way to the Han territory in northern Vietnam.[93]

In monetary terms the volume of this trade was enormous. Literary allusions to massive outflows of specie receive support from a surviving tax document from the second century CE regarding the arrival in an Egyptian port of a ship from Muziris that carried 135 tons of pepper and 84 tons of cinnamon and paid dues in excess of a tenth of a percent of the total annual public revenues of the Roman empire. According to an observer from the Augustan period, when this trade had just taken off, each year 120 ships reached Egypt from the Indian Ocean. The docks at Berenice, a port on the Egyptian east coast, could accommodate vessels that were 120 feet long and displaced 350 tons.[94]

By comparison, in the early sixteenth century Portugal imported between 1,000 and 2,000 tons of pepper from India, and by 1600 Southeast

Asia shipped 4,000 tons a year to Europe—cargo that a small fraction of the 120 ships referenced for the Roman period could have managed. Thus, even though we should be wary of reading too much into flimsy data, there can be little doubt that Roman-era trade flowed on a scale (at least) comparable to that of the early modern period and that Roman merchants were able to move about the Indian Ocean basin unimpeded and often protected by diplomatic relations. With the single exception of Aden, the Romans, unlike the Portuguese, did not normally need to tussle with local potentates and worry about local rivals. The sheer weight of empire and the pull of its market ensured cooperation with exporters that benefited both sides at the expense of intermediaries.[95]

Under these circumstances, any suggestion to sail around Africa or across the Atlantic to access these goods would have been met with bewilderment. This had not always been the case: near the end of the second century BCE, a Greek explorer in the employ of the Ptolemies of Egypt sailed to India and back and then down the eastern coast of Africa. On both occasions, the authorities confiscated the goods he had brought back with him. Their depredations inspired him to seek out an alternative route around Africa, a bold endeavor that appears to have failed. Once the Mediterranean had been united under Roman rule, even this fantastic option became irrelevant: traders faced a straightforward choice between accepting imperial taxation or staying at home. The decision was not difficult: strong demand and the relative smoothness of long-distance trade sustained high volumes of exchange.[96]

The scale of state formation was the critical variable. Imperial unity in the Roman period and abiding fragmentation coupled with relatively low levels of state capacity during the next millennium or so generated dramatically different incentive structures. Even if we were to hold demand for imports constant (itself a dubious proposition, given the enormous concentration of wealth in Roman elite circles), post-Roman polycentrism and the resurgence of Middle Eastern polities in the late Middle Ages and early modern period introduced handicaps that were alien to hegemonic empire. In conjunction with the dynamics of interstate competition that locked parties into open-ended commitments, state-society bargaining that mobilized productive exploitation, and unexpected payoffs (especially in the New World), these constraints sustained growing commitments to overseas expansion.

Geography as such mattered less. The Roman experience refutes the notion that it was inherently difficult for Europeans to access the riches of South and East Asia: it was hard for them only when they were not organized as a single imperial entity. It is true that navigating the Atlantic Ocean required sturdier ships and more sophisticated rigging than riding the monsoon winds did in the Indian Ocean and South China Sea: but that fact alone did not compel Europeans to live up to that greater challenge. Otherwise, Japan would have developed similarly advanced shipping instead of orienting itself toward the imperial behemoth to its southwest. Institutions, not winds, turned out to be decisive: imperial hegemony and its gravitational pull on the one hand, inter- and intrastate polycentrism on the other.[97]

East Is West . . .

This leaves us with the second objection to an institutionalist perspective: that geography may have lent Europeans a helping hand while stymieing others. Testing this notion calls for a rather extravagant counterfactual: it is only by changing the orientation of entire continents that we can hope to gauge the influence of geography as such. The goal is to make it harder for Europeans and easier for the Chinese to reach the New World. (As there is no obvious way to make this possible for South Asia, which is bound to remain remote from the western hemisphere unless we rearrange the world in an even more fantastic fashion, I focus on the traditional contrast between the eastern and western fringes of Eurasia.)

I can think of three different adjustments that serve our purpose. One is to flip the Old World around its axis, so that Europe faces the Pacific and China the Atlantic. This can be done in a manner that preserves the overall integrity of this cluster of continents and their principal adjacent islands (what we might call "Greater Afroeurasia"): by rotating the entire area between 30 degrees West (to include the Azores and Iceland) and the dateline (to include the northeastern tip of Siberia and New

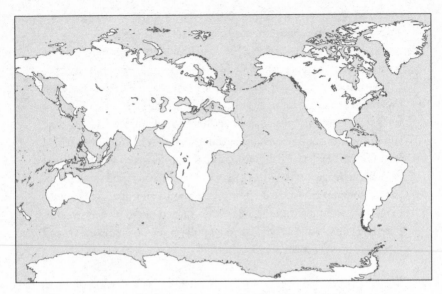

FIGURE 11.1 The world with Greater Afroeurasia rotated around its axis at 75°E.

Zealand) east–west around an axis located at 75 degrees East, halfway between these two boundaries (figure 11.1).

Even though this intervention helps preserve existing connections at the margins of the Old World, it displaces the European coast outward into the Pacific and pushes China and Japan toward the center. This shortens Pacific crossings from Europe to the New World and expands Atlantic crossings for East Asians. Because this conflicts with the main objective of this experiment—to reverse the European advantage—it might make better sense to disregard the integrity of the cluster and focus on relative distance.

In this second scenario, the goal is to approximate the location of central Japan to that of England, and that of the Yangzi Delta region to that of the southwestern Iberian peninsula, even if that adjustment severs connections between the Afroeurasian mainland (here: "Afroeurasia") and peripheral island chains. This adjustment, which ensures that the principal East Asian launch points for voyages to the Americas are as close to their destination as the principal Western European launch

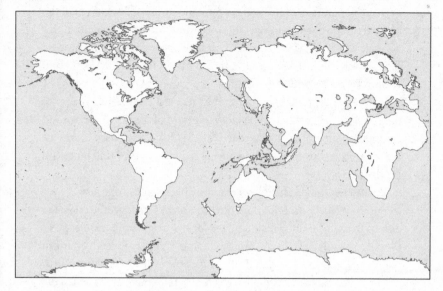

FIGURE 11.2 The world with Afroeurasia rotated around its axis at 63°E.

points are in real life, requires a flip around an axis at 63 degrees East, the midpoint of the averaged distances between London/Lisbon and Tokyo/Suzhou (figure 11.2).

A third and (even) more radical counterfactual would leave the map unchanged but assume that China equals Europe and vice versa. In this case, Japan plays the role of Britain and east-central China serves as the equivalent of the Iberian peninsula. While this may seem to be the least invasive method of substitution, it does rupture the connections between geography, ecology, and state formation: contrary to what I have argued in chapter 8, it forces us to presume that Europe's physical environment could have supported Chinese-style imperiogenesis, and that proximity to the steppe would not have affected European institutions. This also completely transforms interactions between "Europe" and neighboring regions: it no longer abuts the Mediterranean or has access to Africa, whereas "China" does.

This final scenario would alter history in a much more arbitrary and unpredictable fashion, and render it unsuitable for controlled conjecture.

Perhaps paradoxically, leaving geography untouched would entail the most dramatic changes in starting conditions. I therefore abandon this approach in favor of the two axial rotations that change only oceanic distances without interfering with the dynamics of state formation within the Old World.

Rotated around these axes, Europe faces the enormous expanse of the Pacific Ocean, which covers close to a third of the earth's surface and contains about half of all its water. Depending on which sea routes we are looking at, this intervention affects logistics in very different ways (table 11.1).

First of all, the distance between northwestern Europe and the extremities of North America does not significantly change: the relocated city of Bergen (employed as a proxy for the origins of Norse expeditions) is roughly as far away from Anchorage (a proxy for the American mainland) as the real Bergen is from L'Anse aux Meadows at the northern tip of Newfoundland, the site of a Norse settlement at the end of the tenth century. While the historical Norse could (and did) use the Faroe Islands, Iceland, and Greenland as stepping-stones, their rotated counterparts would have been able to sail along the Kuril Islands, the Siberian coast, and the Aleutian island chain: at the time, the latter housed an expanding civilization with sizable settlements. By the same token, a rotated Tokyo is not dramatically closer to Newfoundland than the real Tokyo is to Alaska.[98]

Ian Morris's claim that it was much easier for the Norse than for the Chinese to reach America disregards these basic facts, and gives short shrift to Japan's potential role as a forward base and the presence of elongated island chains. Chinese sailors would by no means have been forced to cover ten times as much open sea in a single stretch than the Norse. As far as the northern seas are concerned, there is little to support the view that it was intrinsically much more difficult to cross the Pacific from East Asia than to cross the Atlantic from Europe.[99]

But neither Newfoundland nor Alaska were particularly profitable destinations. In 1492 Columbus sailed from Palos de la Frontera in Andalusia to San Salvador Island, about 6,500 kilometers as the crow flies.

TABLE 11.1 Minimum distances (in kilometers) and differences between actual and counterfactual distances (in percent)

	Actual	"Greater Afroeurasia" rotation	"Afroeurasia" rotation
Bergen to L'Anse aux Meadows	3,800		
Bergen to Anchorage		3,400 (−11%)	4,500 (+18%)
Palos de la Frontera to San Salvador Island	6,500		
Palos de la Frontera to Todos Santos		8,700 (+34%)	10,600 (+63%)
London to Jamestown	6,000		
London to San Francisco		6,600 (10%)	8,100 (+35%)
Lisbon to Salvador de Bahia	6,500		
Lisbon to Panama	7,700	11,900 (+55%)	13,600 (+77%)
Cádiz to Lima	*11,000	14,100 (+28%)	16,000 (+45%)
Cádiz to Veracruz	8,700		
Cádiz to Acapulco		10100 (+16%)	11,900 (+37%)
Cádiz to Panama	8,000	12,300 (+54%)	13,900 (+74%)
São Tomé to Salvador de Bahia	9,600		
São Tomé to Panama		15,100 (+57%)	17,700 (+84%)
Tokyo to San Francisco	9,000		
Suzhou to San Francisco	9,900		
Suzhou to Acapulco	13,100		
Tokyo to Anchorage	5,600		
Tokyo to L'Anse aux Meadows		5,400 (−4%)	3,800 (−32%)
Tokyo to Jamestown		7,500 (−17%)	5,600 (−38%)
Suzhou to San Salvador Island		9,900 (0)	6,700 (−32%)
Suzhou to Salvador de Bahia		8,700	6,100

* Includes land crossing.
Geodesic distances in table 11.1 derived from https://www.movable-type.co.uk/scripts/latlong.html.

His actual route via San Sebastian de la Gomera in the Canary Islands was a little longer than that, in excess of 7,000 kilometers. After the rotations, departing from Palos's new location either west or east of Japan, he would have had to cover between one-third and two-thirds as much distance again to reach the American mainland at the same latitude as San Salvador Island, near Todos Santos in Baja California Sur. However, the prevailing winds (the Pacific westerlies) and the North Pacific current would have brought him close to the American mainland well north of that spot. This would have reduced Columbus's travel without landfall to something not dramatically longer (maybe by one-third or less) than his actual voyage from the Canaries to the Caribbean. The Northeast trades and the Californian and North Equatorial currents would then have allowed him to move down the coast and return to rotated Europe.

In terms of access to much of the New World, northwestern Europe would have been very little affected by either one of the axial rotations. London lay some 6,000 kilometers from Jamestown, only up to one-third less than the distance between flipped London and San Francisco, Jamestown's latitudinal equivalent on the West Coast. Similarly, it would not have been much more demanding for Spanish ships to reach Mexico: the trip from flipped Cádiz to Acapulco is only between one-sixth and one-third longer than between actual Cádiz and Veracruz.

This need not have impeded conquest of the Aztec empire, which touched both the Atlantic and the Pacific coasts. Instead of the Tlaxcala, the Tarascans near the Pacific coast might have collaborated with the conquistadores. The lack of islands to be used as staging areas (which the Caribbean provided in abundance) was an inconvenience that could have been overcome by the establishment of coastal positions along the Spanish access route north of the Tarascan-Aztec zone.

Much the same applies to the connections between Spain and the Andean region. Cádiz is 11,000 kilometers from Lima including a land crossing at Panama. Although rotated Cádiz would have been between a quarter and half as far away again, an unobstructed all-sea voyage would have helped make up for this disadvantage. Only Brazil would have become much more remote: the distance from Lisbon to the early Portuguese Brazilian capital of Salvador de Bahia would have tripled from 6,500 kilometers to something closer to 20,000 kilometers plus a land crossing.

Failing as they do to properly account for the varying impact of winds and currents, all these calculations are necessarily exceedingly rough but nevertheless contribute to a more nuanced understanding of geography's role. Rotating the Old World around its axis and the consequent expansion of the ocean that separates Europe from the Americas would have had no substantive impact on the early stages of exploration and exploitation. The Norse could easily have reached Alaska, Columbus California, Cortés and Pizarro Mexico and Peru. Undermined by Old World pestilence, the Pre-Columbian societies would have fallen just the same and their precious metal would have been shipped off.

Even if this process might have taken a little longer and been a little more costly, there is no compelling reason why it would have been aborted altogether. After all, logistical constraints would for the most part have been only moderately greater. The same intra-European rivalries would have played out, albeit sometimes in different terrain; the same hunger for fame and fortune would most likely have sustained colonial development.

This is not a complacent assessment. Even in the sixteenth century, European seafarers were already perfectly capable of mastering challenges much more daunting than Atlantic crossings. As early as 1520–1521, Magellan's ships covered more than 15,000 kilometers in 99 days between Chile and Guam without making landfall. From the 1560s, once it had been discovered how to traverse the Pacific in the opposite direction, Spanish treasure ships undertook twice-a-year passages between Acapulco and Manila, a notional 14,300 kilometers as the crow flies and, on the way back, closer to 18,000 kilometers in practice as eastbound vessels had to swerve far into the North Pacific in order to capture the trade winds. Crew attrition was higher than for Atlantic voyages but not enough to deter.[100]

The proper metric for gauging the implications of our counterfactual is not so much what the historical Europeans did do, but rather what they could do; and what they could do was clearly sufficient to master Pacific routes just as they had mastered Atlantic ones. And we must also bear in mind that by increasing some distances between Europe and the New World, these scenarios reduce the effort Europeans had to make to reach China via the Americas across the Atlantic in order to exchange Andean bullion for trade goods.

Even so, distance is only part of the story. Natural endowments also played an important role, and it is in this respect that the counterfactual creates more serious problems for European development. For one, the plantation system sprang up on the eastern side of the Americas, on the Caribbean islands, and then in Brazil and what was to become the southeastern United States. Had the real cost of shipping goods to Europe been much higher, as it would inevitably have been, this would have been much more difficult to accomplish on a comparably large scale. This casts doubt on the potential for development beyond tributary extraction as practiced by the Spanish crown. If, as has often been argued, it was more advanced features of the New World economy that contributed significantly to the (Second) Great Divergence, this qualification carries very considerable weight.

Triangular trade between manufacturing and staple-consuming Western Europe, slave-exporting and staple-consuming West Africa, and slave-importing and staple-exporting Atlantic America would have faced huge obstacles. Much increased distances between suitable parts of the New World and Europe would have weighed on commercial development. Shipping sugar, tobacco, and cotton around South America would have been expensive, albeit not impossible. Construction of a Panama canal became feasible only once certain breakthroughs had already occurred, not just in civil engineering but also in disease prevention. Reliance on the Strait of Magellan and the Isthmus of Panama would have created chokepoints that protected incumbents and stifled competition, with unpredictable second-order effects on conditions back in Europe.

Africa's novel remoteness would conceivably have represented the biggest obstacle. The distance between the Gulf of Guinea—employed as a convenient stylized proxy for the sources of slave labor—and the American Eastern Seaboard would have been dramatically greater than in real life. Slaves would have had to travel two and a half times as far (including a land crossing) if routed via Central America, or twice as far if routed around South America. Given the grueling nature of the historical Middle Passage, one must wonder how many of them would have survived journeys that long. Considerable adjustments would have become necessary but were practicable in principle. The South Pacific is endowed with enough island chains to break up the journey from the rotated Gulf of Guinea (located roughly where Indonesia is now) to Chile. Stops at some of these locations would have made these trips even longer and considerably more expensive but not necessarily that much deadlier.

Whatever the workarounds, both American geomorphology and distance from Africa were bound to raise costs by a wide margin. This, of course, might have triggered second-order counterfactuals that are hard to predict. One option would have been greater reliance on indigenous forced labor from the Americas to staff plantations, even though hostilities among colonial powers might well have restricted access. More intensive development of California early on is another option. Yet this region's output could not have replaced that of the eastern Atlantic Seaboard. Overall, it seems unlikely that the negative consequences for development arising from our counterfactual rotation could readily have been offset by plausible alternative strategies. In view of this, a deficit in the development of resources that at least some have deemed critical to Europe's economic transformation must count as the most probable outcome.

Easy fixes will not do: questioning the significance of New World resources, or envisioning substitution of Indian for American cotton. This chapter is built on the premise that we need to take seriously arguments that emphasize external inputs to early modern Europe's most advanced economies, if only for the sake of evaluating the relevance of the polycentrism thesis to this line of reasoning.

At the same time, it is important to be clear about what matters for our present purposes. We cannot rule out the possibility that different geographical conditions might have derailed the (Second) Great Divergence by restricting colonial development and the flow of critical resources to Europe. But this has no bearing on the idea that Europe's multiple fragmentations were required to bring about modernization. Even if counterfactual environmental restraints had blocked the latter, the underlying argument would remain unaffected: even in that case, competitive dynamics would still have favored transformative change.

. . . But China Is Still China

Most importantly, the plausible notion that higher geographical hurdles might have obstructed Europe's exploitation of the New World and West Africa and thus curbed Triangular Trade effects does not translate to the inverse regarding China: a counterfactual environment that crimped European opportunities would not automatically boost China's economic development. For the latter, improved access to the New World was hardly enough.

The main point is not that these logistical gains would have been fairly modest. It is true that the distance between Japan and Alaska is not that much greater than that between a repositioned Japan and Newfoundland, or that after the rotation, Japan would not have been much closer to Virginia than actual Japan is to California.

But is there any reason to believe that smaller distances would actually have mattered? If China never showed any particular interest in Japan or the Philippines or, for most of its history, even nearby Taiwan, why would reducing its distance from a desirable spot on the American mainland from 10,000 kilometers to 6,000 or 7,000 kilometers have made the slightest difference? On this scale, distance is utterly meaningless once we take account of the underlying institutions. That "China had the misfortune to lie twice as far from the New World" (or rather, Mexico) as Spain, as Morris puts it, is both factually correct and substantively irrelevant.[101]

For all we can tell, the New World could have lain just a couple of thousand kilometers east of China without ever being discovered, let alone colonized, as long as there were no structural incentives to take any steps in that direction. Nothing that we know of Chinese history suggests that such incentives existed, waiting to be activated by fortuitous discovery. In one respect, the (in)famous fantasies of the British former submarine commander Gavin Menzies, who has Zheng He's treasure fleets discover terra incognita from Australia and New Zealand to the Americas and circumnavigate the whole world, turn out to be right on the mark: in his telling, Zheng He discovered everything but nobody cared, and the imperial court suppressed all records.[102]

Arguments derived from distance are based on a triple fallacy: the assumptions that distance determines the odds of discovery, that it determines the real cost of exploration and colonization, and that discovery equates to colonization and development. None of this is obvious. Pacific history conveniently provides us with a real-life alternative to the Chinese default position of indifference: the Polynesian expansion I referred to above. If the Pacific Ocean is wider than the Atlantic, it is also, in the southern hemisphere, far less empty. If ancient Polynesians, disposing of incomparably smaller resources than the average Chinese empire, were able to spread out across 25,000 kilometers, what kept more advanced civilizations from doing the same?

And, more specifically, what prevented China from piggybacking on this process once it was under way? The Song empire, the most sea-friendly Chinese polity thus far, coincided with a period of extensive connectivity among the different clusters of Polynesian-settled islands during the first half of the second millennium. Had there been any genuine interest in overseas exploration, it would hardly have been beyond Song capabilities to exploit this extraordinary network for China's own purposes.[103]

Distance does not equal true cost. In a sense, it was costlier for any one European state to become involved in the Americas than it would have been for imperial China. European colonizers competed with their peers. If China had arrived first, it would have had the New World to itself. Any comparative accounting of "cost" needs to factor in this crucial difference. Nor were other financial considerations decisive: although it is true that China needed to focus on the steppe while Europe could afford to "face away from it," the outlays for sustainable overseas initiatives were so modest that the Middle Kingdom could easily have afforded them on the side: no pricey treasure fleets were required.[104]

As far as China is concerned, geographical explanations of its lack of exploration and colonization are red herrings. Given its hegemonic position, institutional structure, and configuration of social power, China's empires thoroughly lacked adequate incentives for embarking on any such projects. In this case, greater distance, however real, was entirely coincidental to observed outcomes.

Geography played a different role for Europe. Our counterfactual indicates that initial overseas development would not have been overly burdened had Europe faced the same oceanic distances as China. Conversely, the buildup of the slave-based plantation economy would have had to contend with more formidable barriers. Whereas Andean silver would have been shipped to Europe and (some of it) on to India and China, the Triangular Trade that so stimulated British economic, financial, and technological innovation might have been much smaller in scale or not have occurred at all.

Thus, while geography had the potential to hamper transoceanic colonization, it could not act as a driving force: on its own, it could only discourage, not stimulate. Political economy was of paramount importance, exemplified by the stark contrast between Britain as a fiscal-naval, mercantilist, and colonizing state on the one hand and China as a traditional agrarian empire on the other. The former was a product of the competitive extraversion of European states that embraced capitalism, militarism, and protectionism. This dynamic divided the globe into core and peripheries and created the overseas ghost acreages that helped fuel industrial takeoff.[105]

Even as they added territory, most notably during the massive Qing expansion, China's empires never sought to reorder lands, peoples, and resources in this manner. Outlying areas were not turned into producers of raw materials for processing in a core that would have reaped benefits from the added value. Instead, the empire sought to control migration and neglected or on occasion even obstructed the development of natural resources in border regions such as Manchuria, Xinjiang, Taiwan, and Tibet. If the Americas had been handed to the Ming or Qing rulers on a platter, would their attitude have been any different?[106]

One way or another, Europeans were bound to make it to the New World. As James Belich reminds us, "By the late fifteenth century, with or without Columbus . . . Europeans were on their way to the Americas on three trajectories: across the South Atlantic after slaves and sugarlands, across the North Atlantic in pursuit of cod and whales, and across Siberia in search of furs." By contrast, mighty empires such as that of the Ming "did not need to chase furs or fish" for the simple reason that others were happy to do it for them. Not all exploratory initiatives were driven by power fragmentation, but all of them could be checked by imperial hegemony and wealth.[107]

In the end, access to overseas resources was inextricably bound up with institutional development, the subject of chapter 10. We now move on to the final piece of the puzzle: technological innovation, which determined the benefits that such resources delivered. In its absence, Europeans might have ended up taking over the New World without being able to capitalize on this tremendous windfall.

CHAPTER 12

Understanding

CULTURES OF KNOWLEDGE

ALONGSIDE POLITICAL and economic institutions and access to overseas resources, the (Second) Great Divergence and more specifically the Industrial Revolutions are commonly attributed to the culture and ideas that promoted and sustained scientific inquiry, technological innovation, and the valorization of attitudes and norms that fostered economic progress—or, more generally, the way people viewed and understood the world. I therefore place this final chapter under the heading of "understanding," an aptly multivalent term.

Here it covers the way we improved our understanding of the workings of the physical universe and harnessed it for economic development and human welfare; the way societies understood the role and status of certain practices and constituencies, such as commercial enterprise and the bourgeoisie; and finally, the way modern observers seek to understand the clustering of different types of factors in bringing about the modern world. This and the following two sections draw on these different meanings one by one.

I begin by reviewing, in utmost brevity, the institutional underpinnings of critical changes in engaging with the world that are associated with the European Enlightenment, the emergence of a culture of scientific knowledge, and the practical application of new insights in technological

experimentation. As before, I also consider contrasting features elsewhere, above all in China, and, where applicable, in other Asian cultures
so as to throw the European trajectory into sharper relief.

Preindustrial Enlightenments and Their Alternatives

POLYCENTRISM AND ENLIGHTENMENT

In recent years, Joel Mokyr has been the foremost champion of the role
of what he calls a "culture of knowledge" in driving Europe's—and especially Britain's—transformative economic development. For him as for
many others, this phenomenon is rooted in the early modern period.[1]

In this telling, Enlightenment culture grew out of the commercial
capitalism of the late Middle Ages and the sixteenth century, and the
"individualism, man-made formal law, corporatism, self governance,
and rules that were determined through an institutionalized process."
All of these putatively significant traits were the result of the institutional
arrangements discussed in chapter 10 that were predicated on the post-
Roman fragmentation of social power.[2]

A fortuitous blend of pervasive political splintering and overarching cultural integration created a viable marketplace of ideas. Polycentrism opened up space for cultural innovation by reducing "coercion
bias," the ability of powerful incumbents to suppress innovation and
heterodoxy. Whereas monopolistic systems tend to preserve the status
quo, a fragmented political ecology is less likely to impose this
outcome.[3]

Rather than by serving as an active driver of competitive innovation,
the European state system facilitated ideational change by preventing
conservative forces from consistently coordinating resistance to and
suppression of innovation. This insight dates back at least to David Hume,
who observed in 1742 that "the divisions into small states are favorable
to learning, by stopping the progress of authority as well as that of power."[4]

Productive fragmentation deepened in the sixteenth century:
whereas post-Roman Europe had always been politically fractured,
the Reformation became a novel means of undermining the Catholic

Church's transnational capacity to quell dissent. As a result, "the power of authorities in charge of defending the orthodoxy was increasingly constrained by their inability to coordinate their actions across different political entities." This lack of efficacy should not be mistaken for growing tolerance: at first, and indeed for some time, secular and clerical leaders were hamstrung solely by their inability to fully implement reactionary responses.[5]

Owing to the manifold rivalries among Catholic and Protestant countries and between secular rulers and the papacy, coordinated repression eventually became unfeasible. Thus, whereas Jan Hus was burned at the stake in 1415 because the king of Germany, who had initially guaranteed his safety, abandoned him to the pope and his council, a century later Martin Luther operated under the protection of three consecutive Electors of Saxony whom neither emperor nor pope managed to rein in. Ulrich Zwingli exploited divisions among the Swiss cantons to establish his reform movement, and Jean Calvin found refuge from France in Geneva.

Famous émigré scholars included Paracelsus, Comenius (who fled Bohemia to live in Poland, Sweden, and England, among other places), René Descartes, Thomas Hobbes (who found refuge in Paris), John Locke (who escaped to the Netherlands until the Glorious Revolution allowed his return to England), and Pierre Bayle (who fled France twice, first to Geneva and then to the Netherlands). Later Voltaire, beset by trouble in France, spent a lot of time in various European countries. Others played different powers off against each other, most notably Galileo Galilei and his onetime defender Tommaso Campanella, who wrote his most important works in prison, published in Germany and France, was freed from Spanish detention thanks to papal intervention, and eventually ended up in France. Polycentrism played an essential role in allowing thinkers to change patrons and protectors.[6]

Fragmentation of power within states also mattered. Self-governing corporations such as monasteries and especially universities could enjoy considerable autonomy. The communal movement of the Middle Ages—a consequence as well as a driver of polycentrism—had created corporations that elected leaders by consent and set rules that governed their conduct. Universities were a product of this process, legally autonomous corporate entities with rights and privileges that opened up a neutral space for discourse rather than religious foundations (as in Islamic societies) or state-sponsored entities (as in China). Pluralism broadened horizons. Even though most universities had long tended to uphold existing authority, not all of them did so in equal measure: from the sixteenth century, outliers such as Padua and Leiden acquired a reputation for greater innovativeness.[7]

At the time, the positive contribution of the state system was much narrower. Only in certain respects did interstate rivalries encourage the authorities to embrace innovators—mostly by competing for artists who conferred status on their patrons as well as for craftsmen, captains, and armorers who contributed to military and nautical capabilities. Yet competitive pressures also made Europeans willing and indeed eager to adopt and adapt foreign inventions, most consequentially gunpowder and paper.[8]

In addition, the English and French crowns in particular promoted innovative research. In the seventeenth century, the establishment of the Royal Society of London for Improving Natural Knowledge and the Académie royal des sciences in Paris for the first time created bodies dedicated to the autonomous study of the natural world by cohesive groups of scholars.[9]

Fragmentation between and within polities was coupled with a high degree of mobility among European intellectuals, both in person and even more so through communications. This connectivity greatly boosted the size of the market for ideas. Yet even in this arena, systemic competition played a central role: the transnational intellectual community famously known as the "Republic of Letters" transcended political fractures by creating a "competitive marketplace not only for ideas but also for the people who generated them in their struggle to gain recognition, fame, and patronage."

This market connected people with new ideas with potential customers who needed to be persuaded of the merits of these ideas. Insofar as competitive patronage served as an incentive mechanism, Europe's political fragmentation once again emerged as a crucial precondition. It

dispersed patronage opportunities that might otherwise have been concentrated at a bloated imperial center or court such as Alexandria,
Rome, or the various capitals of imperial China. That, in turn, helped
ensure diversity.[10]

The "Respublica Literaria," a term first attested in 1417 and in common
use by the seventeenth century, served to diffuse useful knowledge. Governed by basic rules—freedom of entry, contestability, transnationality,
and the commitment to make results accessible—it fostered standards
of rigor, argument, and proof unencumbered by centralized political or
religious fiat or patronage. It was cumulative and converged toward consensus based on the merit of the ideas. This was not a given: if Habsburg
Spain or the Jesuits had prevailed, this dynamic might have been
aborted. Mokyr thus plausibly contends that "had a single, centralized
government been in charge of defending the intellectual status quo,
many of the new ideas that eventually led to the Enlightenment would
have been suppressed or possibly never even proposed."[11]

But these networks effects also highlight the limits of fragmentation:
although political pluralism was essential in ensuring free discourse, so
was the relative ease of transnational intellectual communications. In
the absence of some degree of underlying cultural unity, the costs of
catering to a larger market of ideas would have been higher, limiting
entry and competition and protecting incumbents from disruptive innovation. This cultural unity—manifest above all in the use of Latin and
Christian norms—was a legacy of the Roman empire: later polycentrism
was made more productive by a shared background of antecedent, if
safely distant, hegemonic empire. I revisit this issue in the Epilogue.

For now, suffice it to note that whereas the widespread use of Latin
as an elite language undeniably served to maintain and reinforce connections beyond individual polities, persistence of its privileged position would have limited access to useful knowledge beyond refined
circles. Thus, the gradual shift to vernacular languages—which was itself
driven in part by polycentric state formation—not only fractured this
ecumene but broadened the base of participants: use of regional languages made writings more approachable while recourse to translations
mitigated the decline of hegemonically monoglot publication.[12]

Many of these developments unfolded all over Latin Europe. This raises the question of whether the North Sea region and particularly England stood out in ways that can be meaningfully linked to their later leading role in bringing forth industrialization and modern economic growth. Spatial-temporal variation does suggest a trend: whereas scientists from Italy had been the most prominent during the fifteenth and sixteenth centuries, they were eclipsed by those from Britain (alongside the Netherlands and Paris) during the following two centuries.[13]

The Reformation arguably played a major role in opening up Europe north of the Mediterranean to fresh ideas. Numerous studies of persistence effects—based mainly on German and Swiss data—have tracked the beneficial consequences of the adoption of Protestant denominations over the long run, as they became visible from the nineteenth century to the present. These benefits include greater human capital accumulation with higher literacy rates and smaller gender gaps in schooling and reading scores. Protestant cities with formalized public mass education both produced and attracted more high-level human capital than others. These effects reflect payoffs from early Protestant emphasis on Bible reading and education more generally. Other persistence effects pertain to work ethic, with Protestants working longer hours, achieving higher incomes, and displaying less preference for leisure. Protestantism is also positively correlated with proxies of economic development such as tax revenue, sectoral distribution of the labor force, and urban growth.[14]

Other payoffs are already documented for the more distant past. In the sixteenth century, printing for the Reformation made the Swiss the European leaders in book production. Afterward, the Netherlands and Britain took the lead. By the seventeenth century, half of the adult Dutch and English populations were literate, a much larger share than in other European societies. This contributed to the growth of a skilled apprentice class. Cultural specifics mattered: high literacy rates were not simply a function of elevated real wages but acted independently on development. Well before the nineteenth-century onset of mass schooling, human capital formation already had a strong impact on economic performance.[15]

More specifically, the various types of Protestantism appear to have differed in their capacity to foster an environment that was congenial to technological creativity. In this respect, the Reformed Church in England did better than the Dutch Radical Enlightenment, which retarded the utilitarian turn in natural philosophy. Besides, the Dutch Reformed Church became increasingly less tolerant of other denominations. Once again, political polycentrism was critical in sustaining diversity in outcomes.[16]

The growth of science coevolved with local culture and institutions. In Britain's case, Puritanism proved influential by enhancing the prestige of experimental science, focusing on empiricism and utility, condemning leisure, valuing education, and accepting scientific pursuits as a form of worship. Even if this movement did not directly benefit the mechanical arts and was separated by a considerable time lag from the Industrial Revolution, it nevertheless helped raise the social standing of empirics and science.

Puritanism was itself an outgrowth of the Reformation, which in England had been made possible in the first place by the country's political sovereignty. Domestic conflicts with that country first brought Puritans to power in the 1640s. Renewed struggles after Restoration led to a liberalization of Anglicanism: the national church endorsed experimentalism and the notion of material progress, and accommodated Newtonian principles as a symbol of divine harmony under natural laws.[17]

When compared to other European societies, the British Enlightenment has been credited with greater emphasis on "empiricism, pragmatism, and individual utilitarianism." These preferences go back to the Baconian premise that knowledge ought to be useful. A growing divide thus separated Cartesian rationalism in continental Europe and Baconian empiricism in Britain. The latter prioritized instrument-based experimental research and promoted the adoption of the experimental method more widely, most notably in industry.[18]

Over the course of the seventeenth century, this helped foster a culture of improvement that expressly valued and encouraged economic progress driven by the accumulation of investments and skills. Systemic expectations of progress were embodied in the notion that current levels of knowledge exceeded anything that had come before. Constraints on scientific endeavor gradually fell away, to be replaced, in Chris

Bayly's words, by new "routines of intellectual behavior" that turned science into a "modern integrated doctrine."[19]

Incrementally, these developments prepared the ground for ongoing and self-sustaining changes that underpinned the transitions to modernity: a commitment to useful knowledge not only as a good in and of itself but as a means of economic development, the improvement of human welfare through aggressive manipulation of nature, and the conception of the universe as a mechanistic and intrinsically intelligible order.

HEGEMONY AND CONSERVATISM

This outlook differed quite systematically from the experience of a persistently imperial culture such as China. We must be careful to be precise about the differences that mattered. It was certainly not the case that Chinese society did not produce useful knowledge, or that rulers did not sponsor such production, at least at times. But two particulars merit attention.[20]

One concerns process. Inasmuch as state support was contingent on centralized preferences and sensitive to turnover at the very top, it could be supplied or withdrawn at will: monopolistic decision-making shaped expectations and outcomes in ways that were alien to conditions in a competitive state system. Just as one regime (say, the Mongols) wished to invest in engineers and mathematicians, another (say, the Qing) could make different choices. In some sense, it may well have been coincidence that disincentives to scientific and technological progress strengthened in late imperial China at the same time as they weakened in much of Latin Europe: the Chinese authorities could just as readily have followed a different track. What is crucial here is not so much actual outcomes but the potential for centralized intervention and regulation across a large territory that contains within it, however latently, the option of discouraging innovation: in Mokyr's pithy judgment, under conditions of monopoly "the government can flip the switch off."[21]

The other is about content. Recurrent and deepening imperial unity and continuity reinforced respect for ancient, foundational authorities.

A very long time ago, the Warring States period had sustained a flowering diverse schools of thought that encouraged argument and debate. Confucius is portrayed as having resented this approach, and it was later consequently regarded as undesirable: only the Mohists continued to regard argumentation as a path toward the truth. The violent demise of Warring States pluralism discouraged "intellectual vigor and élan": a key proponent of Confucian thought under the Western Han, Dong Zhonshu, called for the suppression of "perverse teachings" so as "to unify governing principles, to clarify laws and measures; and the people will know what to follow."[22]

As already noted, serial imperial reconstitution gradually cemented the hegemony of neo-Confucianism over the course of the second millennium. Upholding an orthodoxy that valued stability and continuity above all else, it was structurally inimical to disruptive innovation. The fact that Confucian thought was primarily social, more interested in human relations than in nature, contributed to its utility as a means of preserving the established order but not to scientific curiosity.[23]

In late imperial China, the canonization of neo-Confucian compendia furthered a closing of the literati elite's mind. Engagement with classical texts, always a cornerstone of this tradition, was stepped up under the Ming and Qing. Critiques increasingly focused on putative misreadings of these privileged texts. Even before they were dropped from the reading lists for the civil service examinations, natural studies had been based on a fixed classical canon. Literature dominated over technical fields, and the study of science did not bring the same rewards to candidates. The whole edifice of learning was overshadowed by "conservative giants."

More generally and regardless of content, the examination system favored incumbents by encouraging rote learning and focusing on refined literacy and calligraphy. The incentive structure diverted intellectuals away from science, especially the mathematization of hypotheses and controlled experimentation, in favor of memorization of the 431,286 characters of the Confucian "classics." It is hardly an exaggeration to call this system "a prescription for stagnation" that misallocated human capital. Moreover, the impact of this canonization was amplified by the fact that commercial elites tended to emulate the lifestyle and tastes of the conservative literati elite, for the reasons discussed in chapter 10. This prevented alternative spaces of discourse from opening up.[24]

While scholars competed for imperial patronage, the absence of interstate competition removed incentives for monopolistic patrons to encourage or adopt innovation. The rivalries of the Warring States had generated mobility and competitive patronage of scholars and experts much in the same way as they much later existed in Europe. Demand for specialized services ensured a degree of protection from persecution. Later, under hegemonic empire, exit options had vanished: the system was all-encompassing and anyone who managed to leave was effectively shut out from future interactions—the exact opposite of the experience of footloose dissidents in Latin Europe. The lack of productive competitiveness in the market of ideas was a faithful reflection of the lack of competition for political power.[25]

Science was more strongly affected by this than engineering, which helps account for the fact that technological innovation continued to take place. In the end, however, the weakness of incentives for scientific research robbed practitioners of the opportunity to develop more ambitious applications.[26]

In imperial China, the "classics" were endlessly commented on but never overthrown. In Western Europe, by contrast, the "rise of modern science and technology" was "not just . . . the natural continuation of ancient, medieval and Renaissance culture but also . . . its repudiation." The sixteenth and seventeenth centuries were rife with such challenges, from the discovery of the New World to advances in anatomy, the conceptualization of the solar system and elliptical orbits, and the Baconian rejection of Aristotelian deductive logic, all of which openly contradicted established classical authorities. As long as centralized power persisted, this was not a viable route in an empire that derived legitimacy not least from its guardianship of ancient traditions.[27]

China did not host independent institutions of higher learning for disinterested scholars akin to Europe's universities, the enduring products of social power fragmentation. Nor were there scientific academies: the state sponsored only institutionalized reflection of affairs that were of concern to Confucians, namely, political and moral ones. The imperial center invested in education but not in specialist, technical training, which was left to family tradition. Little was published on machines and mechanics, unlike on farming. Scholarship and technology, scholars and artisans were hardly connected.[28]

It is telling how Chinese scholars responded to Western knowledge: they continued to adhere to dominant values, a choice Nathan Sivin explains with reference to the persistent unification of Chinese society in which the classic mode of education involved strong identification with elite culture, and few scholars gravitated toward the margins. This sidelined those "for whom science was not a means to conservative ends, for whom a proven fact outweighed the whole body of millennial values." That these preferences survived into the late nineteenth century shows how powerful traditions rooted in monopolistic empire were not only in stifling domestic innovation but even in shaping the reception of external knowledge.[29]

Are there plausible counterfactuals? Even a champion of later imperial China's development such as Kenneth Pomeranz finds it hard to conceive of European-style breakthroughs had China been left alone. Even as elements of a culture of shared scientific inquiry emerged in the seventeenth and eighteenth centuries, characterized by collaboration among scholars in different fields who circulated letters and debated intellectual priority and citation practices, it is unclear whether this process would have continued and where it would have turned. For a variety of reasons, several modern observers have deemed the counterfactual of an indigenous Chinese steam engine unlikely.[30]

And what was true of imperial China also applied, to varying degrees, to other imperialized societies. Abatement of scientific inquiry and genuine technological innovation was already visible in the mature Roman empire, compared to initiatives in the preceding centuries of competitive polycentrism in the Greek and Hellenistic worlds.[31]

In the Islamic sphere, science research, writing, and teaching—which had indeed flourished and received support under the first two caliphates—declined after the eleventh century in the wake of the Sunni revival. Madrassas proliferated, funded by religious endowments that prohibited teachings contrary to Islamic doctrine and turned scholars into employees. This fashion, which gradually spread from Central Asia westward and intensified over time, cannot readily be related to imperiogenesis per se, for instance, to the rise of the Seljuqs. Even so, it appears to have been associated with state formation in a more general way.

As military rule—most notably under slave soldier regimes—expanded and civilian bureaucracies dwindled, religious leaders became the principal representatives of civil society and providers of public goods. This raised their overall profile, turning them into invaluable allies for foreign conquest regimes. In this case, the critical variable was not so much the degree of political fragmentation—after all, these processes preceded the later Ottoman-Safavid-Mughal triopoly—but the lack of diversity in regime type, a state of affairs that contrasts starkly with conditions in Europe where a variety of institutional orders sustained considerable plurality of outcomes.[32]

Eventually, hegemonic empire also came to play a role in reinforcing this trend. In the seventeenth century, Ottoman religious elites promoted purity in response to internal rebellions. Their Turkic overlords demonstrated commitment to their religious obligations, not just in waging war against infidels but also in curbing contact with Christian Europe: travel to and trade with Europe as well as engagement with European scholarship generally met with disapproval.

Except for Jews and Christians, printing was banned until the early eighteenth century. Just as in imperial China, the potential for random intervention was significant. In 1580 the religious leadership persuaded the sultan to destroy a newly built observatory in Istanbul—in the same year that the king of Denmark had built one for Tycho Brahe, which was to provide Johannes Kepler with valuable data that in turn contributed to Isaac Newton's discovery of the laws of gravity and motion. And all of these European scholars accessed information in printed works. Restraints loosened only after Napoleon's invasion of the Middle East, as Ottoman hegemony began to erode.[33]

This was not a unique outcome. In India, Mughal rulers such as Aurangzeb had championed adherence to orthodox Islam. The decline of the Mughal empire in the eighteenth century and the emergence of a violently competitive cluster of polities coincided with growing interest in sponsorship of scientific knowledge and technology. Rulers sought to attract skilled workers and showed themselves to be receptive to foreign ideas, funding imports of European experts and scientific literature. The kings of Mysore acquired a large collection of technical treatises from India and Arabia alongside some translations of Western works, and other libraries and observatories were set up elsewhere. The pressures of war precipitated advances in the manufacture of guns and artillery.[34]

In the end, investment in foreign knowledge was of limited consequence. As Sheldon Pollack puts it, "No Indian Enlightenment lies hidden from view." Library stocks would have little if any effect on practical application. Notwithstanding the presence of skilled workers, information flows across industries were more limited than in Europe because they were family-based and subject to strong collective social control. Nothing like the European "package," with its incentives and opportunities, was available.[35]

Imperial hegemony as such did not foreclose innovation: empires were "not necessarily antithetical to technological progress." Even if, empirically, "a negative correlation between the two has been observed," what mattered most was what empires were *not*. Large-scale imperiogenesis, however intermittent, fatally interfered with the development of the kind of stable state system whose cumulative competitive dynamics, cross-fertilization, and exit options supported European development.[36]

It is worth remembering that even in Latin Europe, powerful bodies strove to uphold the status quo, and failed only in the face of persistent polycentrism. During the seventeenth century, when Ottoman, Mughal, and Qing rule obstructed intellectual innovation, many European rulers tried to do the same. In Spain, conservative attitudes had been hardening, and the Counter-Reformation provided pushback on a broad front. In the late seventeenth century, only England, Denmark, and Prussia promoted religious toleration.[37]

The flowering of knowledge in early modern Europe was only as robust as the fragmentation of power within and between polities. These advances were by no means a foregone conclusion: greater consolidation of reactionary forces might have blocked them. At the same time, these advances, and the transformative transitions that depended on them, could not plausibly have taken place elsewhere.[38]

Industrial Enlightenment

Conditions differed greatly even within Latin Europe. Britain's Industrial Revolution was rooted in a very particular configuration of circumstances, which Mokyr labels the "Industrial Enlightenment." It was predicated on general Enlightenment premises—measurement, experimentation, replicability, intelligibility of nature—but also and crucially on their application to practical and economically profitable matters.[39]

Applied scientific learning was a key part of this process. The Industrial Enlightenment promoted material progress by harnessing the growing understanding of nature and making it accessible to those who could employ it for productive purposes. Concrete problem-solving and cost-cutting results were key objectives.[40]

Democratization of scientific knowledge drove progress. Eighteenth-century France alone boasted about 100 local academies. Many such entities published proceedings. Universities became less important for the advancement of useful knowledge: fewer scientists attended top institutions, and engineers generally owed little to higher education. Instead, knowledge was widely diffused by technical journals, proceedings, newspapers, public lectures, and academies, "many of which were hardly affected by restrictive legislation imposed by religion or state."[41]

The ongoing expansion of such outlets disseminated information among lower-class men and enabled them to participate meaningfully in the scientific enterprise, which in turn favored inquiry oriented toward practical application. This opening-up unfolded unevenly across countries. By all accounts, Britain was a pioneer. Its traditional elite education had little to offer to scientists or engineers. Yet science was still basic enough to be understood by the moderately educated. This redounded to Britain's benefit: primary school enrollment and literacy rates were high and created a large pool of sufficiently skilled men. Even ordinary workers such as millwrights had access to mechanical theory and applied knowledge. High levels of literacy and numeracy, themselves rooted in the Reformation and the region's antecedent regional economic development, were crucial preconditions.[42]

The resultant group of knowledgeable actors in Britain was small—a few thousand engineers, chemists, physicians, and natural philosophers—but influential. Their success relied on the presence of a few tens of thousands of skilled workers who provided tools and craftsmanship, such as mechanics, instrument makers, and metalworkers. Declining wage premiums associated with these skills reflect adequate supply in these areas already by the late eighteenth century. This favorable environment ensured that "macroinventions"—changes that represented a clear break with prior practice—were complemented and calibrated by much more numerous "microinventions" driven by continuous tinkering for the sake of improvement.[43]

That formal science did not make a great direct contribution to the earliest stages of industrialization suited this practical-minded approach. Whereas development of the steam engine relied on insights into facts that could not be derived from mere observations, advances in cotton and iron processing owed little to improved scientific understanding. Insofar as science contributed, it did so above all in terms of style: the culture of controlled experimentation was carried over from science to technology.[44]

The early Industrial Revolution was greatly aided by the free flow of information in critical sectors, via mechanical journals, patent specifications, manuals, and more generally technical literature that was accessible to nonelite audiences. This openness did not merely sustain continuing expansion of useful knowledge but also raised Britain's appeal to skilled immigrants. Long a haven for intellectual or religious refugees from the continent, it now also attracted foreign patent holders and businessmen who benefited from the supply of capital and the mechanisms for the registration and protection of property rights.[45]

Political economy mattered. Patent law went back to the early seventeenth century and helped ensure that inventors could enjoy the fruits of their labors. Patents simultaneously protected and publicized innovation. The British authorities, a thoroughly materialist elite, generally sided with industrial interests even if they entailed unpopular change. They were ready to reject new regulations and rescind existing ones that obstructed change, and resisted anti-machine lobbying: more than anything else, the Luddite riots were a sign of powerlessness.

In explicit acknowledgment of the role of Europe's competitive state system, the government even claimed that machine business might depart if operations were blocked at home. Political will thus helped create an environment in which useful and disruptive knowledge "was indeed *used* with an aggressiveness and a single-mindedness that no other society had experienced before."[46]

Technology innovators' influence rested in no small measure on their interaction with business. Industry played a greater role in supporting their endeavors than public patronage. The fusion of a dominant ideology of commercial development with mechanical applications connected capital and applied science. This process not only fostered an environment that valued improvement and progress but also brought engineers and investors together. Businessmen were exposed to mechanical knowledge in schools and publications and were welcome to participate in scientific culture. Both entrepreneurs and engineers operated in a shared value and knowledge system of "industrial culture wedded to scientific knowledge and technology." Barriers between crafts, business, and science were lower than on the continent, and the focus on practical application was stronger.[47]

Interest in science, whether genuine or faked, became part of "polite society," just as an "improving frame of mind" had already become fashionable. The resultant links "between the savants and the fabriquants" were rare in other societies where class and status distinctions acted as brakes. In Spain, for example, aristocratic culture proved resistant to novelties, and in France a rigid status pyramid separated land and trade.[48]

Such alternatives highlight once again the critical importance of political pluralism within Europe. The prerevolutionary French elite maintained a stronger grip on learning while state funding created a new elite of scientists under state direction. Engineering knowledge was regarded as "property of the state, in the service of national interest." Though potentially promising, this approach subordinated science to political preferences, which tended to incline toward preservation of the social status quo. Scientists' ties to the state forced them into personal relationships with the political establishment, as opposed to the deepening cooperation with industrialists that occurred in Britain. Whereas Britain was run by a pro-business elite, French kings were too weak to overcome vested interests even if they desired reform.[49]

Far from bringing relief, the travails of the revolutionary period and of restoration further retarded progress. All-out war stalled diffusion of British innovation into France at a critical juncture. Scientific academies were abolished in 1793, even if the Paris academy soon reopened. After 1815, clergy were restored to a prominent position within the education system, charged with promoting "religion and love of the king": primary school teachers faced religious probity tests and science education retreated despite continuing public interest. Books were censured for inspiring "sentiments of animosity toward the elevated classes," and industrial development attracted suspicion of political subversion. Higher education likewise fell under clerical influence. Only renewed revolution in 1830 ended obstruction.[50]

Sovereignty was key. In Britain, security—both vis-à-vis foreign opponents and domestically in terms of property rights—and the specific political economy it sustained were as important in facilitating transformative technological innovation as in ensuring access to international trade and domestic coal: all of these inputs were required to support ongoing development. Even if the British state did not contribute much directly to scientific and technological progress, it did not obstruct it either. Overall, it helped create a climate that was favorable to innovation and its practical application. In this regard, it differed from many other states at the time. Had a single hegemonic political economy dominated Latin Europe, no comparable outliers could have emerged.[51]

VALUES

The ascent of an enlightened culture of knowledge and its practical application for economic gain inevitably involved adjustments in the valuation of entrepreneurship and the dignity of work and craftsmen. This raises the question of the extent to which changes in values were instrumental in fostering transformative economic development.

Deirdre McCloskey has advanced a bold thesis that places values at the center of modernization and the Great Escape. In her telling, "liberal ideas caused the innovation" necessary to sustain this process. By 1700, talk and thought about the middle class began to change. As "general opinion shifted in favor of the bourgeoisie, and especially in favor of its marketing and innovating," commerce and investment in human capital expanded as a consequence of this shift, rather than precipitating it. This led to a sweeping "Bourgeois Revaluation" embodied in a new rhetoric that protected the pursuit of business: whereas aristocratic-inflected discourse had previously stigmatized it as a vulgar pursuit, it now garnered acceptance and even admiration. This new mode of thinking permitted the bourgeoisie to join the ruling class and to infuse and enrich it with innovative and competitive traits. In the final analysis, the idea of liberty and dignity for ordinary people was the principal driving force behind this change.[52]

According to McCloskey, this process unfolded in a series of steps. The Reformation together with the growth of commerce, the fragmentation of Europe, and the freedom of their cities enabled the Dutch bourgeoisie to enjoy freedom and dignity. Over time, Dutch influence that encouraged emulation of their practices regarding trading, banking, and public debt converged with the spread of printing and English liberties in similarly liberating and dignifying the British bourgeoisie, whose efforts subsequently unleashed modern economic growth.[53]

Thus, "the Four Rs"—reading, reformation, revolt (in the Netherlands), and revolution (in England in 1688)—culminated in late seventeenth-century England in the fifth and ultimately decisive "R," the revaluation of the bourgeoisie, an "R-caused, egalitarian reappraisal of ordinary people." Democratic church governance introduced by the Reformation emboldened the populace, and northern Protestantism encouraged literacy. McCloskey regards political fragmentation as vital to these processes: these forms of improvement worked better on a small scale. But political ideas, and ideas more generally, took the lead:

"rhetorical change was necessary, and maybe sufficient." She consequently documents at great length the emergence of a pro-bourgeois
rhetoric in Britain during the eighteenth century.[54]

This idealist perspective, however unusual for a professional economist,
is once again fully compatible with the notion that political polycentrism
was essential. Just as the success of the Reformation was contingent on
the absence of hegemonic empire, and the state system protected the
growth of commercial wealth, the expansion of international commerce
was rooted in overseas expansion driven by competitive fragmentation.
The same is true of changes in rhetoric. As McCloskey avers, insofar as
social regulation of business and attitudes toward it were controlled by
aristocratic or Christian or Confucian elites, this dominance represented a "chief obstacle preventing the march to the modern, namely,
the withholding of honor from betterment and of dignity from ordinary
economic lives."[55]

Throughout, she emphasizes "liberty" as a concept that allowed a previously subaltern class to achieve hegemonic status. It is hard to see, on
a priori grounds, how large traditional empires with entrenched ruling
classes—whether hereditary aristocrats, conquest elites of warriors, or
gentry bureaucrats—would or could ever have allowed comparable shifts
in values to occur, most notably the liberation and dignifying of a mercantile bourgeoisie. Late Roman and medieval Christianity were hardly
fertile ground for such revalorization, nor was the neo-Confucian intellectual and moral hegemony that constrained commercial interests.[56]

It is hard to prove a negative: we cannot conclusively show that empire per se ruled out such shifts. Historically, they only took place in
northwestern Europe under very specific conditions that had been profoundly shaped by the polycentric nature of state formation and social
power: in McCloskey's enumeration, in the Netherlands from the late
sixteenth century, in England from the late seventeenth century, in New
England and Scotland in the eighteenth century, and in France after
1789. She is careful to note that this does not mean that other cultures
"faced permanent and insurmountable obstacles to rapid betterment":
it is just that the appropriate preconditions were not present there.
Competitive fragmentation was the critical variable.[57]

I stop here. In principle there is nothing to keep us from expanding into even more overtly idealist approaches, most famously Max Weber's thesis of a Protestant ethic, but that would simply take us back to the same lines of reasoning. The proliferation and success of any such attitudes and value systems were necessarily contingent on the same set of circumstances that made the revaluation posited by McCloskey possible: they cannot be treated as autonomous, let alone exogenous.[58]

SYNTHESIS

Any one way of organizing the numerous competing and complementary arguments about the origins and principal causes of the (Second) Great Divergence and the Industrial Revolution(s) is inevitably somewhat arbitrary. Grouping them in clusters, as I have done in chapters 10–12, tends to sever connections between the different elements of more complex explanations. Realistic accounts are multifactorial. How well can they be reconciled with the thesis that Europe's multifaceted polycentrism was of paramount importance in transforming the world?

Robert Allen and Britain's Path to the Industrial Revolution

I begin with a particularly detailed and influential model that seeks to identify and weigh the main factors that made the First Industrial Revolution in Britain possible. For Robert Allen, the key drivers of British economic development up to that transition were textile exports, the growth of international trade, and cheap energy supplied by coal.

Textile exports owed much to the Black Death of the Late Middle Ages, which undermined serfdom and raised real wages. It carried off so many people that farmland was converted to pasture, which fed a larger number of more productive sheep. This output supported British exports of competitive cloths—the "new draperies"—initially to continental Europe. Elevated real incomes were preserved or rather revived by the expansion of international trade, which shifted from the Mediterranean to the North Sea (in the sixteenth and seventeenth centuries) and beyond (in the seventeenth and eighteenth centuries). This commerce boosted urban growth, on a scale that eventually outpaced that in other countries.

The growth of London, driven by booming trade with the Americas and Asia, the emulation and eclipse of Britain's Dutch rivals, increases in efficiencies and wages associated with urbanization, and the ready availability of coal offered uniquely favorable conditions for early industrialization. For good measure, all of this was "underpinned by favorable institutions and cultural developments" that raised literacy and numeracy rates and by a strong work ethic that responded to the demands and inducements of commercial development.[59]

Allen's approach privileges the role of economic forces acting in concert. Some of these phenomena were facts of nature: bubonic plague and the location of coal deposits. Yet what the British made of them was not. The impact of mass mortality—which made room for sheep that were better fed and grew longer wool fibers—was decisively mediated by political fragmentation. England had long exported raw wool for processing on the continent, but starting in the late thirteenth century it imposed growing export tolls on wool that protected the domestic textile industry.

Meanwhile, the Low Countries pioneered "new draperies," light worsteds that eclipsed hitherto dominant Italian textile production. As England adopted this innovation, its East Anglian cloth manufacturers benefited from the inflow of Flemish refugees from the conflict with Spain that commenced in the mid-sixteenth century. Production of the "new draperies" was likewise protected by export taxes on raw wool. In fact, complete bans of wool exports (albeit circumvented by smuggling) were introduced in 1614 and 1660 and remained in force until 1824.[60]

English sovereignty was a crucial precondition. As Allen himself notes, "In the absence of that tax, England's high wages would have meant that cloth production was uncompetitive and unprocessed wool would have been exported instead of worsted cloth." The implicit counterfactual is that of a Britain in a position akin to that of the Roman province Britannia, which would not have been able to control its exports. The rivalries immanent to a competitive state system guided the injection of know-how from across the Channel. Jean-Laurent

Rosenthal and Bin Wong put it best: "Had England and the Low Countries been in the same polity (as would have been the case in a China-like empire), the rise of the new draperies in England would have been unlikely at the very least."[61]

Given the growing role of textile exports in the British economy and the lead-up in the Industrial Revolution, this rise mattered. By the late seventeenth century, 40 percent of Britain's woolen cloth was sold abroad: it accounted for more than two-thirds of all exports of British manufacturers and three-quarters of London's exports and reexports. A quarter of the population of that high-wage city was sustained by shipping, port services, and related functions.[62]

In the eighteenth century, this system expanded further thanks to protectionism, colonies and growing trade with the Americas, Africa, and Asia—in short, "aggressive mercantilism and empire." As discussed in chapters 10 and 11, both were rooted in European polycentrism. Mercantilism was a response to interstate competition, and intercontinental maritime trade had been made possible by ventures from exploration to the creation of chartered trading companies that were similarly driven by conflict and the balance of power within polities.[63]

Allen devises a quantitative model that simulates the effects of rising urbanization, growing agricultural productivity, and high real wages in England. It suggests that international trade growth was the most important determinant of development, closely followed by the "new draperies" and coal. In this scenario, more than half the growth of the urban and nonagricultural sectors was caused by expanding trade: between 1500 and 1800, the share of the urban population rose from 7 percent to 29 percent, that of the agricultural population shrank from three-quarters to one-third, and the rural nonagricultural share doubled. The "new draperies" played a key role in increasing agricultural factor productivity and propping up real incomes. And while higher productivity in domestic food production was critical in enabling this urban growth and the expansion of the secondary and tertiary sectors, it materialized in no small measure in response to stronger urban demand.[64]

Britain could not have been successful in international trade in general and textile exports in particular had it not been an independent country that benefited from the dynamics of an overseas expansion that was itself a product of interstate competition. Moreover, its success was mediated by the intensity of political fragmentation. As Allen points out, France's much larger population meant that "intercontinental trade would have had to have been larger by the same proportion to have the same per capita effect" there. Thus, more modestly sized polities such as Britain and the Netherlands found it easier to capitalize on these developments than quasi-imperial kingdoms.[65]

Coal also occupies a central position in Allen's account. London's rapid growth encouraged coal mining in Northumbria, which had the potential to produce "unlimited fuel at a reasonable price." Eventually, coal's (even) lower cost in northern England led to the expansion of northern industrial cities in which the metal and textile industries took off on a large scale. More specifically, the early steam engine was useful only in coalfields where deep shafts near mines required drainage.[66]

Coal literally fueled industrialization: as its share in global energy consumption rose from 2 percent in 1700 to 20 percent in 1850, more than 70 percent of this increase was captured by Britain. British coal production per capita increased more than twentyfold between the mid-sixteenth century and 1800, almost reversing the ratio of traditional energy sources such as human and animal muscle and firewood to energy from coal from 9 to 1 to 2 to 4. The significance of poorer access to coal in China as a constraint on an economic takeoff has been much discussed.[67]

Just as pasturage, coal needed to be locally available to ensure widespread use: the threat of warfare would have disrupted supply chains from abroad. In that sense, Britain had been lucky: its coalfields had existed for 300 million years. Yet their mere presence was not enough. Allen argues that the trade in coal "was only activated by the growth of the international economy," which made the former "a social artifact as well as a natural fact." London's growth raised demand for wood fuel, which in turn created a market for cheap coal.[68]

Interstate competition and ensuing interventionism also affected coal production. Export duties and measures against price-fixing limited consumer prices, and the French Wars launched a push for autarky that favored the substitution of British coal for Baltic wood fuel.[69]

Conflict, latent or actual, was a crucial prerequisite of concentrated economic innovation. Rosenthal and Wong consider it

> doubtful that English entrepreneurs would have deployed their textile devices in high-wage northern England rather than in the cheaper continental settings had that been an option. Even more likely, they would have avoided the costs of developing such devices if they could have relied on the cheaper wages that prevailed on the Continent. Such traitorous outsourcing was precluded by politics.[70]

It is not necessary for every single component of Allen's model to have been conditioned by interstate conflict and fragmentation. All that is needed to confirm the paramount significance of European polycentrism is the demonstration that enough of the model's driving factors were sufficiently contingent on it to make overall outcomes depend on it as well. The way Allen's argument is configured, it readily clears this threshold. The dynamics he envisions operate only under the right political conditions: what is presented as an economic model with some environmental inputs is therefore derived from specific power structures. Even when—as in Allen's case—it is not expressly acknowledged, interstate fragmentation takes center stage.[71]

Complementarity, Mutual Reinforcement, and Independence

Allen belongs to a long line of scholars who have bundled various factors in their quest to explain the transition to modern economic and more generally human development. The thematic layout of my discussion has forced me to treat many of these factors in isolation. It is thus worth sketching out some of the most prominent scenarios in toto.

In addition to features that were not mediated by state formation, such as Europe's environmental diversity and protection from the steppe, Eric Jones invokes several that were: discoveries, ghost acreages, property rights protection, mercantilism, and, expressly, the existence of a state system that provided exit options and fostered an "arms race" that both sustained innovation. Others have also focused on competitive fragmentation, most notably Rosenthal and Wong. In their view, conflict pushed Europe, at great cost, toward urbanization and capital-intensive technologies.[72]

Others paint on an even bigger canvas. Michael Mitterauer emphasizes a combination of feudal relations and estates that gave rise to parliamentary traditions, the separation of secular and clerical powers, the commercial protocolonialism of the High and Late Middle Ages in the Mediterranean, and the diffusion of printing as crucial preconditions for later development. Jan Luiten van Zanden, who likewise traces the roots of the success of the North Sea region back to the medieval period, cites the influence of relatively democratic institutions that arose at various levels, from households to corporate bodies such as communes, guilds, and universities. In an environment riven by power struggles between secular and clerical constituencies, their ascent "occurred in a political vacuum" of "weak or non-existent states" resulting from failed imperial projects.[73]

Erik Ringmar's list of European features that enabled change ranges eclectically from mirrors, printing, and news media to universities, scientific academies, parliaments, and stock companies. Ricardo Duchesne ticks off printing, navigation, the mercantilistic-militaristic state, and the division of power within states as key factors underlying Western exceptionalism. One way or another, almost all of these can be traced back to polycentric arrangements. Similarly, what Robert Marks thinks of as contingencies that permitted Europe's ascent—Ming China's retreat from the high seas, New World silver production, and the Habsburgs' failure to subdue Europe—share the same root: the difference between hegemonic empire and competitive fragmentation.[74]

Daron Acemoglu and James Robinson invoke improved property rights, aggressive protection of traders and manufacturers, and the expansion of Atlantic trade as key factors in the processes leading up to the Industrial Revolution, all of them rooted in political diversity and interstate rivalries. Chris Bayly considers a wide range of attributes from stable institutions, access to New World resources, a culture of vigorous critique, and a symbiotic relationship between warfare, finance, and commercial innovation born of intense conflict.[75]

Focusing more narrowly on Britain, Jack Goldstone singles out the survival of common law, parliamentarianism, tolerance amid intolerant societies, and the consequent flourishing of a culture of science and innovation. Hegemonic empire would likely have stifled all of these.[76]

In his inquiry into the causes of Britain's success, Peer Vries accepts the relevance of high wages, cheap energy, and low interest rates but insists that without sustained technological and scientific progress, modern development would have been impossible or fizzled out. He also emphasizes the critical role of the mercantilist and fiscal-naval state in enabling imports and exports in sectors that proved critical for industrial takeoff.[77]

According to Joel Mokyr, increases in the stock of knowledge and its practical application go a long way in accounting for Britain's success. But he also assigns key roles to the country's peculiar political economy that helped protect property rights and favored entrepreneurs and innovators, as well as to mercantilism—all of them functions of national sovereignty. And Europe's fragmentation had been conducive to the earlier spread of the Enlightenment.[78]

In sum, all these multifactorial accounts rest, to varying but consistently large degrees, on inputs provided by power polycentrism both between and within polities. Without a durable state system that sustained institutional variety, competition for resources and innovation, none of these scenarios would have emerged.

This raises one final question: Are there any explanations of the (Second) Great Divergence and its consequences that are substantively independent of polycentrism, and how plausible are they? The list is short, in the first instance because even those scholars who adduce factors unrelated to the distribution of social power commonly pair them with those that are linked to it.[79]

Demography is the most prominent candidate. Gregory Clark positions himself against popular explanations from coal and colonies to institutions and the Enlightenment. Regarding England, he prioritizes long-term cultural and, indeed, genetic diffusion of traits that favored hard work, literacy, numeracy, and delayed reproduction. As the more successful outbred others, society reached a tipping point of breaking free from Malthusian constraints.

It is fair to say that this idiosyncratic approach has not stood up well to peer criticism. In any case, even if we were to accept that such a process took place and that it was pioneered in England, we would also have to ask whether this would have been feasible had Britain been part of a larger imperial entity that might have interfered with regionalized evolution of norms and behaviors.[80]

More substantive demographic explanations are on offer. The so-called Northwestern European marriage pattern, characterized by late male and female marriage, counts as a positive influence on economic development that reduced inequalities between spouses and opened up access to formal labor markets for both genders. Even households that lacked substantial resources benefited from work opportunities for its younger members.

This shifted power away from parents, boosted the role of wage labor, and led to the proletarianization of the workforce. Households' growing dependence on market transactions and wages encouraged job training and generally investment in human capital. Moreover, under conditions of neo-local household formation (that is, away from parental households), smaller nuclear families were in greater need of protection that could be provided by larger non–kin-based associations, and the elderly had to save for old age.

Yet once again, state formation mattered. When real wages fell after the abatement of the Black Death, more patriarchal structures were prone to reassert themselves, most notably among Catholics and even continental Protestants. Meanwhile, for reasons closely associated with its sovereignty and success in interstate competition, England managed to sustain elevated levels of real income for workers. Moreover, it was spared the widespread revival of Roman law that gave greater powers to fathers. English common law, by contrast, stressed the contractual and consensual nature of marriage.[81]

The obvious counterfactual is Britain's inclusion in a larger polity that imposed a more uniform legal tradition, whether revived Roman law or something else that differed from local norms. Thus, even if the emergence of the Northwestern European marriage pattern cannot be meaningfully linked to the absence of hegemonic empire (unless land abundance after the fall of Rome contributed to its appearance), its persistence depended at least in part on sovereignty and cognate effects. Most important, reference to these practices could at best complement but not replace alternative explanations of the (Second) Great Divergence.

A different demographic argument stresses the role of the Black Death. The scarcity of manpower it created prompted the development of labor-saving devices and raised real wages. Even as these shortages faded, they left behind more yeomen and craftsmen with memories of a more affluent world. More specifically, the great plague may have contributed to the decline of sugar production in Egypt, Palestine, and Syria by disrupting irrigation. This helped Genoa establish plantations at various Mediterranean locations and to revive chattel slavery by extending the slave trade along the African coast and setting up slave estates on Atlantic islands, which served as a template for later New World ventures.[82]

However, even if this adds to our understanding of the genealogy of colonial development, much of the latter depended on factors that were unrelated to the Black Death as such and rooted instead in the competitive polycentrism that produced commercial city-states and had rulers vie for novel resources. As Allen has already noted, the dislocations wrought by the plague may very well have been a necessary condition for the most promising forms of economic growth: but no one would claim that they were anywhere near sufficient.

In a series of studies, Nico Voigtländer and Hans-Joachim Voth regard plague-induced shifts in real incomes and the Northwestern European marriage pattern as sources of surplus that funded warfare and drove urbanization. By raising mortality and reducing population pressure, these two phenomena sustained economic growth up to 1700. Whatever the merits of this model, it critically depends on high levels of polycentrism that triggered interstate warfare and religious strife.[83]

I conclude with Terje Tvedt's perceptive study of the contrasting ways in which waterways contributed to economic development in England, China, and India. In this respect, England enjoyed unearned advantages. Endowed with reliable small, silt-free rivers and a perennial water supply that could be used to power devices, it was well positioned to employ inventions such as Arkwright's water frame and Crompton's mule. Its waterways were especially useful for the cotton industry and the operation of furnaces. Moreover, coal and iron deposits happened to be located within easy reach of the water transport system.

By contrast, Chinese rivers experienced extreme seasonal fluctuations in water levels and high rates of bank erosion and sedimentation. Navigable river outlets into the ocean were scarce, and all major river basins were exposed to catastrophic floods. Silt and flooding would have posed a serious threat to waterwheels and factory equipment. India faced similar challenges in terms of flooding and changes in riverbeds. For all these reasons, it was harder to develop dependable water systems in China and India than in England.

State intervention exacerbated this difference. The Chinese authorities were primarily concerned about flood control and the shipment of vital tribute such as grain at certain times of the year. The system they supported was thus designed more for drainage and tribute than for year-round exchange. Water use in England was more pluralistic and geared toward business activities, unconstrained by uniform elite interest and guidance. Even so, in this regard, nature was the decisive variable, even if its impact was mediated by state power.[84]

What these demographic and environmental perspectives have in common is that they tend to be rather vague in identifying factors that led to modern economic growth. They are best seen as contributions to our understanding of general conditions that made this particular outcome more likely to occur in northwestern Europe than elsewhere—as impulses to what are commonly regarded as the early stages of the (Second) Great Divergence. (In this regard they do not differ from some of the points made in this and the previous two chapters.)

Yet even these ostensibly nonpolitical explanations are generally predicated on specifically European modes of state formation and the configuration of social power that mediated the way in which demographic regimes and environmental features acted on economic development. Most important, none of them propose anything even remotely approaching an alternative chain of causation independent of the effects of variegated fragmentation.

Why We Escaped

In this book, I have identified two robust features of European history: post-Roman polycentrism between and within states, and causal linkages between this polycentrism and transformative developmental outcomes. As I argued in Part III, once Rome had fallen, Europe's political fracturing proved impossible to overcome: its state system was highly durable and increasingly resilient. This persistence owed much to the balancing of different sources of social power within individual polities that constrained large-scale state formation. But it also had deeper roots: in Part IV, I sought to make the case that the physical environment greatly influenced the odds of successful imperiogenesis. Interstate and domestic fragmentation sustained the competitive dynamics and constraints on authority that lie at the heart of the principal and often overlapping explanations of modern economic growth, industrialization, and subsequent improvements in human welfare. Part V shows that this is true no matter which factors—institutions, overseas resources, science and technology, or values—we choose to prioritize.

This does not mean that these outcomes were themselves a foregone conclusion. My survey merely suggests that they could not just as readily have occurred elsewhere. If European styles of polycentrism were essential and foundational to the creative destruction that spawned modernity, the (Second) Great Divergence and the Industrial Revolution(s) were unlikely to take place in Asia or Africa. And even Europe—Latin, Western, or otherwise—is far too broad a concept: we may take a step further in concluding with Robert Allen that "there was only one route to the twentieth century—and it traversed northern Britain."[85]

Given current and entirely justified sensibilities about Eurocentrism, I ought to stress that this observation does not seek to essentialize certain features as "Western European," let alone "British." The factors that (eventually) promoted transformative development were "Western European" or "British" only insofar as enduring productive polycentrism happened to be specific to these areas and shaped their political, social, economic, cultural, and intellectual evolution. Had comparable conditions surfaced in some other part of the world, they might very well have produced similar results. By the same token, had these conditions been absent from Europe, we would not have to worry about the origins of the modern world because it most likely would not exist in any recognizable form.[86]

At the same time, the fact that these vital preconditions arose in Latin Europe rather than elsewhere was not the product of mere chance. European polycentrism was inadvertent but not accidental. Comparative analysis suggests that its endurance cannot be fully separated from the physical environment. Thus, if certain Europeans were the first to nudge humankind toward vast areas of new knowledge, unprecedented levels of material prosperity, and longer, healthier, safer and freer lives, they found themselves in that position in no small measure because of where they lived. This fortuitous association must not be mistaken for geographical determinism: over the long run, geography and ecology merely rendered some outcomes more likely than others.

Existing perspectives run the gamut from triumphalist narratives of "Western" exceptionalism to opposing denunciations of colonialist victimization. None of them captures more than a fraction of the underlying dynamics. Europeans were not somehow special, and the question of who did what to whom takes us only so far: precisely because competitive fragmentation proved so persistent, Europeans inflicted horrors on each other just as liberally as they meted them out to others around the globe. Humanity paid a staggering price for modernity. In the end, although this may seem perverse to those of us who would prefer to think that progress can be attained in peace and harmony, it was ceaseless struggle that ushered in the most dramatic and dauntingly open-ended transformation in the history of our species: the "Great Escape." Long may it last.

Epilogue

What Have the Romans Ever Done for Us?

TOO BIG TO SUCCEED

Rome as Status Quo

I HAVE OFFERED a simple answer to the question posed in the chapter heading: the Roman empire made modern development possible by going away and never coming back. This rupture ushered in enduring polycentrism both within and between states that sustained development-friendly institutional arrangements, encouraged overseas exploration and expansion, and allowed a culture of innovation and bourgeois values to take hold. As I have repeatedly sought to show, the persistence or return of quasi-monopolistic empire would have been antithetical to any and all of these trends.[1]

This assessment should not be mistaken as a judgment of the Roman empire and its contribution to human welfare *at the time*. When the Monty Python crew answered this question in their 1979 movie *Life of Brian*, they homed in on Rome's putative infrastructural achievements—"the sanitation, the medicine, education, wine, public order, irrigation, roads, a fresh water system, and public health"—capped by "peace."[2]

With some qualifications—medical services and mass schooling were not exactly hallmarks of Roman rule—a similar perspective has long prevailed in academic circles, and for good reason. The mature

Roman empire produced the most prolonged period of almost continuous internal peace that this particular part of the world has ever experienced. Urbanization, while unevenly distributed, reached unprecedented and long unrivaled heights, and population density rose to levels that were not reattained until the High Middle Ages—or, in some parts of the Middle East and North Africa, not until a few generations ago.

Market integration, however imperfect, advanced in the absence of political boundaries, uncontrolled rent-seeking, severe tariffs, and disruptive conflicts: the Mediterranean basin, formally united for the only time in history, served as a reliable conduit for the untrammeled flow of goods, people, and information. Even bulk goods were shipped over long distances—most famously several hundred thousand tons of Egyptian and North African grain each year to feed the city of Rome—and a wide range of supplies for the military (including Indian pepper) reached the remotest frontiers. Monetization boomed on a scale not found again until the early modern period, driven both by massive mining operations that left their mark on Greenlandic ice cores and by sophisticated credit institutions.[3]

At the same time, the Roman economic expansion rested on Smithian growth, driven in the first instance by integration and stable governance, specialization, and the refinement and broader application of existing technologies. This limited productivity gains. We may never be able to reconstruct trends in gross domestic product (GDP) in more than the most cursory fashion. Yet if we are prepared to interpret a variety of archaeological proxy data as a rough reflection of output or consumption trends—admittedly a big and rightly contested "if"—the overall impression we gain is one of intensive economic growth that was concentrated in the last couple of centuries BCE, during the final stages of political unification and growing civil strife, followed by gradual abatement during the more stable monarchy and, depending on the region, further attenuation of development or even contraction in the final phases of imperial rule.[4]

Roman rule did not yield major breakthroughs in productive technology. Most innovations of the era had originated in the Hellenistic East during the last three centuries BCE, such as water-lifting devices, water mills, and glassblowing, as well as others that could have been commercially exploited but were not, most famously a playful version of the steam engine and perhaps also the windmill. The mature Roman empire was characterized by diffusion and incremental improvement rather than ongoing and similarly influential innovation.

Sophisticated precision instruments such as the famous Antikythera device did not spawn a machine revolution. Science and engineering—the latter applied on a grand scale in military affairs and civil engineering—largely moved on separate tracks. Glassblowing did not yield eyeglasses, and even the wheelbarrow appears to have been unknown. Moreover, in keeping with imperial traditions elsewhere, overseas exploration did not attract significant interest or resources.[5]

The very notion that Rome might have had the potential to industrialize is thus hardly worth considering and best left to novelists, who have indeed on occasion tried their hand at developing such scenarios.[6]

In many ways, the baseline conditions that framed economic development and overall outcomes in the Roman imperial economy resembled those in imperial China. This helps account for striking similarities in the debates concerning the economic impact of imperial rule in Rome and China, even if scholars on either side of this particular fence of academic specialization tend to remain unaware of this overlap. Thus, just as scholarly positions on Chinese development have shifted back and forth between notions of stifling despotism, corrupt laissez-faire, and selective benevolent state intervention aimed at ensuring social stability, students of the Roman economy have focused on comparable features. The main difference, if only in terms of style, lies in the fact that its "Western" connotations helped protect the Roman empire from overt charges of "Oriental" despotism: inasmuch as the latter was once invoked in discussions of the Roman case, it used to be confined to the later phases of imperial history. Meanwhile, even this position has been greatly modified in favor of greater continuities over time.[7]

As a result, when it comes to economic development, Roman rule is commonly regarded favorably. A whole minischool—the Oxford Roman Economy Project—has sprung up to document and, in essence, celebrate the expansion of the Roman imperial economy. Among the very few professional economists who care about Roman history, adherents to a neoclassical perspective have moved in the same direction. What these different strands of research have in common is their emphasis on the beneficial role of market integration and other consequences of imperial unity that lowered transaction and information costs.[8]

This view that empire promoted economic activity is available in two complementary flavors, one emphasizing the role of market forces unleashed by political order and stability, the other placing greater weight on the impact of state demand—for provisioning the capital and the military—in spurring economic development. A broad model of how taxation boosted interregional trade seeks to capture this latter dynamic, just as the eventual decline of the late Roman economy has been interpreted as a function of the abatement of state power.[9]

These readings are reminiscent of assessments of the economic influence of the Chinese imperial state, as it created a favorable environment for market activity while intervening to secure supplies for the court and capital cities. Structural parallels also extend into the fiscal sphere. After costly upheavals at the end of the republic that required massive mobilization of resources (not dissimilar to efforts undertaken to establish new dynasties in China), for about a quarter of a millennium the Roman monarchy made do with revenues that were relatively modest in per capita terms, just as mature Chinese regimes were inclined to do.

The underlying rationale was the same: a de facto compromise with rent-seeking elites on whose cooperation distant centers depended. As a result, enough revenue reached the Roman central authorities to fund army, court, and capital, but little else. Much was retained at the local level, through municipal taxation, or withholding by self-taxing elites. While steep tolls on imports from the Indian Ocean region and intensive gold and silver mining subsidized the treasury, formal demands on domestic taxpayers were effectively open to negotiation.[10]

It should go without saying that in Rome as well as in China, moderate tax receipts went hand in hand with high corruption incomes as officials preyed on ordinary taxpayers. The predatory dimension of the ostensibly benevolent weak state—a commonplace regarding China—is now also attracting greater attention among Roman historians, even

if realistic accounts continue to struggle to break through the more up-
beat neoclassical and Smithian growth narrative. In both empires, centralized authoritarianism coupled with delegational oligarchy generated
growing income and wealth inequality.[11]

The Roman empire thus trended toward an equilibrium comparable
to that experienced under several Chinese dynasties: while periods of
peace and stability generated sufficient revenue to maintain the state
apparatus, the latter lacked reliable mechanisms for raising revenue in
times of stress. Public debt was not an option, and higher demands were
bound to be met with strong elite resistance. Aggressive state intervention, though it was sometimes attempted—compare the scope of the
early Ming reforms with the efforts of late Roman juntas to streamline
fiscal and administrative arrangements—unfolded within rather tightly
circumscribed practical limits.[12]

The general template was one of some degree of market integration
and unevenly distributed (extensive as well as—modest—per capita)
growth that was eventually constrained by low state capacity, pervasive
elite encroachment and secular lack of innovation, human capital formation, and Schumpeterian growth. In these respects, as in many others,
it is not hard to recognize in the Roman empire yet another version of
the great Asian empires that have long served—and for me continue to
serve—as a foil to post-Roman European exceptionalism.

The Roman and Chinese imperial economies shared a baseline preference for laissez-faire enlivened by narrowly focused state demand and
interspersed with occasional spurts of more ambitious interventionism.
Both systems excluded commercial elites from political power. Fiscal
strictures triggered runaway coin debasement in Rome and paper
money inflation in Song and Yuan China. In terms of tributary mobilization and stimulation of exchange through state demand and a voracious
military sector, Rome had more in common with Mughal India. And
just like the Ottomans, the Roman authorities were heavily invested in
provisioning both the capital and the army.[13]

At the same time, all of these imperial entities lacked the same array
of features: mercantilist protections; powerful stock companies (notwithstanding Roman antecedents, tied to tax farms); public debt and

resultant credit markets; a culture of sustained technological and scientific innovation geared toward practical applications; and, perhaps most important, a strong dispersion of the different sources of social power.

Likewise, there was no sustained productive competition of the later European type; no institutionalized bargaining with civil society; no secure niches and powerbases for commercial capital, artisanal activity, and finance; few if any viable exit options for dissenters; no enduring corporations; and little interest in developing resources external to the empire's contiguous territory. However benevolent, restrained, or feeble the state, the specter of asset requisition never went away, and both endemic corruption and maintenance-oriented traditionalism were the norm.

In fact, the Roman empire earns top marks for the latter: witness the charade of passing off military dictatorship as a revival of the republic, and Constantine's desire to extend his chief-priestly powers to govern Christian affairs. Even when change did occur, it did so under the cloak of continuity. In all these respects, post-Roman Europe's polycentrism in the political, social, economic, military, and ideological domains not only opened up an enduring divide to other parts of the Old World but also represented an increasingly dramatic break from its own past.[14]

Status Quo, Continued

But what of the alternatives? Although we can only guess what counterfactual post-Roman empires in Europe might have looked like, it is tempting—and not entirely hopeless—to try. The Byzantine empire conveniently provides a real-life model. Centered on Constantinople, the Roman state, however much diminished in scale, continued for fully another millennium. In striking contrast to developments in medieval Latin Europe, it preserved its trademark military-monarchical style of governance and kept the church in check.

If we were to envision Roman-scale empire in post-Roman Europe, some version of the Byzantine model would seem the most plausible candidate: elite adherence to classical traditions coupled with a Caesaropapist fusion of political and ideological power; cycles of waxing and waning central state power locked into perennial competition with landed elites, yet without the pervasive erosion of central authority that characterized the European Middle Ages.

In Chinese fashion, the mature Byzantine state has been said to have "restrained" the economy, tempering market transactions with interventions meant to preserve social stability and curb the worst inequalities. Strong administrative centralization overshadowed a decentralizing economy. From the ninth through the eleventh centuries, features of a command economy were in place. The state remained dominant in economic affairs in the eleventh and twelfth centuries, and the price of capital rose. When the central state splintered after the Fourth Crusade of 1204, its constituent elements were drawn into an international economy under unfavorable circumstances. In the following centuries, the regime shifted to an "economy of privileges" that helped elites avoid taxes, privatized state revenue, and burdened peasants, in keeping with similar developments in aging empires elsewhere.[15]

Tellingly, none of medieval Europe's more influential innovations, from chartered communes, universities, and guilds to parliaments and public debt, were meaningfully associated with Byzantium. The asymmetries between the economically most vibrant parts of Latin Europe and Byzantium are also reflected in the fact that it was Italian city-states that pioneered institutional innovations later adopted in Byzantine commerce, and more brutally in the wide-ranging trade concessions the Byzantine state granted to leading Italian city-states—first Venice and later Genoa—from the late eleventh century onward, which were followed by an Italian takeover of trade in the thirteenth century. Small-state Italians were responsible for Byzantium's integration into wider commercial networks.[16]

Quasi-Byzantine iterations of hegemonic empire in Europe would likely have shared at least some of these traits. To be sure, the Roman-Byzantine template was not the only option, and great imperial powers founded on different principles might perhaps have emerged over time. Yet the larger and more durable those powers might have become, the more their success would have suppressed the peculiarly European trajectory of polycentric development that underpinned the continent's long march toward modernity. From a global comparative perspective, there is no compelling reason to assume that any such formation would have broken the mold that was common to all real-life Old World empires by managing to marry imperial unity with transformative innovation. Some variant of the Roman or Asian imperial tradition and its attendant economic conservatism is thus by far the most economical counterfactual.[17]

The answer to the question of what the Romans ever did *for them* is therefore more or less the same as for other traditional empires. This is also true for the answer to the question of what the Romans would *not* have done for later generations had their empire persisted or returned in a similar guise: business as usual would have been the order of the day, with far poorer odds of transformative change. But what *did* they do for *us*?

ROMAN LEGACIES

This is a valid question: even if the Roman empire's failure to persist or return was its most consequential contribution to much later breakthroughs, it need not have been the only one that mattered in bringing about these unexpected outcomes. The absence of Roman-scale empire from post-Roman Europe is not the same as the absence of any such empire from all of Europe's history. Did the Roman empire's existence help us along on our "Great Escape"?

The Roman cultural legacy is famously rich and varied—from Romance languages, the Roman writing system, and many proper names to the Julian calendar, Roman law, the urban grid and architectural styles (widely disseminated by Rome even if Greek in origin), and the Catholic and Orthodox Churches. Even so, in the present context, only those influences that can be shown to have been foundational to European polycentrism and its attendant windfalls merit consideration. In principle, such influences could have made themselves felt in two different ways: by reinforcing polycentrism and by counterbalancing it by adding to a measure of cohesion that created a more *productively* competitive environment.

Division

Christianity was the paramount divisive trait passed down from the Roman period. As I noted in chapter 9, its foundational autonomy endowed it with considerable potential for divisiveness. Thus, it had not only evolved outside state control or cooperation for three centuries, it had also from very early on envisioned both clear boundaries between its community and the secular authorities—the synoptic gospels' "render to Caesar the things that are Caesar's, and to God the things that are God's." Intimations of supremacy followed in due course, such as Gelasius's famous distinction four centuries later (proffered at safe remove from the seat of imperial power) between the clergy's "sacred authority" and "royal power," of which the former is "the more weighty." Its standing was enhanced by the divine nature of the founder, a notion late Roman rulers readily (if somewhat perversely, given that founder's terrestrial fate) embraced.

In practice, these normative principles were backed up by an autonomous administrative apparatus and growing wealth. From this powerful position, church leaders, however closely their affairs were enmeshed with those of secular rulers, generally managed to keep the latter at arm's length. It was these capabilities, alongside the weakness of the medieval polity, that later encouraged the politicization of the Gelasian premise of the "two powers"—that "spiritual activities have been separated from earthly affairs" by Christianity and "none is so proud as to take on both at the same time"—in conjunction with Augustine's "two cities" template.[18]

Much of this was contingent: as Byzantine and then Russian history show, there was nothing to keep imperial regimes from taming the church. Post-Roman state (de)formation made it possible for Latin Christianity to preserve and expand its autonomy. Yet as we have seen in chapter 7, this process of (de)formation, even if Christianity contributed to it, was in the first instance driven by factors other than the church, most notably specific characteristics of the successor regimes: it cannot in any meaningful way be considered primarily the result of Christian influences. Thus, for Christianity's divisive traits to come to the fore, the political landscape already had to be changing in a certain direction that undermined state power. Universal empire had to fade for good before the papacy could flex its muscles or the Reformation could take off. Roman-style Christianity reinforced this fading but was not its root cause.

It might be more productive to ask at which junctures when European empire-building on a larger scale might conceivably have been an option can Christianity be credited with a significant role in preventing this outcome. The yield is modest at best. It would seem a stretch to assign Christianity much weight in the Frankish repulsion of the Arabs and Berbers: as I argued in chapter 5, these incursions held little promise to begin with. More importantly, as its reach across the Levant and the Maghreb into the Iberian peninsula makes clear, Islamic rule over Christian populations did not encounter serious obstacles at that time. It is hard to see why the Christian communities of France or Italy should have proven less accommodating.[19]

The Catholic Church was somewhat more effective in undermining the position of German emperors, culminating in Henry IV's and Frederick II's unsuccessful power struggles with the ascendant papacy. Even so, this effectiveness critically depended on the configuration of power both within the German "empire" and more specifically in the Italian peninsula: it was the dispersion of powers and the capacity of city-states to marshal and pool resources that made resistance against feeble imperial centers viable in the first place. Once again, while the church had helped shape the evolution of these power relations, it could not claim a leading or crucial role in this process.[20]

The most promising scenario of Christianity's divisiveness having a powerful effect on imperial ambitions dates from the early modern period. Imagine a counterfactual world in which the sixteenth-century Habsburgs had managed to gather diverse realms and to gain access to New World bullion but did not face Protestantism. What difference would that have made? There can be no doubt that this schism contributed to the failure of imperial hegemony at the time. However, two questions complicate the issue, for there are two ways in which schism could have been avoided: through unity, or by removing Christianity altogether.

The first question is whether Catholic unity by itself would have been enough to enable the Habsburgs to overcome other sources of resistance, from German nobles and Dutch councils to international competition and balancing strategies. As I pointed out in chapter 6, a lot hinges on how much autonomous force we are prepared to assign to religious beliefs as such—on whether we view them more as a genuine driver of collective action or more as a reflection of underlying divisions that would have played out regardless. Only in the former case might the absence of religious conflict have presented the Habsburgs with a more compliant England and Netherlands, and with less intractable German princes. But even then, France would still have been a separate large kingdom, unencumbered by religious strife of its own: thus, the Habsburgs would not have been the only ones to benefit from religious concord.

The second question is more fundamental, if intrinsically unanswerable: if Christianity had not been unified but instead had not existed at all, would it be legitimate to envision a sixteenth-century Europe more or less the way it was, just without religiously motivated conflict? This would surely be an overly simplistic counterfactual that, at the very least, neglects the positive role of the church in holding the Habsburg domain together. In a non-Christian Europe, would it have been as easy for princes to inherit diverse lands? And would the Reconquista of the Iberian peninsula have unfolded in a comparable way? Ultimately, just how different would early modern Europe have turned out had Christianity never existed at all?

It is thus only by suspending disbelief and accepting the dubious premise that such crude counterfactuals free of second-order effects have any merit at all that it becomes possible to contemplate the consequences of a schism-free Europe for Habsburg imperial designs. And even if we were prepared to go down that road, it would by no means be a given that this alone would have sufficed to dislodge polycentrism in favor of sustainable hegemonic empire.

Overall, the case for attributing any critical importance to Christianity in accounting for the failure of empire-building in Latin Europe is therefore extremely weak. It is telling that we need to wait for an entire millennium after the collapse of the sixth-century imperial restoration attempt for an even halfway plausible critical juncture to appear where Christianity might have played a major role in preventing imperiogenesis. This alone casts serious doubt on the notion that Christianity had somehow been necessary for the preservation of European polycentrism, rather than merely reinforcing existing trends in that vein.

Much the same is true of canon law. Developed during the papal revolution of the eleventh and twelfth centuries, it enshrined the plurality of legal traditions by demarcating church law from fragmented secular—urban, feudal, manorial—laws. But once again, this demarcation reflected the existing diffusion of power at least as much as it strengthened it.[21]

Roman law, by contrast, could be used to reassert royal power. It did not effectively constrain it: this was, after all, why from the 290s CE onward, late Roman emperors desirous of shoring up central authority had found it expedient to sponsor successive codifications. In and of itself, there was nothing in Roman law that would have turned it into a driver of European polycentrism: it contributed to it only in contradistinction to canon law. In Joseph Strayer's judgment, "While the revival of Roman law facilitated and perhaps accelerated the process of state-building, it was certainly not the primary cause and probably not even a necessary condition."[22]

Unity

The search for powerfully divisive legacies of the Roman empire thus comes up short. By contrast, the second option raised above appears more promising: the idea that Roman traditions softened post-Roman fragmentation in ways that rendered it more productive in regard to long-term developmental outcomes. This notion is worth considering since competition as such need not have been enough to ensure these outcomes.

Existing scholarship tends to endorse this idea in somewhat apodictic fashion, usually in the form of what we might call the "goldilocks scenario" of a Europe that was not united but not too splintered either. "Unity in diversity gave Europe some of the best of both worlds," in Eric

Jones's pithy phrasing, allowing it, according to Joel Mokyr, to "combine the best of fragmentation and consolidation": "the key to Europe's success was its fortunate condition that combined political fragmentation with cultural unity."[23]

Impressionistic judgments of this sort are complemented by more strident observations *ex cathedra*, such as Jean Baechler's claim that commercial development toward capitalism requires an environment *"where sovereign political units coexist within a culturally homogeneous area,"* echoed in John Hall's view that "competition between strong states inside a larger culture encouraged the triumph of capitalism" and Jan Luiten van Zanden's slightly more refined assertion that "the combination of political competition and economic cooperation (through trade)" was "crucial" for long-term development.[24]

There is no shortage of evidence for transregional integration: the movement of labor and capital across Europe's many borders, or more specifically the rapid dissemination of book printing. Even so, indeterminate claims of causal significance can come dangerously close to just-so stories.[25]

As before, we need to concentrate on Roman-era legacies that not only fostered cohesion but meaningfully contributed to the developmental dynamics identified in chapters 10 through 12. Two candidates stand out: Latin as a shared elite language that transcended political divisions, and—once again—Christianity, as the one commonly shared belief system, backed by a single transnational organization. Latin, followed later by exchange in the influential Romance languages of Italian and then French, facilitated communication among the educated. Christian norms are thought to have helped pacify the medieval lords and to have lowered transactions costs, most notably in interregional trade.[26]

The "idealist" school of thought regarding the underpinnings of modernity puts the greatest emphasis on the importance of cultural cohesion. If we follow those who ascribe a central role to the emergence of a European culture of knowledge and science and view it as being rooted in transnational exchange and competition, anything that assisted in this process would have been beneficial to transformative development.

Thus, for Mokyr, Western Europe profited from "a disconnect between the size of the political unit and the intellectual community" because it created space for a Republic of Letters. The lack of such networks would have raised the cost of access to a transnational market of ideas and helped incumbents—defenders of entrenched tradition—fend off challengers.[27]

This relatively narrow perspective is bound to disappoint champions of the long-term legacy of Roman law or ancient political discourse. Yet inasmuch as Roman law exerted influence, it did so because the medieval church had kept it alive, not just by ensuring the survival of Latin but also by applying elements of this tradition for its own purposes and drawing on it in the training of clergy. Moreover, even though the revival of Roman law in the High Middle Ages boosted its standing in learned discourse and in debates of current affairs, and later left its mark on law and court procedure both in the Protestant North and the Catholic South, it did not act as some form of transnational glue.[28]

Most tellingly, medieval and early modern merchants—groups that straddled regional customs and were perhaps most in need of a unifying set of rules—preferred to rely on peer panels to arbitrate disputes rather than on local courts, and came to develop their own body of customary law. England, the eventual spearhead of modernization, privileged common law, and its political system, inasmuch as it had not been influenced by Carolingian traditions (at the time or later via the Normans), was grounded in local practice and bereft of any substantive Roman legacy. And even where the Roman legal tradition was adopted and adapted, this process was governed by contemporary concerns: practitioners approached it, in Peter Stein's words, as "a kind of legal supermarket, in which lawyers of different periods have found what they needed at the time."[29]

What we are looking for in the present context is solid evidence of a Roman tradition's critical impact on the later European path to modern development: mere residual presence or influence will not do. Christianity and Latin may well be the only factors to clear this threshold.

Without Christianity

How can we tell? Any claim that such unifying traditions were instrumental in making competitive fragmentation yield developmental benefits over the long run implicitly entertains a counterfactual: a world from which these features were missing. What would it have taken to remove them, and what difference would that have made?

West of the Balkans, post-Roman Christianity and Latin were joined at the hip. It is doubtful whether the latter could have survived as a single elite lingua franca without the Catholic Church. The timing of the onset of linguistic diversity within Latin remains contested but was certainly under way by the sixth century and perhaps already several centuries earlier. During the sixth and seventh centuries, the negative effect of the Roman empire's fall on Latin usage and literacy was partly offset by the growing influence of the church and its efforts to maintain a recognizably "Latin" language in the face of growing differences between a standard high-register version and popular (or "vulgar") Latin.

In the eighth century, the shift of political power to the Carolingian realm and the challenge of Islamic expansion prepared the ground for more significant change in the following two centuries. The renewal of formal Latin in ecclesiastical contexts that focused on spelling, pronunciation, and antiquated grammar based on late Roman primers meant that popular styles of Latin were no longer recognized as such but increasingly treated as separate languages.[30]

This in turn encouraged experimentation with written vernacular versions: in the ninth century in France, from the late tenth century in Italy, and in the late eleventh century in the Iberian peninsula. Regional clusters began to diverge: the difference between Italian and French versions of "post-Latin" was already recognized in the tenth century. In the twelfth century, competitive state formation favored the concept of separate Romance languages, complemented in the thirteenth century by distinct writing systems. By then, most writing was no longer done in Latin, even as it had survived long enough to witness a revival in elite circles during the High Middle Ages.[31]

In the absence of the Catholic Church, the use and coherence of Latin would presumably have faded more rapidly from the fifth and sixth centuries onward. Vernacular variants would gradually have gained ground as part of ongoing linguistic evolution rather than in reaction to a church-driven renewal of Roman-style Latin. Latin would not have proven as resilient as regional usages continued to diverge, and would have found it much harder to reclaim a prominent position. In the most extreme scenario, it might even have disappeared altogether except as a pursuit for learned antiquarians.

In the absence of a viable foundation—ecclesiastical formal Latin coupled with formidable clerical power—there is no good reason why the revival of state power and the attendant shoring up of regional languages and scripts should have been accompanied by a renewal of Latin in elite circles: the appeal of emerging regional identities might well have been too strong. This highlights the crucial role of Christianity not just in creating and maintaining a unifying system of norms and beliefs but also in helping to preserve a modicum of linguistic unity. Both directly and indirectly, therefore, religion and the church acted as the most significant integrative force.

But what would it have taken to erase Christianity—and thus probably also (high-register) medieval Latin—from post-Roman Europe? In principle, very little. Regardless of what we make of the canonical stories, there can be no doubt that Christianity grew from very small beginnings, and might just as well not have done so at all. When in the early 60s CE, one Jesus, son of Ananias, made a nuisance of himself by predicting a judgment "against Jerusalem and the sanctuary . . . and against all the people," the local authorities handed him over to the Roman governor, who had him "flayed to the bone": yet even after Jesus failed to respond to the governor's queries, the latter chose to dismiss him as a harmless madman. Except for the final outcome, the other elements of this tale closely resemble those attributed to his more famous namesake.[32]

What if the latter had also been let go? The Savior's sacrifice on the cross was essential, especially for his greatest popularizer, Paul of Tarsus. But what if no Paul had stepped in to market this new sect to a wider, non-Jewish audience? Or if different versions of this tradition, or some

Gnostic variant, had gained the upper hand? Or if rival churches had splintered among irresolvable schisms, beginning with Marcionite rejection of the Old Testament tradition? And what would the late Roman church have looked like without the emperor Constantine's unexpected embrace? Or without the Nicene creed: it was the uncompromising affirmation of Jesus's divinity that was to set Christendom apart from other civilizations, ruling out divine kingship, making it harder to check the claims of the church and setting the scene for formative conflicts between popes and secular rulers. There are so many ways in which Christianity could have failed to get off the ground or developed differently even if it had. And we cannot blithely assume that some comparable movement might seamlessly have taken its place, least of all Judaism.[33]

A mature Roman empire without Christianity or anything like it is thus perfectly plausible, and arguably more plausible than what actually happened. This, in turn, would have deprived post-Roman Europe of a shared belief system as well as Latin, alongside an important means of co-opting the Germanic successor regimes into an existing cultural ecumene. All of these absences would inevitably have deepened the divisions emerging from the wreckage of universal empire: after a while, there might no longer have been a single elite language to be used across borders; there would have been fewer and less specific widely shared beliefs and norms, and less-"domesticated" successor kings; and fewer if any classical texts written in Latin would have survived. Without Roman-style Christianity, postimperial spatial polycentrism would have asserted itself with even greater intensity than in real life, whereas individual societies might have ended up less fractured within.

Could that have diverted Europe from its trajectory toward competitive modernization? If that had been the case—if the lack of unifying features had made fragmentation less productive—we would find ourselves in the remarkable position of having to attribute the emergence of the modern world to a highly contingent chain of events, from the Disciples who spread the faith to Paul of Tarsus who made it more accessible and on to the emperor Constantine and his sons. Then again, if polycentrism without Christianity had, in the end, been "good enough," we would be forced to conclude that Roman tradition in general did not really matter: after all, if it were possible to remove what was by far the most influential of these legacies—Christianity—without aborting modernity, it would seem exceedingly unlikely that the erasure of any less potent legacies (say, in law or political thought) would have made a critical difference.

It seems to me impossible to decide between these two stark alternatives, not least because they involve the kind of brazen counterfactual conjecture that gives the whole exercise a bad name: a sweepingly maximalist rewriting of history that opens up so many second-order counterfactuals that the simulation becomes impossible to control. The best we can do is to acknowledge that there is at least a good chance that imperial Christianity was in fact essential in bringing about much later breakthroughs.

This position preserves a space for the notion that the Roman empire contributed meaningfully and perhaps decisively to modernity. However, it would have done so in a much narrower and more specific manner than the richness and variety of Roman legacies might lead us to suspect. *If* it did contribute to this end, it did so in the spirit of "no man cometh unto the Father, but by me"—in the sense that there might not have been a path to the modern world except through the imperialized Catholic Church. Nothing else that Rome handed down to later generations would have mattered nearly as much, or—most notably Latin—mattered only because Christianity allowed it to.[34]

Without Rome

But what if there had never been a Roman empire to begin with? This question makes even the scenario of a Roman world without Christianity appear moderate by comparison: a concern fit only for the foolhardy, if not the outright foolish. Even so, the very idea is far from exotic. As we have seen, the Roman empire was a unique formation in that part of the world (chapter 1). Many conditions had to come together in just the right way to make it succeed (chapters 2–4). And it not only never returned, it was never even likely to (chapters 5–9). For all these reasons, a Europe without the Roman empire is more plausible than one with it. This alone makes this counterfactual less pointless to pursue. What, then, might Europe have looked like had the Romans never taken over?

Just as in the case of the church, it would not take any dramatic modifications of history to produce this alternative outcome. In the fifth and early fourth centuries BCE, defeat by its neighbor Veii, destruction by Gauls, or failure due to internal strife were all perfectly plausible events that could have prevented Rome from ever becoming a major power. Nor was it a given that some other Italian entity, such as the Samnitic confederation, would have taken its place and, above all, would have proved as adept at setting up a comparably effective war machine.

In the absence of large-scale expansionist state formation in the Italian peninsula, the most likely short-term outcome in the western Mediterranean would have been some form of stalemate between Carthage and the western Greeks. While the former would have been better able to access additional manpower and resources by expanding farther west (as they eventually did in actual history), the latter could balance this with the help of other Greeks polities to the east. Although a variety of shocks might have upset this uneasy equilibrium—a successful Greek or Hellenistic attack on Carthage, or conversely Italian encroachment on the Greeks—the lack of Roman-scale mobilization capabilities speaks against a scenario of stable imperial consolidation in the western Mediterranean.[35]

In the eastern Mediterranean, meanwhile, the Hellenistic successor states would have remained locked in conflict. Absent Rome's intervention against Macedon, the Seleucids would have found it difficult to expand westward. Although Seleucid conquest of a Ptolemaic Egypt shorn of Roman support might well have been feasible, long-term control would have been an elusive goal, just as it had been for Assyrians and Achaemenids and was again to be for the Abbasids later. Parthian pressure, which in actual history subdued much of the Seleucid territories, posed a further constraint. In the longer term, renewed Iranian expansion was a plausible outcome, with the Parthian empire eventually absorbing the remaining Seleucid domains and perhaps advancing into Asia Minor and Egypt as well. Yet in that case, they too would have faced the same challenges as the Achaemenids before them, struggling to hold on to the Nile valley or the Aegean region.[36]

Over time, an Iranian empire centered on Iran and Mesopotamia might have been balanced by Hellenistic states in the eastern Mediterranean basin. In this context, Hellenistic culture could have survived and even prospered, just as it did under Roman rule. The major centers of Greek learning—the Aegean and Alexandria—were relatively far removed from Iranian power bases, and might have endured as long as they did in real life.[37]

Would Hellenistic culture have spread as widely as it did under the aegis of Roman power? The use of Greek language and writing is a critical issue. They were successful where Macedonians ruled but also made inroads beyond: Roman historians writing in Greek are the best-known example. Latin literature arose only when Rome was already on its way to empire and initially involved a great deal of translation from Greek into Latin. In the absence of Roman rule, would other societies in Western Europe have done the same as political and socioeconomic complexity increased and state-level polities formed?[38]

Real-life evidence gives little cause for optimism. During the last half of the first millennium BCE, local populations tended to adapt existing scripts of Phoenician, Etruscan, and Greek origin to record their own languages. Without a later Roman takeover and the concomitant spread of its script and language, this trend would not have been conducive to cultural unity. Most Iberian groups that left written material wrote in Iberian languages using Iberian scripts, influenced by the Phoenician alphabet. The spread of the Greco-Iberian script remained minimal, to say nothing of Greek itself. In Gaul, despite a long-standing Greek presence in Marseille and trade links up the Rhone, Greek inscriptions are rarely found outside the extreme south, even if they were on occasion set up to record texts in native languages. Evidence of the use of Greek as a lingua franca among the Celtic Gauls is exiguous as well as ambivalent, reflecting weak penetration overall.[39]

What is now the most visible sign of influence, Celtic coinage, was originally closely modeled on Greek types but gradually diverged into native designs. Only Greek lettering was frequently used in this context, not just in Gaul but even, if rarely, in Britain: even so, Gallo-Greek coin appeared only late (dating from period of Roman advance) and remained highly limited in scope.[40]

The picture is complicated by the observation that Iberian and Celtic—as well as Illyrian and Germanic—societies at the time had not yet reached levels of development that would have provided strong impetus for more systematic literacy. Before the Roman conquests, writing had been optional—or at least that is the most economical conclusion to derive from the patchy nature and uneven density of writing practices.[41]

Thus, continued development without Roman intervention might eventually have opened up opportunities beyond what the actual pre-Roman record shows. Even so, the Iberian case should give us pause: given the established dominance of local writing and language, the most plausible longer-term outcome would seem to be the intensified use of local scripts to record local languages. Much the same would have been true of Italy, with its profusion of local letters and languages, and even future Gallic state elites might well have elected to adapt rather than copy Greek writing. Under these circumstances, it is highly doubtful that Greek cultural traits would eventually have come to be shared across the diverse societies of continental Europe. This matters because in view of the differences between Iberian, Celtic, Germanic, and Illyrian languages, Hellenization without empire would have been the only available means of creating some degree of coherent linguistic and cultural framework for a politically divided Europe, at least in elite circles.

Yet even in the most optimistic scenario, there is no plausible way to imagine Greek becoming anywhere near as influential as Latin was under Roman rule. Whether a thin veneer of Hellenistic elite culture, insofar as it would have developed at all, would have left much of a mark on later European civilization is questionable. This is not a trivial issue: some of the most important Greek influences on later Europe could in theory have occurred without Latin-Roman mediation. Key texts of the medieval canon—Aristotle, Ptolemy, and Galen—were of Greek and Hellenistic origin, as were the gospels and the letters of Paul. Absent Roman rule, such writings—or rather, in most of these cases, their putative counterfactual Hellenistic equivalents—could have been accessed in the original, even if only by the very few. The same is true of technical texts—most notably by Archimedes—that stimulated early modern advances in mathematics and physics and may arguably have made a vital contribution to the eventual scientific revolution.[42]

In this Rome-less environment, trade and religion would have served as the main conduits for the dissemination of Greek. Even without Pontius Pilate, the Hellenistic Levant might very well have produced belief systems that were not wholly dissimilar from Christianity: the famous "Dead Sea Scrolls" from Qumran show the potential. And even if that had not happened, plenty of other regional religions from Isis worship to Mithraism and Manichaeism that were successful in the actual Roman west could have made inroads, and indeed perhaps even more so if unconstrained by Christian competition. Given enough time, a Greek-inflected intellectual and cultural superstructure could have helped build bridges in a Europe without hegemonic empire.

Just how fractured would that Europe have been? There were no plausible substitutes for the Roman empire. Even if it had managed to overcome the western Greeks, Carthage, centered on Tunisia and constrained by lower mobilization capacity, would not have been in a position to advance anywhere near as far into continental Europe as the Romans did. Greek- or Macedonian-led imperial state formation—another Alexander-style eruption, this time directed westward—was made unlikely by the multiple weaknesses of the Hellenistic state system around 200 BCE that I discussed in chapter 3. Thus, given the limitations of the major powers along the Mediterranean rim, indigenous state formation among Iberians, Gauls, and Germans seems by far the most realistic long-term scenario.[43]

Given the tremendous scope of this counterfactual, there is simply no sound way of guessing what this world might have looked like in the second half of the first millennium CE. All we can say is that it need not have been dramatically different from the real one. If we accept my argument in chapter 8 that Europe was inherently less suitable for large-scale imperiogenesis than other core regions of the Old World, the emergence of sometimes sizable but not vast regional polities, endowed with kings, cities, writing, and currencies, might well have been the most realistic outcome.

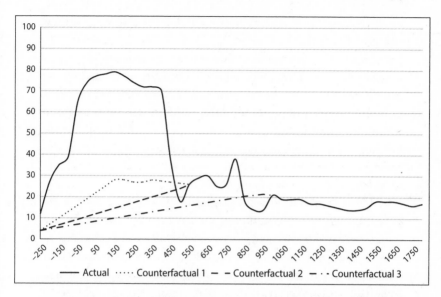

FIGURE E.1 Actual and counterfactual concentration of state power in Europe, 250 BCE–1800 CE (in terms of the population of Europe ruled by the largest power, in percent).

In this case, at least in the broadest terms, the political map of Europe in 500 or 1000 CE need not have diverged widely from that of post-Roman Europe, dominated by some large but not particularly capable states interspersed with more highly fragmented regions. There was more than one path to that point: the historical trajectory, which involved an enormous detour from tribes, chiefdoms and city-states to near-monopolistic empire to weak regional polities, and alternative counterfactual trajectories charting a more gradual but also more linear progression from the first to the third of these stages (figure E.1).[44]

The plausible counterfactual of indigenous state formation makes it unnecessary to consider Roman legacies of centralizing statecraft an essential precondition for the later rise of what Daron Acemoglu and James Robinson call the "Shackled Leviathan" in Western Europe—the powerful yet nondespotic type of state that came to protect liberties and promote human flourishing. Even if centralizing governmental traditions needed to balance localized consensual decision-making for such productive polities to emerge, imperial Rome was by no means their only possible source.[45]

Just how interconnected elite culture would have been across Europe's counterfactual societies of the mid- and late first millennium CE, so many centuries after we diverge from actual history, is obviously impossible to divine. At one—and admittedly far-fetched—end of a broad spectrum of possibilities, we might encounter a world of kingdoms run by bilingual (local-language and Hellenophone) elites, supplied and educated by equally bilingual traders and scholars, and tended to by the Greek-speaking priests of some Levantine salvation religion. At the opposite extreme, vernacular languages and concurrent writing systems of the Paleo-Hispanic, Celtic, Italic, Illyrian, and Germanic varieties would have suppressed transregional modes of communication, and a wide range of indigenous animistic and polytheistic beliefs would have coexisted with Hellenistic imports. In the latter case, deeply entrenched fragmentation would have sustained political polycentrism and institutional variety while impeding the flow of people, goods, and ideas within Europe.

Only if, in a world without Rome, outcomes had come to be concentrated near that end of the spectrum could the Roman empire be credited with a contribution that might have been vital to later European development. And even this view is predicated on a premise that cannot be accepted a priori, and therefore remains little more than a guess: that without empire, there would not have been enough connectivity and cohesion later to make fragmentation developmentally productive and nurture eventual breakthroughs.

• • •

What, then, were the root causes of the onset of modernity? Two circumstances, one exceedingly remote and the other far less so, were critical for European fragmentation and polycentrism. From the late Cretaceous onward, the collision between the African and the Eurasian tectonic plates caused the Alpine orogeny, a process that formed the Carpathians and Alps and raised them ever higher. Without the former, Transylvania would not have appeared and the great Eurasian steppe would extend to Vienna; and without the Alps, it might stretch even farther west. Tens of millions of years later, mounted warriors might have pushed state formation in a different direction, toward serial empire.[46]

In actual history, at roughly the time when such influences would have made themselves felt, Germanic warriors in the Iberian peninsula, Gaul, Italy, and Germany gained control over their means of subsistence and lordly autonomy undermined central state power. Had taxation and centralized governance been sustained, the odds of imperial restoration would have been improved, and a rerun of the Roman experience might no longer have been impossible.

A third factor arguably contributed as well, albeit in a more ambiguous way: the perseverance of the followers of an obscure Jewish prophet in building up a far-flung network that evolved into a hierarchical and fairly cohesive transnational organization. Its presence simultaneously contributed to and helped offset post-Roman fragmentation.

Plate tectonics, warriors, and—perhaps—preachers interacted in very specific ways to create the environment that gave birth to modernity. But where does all this leave the Romans? What did they ever do for us *before* their empire fell apart? What seems to me the most honest answer is also disappointingly vague: that they quite possibly may have done something very important for us—if, but only if, their empire, by turning to Christianity, laid some crucial foundations for much later development—but that they just as likely may not have contributed anything essential at all to this eventual outcome and thus failed to shape the general appearance, if not some of the finer points, of the world we live in today.

In the end, competitive fracture may well have mattered more—or rather, *even* more—than residual cultural unity: the unanswerable question is whether the former, on its own, would have been enough. Rome's unreversed demise was an indispensable precondition of modernity. But when it comes to explaining this breakthrough, does it really matter that its empire ever existed at all?

GLOSSARY

Some of the key terms employed in this book are bound to mean different things to different people. Explaining my own usage of the most common ones should help avoid misunderstandings.

CHINA Depending on context, China refers to the (fluid) geographical area that was controlled by the main dynasties from the Qin onward, as well as to the territory of the current People's Republic of China (PRC). Where applicable, I differentiate China from "core China" or "China proper," shorthand for the PRC exclusive of Manchuria, Inner Mongolia, Xinjiang, Tibet, and Taiwan. For the sake of convenience, if anachronistically, I loosely apply the terms "China" and "Chinese" to these core areas going back to the second millennium BCE. I do not use China and East Asia interchangeably; the latter includes Korea and Japan. My use of any of these terms is not intended as commentary on ethnic identity or current affairs.

EMPIRE A generally large, composite, and often multiethnic state organized around a dominant center that controls subordinate and sometimes distant territories and populations (or "peripheries"). Even this conservative definition is far from precise: imperial formations did not have to be particularly large and varied greatly in terms of heterogeneity and intensity of demarcation between dominants and subordinates. In practice, I apply this term only to physically and demographically substantial polities that covered from several hundred thousand to tens of millions of square kilometers and claimed between millions and hundreds of millions of subjects. Where applicable, I employ characterizations such as "agrarian," "traditional," or "tributary" to highlight salient attributes. "Hegemonic" empires were states that effectively dominated territory and population on a subcontinental scale by a combination of direct rule and often highly asymmetric relations with neighboring political entities, in periods when their existence and overall territorial integrity were not systematically at risk from challengers. Whenever I use the term "empire" without further specification, I refer to contiguous land empires (based in agrarian areas, the steppe, or both). I distinguish as "colonial empires" the overseas territories European powers acquired from the late fifteenth century onward. I employ the term "imperiogenesis" to describe state formation on a large scale.

EUROPE I adopt the conventional definition of Europe as comprising the lands west of the Urals, the Ural River, the Caspian Sea, the Caucasus, and the Black Sea. I also single out specific parts thereof. "Latin Europe" refers to Europe west of the areas traditionally dominated by the Orthodox Church (currently west of Russia, Belarus, Ukraine, Romania,

Serbia, and Greece, a line that has not substantively shifted since the Schism of 1054). "Western Europe" is a slightly smaller portion from the Atlantic to the Germanic- and Italian-language areas in the east. "Northwestern Europe" encompasses the British Isles, the Scandinavian Peninsula, the Low Countries, northern France, and northern Germany. More narrowly but somewhat poorly defined, the "North Sea region" centers on Britain and the Low Countries. I have sought consistency in usage but may use "European" as shorthand if the context is clear. I generally avoid the labels "West" and "Western": when they are used, they refer in the first instance to Europe (and especially Latin Europe) plus its main colonial settler societies in North America and the Antipodes.

FIRST GREAT DIVERGENCE As explained in chapter 7, I use the term "First Great Divergence" to describe the secular divergence in patterns of state formation between Latin Europe on the one hand and the Middle East, South Asia, and especially East Asia on the other, which commenced and solidified during the second half of the first millennium CE. Unlike the Second Great Divergence, this process was political in nature: it witnessed the emergence of a durable polycentric state system in Latin Europe as opposed to the serial constitution of very large empire in other parts of the Old World.

POLYCENTRISM A polycentric system is characterized by multiple centers of power, authority, and control. Polycentric arrangements exist between polities within state systems that are not dominated by a single hegemon as well as within any given polity in which different constituencies autonomously exercise power that balances that of the central political leadership. With regard to both types of arrangements, I use polycentrism and fragmentation as effectively interchangeable terms. They serve as an ideal-typical antithesis to the (equally ideal-typical) monopolistic exercise of power within a given polity or the hegemonic status of an imperial state within a very large catchment area. Monopoly, hegemony, and polycentrism are inevitably a matter of degree, and I spend much time in this book exploring their relative preponderance in different historical settings.

SECOND GREAT DIVERGENCE I employ this term as the equivalent of what is generally called *the* "Great Divergence," the process whereby the most advanced economies of Western Europe pulled ahead of other parts of the world in terms of economic productivity. Definitions of this divergence vary: while some apply it broadly to relatively subtle differences in output and welfare that can be traced back to the Middle Ages, others use it in a more focused manner to contrast the onset of industrialization and sustainable economic growth in eighteenth-century northwestern Europe with the persistence of more traditional modes of economic activity and technological development elsewhere, most notably in Asia. I generally call this process the "(Second) Great Divergence," a compromise that seeks to reconcile standard usage (which recognizes only a single "Great Divergence") with my introduction of the term "First Great Divergence." When mentioned without qualifiers, "Great Divergence" refers to the "Great Divergence" as conventionally defined.

STATE For the purposes of a wide-ranging comparative study that reaches far back in time, I define the state very loosely as a somewhat durable and hierarchical political organization that claims and at least to some degree exercises authority over territory, people, and resources, and does so by asserting priority over certain claims of other groups within or outside that territory and through its ability to establish this priority by coercive means, at the very least on an occasional punitive basis. This minimalist definition omits features commonly associated with more mature states, such as legitimacy, sovereignty, or a monopoly of legitimate violence in the enforcement of rules and the legal order. Historically, such political organizations greatly varied in their level of centralization and effectively shared many claims, prerogatives, and functions with other constituencies. Unless we apply formally Eurocentric and modernizing concepts of statehood, these common characteristics should not deter us, however, from labeling such polities "states." I use the more neutral term "polity" interchangeably with the term "state" and also to describe political entities that might not have met even the basic requirements set out here, such as chiefdoms, tribal confederations, or particularly decentralized or ephemeral political organizations. I do not employ the term "nation" as a generic equivalent of "state" but occasionally switch between "interstate" and "international" to avoid repetitiveness.

STATE FORMATION I use this term in a very general sense to refer to any developments that create and modify institutions of governance over people and territory beyond the level of small-scale communities. I envision state formation as an ongoing process of structural change that may (but need not) lead to increased centralization or state capacity: historically, state power within given polities waxed and waned over time. Very occasionally, I refer to "state (de)formation" to emphasize the decentralizing and regressive character of a particular process.

STATE SYSTEM A cluster of several adjoining independent states that systematically interact over the long term in the political, military, economic, and cultural domains. I use this concept as the stylized opposite of "hegemonic empire" as defined above. The "Warring States" of fifth- to third-century BCE China and the post-Carolingian states of Latin Europe are the most straightforward historical examples and are frequently referenced in this book. Others that are beyond the scope of my study, such as various city-state cultures from Sumerians to Maya, also qualify.

STEPPE FRONTIER I apply this term to the shifting borderlands and intermediate zones between grasslands that primarily sustained herding and hunting on one side and settled agricultural areas on the other. These frontiers could be wide or narrow depending on local circumstances, and their extent was sensitive to ongoing changes in climate and land use. They served as interaction zones between nomadic or seminomadic pastoralists and sedentary agriculturalists. The most extensive steppe frontier in history was that between the great Central Eurasian grasslands and agrarian regions to the south.

TECHNICAL NOTE TO CHAPTER 1

IN CHAPTER 1, I seek to determine the share of the largest power in the population of a given region at a certain point in time. This approach requires information about the territorial extent of the principal polities and the probable size of their population. The former can readily be obtained from standard historical atlases. Although these may differ in points of detail, such differences are fairly trivial compared to the much greater uncertainty surrounding population number. Specialized historical scholarship, inasmuch as it exists at all, is of highly uneven quality, and so is the evidentiary base (such as it is). For present purposes, the single most important objective is to ensure consistency across time and space in order to facilitate systematic comparison.

The *Atlas of World Population History* compiled by Colin McEvedy and Richard Jones in 1978 is the only resource that provides the required level of internal coherence and consistency. McEvedy and Jones give estimates of the population of modern countries (or clusters of countries), a few historical entities (such as the Ottoman and Russian empires), and entire continents and the whole world. Their time series commences in 400 BCE and ends in 1950, with projections offered for 2000. The level of resolution is 200-year intervals between 400 BCE and 1000 CE, 100-year intervals from 1000 to 1500, and 50-year intervals thereafter.[1]

In arriving at their figures, they rely on an eclectic mix of earlier scholarship and they frequently extrapolate backward when there are no data at all. Their extrapolations are undergirded by key assumptions about the overall direction and relative scale of long-term change, which are open to debate. Based on my own research experience, I can say with confidence that their numbers systematically underestimate population density in the ancient world. For example, a tally of 60 million–70 million inhabitants for the Roman empire at its peak in the mid-second century CE is much more realistic than their minimalist estimate of 45 million. The ancient Greek world was also more heavily populated than they allow for.[2]

Similar problems undermine their results for East Asia. They assume a population of 50 million in China (within its current borders plus Taiwan) in 1 CE, although the Han census for 2 CE refers to 59.5 million, even as not all of China was actually under Han rule and not everyone who was a subject can be expected to have been counted. Their claim of dramatic demographic growth after 1000 stems at least in part from their tendency to underestimate earlier Chinese population size, which then requires an unrealistically rapid catching-up to match documented census totals from the Song period. Their figures for South Asia are inevitably even more conjectural and may likewise underestimate earlier population densities.[3]

All of this is intentional, given that McEvedy and Jones operate on the assumption of a strong global net increase in population number during the first millennium CE, whereas other scholars favor a boom-and-bust scenario with little if any net increase overall. More recent research lends greater support to the latter view. As McEvedy and Jones correctly observe, their estimates for the second millennium CE are for the most part less controversial and the margins of uncertainty keep shrinking as we approach the present.[4]

What matters most for us is that insofar as their premodern population figures aim too low, they do so in a consistent fashion. This would be a concern if we were interested in actual population size, but it is of no particular relevance to the computation of population *shares* as undertaken in chapter 1. Thus, if a given polity covered an area whose population had in fact been 25 percent or even 50 percent larger than McEvedy and Jones believe it was, this undercount would not affect the ratio of imperial to macro-regional population size. I have therefore generally refrained from adjusting their figures so as not to introduce imbalances into their internally coherent edifice of guesstimates.

A more serious problem arises from the need to break down national population totals into smaller elements that can be assigned to imperial states that held only portions of the territory of particular modern countries. In Europe and the MENA region this is a minor issue, given that modern countries there tend to be of fairly moderate size. This makes it relatively easy to come up with plausible fractional estimates, and modest margins of error do not greatly affect overall outcomes for polities that extended across a number of modern states. South and East Asia, by contrast, present us with formidable challenges, dominated as they are by just two massive modern states that form the basic units for McEvedy and Jones's estimates.[5]

In those two cases I had to employ (even) cruder ways of apportioning historical population to parts of modern states. For China, I drew on the distribution of Han census results for 140 CE to establish rough proportions for northern and southern China and Sichuan. I also used the present distribution of population among China's various provinces to extrapolate a gradual shift over time from the ancient to the current pattern. Broadly speaking, northern China, which was demographically heavily dominant in antiquity, gradually lost out to other areas, above all to the South, which witnessed substantial development especially from the Song period onward. Although it might be possible to devise a somewhat finer-grained adjustment method by taking account of historical census data from the second millennium CE, this is made redundant by the fact that China was for the most part either united or split in two. This pattern greatly facilitates estimation of the population share of the largest polity in East Asia.[6]

My estimates for South Asia remain much more problematic, both because of the dubious nature of any early population guesstimates and because of our ignorance regarding the spatial distribution of the population in the more distant past. In the most general terms, early India—not unlike China—would have been characterized by greater demographic concentration in the north, in the Indus and Ganges basins, than it is today. In the absence of information comparable to the ancient Chinese census records, there is no obvious way of quantifying this shift even in a crude manner. I have therefore relied on the current distribution of the population of India and Pakistan in order to estimate population shares in the past, an uncomfortably simplifying approach that produces a good fit for the recent past but inevitably becomes increasingly shaky the farther we move back in time.[7]

This is significant because the largest South Asian empires commonly originated in the north, either indigenously in the Ganges basin (Maurya and Gupta) or as the result of incursions from the northwestern frontier (Saka, Kushan, and a series of Muslim polities). Only some of them arose in central India (Satavahara, Chalukya, and Rashtrakuta), and Vijayanagara and Chola remained the only major empires in the far south. My population shares likely underestimate the relative demographic dominance of northern empires and somewhat inflate the weight of more southerly ones, a problem I duly note in chapter 1. This problem is limited to amplitude and does not affect measurement of the duration of the dominant imperial formations. Thus, although my reconstruction of the South Asian profile ought to be approached with greater caution than that for the other macro-regions, it is nevertheless defensible in its general outlines.

Overall, the charts provided in chapter 1 serve as a means to a very specific end, which is to establish and compare long-term patterns in imperial state formation in different parts of the Old World. For them to be substantively misleading, they would have to be wrong in ways that seem incompatible with the historical record. Nonetheless, I advise readers not to use these tentative reconstructions in ways that go too far beyond this limited objective: they are based on controlled conjecture, and are not to be mistaken for historical "facts."[8]

INTRODUCTION

1. The simile of an "escape" has been employed before, most notably by Fogel 2004, Deaton 2013, and Vries 2013. I use it here in part to continue the cinematic theme of this book's motto; cf. also Deaton 2013: 2–3 for a reference to the 1963 movie *The Great Escape*.

2. For notable premodern growth phases, see, e.g., Goldstone 2002 (cross-cultural); Saller 2002 (ancient Rome); Scheidel, Morris, and Saller 2007 (ancient Greco-Roman world); Jursa 2010 (ancient Babylonia); W. Liu 2015a (Song China); Ober 2015 (ancient Greece). For the underlying methodology of the Maddison Project Database 2018, see most recently Bolt et al. 2018.

3. In terms of the world's economic center of gravity, the West's preeminence peaked around 1950, see https://www.economist.com/graphic-detail/2018/10/27/the-chinese-century-is-well-under-way for a visualization.

4. See Bourguignon and Morrisson 2002.

5. I. Morris 2013b, expanding on I. Morris 2010. Eastern Eurasia shows a similar upturn after a time lag. Morris's scoring (not shown here in full) reaches back to the beginning of the Holocene.

6. I. Morris 2013b: 239–48 defends the broad validity even of earlier variations by discussing margins of error. Quote: Landes 2003: 5.

7. I. Morris 2013b: 53–143 (energy capture), 249, table 7.3 (role of energy capture), 63–65 (eighteenth and nineteenth centuries); see 66, fig. 3.4 for a visual. Energy capture refers to energy flows to humans from food (consumed by humans or by animals used or consumed by humans), fuel (including wind and water power) and raw materials (I. Morris 2013b: 53). Lower estimates of premodern energy capture in other studies are to some extent the result of narrower definitions (76–80). Even though Morris appears to underestimate the contribution of coal to the nineteenth-century expansion (compare I. Morris 2013b: 63 to Warde 2007: 117–20 and Warde 2013: 133, table 5.1), his totals are sufficiently similar to other estimates to support their inclusion in his development index.

8. Warde 2007: 127–28, accepted by Wrigley 2016: 34. See also Warde 2013: 134, fig. 5.2 for an analogous tripling of per capita energy consumption in a larger sample of Western and Southern European countries. For England's pioneering role in the fossil fuel transition, see, e.g., Warde 2013: 131–41 and chapters 10 and 12 in this volume. For the transformative shift from organic and fossil fuel economies, see most recently Wrigley 2016: 1–3.

9. On life expectancy, see Norberg 2017: 43; Pinker 2018: 54. See Roser 2019 for more detail. See Deaton 2013: 29–41 for the link between GDP and life expectancy. On global per capita

GDP growth, see Maddison 2010. On poverty and malnourishment, see Norberg 2017: 9, 20, 65, 76.

10. Floud et al. 2011: 69, table 2.5 (heights), 364 (quote).

11. On literacy, see Norberg 2017: 131–33; Roser 2018. On freedom, see Pinker 2018: 202–3; Roser 2018. Fifty-six percent of the world's population currently lives in democracies. On happiness and "life evaluation," see Deaton 2013: 18, 21, 53; Pinker 2018: 269. On global economic inequality trends, see Milanovic 2016: 118–32. On resilience of within-society economic inequality, see Scheidel 2017: 405–23.

12. For a taste of the growing literature on the risks the future holds, see Rees 2003, 2018, and, more specifically, http://www.ipcc.ch/, https://www.globalchange.gov/, and http://www.lancetcountdown.org/ for the fossil-fuel economy's impact on the climate and human welfare.

13. McCloskey 2010: 125–384 (with 2016: 83–146) and Vries 2013: 153–438 are the most comprehensive (and strident) surveys-cum-critiques. Daly 2015 offers a scrupulously neutral survey of the main approaches, primarily aimed at students.

14. When empire once again emanated from Europe, from the sixteenth century onward, it did so by exporting it to an increasingly global periphery while coexisting with and arguably even reinforcing fragmentation in Europe itself. Russia's initial lack of demographic heft long offset its massive spatial expansion. Thus, neither colonial empire nor Russia (which Lieven 2000 and Burbank and Cooper 2010: 185–99 put into comparative context) represent deviations from this pattern.

15. This observation cannot be undone simply by calling ancient Rome a "Mediterranean" rather than a "European" empire (e.g., Gat 2006: 392–93): Rome ruled most Europeans at the time, well more than half of the empire's population was located in Europe, and the empire controlled almost all of Western Europe, which is at the center of this book's attention.

16. For the nomenclature, see chapter 7 in this volume.

17. I refer to empire *within*—above all, Western—Europe. Colonial empires overseas were extensions of competing European polities.

18. See chapter 10 in this volume for "long-term" and "short-term" explanations of modern economic development and for the "Little Divergence," and see chapter 7 for definitions of various "divergences."

19. With no claim to completeness: among the chief proponents are J. Hall 1985: 111–44 and J. Hall 1988: 33–38; Landes 1998: 37–39; E. Jones 2003: 104–26, 225, 233; Mokyr 2007: 23–26 and Mokyr 2017: 165–78; Cosandey 2008: 175–316; van Zanden 2009a: 32–68, 295; Rosenthal and Wong 2011, e.g., 124–25, 145, 198–99, 208–10, 225–30; Vries 2013: 379–82, 434–35; Vries 2015, e.g., 363, 430. Among the many others, see, for various aspects, Wallerstein 1974: 60, 63; Baechler 1975: 74–77; Mann 1986: 376; Macfarlane 1988: 191; Diamond 1997: 416; Wong 1997: 148; Abernethy 2000: 206–24; Crone 2003: 161–63; Chaudhry and Garner 2006; Mann 2006: 383; Arrighi 2007: 315; Ringmar 2007: 289; Karayalcin 2008: 977; Chu 2010; Voigtländer and Voth 2013a, 2013b; Hoffman 2015, esp. 213; McCloskey 2016: 396–400; Cox 2017: 746–47; Roeck 2017: 22; Dincecco and Onorato 2018; Ko, Koyama, and Sng 2018: 310–11; and cf. also Mielants 2007: 154–62 and Stasavage 2011: 47–109 for the role of city-states and small polities.

20. I develop this approach in chapter 1.

21. Bang, Bayly, and Scheidel (in press) offer a more systematic survey than the very substantial collection of Rollinger and Gehler 2014. For the nature of empire and the debate, see the introductory chapter by Bang (in press), and notably also Haldon (in press), with references. For partial syntheses and/or theory, see Eisenstadt 1963; Kautsky 1982; Doyle 1986; Lieven 2000; Motyl 2001; Wood 2003; Chua 2007; Münkler 2007; Darwin 2008; Burbank and Cooper 2010; Leitner 2011. See also, among collaborative works, Tracy 1990, 1991 (early modern merchant empires); Alcock et al. 2001 (eclectic); Morris and Scheidel 2009 (antiquity); Scheidel 2009d, 2015c (on the two largest ancient empires, Rome and Han China).

22. Not on its own: Mokyr 2009: 83–84. Quote: Landes 2003: 12. See also Vries 2013: 22–27, for the breadth of the process but also the key role of industrialization.

23. As Wickham rightly observes regarding the survival of states (and not just large empires, but state structures as such), "It is survival that is the norm, failure that is the deviation" (1994: 74), and that this poses a challenge to scholars of post-Roman Western Europe. I hope to have reduced this challenge.

24. Quotes: Johann Wolfgang von Goethe in *Italienische Reise* (ch. 24, December 3, 1786, on the city of Rome); Gibbon 1788b: 645.

25. Paired by Campbell 2004: 167. The inscription appears as no. 138 in Sartre 1993, and Virgil's quote is from the *Aeneid* 1.279.

26. "Getting to Denmark" is a metaphor for establishing political and economic institutions that are highly conducive to human welfare, a concept that goes back to Pritchett and Woolcock (2002: 4) and that has since been popularized especially by Fukuyama 2011: 14. Metaphorically, the escape from Rome was also an escape from China, and indeed from rule by any large agrarian empire.

27. This imbalance was already noted more casually by Klein 2017: 302. My sample, with due apologies for unconscionable omissions and idiosyncrasies: Economists (19): Daron Acemoglu, Robert Allen, Stephen Broadberry, Kent Deng, Ronald Findlay, Bishnupriya Gupta, Eric Jones, Cem Karayalcin, Mark Koyama, Timur Kuran, Deirdre McCloskey, Joel Mokyr, Patrick O'Brien, Kevin O'Rourke, Jean-Laurent Rosenthal, Jared Rubin, Jan Luiten van Zanden, Nico Voigtländer, and Hans-Joachim Voth. Sociologists (9): Jean Baechler, Joseph Bryant, Ricardo Duchesne, Jack Goldstone, John Hall, Toby Huff, Eric Mielants, Immanuel Wallerstein, and Dingxin Zhao. Historians (8): Philip Huang, Margaret Jacob, David Landes, Michael Mitterauer, Prasannan Parthasarathi, Kenneth Pomeranz, Peer Vries, and Bin Wong. Political science is only marginally represented by Gary Cox, Erik Ringmar, and David Stasavage, and the list is rounded off by the physicist David Cosandey, and Ian Morris, a classical archaeologist turned world historian. One could have added Joseph Needham, trained as a biochemist. If one wanted—even more idiosyncratically and thus anonymously—to single out the dozen most influential scholars in this sample, ratios would change only a little, with two-thirds of the putative top spots held (mostly) by economists and a couple of sociologists, and the remainder by historians. What is even more striking, of course, is that 95 percent of the full sample is (now) male: this is not by any means an inclusive domain of research.

28. Fowden 2011: 172 (quote). See 168 for the "first millennium" (CE) as a meaningful unit of analysis, a notion that is borne out in my book: all of the critical events—the fall of the

Roman empire and the inexorable early medieval dismantling of its institutions, as well as the revival of empire in China (Sui-Tang and Song) and elsewhere in the Old World—took place in precisely that period.

29. Quote: Kocka 2009: 15. For comparison in history and cognate social sciences more generally, see Bonnell 1980; Skocpol and Somers 1980; Tilly 1984; Ragin 1987; Goldstone 1991: 50–62; Haupt and Kocka 1996a (esp. Haupt and Kocka 1996b; Osterhammel 1996); Mahoney and Rueschemeyer 2003 (esp. Mahoney 2003; Rueschemeyer 2003); Kocka 2009. There does not seem to be an introduction specifically to comparative history: for now, Lange 2013 offers the closest approximation. Specifically for comparative ancient history, see Mutschler and Scheidel 2017; Scheidel 2018.

30. Quotes: Lloyd and Sivin 2002: 8; Rueschemeyer 2003: 332.

31. Quote: Kocka 2009: 15.

32. Quote: Kocka 2009: 15.

33. Quote: Kocka 2009: 17.

34. Weber 1920–1921.

35. For analytical comparisons, see Bonnell 1980: 164–65.

36. For these concepts, see Skocpol and Somers 1980: 175–78; Ragin 1987: 17.

37. Tetlock and Parker 2006: 15 (quotes) and 17–28 for a forceful statement of this position. See also Demandt 2011: 51 for the same point. For counterfactual history, see Hawthorn 1991; Tetlock and Belkin 1996; Ferguson 1997; Cowley 1999, 2001; Tetlock, Lebow, and Parker 2006b; Demandt 2011.

38. Tetlock and Parker 2006: 18–19 for these two approaches; Demandt 2011: 28–31 for causality.

39. Tetlock and Parker 2006: 33–36 on procedure, esp. 34 (quote). See also Tetlock and Belkin 1996: 1–31 on criteria for judging the quality of counterfactuals, esp. 23–27 on consistency with historical facts and theoretical laws.

40. Imperative: Tetlock and Belkin 1996: 19–23. Problems: Tetlock and Belkin 1996: 21; Tetlock, Lebow, and Parker 2006a: 10; Tetlock and Parker 2006: 34–35.

41. Junctures: Tetlock and Belkin 1996: 7–8; Tetlock and Parker 2006: 33–34.

42. Tetlock and Parker 2006: 35–36 consider this risk the greatest challenge of counterfactual reasoning.

43. Tetlock, Lebow, and Parker 2006a: 10–11 (change over time); Tetlock and Parker 2006: 21 (question).

44. "The reader should remember that to describe a phenomenon is not to praise it" (Strayer 1970: xxviii, on the creation and strengthening of European states). The same applies to inter-state competition (a euphemism for pointless warfare and consumer-unfriendly protectionism), religious strife, colonization, plantation slavery, and so much more.

Not least because of its wide scope, this is not designed to be a book of overt controversy. I note disagreements rather than seek to arbitrate them as long as they do not materially affect my argument, and I focus on the plausible and on positive contributions as I try to build my case. On rare occasions when I do engage, I tend to do so in dialogue with fellow Princeton University Press authors, in what I hope will be understood as a gesture of collegial respect: e.g., Beckwith 2009; Pines 2012; Hoffman 2015.

CHAPTER ONE

1. I draw here on Scheidel in press-b.

2. Taagepera 1978a, 1978b, 1979, 1997; Turchin 2009; Scheidel in press-b.

3. Translated from Braudel 1966: 326. For an analysis of cost constraints on the functioning of the Roman empire, see Scheidel 2014, based on http://stanford.orbis.edu.

4. For the "shadow" empires of the steppe, see Barfield 2001 and chapter 8 in this volume.

5. The "most populous polity" of a given region is defined as the polity with the largest number of people who were located *within that region*, rather than as the polity with the largest total population that extended into that region. In practice there is hardly any difference between these two criteria. A few exceptions occurred in the Middle East and North Africa region, where the Roman empire would have been the most populous power overall in 150 and 100 BCE and the Mongol empire in 1250; in Europe, where the Mongols were the most populous power overall in 1250; and in the "Roman empire region," where the most populous powers overall were the Seleucid empire in 300, 250, and 200 BCE and the Abbasid caliphate in 800 and 850 CE.

6. For Chinese censuses, see Bielenstein 1987. I have firsthand experience with ancient Roman population numbers: see esp. Scheidel 2001: 181–250 (Roman Egypt) and 2008b (Italy). Uncertainties are particularly extreme when it comes to the Pre-Columbian and early colonial Americas: see, for example, Henige 1998; McCaa 2000; and the technical note to this chapter.

7. I include Afghanistan in the MENA region because from the perspective of historical state formation that is where it (most) belongs. The other regions are defined in keeping with standard conventions.

8. According to the figures in McEvedy and Jones 1978, these regions accounted for approximately 92 percent of the global population in 1 CE, 83 percent in 1000, and 81 percent in 1500. Their share in 2012–2013 amounted to 62 percent (or 4.45 billion out of 7.1–7.2 billion).

9. The former Spanish Sahara that is currently claimed by Morocco is omitted from these tallies. Omission of the Algerian and Libyan deserts reduces the total to roughly 9.5 million square kilometers, and further adjustments for outlying portions of western Egypt and the Rub' al Khali in Saudi Arabia would lower it to 8–8.5 million square kilometers.

10. The rather severe fluctuations in the early second millennium CE are in part a function of McEvedy and Jones's specific assumptions (see the technical note) and need not be taken at face value. Once again it is only the overall pattern that matters.

11. Here and in the following, the combination of a polity followed by another polity in parentheses refers to a scenario in which the leading empire was closely followed by the runner-up; de facto they might be considered roughly equivalent. If two polities listed for the same year are divided by a slash (/), the demographic estimates do not allow even tentative ranking. For the data, see the technical note. I consider the Roman empire in 400 CE to be united even though it effectively (though not formally) split up five years earlier, and I treat the medieval German empire (eventually known as the Holy Roman Empire) as a single polity until the death of Frederick II, a somewhat arbitrary cut-off point but necessary to account for the progressive internal segmentation of this peculiar entity. To be sure, both the German empire and the kingdom of France (the runner-up) were strongly decentralized during this period.

12. Even this may well be a slight underestimate. A Roman share of around 85 percent at its peak in the second century CE is perfectly possible and indeed plausible once we adjust for the underestimate of the Roman imperial population found in McEvedy and Jones 1978 (see the technical note) in keeping with my (fairly conservative) estimates in Scheidel 2007a: 48, table 3.1. Even if we upgrade the non-Roman European population to the levels of 800 CE given by McEvedy and Jones 1978 in order to compensate for some of this adjustment, the Roman share still reaches or exceeds 80 percent in the mid-second-century CE.

13. See the technical note.

14. For specifics, see chapter 8 in this volume.

15. See the introduction and chapter 10 in this volume.

16. Minor discrepancies for several maxima in figure 1.10 are a function of the juxtaposition of two imperfect data series, for the census population and for the estimated actual population. Moreover, for the Northern and Southern Song, the census population had to be extrapolated from the number of households: records from that period list only adults whereas censuses from other dynasties tend to cover all individuals. See Bielenstein 1987: 49, 78.

17. The scale of the latter effect is probably somewhat exaggerated by underestimates of the relative demographic prominence of pre-Islamic empires that were based in the north of the subcontinent, for the reason given above.

18. For a comparison between ("Western") Europe and China ("proper") in terms of the number of sovereign states from 1 to 1800 CE, see Ko, Koyama, and Sng 2018: 288–89, esp. 288, fig. 2 and 289n7 (problematic because their source—https://www.euratlas.net/history/europe/index.html—counts polities within the Holy Roman Empire as "sovereign" or "independent" (288–89, esp. n7), yet omits many of the smaller ones of these formally subordinate entities). Tilly 1992: 45 reckons with between 80 and 500 formally autonomous polities in Europe by 1500. Comparison of the size of the largest cities (generally imperial capitals) in eastern and western Eurasia in I. Morris 2013b: 171, fig.4.7—largely a function of state size—shows a similar divergence after the mid-first millennium CE.

CHAPTER TWO

1. See esp. Doyle 1986: 22 (metrocentric views of empire) and 25–66 (pericentric views). I take for granted the premise—a cornerstone of international relations theory—that international power politics are driven by imbalances in power within state systems as actors (i.e., polities) seek to increase their power for the sake of protection or gain; see 26–30 (systemic views of empire). Doyle 1986: 123–27 discusses merits and weaknesses of these perspectives. Champion and Eckstein 2004: 4–6 briefly survey applications of these categories to the study of Roman expansion.

2. I agree with Doyle 1986: 127 that the drive for empire-building must emanate from the metropole, even though metrocentric approaches are "at best incomplete" (124). For the need to combine different perspectives, see, e.g., Eckstein 2006: 35; Morley 2010: 29–30.

3. See Cornell 2000: 212–13, 217, 219–20 for a concise summary. See also C. Smith 1996.

4. Model: Armstrong 2016: 47–128, esp. 47–49, 73. Beard 2015: 117 calls these groups "chiefdoms and warrior bands," an apt characterization. See C. Smith 2006 on the nature of clans and how little we can hope to know about them. Land: Armstrong 2016: 129–82.

5. Barker and Rasmussen 1998: 175–76; Torelli 2000: 195–96.

6. Hansen 2000a, 2002.

7. In other cases, the origins of city-state–based empires are more opaque, as in the case of Akkad and Ur III in Sumer or later in Assyria, Carthage, and the Srivijaya empire in Sumatra. Hansen 2000b: 602, 613–14; Gat 2006: 310–13. Scheidel 2016 compares the Roman and Aztec cases.

8. See Cornell 1995: 127–214 for tradition concerning the sixth century BCE; he believes in an Etruscan-led Roman hegemony (309–10). Rome's territory compared well with those of the southern Etruscan city-states of Veii (562 square kilometers), Caere (640 square kilometers), and Tarquinii (663 square kilometers) (Cornell 2000: 215), as does the size of its capital city (215–16, esp. 216, fig. 5). On the question of Rome's early size, see Woolf 2012: 35–37, stressing location and proximity to the Etruscans, which produced some form of "hybrid . . . vigour" (36). In more formal terms, this meshes well with meta-ethnic frontier theory as propounded by Turchin 2003: 50–93; and see chapter 8 in this volume.

9. By 495 BCE, Rome had scaled-up to closer to 950–1,000 square kilometers, or 40 percent of Old Latium, by swallowing three of the other fifteen Latin polities: Cornell 1995: 205.

10. Alliance with Latins: Cornell 1995: 299–301; Cornell 2000: 220. Colonies: Oakley 1993: 19; Cornell 1995: 301–4; Cornell 2000: 213. Volscians and pressure from the interior: Cornell 1995: 304–9; Cornell 2000: 213 (five cities). Character of conflict: Cornell 1995: 309. Plunder and prestige: Woolf 2012: 72.

11. Shift to expansionism: Cornell 1995: 309, 311–13, 319–20. Growing internal cohesion: Armstrong 2016: 183–232. Later reports of the introduction of some form of compensation for military service around 400 BCE, possibly in kind, may well be correct (211–14): if true, this would have facilitated more sustained and broadly based military campaigning.

12. For the sack of Rome, see Cornell 1995: 313–18. The scale of later attacks remains unclear (see 324–25). This makes it hard to gauge the significance of meta-ethnic frontier dynamics in later Roman-led alliance-building.

13. Cornell 2000: 213; Harris 2016: 29 on "oppressive bilateral treaties." For the image of empire as a rimless wheel, see Motyl 2001: 16–17.

14. For this system, see, e.g., Cornell 1995: 351, 365. The nature and scope of citizenship without vote are not well understood: see Mouritsen 2007.

15. Eckstein 2006: 252 (quote). This created what de facto resembled dual citizenship (of Rome and one's native local community): see Beard 2015: 165. For Roman openness and the contrast to Greece, see, e.g., Raaflaub 1991: 578; Champion and Eckstein 2004: 7; Eckstein 2006: 246–47, 256, and from a comparative perspective see also Mann 1986: 254.

16. For the crucial importance of scaling-up military cooperation, see Eckstein 2006: 245–57; Beard 2015: 163–68.

17. See Nicolet 1980: 153–69 on the exiguous record, esp. 158: a rate of 0.1 percent might have represented a penalty, and one of 0.3 percent could be imposed on luxuries, which suggests that regular rates may have been very low indeed. However, multiples of the base rate could be levied in times of crisis. Assuming 5 percent annual return on investments, a base rate of 0.1 percent would translate to a 2 percent income tax, or rather 3 percent if two-thirds of assets were productive. Refunds: Nicolet 1980: 156.

18. See J. North 1981: 7 for this point about "complicity."

19. For low rates of compensation for Roman and Italian soldiers, see the next section.

20. Service: Hopkins 1978: 33–35; Harris 1985: 44–45; 2016: 67. After 200 BCE, half of all men under the age of thirty would have had to serve for ten years to fill the attested military units: Rosenstein 2004: 89–91. Population: Brunt 1987: 44–130 used to be accepted as the canonical reconstruction, which I follow here. His work has now been reinforced and enhanced by de Ligt 2012, who offers the most convincing version of Roman population history. For an argument in favor of somewhat higher tallies in the late Republic, see Hin 2013: 261–97. Much higher totals as suggested by a few revisionists, while not strictly speaking impossible, are less likely overall: for detailed discussion, see Scheidel 2008b and the update in Scheidel 2013a.

21. Mobilization rate: de Ligt 2012: 72–77, at 74.

22. See Tilly 1992: 30 for the two quotes. See 17–20 on his definitions of capital and coercion. He accords the environment a crucial role in determining a given mode of state-building (30). His model applies similarly well to Warring States China. Eich and Eich 2005: 15–16 correctly note the relative suitability of the coercion-intensive mode in much of fifth- and fourth-century BCE Italy. See also Eich and Eich 2005: 25 for the relative lack of intensification of exploitation in the Roman core beyond military labor obligations.

23. Eich and Eich 2005: 24. Terrenato 2019 emphasizes the role of elite co-optation by non-military means.

24. Fronda 2010: 300–307 judiciously stresses how difficult it was to manage these tensions. See Mouritsen 1998 on the limits of integration in Italy down to the early first century BCE.

25. Scheidel 2006: 217–20, esp. 218, fig. 4. Due to the rapid growth of the capital, the potential for voter participation quickly shrank even in the metropolitan core: 219, fig. 5. See also Linke 2006: 71–73. Mouritsen 2001: 18–37 demonstrates the critical importance of public space for our understanding of the Roman political system, which was thoroughly oligarchic and aristocratic (e.g., Hölkeskamp 2010, and now in general Mouritsen 2017).

26. See Hopkins 1991, on levy, census, and voting as rituals. On mixing, see esp. Jehne 2006: 250–55, 264–66, and also Eich and Eich 2005: 17.

27. Pfeilschifter 2007 is the best discussion. On material benefits see the "Wages of War" section.

28. Estimates in Scheidel 2004: 10–13, and see 21–24 for integrative effects. See also Pina Polo 2006 just for the second century BCE.

29. Scheidel 2006: 224.

30. Tilly 1992: 96–97.

31. Eich and Eich 2005: 19–20. The logistical requirements of near-continuous large-scale campaigning also helped create various types of networks: see Beard 2015: 168. For the question of the degree of state-ness of the Roman Republic, see Lundgreen 2014a, and esp. Lundgreen 2014b. The argument that Roman acceptance or reinforcement of patriarchal power in autonomous households offered a strong reason for men to support Rome (Linke 2006: 74–83; 2014, esp. 85–86) is predicated on the dubious notion that Rome was in a position strongly to affect local social mores, which seems unlikely. No monopoly: contra Eich and Eich 2005: 14.

32. Making states and war: on this process in postmedieval Europe, see Tilly 1992: 67–95. For the concept, see B. Porter 1994: 11–19; Kasza 1996: 364–68; Thompson and Rasler 1999. For

application of Tilly's concepts to Rome, see Eich and Eich 2005: 7–15, esp.14–15. Spin-offs: Eich and Eich 2005: 18. For the segmentation of the citizenry between an urban core and the rest, see Scheidel 2006: 214–17: the share of citizens outside the core rose from zero in the mid-fourth century BCE to 80 percent in the mid-first century BCE (216, fig. 3).

33. Concentration: Eich and Eich 2005: 30–31. Resources: Tan 2017, a vital complement to the narrow view that elaborate state structures were merely unnecessary.

34. See Mann 1986: 22–28 for the concept of social powers (the IEMP model).

35. See Cornell 1995: 327–44; Armstrong 2016: 183–289, esp. 231–32, 287–89. Cf. also Torelli 2000: 196–97 for exclusion of Etruscan bondsmen from military service. Enslavement: Harris 1985: 59, 63; Oakley 1993: 23–25. Slaves replacing bondsmen: Oakley 1993: 26.

36. Mann 1986: 252. Andreski's 1968 thesis that military participation ratios are inversely correlated with social stratification (39–73) is not well supported by the Roman case: for discussion, see Patterson 1993: 95–97. However, it is certainly true that Roman conquests led to interstratic social mobility (cf. Andreski 1968: 134–38). Religion and war: Rüpke 1990. Temples: Cornell 1995: 381, 384, and now in detail Padilla Peralta 2014: 36–110.

37. Harris 1985: 10–41 is essential. See also the brilliant précis by J. North 1981: 6 (quote) and Morley 2010: 27–29.

38. Harris 1985: 74–93 on senatorial enrichment. Shatzman 1975: 53–67, and esp. 107, in a detailed survey of senatorial fortunes, considered war spoils crucial. See also Rosenstein 2008: 23–24. On the abatement of imperialism after the 160s BCE, see Rich 1993: 46–55.

39. On the question of allied leadership, see Oakley 1993: 17–28; Cornell 1995: 366–67, where he also reports a few concrete examples of direct backing. By and large, however, allied elites were on their own. See J. North 1981: 7 for the point about "complicity."

40. Harris 1985: 54–104 discusses economic motivations for war, and specifically 101–4 those for ordinary people. See also Morley 2010: 25–29 on the question of motivation. Compliance: Harris 1985: 46–47; Eich and Eich 2005: 25. For this reason the general population had to experience or perceive benefits: Harris 2016: 22–23.

41. See Harris 1985: 60 for these figures.

42. Or *propugnacula imperii*; see Cornell 1995: 380–83. Subsequent programs from 200 to 177 BCE covered another 40,000–65,000 adult men plus dependents (Scheidel 2004: 10–11), and much more massive state-sponsored relocations both within and outside Italy occurred from the 80s to the 20s BCE, displacing more than half a million Romans.

43. Roselaar 2010: 71–84 considers the fate of the previous owners, and see esp. 79 for ownership by locals. Debt: Oakley 1993: 21–22. Analogy: Woolf 2012: 73. For Qin, see M. Lewis 1990: 61–64.

44. Share: Pfeilschifter 2007: 27. Security: Fronda 2010: 300–307.

45. Requirement: Cornell 1995: 366. Tax rebate: see J. North 1981: 7 for this analogy, followed by Morley 2010: 26. Resources: Eich and Eich 2005: 21, 25–26.

46. For versions of this argument, see Momigliano 1971: 44–46 (allies); J. North 1981: 6–7 (without war the whole system "would have lost the medium through which it existed and hence . . . would itself have ceased to exist": 7); Raaflaub 1991: 576; Oakley 1993: 17; Cornell 1995: 366; Eich and Eich 2005: 21. Quote: J. North 1981: 7. Harris's 1984: 91–92 dissent is baffling.

47. Quote: Bickerman and Smith 1976: 149 via Cornell 1995: 367.

48. Eich and Eich 2005: 24–26.

49. Rosenstein 2004: 63–106, esp. 82–84, on age at first marriage. However, these inscriptions predominantly reflect urban customs and need not be representative of the rural majority: Scheidel 2007c: 400–401 (but cf. Rosenstein 2004: 238n105 and Hin 2013: 178–79). Hin 2013: 169–71 argues that we should not overestimate the negative effects of war losses: military service that focused on unmarried draftees addressed structural underemployment. Older men: Rosenstein 2004: 89–91 on the Second Punic War.

50. Harris 1985: 49–50; Morley 2010: 33–35. In the second century BCE rural citizens largely displaced their urban peers from the military (Jehne 2006: 256), which widened the gap between political and military participation (even) further.

51. Slavery and mobilization: see Finley 1998: 152 on this point; and also Harris 2016: 21–22, 67. Expansion of slavery: Scheidel 2008a: 115–23, esp. 119 for this process in Rome and elsewhere.

52. Scheidel 2011c on the scale of Roman slavery and its supply, and 294–97 for capture in war; Scheidel 2005: 64–71 on Italy in particular; Scheidel 2011c: 292 for their share in the overall population. Hopkins 1978: 99–115 discusses the growth of Roman slave society.

53. I borrow the term "expansion-bearing structures" from J. North 1981: 9.

54. Cornell 1995: 345–47.

55. Samnite vs. Roman manpower: Afzelius 1942: 138–41 (twice as many Samnites on four times as much territory in the 340s BCE), 158 (similarly sized populations in 326 BCE), 171 (2½ times as many people on Rome's side by 304 BCE). For these conflicts and their consequences, see most recently Scopacasa 2015: 129–58. The specifics of Samnite organization remain opaque: Grossmann 2009: 21–22, and, for the limits of their capabilities, 317–18. But Grossmann goes too far in doubting the existence of more extensive alliances against Rome (134–47); cf. Scopacasa 2015: 138–40.

56. Conquest of Italy: Afzelius 1942: 136–96 (numbers), Cornell 1995: 345–68 (general account); most recently Harris 2016: 23–33. Battle of Sentinum in 295 BCE: Cornell 1995: 361.

57. The section caption is a reference to a famous maxim of the early Roman poet Ennius, *moribus antiquis res stat Romana virisque*. Although many southern allies defected in the early 270s BCE in response to the Epirote campaign, Rome retained control over twice as many Italians as the opposing side (Afzelius 1942: 187), and was able swiftly to replace battlefield losses in a way that neutralized the tactical skills of the Epirote king Pyrrhus—hence the famous notion of a "Pyrrhic victory." Conflict with Carthage: our main source, the Greek historian Polybius, claims that 700 Roman warships were lost, and while the actual number may have been closer to 500, both of them are enormous: average crew size per vessel ranged in the hundreds.

58. Levies: Polybius 2.23–24. For discussion, see Afzelius 1942: 15–135; Brunt 1987: 44–60; Baronowski 1993; de Ligt 2012: 40–78, esp. 54–55 and 69 for adjustments to 340,000 Romans and 540,000 allies capable of bearing arms out of a free population of close to 3 million (71). For Carthaginian capabilities, see chapter 3 in this volume.

59. Brunt 1987: 416–512, esp. 417–22 (Second Punic War), 423–26 (200–168 BCE). Possible inflation of infantry numbers is offset by the omission of naval levies from these tallies. For the demographic consequences of the Second Punic War, see Hin 2013: 142–54.

60. Brunt 1987: 439, 445, 449, 487, 511.

61. European levies: Parker 1996: 45–46. Effective distance between Rome and Philipp calculated from Scheidel and Meeks 2014. European population number: McEvedy and Jones 1978: 18 (whose numbers for antiquity may be a bit too low; see the technical note to chapter 1).

62. Harris 1985: 51–53 on Roman brutality, with reference to Andreski 1968: 117–18, who argues that high military participation rates translate to greater ferocity in war. On pathological violence in different domains of Roman culture, see Harris 2016: 42. Trade-off: Löffl 2011: 48–51, esp. 48. Rosenstein 1990: 179–204 identifies ninety-two Roman commanders between 390 and 49 BCE who suffered defeats against foreign enemies and lived to tell the tale, plus twelve consuls who were killed in battle in defeats between 249 and 50 BCE.

63. Schumpeter 1919: 33 (quotes). Doyle 1986: 156n37 explains the meaning of "objectless disposition," which applies to much of Roman history, even if Schumpeter himself (correctly) did not classify Rome as a "warrior nation" in his own very narrow definition that in such a state "life and vocation are fully realized *only* in war" (Schumpeter 1919: 65–69).

64. Taylor 2017: 169–70.

65. Polybius 32.13.6–8. Cf. also Livy 10.1.4, on a much earlier incursion into Umbria "lest they should pass the whole year entirely without fighting": Oakley 1993: 16. Neither one of these passages betrays a sense of irony.

66. Harris 1985: 10 (at most thirteen years without war between 327 and 101 BCE); Oakley 1993: 14–16 (eleven years without war from 410 to 265 BCE; but cf. twelve years from 440 to 411 BCE, when the record is even poorer but war-making might also have been less intense before Rome ramped up its capabilities). China: data for Qin (186 years) and Chu (185 years) are drawn from a database compiled and kindly shared by Dingxin Zhao. Years of peace 722–221 BCE: Hsu 1965: 56, 64. Cf. Deng 2012: 336, table 4.1 for the disproportionate belligerence of the Qin state. (Adding the entire first century CE to the Roman count to match the 502 years of the China count would not substantively alter the picture.) The claim that Hellenistic powers were (also) always at war (Chaniotis 2005: 5–12) is facile in its imprecision: it can be empirically substantiated only for a century or so of Macedonian history. On Roman continuous war in general, see Hopkins 1978: 25–37.

67. Thus, evidence of warlike behavior of other ancient states does not show that they were more or less the same (*contra* Eckstein 2006: 118–80; and cf. also Eich and Eich 2005: 1, 4, 14, 33), even if the vitriol Harris 2016: 42 expends on this notion is unhelpful. For Rome's greater bellicosity, see also Harris 2016: 37. From this perspective, Eckstein's 2006 critique of "unit-attribute explanations" of Roman success that focus on domestic conditions must be judged excessive, even though his emphasis on systemic relations is well taken (see esp. 35). Domestic conditions did in fact account for Rome's ability to project power on an unprecedented scale. More specifically, the Schumpeterian "war machine" dynamics of Roman conduct deserve more attention than they have generally received.

68. See Scheidel (in press-a) for this pattern.

69. See chapter 3 in this volume, and esp. Doyle 1986: 88–92.

70. Campaigning beyond Italy had always bestowed greater autonomy to generals (Eckstein 1987; Woolf 2012: 74): coupled with political clout, their powers grew with increasing distance from the center. Vervaet 2014: 214–92 offers a formalistic perspective of this shift.

71. See, e.g., Löffl 2011: 133–34 on the Alpine campaigns, which were risky and unprofitable and had therefore been unappealing to more vulnerable Republican commanders (135–36).

72. From 61 to 59 BCE, the Roman state got by with 15 legions, some 80,000 men—4 legions in Spain, 4 in Provence and Northern Italy, 3 in the Balkans, and 4 in the eastern Mediterranean (Brunt 1987: 449). If we move 3 legions from Spain (1 legion remained after conquest there had been completed) to North Africa and Egypt and put an extra one in the East, we end up with 16 legions, compared to the 28 that actually existed under Augustus, the 25–28 from 9 CE to the 160s CE, and the 30–33 in the late second century CE. This suggests that without the massive expansion into the European periphery that commenced with Caesar and Augustus, military forces only a little over half as large as they came to be could have secured the empire if it had remained confined to the Mediterranean basin.

73. Service: Scheidel 1996: 93–94. Roman emperors' exposure to challenges from within the military domain is just one of these consequences, a theme I explore in forthcoming work.

74. Economic perspective: Harris 2016: 130–32.

75. Not rational: Mattern 1999: 123–61. Question: *contra* Cornell 1993: 145–49. Quotes: Strabo, *Geography* 4.5; Appian, *Preface* 5. In the second century CE Britain received around 15 percent of total Roman military spending (Mattingly 2006: 493). If second-century-CE Britain accounted for 10 percent of Rome's military budget, or 6–7 percent of overall public expenditure, if two-thirds of the troops stationed there would not otherwise have been deployed elsewhere, and if the province comprised 3 percent of the population of the empire (see Mattingly 2006: 368 for a population of 2 million) and was slightly poorer than the imperial average, regional military expenditure could easily have been double the amount of regional tax revenue. Its share in Rome's military budget may have been even higher (Mattingly 2006: 493 reckons with 15 percent); and although its population may also have been larger (Millett 1990: 185 posits 3.7 million), if that had been the case it would have been even more rural and poorer. Therefore, quite simply, in no way could Roman Britain ever have paid for itself. Limits: Mattingly 2006: 491–96.

76. Motivation: Morley 2010: 37. Service: Harris 2016: 133–36. Political restraints on commanders: Cornell 1993: 162–64; demilitarization of elite: 164–68. See Scheidel 1996: 95–96n18 on the evolution of recruitment patterns.

77. Harris 2016: 112–36 gives a good account. Transition: Morley 2010: 36–37.

78. Gellner 1983: 9.

CHAPTER THREE

1. On the concept of semiperipherality, see Chase-Dunn and Hall 1997: 78–98. Italy conforms to their definition as a region that mixed both core and peripheral forms of organization and was spatially located between core and periphery (78); see also 19, 201, and 274 for definitional issues. Different types of networks (bulk- and prestige goods, political/military, and information networks) coexisted (52). For the emergence and expansion of the Near Eastern PMN, see 201, and the visualization 203, fig. 10.1, derived from Wilkinson 1987, who labeled this network the "Central Civilization" that eventually expanded to encompass the entire globe.

2. See Broodbank 2013, esp. 508–9, fig.10.2, for Mediterranean integration before the Roman period.

3. I. Morris 2009: 159–63, esp. 163, on capital-intensive state formation featuring mercenaries and navies but concurrent institutional underdevelopment due to autocrats' (i.e., tyrants') lording it over fragmented citizen communities; and I. Morris 2013a: 283–86 for Syracuse as a hybrid case. The Sicilian boom-bust cycle of war and peace that was sustained by large levies until funds ran out "reflects shallow state capacity" (292).

4. Ameling 1993 is the most penetrating account of the nature of the Carthaginian state, stressing its militarism and domestic mobilization capacity against earlier (ancient and modern) myths of mercantile proclivities.

5. Hansen 2006: 98 reckons with 750,000 people living in poleis (or Greek-style city-states) from Spain to the Adriatic, most of them located in Sicily and southern Italy. This fits De Angelis's 2006: 139 suggestion of a possible Sicilian population of 600,000, compared to a potential maximum of 1.2 million or more. This number would have been equivalent to maybe 15 percent of the (highly mobilizable) population of the area under Roman control in the mid-third century BCE (see above). For Sicilian troop sizes, see Beloch 1886: 290–94, who rightly discards the unique outlier of 83,000 troops mentioned by Diodorus 14.47 that is still kept alive by I. Morris 2013a: 291.

6. The population of the Roman Maghreb in 14 CE may have been around 3.5 million (Frier 2000: 812, table 5), which need not have been very different from conditions in the Carthaginian period: compare the 3 million–4 million conjectured by Beloch 1886: 470 and Hoyos 2010: 199 for the time of the First Punic War. By 218 BCE, both sides had increased their populations by maybe another half, in Northern Italy, Sicily, Sardinia, and Corsica in the case of Rome and in the Iberian peninsula in the case of Carthage. In this regard they were quite evenly matched. Concerning Carthage's martial disposition, Ameling 1993 is fundamental: see pp. 155–81 for elite militarism and pp. 190–210 for citizen participation. For citizen levies of 20,000, 30,000, and 40,000, see pp. 190–94. Normal naval strength was 120–130 ships, which could have been manned by fewer than 40,000 citizens (198).

7. Ameling 1993: 210–12 for allies (Libyans). For the various layers of Carthaginian rule, see Huss 1985: 467–74. Either navy or army: Ameling 1993: 209–10. Carthage supposedly lost at least 450 ships and 100,000 crew in the First Punic War, fewer than Rome if reported figures (or at least the ratios they imply) are to be believed, but it also lost the war. On mercenaries, see Ameling 212–22, and in great detail, see Fariselli 2002.

8. Hoyos 2010: 145, 185–86, 190–92 on Libyan risings in 396, 309–307, 256–255, and 241–238 BCE, the last case compounded by a mercenary revolt that pushed Carthage to the brink. Unlike in Rome, there is no sign of an integrative reward system beyond the metropolitan citizenry: Ameling 1993: 225, 262. See Barcelo 1988 for involvement in Spain before 237 BCE.

9. Ameling 1993: 199–203 argues for a maximum of 200 vessels, while Lazenby 1996: 82–87 sides with the maximalists. Either way, Carthage's naval levies were very large by the standards of the time. My own estimates in unpublished work, based on a mix of ancient sources and conjectures, suggest, very crudely, shifts from around 25,000 mean military strength in the fourth century BCE, to around 50,000 in the First Punic War, to around 75,000 in the Second Punic War, and peaks of 50,000+, 70,000–80,000, and 100,000, respectively. Figures given by Roman sources (such as 120,000–150,000 in the Second Punic War, Hoyos 2010: 199, 205) tend to be inflated, just as they were later for the Hellenistic kingdoms.

10. Manpower: Chaniotis 2005: 20–24, 46–51. On professional warfare, see 78–101. Doyle 1986: 89, 91, and 134–36 defines these polities as "fractionated republics" that were a source of collaborators. Aitolians: Grainger 1999: 202–14, esp. 213. In 279 BCE, Boiotia, Phokis, Aetolia, Lokroi, and Megara sent 22,100 men to Thermopylae to stop a Galatian invasion (Chaniotis 2005: 23). In 225 BCE, Rome mobilized no fewer than 160,000 troops to deal with a similar event.

11. Doyle 1986: 89, 91, and 133 defines them as patrimonial monarchies.

12. This is consistent with the maximum number of Macedonian soldiers that were available after the end of Alexander's reign, of some 40,000 in 321–320 BCE (Bosworth 2002: 86).

13. Armies: Aperghis 2004: 191; Fischer-Bovet 2014: 73. Navies: Aperghis 2004: 197–99; Fischer-Bovet 2014: 71–72. As noted above, Rome lost some 500 to 700 ships in the First Punic War alone.

14. Grainger 2010 for the Syrian Wars, esp. on competitive development (89–115), Seleucid internal strife and fragmentation from the 240s to the 220s BCE (171–94), and domestic turmoil in Egypt from 207 BCE onward (219–43).

15. Parallel wars: Grainger 2010: 245–71.

16. Sekunda 2007: 336 for risk of losing core troops.

17. Bar-Kochva 1976: 7–19 (army size), and 20–48 on military settlers as "hard core." See also Fischer-Bovet 2014: 199–237 for Egypt. Sekunda 2007: 335–36 for this vital contrast.

18. Armies: Brunt 1987: 423–24. These Roman numbers might be a bit too high (p. 423), but then so are the Hellenistic ones (cf. Grainger 2002: 322, 359–61 on the battle of Magnesia). Potential: Brunt 1987: 422. Manpower was lower right after 200 BCE than it had been in 225 BCE, but recovery was swift: Hin 2013: 142–54. In any case, the original total pool may well have been closer to 900,000.

19. Numbers from Afzelius 1944: 47, 78–79, 89. Ships: Afzelius 1944: 83–84 and W. Murray 2012: 209–25. Even if Afzelius's numbers are a little inflated (cf. Brunt 1987: 423), this does not (much) affect ratios between theaters.

20. Roman citizen infantrymen were paid the equivalent of one-third (or perhaps rather only 0.3: Taylor 2017: 146) of a drachma per day (which covered food as well), and those of the Italian allies received 34.5 liters of grain per month, equivalent perhaps to one-tenth of a drachma per day (Taylor 2017: 150 estimates one-twelfth). Hellenistic soldiers could expect five-sixth or a full drachma per day plus another one-third of a drachma for food (Launey 1950: 725–80, at 763; Aperghis 2004: 201–5). This yields a ratio of approximately 1:6 (if Roman forces were evenly split between citizens and allies), or closer to 1:3 if Romans were granted double (combat) pay and grain was dearer in wartime. Taylor 2015 discusses military finances more generally.

21. Fischer-Bovet 2014: 76, table 3.5. See T. Frank 1933: 145 and Taylor 2017: 165 for average annual military outlays of between 1,550 and 1,800 talents in Rome (200–157 BCE), compared to 5,000 talents for the Ptolemies and 7,000–8,000 talents for the Seleucids in peacetime and 10,000+ talents for each in time of war (Fischer-Bovet 2014: 76, table 3.5). Orders of magnitude are all that matter here.

22. Reported fatalities on the Roman side for these four engagements add up to merely 1,350, about 1.3 percent of the forces deployed, compared to up to 90,000 enemy deaths. Even if actual Roman totals were higher and the others lower (cf. Grainger 2002: 249–50, 328 for rather arbitrary adjustments), the overall imbalance is not in doubt.

23. Sekunda 2001 on reforms in the 160s BCE, though their actual extent remains unclear; and see 115 on manpower. Quote: Livy 9.19.

24. Rome scored decisive victories at Chaeronea (86 BCE) and Orchomenos (85 BCE) in Greece, at Tigranocerta (69 BCE) and Artaxata (68 BCE) in Armenia, and in Pontus (66 BCE and, at Zela, 47 BCE). There do not seem to have been substantial numbers of Roman soldiers in western Asia Minor when Pontus defeated Rome's local allies and overran its province in 88 BCE (Brunt 1987: 435). Two Roman legions (or roughly 10,000 men) were defeated in 81 BCE but survived, and were later crushed at Zela in 67 BCE. For these wars in general, see Mayor 2010.

25. Later it took centuries of interaction with the Roman empire and gradual scaling-up of capabilities for Germanic populations to become capable of threatening Roman territory: see chapter 5 in this volume.

26. See Doyle 1986: 89–90, 132–33, 135 for the characteristics of tribal peripheries: fierce but small and undifferentiated, and to be ruled directly. J. Williams 2001: 187–207 on the Po Valley (where appearance of La Tène—i.e., "Celtic"—burials coincided with a general decline in nucleated settlements followed by a dispersed settlement pattern: 198–99, 205; and see 207–18 on the impact of Roman conquest); Richardson 1986 on Spain, esp. 16–17 on the indigenous population (ranging from pastoral seminomads to large villages and fortified towns on hilltops).

27. See Johne 2006: 83–198.

28. Summaries in Doyle 1986: 91, 130, table 3.

29. Roman scores: until the late third century BCE, the Warring States of China and then the Qin empire had belonged in the same category. The early Western Han empire maintained a smaller active military than its predecessors.

30. The underlying calculations are necessarily tentative. I focus on overall population size and maximum troop numbers (excluding rowers), and all estimates are rounded off and deliberately conservative. I reckon with 4 million people in Italy and 200,000 peak troops for Rome in the Second Punic War, and 5.5 million people including provincials and 180,000 troops for the early second century BCE; with 5 million people and 100,000 troops for Carthage; 600,000 people and 30,000 troops for Syracuse; 9 million people and 100,000 troops for the Seleucids; 4.5 million people and 100,000 troops for the Ptolemies; and 1.5 million people and 40,000 troops for the Macedonians and their Greek allies. I also assume 600,000 people for Aetolia (in analogy to Epirus as calculated by Corvisier 1991: 289) and 15,000 troops. For these numbers, see McEvedy and Jones 1978; Fischer-Bovet 2014: 76, 170 (Hellenistic military forces); Corvisier 1991: 252, 271 (Thessaly and Macedonia); above (Sicily, Rome, Carthage, Macedon). Aperghis 2004: 57 proposes a larger Seleucid population of 11 million to 15 million, but that is highly uncertain.

31. Balancing failure: Macedon joined Carthage's war against Rome in 214 BCE but to little effect. The Ptolemies stayed neutral, perhaps to balance Rome against Carthage (thus Lampela 1998: 56–63). See my discussion of counterfactuals in chapter 4 of this volume.

32. E.g., Fischer-Bovet 2014: 65–66. See W. Murray 2012: 192, map 6.1 for Ptolemaic dependencies across the entire eastern Mediterranean and in the Aegean.

33. Terms: Lampela 1998: 33–56, esp. 33–37 on an embassy exchange in 273 BCE that led to diplomatic "friendship" or perhaps even a treaty. Geographical distance as a defining

geopolitical feature: 20–21. On the Ptolemaic navy, see W. Murray 2012: 188; Fischer-Bovet 2014: 71–72. King Ptolemy IV (r. 221–204 BCE) was said to have built a 420-foot-long ship that held over 7,000 crew (W. Murray 2012: 178–85).

34. De Souza 1999: 97–178 on the Cilician pirates, born of Seleucid state failure from the 140s BCE onward, down to their demise at the hands of Rome in 67 BCE.

35. See Erdkamp 1998: 62–62 and Roth 1999: 158–65, 189–95. In the campaign against the Seleucids, grain from Sicily, Sardinia, Numidia, and even semidependent Carthage was shipped to the Aegean to provision Roman and allied forces: Roth 1999: 161–62; 228, table V. Simulation: Artzrouni and Komlos 1996: 127–33, esp. 132.

36. I owe these observations to James Bennett, based on his independent re-creation of the Artzrouni and Komlos model (personal communication March 8, 2017). Within the specifications of this simulation, low coastal defense costs on their own do not guarantee success because the algorithm randomly selects polities across Europe to attack their neighbors. As states become larger, they have a growing chance of being selected, which means that even polities with very small coastal defense savings come to dominate only if they start early and amass enough power to succeed against Italy when they collide. A head start by Italy, on the other hand, reinforces its initial advantage.

37. Scheidel 2014, esp. 21–23. For Orbis, see Scheidel and Meeks 2014.

38. "Economic" refers to the movement of goods, "military" to (fast or slow) troop movements. Steps of expansion: Scheidel 2014: 13–14, with 17, figs. 1–2.

39. For the localized nature of Roman fiscal extraction under the mature empire, see Scheidel 2015a: 248, 251.

CHAPTER FOUR

1. For the case for counterfactuals, see the final section of the introduction.

2. Demandt 1999: 75 invokes the counterfactual of an early "Etruscization" of Rome and consequent lack of Latin support as a potential obstacle to imperial state formation.

3. On the Akkadian imperial project, see Foster 2016: 80–83; on its fall, 22–25. For Neo-Assyrian state-building, see Bedford 2009.

4. Briant 2002 is the most comprehensive account of Achaemenid history.

5. On the war from a Persian perspective, see Briant 2002: 146–61, 525–42; Cawkwell 2005. Several historians have explored the counterfactual of Persian victory in Greece in 480 BCE. Strauss 2006: 99–106 argues for a scenario of a failed Persian invasion of southern Italy followed by revolt and liberation in mainland Greece. Demandt 2011: 83 similarly considers a later revolt the most plausible outcome. Hanson 2006: 71–72 downplays Persian problems of holding on to various peripheries. For Persia's persistent problems with Egypt, which was lost or only partly controlled by the former for approximately 83 of the 194 years from 525 to 332 BCE, or 43 percent of the time, see Ruzicka 2012: 23 (c. 522–c. 518 BCE), 27–29 (c. 487–484 BCE), 29–33 (462–454 BCE), 35–198 (c. 405–342 BCE), 199–205 (338–335 BCE). Persia's rule also frayed in Cyprus (380s, c. 348–344 BCE), Asia Minor (366–360 BCE), and Phoenicia (c. 348–345 BCE), and the extent of its control in the Indus Valley remains obscure (Briant 2002: 754–57). See Hansen 2006 for Greek manpower, and Ober 2015: 21–44 on city-state

ecology and esp. 71–122 on economic development. Ameling 1993: 15–65 tracks Carthaginian state formation.

6. Athens's ambitious (if unsuccessful) intervention in Egypt in the 450s BCE in support of a local revolt highlights the scope of its designs on Achaemenid possessions (Ruzicka 2012: 30–32); it was accompanied by operations in Cyprus and on the eastern Mediterranean coast (Biondi 2016). In the 420s BCE, Athenian comedy could at least joke about the possibility of a campaign against Carthage: Aristophanes, *Knights* 1300–1304. The massive Sicilian expedition in 415 BCE, which in a counterfactual world might have succeeded instead of ending in disaster, would have opened the door to involvement in Italy.

7. *Contra* I. Morris 2009. The substance of Runciman's 1990 argument—that Greek city-states were too inclusive and democratic to form viable larger states—has not been refuted: Athenian direct democracy in particular would have militated against the formation of a Gellnerian ruling class that transcended individual communities (Gellner 1983: 9, fig. 1, pictured in chapter 2, figure 2.6 [a] of this volume). For criticism of Morris's thesis, see Raaflaub 2016: 120–25; Scheidel in press-a.

8. A large army of Macedonian and Asian, mostly Iranian troops, had been assembled at the time, and he had appropriated large quantities of gold and silver from the Achaemenids and other sources (Holt 2016).

9. Diodorus 18.4.4. For contrasting positions regarding its reliability, see the contributions by Fritz Hampl and Fritz Schachermeyr in Griffith 1966: 308–34. Bosworth 1988: 185–211 defends the veracity of this account; see esp. 190–202 for evidence in support of massive war preparations in the Mediterranean.

10. Bosworth 1988: 83–93 analyzes the ancient tradition.

11. Demandt 2011: 86, however, considers Macedonian expansion beyond the Adriatic unlikely: the western regions would have been left to Romans, Celts, and Germans. But see also Demandt 1999: 75–76 for Alexander's chance of preventing the Roman empire.

12. Toynbee 1969: 441–86, at 467–70. Cf. Ober 1999: 46–47 against Toynbee's anachronistic model of an enlightened super-state: given Alexander's earlier conduct, further campaigning would most likely have resulted in more carnage and predation.

13. Livy 9.17–19. Oakley 2005: 184–99 provides painstaking commentary.

14. Seleucus: Grainger 1990: 76–94. Billows 1990: 158–59 argues that Antigonus did not aim to be Alexander's successor, but compare 183 for the view that an Antigonid victory in 301 BCE would have paved the way for imperial reunification. See also Grainger 1990: 215–17 for powerful constraints on Seleucid expansion.

15. Fronda 2010: 288–300 discusses several counterfactual scenarios, noting Hannibal's inability to win over enough allies to overcome Rome's manpower advantage (50–52, 299).

16. Demandt 1999: 76 and 2011: 94 also deems Hannibal's efforts too late and Carthaginian manpower insufficient.

17. I discussed the alternative counterfactual of a durable Macedonian-Persian empire from Alexander's rule onward earlier in this chapter. It would also be possible to envision an intermediate scenario of more rapid reunification, in time to intervene against Rome on Carthage's side, but this would effectively be largely indistinguishable from the first one.

18. Partly based on Fischer-Bovet 2014: 76 and Murray 2012. I reckon with 90,000 soldiers each for the Ptolemies and Seleucids, 40,000 for Macedon, and 15,000 each for the two major

Greek leagues, and with 300 warships for the Ptolemies, 100 for the Seleucids, and 100+ for the Aegean powers.

19. Mouritsen 1998 is the best analysis of the relationship between Romans and allies.

20. Irrelevant: unless we assume that Roman expansion into the European periphery depended on material resources from the east, which is a valid concern.

21. Much the same was true of the short-lived civil war of 69 CE, at a time when the legions still heavily relied on recruitment in Italy and Spain.

22. Enduring fragmentation (and just conceivably wholesale failure) first became an option again in the 260s CE but was averted by peripheral military rulership, a development I discuss in forthcoming work.

23. For documentation, see chapters 1 and 8 in this volume.

CHAPTER FIVE

1. Unless noted, all dates in this chapter are CE.

2. Demandt 1984: 695.

3. Quotes: Gibbon 1781: 631.

4. Cross-cultural approaches include Toynbee 1934–1961; Tainter 1988; Yoffee and Cowgill 1988; Randall Collins 1995: 1554–67; Motyl 2001; R. Li 2002; Turchin 2003, 2006; Turchin and Nefedov 2009; S. A. Johnson 2017; Middleton 2017. For commentary, see briefly Scheidel 2013b: 38–40; Middleton 2017: 29–46.

5. Paradigmatically, out of a vast literature, contrast Heather 2006 (external forces) and Goldsworthy 2009 (internal problems). On environment, see Harper 2017.

6. Demandt 1984: 597–600 offers an elegant objection to traditional blends of internal and external causes that seek flaws in entities that fail, and prioritizes external factors (588–97). But this is a problem separate from that of distinguishing internal from external factors.

7. On the mechanisms of migration and settlement, see most lucidly Halsall 2007: 417–54; and cf. also Heather 2009: 335–59; Sarris 2011: 33–40. For the role of the Huns, see Kelly 2009. For the fiscal interdependence of the empire's regions, see Hopkins 2002; Scheidel 2015a: 251–52.

8. For the use of counterfactuals, see the final section of the introduction in this volume.

9. See chapter 8 in this volume.

10. See Sarris 2011: 127–34 for the various frailties of the East Roman state.

11. Gold reserves had risen from 32 tons in 457 CE to 129 tons in 527 CE (Scheidel 2009c: 175).

12. Summaries in Haldon 1990: 21, 33–34. For the Balkans see now esp. Sarantis 2016.

13. Summaries by Haldon 1990: 20, 34–46; Sarris 2011: 146, 239–54.

14. Haldon 1990: 50–84 and now esp. 2016: 31–55. Picard 2018 describes the rise of caliphal naval power.

15. Harper 2017: 199–245 is the latest analysis.

16. Survival: Haldon 2016: 55–57; for an answer, see 282–94. Attrition: Decker 2016: 8, 22 (maps); Treadgold 1995: 42–75 (army); Haldon 2016: 27–29 (revenue). Archaeology: Decker 2016: 191–94, in an account that is scrupulously wary of declinist narratives of the Byzantine "Dark Ages" in the seventh through the ninth centuries.

17. See chapter 4 in this volume.

18. H. Kennedy 2007 is a standard narrative of the Arab conquests.

19. Size: Taagepera 1997: 496 (but cf. Scheidel in press-b). Population estimated from McEvedy and Jones 1978, adjusted for these authors' undercount (see the technical note to chapter 1). Population shares: see chapter 1 in this volume.

20. See H. Kennedy 2007: 366–70 for a good survey, and also Sarris 2011: 272.

21. Quote: H. Kennedy 2007: 370. Early successes: see H. Kennedy 2001: 2 for another counterfactual.

22. See Stathakopoulos 2004 for a dossier and discussion of the various episodes. H. Kennedy 2007: 366–67 on plague-induced depopulation as a factor.

23. H. Kennedy 2001: 6; H. Kennedy 2007: 370–74; Sarris 2011: 273–74.

24. Quoted from H. Kennedy 2007: 1, in Sebastian Brock's translation from the original Syriac.

25. H. Kennedy 2001: 4, 8–9, 18–19, 30–51 for elements of this summary.

26. Wickham 2009: 322–23, 325, 331–33. See Gordon 2001 for the rise of Turkic forces in the Samarra period, and more generally chapter 7 in this volume.

27. For divergent fiscal evolution under the Germanic successor regimes and the Arabs, see chapter 7 in this volume.

28. H. Kennedy 2001: 59–95 on military payments, esp. 59, 62–64, 74–78; H. Kennedy 2015: 393–94, 397; and also Haldon 2016: 75–77.

29. H. Kennedy 2001: 19–21, 76–78.

30. As noted by Wickham 2009: 334–35.

31. H. Kennedy 1995: 256–58.

32. Quote: Gibbon 1788a: 408–9.

33. Strauss 1999: 85–89.

34. H. Kennedy 1995: 259–69; Wickham 2009: 338–47.

35. H. Kennedy 1995: 251–54.

36. Parker and Tetlock 2006: 378–79 also stress the likelihood of fragmentation in the event of Arab success.

37. Kasten 1997 is an exhaustive study of the succession of Frankish rulers and the attendant partitions of power and territory. See esp. 9–14 for the origins of this practice.

38. For the mode of succession specifically in this period, see Kasten 1997: 136–98.

39. For summaries, see Nelson 1995a; Roger Collins 1999: 333–63, as well as Costambeys, Innes, and MacLean 2011: 379–427, on fragmentation after 843, and Wickham 2009: 427–52, on the successor states of Carolingian France, esp. 439–44 on West Francia; also Wickham 2016: 102, 105. See also Tabacco 1989: 144–81 for anarchy in post-Carolingian Italy.

40. Kasten 1997: 574 concludes that shifts to more primogenitural arrangements were generally limited to periods of political and material weakness.

41. See chapter 7 in this volume. I sidestep the debate over whether these developments ushered in "feudalism": see Patzold 2012 for a recent survey of the controversy, esp. 14–43 on eighth- and ninth-century Francia. Cf. also Costambeys, Innes, and MacLean 2011: 317–19; Wickham 2016: 10. Reynolds 1994 remains the classic challenge to the application of the feudal model to the early Middle Ages. In the present context, this issue is not of critical importance.

42. Halsall 2003: 25–27, 31; Halsall 2007: 492–97.

43. Wickham 2005: 102–15 is the classic analysis.

44. Halsall 2003: 54–56, on the pre-Carolingian period.

45. Fouracre 1995: 86, 89, 93; Halsall 2003: 73–77.

46. Wickham 2001: 72 (quote); Nelson 1995b: 387, 394.

47. Roger Collins 1999: 295–98.

48. Airlie 1995: 448–49; Nelson 1995b: 394; Halsall 2003: 92.

49. Wickham 2001: 91; Halsall 2003: 93–95, 99–101.

50. Fouracre 1995: 108–9.

51. Successor states: Halsall 2007: 508–12; S. F. Johnson 2012: 50. Government: S. F. Johnson 2012: 48, 550. Charlemagne: Fouracre 1995: 107.

52. Halsall 2003: 119–33; Barbero 2004: 249–71, esp. 252, 256–59, 265–68.

53. McCormick, Dutton, and Mayewski 2007, esp. 875–89; Newfield 2013: 169. "Charlemagne was more than vigorous and smart: he was, with respect to volcanic aerosols and rapid climate change, a very lucky ruler" (McCormick, Dutton, and Mayewski 2007: 892).

54. See Moreland 2001: 404–6, 414–17 for an admirably sober account.

55. Most remarkable: thus Fouracre 1995: 86.

56. Wickham 2009: 430–32.

57. See C. Morris 1989: 113–21, 154–73 for the conflict over lay investiture.

58. E.g., Tabacco 1989: 182–236, esp. 220, and chapter 10 in this volume. Lombard League: Raccagni 2010. The Mediterranean disease environment also played a role: both Otto II and Otto III succumbed to malaria, which repeatedly ravaged invading armies.

59. P. Wilson 2016, esp. 9–11, 44–45, 343–44, 348–52, 356–61.

60. P. Wilson 2016: 365–77 (quote: 366).

61. France 1999: 77–106, esp. 85–87, 107, and 230–34 (quote: 232). See also Brauer and van Tuyll 2008 for the underlying economics: 45–79.

62. P. Wilson 2016: esp. 325–27, 332, 372, 389–90, 404.

63. P. Wilson 2016: 87, 319, 324. Analogy to sovereign rulers: Arnold 1991: 284.

64. Angelov and Herrin 2012: 167–71; P. Wilson 2016: 46–76.

65. Arnold 1991: 281 notes that "if the experience of other west European kingdoms, Angevin England, Hauteville Sicily, and Capetian France, is anything to go by, then the regal machinery equal to overturning the local rule of the princes would have had to include regular taxation throughout Germany, annual judicial assizes, and a capital residence gradually enforcing political centripetence." None of these features was on the horizon (280–84).

66. P. Wilson 2016: 380 (quote), 385–87.

CHAPTER SIX

1. From the rich literature, see, e.g., May 2012; Man 2014. For the role of climate in the rise of the Mongols under Genghis, see Pederson et al. 2014 (unusual warm and wet conditions from 1211 to 1225), and cf. also Putnam et al. 2016 for the southward spread of grasslands more generally.

2. For the European campaigns, see Chambers 1979; Hartog 1996: 29–41; Jackson 2005: 58–86; Man 2014: 138–45; Sverdrup 2017: 293–327. Medieval reports and modern estimates

regularly posit Mongol forces in excess of 100,000 men including auxiliaries (e.g., Hartog 1996: 29; Sinor 1999: 19); but see Sverdrup 2010: 114 and 2017: 297, who argues for 40,000 Mongols, an estimate that, however, neglects the potential for drawing in allies from the western Eurasian steppe.

3. E.g., Chambers 1979: 70–82. For more on Kievan Rus', see chapter 8 in this volume.

4. For conditions in Europe, see the previous section, and briefly Chambers 1979: 87–90; Hartog 1996: 34–35; Jackson 2005: 9–10. Army sizes: France 1999: 13, 128–30.

5. Specifically for Central Europe, see Chambers 1979: 86–113; Jackson 2005: 63–74. Co-optation of Turkic warriors: Hartog 1996: 29, who gives a total of 120,000–140,000 men; but see note 2 above.

6. Chambers 1979: 110–11; Jackson 2005: 65–67; Man 2014: 143–44.

7. For discussion of divergent scholarly positions on this matter, see especially the surveys by Rogers 1996 and Pow 2012: 12–45; and cf. also more briefly Jackson 2005: 71–74. Raid: Jackson 2005: 73–74, who also considers other reasons. Sverdrup 2017: 325 notes the disposition of Batu's forces in early 1242.

8. See Pow 2012: 34–41 for critical discussion of this position.

9. See Rogers 1996: 12–14 and Pow 2012: 41–45 for discussion. For a cold and wet spell in the winter of 1241–1242 that reduced pasture and mobility, see Büntgen and Di Cosmo 2016, rejected by Pinke et al. 2016. The signal is not strong, and does not explain why the Mongols did not return sooner.

10. Accepted by Strauss 1999: 92; Parker and Tetlock 2006: 380. Jackson 2005: 72 assigns some significance to this event, noting the conflict between Batu and Guyuk. Cf. also Mielants 2007: 159, who claims that the Mongols could easily have overrun Europe.

11. See Rogers 1996: 8–9, 15–18; Pow 2012: 12–24 for discussion and criticism. Their reference to continuing operations in Anatolia and Syria is not compelling, for the reason given in the text.

12. Pow 2012: 46–77 is by far the best discussion of this issue in relation to Mongol expansion.

13. Jackson 2005: 69; Pow 2012: 59. Quote: *Annales S. Pantaleonis* in Jackson 2005: 64.

14. Jackson 2005: 69 (Esztergom); Pow 2012: 70 (Silesia and Moravia); Jackson 2005: 65 (Croatia); Pow 2012: 75 (Serbia and Bulgaria).

15. Chambers 1979: 164–65; Pow 2012: 76–77.

16. Pow 2012: 46. France's 1999: 234 verdict that the Mongol retreat owed nothing to European military prowess is correct as far as battles are concerned but neglects the role of fortifications, which he himself discusses at length (77–106).

17. Sinor 1972: 181–82; Sinor 1999: 19–20; and, in general, Lindner 1981. Criticism in Pow 2012: 24–34. For 1918, see Sinor 1972: 181. Total Mongol forces probably numbered a little over 100,000 in the early thirteenth century, which is consistent with these figures: Sverdrup 2017: 110.

18. Estimates vary. See Lindner 1981: 14–15 for 42,000 km^2 of grassland in Hungary and a maximum of 320,000 horses, or closer to half that in real life, and a 1:10 man:horse ratio for Mongols (i.e., 16,000–32,000 men). Sinor 1999: 19–20 allows for a theoretical maximum of 415,000 horses and 83,000 men at a 1:5 ratio (superseding 1972: 181–82, for 205,000 horses and

68,000 men). Man 2014: 144 estimates that 24,000 square kilometers of grassland could have supported 150,000 men with 600,000 horses.

19. Lindner 1981, for this adaptation among Huns, Avars, and Magyars, a thesis that has stood up reasonably well to later criticism. Dynamics: see chapter 8 in this volume.

20. Mongols in unsuitable terrain: Pow 2012: 33–34. For comparative analysis of how Mongols dealt with fortifications elsewhere, see Pow 2012: 79–121, emphasizing their use of artillery against mud and brick walls and the role of collaboration and defection (120–21). Russian craftsmen: Hartog 1996: 163. See Allsen 2002: 268–71, 278–80 for the use of Chinese gunpowder weaponry (rockets) during the conquest of Central Asia and Iran (1220s–1250s) and the subsequent transfer of counterweighted catapults from Syria to China to assist in the final stages of the conquest of Song China in the 1270s.

21. May 2012: 67–80 gives a summary of fragmentation and hostilities between the khanates in the late thirteenth century.

22. For the importance of alternative targets, see, e.g., Jackson 2005: 74; Pow 2012: 121.

23. See Jackson 2005: 113–34 for the halting of Mongol advances.

24. For these later attacks, see Chambers 1979: 164–65; Jackson 2005: 123, 203–6, 210, 212.

25. Pow 2012: 122 and Sverdrup 2017: 327 share this view.

26. See chapter 8 in this volume.

27. For Otto I, see chapter 5 in this volume.

28. Allsen 1987: 207–9; Hartog 1996: 54–56 (census in Russia), 55–56 (tax), 162–67 (influence); Ostrowski 1998: 133–248 (ideology).

29. Holland 1999: 102 (quotes), 104. See also Parker and Tetlock 2006: 381 for a consequent halt to "Western" development. Cf. Hartog 1996: 166 for the Mongol invasion's initially disastrous effect on the Russian economy, which was later partly offset by the expansion of long-distance trade.

30. Blame: cf. Pow 2012: 127–33. See Allsen 1987: 190–94 for mobilization practices, esp. 191 on drafting for sieges. It is not explicitly recorded that Russians provided troops, though it is highly likely (209n73). Pow 2012: 133 employs this scenario as a counterfactual for Latin Europe.

31. See chapter 8 in this volume.

32. Watts 2009 offers a recent survey.

33. Blockmans 2002: 36.

34. Pagden 2001: 43–44; also Blockmans 2002: 25–26 for the intensity of fragmentation.

35. Empire: König 2002: 200–209; Pagden 2001: 43–44. Christendom: König 2002: 199–200, 209–12; Luttenberger 2002.

36. P. Wilson 2016: 172–73, 422–82, esp. 423, 436, 448.

37. Reinhard 2002.

38. Babel 2002; Durchhardt 2002; Tracy 2002a; Kleinschmidt 2004. For the contribution of Ottoman pressure on the success of the Reformation, see Iyigun 2008.

39. Pietschmann 2002: 537–38; H. Thomas 2010: 315–36.

40. Brendle 2002, on the opposition of the German estates to Charles V.

41. Brendle 2002: 702–3; Kleinschmidt 2004: 208–10. See Blockmans 2002: 80–99, 108–13 on Charles V and the Reformation.

42. Kleinschmidt 2007: 225.

43. Tracy 2002b: 242 (Metz). This estimate is based on the following values: 0.2 grams of silver per liter of barley in Augsburg in 1552 (nine-year average) ~0.3grams of silver per liter of wheat; 1 ducat (3.5gram of gold at 13:1 gold:silver) ~45 grams of silver; 3.25 million ducats ~150 tons of silver ~490 million liters of wheat. For Roman military compensation, see chapter 3 in this volume.

44. Tracy 2002b: 50–90 (sources of revenue), 91–108 (credit), 109–248 (campaign funding). 248; 2002a: 159 (rising costs). See also Blockmans 2002: 139–68, esp. 154–60 on financial pressures.

45. Tracy 2002b: 182, 247; cf. 2002a: 158. Kleinschmidt 2004: 146.

46. Tracy 2002b: 229, 247.

47. Blockmans 2002: 25–46 gives a pithy overview.

48. Eire 2006b: 150–56.

49. Ibid. 159–61, 164–65.

50. Ibid., 162–65.

51. Parker 1998, esp. 143, 181, 202, 273–75, and 280 for unfavorable outcomes overall. Dutch Revolt: Black 2002: 107–17. Philip as king of Spain: Kelsey 2012.

52. For these three counterfactuals, see Parker 1998: 292–94 and 2014: 372–73, and Parker 1999: 144–53 specifically on the events of 1588.

53. Murphey 1999: 36–49. For the nature of Ottoman rule, see, e.g., Lowry 2003; Barkey 2008.

54. Ibid., 30–32 on the limits of Ottoman state power and control; Karaman and Pamuk 2010: 603–9 (flat tax take), 609–12 (comparison with Europeans). Population: McEvedy and Jones 1978: 18, 79, 97, 111, 137.

55. A truce with Persia—envisioned by Parker and Tetlock 2006: 374–75 as a prerequisite for taking Vienna and the downfall of Habsburg power—would hardly have been enough: the more the Ottomans had been involved in Latin Europe, the stronger the incentive for attacks in their rear would have become.

56. Troop numbers: Karaman and Pamuk 2010: 610, fig. 4 and 612, table 1.

57. Goldstone 2006: 172–73.

58. England: Pestana 2006: 199.

59. Goldstone 2006: 173–78, 184–85 for this scenario's negative effects on science and technology. Mokyr 2006 disagrees. For these factors, see Part V.

60. Horne 1999 considers this counterfactual.

61. For the contrast with East Asia, see chapter 10 in this volume.

62. Horne 1999: 208, 210–12, 214–16; Roberts 2014: 445, 625.

CHAPTER SEVEN

1. See chapter 1 in this volume. For the term "First Great Divergence," see note 17 below.

2. Visualized in chapter 1 of this volume.

3. For parallels, see Gizewski 1994; Scheidel 2009a: 13–15. For the comparative history of Rome and China, see Scheidel 2009d, 2015c; Auyang 2014; and my website, https://web.stanford.edu/~scheidel/acme.htm.

4. In contrast to Rome's experience, Qin's fairly rapid conquest of its main competitors had been preceded by close involvement in several centuries of intensifying competition within an integrated state system not unlike that of post-Roman Europe: see Hui 2005 for a comparative study of why the Chinese Warring States eventually succumbed to a hegemon whereas early modern Europe did not.

5. By then, just four empires—Rome, Parthia, Kushan, and Han—laid claim to at least two-thirds of the entire world population: the global heyday of empire. For the numbers and later parallels, see Scheidel in press-b.

6. For convergent evolution and lasting differences, see Scheidel 2009a: 15–20.

7. M. Lewis 1990 is fundamental. Fukuyama 2011: 110–24 provides a clear outline.

8. Scheidel 2009a: 16–17 (general); Tan 2017 (taxes). For warfare, see Rosenstein 2009. Asymmetries: see chapter 3 in this volume.

9. Scheidel 2009a: 17–19. For a comparison of administrative structures, see Eich 2015 and Zhao 2015b.

10. Bureaucracies: see previous note, and for budgeting see Scheidel 2015d. Urban development: M. Lewis 2015; Noreña 2015; Scheidel 2015b: 9–10; and Noreña forthcoming.

11. See chapter 1 in this volume. Dincecco and Onorato 2018: 3, 5, 20–21 emphasize the role of the fall of the Carolingian empire.

12. Updated from Hui 2015: 13, for the area controlled by the Qin at the height of their power in 214 BCE, dubbed the "interior."

13. Kaufman, Little, and Wohlforth 2007: 231, table 10.1 calculate that East Asia was characterized by a unipolar/hegemonic system for 68 percent of the years between 220 BCE and 1875 (adjusted from their own virtually even split for the longer period from 1025 BCE to 1875), and South Asia for half of the time between 400 BCE and 1810, compared to 2 percent for Europe from 1500 to 2000.

14. According to Lorge 2005: 181, "The period between 907 and 979 was the last moment of a real multi-state system before the chaotic warlord period in the early twentieth century."

15. Sinocentric order: M. Lewis 2009b: 146, 153.

16. The quote is taken from the title of Rossabi 1983, whose editor claims that "a true multi-state system operated during Sung times" (11). This notion is common in modern scholarship on East Asia from the Tang period onward. Contrast Ringmar 2007: 289, who sensibly notes the lack of a balancing state system in China: imperial hegemony was the only game in town. Cf. also Lang 1997: 26, for the lack of serious state-level competitors of China-based empires. Rosenthal and Wong 2011: 22 stress, *contra* Rossabi 1983, the differences between the Song era and European multistate systems. The same reservations apply to the strawman position taken by Goldstone 2009: 100 that "it is a misleading oversimplification to say that from 1500 onward Europe had a system of competing states whereas Asia had empires without competition" and "it is wrong to see the major empires as always dominating their neighbors and being free of military competition." These statements are both correct and irrelevant in that they misrepresent most existing scholarship. Cf. Hoffman 2015: 175–78 for the counterfactual of lasting divisions in China had the Mongols failed to take over the Southern Song, and the possible developmental consequences of a resultant genuine state system.

17. I initially used the term "First Great Divergence" in Scheidel 2009a, echoing the title of Pomeranz 2000 (which contrary to claims on the internet is not indebted to Huntington 1996).

For the concept of the "Little Divergence," see van Zanden 2009a, referred to as a "First Great Divergence" by Karayalcin 2016. See also Davids 2013, an entire book devoted to "great and little divergences." Moore 2009: 577 introduced the notion of an eleventh/twelfth century CE "First Great Divergence," and elaborates on this in Moore 2015 (with a gracious reference (20) to my own use of this term). For the deemphasizing of extended kinship networks in northwestern Europe, cf. chapter 12 in this volume.

18. Cicero, *In Defense of the Manilian Law* 7.17 (66 BCE); Schumpeter 1954 [1918]: 6 (from Goldscheid 1917); *All the President's Men* (Warner Bros., 1976); Tilly 1992: 96–97.

19. For the history of taxation in the long term, see Ardant 1971–1972; Bonney 1995, 1999; Cavaciocchi 2008; Yun-Casalilla and O'Brien 2012; Monson and Scheidel 2015a. For evolutionary taxonomy, see esp. Bonney and Ormrod 1999; for theory, Levi 1988; for a model of variation in contractual forms of revenue collection, Cosgel and Miceli 2009. Articulation: Motyl 2001: 13–20, for a spoke model of empire.

20. For repeated empirical demonstration of these basic trends, see the contributions in Monson and Scheidel 2015a, and esp. Monson and Scheidel 2015b: 19–20. See also Wickham 1994: 43–75 and Haldon in press. Haldon 1993 provides the most extensive discussion.

21. See chapters 2, 5, and 6 in this volume.

22. For conditions during the reconsolidation phase, see chapter 10 in this volume.

23. For a comparison of the fiscal regimes of the Roman empire and Han China, see Scheidel 2015d. For the late Roman tightening of the earlier more-relaxed regime (Scheidel 2015a), see Bransbourg 2015.

24. Institutional decentralization was a function of the paramount importance of the self-governing city as the focal point not just of taxation but of society in general, and of the involvement of rent-seeking local elites in state revenue collection: Wickham 1994: 50, 73–74. Tax remissions: see, e.g., Bransbourg 2015: 275–76.

25. Land distributions: Wickham 2005: 84–86. Initial tax shares: Goffart 1980 (228–29 on the eventual conversion to land assignments); Goffart 2006: 119–86 (quotes: 183). Cf. also Halsall 2003: 42–43. Tedesco 2013 references recent scholarship.

26. Halsall 2003: 64; Wickham 2005: 92–93, 115–20; and Tedesco 2015: 104–12, 166–87 (Italy); Wickham 2005: 87–93; and Modéran 2014: 167 (Vandals).

27. Wickham 2005: 93–102; and see chapter 5 in this volume.

28. Halsall 2003: 54; Wickham 2005: 102–15.

29. Wickham 2009: 553–54. See also Wickham 2005: 146–48. For late imperial China, see chapter 10 in this volume.

30. Wickham 2005: 84 (state size and military status), 149 (localization), and also 830 for the "crucial importance of the end of Roman imperial unity."

In this context, the cultural dimension of the observed shift toward decentralized support for followers that was based on direct access to land yields is also worth considering: we must ask to what extent it might reflect compromises between rulers whose position had grown out of leadership of diverse and mobile warrior confederations and the expectations of their members. Here one must tread carefully: this approach does not merely entail conjecture but also invites charges of essentializing traits of the successor regimes by an academic tradition that has increasingly sought to deconstruct the very notion of "Germanic." Even so, while acknowledging the considerable diversity and fluidity of these conquest groups, we should be open to the possibility that they prioritized certain types of rewards: at the very least, this notion deserves an outsized endnote. (Wickham 2005: 82–83 rejects the notion that cultural differences between old and new ruling classes were responsible for the observed fiscal changes: but more deeply rooted factors might have played a role. Wickham 2016: 29 notes that senior Germanic officers preferred land to pay.)

The tradition that ancient Germans (or "Germans") sought farmland goes back a long way. When Caesar, the highly indebted and wildly ambitious governor of Provence in 58 BCE, was in need of an excuse to intervene in free Gaul, he found one (of several) in the encroachment of Germans from across the Rhine on the Gallic Sequani in what is now eastern France: "Ariovistus, the king of the Germans, had settled in their territory and seized one-third of their land" (Caesar, *War in Gaul* 1.31).

Taken on its own, it would surely be unwise to put much weight on his self-serving account that cast Romans as defenders of soon-to-be-conquered Gauls. But this was part of a much larger pattern. More than half a millennium later, in the dying days of what was left of the western Roman empire, unruly Germanic mercenaries put pressure on the renegade general Orestes, who had just placed his teenage son Romulus (nicknamed Augustulus) on the throne: they "demanded that they [the Romans] should divide with them the entire land of Italy; and indeed they commanded Orestes to give them the third part of this, and when he would be no means agree to do so, they killed him immediately. Now there was a certain man among the Romans named Odoacer . . . and he at that agreed to carry out their commands . . . giving the third part of the land to the barbarians" (Procopius, *Gothic Wars* 5.1.3). While we do not know whether this scheme was actually implemented, the fact that Odoacer managed to hold on to Italy for the next thirteen years until the Ostrogoths invaded and overthrew him and his followers suggests that he did something right: some form of land grants might well have been part of it. Goffart 1980: 62–70 questions Procopius's credibility. However, the Eugippius quote in the main text, referring to Odoacer's great gifts to many, might reflect an actual land distribution.

This would fit well with what had repeatedly happened during the intervening centuries: on dozens of occasions, "barbarians"—mostly of Germanic origin—had been settled within the confines of the Roman empire, beginning with the resettlement of the Ubii in Gaul in 38 BCE. Sometimes they were accommodated once defeated and at other times simply received as settlers. Land features as an explicit objective: in the 160s CE, Germanic groups supposedly threatened war "unless they were accepted" (Historia Augusta, *Life of Marcus* 14.1). Self-governing settler communities are recorded from the 380s onward and became the norm in the early fifth century, thereby precipitating the demise of the western empire. Ste. Croix 1981: 509–18 lists cases from 38 BCE to the 590s CE.

The inhabitants of free Germany were primarily farmers, and many groups that later arrived in former Roman provinces were linked to populations that had long led a settled lifestyle. In view of this, purely functionalist explanations of the later abatement of taxation might be too narrow: the characteristics of the conquest groups and of consensus-building between leaders and followers may also have played a role. The Germanic experience invites comparison with the contrasting preferences of invaders from less settled areas north of China or Arabia, who for the most part did not seem to share this interest in taking over land directly but preferred to be compensated by means of a centralized tax system, keeping primary producers at greater remove.

It is true that steppe conquerors sometimes received land allotments, the Mongol forces in China and Iran among them. This, however, did not end taxation: tax-farming was reintroduced under the Ilkhans, and while the Timurid system was based on land grants coupled with fiscal immunity to local elite allies and senior Turkic military, this did not relieve subject populations from obligations (Potts 2014: 209–13). What we do not see in these cases is a creeping assimilation of the tax status of these populations to that of their privileged conquerors. One explanation would be the overall degree of difference, in culture and mode of subsistence, between these groups: the gap between mounted steppe warriors and sedentary farmers was larger than that between Germans and locals elsewhere. I discuss the impact of these differences in more detail in chapter 8 of this volume.

31. Halsall 2003: 45–110.

32. Halsall 2003: 119–33 (army size), 134–62 (nature of campaigning).

33. *Contra* Rosenthal and Wong 2011: 32, the succession system Frankish lack of primogeniture was not the key determinant of this process: even though this custom contributed by encouraging internal divisions among princely brothers, the roots of local empowerment were deeper than that.

34. Nelson 1995b: 385–86 (quote: 386, from Nithard, *Histories*, 4.3); Costambeys, Innes, and MacLean 2011: 319; Wickham 2016: 11.

35. Wickham 2009: 529–51 on the "caging of the peasantry"; Halsall 2003: 31 on armies as assemblies.

36. Airlie 1995: 448–49; Roger Collins 1999: 361–62, 395–96; Wickham 2001: 91–94.

37. Wickham 2001: 88–89; Wickham 2005: 154–258; Wickham 2009: 508–28; Wickham 2016: 102–9.

38. Strayer 1970: 15 (quote); Wickham 2009: 555–56, 564 (quote). See also Wickham 2016: 78–79, 254–55 for the time around 1000 or the eleventh century as a crucial tipping point.

39. Graff 2002: 39–51; M. Lewis 2009a: 51, 59–62. Inflow of "barbarians" under the Jin: Holcombe 2001: 121–22.

40. Graff 2002: 54–69; M. Lewis 2009a: 73–85.

41. Graff 2002: 59–60; M. Lewis 2009a: 77.

42. Graff 2002: 61; M. Lewis 2009a: 78–79, 114, 118.

43. R. Huang 1997: 76–77 (quote: 77).

44. See Scheidel 2011b: 197, based on Bielenstein 1987: 12 (Han: 9.2–10.8 million households with 47.6–56.5 million residents), 15–17 (third century CE). For strong evidence in support of the notion that state (registration) capacity was the critical variable, see Scheidel 2011b: 203n18, and cf. also Graff 2002: 35–36, 127.

45. Bielenstein 1987: 17 (census), with Scheidel 2011b: 197–99; Graff 2002: 67 (offensive). Europe: McEvedy and Jones 1978: 41–118.

46. Dien 2001: 108–13 (Western Liang). Some exam questions (from fifth- to sixth-century northern China) survive in literary texts (105–7); the examination system continued in southern China (103–4). M. Lewis 2009a: 145–48 (Xiongnu and Murong Xianbei).

47. Graff 2002: 69–73, 97; M. Lewis 2009a: 79–81, 148. The Tuoba were probably a Turkic-speaking group: S. Chen 2012: 183–91.

48. Eberhard 1949: 209–11; Yang 1961: 146–47; Huang 1997: 89. Tuoba military strength attracted Chinese collaborators to their administration: Barfield 1989: 118–19. Von Glahn 2016: 175

suspects that the reclamation of deserted land reduced the state's pressure on these clan communities.

49. Graff 2002: 72; M. Lewis 2009a: 149.

50. Huang 1997: 90–91; M. Lewis 2009a: 139–40; von Glahn 2016: 173–74. The census total of 3.4 million households reported for 528–530 CE (Bielenstein 1987: 17) cannot represent more than a fraction of the actual number; Graff 2002: 127 and 13n19 provides a reference to a more respectable tally of 5 million households and 32 million people at about that time.

51. Kang 1983: 116–75; Huang 1997: 93; Graff 2002: 98–100; M. Lewis 2009a: 81.

52. Kang 1983: 176–216; Graff 2002: 100–106; M. Lewis 2009a: 82–83.

53. Pearce 1987 is fundamental: see esp. 463–74, 480–83, 507–18, 561–66, 734. See also Kang 1983: 222; Graff 2002: 107–10. 114; M. Lewis 2009a: 84–85; von Glahn 2016: 180–81. Army size: Graff 2002: 108–9.

54. Kang 1983: 220; Graff 2002: 107, 115.

55. Graff 2002: 111–13; M. Lewis 2009a: 62–73, 117.

56. Graff 2002: 76–96, esp. 82–83, and 127; M. Lewis 2009a: 138.

57. In the late Eastern Han period, about one-third of the registered population had resided south of the Central Plain region (demarcated by the Huai River) (Graff 2002: 76, 93n1), and about 10 million people south of the Yangzi (de Crespigny 2004: table 2). These shares are likely to have risen between the second and fifth–sixth centuries CE as southward migration occurred, the North suffered devastation, and the South became more developed. In 609 CE, the unified Sui empire produced a census tally of 8.9 million households with 46 million people (Bielenstein 1987: 20, who prefers 9.1 million households), but even that count appears to have missed households in the south, as suggested by comparison with the geographical distribution of the 140 CE census; the actual total would thus have been higher still. Consequently, the southern tallies for 464 (equivalent to one-tenth of the 609 total of households, rather than the expected value of more than one-third) and 589 (equivalent to one-eighteenth of the 609 households instead of more than one-sixth and one-twenty-third of people instead of more than one-fifth) are inevitably far too low. Xiong 2006: 251 bizarrely accepts all reported tallies at face value.

58. Graff 2002: 122–30.

59. A. Wright 1978: 139–56; Graff 2002: 132–35.

60. Von Glahn 2016: 182 (statuses); A. Wright 1978: 85 (Chang'an); Xiong 2006: 134 (Luoyang), 95–105 (palaces).

61. A. Wright 1978: 173 (Sima Guang). Canal: A. Wright 1978: 178–81; Xiong 2006: 86–93; M. Lewis 2009a: 254–55.

62. Graff 2002: 138–59, esp. 145–49 (149 for an estimate of c. 600,000 men).

63. Bielenstein 1987: 20; Graff 2002: 183, 190; M. Lewis 2009b: 44; von Glahn 2016: 187–90.

64. M. Lewis 2009a: 54. Unlike Lewis, who places military power and elite cooperation side by side, I give priority to the former, for the reasons presented in chapters 8 and 9 of this volume.

65. Census: Bielenstein 1987: 20. Decentralization: M. Lewis 2009b: 58–84. Tang collapse: Tackett 2014.

66. Standen 2009 (North); H. Clark 2009 (South).

67. Bielenstein 1987: 47–48 (the multiplier of about 2.2 people per household implied by Northern Song census totals is far too low and probably limited to adults; a mean of about 5 is

more plausible and in line with earlier census tallies that aimed to register all household members); W. Liu 2015a: 266, table F-4 (tax rate); W. Liu 2015b: 64–65 (tax system); von Glahn 2016: 240–41, 245 (tax yield and capital city). Soldiers: Deng 1999: 305. For the Roman empire, cf. Scheidel 2015a: 243. On the Song economy in general (starting with late Tang), see von Glahn 2016: 208–78, alongside the classic survey by Elvin 1973: 111–99.

68. Eugippius, *Life of St Severinus* 6. It does not matter much what exactly Odoacer actually did: as we saw before, this story is part of a larger pattern. The shift from taxation to landowning was a defining characteristic of this period: Wickham 2016: 29.

69. Maier 2005: 62 (Ostrogoths); Wickham 2005: 105–6 (Franks).

70. For Middle Eastern fiscal systems, see Wickham 1994: 56–66. For relations between Rome, Iran, and the Arabs, see most recently Fisher 2011. Between 1984 and 2010, a monumental seven-volume history of Roman-Arab relations was published by Irfan Shahid (https://www .doaks.org/newsletter/byzantium-and-the-arabs).

71. H. Kennedy 2001: 59–95 on military compensation, esp. 59; H. Kennedy 2015: 390–97. Practices in Egypt were similar to Iraq's, whereas those in Syria are less well known (396–97).

72. H. Kennedy 2001: 62–64, 74–78; Wickham 2009: 331–34; H. Kennedy 2015: 398–401; Haldon 2016: 75–77.

73. Wickham 1994: 57–61 remains a classic summary. For the evolution of *iqta'* and similar arrangements, see, e.g., Lambton 1968: 230–39 and Cahen 1975: 311–14 (up to the Seljuqs); Basan 2010: 169–71 (Seljuqs); Petrushevsky 1968: 516–20 (Il-Khanids); Jamaluddin 1995: 154 (Timur); Savory 1986: 364–66 (Safavids). The Ottoman regime in Anatolia and the Balkans likewise insisted on tax payments by peasants, which were initially assigned to military beneficiaries who were then replaced by a salaried army sustained by tax farmers. When the latter turned into lords with private armies, the center moved to suppress them (Wickham 1994: 63–64).

74. Asher and Talbot 2006: 35–41, 128, 152; Lieberman 2009: 640, 643, 740. For the Mughal tax system, see Richards 2012: 411–16.

75. For this taxonomy of developmental correlations, see chapter 9 in this volume. States that collected tax were generally more stable than those based on gift exchange or control over farmland: Wickham 2016: 11, 29.

76. For China, see Lorge 2005: 178. Relaxation: Deng 2015: 314–21 (Qing); M. Lewis 2015: 300–304 (Tang).

CHAPTER EIGHT

1. Quote: Montesquieu 1750 [1748]: 384 (*De L'Esprit des Lois*, book XVII, ch. VI).

2. Adapted from Diamond 1997: 414 (quote). The "peninsular" portion of Korea is roughly three times the size that of Shandong. Cf. also Keay 2000: xxiii, contrasting Europe's mountains and coastlines with India, which lacks real barriers. Cosandey 2008: 499–581 considers the coastline critical for Europe's development, as will be discussed later.

3. Criticism: Hoffman 2015: 112–14. European coastline: Cosandey 2008: 509–33.

4. Cosandey 2008: 533–69, esp. 558: Europe (46 percent peninsulas, 10.2 percent islands), Islamic zone (0.9 percent peninsulas and no islands), India (1.7 percent peninsulas and 1.9 percent islands), and China (1.1 percent peninsulas and 2 percent islands).

5. Cosandey 2008: 561, 567–68. For him, European development is rooted in the resultant system of smaller states: 75–312.

6. Mountains: Montesquieu 1750 [1748]: 384 (*De L'Esprit des Lois*, book XVII, ch. VI) (quote); Diamond 1997: 414. Europe not more rugged: Hoffman 2015: 109–12. Elevation in China: Marks 2012: 17, map 2.4; Auyang 2014: 339 (terrain above 400 and 1,500 meters).

7. Diamond 1997: 414 (quote). See also very briefly Lang 1997: 24.

8. See Tvedt 2010: 37 for the weakness of China's river-coast connections.

9. J. McNeill 1998: 32 (quote), 36.

10. J. McNeill 1998: 36–37 (quotes). See Tvedt 2010: 35–37 for very perceptive observations on the nature of the Chinese river and irrigation system, stressing the risk of flooding, and the drainage and tributary focus of the canal system. See chapter 12 in this volume. Note the partial decay of this system between the Song and Qing periods: W. Liu 2015a: 94–95.

11. Wittfogel 1957. Review of Google Scholar yields studies, too numerous to list here, both supporting and conflicting with Wittfogel's main claims. Europe: Chirot 1985: 183; Diamond 1997: 414 (size and connectivity). For the importance of riverine connectivity in general, see Scheidel and Meeks 2014.

12. Marks 2012: 29, with map 2.7.

13. See the maps of census results in 2, 140, 609, 742, and c. 765 CE in Bielenstein 1987: 193–94, 199, 202–3. Only in the Northern Song period do we see a more even distribution of the registered population between North and South: Bielenstein 1987: 207–12. See, e.g., Lieven 2000: 37. De Crespigny 2012 asserts that "the wealth and population of the North China plain means that the ruler who holds it may dominate East Asia, and this fact of geography . . . explains much of China's continuing capacity for reunification."

14. E. Jones 2003: 105–7, 226; earlier J. Hall 1985: 111; P. Kennedy 1987: 17; and later Lieberman 2009: 738. Quote: Montesquieu 1750 [1748]: 384 (*De L'Esprit des Lois*, book XVII, ch. VI). See also Kiesewetter 2006: 47–52. Lieven 2000: 33 misses the point by noting that China was divided into semi-enclosed regions: *comparative* metrics are key.

15. E. Jones 2003: 105–7 (quote: 107). Remarkably, the Roman empire is not even mentioned in the book's index.

16. Keay 2000: xxv (farm belt); Lieberman 2009: 738–39.

17. Keay 2000: xxv–xxvi; Asher and Talbot 2006: 12; Lieberman 2009: 739.

18. My estimate for the Roman empire schematically draws on the length of Hadrian's Wall, of the Rhine and Danube, and Turkey's, Syria's, and Israel's eastern borders.

19. Needham 1969: 151, fig. 20 (quote, with map visualization). For another map visualization considering altitude and precipitation levels, see Ko, Koyama, and Sng 2018: 288, fig. 1. Elvin 1973: 21 and Pines 2012: 8 note isolation as a contributing factor to China's imperial cohesion.

20. Hui 2005: 160, despite her overall resistance to geographical arguments, notes that the European state system was "more expansive and dispersed" than China's and that Napoleon "faced the tyranny of distance in the Russian campaign." Capitals in the Warring States period—which ended in imperial unification—were much closer together than Paris and Moscow (160).

21. For Rome, see chapter 2 in this volume. In 9 BCE, the Roman commander Drusus reached the Elbe, and the short-lived trans-Rhenanian Roman province of Germania appears to have reached as far as the lower Elbe. For Charlemagne's expansion, see chapter 5 in this volume.

22. Heather 2009: xv (quotes); 386–451 (spread of Slavs), 520–76 (later state formation and development); Wickham 2009: 472–507, esp. 480–91, 505–7, 556 (tenth century); Wickham 2016: 81. Brown 2003 is a classic account of the "rise of Western Christendom" up to 1000 CE.

23. Bartlett 1993, esp. 295, 298–99, 303–4, 306, 308–9; and also 24–59 on the "aristocratic diaspora." Quote: Heather 2009: xv.

24. For a crude guide, see https://www.euratlas.net/history/europe/index.html. Latin Christendom: Bartlett 1993: 292.

25. See, e.g., Lieven 2010.

26. Gat 2006: 394 makes the same point in his (highly superficial) discussion of environmental factors (391–95). In his massive survey of modern explanations of the (second) "Great Divergence," Vries 2013: 153–61, though unsympathetic to geographical reasoning, offers no compelling arguments against it. I fully agree with his view that geography, being static, can never be more than a necessary precondition, and not a sufficient one (413). At the same time, I object to his classification of geography and natural resources as "proximate causes" (409), except insofar as this term is used in a technical economic sense as denoting endogeneity to the economy (as Peer Vries kindly informs me it is). I also find it hard to understand why Hoffman 2015: 109–14, in his rejection of geographical arguments for explaining European exceptionalism, limits himself to mountains and coastlines but ignores features such as compactness and natural cores.

27. Steppe ecology: e.g., Barfield 1989: 20–24; Taaffe 1990: 33–37.

28. See Turchin 2009: 202–3, table 2, for a list of empires, and Scheidel in press-b: table 2.1 for a lightly augmented and revised tabulation that I use here. The fifty-four empires are Abbasid, Almohad, Almoravid, Ayyubid, Bactria, Buyid, Chagatai, Delhi, Fatimid, Former Qin, Ghaznavid, Ghurid, Gokturk, Golden Horde, Hephthalite, Huns (Attila), Il-Khans, Jin, Jurchen, Khazar, Khorezm, Kushan, Kiev, Liao, Lithuania-Poland, Mali, Mamluk, Media, Ming, Mongol, Mughal, Northern Song, Northern Zhou, Ottoman, Parthia, Qara Qitai, Qin, Qing, Rouran, Russia, Safavid, Saka, Samanid, Seljuq, Sui, Tang, Timurid, Tufan, Uigur, Umayyad, Western Han, Xianbei, Xiongnu, and Zhungar. The nine intermediate cases are Achaemenid, Assyria, Egypt, Gupta, Harsha, Maurya, Pratihara, Sasanian, and Shang; and the remaining ten are Axum, Byzantine (high medieval), Franks, Holy Roman empire, Inca, Khmer, Macedonian, Maratha, Roman, and Seleucid.

29. Turchin 2009: 201; Scheidel in press-b.

30. Turchin et al. 2013: 16386 provide analogous heat maps for states of greater than 100,000 square kilometers.

31. Scheidel in press-b: table 2.2. The twenty empires are Delhi, Former Qin, Former Yan, Ghurid, Hephthtalite, Jin, Jurchen, Kushan, Later Zhao, Ming, Mongol, Mughal, Northern Song, Northern Wei, Northern Zhou, Qin, Qing, Tang, Western Han, and Umayyad. The seven intermediate cases are Achaemenid, Gupta, Harsha, Maurya, Nanda, Pratihara, and Sasanian; and the five remaining ones are Macedonian, Maratha, Pala, Roman, and Seleucid. By contrast, the largest South Indian polities, Chola and Vijayanagara, each captured only around 4 percent.

32. Quote: Turchin 2009: 201.

33. Antagonistic relationship: Turchin 2009, esp. 191, 194–97. On conflict giving impetus to state formation, key contributions include Carneiro 1970, 1988; Lane 1979; H. Lewis 1981;

W. McNeill 1982; Tilly 1985, 1992; B. Porter 1994; Spruyt 1994; Kasza 1996; Ertman 1997; Turchin et al. 2013; I. Morris 2014. I summarize this concisely in Scheidel 2013b: 11–12 (conflict theories of state origin), 20–22 (role of violence in state formation), 33–38 (warfare as a driver of state formation).

34. See, e.g., Sunderland 2004: 5–8 for a standard summary of central features, with reference to earlier literature on the emergence of steppe pastoralism. See also Khazanov 1994. Lack of steppe self-sufficiency: Jagchid and Symons 1989; Golden 1998: 20–21. Christian 1998 covers the broad sweep of premodern Central Asian history.

35. Sedentism was a precondition for large-scale farming, mining, and manufacture, and agrarian states arose to protect and acquire such resources. Quote: Khodarkovsky 2002: 5, and cf. 7–75 on "why peace was impossible" on the (Russian) steppe frontier.

36. Lattimore 1988 [1940] on agriculturalists' interaction with steppe peoples and the impossibility of the latter's integration. Theory: Turchin 2003: 50–93, esp. 53–55, 79–81. For an empirical test for post-Roman Europe, see Turchin 2003: 79–93, esp. 83–89.

37. Lieberman 2009: xxi–xxii, 85, 92–93, 97, 100–101n144. Quote: 97.

38. For the Pannonian plain, see chapter 6 in this volume and in the present chapter.

39. See Barfield 1989 and more briefly 2001. On the distinction between primary and shadow empires, see 2001: 28–39 (quote: 33). Correlation of complexity: Barfield 2003: 461 ("In general nomadic polities tend to match the degree of political complexity of the sedentary societies with which they interact"); Turchin 2009: 194. Challand 2004 gives a broad overview of steppe empires, and see more generally Golden 1998. Sinor 1990 covers Central Asian history prior to the Genghisid expansion.

40. Beckwith and Nicola di Cosmo are among the most vocal critics of the "shadow empire" model. Both sides seeking resources from the other: Di Cosmo 2002a: 169–70. Encroachment: Di Cosmo 2002a: 142–43, 174–75, 186–88. Both note that the unwillingness of agrarian societies to grant steppe peoples access to resources led to violence: for nomad raids as a response to encroachment, aggression, and trade restrictions, see Di Cosmo 1999b: 12; Beckwith 2009: 330, 334–38, 345–48. Beckwith 2009: 320–22, in an impassioned diatribe against the denigration of nomads in ancient and modern sources, accepts that pastoralists were familiar with horses and use of the compound bow (322), greatly relied on trade (325, 345), resorted to shock tactics because they had to be careful to preserve manpower and could not easily seize fortified cities (339–40), and that both sides sought to expand at the expense of the other (350–51). None of this contradicts Barfield's reasoning: I fully agree with T. Hall 2010: 109–10, who notes the "broad overlap" of Barfield's and Beckwith's positions, notwithstanding the latter's "very puzzling" attacks on the former. Shared responsibility for conflict along the steppe frontier is a given: see, e.g., Jagchid and Symons 1989: 23 for lack of trust and stability at the frontier, and 24–51 for the options of raiding and trading; likewise Golden 2002: 106.

41. Correlation: Bai and Kung 2011; Zhang et al. 2015. Cf. the earlier prescient piece by Hinsch 1988, written before much of the data became available. Turks: Bulliet 2009: 96–126; Peacock 2010: 45; cf. also Peacock 2010: 53–61 for context. Better resources: Büntgen et al. 2016: 235 (Arabs); and chapter 6 in this volume (Mongols).

42. Denunciation by literati: Beckwith 2009: 355–62, who rightly objects to the use of the term "barbarian." Farming at steppe rims (Inner Mongolia, Northern Mongolia, Southern

Siberia, Manchuria, Xinjiang): Di Cosmo 1994; Beckwith 2009: 341–43. See also Di Cosmo 1999b: 8–13 on the formation of steppe empires.

43. Khodarkovsky 2002: 76–183; Sunderland 2004 (steppe colonization by Russians); Perdue 2005: 133–299 (Qing suppression of nomads).

44. For the emergence of Eurasian pastoralism, see Di Cosmo 2002a: 13–43. Abstract model: Turchin 2009: 196–97. Quote: Deng 2012: 339. The same is true of the notion that steppe invasions were so catastrophic that they acted as a "centripetal force" on China (Ko, Koyama, and Sng 2018: 290), which overestimates their impact: see chapter 10 in this volume.

45. Lattimore 1988 [1940] 542–51 ("marginal zone," for China), 238–51, 547 ("reservoir" and "marginal zone"), 541 (conquests from that zone). Critical importance of borderlands: see, e.g., Barfield 1989: 100, 104, 2001: 22; Skaff 2012: 15–17. With respect to China, Mair 2005: 81 singles out the arid loess- and sand-covered Ordos plateau as the locus of the most intense interaction: "As the zone of consummate interface between the settled and the steppe, the Ordos is the true homeland of 'China.'" Skaff 2012: 16 rejects Fletcher's 1986: 41 claim that geography separated pastoralists from farmers ("At the eastern end of the steppe zone, where the lines between nomad and sedentary were most sharply drawn, Mongolia and China confronted one another through much of history as worlds apart"). In reality, the contact zone was an essential meeting ground.

46. Turchin et al. 2013. For criticism, see R. Thomas 2014, who suggests that seeding of traits in lowland civilizational cores that had already attained high complexity by 1500 BCE—Egypt, Mesopotamia, the Indus Valley, and northern China—might produce identical simulation results. Turchin et al. 2014 fail to address this point, which receives some support from preliminary modeling (James Bennett, personal communications May 28 to June 1, 2017). This underlines the need for concrete case studies of how equine warfare and state formation were related in order to assess the validity of Turchin et al.'s interpretation, which is discussed later in this chapter.

47. This tendency, as well as a profusion of anthropological jargon de jour, bedevils the attempt by Honeychurch 2015 to offer an alternative to existing reciprocal feedback models.

48. Adapted from Turchin 2009: 193, table 1. Ming is an outlier in more ways than one: its rise was the only indigenous (Han) reaction to outright conquest from the steppe (by the Mongols) rather than from the border zone. This was the only time steppe forces had intruded more deeply, effectively pushing the steppe frontier into southern China, as it were. This might make us wonder to what extent the Ming regime, which responded to the Mongol presence within China, should count as a genuine exception. Even so, this might be taking it too far: after all, revolts against established dynasties were common regardless of the latter's ethnic origin.

49. Mair 2005: 56–64 (quotes: 46, 64). Only modern China broke with that paradigm: its leadership had southern roots (83). For the heavy Turco-Xianbei element of the Tang dynasty ("a Särbo-Chinese regime"), see S. Chen 2012: 4–38 (quote: 36).

50. Di Cosmo 1999a: 902–8; Mair 2005: 69–75; Turchin 2009: 198.

51. Pastoralism: Di Cosmo 1999a: 909–14, 924–26; Di Cosmo 2002a: 13–43; Graff 2016: 153. Emergence of mounted warfare: Drews 2004: 31–98. Interstate warfare: M. Lewis 1999; Zhao 2015a: 222–61. See M. Lewis 1990 and Zhao 2015a: 169–221 on the internal restructuring prompted by these conflicts.

52. Offensives: Deng 2012: 336, table 4.1: from 475 to 221 BCE, Qin launched 102 of 244 major offensives, compared to 35 by Zhao, 26 by Chu, and 23 by Wei. Very briefly but to the point: Zhao 2015a: 99, esp. n101 on Qin's origins. See also Teng 2014 for the early weakness of local kinship ties. Conflicts with Rong from the ninth through seventh centuries BCE: Di Cosmo 1999a: 921–24. In the end, the Western Zhou fought and were brought down by Rong and had to abandon the Wei valley.

53. Di Cosmo 1999a: 947–51 (loss of buffer). Warring States–era contacts: Di Cosmo 1999a: 951–52, 960–62; Di Cosmo 2002a: 127–58, esp. 140–43 on attacks and border walls; also Deng 2012: 339; Graff 2016: 154–55. Xiongnu expansion in response to Qin aggression: Di Cosmo 2002a: 174–75, 186–88. The question of whether the Xiongnu empire predated this particular conflict (thus Di Cosmo 2002a: 167–74) remains controversial: e.g., Barfield 2003: 462–63.

54. See Chang 2007 for an account of the enormous cost incurred by these campaigns, even if he takes the sources too much at face value. For the attendant domestic reforms, see Loewe 1986: 152–79, and generally Lelièvre 2001. Xiongnu federation: Barfield 1989: 32–84. Di Cosmo 2002a: 205 acknowledges that steppe demand for Han resources became critical once the Xiongnu empire had been established.

55. Han Chinese ran Former and Western Liang, Northern Yan, and Former Qin; and the Ba ruled Cheng Han. Military contingents from the steppe had already become prominent under the Jin, which they then overthrew: Holcombe 2001: 121–22.

56. Barfield 1989: 123–24; Graff 2002: 72; M. Lewis 2009a: 149; Graff 2016: 145. The Di state of Former Qin must already have enjoyed similar access: large cavalry forces were reported for its failed invasion of the South up to 383 CE (Graff 2002: 67).

57. Graff 2016: 161.

58. See esp. W. Liu 2015b, and chapter 10 in this volume.

59. See chapter 6 in this volume.

60. Barfield 1989: 266–96; Perdue 2005: 133–299.

61. Deng 1999: 363–76, in a survey of mass rebellions since the Qin period, identifies 103 cases over 2,106 years. With very few exceptions, they broke out close to the end of dynastic eras: in 208 BCE (fall of the Qin regime), 17 CE, lasting for seven years (end of the intra-Han interlude of the Wang Mang usurpation), 184–191 CE, lasting for up to three decades (decline and fall of the Eastern Han), 294–311 CE, lasting for up to half a century (fall of Western Jin), 611–623 CE (fall of Sui), 863 and 875 (decline of the Tang), 1119–1130 (multiple cases at the end of Northern Song), 1351–1353, lasting for up to 16 years (expulsion of the Mongols), 1641–1646, lasting for up to 2 decades (fall of the Ming), and finally an uptick in the 1780s followed by bigger disruptions in 1795–1796, lasting for up to 12 years, and the Taiping and other rebellions 1851–1861, lasting for up to 15 years, which seriously challenged the late Qing.

62. For the structural link between unity/disunity in China and the presence of steppe empires, see esp. Barfield 1989: 10–11 and 13, table 1.1, and Barfield 2001: 23, table 1.1; and see 1989: 12–16 on parallel cycles. This elaborates on Lattimore's observation of the existence, over 2,000 years, of "two cycles, distinct from each other as patterns but always interacting on each other as historical processes—the cycle of tribal dispersion and unification in the steppe and the cycle of dynastic integration and collapse in China" (1988 [1940] 512); see Barfield 1989: 11 for acknowledgment of his indebtedness to "Lattimore's tradition." See also Jagchid and

Symonds 1989 for an overview of the key features of 2,000 years of interaction between China and the steppe.

63. Fletcher 1986: 21; Di Cosmo 1999b: 29–37. As discussed, dual administration was already pioneered in the Period of Disunion.

64. Turchin 2009: 199 notes the underlying feedback loop.

65. Mote 1999: 26; cf. also Barfield 2001: 15.

66. See, e.g., Golden 2002: 130–32; Graff 2016: 154. For female involvement, see Golden 2002: 130–31; Mayor 2014: 395–410.

67. Bai and Kung 2011: 974, table 1, with 975, fig. 3 (broad survey; adopted by Ko, Koyama, and Sng 2018: 300–304); Skaff 2012: 40–41, table 1.2, with a complete list 301–12 (599–755 CE, based on Sima Guang's *Zizhi tongjian*).

68. Border walls have already been discussed. City walls: Ioannides and Zhang 2017: 79–81 (taller, $n = 1,436$; thicker, $n = 934$). Unity: Ko, Koyama, and Sng 2018: 300–304.

69. Gaubatz 1996: 13–44, esp. 19–21 (20 for the term).

70. Shifting control: Skaff 2012: 17, 26, 50–51, 291–94. It was rare for the border zone to be controlled by one separate power that did not engage in further expansion, as was the case with the Qidan pastoralists that formed the Liao state in the tenth century CE and sought to exercise but failed to maintain hegemony over northern Chinese states that rose and fell in rapid succession. See Standen 2007 on Liao frontier state formation. Cession: Huang 1997: 124; Standen 2009: 86–87.

71. Perspective: see, most recently, e.g., M. Lewis 2009a: 151; Skaff 2012: 3–4; Rawski 2015: 225.

72. For the shadowy Rus' khaganate, see Franklin and Shepard 1996: 31–70, and the recent summary in Neumann and Wigen 2018: 165–72 (and 163–98 on the general context). Large empires: Lithuania rivaled Carolingian Francia and Germany in size, and Rus' claimed territory twice as large. Russia gradually grew to be much larger still: by the late fifteenth century, it exceeded the size of the two earlier polities, and by the late sixteenth century it was as large as all of Latin Europe (see Taagepera 1997: 494, 497–98).

73. Franklin and Shepard 1996: 81–83, 97, 113, 143–45; Golden 2002: 115, 119.

74. Franklin and Shepard 1996: 170 (quote), 170–72 (500 kilometers of ramparts and 100 forts), 326 (power), 369–70 (lack of unity); Golden 2002: 121–23 (Cumans); cf. also Neumann and Wigen 2018: 174–78 for Rus' enmeshment with steppe peoples and practices.

75. See chapter 6 in this volume. Hartog 1996: 55–56 (tax), 162–67 (influence); Ostrowski 1998: 36–63 (borrowings), 133–248 ("Tatar yoke" ideology in the fifteenth and sixteenth centuries); Knobloch 2007: 173, 177 (borrowings); Neumann and Wigen 2018: 184–86 (early Tatar support); Lieberman 2009: 113 (size), 212–38 (evolution).

76. See chapters 5 and 6 in this volume, and very briefly Challand 2004: 53–58.

77. See chapter 6 in this volume.

78. See in the next section.

79. See chapters 5 and 10 in this volume.

80. Remoteness: see also Lévy 1997: 36–40. Golden 2002: 108 and Graff 2016: 157–59 note Rome's limited contact with steppe warriors. In addition, imperial allies kept steppe groups at arm's length. The Bosporan kingdom on the Crimean and Taman peninsulas, formed by Greek colonies in the fifth century BCE in response to steppe tribes but increasingly accommodating

them, was sustained as a buffer client state by the Romans, propped up by garrisons and occasional military intervention. In the Sarmatian-populated Hungarian Plain and Wallachia, diplomacy alternated with episodic clashes, but the limited grasslands did not support any larger confederations. Later, the Byzantine empire proved adept at containing steppe powers through diplomacy and subsidies.

81. Taaffe 1990: 37 (conduits); Asher and Talbot 2006: 12 (pastoralists); Roy 2015: 50 (Maurya).

82. Roy 2015: 56–64, 70–73, 87–90.

83. Asher and Talbot 2006: 26–28 (critical role of cavalry); K. Roy 2015: 93.

84. K. Roy 2015: 95–99, 104–6. Chagatay nomads formed the backbone of Timur's forces: Jamaluddin 1995: 165–67.

85. B. Stein 1989: 22; Asher and Talbot 2006: 54–59; K. Roy 2015: 117–19.

86. Asher and Talbot 2006: 123–28, 152; K. Roy 2015: 120–26. Mughal identity focused on descent from Timur in particular and from Mongols in general: Foltz 1998: 21–27.

87. Lieberman 2009: 102 (quote), 637, 643. See chapter 1, figure 1.7 in this volume.

88. K. Roy 2015: 212–16. Mughal imports: Foltz 1998: 63. As noted later, this practice first appeared in the Neo-Assyrian empire.

89. Cf. Lattimore 1988 [1940] 242–47 for the relevance of the "reservoir"/"marginal" zone model for India's northwestern tribal frontier. South Asian empires tended to be less durable than those in China for reasons that need not concern us here (see chapter 10 in this volume); but that they existed at all owed much to these direct and indirect steppe inputs.

90. Bulliet 2009: 101 (rivers); Potts 2014: 47–87, esp. 78–81, 84–85. Drews 2004: 123–38 is essential.

91. Potts 2014: 88–119, esp. 93, 98, 113–17. Cf. also Challand 2004: 35–36 (italicized in original): "Responding to pressure from the nomads in the north was one of the constant features of Iran's external policy."

92. Potts 2014: 124–56, esp. 144–48, 156; Payne 2016: 7–10; Rezakhani 2017: 87–146.

93. Iran/Turan: Payne 2016: 5. Historiographical bias: Rezakhani 2017: 4.

94. Arabs: Potts 2014: 169–72. Turks and Mongols: Barfield 2002: 61. See more specifically Peacock 2010: 72–98 and Basan 2010: 165–69 for the characteristics of the Seljuq military. Rezakhani 2017: 187–91 argues that Sasanian-Central Asian interactions at the eastern frontier laid the foundations for Khorasan's pivotal role in state formation after 750 CE. Central Asian steppe people proved more accepting of hierarchy than the Arab Bedouin, in no small part thanks to more sustained contact with state-level polities: Barfield 2002: 65–66.

95. See Kuhrt 1995: 71, 75, and esp. Porter 2012, on the identity of the Amorites. Mitanni: Kuhrt 1995: 283–89, 298.

96. See Spalinger 2005: 8–9, 12–15, and 32–69 on New Kingdom militarism; and also briefly Kuhrt 199: 189–90.

97. Kuhrt 1995: 393–401; cf. also 432 for the Israelites.

98. Barfield 2002: 65; Turchin 2009: 207.

99. Territorial evolution: summaries in Lieberman 2003: 23–31; Lieberman 2009: 12–22. Secular shift: Lieberman 2009: 22–30.

100. Lieberman 2009: 763–894. On horses in Southeast Asia, see Bankoff and Swart 2007, esp. 33, 68 for their size.

101. I am not aware of academic comparisons between Roman and Andean state formation. For culture change, see DeMarrais 2005. For a later New World steppe empire (that of the Comanche) sustained by Old World horses, see Hämäläinen 2008.

102. Hoffman 2015: 115 (block quote), 142 ("nomads were China's enemy, for like most big states, China had expanded into areas where nomads lived"), 172 ("different political geographies"), 206–7 (politics vs. geography). He refers in passing to Turchin's "steppe effect" model (115n15) but appears to misunderstand its gist, and notes only casually that "China would have been different without the steppe" (115) without elaborating on this crucial point. The statistics in Ko, Koyama, and Sng 2018: 302–3 show that nomadic attacks on China were not "merely . . . a product of the tendency for the autocratic Chinese state to expand till it bordered the steppe and encountered conflicts with the nomads."

103. Lieberman 2009: 111.

104. Ko, Koyama, and Sng 2018: 292–99, 300–309.

CHAPTER NINE

1. Xigui 2000 is fundamental. See also Boltz 1994; Zhou 2003.

2. See Dong 2014 for a recent account.

3. Chiang et al. 2017, esp. fig. S4.

4. For instance, Lieven 2000: 33–34 and H. Lin 2014: 487–88 consider China's uniform writing system and the lack of vernacular literatures (unlike in Europe) sources of unity. Lieberman 2009: 535–36 holds that the logographic system did not encourage regional identities as much as the phonetic alphabets used in the Roman empire and in South and Southeast Asia. For China's variety within unity, see Moser 1985.

5. MacMullen 1966; Millar 1968; Neumann and Untermann 1980; Adams 2008; Visscher 2011. For the continuing split between governmental Latin and common Greek in the East in the fifth century CE, see Millar 2006: 13–25, 84–97. For the Roman Near East in general, see Millar 1993, esp. 503–4 on the role of Aramaic.

6. Duncan-Jones 1990: 48–59; Scheidel 2014: 26. "In broad terms," the Eastern empire of the fifth century CE "was not only *a* Greek-speaking world, it was *the* Greek-speaking world" (Millar 2006: 15).

7. See the epilogue in this volume.

8. I sidestep the thorny question of the extent to which cultural unity and state formation were in fact meaningfully correlated in premodern societies. In second-millennium-CE India, for example, growing regionalization at the expense of an earlier Sanskrit ecumene, combined with the inflow of Persian and Middle Eastern elements, coincided with the creation of more rather than less powerful empires: Asher and Talbot 2006: 9.

9. "Render": Mark 12.17; also Matthew 22.21; Luke 20.25. This was, however, more accommodating than the Islamic notion that rulers were to be obeyed only in keeping with Allah's command: Rubin 2017: 52–53.

10. Very briefly, e.g., Mitterauer 2003: 177–78; Drake 2007: 412–17; Gwynn 2012: 878–87. Gelasius: Letter 8, "To the Emperor Anastasius" (PL 59:42AB); and Dagron 2003: 295–306 on the "two powers" theory. See the epilogue in this volume. When the Constantinopolitan patriarch Nicholas I excommunicated the Byzantine emperor Leo VI for entering a fourth marriage,

he was dismissed and kept in exile until Leo's death: Tougher 1997: 156–63. The contrast to Ambrose or papal activities in the High Middle Ages is instructive.

11. See chapters 5 and 10 in this volume. Papal detachment: Mitterauer 2003: 153.

12. Mitterauer 2003: 178; Angelov and Herrin 2012: 151–52, 166–69. For the complexities underneath the surface, see Dagron 2003, esp. 282–95 on the concept of "Caesaropapism," and 309–10 for the hybrid (political-religious) character of the patriarchate.

13. For this counterfactual, see J. Hall 1985: 135. Cf. also Hoffman 2015: 174 for the notion that a more enduring Frankish empire would have managed to suppress the papacy. See Goldstone 2009: 40–41; Hoffman 2015: 133 for the pliant Eastern Church. Causation: *contra* Hoffman 2015: 134 ("western Christianity and cultural evolution are the ultimate cause behind Europe's fragmentation"). Hoffman's judgment runs counter to his own emphasis on the primacy of political history.

14. Berkey 2003: 12 (Muslim majority in Egypt by the tenth century); O'Sullivan 2006: 74–78 (Muslim majorities in Egypt by the ninth century and larger ones in Iran by the tenth century and in Anatolia by the sixteenth).

15. Lieven 2000: 35 claims that the expansion of Islam and resultant division between Christendom and Islam "undermined this possibility of empire renewed." It might be more sensible to think of this as a coincidence than a causal relationship. As noted in chapter 6 of this volume, by the time of the Ottoman expansion, deepened European commitment to Christianity may have mattered more.

16. Origins: M. Lewis 2009a: 162, 19, 204–12. Patronage: M. Lewis 2009a: 113, 205.

17. Janousch 1999; M. Lewis 2009a: 206. Potential: Pines 2012: 61.

18. M. Lewis 2009a: 207; Pines 2012: 61.

19. M. Lewis 2009a: 208.

20. M. Lewis 2009b: 214–17 (quote: 215); Gernet 1995: 5–43, esp. 7–12, 39–40.

21. Pearce 1987: 700–703.

22. Weinstein 1987: 114–36 (suppression), 136–44 (restoration).

23. Zhao 2015a: 13–14, 274–93.

24. Zhao 2015a: 280, 293 (quotes). See also M. Lewis 2009a: 206. Legalism: Fu 1996.

25. Zhao 2015a: 297–313. Neo-Confucianism: Bol 2008. See Chaffee 1995 for the Song examination system, and Elman 2000 for later dynasties.

26. Pines 2000, esp. 282, and Pines 2009, esp. 220, for the Warring States; and Pines 2012 for the whole of Chinese history.

27. Pines 2012: 16–19. Mair 2005: 50 attacks teleological acceptance of ancient texts that think in terms of Chinese unity early on, possibly as the result of later redactions.

28. Pines 2012: 33 (limited horizons). Pines 2012: 4 (quote), 37–41 (nomadic rule). But note that both Levine 2013: 576 and Wang 2014 criticize Pines's neglect of evidence regarding the most momentous regeneration events, the Sui and Northern Song unifications. Note also that it was possible, during the divisions of the third and fourth centuries CE, to write "against the state" (Declercq 1998).

29. Quote: *Mengzi* "Wan Zhang A" 9.4:215, in Pines 2012: 31, with 189n43. God: Pines 2012: 58, and 44–75 on the monarch in general. Contrast Loewe 2014: 336 for trenchant criticism of the analogy.

30. Pines 2012: 85–92 (homogenization attempts), 101 (gentry longevity).

31. Thus, cogently, Pines 2012: 6–7.

32. See Levine 2013: 576 for some of these points.

33. Pines 2012: 3, 8 (other factors), 11 (quotes). As I understand it, Pines 2000: 321–24 obliquely suggests that state formation in the Warring States period was driven by the ideological imperative of unity.

34. Pines 2012: 11 (quote).

35. Pines 2000: 282 (quote).

36. Pines 2012: 19. I leave aside the question of whether elite authors whose writings survived into the unity phase can be called "everybody."

37. Pines 2012: 31 (quote), 11 (quote from *Romance of the Three Kingdoms*).

38. Pines 2012: 42 (quote), 43 (state system).

39. Pines 2012: 103 (quote).

40. Contribution: Pines 2009: 222.

41. Comparanda: Stoicism in the Roman empire did not fulfill this role (cf. Shaw 1985); Christianity transcended empire; and for later notions, see chapter 6 in this volume.

42. Hoffman 2015: 120–32 (Europe), 144–45 (China). See also Wickham 2016: 12, 232.

43. Lorge 2005: 9 (quote).

44. Levine 2013: 577 (quote), and see also 575 ("one wonders . . . whether Pines is looking in the right place for an explanation of the longevity of the imperial project . . . [he] does not rigorously distinguish between political imaginaries and state capacities"). See also de Crespigny 2012 ("this fact of geography [i.e., the dominance of the North China plain], rather than any philosophical approach, explains much of China's continuing capacity for reunification"), echoed by Lin 2014: 488.

45. For the last points, see Lieberman 2009: 743.

46. Spread of ecumene: Pollock 2006. Ethnic loyalty: Lieberman 2009: 105. One should add, though, that the same happened in Russia in opposition to steppe encroachment: and imperialism was possible, in this rare case, by displacing existing cultures.

CHAPTER TEN

1. For surveys of the debate, see the introduction in this volume. I remain unconvinced by— and offer this book as a response to—what we might call "short-termist" scholarship (often labeled the "California school," a term coined by Goldstone 2000: 179 that ascribes divergence and modernity to fairly recent and putatively contingent factors [e.g., Goldstone 2000; Pomeranz 2000; Marks 2002]). This puts me in good company, such as North and Thomas 1973; Baechler 1975; Chirot 1985; J. Hall 1985, 1988; Qian 1985; Sivin 1991; Soucek 1994; Landes 1998: 29–44; Deng 1999; Huang 2002; Huff 2003; E. Jones 2003, esp. 225–38; Landes 2003: 12–39; Mitterauer 2003: 274–96; Bayly 2004: 81–82; Bryant 2006: 409–18; Mann 2006: 380–83; G. Clark 2007; Findlay and O'Rourke 2007, esp. 362; Mielants 2007: 154–62; Mokyr 2007; Bryant 2008; Cosandey 2008: 175–316; Elvin 2008; van Zanden 2009a; Appleby 2010: 14; Duchesne 2011; Huff 2011: 301–19; Rosenthal and Wong 2011, most explicitly 8; O'Brien 2012b; Voigtländer and Voth 2013a, 2013b; Vries 2013, e.g., 50–51, 57, 434–35; Hoffman 2015: 213–14; Studer 2015; Zhao 2015a: 349–70; Gupta, Ma, and Roy 2016; Karayalcin 2016; Broadberry, Guan, and Li 2017; Greif and Tabellini 2017: 32; Mokyr 2017; Roeck 2017: 24–26; Rubin 2017, esp. 212; Ko, Koyama, and Sng

2018; Wrigley 2018: 41. Moreover, as I argue in chapter 11 of this volume, the role that New World resources—one of the short-termists' principal "contingencies"—may have played in Europe's ascent was itself a result of the long-term dynamics of European polycentrism.

2. Quotes: Montesquieu 1750 [1748]: 385 (*De L'Esprit des Lois*, book XVII, ch. VI); Kant 1903 [1795]: 155 (*Zum ewigen Frieden, Erster Anhang*).

3. Mao Zedong as quoted in Moser 1985: 136.

4. For the concept of the "capstone" state, see J. Hall 1985: 52 ("Its concern was less with intensifying social relationships than in seeking to prevent any linkages which might diminish its power") and J. Hall 1996: 35, 42–43, followed by Crone 2003: 57 (quote).

5. This contrast has a long pedigree: the best and most detailed comparisons can be found in Rosenthal and Wong 2011 and Vries 2015. See also J. Hall 1985: 33–57; Wong 1997: 142–49; Pomeranz 2000; E. Jones 2003, esp. 202–22; Landes 2006; Arrighi 2007; Mielants 2007: 47–85; Ringmar 2007: 275–89; O'Brien 2012b; Vries 2013: 401–8; Zhao 2015a: 357–70; and more generally I. Morris 2010.

6. In keeping with the focus of this book, I consciously and deliberately privilege social science literature that explicitly engages with the questions of developmental divergence rather than with the gigantic specialized scholarship on the history of the institutions I refer to. What will be lost in nuance should be offset by that focus.

7. Vries 2002: 126 (quotes); E. Jones 2003: 104. Vries himself attempts to do so in Vries 2015. The section subheading is a play on the idea of the "long march through the institutions" promoted by German student activist Rudi Dutschke after 1968, envisioned as a process of subverting state and society from within. This did not in fact create conditions for revolution; Dutschke himself died of long-term health complications caused by an assassination attempt.

8. Bosker, Buringh, and van Zanden 2013: 1425 (hubs); Dalgaard et al. 2018 (various persistence metrics in Roman Europe); and especially Wahl 2017, who carefully argues for (a small degree of) higher contemporary development (proxied by luminosity) in southwestern Germany on the Roman side of the *limes* associated with the Roman road network and its later effect on urbanism. For the difference between urban locations in post-Roman England and France, see Michaels and Rauch 2018.

9. Reforming of the papacy: see, e.g., C. Morris 1989: 79–108; briefly Mitterauer 2003: 157–60; Cushing 2005, esp. 55–90; van Zanden 2009a: 46–47; Wickham 2016: 113–17. Investiture: C. Morris 1989: 154–73, 527–28.

10. See, e.g., Wickham 2016: 141–42.

11. Van Zanden 2009a: 43–44.

12. See chapter 5 in this volume.

13. Thus also J. Hall 1996: 48: "The church did [the] most to make empire impossible."

14. C. Morris 1989: 582; Wickham 2016: 212–13, 256; see also chapter 6 in this volume.

15. Wickham 2017 provides an incisive comparative survey (quotes: 391–92); also briefly Wickham 2016: 33–34.

16. Wickham 2017: 397–424. See also Barnwell and Mostert 2003, esp. Barnwell 2003; Mitterauer 2003: 137–39; Reuter 2018; and Roach 2013 specifically for Anglo-Saxon England (to which I will return).

17. Mitterauer 2003: 137–40.

18. Ibid., 141–47. Rise of taxation and its consequences: Watts 2009: 224–33.

19. Watts 2009: 233–38; Maddicott 2010: 377–78; van Zanden, Buringh, and Bosker 2012: 837–39.

20. Duchesne 2011: 481–88; Maddicott 2010: 378.

21. Van Zanden, Buringh, and Bosker 2012: 840–44 (spread), 846 (access), 847 (communes). See Hébert 2014 for a survey of late medieval parliamentarianism across Western Europe.

22. Quote: Duchesne 2011: 484.

23. Mitterauer 2003: 149–51; van Zanden, Buringh, and Bosker 2012: 848–49.

24. Van Zanden 2009a: 50–51; Greif and Tabellini 2017: 15–16, also for the dominance of corporate bodies in high medieval Europe. Cf. also Mitterauer 2003: 284–87. Specifically for Italy, see Tabacco 1989: 182–236; Jones 1997; Menant 2005; and Wickham 2015, esp. 15–16, 196–204. See also chapter 5 in this volume.

25. Van Zanden 2009a: 52–55, 65–66, 68.

26. Ibid., 295–96; Greif and Tabellini 2017: 3, 32.

27. Chronology: Stasavage 2014: 344–45. For the city-states of Europe in general, see Hansen 2000a; Parker 2004: Scott 2012.

28. Stasavage 2011: 94–109, esp. 104 for 59 percent probability of urban autonomy within 100 kilometers from the line to 39 percent and merely 13 percent within 250 and 500 kilometers, respectively. See chapter 5 in this volume. For Italy, see the references in note 24 above.

29. Stasavage 2014: 337–41. See now Ogilvie 2019, the most detailed analysis of the economic impact of guilds, which came out too late to be considered here.

30. Blockmans 1994: 244–45; Spruyt 1994, esp. 184–85; Mielants 2007: 83–84, 155.

31. Mielants 2007: 160 (quote); see also chapter 11 in this volume.

32. Stasavage 2011: 51–53, following Blockmans's work.

33. Stasavage 2010, esp. 626–27.

34. Stasavage 2011: 58, 63.

35. Bosker, Buringh, and van Zanden 2013: 1432–34; Cox 2017: 744–46.

36. Stasavage 2003: 51–67; Stasavage 2011: 1–2, 31–32, 39–41. For the concurrently growing sophistication of the banking system in the Italian communes, see Menant 2005: 304–12.

37. Stasavage 2011: 3–4, 150–54. Tracy 1985 is a classic account of the Dutch financial revolution.

38. See Mackil 2015 for public debt in ancient Greek city-states and leagues. Empires: see later in this chapter, on China.

39. See briefly Wickham 2016: 143, 145–46, 218–19.

40. See, e.g., Mitterauer 2003: 148; Hoffman 2015: 120–32 (martial ethos).

41. Quote: J. Hall 1988: 37–38.

42. Rosenthal and Wong 2011: 101–5, 115–19; Hoffman 2015: 210–11; Dincecco and Onorato 2018, esp. 9–10, 33–49, 52, 59, 75, superseding Dincecco and Onorato 2016.

43. For criticism of the "safe harbor" model, see Vries 2013: 184–86.

44. Van Zanden 2009a: 39–41 (cities), and 69–91 and Buringh and van Zanden 2009: 419 on medieval book production. Exit: J. Hall 1985: 139; J. Hall 1988: 35; J. Hall 1996: 56 (state system with a "built-in escape system").

45. Quotes: Landes 1998: 38; E. Jones 2003: 118. Karayalcin 2008: 977–85 for a model, and 985–91 for supporting evidence; likewise Chu 2010, esp. 182.

46. E. Jones 2003: 233.

47. J. Hall 1985: 126–28; van Bavel, Buringh, and Dijkman 2018: 47.

48. Cox 2017: 726–29, who shows that tolls on fixed Ottoman caravan routes were much higher than on flexible English trade routes.

49. Mann 1986: 376–77 (quote: 376).

50. This last feature prompts Baechler 1975: 77 to observe that "the expansion of capitalism owes its origins and its raison d'être to political anarchy" (quote italicized in original).

51. Van Zanden 2009a: 48–49. My specifications in italics add much-needed precision to his own underlying trifecta (49). For the difference between despotic and infrastructural power, see Mann 1984. Unlike traditional emperors, medieval rulers were "hemmed in by what Stephan Epstein has aptly called "freedoms," a host of particularistic privileges that limited the prince's capacity to tax, to regulate the economy, and to provide public goods" (quote from Rosenthal and Wong 2011: 25). As Wickham 2016: 240 stresses, "Any successful ruler had to and did negotiate with the different types of community which made up his or her realm."

52. See J. Hall 1996: 35 for the distinction between "capstone" state (strong in arbitrary power but weak in penetrating society) and "organic" state (less despotic but with greater reach into social relations).

53. Watts 2009: 424; Wickham 2016, esp. 99, 109, 160–61.

54. Watts 2009: 421; Wickham 2016: 236–38, 243, 256 (quote).

55. Wickham 2016: 233 (pathways). Variation: J. Hall 1985: 136–37, 142; also J. Hall 1988: 33–34, esp. 33: "Why should an imperial Europe have been any different" from conventional capstone empires? For counterfactuals, see chapter 6 in this volume.

56. For the severity of the collapse, see Wickham 2005: 306–14; Fleming 2010: 22–29. The section title is a quote from Gildas, *On the Ruin and Conquest of Britain*, ch. 3 (sixth century CE).

57. A. Williams 1999: 1–21, 33–36, 54, 88–89; Fleming 2010: 270–74; Wickham 2016: 83–87. For the timing of cohesion-enhancing reform in the late tenth century, see Molyneaux 2015.

58. Maddicott 2010: 1–56; Roach 2013, esp. 44, 77–160, 212, 235–38 (quote: 238); Wickham 2017: 415–18. There is no need to assume that this format had been imported from Carolingian France: Wickham 2016: 89 and 2017: 416 *contra* Maddicott 2010: 31–32.

59. For these developments since the tenth century, see Maddicott 2010, esp. 57, 64–65, 102–4, 119, 136–40, 382–86, 393, 407–8, 413–31, 435–37, 440–53 (quote: 452). Genesis of gentry: Coss 2003. Wickham 2016: 88–89, 100 stresses the importance of England's modest size, comparable to that of a large German duchy, and the aristocratic cohesion this facilitated. Fukuyama 2011: 428–31 offers a valuable comparative perspective.

To be sure, English state-building did not follow a smooth or linear path: opposition to royal power caused taxation to decline after the Hundred Years' War, and after 1455 conflict among aristocrats and Parliament resulted in civil war. Yet even when the elites fought, they remained committed to the state instead of relinquishing their status as "co-participants in government." Thus Wickham 2016: 219–20 (quote: 219), who (233) emphasizes the importance of "oligarchic involvement in policy-making and a tradition of justice based on assemblies which went back to the early middle ages without a break, the only example of this among the more powerful polities of the period." Scandinavian polities, which shared these traits, were comparatively weak.

60. Ertman 1997, esp. 34, 88–89, 163, 168–69, 318–19.

61. Tilly 1992: 72; Voigtländer and Voth 2013a: 174, 180 (wars); Dincecco and Onorato 2018: 19–30, esp. 27–29 (122 conflict events in the sixteenth century, 164 in the seventeenth, and 323 in the eighteenth), and 78, fig. 5.1 for their spatial concentration in northern France, the Low Countries, southwestern Germany, northern Italy, Scotland, and Poland, followed by southern England and the remainder of Germany.

62. Hoffman 2015: 15–18, 29–34 (progressive nature), 49–63 (model). The chronology of these specifications remains somewhat opaque: some additional requirements that I omit here (such as high cost of warfare and low variable costs) may have been more recent developments that did not predate the seventeenth century or so. For the relationship between European war-making and state-making, see esp. Tilly 1992 alongside B. Porter 1994; Spruyt 1994; Ertman 1997; Glete 2002.

63. Vries 2015: 276–81 offers a concise and useful summary. This growth was a more gradual process than the "military revolution" envisioned by Parker 1996, but the overall result was dramatic. Black 2002 covers the early stages. State system and innovation: see, e.g., E. Jones 2003: 118–19, 124–25; Bayly 2004: 81. See I. Morris 2014: 165–234 for the nature of war in and beyond Europe from 1415 to 1914, which he labels "productive war."

64. For the rise of the fiscal-military state, see esp. Bonney 1995; Glete 2002; Cavaciocchi 2008; Yun-Casalilla and O'Brien 2012. Competition: Rosenthal and Wong 2011: 178–79; B. Porter 1994: 111 (quote).

65. Tax rates from Karaman and Pamuk 2010: 611, fig. 5 and 615, fig. 6. Dutch rates doubled in real terms and tripled in silver terms between 1600 and the 1780s. Budgets: Rosenthal and Wong 2011: 181.

66. Karaman and Pamuk 2010: 611, fig. 5 and 623, fig. 9. In the early eighteenth century, Venice ranked third.

67. Rosenthal and Wong 2011: 173–78, 185, 193, 197–98.

68. Damage: De Long 2000: 150–57. Finance: Rosenthal and Wong 2011: 140–48.

69. O'Brien 2012b: 545–47.

70. See, e.g., Ringmar 2007: 170; Goldstone 2009: 97–119, who cites England as the only exception (see below); Dincecco 2011.

71. For the concept of the "North Sea region"—centered on the Netherlands and Britain—see van Zanden 2009a: 233–66.

72. I am grateful to Şevket Pamuk for sharing these data with me. Pamuk 2007: 297, fig. 2, also shows the preceding plague-induced improvements; see Scheidel 2017: 293–313 for a recent overview. The "continental Europe" sample is based on data from Paris, Strasbourg, Augsburg, Milan, Valencia, Vienna, and Kraków, which provide the longest relevant time series. Trends were very similar for skilled urban workers: Pamuk 2007: 297, fig. 3. "Welfare ratios" are determined by relating nominal wages to stylized consumption baskets.

73. The "Continental Europe" metric is based on data from France, Germany, Italy, Spain, Portugal, and Sweden. For similar comparisons over an even longer term, see Broadberry et al. 2015: 423 fig.11.05.

74. In figure 10.4, the "English share" metric covers the half centuries before the stated dates.

75. For England/Great Britain, see also Broadberry et al. 2015: 410–11.

76. Cf. similarly Allen 2003: 415, table 2.

77. For the Little Divergence, see chapter 7 in this volume. The best accounts of the pioneers are De Vries and van der Woude 1997 (Netherlands) and Broadberry et al. 2015 (Britain). With respect to other proxies of improved access to financial and human capital and of commercial integration, such as falling interest rates, skill premiums, and price variability, Europe more generally had scored well compared to other parts of the world from the Late Middle Ages onward: see esp. van Zanden 2009a: 17–31 and van Zanden 2009b.

78. Van Zanden 2009a: 262 (legacy), 296 (quote), and 203–66 for the underlying dynamics in general. Specifically for the benefits of the Reformation, see chapter 12 in this volume. Advantages: Downing 1992, esp. 239–42 for comparative analysis.

79. De Long and Shleifer 1993, esp. 689–90, 697; Acemoglu, Johnson, and Robinson 2005: 562–63, 569–72; Findlay and O'Rourke 2007: 351; van Zanden 2009a: 263, 291–93.

80. Van Zanden, Buringh, and Bosker 2012: 840–44, esp. 843, fig. 4 (trends), 849–52 (conflicts), 852–58 (economic effects). Stasavage (in press) tracks the evolution of democratic institutions over the very long run: see esp. ch.5, on medieval Europe.

81. For Dutch innovations, see North and Thomas 1973: 132–45, esp. 134–35, 139–42. De Vries and van der Woude 1997 is the classic account of the early modern Dutch economy. Traditions: van Zanden 2009a: 207–10. National citizenship: Mielants 2007: 156.

82. Growth: van Zanden 2009a: 215–26. (Contrast Philip II's multiple defaults: Drelichman and Voth 2014.) Association: Voigtländer and Voth 2013a: 177–79, esp. 179, fig. 4: this correlation for Europe overall (from 1300 to 1700 for urbanization and from 1500 to 1700 for GDP) is driven above all by the Dutch data, and the trend more or less disappears when the Netherlands and England are excluded: see 179, fig. 4B. Cf. Voigtländer and Voth 2013b: 806, fig. 10 for a somewhat different but fundamentally similar depiction of trends.

83. See, e.g., Magnusson 2009: 19–25. Dutch cities: t'Hart 1994: 211–12. For Dutch influence on British development more generally, see Jardine 2008.

84. See, e.g., Macfarlane 1988: 192, 201–2. The caption quotes A. Smith 1776: 221.

85. Goldstone 2009: 110–11.

86. See, e.g., Neal 1990: 10–12; Landes 1998: 223. For the role of Huguenots in later British development, see most recently Beaudreau 2018.

87. Kelly, Mokyr, and Ó Gráda 2014: 369–84 emphasize these factors, which in their view generated high real wages rather than being their result (*contra* Allen 2009b: see chapter 12 in this volume).

88. Van Zanden 2009a: 228–29; Johnson and Koyama 2017: 3–6.

89. Angelucci, Meraglia, and Voigtländer 2017.

90. E. Jones 2010: 244; O'Brien 2011: 426; Acemoglu and Robinson 2012: 209–11.

91. See, e.g., Acemoglu, Johnson, and Robinson 2005: 563–66; Acemoglu and Robinson 2012: 208.

92. North and Weingast 1989, esp. 805, 821–27.

93. Cox 2012, esp. 568, 594, 596. Cf. also Vries 2013: 325–27 for criticism of the widespread academic focus on 1688 in relation to property rights. Quote: North and Thomas 1973: 155–56.

94. Van Zanden, Buringh, and Bosker 2012: 844, fig. 5; Pincus and Robinson 2014, esp. 201–22; Hoppit 2017: 308–9.

95. Bogart and Richardson 2011; Hoppit 2017: 318–19, 322–33; and chapter 12 in this volume.

96. Hoppit 2017: 310, 312, 320.

97. Ibid., 312 (quote); Mokyr and Nye 2007: 60–61.

98. Bogart and Richardson 2011: 270.

99. North and Thomas 1973: 146–56, esp. 155–56; and earlier North and Thomas 1970, as well as North 1981: 164–67. Appleby 2010: 13 (quote), where she also notes that only England succeeded in "sustaining innovation through successive stages of development." Epstein 2000: 37, 173–74. During the seventeenth and eighteenth centuries, economic intercity competition—driven by growing urban density and falling distance to consumers in other cities—became so strong that guilds no longer resisted innovation: Desmet, Greif, and Parente 2017.

100. See, e.g., O'Brien 2011: 428–30; Vries 2015: 69–179, esp. 121, 164, 175–78, with a comparison to low-tax China (more on this later in this chapter).

101. Vries 2015: 181–217, esp. 184, 187, 207, 210–11.

102. He 2013: 63–77; Vries 2015: 219–22, 228–29. Brewer 1988 is a classic account of the relationship between warfare, taxation, public debt, and financial innovation. Much the same was true of the Netherlands, which had pioneered large-scale public debt by building on (much more modest) medieval Italian precedent: in the seventeenth and eighteenth centuries, debt rose while interest rates fell, and more than a tenth of Dutch households invested in the war against Spain: Vries 2015: 224 (65,000 individuals out of a population of 2 million).

103. Bayly 2004: 62–63; Goldstone 2009: 114. For the role of credible commitments, see esp. Coffman, Leonard, and Neal 2013. This had deep roots: in the late Middle Ages, English kings had come to depend on credit from domestic capital, which could only be accessed if political support was granted: Grummitt and Lassalmonie 2015: 135–37.

104. Vries 2015: 282–89, 321.

105. Brewer 1988: 34–35; Vries 2013: 236–39.

106. For the more general issue of the relationship between state capacity and modern economic growth, see the survey by Johnson and Koyama 2017: 8–12.

107. Findlay and O'Rourke 2007: 352; Vries 2015: 314–35.

108. Hoffman 2015: 210; and see chapter 12 in this volume on Allen's model.

109. "Mercantilist states were warfare states rather than welfare states": Vries 2015: 332. For the system, Vries 2015: 325–47.

110. Thus Magnusson 2009: 26–50, esp. 45–49. See in general Ormrod 2003 for mercantilism in the Netherlands and Britain. See also Reinert 2011 for the creation of political economy as a science in the eighteenth century. Nevertheless, as Hoppit 2017 reminds us, the cohesiveness even of English policymaking should not be overrated.

111. O'Brien 2011: 439; Mokyr and Nye 2007, esp. 55–60 (quote: 58–59).

112. Jha 2015.

113. Vries 2015: 344–46, 433.

114. Ibid., 339–44.

115. Parthasarathi 2011: 125–35. The Indian textile export industry was duly ruined in the nineteenth century (223–62). For medieval protections, see chapter 12 in this volume. Textile machinery could not legally be exported until 1843, even if enforcement proved unfeasible.

116. Parthasarathi 2011: 164–68; O'Brien 2017: 50–54. Real prices: Allen 2009b: 87, fig. 4.3, also 95, fig. 4.4.

117. Parthasarathi 2011: 168–70.

118. Magnusson 2009, esp. 8, 85–86; Vries 2012: 654–61 (656 and 660 for the simile of the crutch, borrowing from Herbert Norman).

119. An important point made by Vries 2013: 418–19. For the Industrious Revolution, see chapter 11 in this volume.

120. Heavy hand: thus Vries 2013: 336, also 433–34; and in great depth Vries 2015. Mobilization: Vries 2015: 317–18.

121. O'Brien 2017: 19–58, and 79: "My rhetorical and debateable [*sic*] perception is that in significant respects the First Industrial Revolution can be plausibly represented as the paradigm example of successful mercantilism and that the unintended consequences of the Revolution in France contributed positively and perhaps 'substantially' to its ultimate consolidation and progression." Patenting: Billington 2018.

122. Satia 2018: 147–61 is the latest summary.

123. Vries 2015: 409–13 (quote: 413); E. Jones 2003: 234 (question).

124. E. Jones 2003: 235 (quote).

125. War: Rosenthal and Wong 2011: 185. For the costs and benefits of colonial empire, see chapter 11 in this volume. By-product: Rosenthal and Wong 2011: 225–30 (for war-induced policies yielding "unanticipated positive conditions for economic change" [230]), who stress the contrast to China, where, as we will see later in this chapter, benign policies were pursued that did not similarly stimulate development. Vries 2013: 382 follows their assessment.

126. Vries 2015: 435.

127. Ibid., 434–36.

128. Cf. also de Long 2000: 158–65 for another summary.

129. From this perspective, it makes little sense to ask whether the onset of industrialization was a British or a European phenomenon (e.g., Pomeranz 2000: 6): it was both.

130. Bayly 2004: 82 (quote). Cf. also E. Jones 2003: 127–49.

131. Vries 2013: 358–79 is fundamental. Intervention and its roots: Vries 2013: 381 and most clearly 382: "Competition and the way it was institutionalized in all its varieties *in the end*, in my view, were fundamental to the rise of the West."

132. Quote: Vries 2013: 434–35. Van Zanden 2009a: 15–91, esp. 31 and also 294, stresses the medieval foundations of later North Sea region development.

133. Institutions and modernity: Ringmar 2007: 34, 38 (quote); Vries 2013: 319. Experiments: Ringmar 2007: 289: "If one European society temporarily stagnated, there would be elsewhere in Europe another society that continued to change." Ringmar 2007: 38 (quote).

134. Ringmar 2007: 283–89, esp. 287; Vries 2013: 336. For a complementary perspective, see also North, Wallis, and Weingast 2009: 240–50.

135. Quotes: Bryant 2006: 407–8 (italicized in original); Wong 1997: 151; see also Baechler 1975: 114.

136. Vries 2013: 318–22 considers institutions the ultimate cause of transformation; see also 429–35. Cf. chapter 8 in this volume. Hoffman's 2015: 213 conclusion that "political history is then one of the ultimate causes behind both the European conquest of the world and the 'great divergence'" applies (only) in this very broad sense.

137. The quote in the section heading is from line 29 of the Mount Yi inscription honoring Qin unification, supposedly dating from 219 BCE (Kern 2000: 12–13).

138. Lists: see, e.g., Landes 2006. E. Jones 2003: 153–222 is perhaps the most massive recent indictment of Asian empires and their economies (quote: 231); for even more blatant Orientalizing, see 110: "Excessive consumption and debauchery and terror were much more prevalent in the empires of Asia and the Ancient World than in the states of Europe."

139. Criticism: Parthasarathi 2011: 53–55; Rosenthal and Wong 2011: 167–68 (quote: 168); Vries 2013: 59; Brandt, Ma, and Rawski 2014: 59–61.

140. Pines 2012: 107 deems it "highly significant that during the formative stage of Chinese political thought and political culture, no powerful independent elite existed on Chinese soil."

141. See Zhao 2015a: 11–16 for a summary of the argument, and esp. 274–93 for the rise of the Confucian-Legalist state. Arrighi 2007: 318 also notes that political, economic, and cultural power was much more concentrated in East Asia than in Europe. See, furthermore, Pines 2012: 76–103 on the literati class, esp. 89, and 101 on the absence of divisions between spiritual and political authority.

142. Zhao 2015a: 18 (quote): spatial and temporal variations in Chinese history "do not fundamentally challenge the historical patterns based on comparisons between different historical periods of China and between Chinese and other major civilizations."

143. Revival and characteristics: Bol 1992; Pines 2012: 102, 113–14; Zhao 2015a: 331–46. Bol 2008 is fundamental for our understanding of neo-Confucianism since the Song.

144. Arrighi 2007: 333 (quote). See Zhao 2015a: 348 on merchants' inability to "counterbalance the state negativity" due to the "*higher-order* structural condition" of the political-ideological system. See also Chen 2012: 58 for merchants as a politically disadvantaged group; and likewise Vries 2015: 358.

145. Zhao 2015a: 369–70.

146. Brandt, Ma, and Rawski 2014: 61–80 on China's political economy, see 64–66.

147. Ibid., 66–75 (quote: 75).

148. Ibid., 75–76.

149. Ibid., 76–80 for this summary and quotes.

150. Wong 1997: 281–83 (quotes). See also Rosenthal and Wong 2011: 212–13.

151. Baechler 1975: 82. See also Ringmar 2007: 269–73 and, if very superficially, Hui 2015: 20–22.

152. See chapters 7 and 12 in this volume. Desirability: Fu 1996: 39–40. For economic development in this period, see von Glahn 2016: 44–83.

153. Von Glahn 2016: 85, 96, 118.

154. S. Liu 2001; von Glahn 2016: 160, 227 (quote), 232.

155. W. Liu 2015b: 51; von Glahn 2016: 214.

156. G. Wang 1990: 402–3; Clark 2009: 177–78, 191–93.

157. Von Glahn 2016: 229. For the concept of a state system and its applicability to China, see chapter 7 in this volume. The counterfactual developed by Yates 2006, which supposes further Song advances after victory over the Xi Xia in the 1080s, runs counter to the logic of competitive pressures: greater military successes might well have reduced the incentive for further development. Hoffman 2015: 175 raises a similar objection.

158. W. Liu 2015b: 53–57. For the late Tang/Song economic transition in general, see von Glahn 2016: 208–554.

159. W. Liu 2015b: 67–72 (quote: 73, on the mid-eighth through mid-tenth centuries).

160. See chapter 8 in this volume.

161. Arrighi 2007: 314–21; Hoffman 2015: 70, 74–75, and in general 69–81 on the differences between Chinese and European styles of war.

162. Qing martial culture: Waley-Cohen 2006. See Perdue 2005 for their subjugation of the steppe, noting (549) that the end of expansion in the mid-eighteenth century "meant that both the incentives for innovation and the means of control slackened." Andrade 2016 makes a similar case. See also Lorge 2005: 158–74 for the Qing victories between 1684 and 1795. Military participation decreased as a share of population: Lorge 2005: 183. Shift after 1368: I. Morris 2014: 176. Retardation: Hoffman 2015: 71, 79–81.

163. Von Glahn 2016: 285–93.

164. See von Glahn 2016: 293–94 for this contrast (quote: 293).

165. W. Liu 2015a: chs. 3, 5, and 6.

166. W. Liu 2015a: 106–13, 119, 195, 199–200; von Glahn 2016: 286.

167. Von Glahn 2016: 289 (quote).

168. W. Liu 2015a: 134 finds that by the late nineteenth century, real per capita income was lower (in terms of rice) than it had been 800 years earlier, and about the same in silver terms. By contrast, Broadberry, Guan, and Li 2017 doubt a Song peak but observe a decline after 1700. See von Glahn 2016: 354–58 for critical discussion.

169. See chapter 11 in this volume.

170. Elvin 1973: 217–18.

171. Levathes 1994: 174–75; Elvin 1973: 218, 224–25. Japan was able to pursue similar policies because it did not face any serious international security threats.

172. Elvin 1973: 219, 222 (quote), 224; Deng 1997: 88–93; Mielants 2007: 66; Vries 2015: 354.

173. Elvin 1973: 292.

174. So 2000: 227–52 on formal constraints (quote: 251), and 253–79 on informal constraints.

175. Lack of support: Deng 1999: 210 (also for the term "state-pulled"). Empires: Mielants 2007: 111–12.

176. Pomeranz 2000: 173 (quote); Vries 2002: 87; 2015: 349–51, 356–57.

177. X. Zhang 2010 (Ming); Zhao 2015a: 368 (Qing).

178. For the First Emperor of Qin, see Petersen 1995, who defends the historicity of the tradition (11–12). Proscription: Bodde 1991: 187, and 186–90 for the difference in intensity of persecution in East and West and its putative causes.

179. Vries 2015: 353 (quote), and earlier Vries 2002: 111.

180. On Wang Mang, see Thomsen 1988, esp. 117–40 for his economic reforms.

181. Von Glahn 2016: 236–42; also Bol 1993; Pines 2012: 92.

182. J. Hall 1985: 53; Wong 1997: 144; Vries 2002: 113–14; 2015: 347–48.

183. *Analects* 16.1, quoted from T. Zhang 2017: 267. For revolts, see chapter 8 in this volume.

184. Deng 1999: 122–24 for the model (quote: 122), 128–47 for its origin, 299–324 (Song anomaly).

185. Van Zanden 2009a: 288 contrasts the European path of accelerating commercial development in a fragmented state system with the laissez-faire approach of large empires. Capstone state: J. Hall 1985: 33–57 and 1996: 35–44 on China; also Vries 2015: 414. Cf. in general Crone 2003: 35–80, esp. 56–57. Learning: Rosenthal and Wong 2011: 23: "The history of China before 1350 (from the Qin through the Mongols) can in fact be seen as a long apprenticeship in the strategies of internal rule." Similarly, Pines 2012: 105–33, for the long process of trying out different strategies—from excessive centralization to tolerance of overly powerful aristocracies—from the Qin to the Tang before more stable arrangements emerged in the second millennium.

186. Benign neglect: Ringmar 2007: 286–87; see also Parthasarathi 2011: 170–71 on iron production. Rights: Rosenthal and Wong 2011: 96.

187. Rosenthal and Wong 2011: 151–63 (also 165: "traditional empires do not borrow"); Wong 2012: 365; Vries 2015: 212–13, 233–40.

188. Rosenthal and Wong 2011: 163–65.

189. Levels: Rosenthal and Wong 2011: 173–82, 195. The Qing spent maybe 50 percent of state revenues on war, compared to 70–90 percent in some European states (181–82), and even less as a share of GDP. See also Vries 2015: 183–90. Qing: W. Liu 2015a: 266, table F-4; von Glahn 2016: 314–16 (declining tax rates); Hoffman 2015: 50–51; Vries 2015: 102–3, 121–22; and Ko, Koyama, and Sng 2018: 307 (comparative tax rates); Sng 2014: 108–9; Vries 2015: 138–45 (inefficiencies in collection), 151–58 (corruption).

190. Pines 2012: 131: "The perennial cycle of the government's aggravating impoverishment under any lengthy dynasty clearly related to the elite's ability to shield its wealth by minimizing transfers to the state's coffers." Exceptions: Sng 2014: 123; Deng 2015.

191. Von Glahn 2016: 10, 320 (quotes). Welfare schemes: Parthasarathi 2011: 173–74 thinks that the combination of low tax revenue and massive commitment to a vast and costly granary system left the Qing state unable to intervene in other sectors of the economy.

192. Q. Chen 2012: 46–49. E. Jones 2003: 208 sardonically likens the Chinese elite system to being "allocated hunting-licences subject only to a bag limit and a fee," entitling officials to make money off their charges.

193. Q. Chen 2012: 51–58; and also Ni and Van 2006: 318–23; Karayalcin 2008: 990–91 for high corruption income.

194. Q. Chen 2012: 57–60. See Ni and Van 2006: 323–34 for a model of corruption with detrimental consequences for the economy (also 317n3, 335).

195. Thus Ni and Van 2006: 322–23; Q. Chen 2012: 57. For low state capacity in Qing China, see the recent literature survey by Johnson and Koyama 2017: 6–7.

196. Governmental intent—with regard to economic development—was irrelevant to these outcomes: Rosenthal and Wong 2011: 199–200.

197. Osborne 2004; Zelin 2009.

198. Greif and Tabellini 2017; T. Zhang 2017. Trusts: Zelin 2004: 32–33; and see chapter 12 in this volume.

199. T. Zhang 2017: 196–219 analyzes competing explanations; see esp. 206–10, 212, 218. Greif and Tabellini 2017 likewise acknowledge the centrality of the Song period (14–15), although their own explanation (lower state power coupled with migration: 19) does not mesh well with conditions in this particular period: by Chinese standards, state capacity was unusually high.

200. Von Glahn 2016: 295–347 is the most recent, and insistently optimistic, account. Comparisons: Shiue and Keller 2007, esp. 1205; von Glahn 2016: 346–47.

201. The question of real wages has generated a lot of discussion, but the overall trends are now pretty clear: Broadberry and Gupta 2006, esp. 19; Allen 2009a: 546–49; Allen et al. 2011, esp. 27–28; Li and van Zanden 2012; Broadberry, Guan, and Li 2017, esp. 49. Deng and O'Brien 2016 voice methodological concerns. Capitalistic features: Vries 2002: 117–20; 2013: 340. Integration: von Glahn 2016: 334.

202. Thus Brenner and Isett 2002, in their detailed critique of Pomeranz 2000.

203. Von Glahn 2016: 336–37, 343–45.

204. Zhao 2015a: 353–55.

205. Based on the catalog in Deng 1999: 363–76, the respective intervals were 218 years for the Western Han, 159 years for the Eastern Han, 245 years for the Tang, 159 years for the Northern Song, 80 years for the Yuan (perhaps sped up by foreign rule), 273 years for the Ming, for a mean of 201 years excluding the Yuan (and less with them). The Qing intervals were 151 years (White Lotus) and 207 years (Taiping). For the frequency and pattern of popular revolts, see chapter 8 in this volume. See very briefly J. Hall 1996: 36–38 for the underlying cyclical dynamics.

206. Von Glahn 2016: 347 (quote), also 361: "No new institutions, public or private, were developed to mitigate these pressures." For Britain, see chapter 12 in this volume.

207. See Rosenthal and Wong 2011: 208–27 for an argument that China since 1500 was more geared toward fostering (Smithian) economic growth while Europe benefited from "unanticipated positive conditions for economic change" rooted in the chronic threat of war (esp. 209, 230 [quote]).

208. Pines 2012: 132–33; von Glahn 2016: 385 (quote), 397. The contrast to Japan is striking. For Japan's modernization, see Vries 2020.

209. Quote: Vries 2015: 364.

210. Divergence: Rosenthal and Wong 2011: 9 (quote). Wong 1997: 279–80, 149 (quotes: 280, 149). See also Hall 1985: 56–57; Deng 1999: 3, 15; Vries 2015: 432. Political economy: Wong 1997: 142–49; Brandt, Ma, and Rawski 2014: 61–80.

211. Size: Elvin 1973: 18–20. Quote: J. Hall 1988: 33.

212. Constraints: Vries 2002: 110 (quote); O'Brien 2012a: 451–53. Even in Europe, diverse polities fared less well: O'Brien 2012b: 547. Zones: Lieberman 2009: 110–13.

213. Elvin 1973: 313–14; Vries 2002: 112; Rosenthal and Wong 2011: 99; Vries 2013: 351–54. See also chapter 12 in this volume.

214. R. Huang 1974: 2 (Ming); Wong 1997: 148; Vries 2015: 400, 405–7.

215. For a good survey, see Vries 2002. I disagree with Rosenthal and Wong's (2011) narrow definition of empires as "polities . . . where a central ruler exercised effective authority over a large fraction of a contiguous region," which by their own reckoning excludes not only modern colonial empires but even that of the Ottomans (13). See the Glossary. Shared feature: see, e.g., E. Jones 2003: 161, 171, 228–29. Their earlier history scarcely matters here: any ancient societies, whether in those regions or elsewhere, were a priori unlikely to spawn modern economies.

216. Goldstone 2009: 100–101 badly misses this crucial point when he deems it "a misleading oversimplification to say that from 1500 onward Europe had a system of competing states

whereas Asia had empires without competition" and "wrong to see the major empires as always dominating their neighbors and being free of military competition." This is a straw-man argument that elides fundamental differences between empires at war and an enduring state system.

217. See chapter 8 in this volume.

218. By contrast, the Manchu in China integrated more readily into existing bureaucratic structures: Rosenthal and Wong 2011: 213. This fostered static continuity.

219. Blaydes and Chaney 2013: 16 (quote), 23–24; Crone 1980: 91 (quote), drawing on Ibn Khaldun's vision of the Islamic (conquest) polity as tribal. Crone 1980: 82–91 brilliantly captures the underlying dynamics. See also Fukuyama 2011: 189–213. Durand-Guédy 2010 provides a detailed case study of the relations between Turkic rulers and the local elite of Isfahan in the eleventh and twelfth centuries. While elite wealth and their fiscal capacities mattered greatly, their local politics were repeatedly checked by Turkic intervention. Then the Mongol sack of the city produced a major rupture. All these elements—local elite power, intervention by a military conquest elite, and sporadic exposure to catastrophic violence—were typical of this environment and converged in stymieing inclusive and sustainable institutional development.

220. Crone 2004: 145, 263–64, 276, 395. The Greek libertarian heritage had been lost: democracy was portrayed as abhorrent and the virtuous polity as autocratic (279–81).

221. Vries 2002: 100–104; Hoffman 2015: 147–51; and specifically for the Ottomans, see Karaman and Pamuk 2010, esp. 625 (reform). Parthasarathi's observation (2011: 53–55) that the Mughal state (just as the states of the Ottomans and Qing) did not enjoy extreme power concentration and ruled with the "consent" of multiple powerholders is not nearly as novel as he makes it out to be, flogging as he does the dead horse of Orientalism. It is also untrue that the state systems thesis (as represented in this book) "rests upon an inflated sense of the centralization and administrative and coercive capabilities of imperial states in Asia" (56), even though—as noted earlier—such arguments were admittedly sometimes made in the past: conversely, it focuses on the logic of empire and the developmental benefits of a state system. Parthasarathi's own observation (56–57) that the more the Mughal empire came under pressure in the seventeenth and eighteenth centuries, the greater the impetus for developmental change was, is consistent with these premises. For the intellectual dimension, see chapter 12 in this volume. Studer 2015 discusses lower levels of market integration in India compared to Europe.

222. Compromise: Gupta, Ma, and Roy 2016. Finance: that is the conclusion of O'Brien 2012b, a grand survey of the fiscal systems of Europe, the Mughals, Ottomans, and Ming/Qing (quote: 546).

223. Vries 2002: 88–89, 115; Parthasarathi 2011: 115 (quote), 131–33, 137.

224. See Ko, Koyama, and Sng 2018: 308–9 for the notion of massive demographic contractions in China when empires fell, which is, however, based on arbitrary adjustments of even more dramatic swings suggested by the population registers (308n33): for this problem, see chapter 7 in this volume.

225. Ko, Koyama, and Sng 2018: 310. The argument that Europe's better protection from invasions was beneficial to its economic development is a popular one: see, e.g., Chirot 1985: 182;

J. Hall 1985: 112; P. Kennedy 1987: 17; E. Jones 2003: 36, 227, 233; Landes 2003: 33–34; Findlay and O'Rourke 2007: 360; Mielants 2007: 159. South Asia: Bayly 2004: 61; Mielants 2007: 114–16.

226. Kuran 2011, esp. 110–15, 282–83; but cf. van Bavel, Buringh, and Dijkman 2018: 50. See also Kuran 2011: 281, 291–92 on the limitations of commercial partnerships, and 43–166 on organizational stagnation overall. Not all of these features were meaningfully rooted in imperial rule: see Kuran 2018 for a survey of scholarship on the negative effects of Islam on economic development.

227. Rubin 2017, esp. 12–13, 49–54, 75–118, 203–13; and see chapter 12 in this volume.

228. See the epilogue in this volume.

CHAPTER ELEVEN

1. Wallerstein 1974, 1980, 1989, 2011. For convenience, see the brief summary in Daly 2015: 79–87.

2. See, e.g., Frank 1998: 134, 277.

3. Wallerstein 1989: 131–37; Marks 2002: 156; Goldstone 2009: 58. Scale: Vries 2013: 252n802 (contra, e.g., Marks 2002: 80). Dependence: Inikori 2002: 479. Baltic: O'Brien and Prados de la Escosura 1998: 56.

4. Mediterranean: Inikori 2002: 479. Growth: Acemoglu, Johnson, and Robinson 2005.

5. Allen 2009b: 106–31, esp. 125–28; Palma 2016: 140, 144. See also chapter 12 in this volume.

6. De Vries 2008; Allen and Weisdorf 2011.

7. Inikori 2002: 479–81.

8. Cuenca Esteban 2004: 62–64 (contributions); Inikori 2002: 265–313 (shipping), 314–61 (financial institutions), 362–404 (raw materials and industrial production).

9. Cuenca Esteban 2004: 58 (stimuli), 60 (extra output exported); Inikori 2002: 405–72 (British manufacturing), 477–79 (summary); Findlay and O'Rourke 2007: 345.

10. Inikori 2002: 156–214 (slave-based commodity production), 215–64 (British slave trade), 481 (summary). See also Parthasarathi 2011: 134–35 for West African demand for cotton cloth—in the third quarter of the eighteenth century, about half of British exports went there in exchange for slaves—that spurred technological innovation in the British textile industry: see chapter 10 in this volume.

11. Pomeranz 2000: 264–97.

12. Pomeranz 2000: 275–76; Vries 2013: 296. Total acreage: Overton 1996: 76. Coal: Cuenca Esteban 2004: 55, against the estimate by Pomeranz 2000: 276, that by 1815, coal substitution for timber was worth an extra 6 million–8.5 million hectares. For coal (whose contribution was vital not just for heating but for providing steam power), see chapter 12 in this volume. See also E. Jones 2003: 83–84 for the importance of ghost acreages more generally.

13. See Findlay and O'Rourke 2007: 330–45 for the role of overseas trade in industrialization, esp. 334. For a model of this role that matches historical outcomes, see Findlay and O'Rourke 2007: 339–45. U.S. share of British cotton imports: Olmstead and Rhode 2018: 4, fig. 2.

14. Vries 2013: 253.

15. See Morgan 2000; cf. Vries 2013: 257.

16. O'Brien and Prados de la Escosura 1998: 37–59, esp. 50–54, 58 for Britain; Magnusson 2009: 85 (entrepreneurs).

17. Eltis and Engerman 2000, esp. 124, 141 (Caribbean sugar and the slave trade did not add much value and growth, probably helped industrialization but not more than other factors, and were not essential); Vries 2013: 258–62, on Blackburn 1997: 541. See Blackburn 1997: 509–80 on primitive accumulation and British industrialization; esp. 540–42 for the estimate that profits from the triangular trade could have provided between 20 percent and 35 percent of British gross fixed capital formation in 1770. Profits went to wealthy individuals who saved a higher proportion of their incomes.

18. Goldstone 2009: 67; Vries 2013: 297–98, 301, 303. See, in general, Bryant 2006: 438, who stresses that contingencies are context-dependent, and thus external resources mattered only thanks to "their 'timely activation' by human agents whose technical skills, culturally informed ambitions, and organizational powers had reached an enabling level of development."

19. Pomeranz 2000: 283 (quote). For critiques of Pomeranz, see Vries 2001; Huang 2002; Bryant 2006: 418–35; Duchesne 2011: 117–63; Vries 2013: 290–98. Van Zanden 2009a: 250, 255–56 thinks the role of ghost acreages in overall development was small even in Britain, just as it was in the Netherlands.

20. Access: Beckert 2014: 81. Cf. Belich 2009: 50: American independence did not cause a big rift in transatlantic economic relations. Substitution: Findlay and O'Rourke 2007: 336, 342; Beckert 2014: 255–57; Hanlon 2015: 76–78 (India and Egypt saved the British cotton industry in the 1860s). Cotton quality: Hanlon 2015: 75–76. Only in the 1860s did technological innovation respond to the challenge of processing lower-quality Indian cotton (Hanlon 2015: 81–97). See Olmstead and Rhode 2018 against some of the more sweeping claims regarding modern capitalism's dependence on New World slave labor and other forms of coercion. Endowments: Pomeranz 2000: 277–78. Arguably, higher costs from other sources of cotton could have been borne given that technological change in Britain itself produced the largest benefits: Brenner and Isett 2002: 646. Eastern Europe (Baltic): Pomeranz 2000: 261–63.

21. Ghost acreages explain breakthrough: Pomeranz 2000: 296–97. Vries 2013: 301 somewhat grudgingly concedes that ghost acreages were "a necessary condition at best but never a sufficient one."

22. O'Brien and Prados de la Escosura 1998: 58 (quote), even though they note that British agricultural productivity, coal, and skills mattered (even) more (59): for these factors, see chapter 12 in this volume. Innovation: Findlay and O'Rourke 2007: 338, 343–44. Even Vries 2013: 284 agrees.

23. Inikori 2002: 479 (quote). But Inikori himself stresses the role of complementary factors.

24. See Férnandez-Armesto 2006: 119–20 for this premise.

25. Roller 2006: 22–50, esp. 23–27 for circumnavigation of Africa.

26. Roller 2006: 57–91 (Pytheas), 51 (scholars).

27. Férnandez-Armesto 2006: 43–50.

28. Ibid., 51–59 (Norse), 122–37 (Middle Ages). These endeavors are best understood as analogous rather than homologous to ancient Phoenician and Greek seafaring: the enormous hiatus speaks against potent legacies.

29. Roller 2006: 20–21, 26.

30. Ibid., 112–32, esp. 112–13 (Iuba), 119–22 (Baltic), 123–24 (Britain), 125–27 (rhetoric).

31. See Garza 2014: the Mughal empire acquired naval assets by absorbing existing smaller naval states in Gujarat and Bengal, and employed its navy to fight the Marathas and other regional challengers.

32. Tsai 2001: 113, table 3.1 (census), 114 (land), 119 (canal), 123 (quote from *Mingshi*), 125 (palace); Dreyer 2007: 8 (undercount).

33. Tsai 2001: 201 (ships); Dreyer 2007: 99–134, esp. 105, 112 (ships and personnel). Church 2005 offers a penetrating deconstruction of the tradition regarding ship size.

34. Levathes 1994: 87–153; Tsai 2001: 201–8; Dreyer 2007: 46–97, 150–63.

35. For the expenditure estimate, see Tsai 2001: 121–22; for revenue, see 123.

36. Yield: Tsai 2001: 206; Dreyer 2007: 82, 90.

37. For the fading of the program, see Levathes 1994: 173–81; Dreyer 2007: 166–71. See also Dreyer 2007: 91 (suspension and rescinding), 171 (1436), 172–73 (rival traditions).

38. Tsai 2001: 57–76.

39. Tsai 2001: 123–24, 186–98.

40. Dreyer 2007: 3, 33 (quote from the *Mingshi*); see also 2–4, 28–35 on the purpose of the voyages. Glory: Elvin 1973: 220; Qian 1985: 111–12; Férnandez-Armesto 2006: 109 ("Perhaps because he was a usurper with a lot to prove, China's Yongle emperor was willing to pay almost any price for glory"); Dreyer 2007: 208. Finlay 2000: 296 is more sanguine, contemplating militarization of the tribute trade system and the conversion of Siam and Java into client states as possible objectives. Yet even if true, it is not clear what benefits this would have brought.

41. Not exploration: Finlay 2000: 297–99; Dreyer 2007: 3, 30.

42. Elvin 1973: 220; Levathes 1994: 43, 55; Dreyer 2007: 3, 26. No benefit: Hoffman 2015: 171.

43. Tsai 2001: 179–86 (Annam), 148–77 (Mongols).

44. Elvin 1973: 220; Dreyer 2007: 167–68, 173 (quote); Ringmar 2007: 251–53.

45. Dreyer 2007: 25.

46. Tsai 2001: 177, 186, 190

47. Levathes 1994: 175–77; J. Hall 1996: 41–42.

48. Dreyer 2007: 175–77.

49. For the importance of monopolistic power in this process, see Qian 1985: 112; Diamond 1997: 412. Critics: Dreyer 2007: 173 (quote from *Shuyu Zhouzilu*).

50. See, e.g., Diamond 1997: 412–13; E. Jones 2003: 67; McCloskey 2016: 397. For context, see Wey Gómez 2008.

51. Diamond 1997: 416 (quote). Mokyr 1990: 231: "No single European government could have stopped exploration"—although this mischaracterizes the purpose of the treasure fleets.

52. Wallerstein 1974: 60 (quote).

53. E. Jones 2003: 205.

54. I. Morris 2010: 429 (quote). Rational response: Férnandez-Armesto 2006: 114–15; Findlay and O'Rourke 2007: 363. Marks 2002: 48, 156 fails to understand this fundamental point by treating China's turn away from the sea as one of many "contingencies," in the sense of outcomes that could just as well have been quite different (cf. 10).

55. *Contra* Cook 2001: 99–101, who develops this fanciful counterfactual scenario.

56. See, e.g., Férnandez-Armesto 2006: 116–17. Ratios: Deng 1997: 96, 161. State size: Hoffman 2015: 169.

57. State: e.g., Vries 2015: 347–48, and see chapter 10 in this volume. Cities and social order: Abernethy 2000: 203–4. Quote: Wong 1997: 147. Power bases: Elvin 1973: 221; Hoffman 2015: 168.

58. Waley-Cohen 1993: 1541–44 explores the complexities of this text. For a comparative perspective on the attributes of universal empire, see, e.g., Bang and Kolodziejczyk 2012.

59. See also chapter 10 in this volume. Southern Song: Levathes 1994: 41; Deng 1999: 315–16 (quote 315); von Glahn 2016: 270–73.

60. Levathes 1994: 41–54; von Glahn 2016: 284.

61. K. Roy 2015: 168 (quote). Lack of incentives: Vries 2013: 165. Security: Pomeranz 2000: 203. Bans and restrictions: Deng 1999: 191; von Glahn 2016: 312, 319. See also chapter 10 in this volume.

62. Lack of support: Mielants 2007: 84–85; Vries 2015: 358–59. Malacca: Abernethy 2000: 242–49. Manila and Batavia: Wang 1990: 409–12, 420; Pomeranz 2000: 202–3. Quote: G. Wang 1990: 401.

63. Lorge 2005: 155–56.

64. H. Thomas 2014: 241–58 (operations in the Philippines), 259–84 (plans).

65. Pomeranz 2000: 205; Findlay and O'Rourke 2007: 358–59.

66. Mielants 2007: 109–10, 117.

67. K. Roy 2015: 164–70, 214. For Chola's operations, see in greater detail Kulke, Kesavapany, and Sakhuja 2009. Merchants: Mielants 2007: 100–102, 112.

68. Casale 2010: 114–15, 119–20, 138, 155 on the viziers and their downfall, 163, 177–79 on the shift to Yemen, and 87–88, 114–19, 155–56, 162–63, 182–83 on the "Indian Ocean faction" at the Ottoman court.

69. Ibid., 182–83 (shift to private trade), 199–202 (crisis and losses), 202–3 (quote). For the crisis, see chapter 6 in this volume.

70. Wallerstein 1974: 60 (quote).

71. Abernethy 2000: 173–273, on which I draw in the following, remains the most compelling account of the causes of European colonial expansion.

72. Ibid., 206–8 (quote: 208), and more generally 192–253 for the central role of competitive fragmentation. Cf. also Chirot 1985: 192. Logic: Vries 2015: 382.

73. Constraints on expansion: Abernethy 2000: 184; Rosenthal and Wong 2011: 217. Extension: Vries 2015: 381. Contrasts: Abernethy 2000: 212–13, who speculates that a fragmented China might have behaved differently. Readiness: Wickham 2016: 232.

74. Abernethy 2000: 192–202, 225–42 (quote: 205).

75. Mitterauer 2003: 220–21, 228–33; Mielants 2007: 27–29.

76. Férnandez-Armesto 2006: 157–64.

77. We have already noted the contrast with imperial China's diffidence. Deng 1999: 205–10 stresses the difference between Western and Chinese sea power.

78. Vries 2015: 344–46.

79. Abernethy 2000: 213–24. From early on, the Portuguese state had been strongly involved in trade: Subrahmanyam 2012: 48–52. For the development of the Portuguese overseas empire, see Disney 2009.

80. Thus Hoffman 2015, esp. 7–15 for a summary (quote: 7). Sharman 2019 disagrees. Outgrowth: Mann 2006: 380–83 (quote: 383).

81. Global share: Hoffman 2015: 2n4; see also Etemad 2007: 119–87 for quantitative analysis of the evolution of territory and population under colonial rule. For 1938 (42 percent of territory and 32 percent of population under colonial rule), see Etemad 2007: 123, table 7.1. 1760–1830: Etemad 2007: 125, table 7.2.

82. See, e.g., Darwin 2008; S. Dale 2010; Stanziani 2012.

83. Hoffman 2015: 69–81 (China) (see also I. Morris 2014: 176), 81–85 (Japan), 85–89 (India), 89–94 (Ottomans and Russia).

84. Hoffman 2015: 94, 97–98 (prerequisites), 11–12, 96 (allies); Férnandez-Armesto 2006: 148–49 (withdrawal).

85. Hoffman 2015: 158–66. This qualifies E. Jones's (2003: 169) observation that lack of maritime exploration denied Asian empires "that special European windfall of food, raw materials, colonies, and . . . business opportunities."

86. Abernethy 2000: 205.

87. See, e.g., Abernethy 2000: 180–81.

88. For geographical constraints, see, e.g., Abernethy 2000: 183; Férnandez-Armesto 2006: 149; Findlay and O'Rourke 2007: 361; I. Morris 2010: 421, 427–31.

89. For Rome's eastern trade, see Young 2001; McLaughlin 2010, 2014; Evers 2017; Cobb 2018. For the scope of Roman pepper consumption, which points to the existence of a large nonelite market, see Mayer 2018; and also Evers 2017: 68–82.

90. McLaughlin 2014: 134–38; Speidel 2016: 103–4, 106. Cf. Cobb 2018: 36–37 for doubts about the Aden episode. Sabaean coins of the late first century BCE that depict Roman busts might signal submission, and we cannot rule out some form of Roman military presence: Speidel 2016: 107–9.

91. McLaughlin 2014: 116, 122–27 (East Africa); Speidel 2016: 89–94 and Cobb 2018: 118–20 (Farasan).

92. McLaughlin 2014: 140, 168, 172–95; Speidel 2016: 111–9; Cobb 2018: 155–70.

93. Thus McLaughlin 2014: 196–99, 202–3, 206, a maximalist account. Cobb 2018: 170–78 is more cautious.

94. For discussion of extrapolations from the customs record, see Scheidel 2015d: 160–61, and most recently Evers 2017: 99–109. Volume: McLaughlin 2014: 89, 95, and Cobb 2018: 274–80, a critical assessment of specie outflows.

95. Comparisons: McLaughlin 2014: 93–94.

96. Roller 2006: 107–11.

97. The Atlantic vs. monsoon argument is popular: see, e.g., Deng 1997: 160; Abernethy 2000: 178; Férnandez-Armesto 2006: 116; Hoffman 2015: 171.

98. For the counterfactual of Pacific exploration via the Aleutians by more adventurous Chinese sailors, see briefly Cook 2001: 101.

99. *Contra* I. Morris 2010: 421–22, who states that the Norse never had to negotiate more than 500 miles (800 km) of open sea whereas these Chinese would have had to cover 5,000 or 6,000 miles (8,000–9,000 km) using the Kuro Siwo Drift to reach Northern California, or closer to 10,000 miles (16,000 km) using the Equatorial Counter Current from the Philippines to Nicaragua (cf. also Cook 2001: 101 for the problems open sea routes posed for potential Chinese sailors). This misrepresents the actual trajectories of the most economical North Pacific

crossing from northeastern East Asia, which would not have differed much from that taken by the Norse in the North Atlantic. To his credit, I. Morris, despite his emphasis on geography (2010: 427–31), acknowledges the role of domestic incentive structures.

100. Férnandez-Armesto 2006: 199–203. Mortality: Hoffman 2015: 171.

101. I. Morris 2010: 428 (quote).

102. Menzies 2004. The whole story is, of course, pure nonsense, as has been pointed out ad nauseam.

103. For Polynesian development, see Rolett 2002. The Polynesian example also undermines the idea that Chinese naval design was held back by the ease of conducting trade relations with Southeast Asia and in the Indian Ocean thanks to the monsoon winds (thus Deng 1997: 160): Polynesian outrigger canoes were no carracks either.

104. Cost of competition: a perceptive point made by Vries 2015: 385. Funding: Abernethy 2000: 183 (quote).

105. Vries 2015 is now by far the best account of this contrast.

106. See Vries 2013: 347–50 for the lack of peripheral development under the Qing.

107. Belich 2016: 104, 107 (quotes).

CHAPTER TWELVE

1. Mokyr 2017 is the most recent and comprehensive exposition of his position.

2. Quote: Mokyr 2005: 339.

3. Mokyr 2007, esp. 23–26; Mokyr 2017: 165–78, esp. 165–66.

4. Hume's "Of the rise and progress of the arts and sciences," quoted by Mokyr 2017: 166. Coordination failure: Mokyr 2017: 169.

5. Fragmentation: Mokyr 2007: 23–24 (quote); see also 24: "European political fragmentation created the environment in which dissident and heterodox opinions could be put forward with increasing impunity." Lack of efficacy: Mokyr 2017: 177. In absolutist states it took until the eighteenth century for suppression to morph into a largely "ritualized formality" (177–78).

6. Playing off: Mokyr 2005: 342. Cf. for some of these examples Mokyr 2007: 24; 2017: 169–71. Polycentrism: Mokyr 2005: 342; Vries 2013: 385.

7. Huff 2003: 133–39, 179, 251, and also 179–89, 317, and 339–45 for the role of universities in the rise of early modern science. Cf. also Lang 1997: 19. Exceptions: Mokyr 2017: 172–75.

8. Mokyr 2017: 169 (competition), 149–50 (innovations). See Hobson 2004 for the scope of borrowing.

9. H. F. Cohen 2015: 173–74.

10. Mokyr 2017: 175–76 (mobility); Mokyr 2007: 5–6 (marketplace); Mokyr 2017: 179–224 (Republic of Letters), 179 (quote), 181 (mechanism). I turn to China later in this chapter.

11. Mokyr 2007: 7–8; Mokyr 2017: 186, 189–91. Counterfactual: Mokyr 2007: 24 (quote); Mokyr 2017: 220–21.

12. Costs: Mokyr 2017: 215 and the epilogue in this volume. Vernacular: Mokyr 2007: 31.

13. See C. Murray 2003: 301–3 for an attempt at a census (see also 113–14, 158, 252, 297–98).

14. Becker, Pfaff, and Rubin 2016: 10–20 provide an excellent survey of relevant social science research.

15. Printing: Buringh and van Zanden 2009: 421–22. Literacy: Van Zanden 2009a: 193–95. Acting: Baten and van Zanden 2008: 226–33. The latter also observe a strong relationship between eighteenth-century human capital formation and nineteenth-century economic performance across a number of European and Asian countries (230–32).

16. Davids 2013: 173–233, esp. 222, 228; cf. also Goldstone 2009: 118.

17. Mokyr 2017: 227–46. For criticism of the role of Puritanism, see Davids 2013: 228. Accommodation: Jacob 1997: 51–72; Goldstone 2002: 370; Goldstone 2009: 156.

18. Mokyr 2009: 37 (quote), 70–98 (Bacon); Goldstone 2009: 150–55 (divide), 158 (priority).

19. Improvement: Slack 2015 gives a rich (and self-proclaimed "Whiggish": 263) account of this mind-set. See also Friedel 2007: 2–5. Trend: Mokyr 2017: 247–66. Bayly 2004: 79–80 (quotes).

20. For comparison, see especially Qian 1985: 90–130; Goldstone 1987: 129–32; Huff 2003: 240–324; Mokyr 2003: 49–63; Goldstone 2009: 136–61; Mokyr 2017: 287–320.

21. See Mokyr 2017: 301–2 for variation in outcomes, and Goldstone 1987: 129–32 and Mokyr 2017: 294 for divergence from the seventeenth century onward. Quote: Mokyr 1990: 237. This fundamental premise obviates the need to go as far as Qian 1985: 103: "A territorially unified autocratic rule was effectively aided by and symbiotically combined with an equally unified system of ideological control. Its philosophical spirit was introspective, its academic scope was officially limited and exclusively politico-ethical, and its basic attitude discouraged innovative practices and rationalistic inquiries."

22. Warring States: see, e.g., Bodde 1991: 178–82; Ringmar 2007: 270–71; Pines 2012: 87 (quote by Dong Zhonshu).

23. Orthodoxy: see chapters 9 and 10 in this volume. The counterfactual is spelled out by Bodde 1991: 364:

> Had China permanently remained a collection of some half dozen competing principalities after 221 B.C. instead of becoming a single empire, the resulting conditions of life for the ordinary person would no doubt have been far more difficult and less secure. On the other hand, had such political disunity continued, and with it the diversity of ideas that had previously been its byproduct, I venture to suggest that the resulting intellectual environment might well have been more conducive to scientific development than that afforded by the orthodox state Confucianism of imperial China.

In terms of content, Confucianism encouraged a holistic worldview, whose dissolution in Renaissance Europe is seen as an important precondition for the Enlightenment: Bodde 1991: 186. Social focus: Needham 1969: 156–66. Other cultural features that are not directly linked to politics have also been invoked: thus Needham's (1969) observation that Chinese lacked the notion of laws of nature: since order resulted from cosmic hierarchy, there were no laws for humans to decipher (36–37, 299–330); contrast Milton 1981 for the ascent of this concept in late medieval and early modern Europe. Bodde 1991: 19–96 views the Chinese writing system as inhibitive to scientific thinking; for its imperial monopoly, see chapter 9 in this volume.

24. Bodde 1991: 365–66; J. Lin 1995: 281–85; Huff 2003: 277–87; Mokyr 2017: 298–300, 303–7 (quotes: 306–7). For the examination system in late imperial China, see Elman 2000, 2013. Pines 2012: 89 summarizes the overall outcome: "Having monopolized the routes of individual advancement, the court could deploy its power to define what kind of expertise and knowledge was required of an aspiring official, thereby directing the educational efforts of the vast majority

of the literati toward desirable ends. In addition, coercive measures could further solidify ideological orthodoxy." Commercial elite: see chapter 10 in this volume.

25. Pines 2012: 84; Mokyr 2017: 298, 311, 317. Cf. Qian 1985: 26 for "the Chinese politico-ideological rigidity—its uniformity over a vast territory fed back strongly to intensify itself."

26. Bodde 1991: 367.

27. Mokyr 2017: 298, 310, 340 (quote); Goldstone 2009: 147–50. Cf. Bodde 1991: 194: "We may speculate that if, in the West, a single state or church had continued indefinitely to exercise the same control over astronomy, for example, as was taken for granted in China, the Copernican-Galilean revolution probably would not soon and possibly would never have taken place."

28. Bodde 1991: 360–61; Huff 2003: 321; Ringmar 2007: 285; Davids 2013: 229–30.

29. Sivin 1991: 63–65 (quote: 65).

30. Pomeranz 2006: 253–63. Steam engine: Deng 2004; H. F. Cohen 2009: 126–27.

31. See the epilogue in this volume. In terms of quality, scientific writing arguably peaked in the third century BCE when it was at its most detached from philosophy (Reviel Netz, personal communication). Cf. Mokyr 1990: 199.

32. Chaney 2016: 5–24 (decline in output and spread of revival), 24–27 (survey of possible causes). In a related context, Koyama 2017b: 552 notes the relevance of the lack of variety in regime types. For the earlier flourishing of Islamic scientific culture, concentrated to some extent in Central Asia (and thus away from the main imperial centers), see Starr 2013.

33. Rebellions: Goldstone 2009: 48, 143. Restrictions and interventions: Soucek 1994: 126–27, 130, 135–36; Acemoglu and Robinson 2012: 213–14. Loosening: De Bellaigue 2017.

34. Goldstone 2009: 49, 143; Parthasarathi 2011: 185–222, esp. 187, 195–201, 212–13, 265. For weapons technology, see also Hoffman 2015: 87, 99. Cf. Foa 2016: 80–106 for institutional change.

35. Pollock 2005: 79 (quote), with Roy 2008: 386; Parthasartahi 2011: 193–94; Yazdani 2017: 100–105, 279–85, 515–22.

36. Mokyr 1990: 236 (quotes).

37. Goldstone 2009: 49–50.

38. In my reading of counterfactuals (see Part III in this volume), European polycentrism was considerably more robust than was envisioned by Mokyr 2017: 341, who claims that "fairly minor rewrites of history could have secured Europe for an obscurantist Catholic regime in which the Republic of Letters would have turned into a benighted theocracy dominated by Jesuits." Only in Europe: Mokyr 2006: 290–311. *Contra* Goldstone 2002: 376–77, it was not necessary for competing "nation-states" to exist for engine science to arise and succeed: what mattered most was simply the absence of the opposite, irrespective of the characteristics of these states. For a basic model of how competition between countries favors innovation, see Chaudhry and Garner 2006.

39. See Mokyr 2002: 35; 2009: 40 for the term, and more generally 2002: 28–77. Premises: Mokyr 2002: 36–41.

40. Mokyr 2009: 40.

41. Inkster 1991: 35–36 (quote: 36); Huff 2011: 314–15.

42. Inkster 1991: 36, 42–43; Moe 2007: 75; Huff 2011: 314–15. Human capital: Allen 2009b: 260–64 (who emphasizes economic development that raised real wages as a driving force).

Conversely, Kelly, Mokyr, and Ó Gráda 2014 emphasize the superior human capital and physical condition of British workers as a driver of high real wages. Literacy was not a sufficient condition: Vries 2013: 225–26 notes that literacy requirements for most jobs remained low well into the nineteenth century, and that the Netherlands, which enjoyed a very high literacy rate, was not at the forefront of innovation in the eighteenth and early nineteenth centuries.

43. Mokyr 2009: 107–13, 121–22. Inventions: Mokyr 1990: 291–92 for these terms.

44. Modest contribution: Mokyr 2002: 46–50, 81; Mokyr 2009: 61–62. Steam engine: Allen 2009b: 252. Goldstone 2002: 367–69 and 2009: 132–34 likewise invokes the case of the steam engine but is generally more sanguine about the relationship between scientific advances and the Industrial Revolution. Vries 2013: 306–12 follows the Goldstone–Mokyr line concerning an "enlightened economy" and sustained innovation rooted in science and technology (and on 313n949 disagrees with McCloskey's rejection of science as a driver of industrialization). See Landes 1998: 201–6.

45. Inkster 1991: 60–88, esp. 73, 78–80, 87; Mokyr 2009: 93.

46. Patents: Mokyr 2009: 92–93. Exit option: Mokyr 2002: 263–68. On the enlightened political economy, see Mokyr 2009: 63–78. Mokyr 2002: 297 (quote). Cf. also chapter 10 in this volume, for the findings of Hoppit 2017.

47. Jacob 1997: 113–15; Jacob 2014: 7–8 (quote: 8), 221; Inkster 1991: 37–45; Goldstone 2002: 365; Goldstone 2009: 157, 159–60, 169–70; Mokyr 2009: 85–87.

48. Mann 2006: 376; Mokyr 2009: 51, 54 (quote), 57; Slack 2015: 234 (quote), 242–56.

49. Inkster 1991: 44–45; Moe 2007: 76–78.

50. Moe 2007: 77; Jacob 2014: 136–84 (quotes: 163–64).

51. Mokyr 2009: 25–27, 100–105; Vries 2013: 428.

52. McCloskey 2010: 6–25 for a summary (quotes: 10, 7, 24). For an earlier statement, see Baechler 1975: 113.

53. McCloskey 2010: 409, fig.4 for a chart of the causal connections underlying this process, and 406–19 for a more formal presentation of her model.

54. "4 Rs:" McCloskey 2016: xxxiv–xxxvi. By contrast, the aristocratic values of the earlier Renaissance (another potential "R") "were not democratic betterments and did not improve the lives of ordinary people, at any rate not for a long time" (xxxv). McCloskey 2016: 367–76 (church), 388–96 (literacy), 396–400 (fragmentation), 401–23 (ideas; quote: 417), 149–291 (rhetoric).

55. McCloskey 2016: 459 (quote).

56. Liberty and hegemony: McCloskey 2016: 359, 362. For China, see chapter 10 in this volume.

57. McCloskey 2016: 511, 439 (quote).

58. Vries 2013: 398–400 and 435–36 stresses the difficulties of relating cultural features empirically to economic outcomes, as the former often include such a high level of generalization that it becomes "impossible to use them as operational variables in concrete . . . explanations" (quote: 435). Even so, he considers the Weberian maxim that the rationalization of economic life (in capitalism), public life (in the state), and mastery of nature and society (through science and technology) had been pushed farther in the West than elsewhere to be respectable and worthy of closer engagement (436; cf. Chirot 1985: 186–91).

59. Allen 2009b: 16–22 summarizes his argument. See also Allen 2011 for another short version. For criticism, see above all Kelly, Mokyr, and Ó Gráda 2014, esp. 364–67; and also Vries 2013: 199–207.

60. Allen 2009b: 19, 109–10, followed by Rosenthal and Wong 2011: 124. For the conversion of arable- to pastureland after the Black Death and the increase in the number of sheep, see Oldland 2014. For the imposition of growing export tolls on wool and measures to pass those extra costs on to foreign buyers rather than to domestic sellers between the 1270s and 1390s, and their unintended consequence of making (less heavily taxed) broadcloth exports more competitive, see Munro 2005: 451–53. For the bans, see Hoppit 2017: 216–48.

61. Allen 2009b: 110 (quote), and also 130; Rosenthal and Wong 2011: 124–25 (quote).

62. Allen 2009b: 109.

63. Ibid., 110–11, 130 (quote).

64. Ibid., 111–31 (model), esp. 123–28 for the key findings. By contrast, representative government and enclosure hardly mattered. Urban/rural shifts: ibid., 17, table 1.1. London's population grew tenfold between 1500 and 1700: 19. For similar statistics, see Wrigley 2016: 45–50, 67–74, who emphasizes that English urban growth in the seventeenth and eighteenth centuries hugely exceeded the continental rates: the urban population in England grew by more than 700 percent compared to 80 percent in continental Western Europe, and the urban share quadrupled in England while rising by one-third in Western Europe overall, with much of the latter growth due to the former's: see chapter 10 in this volume. Cf. Palma 2016 for the observation that international trade boosted real wages in some other Atlantic economies of Europe as well. Agricultural revolution: Overton 1996; Wrigley 2016: 51–60, 65, 67–74.

65. Allen 2009b: 129 (quote); Hoffman 2015: 211–12. See also chapter 10 in this volume.

66. Allen 2009b: 111, 162–63. Also see, e.g., Pomeranz 2000: 61; Cuenca Esteban 2004: 55.

67. Goldstone 2002: 363–64; G. Clark 2007: 242; Wrigley 2016: 34, table 3.2. Coal and China: Pomeranz 2000: 59–68; Pomeranz 2006: 252–56; also Marks 2002: 110–11; Tvedt 2010: 34, 36. Against Pomeranz's emphasis on the contingency of access to coal, see, from different angles, Bryant 2006: 438; Parthasarathi 2011: 162–64; Rosenthal and Wong 2011: 167; Vries 2013: 291–96; Vries 2015: 404. Coal as ghost acreages: E. Jones 2003: 84.

68. Disruption: *contra* Goldstone 2002: 360–61, who avers that if the coalfields had been located in Brittany instead of Britain, coal could simply have been imported—which would hardly have been possible during the French Wars. Activation: Allen 2009b: 84–90 (quotes: 90). Mokyr 2009: 102 notes that coal use was ultimately driven by changes in knowledge that created demand and enabled exploitation. Allen 2009b: 90–96 likewise recognizes collective invention as a driver of demand for coal.

69. See chapter 10 in this volume.

70. Rosenthal and Wong 2011: 125 (quote).

71. Rosenthal and Wong 2011: 7 correctly note that Allen's model does not work without recourse to politics to explain how the necessary economic conditions arose.

72. E. Jones 2003: 3–149, 225–38 (quote: 119); Rosenthal and Wong 2011, esp. 228–40 for their conclusions.

73. Mitterauer 2003: 274–98; van Zanden 2009a: esp. 291–300 (quotes: 294–95), and also 295: "The big wave of institutional design of the 10th–13th centuries occurred in a political

vacuum resulting from the disintegration of the Carolingian empire, and more generally, the weakness of earlier Greco-Roman traditions."

74. Ringmar 2007: 61–92, 131–48; Duchesne 2011: 165–229; Marks 2002: 156.

75. Acemoglu and Robinson 2012: 197–212; Bayly 2004: 59–82.

76. Goldstone 2009: 108–76. In light of this, his objections to (a crude, even strawman version of) the state system argument (100–102) seems curiously misguided: see chapter 10 in this volume. See also 172: "The unusual characteristics of Britain's social, political, religious, and intellectual life—many of them emerging over many centuries from *Magna Charta* to the Toleration Act of 1689—created an alternative to the dominant tendencies on the continent and created the first society in which innovation and scientific engineering became widespread and firmly integrated into everyday production routines."

77. Vries 2013: 416, 427–28; Vries 2015: 431–36. See also, e.g., O'Brien 2011; Parthasarathi 2011: 264–67.

78. Mokyr 2002: 263–75; Mokyr 2009: 7, 25–27, 63–78. Fragmentation and enlightenment: Mokyr 2005: 342; Mokyr 2007: 23–26; Mokyr 2017: 165–78.

79. Karayalcin 2016: 495 explains the Great Divergence in terms of variation in land regimes in post–Black Death Europe, a diversity that was itself associated with the presence of a multistate system. Wrigley 2016: 201–3 focuses on positive feedback mechanisms within the modernizing English economy without seeking to explain what mobilized and mediated these mechanisms.

80. G. Clark 2007. Reviews are gathered at http://faculty.econ.ucdavis.edu/faculty/gclark/a_farewell_to_alms.html.

81. See van Zanden 2009a: 101–43 for this line of reasoning; and see also Hartmann 2004 for the notion that this pattern undergirded the first Industrial Revolution (231–42), although the actual mechanisms remain unclear. See Dennison and Ogilvie 2014 and 2016 for a sustained critique of the proposed linkage between the Northwestern European marriage pattern and economic growth, *contra* De Moor and van Zanden 2010 and Carmichael et al. 2016, among others.

82. Belich 2016: 99–104. For the notion of labor-saving devices and capital use, see Herlihy 1997: 49–51, doubted by his editor Samuel K. Cohn Jr. (10–12) on chronological grounds.

83. Voigtländer and Voth 2009: 248–51; Voigtländer and Voth 2013a, 2013b. In a shift away from an earlier model (Voigtländer and Voth 2006), war is the most important proximate factor for them: Voigtländer and Voth 2013a: 182; Voigtländer and Voth 2013b: 799. Cf. Edwards and Ogilvie 2018 for criticism of other elements of their argument.

84. See Tvedt 2010 for an illuminating comparative study.

85. Rosenthal and Wong 2011: 200 are right to maintain that "political competition and conflict are not enough to guarantee technological change and economic growth." But these are necessary preconditions for making it happen. Quote: Allen 2009b: 275. See Mokyr 2006 for the view that if the Industrial Revolution had not happened in Europe, it probably would not have happened at all; and more generally Crone 2003: 171–75 (who notes that indigenous modernizing development was unlikely to have occurred in Japan instead, which was not generally part of a competitive state system: 174–75). The contributors to Prados de la Escosura 2004 all agree on the exceptional nature of the British Industrial Revolution.

86. I say "most likely" because we cannot strictly speaking establish whether traditional empire was in principle and invariably inimical to modernizing development or merely usually and in practice. Based on Part V of this book, I do, however, incline toward the former.

EPILOGUE

1. It has not taken much effort to flesh out David Landes's intuition that "Europe's good fortune lay in the fall of Rome and the weakness and division that ensued. (So much for the lamentations of generations of classicists and Latin teachers.)" (Landes 1998: 37). By now, outright praise of the Roman empire has (largely) followed modern colonial empires to the trash heap of history. I touch on the historical merits of Latin near the end. of this chapter.

2. Quoted from http://montypython.50webs.com/scripts/Life_of_Brian/10.htm.

3. The general picture holds true even as the precise scale of these various developments continues to be debated. For urbanization, see Scheidel 2007a: 78–80; Wilson 2011: 179–93; J. Hanson 2016. Population size is a particularly controversial issue but even conservative estimates point to relatively high densities: see Frier 2000: 814, table 6, updated by Scheidel 2007a: 48. For maritime market integration and lowered transaction costs, see Scheidel 2011a; Scheidel and Meeks 2014. For bulk goods, see, e.g., Erdkamp 2005. For a high estimate of monetary value, see Duncan-Jones 1994: 168–70; but cf. Scheidel 2009c: 201–2. For isotopic evidence of silver ore smelting preserved in ice cores, see the references in Scheidel 2009b: 47–48n7, and most recently McConnell et al. 2018. Credit: Harris 2006; Rathbone and Temin 2008.

4. Size of GDP: Scheidel and Friesen 2009. Direction of GDP trends: Scheidel 2009b, with Wilson 2009 and 2014, who not unreasonably casts doubt on the relevance of various proxies. For different interpretations of the economic expansion of the late republican period, see Scheidel 2007b and Kay 2014.

5. On Roman technology, see the survey by Oleson 2008, and specifically Schneider 2007 for its economic dimension. Antikythera device: Alexander Jones 2017. Steam engine: Bresson 2006. See Scheidel 2009b: 69 for the nature and abatement of innovation. For overseas exploration and trade, see chapter 11 in this volume.

6. To the best of my knowledge, Schiavone 2000: 180–86, 190 is the only professional ancient historian to have pondered the possibility of political and economic change at a critical juncture that he locates in the 80s to 60s BCE, when substantial resources came to be concentrated in Italy and the old sociopolitical order was under pressure but transformative change was averted by imperial predation and the stabilization of aristocratic dominance. This counterfactual has little to commend it. From an economics perspective, Koyama 2017a notes that a turn toward a machine culture to satisfy labor demands would have required an absence of slave labor, which is not a plausible counterfactual (given that the imperial elite owned several million slaves), and that conditions were not at all conducive to the emergence of a culture of science or bourgeois values. (Cf. also Tridimas 2018 for ancient Greece's failure to industrialize, which he blames on energy costs, small polity size, and hegemonic attitudes.) Alternative history novels have come up with scenarios of a Roman empire that either experienced industrialization already in antiquity (H. Dale 2017) or survived into our time (Mitchell 1984: significant technological progress without full industrialization; Silverberg 2003: essentially a replay of historical innovation).

7. For China, see chapter 10 in this volume. For the evolution of modern views of the nature of the later Roman empire (from the late third century CE), compare Arnold Jones 1964, Garnsey and Humfress 2001, and Kelly 2004.

8. http://www.romaneconomy.ox.ac.uk/, with the manifesto by Bowman and Wilson 2009. Neoclassical economics: Temin 2012, and numerous papers by Morris Silver. For criticism, see Scheidel 2014: 28–29; Bang 2015. Terpstra 2019: ch. 4 advances a more nuanced view.

9. State institutions and economy: see, e.g., Lo Cascio 2006; Wilson and Bowman 2018, 27–132, and esp. Lo Cascio 2018. Taxes and trade: Hopkins 1980, 2002. Abatement: Wickham 2005: 62–80, 693–824. For the dualism of markets and state demand (predation), see briefly Scheidel 2012: 7–10.

10. For the Roman tax system, see Scheidel 2015a, 2015d. For the logic of abatement, see Monson and Scheidel 2015a. For Chinese taxation, see chapter 10 in this volume. The notion that imperial Rome was a high tax regime (Bowman 2018) is a fantasy that confuses nominal and effective tax rates, and is incompatible with what we know about the limits of public spending (see Scheidel 2015a: 243–44 for a central state share of 5–7 percent of GDP, plus local taxes).

11. Predation: Bang 2007, 2008, 2012. For China, see chapter 11 in this volume. Inequality: Scheidel 2017: 63–80.

12. For the Ming measures and other state interventions, see chapter 13 in this volume. Late Roman empire: Arnold Jones 1964, with Gwynn 2008. For a comparative perspective, see Haldon 2012. See also Terpstra 2019: ch. 7 for institutional stagnation and preference for the status quo under the mature Roman empire.

13. Mughals: Bang 2008. Ottomans: Vries 2002: 115.

14. Insofar as more productively competitive and inclusive societies had developed in the ancient Mediterranean, they were concentrated among the participatory city-states and federated polities (*koina*) of classical and early Hellenistic Greece (see esp. Mackil 2013 and Ober 2015, and cf. also Raaflaub 2018)—potentially promising experiments that did not survive Roman conquest.

15. Laiou 2002: 1153, 1164; Oikonomides 2002: 1020. Oikonomides 2002: 973–74, 990–1026 (command economy), 1026–58, esp. 1042–48 (privileges).

16. Innovations: Laiou 2002: 1152–53. Concessions: Laiou 2002: 1156–59; Oikonomides 2002: 1050–55; Jacoby 2008.

17. Thus also J. Hall 1996: 55–56.

18. See chapter 9 in this volume and Gelasius, *Tractatus* 4 (second set of quotes), from Dagron 2003: 182. Politicization: Dagron 2003: 302–3.

19. See chapter 5 in this volume.

20. See chapter 5 in this volume.

21. Van Zanden 2009a: 45–49; see also chapter 10 in this volume.

22. Strayer 1970: 26.

23. Quotes: E. Jones 2003: 110 (and more generally 110–17, 245); Mokyr 2007: 28; Mokyr 2017: 215.

24. Quotes: Baechler 1975: 76 (and see 76–77, 113 for the importance of a single culture); Hall 1988: 35; van Zanden 2009a: 68. See also J. Hall 1996: 65.

25. E. Jones 2003: 115–17; van Zanden 2009a: 90.

26. Language: E. Jones 2003: 112–13; and cf. Mokyr 2017: 170. Pacification: Mann 1986: 377, followed by J. Hall 1988: 32 and van Zanden 2009a: 36, 45. Trade: Hall 1986: 125. Transnational body: Mitterauer 2003: 154–55. See in general Hall 1985: 123–26. E. Jones (2003: 112) also deems "limited diversity" in religion preferable to "infinite splintering."

27. Mokyr 2002: 76; Mokyr 2007: 28–29 (quote: 29); Mokyr 2017: 179–224, esp. 215 for the counterfactual.

28. P. Stein 1999: 40–41 (survival), 43–68 (revival up to the thirteenth century), 71–101 (spread up to the seventeenth century).

29. Merchants: P. Stein 1999: 106 (quote), and Hilaire 1986. For merchant institutions in general, see Greif 2006. For the English system, see chapters 10 and 12 in this volume. Quote: P. Stein 1999: 2.

30. Adams 2007; Banniard 2013: 75–85; R. Wright 2016: 15, 17, 21.

31. R. Wright 2013: 118–21; R. Wright 2016: 21–23. See Barrow 2015: 170–235 for the education of the medieval clergy. Schools in general were commonly attached to churches (176–78).

32. Josephus, *Jewish War* 6.5.3. Parallels with Jesus, son of Joseph (or God), in the oldest gospel: Mark 13.1–2 (prophecy), 15.1 (handover), 15.5 (silence), 15.15 (torture).

33. For the counterfactual of no Christianity, see Demandt 1999: 77–78 and Demandt 2011: 101–8. For Marcionism, see Moll 2010. The rationale behind the Constantinian policy shift has been endlessly debated: see Girardet 2006 for a guide to the relevant sources and scholarship. Eire 2006a develops the counterfactual of Christianity without the crucifixion or without divinity, and its consequences for European development. Despite some earlier claims, it is doubtful that Jewish proselytizing had great potential: see Baumgarten 1999: 471–76 for the debate.

34. John 14.5.

35. See chapters 2 (Samnites) and 3 (Greek and Carthaginian capacities) in this volume.

36. The Seleucid king Antiochos IV successfully invaded Egypt in 170 and 168 BCE but was stymied by Roman intervention. In 40–38 BCE, the Parthians briefly overran Syria and Judea as Rome was distracted by civil war. For the obstacles Middle Eastern powers encountered in controlling their eastern Mediterranean peripheries, see chapter 3 in this volume.

37. See Netz forthcoming for the spatial concentration of Greek learning and literature production.

38. Feeney 2016, esp. 45–151 (translation), 122–51 (empire), 173–78 (historians).

39. Woolf 1994: 91–92; Mullen 2013: 161–63 on the penetration of Greco-Gallic texts. Strabo, *Geography* 4.1.5 claimed that under Greek influence, Gauls wrote their contracts in Greek, which is impossible to verify (Mullen 2013: 162). Caesar twice refers to use of Greek writing in Gaul, a claim that, whatever its veracity, must at least have seemed plausible to his readers: Woolf 1994: 90.

40. See Woolf 1994: 92–93 on coinage.

41. Ibid., 89, 94.

42. See briefly Netz forthcoming, and in greater detail in his planned history of ancient Greek mathematics. From this perspective, the Greeks may very well have done more for us than the Romans ever did. Yet it is easy to exaggerate: Russo 2004, an often conjectural argument regarding a Greek scientific revolution in the third century BCE and its impact on European science from the Renaissance onward, shows the limits of this approach. (Most of the "Roman" science similarly celebrated by Carrier 2017 was in fact Greek.)

43. For Carthage and the Hellenistic states, see chapter 3 in this volume.

44. Actual based on figure 1.4. Counterfactual 1 takes account of the favorable conditions of the Roman Warm Period whereas the other two are (even) more crudely schematic.

45. Even if the Roman empire had never existed, mid-first-millennium-CE Europe would hardly have been a stateless environment akin to Norse Iceland, Acemoglu and Robinson's (2019) symbolic counterpoint to state formation in post-Roman Europe. They also tend to overestimate the impact of Roman governmental practice on early medieval state formation, which was characterized above all by a secular shift away from centralized state power: see chapter 7 in this volume.

46. I consider this process more fundamental than the flooding of the English Channel in the sixth millennium BCE that turned Britain into an island, thus sheltering it from European competitors. Large-scale imperial state formation on the continent would presumably have outweighed this advantage, as it did during the Roman period.

TECHNICAL NOTE TO CHAPTER ONE

1. McEvedy and Jones 1978. For more ambitious collaborative simulation efforts, see Kaplan et al. 2011; Klein Goldewijk et al. 2011.

2. McEvedy and Jones 1978: 21–22, and my own calculations based on their country values; Frier 2000: 814, table 6 offers 61 million, whereas Scheidel 2007a: 48, table 3.1 considers 59–72 million. Even higher totals are certainly possible. For ancient Greece, see Hansen 2006.

3. McEvedy and Jones 1978: 167, with Bielenstein 1987: 12 (Han census).

4. McEvedy and Jones 1978: 353–54. For skepticism about net growth in that period, see the survey in J. Cohen 1995: 400–401. More recently, see note 2. This position is also consistent with ecologically informed historiography that increasingly takes account of the impact of climate change and epidemics: see, e.g., Harper 2017 for western Eurasia. The Black Death produced a more compressed sequence of demographic contraction and recovery in the fourteenth, fifteenth, and sixteenth centuries: Malanima 2009: 7–9.

5. Although they do distinguish between China proper and China including Xinjiang, Tibet, Inner Mongolia, Manchuria, and Taiwan, low population densities in the latter areas for much of history (and in some cases even today) limit the usefulness of this breakdown. In South Asia, to make matters worse, they lump together India, Pakistan, and Bangladesh into a single unit: McEvedy and Jones 1978: 167, 171, 183.

6. 140 CE: Bielenstein 1987: 194, map 2.

7. For what it is worth, the British census of India in 1871–1872 suggests that while a slightly larger proportion of the total population was concentrated in the Ganges and Indus basins (Punjab, North West Provinces, Oude, and Bengal) than it is today, the overall distribution was already very similar to the current one: Memorandum 1875. Needless to say, this tells us little about conditions one or two millennia ago.

8. Degree of error: I. Morris 2013b uses similar criteria to justify a more ambitious quantitative comparative exercise.

REFERENCES

Abernethy, David B. 2000. *The dynamics of global dominance: European overseas empires, 1415–1980*. New Haven, CT: Yale University Press.

Acemoglu, Daron, Johnson, Simon, and Robinson, James. 2005. "The rise of Europe: Atlantic trade, institutional change, and economic growth." *American Economic Review* 95: 546–79.

Acemoglu, Daron and Robinson, James A. 2012. *Why nations fail: The origins of power, prosperity, and poverty*. New York: Crown.

Acemoglu, Daron and Robinson, James A. 2019. *Balance of power: States, societies and the narrow corridor to liberty*. New York: Penguin.

Adams, James N. 2007. *The regional diversification of Latin 200 BC–AD 600*. Cambridge: Cambridge University Press.

Adams, James N. 2008. *Bilingualism and the Latin language*. Cambridge: Cambridge University Press.

Afzelius, Adam. 1942. *Die römische Eroberung Italiens (340–264 v. Chr.)*. Copenhagen: Ejnar Munksgaard.

Afzelius, Adam. 1944. *Die römische Kriegsmacht während der Auseinandersetzung mit den hellenistischen Grossmächten*. Copenhagen: Ejnar Munksgaard.

Airlie, Stuart. 1995. "The aristocracy." In McKitterick 1995, 431–50.

Alcock, Susan E., D'Altroy, Terence, N., Morrison, Kathleen D., and Sinopoli, Carla M., eds. 2001. *Empires: Perspectives from archaeology and history*. Cambridge: Cambridge University Press.

Allen, Robert C. 2001. "The great divergence in European wages and prices from the Middle Ages to the First World War." *Explorations in Economic History* 38: 411–47.

Allen, Robert C. 2003. "Progress and poverty in early modern Europe." *Economic History Review* 56: 403–43.

Allen, Robert C. 2009a. "Agricultural productivity and rural incomes in England and the Yangtze Delta, c. 1620–c. 1820." *Economic History Review* 62: 525–50.

Allen, Robert C. 2009b. *The British Industrial Revolution in global perspective*. Cambridge: Cambridge University Press.

Allen, Robert C. 2011. "Why the Industrial Revolution was British: Commerce, induced invention, and the scientific revolution." *Economic History Review* 64: 357–84.

Allen, Robert C. and Weisdorf, Jacob L. 2011. "Was there an 'Industrious Revolution' before the Industrial Revolution? An empirical exercise for England, c. 1300–1830." *Economic History Review* 64: 715–729.

Allen, Robert C. et al. 2011. "Wages, prices, and living standards in China, 1738–1925: In comparison with Europe, Japan, and India." *Economic History Review* 64(S1): 8–38.

Allsen, Thomas T. 1987. *Mongol imperialism: The policies of the Grand Qan Möngke in China, Russia, and the Islamic lands, 1251–1259*. Berkeley: University of California Press.

Allsen, Thomas T. 2002. "The circulation of military technology in the Mongolian empire." In Di Cosmo 2002b, 265–93.

Ameling, Walter. 1993. *Karthago: Studien zu Militär, Staat und Gesellschaft*. Munich: Beck.

Andrade, Tonio. 2016. *The gunpowder age: China, military innovation, and the rise of the West in world history*. Princeton, NJ: Princeton University Press.

Andreski, Stanislav. 1968. *Military organization and society*. 2nd ed. Berkeley: University of California Press.

Angelov, Dimiter and Herrin, Judith. 2012. "The Christian imperial tradition—Greek and Latin." In Bang and Kolodziejczyk 2012, 149–74.

Angelucci, Charles, Meraglia, Simone, and Voigtländer, Nico. 2017. "The medieval roots of inclusive institutions: From the Norman conquest of England to the Great Reform Act." NBER Working Paper no. 23606. Cambridge, MA: National Bureau of Economic Research.

Aperghis, G. G. 2004. *The Seleukid economy: The finances of financial administration of the Seleukid empire*. Cambridge: Cambridge University Press.

Appleby, Joyce. 2010. *The relentless revolution: A history of capitalism*. New York: Norton.

Ardant, Gabriel. 1971–1972. *L'histoire de l'impôt*. 2 vols. Paris: Fayard.

Armstrong, Jeremy. 2016. *War and society in early Rome: From warlords to generals*. Cambridge: Cambridge University Press.

Arnold, Benjamin. 1991. *Princes and territory in medieval Germany*. Cambridge: Cambridge University Press.

Arrighi, Giovanni. 2007. *Adam Smith in Beijing: Lineages of the twenty-first century*. London: Verso.

Artzrouni, Marc and Komlos, John. 1996. "The formation of the European state system: A spatial 'predatory' model." *Historical Methods* 29: 126–34.

Asher, Catherine B. and Talbot, Cynthia. 2006. *India before Europe*. Cambridge: Cambridge University Press.

Austin, M. M. 1986. "Hellenistic kings, war, and the economy." *Classical Quarterly* 36: 450–66.

Auyang, Sunny Y. 2014. *The dragon and the eagle: The rise and fall of the Chinese and Roman empires*. Armonk, NY: M. E. Sharpe.

Babel, Rainer. 2002. "Frankreich und Karl V. (1519–1556)." In Kohler, Haider, and Ottner 2002, 577–610.

Baechler, Jean. 1975. *The origins of capitalism*. Oxford: Basil Blackwell.

Baechler, Jean, Hall, John A., and Mann, Michael, eds. 1988. *Europe and the rise of capitalism*. Oxford: Basil Blackwell.

Bai, Ying and Kung, James Kai-sing. 2011. "Climate shocks and Sino-nomadic conflict." *Review of Economics and Statistics* 93: 970–81.

Bang, Peter F. 2007. "Trade and empire in search of organizing concepts for the Roman economy." *Past and Present* 195: 3–54.

Bang, Peter F. 2008. *The Roman bazaar: A comparative study of trade and markets in a tributary empire*. Cambridge: Cambridge University Press.

Bang, Peter F. 2012. "Predation." In Walter Scheidel, ed., *The Cambridge companion to the Roman economy*. Cambridge: Cambridge University Press, 197–217.

Bang, Peter F. 2015. "An economist approaches Roman economic history." *Journal of Roman Archaeology* 28: 637–40.

Bang, Peter F. in press. "Empire–a world history" In Bang, Bayly, and Scheidel in press.

Bang, Peter F., Bayly, Chris A., and Scheidel, Walter, eds. In press. *The Oxford world history of empire*. New York: Oxford University Press.

Bang, Peter F. and Kolodziejczyk, Dariusz, eds. 2012. *Universal empire: A comparative approach to imperial culture and representation in Eurasian history*. Cambridge: Cambridge University Press.

Bang, Peter F. and Scheidel, Walter, eds. 2013. *The Oxford handbook of the state in the ancient Near East and Mediterranean*. New York: Oxford University Press.

Bankoff, Greg and Swart, Sandra. 2007. *Breeds of empire: The "invention" of the horse in Southeast Asia and Southern Africa 1500–1950*. Copenhagen: NIAS.

Banniard, Michel. 2013. "The transition from Latin to the Romance languages." In Maiden, Smith, and Ledgeway 2013, 57–106.

Barbero, Alessandro. 2004. *Charlemagne: Father of a continent*. Berkeley: University of California Press.

Barcelo, Pedro A. 1988. *Karthago und die iberische Halbinsel vor den Barkiden: Studien zur karthagischen Präsenz von der Gründung von Ebusus (VII. Jh. v. Chr.) bis zum Übergang Hamilkars nach Hispanien (237 v. Chr.)*. Bonn: Habelt.

Barfield, Thomas J. 1989. *The perilous frontier: Nomadic empires and China, 221 BC to AD 1757*. Cambridge, MA: Blackwell.

Barfield, Thomas J. 2001. "The shadow empires: Imperial state formation along the Chinese-Nomad frontier." In Alcock et al. 2001, 10–41.

Barfield, Thomas J. 2002. "Turk, Persian, and Arab: Changing relationships between tribes and state in Iran and along its frontiers." In Nikki R. Keddie and Rudi Matthee, eds., *Iran and the surrounding world: Interactions in culture and cultural politics*. Seattle: University of Washington Press, 61–86.

Barfield, Thomas J. 2003. Review of Di Cosmo 2002. *T'oung Pao* 89: 458–66.

Barker, Graeme and Rasmussen, Tom. 1998. *The Etruscans*. Oxford: Blackwell.

Barkey, Karen. 2008. *Empire of difference: The Ottomans in comparative perspective*. Cambridge: Cambridge University Press.

Bar-Kochva, Bezalel. 1976. *The Seleucid army: Organization and tactics in the great campaigns*. Cambridge: Cambridge University Press.

Barnwell, Paul S. 2003. "Kings, nobles, and assemblies in the barbarian kingdoms." In Barnwell and Mostert 2003, 11–28.

Barnwell, Paul S. and Mostert, Marco, eds. 2003. *Political assemblies in the earlier Middle Ages*. Turnhout: Brepols.

Baronowski, Donald W. 1993. "Roman military forces in 225 BCE (Polybius 2.23–4)." *Historia* 42: 181–202.

Barrow, Julia. 2015. *The clergy in the medieval world: Secular clerics, their families and careers in north-western Europe, c. 800–c. 1200*. Cambridge: Cambridge University Press.

Bartlett, Robert. 1993. *The making of Europe: Conquest, colonization and cultural change, 950–1350*. Princeton, NJ: Princeton University Press.

Basan, Aziz. 2010. *The Great Seljuqs: A history*. London: Routledge.

Baten, Joerg and van Zanden, Jan Luiten. 2008. "Book production and the onset of modern economic growth." *Journal of Economic Growth* 13: 217–35.

Baumgarten, Albert I. 1999. "Marcel Simon's *Verus Israel* as a contribution to Jewish history." *Harvard Theological Review* 92: 465–78.

Bayly, Christopher A. 2004. *The birth of the modern world, 1780–1914: Connections and comparisons*. Malden, MA: Blackwell.

Beard, Mary. 2015. *SPQR: A history of ancient Rome*. New York: Liveright.

Beaudreau, Bernard. 2018. "A pull-push theory of industrial revolutions." IISES Annual Conference, Sevilla.

Becker, Sascha O., Pfaff, Steven, and Rubin, Jared. 2016. "Causes and consequences of the Protestant Reformation." *Explorations in Economic History* 62: 1–25.

Becker, Sascha O. and Woessmann, Ludger. 2009. "Was Weber wrong? A human capital theory of Protestant economic history." *Quarterly Journal of Economics* 124: 531–96.

Beckert, Sven. 2014. *Empire of cotton: A global history*. New York: Knopf.

Beckwith, Christopher I. 2009. *Empires of the Silk Road: A history of central Eurasia from the Bronze Age to the present*. Princeton, NJ: Princeton University Press.

Bedford, Peter R. 2009. "The Neo-Assyrian empire." In Morris and Scheidel 2009, 30–65.

Belich, James. 2009. *Replenishing the earth: The settler revolution and the rise of the Anglo-world, 1783–1939*. Oxford: Oxford University Press.

Belich, James. 2016. "The Black Death and the spread of Europe." In James Belich, John Darwin, Margret Frenz, and Chris Wickham, eds., *The prospect of global history*. Oxford: Oxford University Press, 93–107.

Beloch, Julius 1886. *Die Bevölkerung der griechisch-römischen Welt*. Leipzig: Duncker & Humblot.

Berkey, Jonathan P. 2003. *The formation of Islam: Religion and society in the Near East, 600–1800*. Cambridge: Cambridge University Press.

Bickerman, Elias and Smith, Morton. 1976. *The ancient history of Western civilization*. New York: Harper and Row.

Bielenstein, Hans 1987. *Chinese historical demography A.D. 2–1982*. Stockholm: Museum of Far Eastern Antiquities.

Billington, Stephen D. 2018. "'War, what is it good for?' The Industrial Revolution!" Queen's University Centre for Economic History Working Paper 2018-12.

Billows, Richard. 1990. *Antigonos the one-eyed and the creation of the Hellenistic state*. Berkeley: University of California Press.

Biondi, Ennio. 2016. *La politica imperialistica ateniese a metà del V secolo a.C.: Il contesto egizio-cipriota*. Milan: LED.

Black, Jeremy. 2002. *European warfare, 1494–1660*. London: Routledge.

Blackburn, Robin. 1997. *The making of New World slavery: From the Baroque to the Modern, 1492–1800*. London: Verso.

Blaydes, Lisa and Chaney, Eric. 2013. "The feudal revolution and Europe's rise: Political divergence of the Christian West and the Muslim world before 1500 CE." *American Political Science Review* 107: 16–34.

Blockmans, Wim P. 1994. "Voracious states and obstructing cities: An aspect of state formation in preindustrial Europe." In Tilly and Blockmans 1994, 218–50.

Blockmans, Wim P. 2002. *Emperor Charles V, 1500–1558*. London: Arnold.

Bodde, Derk. 1991. *Chinese thought, society, and science: The intellectual and social background of science and technology in pre-modern China*. Honolulu: University of Hawai'i Press.

Bogart, Dan and Richardson, Gary. 2011. "Property rights and Parliament in industrializing Britain." *Journal of Law and Economics* 54: 241–74.

Bol, Peter K. 1992. *"This culture of ours": Intellectual transitions in T'ang and Sung China*. Stanford, CA: Stanford University Press.

Bol, Peter K. 1993. "Government, society, and state: On the political visions of Ssu-ma Kuang and Wang An-shih." In Hymes and Schirokauer 1993, 128–92.

Bol, Peter K. 2008. *Neo-Confucianism in history*. Cambridge, MA: Harvard University Press.

Bolt, Jutta, Inklaar, Robert, de Jong, Herman, and van Zanden, Jan Luiten. 2018. "Rebasing 'Maddison': New income comparisons and the shape of long-run economic development." Groningen Growth and Development Centre Research Memorandum 174. https://www.rug.nl/ggdc/html_publications/memorandum/gd174.pdf.

Boltz, William G. 1994. *The origin and early development of the Chinese writing system*. New Haven, CT: American Oriental Society.

Bonnell, Victoria E. 1980. "The uses of theory, concepts and comparison in historical sociology." *Comparative Studies in Society and History* 22: 156–73.

Bonney, Richard, ed. 1995. *Economic systems and state finance*. Oxford: Oxford University Press.

Bonney, Richard, ed. 1999. *The rise of the fiscal state in Europe, c. 1200–1815*. Oxford: Oxford University Press.

Bonney, Richard and Ormrod, William. M. 1999. "Crises, revolutions and self-sustained growth: Towards a conceptual model of change in fiscal history." In William M. Ormrod, Margaret Bonney, and Richard Bonney, eds., *Crises, revolutions and self-sustained growth: Essays in European fiscal history, 1130–1830*. Stamford, UK: Shaun Tyas, 1–21.

Bosker, Maarten, Buringh, Eltjo, and van Zanden, Jan Luiten. 2013. "From Baghdad to London: unraveling urban development in Europe, the Middle East, and North Africa, 800–1800." *Review of Economics and Statistics* 95: 1418–37.

Bosworth, A. B. 1988. *From Arrian to Alexander: Studies in historical interpretation*. Oxford: Clarendon Press.

Bosworth, A. B. 2002. *The legacy of Alexander: Politics, warfare, and propaganda under the successors*. Oxford: Oxford University Press.

Bourguignon, Francois and Morrisson, Christian. 2002. "Inequality among world citizens: 1820–1992." *American Economic Review* 92: 727–44.

Bowman, Alan. 2018. "The state and the economy: Fiscality and taxation." In Wilson and Bowman 2018, 27–52.

Bowman, Alan and Wilson, Andrew. 2009. "Quantifying the Roman economy: Integration, growth, decline?" In Alan Bowman and Andrew Wilson, eds., *Quantifying the Roman economy: Problems and methods*. Oxford: Oxford University Press, 3–84.

Boyle, John A., ed. 1968. *The Cambridge history of Iran*, vol. 5: *The Saljuq and Mongol periods*. Cambridge: Cambridge University Press.

Brandt, Loren, Ma, Debin, and Rawski, Thomas G. 2014. "From divergence to convergence: Reevaluating the history behind China's economic boom." *Journal of Economic Literature* 52: 45–123.

Bransbourg, Gilles. 2015. "The later Roman empire." In Monson and Scheidel 2015a, 258–81.

Braudel, Fernand 1966. *La Méditerranée et la monde méditerranéen à l'époque de Philippe*. 2nd ed. Paris: Librairie Armand Colin.

Brauer, Jurgen and van Tuyll, Hubert. 2008. *Castles, battles, and bombs: How economics explains military history*. Chicago: University of Chicago Press.

Brendle, Franz. 2002. "Karl V. und die reichsständische Opposition." In Kohler, Haider, and Ottner 2002, 691–705.

Brenner, Robert and Isett, Christopher. 2002. "England's divergence from China's Yangzi Delta: Property relations, microeconomics, and patterns of development." *Journal of Asian Studies* 61: 609–62.

Bresson, Alain. 2006. "La machine d'Héron et le coût de l'énergie dans le monde antique." In Elio Lo Cascio, ed., *Innovazione tecnica e progresso economico nel mondo romano*. Bari: Edipuglia, 55–80.

Brewer, John. 1988. *The sinews of power: War, money and the English state, 1688–1783*. Cambridge, MA: Harvard University Press.

Briant, Pierre. 2002. *From Cyrus to Alexander: A history of the Persian empire*. Winona Lake, IN: Eisenbrauns.

Broadberry, Stephen, Guan, Hanhui, and Li, David D. 2017. "China, Europe and the great divergence: A study in historical national accounting, 980–1850." University of Oxford Discussion Papers in Economic and Social History no. 155.

Broadberry, Stephen and Gupta, Bishnupriya. 2006. "The early modern great divergence: Wages, prices and economic development in Europe and Asia, 1500–1800." *Economic History Review* 59: 2–31.

Broadberry, Stephen et al. 2015. *British economic growth, 1270–1870*. Cambridge: Cambridge University Press.

Broodbank, Cyprian. 2013. *The making of the middle sea: A history of the Mediterranean from the beginning to the emergence of the classical world*. Oxford: Oxford University Press.

Brown, Peter. 2003. *The rise of Western Christendom: Triumph and diversity, A.D. 200–1000*. 2nd ed. Malden, MA: Blackwell.

Brunt, Peter A. 1987. *Italian manpower 225 B.C.–A.D. 14*. Reprint with postscript. Oxford: Clarendon Press.

Bryant, Joseph M. 2006. "The West and the rest revisited: Debating capitalist origins, European colonialism, and the advent of modernity." *Canadian Journal of Sociology* 31: 403–44.

Bryant, Joseph M. 2008. "A new sociology for a new history? Further critical thoughts on the Eurasian similarity and great divergences theses." *Canadian Journal of Sociology* 33: 149–67.

Bulliet, Richard W. 2009. *Cotton, climate, and camels in early Islamic Iran: A moment in world history*. New York: Columbia University Press.

Büntgen, Ulf and Dï Cosmo, Nicola. 2016. "Climatic and environmental aspects of the Mongol withdrawal from Hungary in 1242 CE." *Scientific Reports* 6, 25606. doi: 10.1038/srep25606.

Büntgen, Ulf et al. 2016. "Cooling and societal change during the late antique Little Ice Age from 536 to around 660 AD." *Nature Geoscience* 9: 231–326.

Burbank, Jane and Cooper, Frederick. 2010. *Empires in world history: Power and the politics of difference*. Princeton, NJ: Princeton University Press.

Buringh, Eltjo and van Zanden, Jan Luiten. 2009. "Charting the 'rise of the West': Manuscripts and printed books in Europe, a long-term perspective from the sixth through eighteenth centuries." *Journal of Economic History* 69: 409–45.

Cahen, Claude. 1975. "Tribes, cities and social organization." In Richard N. Frye, ed., *The Cambridge history of Iran*, vol. 4: *The period from the Arab invasion to the Saljuqs*. Cambridge: Cambridge University Press, 305–63.

Campbell, Brian. 2004. "Power without limit: 'The Romans always win.'" In Angelos Chaniotis and Pierre Ducrey, eds., *Army and power in the ancient world*. Stuttgart: Steiner, 167–80.

Carmichael, Sarah G. et al. 2016. "The European marriage pattern and its measurement." *Journal of Economic History* 76: 196–204.

Carneiro, Robert L. 1970. "A theory of the origin of the state." *Science* 169: 733–38.

Carneiro, Robert L. 1988. "The circumscription theory: Challenge and response." *American Behavioral Scientist* 31: 497–511.

Carrier, Richard. 2017. *The scientist in the early Roman empire*. Durham, NC: Pitchstone.

Casale, Giancarlo. 2010. *The Ottoman age of exploration*. Oxford: Oxford University Press.

Cavaciocchi, Simonetta, ed. 2008. *La fiscalità nell'economia europea secc. XIII–XVIII: Atti della "trentanovesimo settimana di studi" 22–26 aprile 2007*. 2 vols. Florence: Firenze University Press.

Cawkwell, George. 2005. *The Greek wars: The failure of Persia*. Oxford: Oxford University Press.

Chaffee, John W. 1995. *The thorny gates of learning in Sung China: A social history of examinations*. New ed. Albany: State University of New York Press.

Challand, Gerard. 2004. *Nomadic empires: From Mongolia to the Danube*. New Brunswick, NJ: Transaction.

Chambers, James. 1979. *The devil's horsemen: The Mongol invasion of Europe*. New York: Atheneum.

Champion, Craige B. and Eckstein, Arthur M. 2004. "Introduction: The study of Roman imperialism." In Craige B. Champion, ed., *Roman imperialism: Readings and sources*. Malden, MA: Blackwell, 1–15.

Chaney, Eric. 2016. "Religion and the rise and fall of Islamic science." Working paper.

Chang, Chun-shu. 2007. *The rise of the Chinese empire*, vol. 1: *Nation, state, and imperialism in early China, ca. 1600 B.C.–A.D. 8*. Ann Arbor: University of Michigan Press.

Chaniotis, Angelos. 2005. *War in the Hellenistic world*. Malden, MA: Blackwell.

Chase-Dunn, Christopher and Hall, Thomas D. 1997. *Rise and demise: Comparing world-systems*. Boulder, CO: Westview Press.

Chaudhry, Azam and Garner, Phillip. 2006. "Political competition between countries and economic growth." *Review of Development Economics* 10: 666–82.

Chen, Qiang. 2012. "The Needham puzzle reconsidered: The protection of industrial and commercial property rights." *Economic History of Developing Regions* 27: 38–66.

Chen, Sanping. 2012. *Multicultural China in the early Middle Ages*. Philadelphia: University of Pennsylvania Press.

Chiang, Charleston W. K. et al. 2017. "A comprehensive map of genetic variation in the world's largest ethnic group—Han Chinese." bioRxiv, July 13. doi: https://doi.org/10.1101/162982.

Chirot, Daniel. 1985. "The rise of the West." *American Sociological Review* 50: 181–95.

Christian, David. 1998. *A history of Russia, Central Asia and Mongolia*, vol. 1: *Inner Eurasia from prehistory to the Mongol empire*. Malden, MA: Blackwell.

Chu, Angus C. 2010. "Nation states vs. united empire: Effects of political competition on economic growth." *Public Choice* 145: 181–95.

Chua, Amy. 2007. *Day of empire: How hyperpowers rise to global dominance—and why they fall*. New York: Doubleday.

Church, Sally K. 2005. "Zheng He: An investigation into the plausibility of 450-ft treasure ships." *Monumenta Serica* 53: 1–43.

Clark, Gregory. 2007. *A farewell to alms: A brief economic history of the world*. Princeton, NJ: Princeton University Press.

Clark, Hugh R. 2009. "The southern kingdoms between the T'ang and the Sung, 907–979." In Twitchett and Smith 2009, 133–205.

Cobb, Matthew A. 2018. *Rome and the Indian Ocean trade from Augustus to the early third century CE*. Leiden: Brill.

Coffman, D'Maris, Leonard, Adrian, and Neal, Larry, eds. 2013. *Questioning credible commitment: Perspectives on the rise of financial capitalism*. Cambridge: Cambridge University Press.

Cohen, H. Floris. 2009. "The rise of modern science as a fundamental pre-condition for the Industrial Revolution." *Österreichische Zeitschrift für Geschichtswissenschaften* 20, no. 2: 107–32.

Cohen, H. Floris. 2015. *The rise of modern science explained: A comparative history*. Cambridge: Cambridge University Press.

Cohen, Joel E. 1995. *How many people can the earth support?* New York: W. W. Norton.

Collins, Randall. 1995. "Prediction in macrosociology: The case of the Soviet collapse." *American Journal of Sociology* 100: 1552–93.

Collins, Roger. 1999. *Early medieval Europe 300–1000*. 2nd ed. Basingstoke: Palgrave.

Collins, Roger. 2004. *Visigothic Spain 409–711*. Malden, MA: Blackwell.

Cook, Theodore F., Jr. 2001. "The Chinese discovery of the New World, 15th century: What the expeditions of a eunuch admiral might have led to." In Cowley 2001, 85–104.

Cornell, Tim. 1993. "The end of Roman expansion." In Rich and Shipley 1993, 139–70.

Cornell, Tim J. 1995. *The beginnings of Rome: Italy and Rome from the Bronze Age to the Punic Wars (c. 1000–264 B.C.)*. London: Routledge.

Cornell, Tim J. 2000. "The city-states in Latium." In Hansen 2000a, 209–28.

Corvisier, Jean-Nicolas. 1991. *Aux origins du miracle grec: Peuplement et population en Grèce du Nord*. Paris: Presses Universitaires de France.

Cosandey, David. 2008. *Le secret de l'Occident: Vers une théorie générale du progrès scientifique*. Paris: Flammarion.

Cosgel, Metin M. and Miceli, Thomas J. 2009. "Tax collection in history." *Public Finance Review* 37: 399–420.

Coss, Peter. 2003. *The origins of the English gentry*. Cambridge: Cambridge University Press.

Costambeys, Marios, Innes, Matthew, and MacLean, Simon. 2011. *The Carolingian world*. Cambridge: Cambridge University Press.

Cowley, Robert, ed. 1999. *What if? The world's foremost military historians imagine what might have been*. New York: Berkley Books.

Cowley, Robert, ed. 2001. *What if? 2: Eminent historians imagine what might have been*. New York: Putnam.

Cox, Gary W. 2012. "Was the Glorious Revolution a constitutional watershed?" *Journal of Economic History* 72: 567–600.

Cox, Gary W. 2017. "Political institutions, economic liberty, and the Great Divergence." *Journal of Economic History* 77: 724–55.

Crone, Patricia. 1980. *Slaves on horses: The evolution of the Islamic polity*. Cambridge: Cambridge University Press.

Crone, Patricia. 2003. *Pre-industrial societies: Anatomy of the pre-modern world*. 2nd ed. Oxford: Oneworld.

Crone, Patricia. 2004. *Medieval Islamic political thought*. Edinburgh: Edinburgh University Press.

Cuenca Esteban, Javier. 2004. "Comparative patterns of colonial trade: Britain and its rivals." In Prados de la Escosura 2004, 35–66.

Cushing, Kathleen G. 2005. *Reform and papacy in the eleventh century: Spirituality and social change*. Manchester: Manchester University Press.

Dagron, Gilbert. 2003. *Emperor and priest: The imperial office in Byzantium*. Cambridge: Cambridge University Press.

Dale, Helen. 2017. *Kingdom of the wicked. Book one: Rules*. Balmain, Australia: Ligature.

Dale, Stephen F. 2010. *The Muslim empires of the Ottomans, Safavids, and Mughals*. Cambridge: Cambridge University Press.

Dalgaard, Carl-Johan et al. 2018. "Roman roads to prosperity: Persistence and non-persistence in public good provision." Center for Economic Policy Research Discussion Paper 12745.

Daly, Jonathan. 2015. *Historians debate the rise of the West*. London: Routledge.

Darwin, John. 2008. *After Tamerlane: The rise and fall of global empires, 1400–2000*. London: Bloomsbury.

Davids, Karel. 2013. *Religion, technology, and the Great and Little Divergences: China and Europe compared, c. 700–1800*. Leiden: Brill.

De Angelis, Franco. 2006. "Estimating the agricultural base of Greek Sicily." *Papers of the British School at Rome* 68: 111–48.

Deaton, Angus. 2013. *The great escape: Health, wealth, and the origins of inequality*. Princeton, NJ: Princeton University Press.

De Bellaigue, Christopher. 2017. *The Islamic enlightenment: The struggle between faith and reason, 1798 to modern times*. New York: Liveright.

Decker, Michael J. 2016. *The Byzantine Dark Ages*. London: Bloomsbury.

Declercq, Dominik. 1998. *Writing against the state: Political rhetorics in third and fourth century China*. Leiden: Brill.

De Crespigny, Rafe. 2004. "South China in the Han period." Internet edition. https://openresearch-repository.anu.edu.au/html/1885/42048/southchina_han.html.

De Crespigny, Rafe. 2012. Review of Pines 2012. *American Historical Review* 117: 1567–68.

De Ligt, Luuk. 2012. *Peasants, citizens and soldiers: Studies in the demographic history of Roman Italy 225 BC–AD 100*. Cambridge: Cambridge University Press.

De Long, J. Bradford. 2000. "Overstrong against thyself: War, the state, and growth in Europe on the eve of the Industrial Revolution." In Mancur Olson and Satu Kähkönen, eds., *A not-so-dismal science: A broader view of economies and societies*. Oxford: Oxford University Press, 138–67.

De Long, J. Bradford and Shleifer, Andrei. 1993. "Princes and merchants: European city growth before the Industrial Revolution." *Journal of Law and Economics* 36: 671–702.

Demandt, Alexander. 1984. *Der Fall Roms: Die Auflösung des römischen Reiches im Urteil der Nachwelt*. Munich: C. H. Beck.

Demandt, Alexander. 1999. "Statt Rom: Ein historisches Gedankenspiel." In Michael Salewski, ed., *Was wäre wenn: Alternativ- und Parallelgeschichte: Brücken zwischen Phantasie und Wirklichkeit*. Stuttgart: Franz Steiner Verlag, 69–80.

Demandt, Alexander. 2011. *Ungeschehene Geschichte: Ein Traktat über die Frage; Was wäre geschehen, wenn . . . ?* New ed. Göttingen: Vandenhoeck & Ruprecht.

DeMarrais, Elizabeth. 2005. "A view from the Americas: 'Internal colonization', material culture and power in the Inka empire." In Henry Hurst and Sara Owen, eds., *Ancient colonizations: Analogy, similarity and difference*. London: Duckworth, 73–96.

De Moor, Tina and van Zanden, Jan Luiten. 2010. "Girlpower: The European marriage pattern and labour markets in the North Sea region in the late medieval and early modern period." *Economic History Review* 63: 1–33.

Deng, Gang. 1997. *Chinese maritime activities and socioeconomic development, c. 2100 B.C.–1900 A.D.* Westport, CT: Greenwood Press.

Deng, Gang. 1999. *Maritime sector, institutions, and sea power of premodern China*. Westport, CT: Greenwood Press.

Deng, Kent G. 2004. "Why the Chinese failed to develop a steam engine." *History of Technology* 25: 151–71.

Deng, Kent G. 2012. "The continuation and efficiency of the Chinese fiscal state, 700 BC–AD 1911." In Yun-Casalilla and O'Brien 2012, 335–52.

Deng, Kent G. 2015. "Imperial China under the Song and late Qing." In Monson and Scheidel 2015a, 308–42.

Deng, Kent and O'Brien, Patrick. 2016. "Establishing statistical foundations of a chronology for the great divergence: A survey and critique of the primary sources for the construction of relative wage levels for Ming-Qing China." *Economic History Review* 69: 1057–82.

Dennison, Tracy and Ogilvie, Sheilagh. 2014. "Does the European marriage pattern explain economic growth?" *Journal of Economic History* 74: 651–93.

Dennison, Tracy and Ogilvie, Sheilagh. 2016. "Institutions, demography, and economic growth." *Journal of Economic History* 76: 205–17.

Desmet, Klaus, Greif, Avner, and Parente, Stephen L. 2017. "Spatial competition, innovation and institutions: The Industrial Revolution and the Great Divergence." Working paper, February.

De Souza, Philip. 1999. *Piracy in the Graeco-Roman world*. Cambridge: Cambridge University Press.

De Vries, Jan. 2008. *The Industrious Revolution: Consumer behavior and the household economy, 1650 to the present*. New York: Cambridge University Press.

De Vries, Jan and van der Woude, Ad. 1997. *The first modern economy: Success, failure, and perseverance of the Dutch economy, 1500–1815*. Cambridge: Cambridge University Press.

Diamond, Jared. 1997. *Guns, germs, and steel: The fates of human societies*. New York: Norton.

Di Cosmo, Nicola. 1994. "Ancient Inner Asian nomads: Their economic basis and its significance in Chinese history." *Journal of Asian Studies* 53: 1092–126.

Di Cosmo, Nicola. 1999a. "The northern frontier in pre-imperial China." In Loewe and Shaughnessy 1999, 885–966.

Di Cosmo, Nicola. 1999b. "State formation and periodization in Inner Asian history." *Journal of World History* 10: 1–40.

Di Cosmo, Nicola. 2002a. *Ancient China and its enemies: The rise of nomadic power in East Asian history*. Cambridge: Cambridge University Press.

Di Cosmo, Nicola, ed. 2002b. *Warfare in Inner Asian history (500–1800)*. Leiden: Brill.

Dien, Albert. 2001. "Civil service examinations: Evidence from the Northwest." In Pearce, Spiro, and Ebrey 2001, 99–120.

Dincecco, Mark. 2011. *Political transformations and public finances: Europe, 1650–1913*. Cambridge: Cambridge University Press.

Dincecco, Mark and Onorato, Massimiliano G. 2016. "Military conflict and the rise of urban Europe." *Journal of Economic Growth* 21: 259–82.

Dincecco, Mark and Onorato, Massimiliano G. 2018. *From warfare to wealth: The military origins of urban prosperity in Europe*. New York: Cambridge University Press.

Disney, Anthony R. 2009. *A history of Portugal and the Portuguese empire: From beginnings to 1807*, vol. 2: *The Portuguese empire*. Cambridge: Cambridge University Press.

Dong, Hongyuan. 2014. *A history of the Chinese language*. Milton Park, UK: Routledge.

Downing, Brian M. 1992. *The military revolution and political change: Origins of democracy and autocracy in early modern Europe*. Princeton, NJ: Princeton University Press.

Doyle, Michael W. 1986. *Empires*. Ithaca, NY: Cornell University Press.

Drake, H. A. 2007. "The church, society and political power." In Augustine Casiday and Frederick W. Norris, eds., *The Cambridge history of Christianity*, vol. 2: *Constantine to c. 600*. Cambridge: Cambridge University Press, 403–28.

Drelichman, Mauricio and Voth, Hans-Joachim. 2014. *Lending to the borrower from hell: Debt, taxes, and default in the age of Philipp II*. Princeton, NJ: Princeton University Press.

Drews, Robert. 2004. *Early riders: The beginnings of mounted warfare in Asia and Europe*. New York: Routledge.

Dreyer, Edward L. 2007. *Zheng He: China and the oceans in the early Ming dynasty, 1405–1433*. New York: Pearson Longman.

Duchesne, Ricardo. 2011. *The uniqueness of Western civilization*. Leiden: Brill.

Duchhardt, Heinz. 2002. "Tunis–Algier–Jerusalem? Zur Mittelmeerpolitk Karls V." In Kohler, Haider, and Ottner 2002, 685–90.

Duncan-Jones, Richard. 1990. *Structure and scale in the Roman economy*. Cambridge: Cambridge University Press.

Duncan-Jones, Richard P. 1994. *Money and government in the Roman empire*. Cambridge: Cambridge University Press.

Durand-Guédy, David. 2010. *Iranian elites and Turkish rulers: A history of Isfahan in the Saljuq period*. London: Routledge.

Eberhard, Wolfram. 1949. *Das Toba-Reich Nordchinas: Eine soziologische Untersuchung*. Leiden: Brill.

Eckstein, Arthur M. 1987. *Senate and general: Individual decision-making and Roman foreign relations, 264–194 B.C.* Berkeley: University of California Press.

Eckstein, Arthur M. 2006. *Mediterranean anarchy, interstate war, and the rise of Rome*. Berkeley: University of California Press.

Edwards, Jeremy and Ogilvie, Sheilagh. 2018. "Did the Black Death cause economic development by 'inventing' fertility restriction?" Center for Economic Studies and Ifo Institute Working Paper.

Eich, Armin and Eich, Peter. 2005. "War and state-building in Roman Republican times." *Scripta Classica Israelica* 24: 1–33.

Eich, Peter. 2015. "The common denominator: Late Roman imperial bureaucracy from a comparative perspective." In Scheidel 2015c, 90–149.

Eire, Carlos M. N. 2006a. "The quest for a counterfactual Jesus." In Tetlock, Lebow, and Parker 2006b, 119–42.

Eire, Carlos M. N. 2006b. "Religious kitsch or Industrial Revolution: What difference would a Catholic England make?" In Tetlock, Lebow, and Parker 2006b, 145–67.

Eisenstadt, Shmuel N. 1963. *The political systems of empires*. New York: Free Press.

Elman, Benjamin A. 2000. *A cultural history of civil examinations in late imperial China*. Cambridge, MA: Harvard University Press.

Elman, Benjamin. 2013. *Civil examinations and meritocracy in late imperial China*. Cambridge, MA: Harvard University Press.

Eltis, David and Engerman, Stanley L. 2000. "The importance of slavery and the slave trade to industrializing Britain." *Journal of Economic History* 60: 123–44.

Elvin, Mark. 1973. *The pattern of the Chinese past: A social and economic interpretation*. Stanford, CA: Stanford University Press.

Elvin, Mark. 2008. "Defining the *explicanda* in the 'West and the rest' debate: Bryant's critique and its critics." *Canadian Journal of Sociology* 33: 168–85.

Epstein, S. R. 2000. *Freedom and growth: The rise of states and markets in Europe, 1300–1750*. London: Routledge.

Erdkamp, Paul. 1998. *Hunger and the sword: Warfare and food supply in Roman Republican wars (264–30 B.C.)*. Amsterdam: J. C. Gieben.

Erdkamp, Paul. 2005. *The grain market in the Roman empire: A social, political, and economic study*. Cambridge: Cambridge University Press.

Ertman, Thomas. 1997. *Birth of the Leviathan: Building states and regimes in medieval and modern Europe*. Cambridge: Cambridge University Press.

Etemad, Bouda. 2007. *Possessing the world: Taking the measurements of colonisation from the eighteenth to the twentieth century*. New York: Berghahn Books.

Evers, Kasper G. 2017. *Worlds apart trading together: The organisation of long-distance trade between Rome and India in antiquity*. Oxford: Archaeopress.

Fariselli, Anna C. 2002. *I mercenari di Cartagine*. La Spezia: Agorà Edizioni.

Feeney, Denis. 2016. *Beyond Greek: The beginnings of Latin literature*. Cambridge, MA: Harvard University Press.

Ferguson, Niall. 1997. "Introduction: Virtual History: Towards a 'Chaotic' Theory of the Past." In Niall Ferguson, ed., *Virtual history: Alternatives and counterfactuals*. London: Picador, 1–90.

Férnandez-Armesto, Felipe. 2006. *Pathfinders: A global history of exploration*. New York: Norton.

Findlay, Ronald and O'Rourke, Kevin H. 2007. *Power and plenty: Trade, war, and the world economy in the second millennium*. Princeton, NJ: Princeton University Press.

Finlay, Robert. 2000. "China, the West, and world history in Joseph Needham's *Science and civilization in China*." *Journal of World History* 11: 265–303.

Finley, Moses I. 1998. *Ancient slavery and modern ideology*. Ed. Brent D. Shaw. Expanded ed. Princeton, NJ: Markus Wiener.

Fischer-Bovet, Christelle. 2014. *Army and society in Ptolemaic Egypt*. Cambridge: Cambridge University Press.

Fisher, Greg. 2011. *Between empires: Arabs, Romans, and Sasanians in late antiquity*. Oxford: Oxford University Press.

Fleming, Robin. 2010. *Britain after Rome: The fall and rise, 400–1070*. London: Allen Lane.

Fletcher, Joseph. 1986. "The Mongols: Ecological and social perspectives." *Harvard Journal of Asiatic Studies* 46: 11–50.

Floud, R. et al. 2011. *The changing body: Health, nutrition, and human development in the Western world since 1700*. Cambridge: Cambridge University Press.

Foa, Roberto S. 2016. "Ancient polities, modern states." PhD diss., Harvard University.

Fogel, Robert W. 2004. *The escape from hunger and premature death, 1700–2100: Europe, America, and the Third World*. Cambridge: Cambridge University Press.

Foltz, Richard C. 1998. *Mughal India and Central Asia*. Karachi: Oxford University Press.

Foster, Benjamin R. 2016. *The age of Agade: Inventing empire in ancient Mesopotamia*. London: Routledge.

Fouracre, Paul. 1995. "Frankish Gaul to 814." In McKitterick 1995, 85–109.

Fowden, Garth. 2011. "Contextualizing late antiquity: The first millennium." In Johann P. Arnason and Kurt A. Raaflaub, eds., *The Roman empire in context: Historical and comparative perspectives*. Malden, MA: Wiley-Blackwell, 148–76.

France, John. 1999. *Western warfare in the age of the crusades, 1000–1300*. Ithaca, NY: Cornell University Press.

Frank, Andre G. 1998. *ReOrient: Global economy in the Asian age*. Berkeley: University of California Press.

Frank, Tenney. 1933. *An economic survey of ancient Rome*, vol. 1: *Rome and Italy of the republic.* Baltimore: Johns Hopkins University Press.

Franklin, Simon and Shepard, Jonathan. 1996. *The emergence of Rus: 750–1200.* London: Longman.

Friedel, Robert. 2007. *A culture of improvement: Technology and the Western millennium.* Cambridge, MA: MIT Press.

Frier, Bruce W. 2000. "Demography." In Alan K. Bowman, Peter Garnsey, and Dominic Rathbone, eds., *The Cambridge ancient history*, vol. 11: *The high empire, A.D. 70–192.* 2nd ed. Cambridge: Cambridge University Press, 787–816.

Fronda, Michael P. 2010. *Between Rome and Carthage: Southern Italy during the Second Punic War.* New York: Cambridge University Press.

Fu, Zhengyuan. 1996. *China's legalists: The earliest totalitarians and their art of ruling.* Armonk, NY: M. E. Sharpe.

Fukuyama, Francis 2011. *The origins of political order: From prehuman times to the French Revolution.* New York: Farrar, Straus and Giroux.

Garnsey, Peter and Humfress, Caroline. 2001. *The evolution of the late antique world.* Cambridge: Orchard Academic.

Garza, Andrew de la. 2014. "Command of the coast: The Mughal navy and regional strategy." *World History Connected* 12, no. 1. http://worldhistoryconnected.press.uillinois.edu/12.1 /forum_delagarza.html.

Gat, Azar. 2006. *War in human civilization.* Oxford: Oxford University Press.

Gaubatz, Piper R. 1996. *Beyond the Great Wall: Urban form and transformation on the Chinese frontiers.* Stanford, CA: Stanford University Press.

Gellner, Ernest. 1983. *Nations and nationalism.* Ithaca, NY: Cornell University Press.

Gernet, Jacques. 1995 [1956]. *Buddhism in Chinese society: An economic history from the fifth to the tenth century.* New York: Columbia University Press.

Gibbon, Edward. 1781. *The history of the decline and fall of the Roman empire. Volume the third.* 2nd ed. London: Strahan.

Gibbon, Edward. 1788a. *The history of the decline and fall of the Roman empire. Volume the fifth.* London: Strahan.

Gibbon, Edward. 1788b. *The history of the decline and fall of the Roman empire. Volume the sixth.* London: Strahan.

Girardet, Klaus M. 2006. *Die konstantinische Wende: Voraussetzungen und geistige Grundlagen der Religionspolitik Konstantins des Grossen.* Darmstadt: Wissenschaftliche Buchgesellschaft.

Gizewski, Christian. 1994. "Römische und alte chinesische Geschichte im Vergleich: Zur Möglichkeit eines gemeinsamen Altertumsbegriffs." *Klio* 76: 271–302.

Glete, Jan. 2002. *War and the state in early modern Europe: Spain, the Dutch Republic and Sweden as fiscal-military states, 1500–1660.* London: Routledge.

Goffart, Walter. 1980. *Barbarians and Romans, A.D. 418–584: The techniques of accommodation.* Princeton, NJ: Princeton University Press.

Goffart, Walter. 2006. *Barbarian tides: The migration age and the later Roman empire.* Philadelphia: University of Pennsylvania Press.

Golden, Peter B. 1998. *Nomads and sedentary societies in medieval Eurasia.* Washington, DC: American Historical Association.

Golden, Peter B. 2002. "War and warfare in the pre-Cinggisid western steppes of Eurasia." In Di Cosmo 2002b, 105–72.

Goldscheid, Rudolf. 1917. *Staatssozialismus oder Staatskapitalismus*. Vienna: Anzengruber.

Goldstone, Jack A. 1987. "Cultural orthodoxy, risk, and innovation: The divergence of East and West in the early modern world." *Sociological Theory* 5: 119–35.

Goldstone, Jack A. 1991. *Revolution and rebellion in the early modern world*. Berkeley: University of California Press.

Goldstone, Jack A. 2000. "The rise of the West—or not? A revision to socio-economic history." *Sociological Theory* 18: 175–94.

Goldstone, Jack A. 2002. "Efflorescences and economic growth in world history: Rethinking the 'Rise of the West' and the Industrial Revolution." *Journal of World History* 13: 323–89.

Goldstone, Jack A. 2006. "Europe's peculiar path: Would the world be 'modern' if William III's invasion of England in 1688 had failed?" In Tetlock, Lebow, and Parker 2006b, 168–96.

Goldstone, Jack A. 2009. *Why Europe? The rise of the West in world history, 1500–1850*. New York: McGraw-Hill.

Goldsworthy, Adrian. 2009. *How Rome fell: Death of a superpower*. New Haven, CT: Yale University Press.

Gordon, Matthew S. 2001. *The breaking of a thousand swords: A history of the Turkish military of Samarra (A.H. 200–275/815–889 C.E.)*. Albany: State University of New York Press.

Graff, David A. 2002. *Medieval Chinese warfare, 300–900*. London: Routledge.

Graff, David A. 2016. *The Eurasian way of war: Military practice in seventh-century China and Byzantium*. London: Routledge.

Grainger, John D. 1990. *Seleukos Nikator: Constructing a Hellenistic kingdom*. London: Routledge.

Grainger, John D. 1999. *The league of the Aitolians*. Leiden: Brill.

Grainger, John D. 2002. *The Roman war of Antiochos the Great*. Leiden: Brill.

Grainger, John D. 2010. *The Syrian wars*. Leiden: Brill.

Greif, Avner. 2006. *Institutions and the path to the modern economy: Lessons from medieval trade*. Cambridge: Cambridge University Press.

Greif, Avner and Tabellini, Guido. 2017. "The clan and the corporation: Sustaining cooperation in China and Europe." *Journal of Comparative Economics* 45: 1–35.

Griffith, G. T., ed. 1966. *Alexander the Great: The main problems*. Cambridge: Heffer.

Grossmann, Lukas. 2009. *Roms Samnitenkriege: Historische und historiographische Untersuchungen zu den Jahren 327 bis 290 v. Chr*. Düsseldorf: Wellem Verlag.

Grummit, David and Lassalmonie, Jean-Francois. 2015. "Royal public finance (c. 1290–1523)." In Christopher Fletcher, Jean-Philippe Genet, and John Watts, eds., *Government and political life in England and France, c.1300–c.1500*. Cambridge: Cambridge University Press, 116–49.

Gupta, Bishnupriya, Ma, Debin, and Roy, Tirthankar. 2016. "States and development: Early modern India, China, and the Great Divergence." In Jari Eloranta et al., eds., *Economic history of warfare and state formation*. Singapore: Springer, 51–69.

Gwynn, David M., ed. 2008. *A.H.M. Jones and the later Roman empire*. Leiden: Brill.

Gwynn, David M. 2012. "Episcopal leadership." In Johnson 2012, 876–915.

Haldon, John F. 1990. *Byzantium in the seventh century: The transformation of a culture.* Cambridge: Cambridge University Press.

Haldon, John. 1993. *The state and the tributary mode of production.* London: Verso.

Haldon, John. 2012. "Comparative state formation: The Later Roman empire in the wider world." In Johnson 2012, 1111–47.

Haldon, John. 2016. *The empire that would not die: The paradox of Eastern Roman survival, 640–740.* Cambridge, MA: Harvard University Press.

Haldon, John. In press. "The political economy of empire: 'Imperial capital' and the formation of central and regional elites." In Bang, Bayly, and Scheidel in press.

Hall, John A. 1985. *Powers and liberties: The causes and consequences of the rise of the West.* Berkeley: University of California Press.

Hall, John A. 1988. "States and societies: The miracle in comparative perspective." In Baechler, Hall, and Mann 1988, 20–38.

Hall, John A. 1996. *International orders.* Cambridge: Polity Press.

Hall, Thomas D. 2010. Review of Beckwith 2009. *Cliodynamics* 1, no. 1: 103–15.

Halsall, Guy. 2003. *Warfare and society in the barbarian West, 450–900.* London: Routledge.

Halsall, Guy. 2007. *Barbarians migrations and the Roman West, 376–578.* Cambridge: Cambridge University Press.

Hämäläinen, Pekka. 2008. *The Comanche empire.* New Haven, CT: Yale University Press.

Hanlon, W. Walker. 2015. "Necessity is the mother of invention: Input supplies and directed technical change." *Econometrica* 83: 67–100.

Hansen, Mogens H., ed. 2000a. *A comparative study of thirty city-state cultures: An investigation conducted by the Copenhagen Polis Centre.* Copenhagen: Royal Danish Academy of Sciences and Letters.

Hansen, Mogens H. 2000b. "Conclusion: the impact of city-state cultures on world history." In Hansen, 2000a, 597–623.

Hansen, Mogens H., ed. 2002. *A comparative study of six city-state cultures: An investigation conducted by the Copenhagen Polis Centre.* Copenhagen: Royal Danish Academy of Sciences and Letters.

Hansen, Mogens H. 2006. *The shotgun method: The demography of the ancient Greek city-state culture.* Columbia: University of Missouri Press.

Hanson, John W. 2016. *An urban geography of the Roman world, 100 B.C. to A.D. 300.* Oxford: Archaeopress.

Hanson, Victor D. 2006. "A stillborn West?" In Tetlock, Lebow, and Parker 2006b, 47–89.

Harper, Kyle. 2017. *The fate of Rome: Climate, disease, and the end of an empire.* Princeton, NJ: Princeton University Press.

Harris, William V. 1984. "The Italians and the empire." In William V. Harris, ed., *The imperialism of mid-Republican Rome.* Rome: American Academy in Rome, 89–109.

Harris, William V. 1985. *War and imperialism in Republican Rome 327–70 B.C.* Expanded repr. ed. Oxford: Clarendon Press.

Harris, William V. 2006. "A revisionist view of Roman money." *Journal of Roman Studies* 96: 1–24.

Harris, William V. 2016. *Roman power: A thousand years of empire.* Cambridge: Cambridge University Press.

Hartmann, Mary S. 2004. *The household and the making of history: A subversive view of the Western past.* Cambridge: Cambridge University Press.

Hartog, Leo de. 1996. *Russia and the Mongol yoke: The history of the Russian principalities and the Golden Horde, 1221–1502.* London: I. B. Tauris.

Haupt, Heinz-Gerhard, and Kocka, Jürgen, eds. 1996a. *Geschichte und Vergleich: Ansätze und Ergebnisse international vergleichender Geschichtsschreibung.* Frankfurt: Campus.

Haupt, Heinz-Gerhard and Kocka, Jürgen. 1996b. "Historischer Vergleich: Methoden, Aufgaben, Probleme. Eine Einleitung." In Haupt and Kocka 1996a, 9–45.

Hawthorn, Geoffrey. 1991. *Plausible worlds: Possibility and understanding in history and the social sciences.* Cambridge: Cambridge University Press.

He, Wenkai. 2013. *Paths towards the modern fiscal state: England, Japan, and China.* Cambridge, MA: Harvard University Press.

Heather, Peter. 2006. *The fall of the Roman empire: A new history of Rome and the barbarians.* Oxford: Oxford University Press.

Heather, Peter. 2009. *Empires and barbarians: Migration, development and the birth of Europe.* London: Macmillan.

Hébert, Michel. 2014. *Parlementer: Assemblées representatives et échange politique en Europe occidentale à la fin du Moyen Âge.* Paris: De Boccard.

Henige, David 1998. *Numbers from nowhere: The American Indian population contact debate.* Norman: University of Oklahoma Press.

Herlihy, David. 1997. *The Black Death and the transformation of the West.* Cambridge, MA: Harvard University Press.

Hilaire, Jean. 1986. *Introduction historique au droit commercial.* Paris: Presses Universitaires de France.

Hin, Saskia. 2013. *The demography of Roman Italy: Population dynamics in an ancient conquest society 201 BCE–14 CE.* Cambridge: Cambridge University Press.

Hinsch, Bret. 1988. "Climatic change and history in China." *Journal of Asian History* 22: 131–59.

Hobson, John M. 2004. *The Eastern origins of Western civilization.* Cambridge: Cambridge University Press.

Hoffman, Philip T. 2015. *Why did Europe conquer the world?* Princeton, NJ: Princeton University Press.

Holcombe, Charles. 2001. *The genesis of East Asia, 221 B.C.–A.D. 907.* Honolulu: University of Hawai'i Press.

Hölkeskamp, Hans-Joachim. 2010. *Reconstructing the Roman Republic: An ancient political culture and modern research.* Princeton, NJ: Princeton University Press.

Holland, Cecilia. 1999. "The death that saved Europe: The Mongols turn back, 1242." In Cowley 1999, 93–106.

Holt, Frank L. 2016. *The treasures of Alexander the Great: How one man's wealth shaped the world.* New York: Oxford University Press.

Honeychurch, William. 2015. *Inner Asia and the spatial politics of empire: Archaeology, mobility, and culture contact.* New York: Springer.

Hopkins, Keith. 1978. *Conquerors and slaves: Sociological studies in Roman history,* vol. 1. Cambridge: Cambridge University Press.

Hopkins, Keith. 1980. "Taxes and trade in the Roman empire (200 B.C.–A.D. 400)." *Journal of Roman Studies* 70: 101–25 (repr. in Keith Hopkins, *Sociological studies in Roman history,* ed. Christopher Kelly [Cambridge: Cambridge University Press, 2018], 213–59).

Hopkins, Keith. 1991. "From violence to blessing: Symbols and rituals in ancient Rome." In Molho, Raaflaub, and Emlen 1991, 479–98 (repr. in Keith Hopkins, *Sociological studies in Roman history,* ed. Christopher Kelly [Cambridge: Cambridge University Press, 2018], 313–39).

Hopkins, Keith. 2002. "Rome, taxes, rents and trade." In Scheidel and von Reden 2002, 190–230.

Hoppit, Julian. 2017. *Britain's political economies: Parliament and economic life, 1660–1800.* Cambridge: Cambridge University Press.

Horne, Alistair. 1999. "Ruler of the world: Napoleon's missed opportunities." In Cowley 1999, 201–19.

Hoyos, Dexter. 2010. *The Carthaginians.* London: Routledge.

Hsu, Cho-yun. 1965. *Ancient China in transition: An analysis of social mobility, 722–222 B.C.* Stanford, CA: Stanford University Press.

Huang, Philip C. C. 2002. "Development of involution in eighteenth-century Britain and China? A review of Kenneth Pomeranz's *The great divergence: China, Europe, and the making of the modern world economy.*" *Journal of Asian Studies* 61: 501–38.

Huang, Ray. 1974. *Taxation and governmental finance in sixteenth-century Ming China.* Cambridge: Cambridge University Press.

Huang, Ray. 1997. *China: A macro history.* Rev. ed. Armonk, NY: M. E. Sharpe.

Huff, Toby E. 2003. *The rise of early modern science: Islam, China, and the West.* 2nd ed. Cambridge: Cambridge University Press.

Huff, Toby E. 2011. *Intellectual curiosity and the scientific revolution: A global perspective.* Cambridge: Cambridge University Press.

Hui, Victoria Tin-bor. 2005. *War and state formation in ancient China and early modern Europe.* Cambridge: Cambridge University Press.

Hui, Victoria Tin-bor. 2015. "The China dream: Revival of what historical greatness?" In Arthur Shuhfan Ding and Chih-shian Liou, eds., *China dreams: China's new leadership and future impacts.* Singapore: World Scientific, 3–32.

Huntington, Samuel P. 1996. *The clash of civilizations and the remaking of world order.* New York: Simon and Schuster.

Huss, Werner. 1985. *Geschichte der Karthager.* Munich: C. H. Beck.

Hymes, Robert P. and Schirokauer, Conrad, eds. 1993. *Ordering the world: Approaches to state and society in Sung Dynasty China.* Berkeley: University of California Press.

Inikori, Joseph I. 2002. *Africans and the Industrial Revolution in England: A study in international trade and economic development.* Cambridge: Cambridge University Press.

Inkster, Ian. 1991. *Science and technology in history: An approach to industrial development.* New Brunswick, NJ: Rutgers University Press.

Ioannides, Yannis and Zhang, Junfu. 2017. "Walled cities in late imperial China." *Journal of Urban Economics* 97: 71–88.

Iyigun, Murat. 2008. "Luther and Suleyman." *Quarterly Journal of Economics* 123: 1465–94.

Jackson, Peter. 2005. *The Mongols and the West, 1221–1410.* Harlow: Pearson.

Jacob, Margaret C. 1997. *Scientific culture and the making of the industrial West.* New York: Oxford University Press.

Jacob, Margaret C. 2014. *The first knowledge economy: Human capital and the European economy, 1750–1850.* New York: Cambridge University Press.

Jacoby, David. 2008. "Byzantium, the Italian maritime powers, and the Black Sea before 1204." *Byzantinische Zeitschrift* 100: 677–99.

Jagchid, Sechin and Symons, Van J. 1989. *Peace, war, and trade along the Great Wall: Nomadic-Chinese interaction through two millennia.* Bloomington: Indiana University Press.

Jamaluddin, Syed. 1995. *The state under Timur: A study in empire building.* New Delhi: Har-Anand Publications.

Janousch, Andreas. 1999. "The emperor as bodhisattva: The bodhisattva ordination and ritual assemblies of Emperor Wu of the Liang dynasty." In Joseph P. McDermott, ed., *State and court ritual in China.* Cambridge: Cambridge University Press, 112–49.

Jardine, Lisa. 2008. *Going Dutch: How England plundered Holland's glory.* New York: HarperCollins.

Jehne, Martin. 2006. "Römer, Latiner und Bundesgenossen im Krieg: Zu Formen und Ausmass der Integration in der republikanischen Armee." In Martin Jehne and Rene Pfeilschifter, eds., *Herrschaft ohne Integration? Rom und Italien in republikanischer Zeit.* Frankfurt a.M.: Verlag Antike, 243–68.

Jha, Saumitra. 2015. "Financial asset holdings and political attitudes: Evidence from revolutionary England." *Quarterly Journal of Economics* 130: 1485–545.

Johne, Klaus-Peter. 2006. *Die Römer an der Elbe: das Stromgebiet der Elbe im geographischen Weltbild und im politischen Bewusstsein der griechisch-römischen Antike.* Berlin: Akademie Verlag.

Johnson, Noel D. and Koyama, Mark. 2017. "States and economic growth: Capacity and constraints." *Explorations in Economic History* 64: 1–20.

Johnson, Scott A. J. 2017. *Why did ancient civilizations fail?* New York: Routledge.

Johnson, Scott F., ed. 2012. *The Oxford handbook of late antiquity.* New York: Oxford University Press.

Jones, Alexander. 2017. *A portable cosmos: Revealing the Antikythera mechanism, scientific wonder of the ancient world.* New York: Oxford University Press.

Jones, Arnold H. M. 1964. *The later Roman empire, 284–602: A social, economic and administrative survey,* 3 vols. Oxford: Basil Blackwell.

Jones, Eric. 2003. *The European miracle: Environments, economies and geopolitics in the history of Europe and Asia.* 3rd ed. Cambridge: Cambridge University Press.

Jones, Eric L. 2010. *Locating the Industrial Revolution: Inducement and response.* Singapore: World Scientific.

Jursa, Michael. 2010. *Aspects of the economic history of Babylonia in the first millennium BC.* Münster: Ugarit-Verlag.

Kang, Le. 1983. "An empire for a city: Cultural reforms of the Hsiao-Wen emperor (A.D. 471–499)." PhD diss., Yale University.

Kant, Immanuel. 1903 [1795]. *Perpetual peace: A philosophical essay.* Trans. M. Campbell Smith. London: Swan Sonnenschein & Co.

Kaplan, Jed O. et al. 2011. "Holocene carbon emissions as a result of anthropogenic land cover change." *The Holocene* 21: 775–91. doi: 10.1177/0959683610386983.

Karaman, K. Kivanc and Pamuk, Sevket. 2010. "Ottoman state finances in European perspective, 1500–1914." *Journal of Economic History* 70: 593–629.

Karayalcin, Cem. 2008. "Divided we stand, united we fall: The Hume-Weber-Jones mechanism for the rise of Europe." *International Economic Review* 49: 973–97.

Karayalcin, Cem. 2016. "Property rights and the first great divergence: Europe 1500–1800." *International Review of Economics and Finance* 42: 484–98.

Kasten, Brigitte. 1997. *Königssöhne und Königsherrschaft: Untersuchungen zur Teilhabe am Reich in der Merowinger- und Karolingerzeit.* Hannover: Hahnsche Buchhandlung.

Kasza, Gregory J. 1996. "War and comparative politics." *Comparative Politics* 29: 355–73.

Kaufman, Stuart J., Little, Richard, and Wohlforth, William C. 2007. "Conclusion: Theoretical insights from the study of world history." In Stuart J. Kaufman, Richard Little, and William C. Wohlforth, eds., *The balance of power in world history*. Basingstoke: Palgrave, 228–46.

Kautsky, John H. 1982. *The politics of aristocratic empires.* Chapel Hill: University of North Carolina Press.

Kay, Philip. 2014. *Rome's economic revolution.* Oxford: Oxford University Press.

Keay, John. 2000. *India: A history.* New York: Grove Press.

Kelly, Christopher. 2004. *Ruling the later Roman empire.* Cambridge, MA: Harvard University Press.

Kelly, Christopher. 2009. *The end of empire: Attila the Hun and the fall of Rome.* New York: Norton.

Kelly, Morgan, Mokyr, Joel, and Ó Gráda, Cormac. 2014. "Precocious Albion: A new interpretation of the British Industrial Revolution." *Annual Review of Economics* 6: 363–89.

Kelsey, Harry. 2012. *Philip of Spain, king of England: The forgotten sovereign.* London: I. B. Tauris.

Kennedy, Hugh. 1995. "The Muslims in Europe." In McKitterick 1995, 249–71.

Kennedy, Hugh. 2001. *The armies of the caliphs: Military and society in the early Islamic state.* London: Routledge.

Kennedy, Hugh. 2007. *The great Arab conquests: How the spread of Islam changed the world we live in.* Philadelphia: Da Capo Press.

Kennedy, Hugh. 2015. "The Middle East in Islamic late antiquity." In Monson and Scheidel 2015a, 390–403.

Kennedy, Paul. 1987. *The rise and fall of the great powers: Economic change and military conflict from 1500 to 2000.* New York: Random House.

Kern, Martin. 2000. *The stele inscriptions of Ch'in Shih-huang: Text and ritual in early Chinese imperial representation.* New Haven, CT: American Oriental Society.

Khazanov, Anatoly M. 1994. *Nomads and the outside world.* 2nd ed. Madison: University of Wisconsin Press.

Khodarkovsky, Michael. 2002. *Russia's steppe frontier: The making of a colonial empire, 1500–1800.* Bloomington: Indiana University Press.

Kiesewetter, Hubert. 2006. *Das einzigartige Europa: Wie ein Kontinent reich wurde.* Stuttgart: Franz Steiner Verlag.

Klein, Herbert S. 2017. "The 'historical turn' in the social sciences." *Journal of Interdisciplinary History* 48: 295–312.

Klein Goldewijk, Kees et al. 2011. "The HYDE 3.1 spatially explicit database of human-induced global land-use change over the past 12,000 years." *Global Ecology and Biogeography* 20: 73–86, doi: 10.1111/j.1466-8238.2010.00587.x.

Kleinschmidt, Harald. 2004. *Charles V: The world emperor*. Stroud: Sutton.

Knobloch, Edgar. 2007. *Russia & Asia: Nomadic & oriental traditions in Russian history*. Hong Kong: Odyssey.

Ko, Chiu Yu, Koyama, Mark, and Sng, Tuan-Hwee. 2018. "Unified China and divided Europe." *International Economic Review* 59: 285–327.

Kocka, Jürgen. 2009. "Comparative history: Methodology and ethos." *East Central Europe* 36: 12–19.

Kohler, Alfred, Haider, Barbara, and Ottner, Christine, eds. 2002. *Karl V. 1500–1558: Neue Perspektiven seiner Herrschaft in Europa und Übersee*. Vienna: Verlag der Österreichischen Akademie der Wissenschaften.

König, Hans-Joachim. 2002. "PLUS ULTRA—ein Weltreichs- und Eroberungsprogramm? Amerika und Europa in politischen Vorstellungen im Spanien Karls V." In Kohler, Haider, and Ottner 2002, 197–222.

Koyama, Mark. 2017a. "Could Rome have had an Industrial Revolution?" https://medium.com/@MarkKoyama/could-rome-have-had-an-industrial-revolution-412671737oa2.

Koyama, Mark. 2017b. Review of Rubin 2017. *Public Choice* 172: 549–52.

Kuhrt, Amélie. 1995. *The ancient Near East c. 3000–330 B.C.* 2 vols. London: Routledge.

Kulikowski, Michael. 2012. "The western kingdoms." In Johnson 2012, 31–59.

Kulke, Hermann, Kesavapany, K., and Sakhuja, Vijay, eds. 2009. *Nagapattinam to Suvarnadwipa: Reflections on the Chola naval expeditions to Southeast Asia*. New Delhi: Manohar.

Kuran, Timur. 2011. *The long divergence: How Islamic law held back the Middle East*. Princeton, NJ: Princeton University Press.

Kuran, Timur. 2018. "Islam and economic performance: Historical and contemporary links." *Journal of Economic Literature* 56, no. 4: 1292–359.

Laiou, Angeliki E. 2002. "The Byzantine economy: An overview." In Angeliki E. Laiou, ed., *The economic history of Byzantium from the seventh to the fifteenth century*. Washington, DC: Dumbarton Oaks Research Library and Collection, 1145–64.

Lambton, Ann K. S. 1968. "The internal structure of the Saljuq empire." In Boyle 1968, 203–82.

Lampela, Anssi. 1998. *Rome and the Ptolemies of Egypt: The development of their political relations 273–80 B.C.* Helsinki: Societas Scientiarum Fennica.

Landes, David. 1998. *The wealth and poverty of nations: Why some are so rich and some so poor*. New York: Norton.

Landes, David. 2003. *The unbound Prometheus: Technological change and industrial development in Western Europe from 1750 to the present*. 2nd ed. Cambridge: Cambridge University Press.

Landes, David S. 2006. "Why Europe and the West? Why not China?" *Journal of Economic Perspectives* 20, no. 2: 3–22.

Lane, Frederick C. 1979. *Profits from power: Readings in protection rent and violence-controlling enterprises*. Albany: State University of New York Press.

Lang, Graeme. 1997. "State system and the origins of modern science: A comparison of Europe and China." *East-West Dialogue* 2: 16–31.

Lange, Matthew. 2013. *Comparative-historical methods*. Los Angeles: Russell Sage Foundation.

Langlois, Rosaire. 2008. "The closing of the sociological mind?" *Canadian Journal of Sociology* 33: 134–48.

Lattimore, Owen. 1988 [1940]. *Inner Asian frontiers of China*. Hong Kong: Oxford University Press.

Launey, Marcel. 1950. *Recherches sur les armées hellénistiques*. Paris: De Boccard.

Lazenby, J. F. 1996. *The First Punic War: A military history*. Stanford, CA: Stanford University Press.

Leitner, Ulrich. 2011. *Imperium: Geschichte und Theorie eines politischen Systems*. Frankfurt: Campus.

Lelièvre, Dominique. 2001. *La grande époque de Wudi: Une Chine en évolution (IIe-Ie av. J.C.)*. Paris: You-Feng.

Levathes, Louise. 1994. *When China ruled the seas: The treasure fleet of the dragon throne, 1405–1433*. New York: Oxford University Press.

Levi, Margaret. 1988. *Of rule and revenue*. Berkeley: University of California Press.

Levine, Ari D. 2013. Review of Pines 2012. *Journal of the American Oriental Society* 133: 574–77.

Lévy, Jacques. 1997. *Europe: une géographie*. Paris: Hachette.

Lewis, Herbert S. 1981. "Warfare and the origin of the state: another formulation." In Henry J. M. Claessen and Peter Skalník, eds., *The study of the state*. The Hague: Mouton, 201–21.

Lewis, Mark E. 1990. *Sanctioned violence in early China*. Albany: State University of New York Press.

Lewis, Mark E. 1999. "Warring States: Political history." In Loewe and Shaughnessy 1999, 587–650.

Lewis, Mark E. 2009a. *China between empires: The Northern and Southern dynasties*. Cambridge, MA: Harvard University Press.

Lewis, Mark E. 2009b. *China's cosmopolitan empire: The Tang dynasty*. Cambridge, MA: Harvard University Press.

Lewis, Mark E. 2015. "Early imperial China, from the Qin and Han through Tang." In Monson and Scheidel 2015a, 282–307.

Li, Bozhong and van Zanden, Jan Luiten. 2012. "Before the great divergence? Comparing the Yangzi Delta and the Netherlands at the beginning of the nineteenth century." *Journal of Economic History* 72: 956–89.

Li, Rebecca S. K. 2002. "Alternative routes to state breakdown: Toward an integrated model of territorial disintegration." *Sociological Theory* 20: 1–23.

Lieberman, Victor. 2003. *Strange parallels: Southeast Asia in global context, c. 800–1830*, vol. 1: *Integration on the mainland*. Cambridge: Cambridge University Press.

Lieberman, Victor. 2009. *Strange parallels: Southeast Asia in global context, c. 800–1830*, vol. 2: *Mainland mirrors: Europe, Japan, China, South Asia, and the islands*. Cambridge: Cambridge University Press.

Lieven, Dominic. 2000. *Empire: The Russian empire and its rivals*. New Haven, CT: Yale University Press.

Lieven, Dominic. 2010. *Russia against Napoleon: The true story of the campaigns of War and Peace*. London: Penguin.

Lin, Hang. 2014. Review of Pines 2012. *Frontiers of History in China* 9: 484–88.

Lin, Justin Y. 1995. "The Needham puzzle: Why the Industrial Revolution did not originate in China." *Economic Development and Cultural Change* 43: 269–92.

Lindner, Rudi P. 1981. "Nomadism, horses and Huns." *Past and Present* 92: 3–19.

Linke, Bernhard. 2006. "Bürger ohne Staat? Die Integration der Landbevölkerung in der römischen Republik." In Martin Jehne and Rene Pfeilschifter, eds., *Herrschaft ohne Integration? Rom und Italien in republikanischer Zeit*. Frankfurt a.M.: Verlag Antike, 65–94.

Linke, Bernhard. 2014. "Die Väter und der Staat: die Grundlagen der aggressiven Subsidiarität in der römischen Gesellschaft." In Lundgreen, 2014a, 65–90.

Liu, Shufen. 2001. "Jiankang and the commercial empire of the Southern dynasties: Change and continuity in medieval Chinese economic history." In Pearce, Spiro, and Ebrey 2001, 35–52.

Liu, William G. 2015a. *The Chinese market economy, 1000–1500*. Albany: State University of New York Press.

Liu, William G. 2015b. "The making of a fiscal state in Song China, 960–1279." *Economic History Review* 68: 48–78.

Lloyd, Geoffrey and Sivin, Nathan. 2002. *The way and the word: Science and medicine in early China and Greece*. New Haven, CT: Yale University Press.

Lo Cascio, Elio. 2006. "The role of the state in the Roman economy: Making use of the New Institutional Economics." In Peter F. Bang, Mamoru Ikeguchi, and Hartmut Ziche, eds., *Ancient economies, modern methodologies: Archaeology, comparative history, models and institutions*. Bari: Edipuglia, 215–34.

Lo Cascio, Elio. 2018. "Market regulation and transaction costs in the Roman empire." In Wilson and Bowman 2018, 117–32.

Loewe, Michael. 1986. "The Former Han dynasty." In Denis Twitchett and Michael Loewe, eds., *The Cambridge history of China*, vol. 1: *The Ch'in and Han empires, 221 B.C.–A.D. 220*. Cambridge: Cambridge University Press, 103–222.

Loewe, Michael. 2014. Review of Pines 2012. *Journal of Chinese Studies* 59: 330–37.

Loewe, Michael and Shaughnessy, Edward L., eds. 1999. *The Cambridge history of ancient China: From the origins of civilization to 221 B.C.* Cambridge: Cambridge University Press.

Löffl, Josef. 2011. *Die römische Expansion*. Berlin: Frank & Timme.

Lorge, Peter. 2005. *War, politics and society in early modern China, 900–1795*. London: Routledge.

Lowry, Heath W. 2003. *The nature of the early Ottoman state*. Albany: State University of New York Press.

Lundgreen, Christoph, ed. 2014a. *Staatlichkeit in Rom? Diskurse und Praxis (in) der römischen Republik*. Stuttgart: Franz Steiner Verlag.

Lundgreen, Christoph. 2014b. "Staatsdiskurse in Rom? Staatlichkeit als analytische Kategorie für die römische Republik." In Lundgreen 2014a, 13–61.

Luttenberger, Albrecht P. 2002. "Die Religionspolitik Karls V. im Reich." In Kohler, Haider, and Ottner 2002, 293–344.

Macfarlane, Alan. 1988. "The cradle of capitalism: The case of England." In Baechler, Hall, and Mann 1988, 185–203.

Mackil, Emily. 2013. *Creating a common polity: Religion, economy, and politics in the making of the Greek koinon*. Berkeley: University of California Press.

Mackil, Emily. 2015. "The Greek *polis* and *koinon*." In Monson and Scheidel 2015a, 469–91.

MacMullen, Ramsay. 1966. "Provincial languages in the Roman empire." *American Journal of Philology* 87: 1–17.

Maddicott, John R. 2010. *The origins of the English Parliament, 924–1327.* Oxford: Oxford University Press.

Maddison, Angus. 2010. "Historical statistics of the world economy: 1–2008 A.D." Maddison Database 2010, https://www.rug.nl/ggdc/historicaldevelopment/maddison/releases /maddison-database-2010.

Maddison Project Database 2018. https://www.rug.nl/ggdc/historicaldevelopment/maddison /releases/maddison-project-database-2018.

Magnusson, Lars. 2009. *Nation, state and the Industrial Revolution.* London: Routledge.

Mahoney, James. 2003. "Strategies of causal assessment in comparative historical analysis." In Mahoney and Rueschemeyer 2003, 337–72.

Mahoney, James and Rueschemeyer, Dietrich, eds. 2003. *Comparative historical analysis in the social sciences.* Cambridge: Cambridge University Press.

Maiden, Martin, Smith, John C., and Ledgeway, Adam, eds. 2013. *The Cambridge history of Romance languages,* vol. 2: *Contexts.* Cambridge: Cambridge University Press.

Maier, Gideon. 2005. *Amtsträger und Herrscher in der Romania Gothica: Vergleichende Untersuchungen zu den ostgermanischen Völkerwanderungsreichen.* Stuttgart: Steiner.

Mair, Victor. 2005. "The north(west)ern peoples and the recurrent origins on the 'Chinese' state." In Joshua A. Fogel, ed., *The teleology of the modern nation-state: Japan and China.* Philadelphia: University of Pennsylvania Press, 46–84.

Malanima, Paolo 2009. *Pre-modern European economy: One thousand years (10th–19th centuries).* Leiden: Brill.

Man, John. 2014. *The Mongol empire: Genghis Khan, his heirs and the founding of modern China.* London: Bantam Press.

Mann, Michael. 1984. "The autonomous power of the state: Its origins, mechanisms and results." *European Journal of Sociology* 25: 185–213.

Mann, Michael. 1986. *The sources of social power,* vol. 1: *A history of power from the beginning to A.D. 1760.* Cambridge: Cambridge University Press.

Mann, Michael. 2006. "The sources of social power revisited: a response to criticism." In John A. Hall and Ralph Schroeder, eds., *An anatomy of power: The social theory of Michael Mann.* Cambridge: Cambridge University Press, 343–96.

Marks, Robert B. 2002. *The origins of the modern world: A global and ecological narrative.* Lanham, MD: Rowman and Littlefield.

Marks, Robert B. 2012. *China: Its environment and history.* Lanham, MD: Rowman and Littlefield.

Mattern, Susan P. 1999. *Rome and the enemy: Imperial strategy in the Principate.* Berkeley: University of California Press.

Mattingly, David. 2006. *An imperial possession: Britain in the Roman empire.* London: Penguin Books.

May, Timothy. 2012. *The Mongol conquests in world history.* London: Reaktion Books.

Mayer, E. Emanuel. 2018. "Tanti non emo, Sexte, piper: Pepper prices, Roman consumer culture, and the bulk of Indo-Roman trade." *Journal of the Economic and Social History of the Orient* 61: 560–89.

Mayor, Adrienne. 2010. *The poison king: The life and legend of Mithradates, Rome's deadliest enemy.* Princeton, NJ: Princeton University Press.

Mayor, Adrienne. 2014. *The Amazons: Lives and legends of warrior women across the ancient world.* Princeton, NJ: Princeton University Press.

McCaa, Robert 2000. "The peopling of Mexico from origins to revolution." In Michael R. Haines and Richard C. Steckel, eds., *A population history of North America.* Cambridge: Cambridge University Press, 241–304.

McCloskey, Deirdre. 2010. *Bourgeois dignity: Why economics can't explain the modern world.* Chicago: University of Chicago Press.

McCloskey, Deirdre. 2016. *Bourgeois equality: How ideas, not capital or institutions, enriched the world.* Chicago: University of Chicago Press.

McConnell, Joseph R. et al. 2018. "Lead pollution recorded in Greenland ice indicates European emissions tracked plagues, wars, and imperial expansion during antiquity." *Proceedings of the National Academy of Sciences* 115: 5726–31.

McCormick, Michael, Dutton, Paul E., and Mayewski, Paul A. 2007. "Volcanoes and the climate forcing of Carolingian Europe, A.D. 750–950." *Speculum* 82: 865–95.

McEvedy, Colin and Jones, Richard 1978. *Atlas of world population history.* Harmondsworth: Penguin Books.

McKitterick, Rosamund, ed. 1995. *The new Cambridge medieval history,* vol. 2: *c. 700–c. 900.* Cambridge: Cambridge University Press.

McLaughlin, Raoul. 2010. *Rome and the distant East: Trade routes to the ancient lands of Arabia, India and China.* London: Continuum.

McLaughlin, Raoul. 2014. *The Roman empire and the Indian Ocean: The ancient world economy and the kingdoms of Africa, Arabia and India.* Barnsley: Pen and Sword Military.

McNeill, J. R. 1998. "China's environmental history in world perspective." In Mark Elvin and Ts'ui-jung Liu, eds., *Sediments of time: Environment and society in Chinese history.* Cambridge: Cambridge University Press, 31–49.

McNeill, William H. 1982. *The pursuit of power: Technology, armed force, and society since A.D. 1000.* Chicago: University of Chicago Press.

Memorandum. 1875. *Memorandum on the census of British India of 1871–72, presented to both houses of Parliament by command of Her Majesty.* London: Her Majesty's Stationery Office.

Menant, François. 2005. *L'Italie des communes: 1100–1350.* Paris: Belin.

Menzies, Gavin. 2004. *1421: The year China discovered America.* New York: HarperCollins.

Michaels, Guy and Rauch, Ferdinand. 2018. "Resetting the urban network: 117–2012." *Economic Journal* 128: 378–412.

Middleton, Guy D. 2017. *Understanding collapse: Ancient history and modern myths.* Cambridge: Cambridge University Press.

Mielants, Eric H. 2007. *The origins of capitalism and the "rise of the West."* Philadelphia: Temple University Press.

Milanovic, Branko 2016. *Global inequality: A new approach for the age of globalization.* Cambridge, MA: Harvard University Press.

Millar, Fergus. 1968. "Local cultures in the Roman empire: Libyan, Punic and Latin in Roman Africa." *Journal of Roman Studies* 58: 126–34.

Millar, Fergus. 1993. *The Roman Near East, 31 B.C.–A.D. 337*. Cambridge, MA: Harvard University Press.

Millar, Fergus. 2006. *A Greek Roman empire: Power and belief under Theodosius II (408–450)*. Berkeley: University of California Press.

Millett, Martin. 1990. *The Romanization of Britain: An essay in archaeological interpretation*. Cambridge: Cambridge University Press.

Milton, John R. 1981. "The origin and development of the concept of the 'laws of nature.'" *European Journal of Sociology* 22: 173–95.

Mitchell, Kirk. 1984. *Procurator*. New York: Ace Science Fiction Books.

Mitterauer, Michael. 2003. *Warum Europa? Mittelalterliche Grundlagen eines Sonderwegs*. Munich: C. H. Beck.

Modéran, Yves. 2014. *Les Vandales et l'empire romain*. Arles: Éditions Errance.

Moe, Espen. 2007. *Governance, growth and global leadership: The role of the state in technological progress, 1750–2000*. Aldershot, UK: Ashgate.

Mokyr, Joel. 1990. *The lever of riches: Technological creativity and economic progress*. New York: Oxford University Press.

Mokyr, Joel. 2002. *The gifts of Athena: Historical origins of the knowledge economy*. Princeton, NJ: Princeton University Press.

Mokyr, Joel. 2003. "Why was the Industrial Revolution a European phenomenon?" *Supreme Court Economic Review* 10: 27–63.

Mokyr, Joel. 2005. "The intellectual origins of modern economic growth." *Journal of Economic History* 65: 285–351.

Mokyr, Joel. 2006. "King Kong and cold fusion: Counterfactual analysis & the history of technology." In Tetlock, Lebow, and Parker 2006b, 277–322.

Mokyr, Joel. 2007. "The market for ideas and the origins of economic growth in eighteenth century Europe." *Tijdschrift voor sociale en economische geschiedenis* 4: 3–38.

Mokyr, Joel. 2009. *The enlightened economy: An economic history of Britain, 1700–1850*. New Haven, CT: Yale University Press.

Mokyr, Joel. 2017. *A culture of growth: The origins of the modern economy*. Princeton, NJ: Princeton University Press.

Mokyr, Joel and Nye, John V. C. 2007. "Distributional coalitions, the industrial revolution, and the origins of economic growth in Britain." *Southern Economic Journal* 74: 50–70.

Molho, Anthony, Raaflaub, Kurt, and Emlen, Julia, eds. 1991. *City states in classical antiquity and medieval Italy*. Ann Arbor: University of Michigan Press.

Moll, Sebastian. 2010. *The arch-heretic Marcion*. Tübingen: Mohr Siebeck.

Molyneaux, George. 2015. *The formation of the English kingdom in the tenth century*. Oxford: Oxford University Press.

Momigliano, Arnaldo. 1971. *Alien wisdom: The limits of Hellenization*. Cambridge: Cambridge University Press.

Monson, Andrew and Scheidel, Walter, eds. 2015a. *Fiscal regimes and the political economy of premodern states*. Cambridge: Cambridge University Press.

Monson, Andrew and Scheidel, Walter. 2015b. "Studying fiscal regimes." In Monson and Scheidel 2015a, 3–27.

Montesquieu, Baron de (M. de Secondat). 1750 [1748]. *The spirit of laws*, vol. 1. Trans. Thomas Nugent. London: J. Nourse and P. Vaillant.

Moore, Robert I. 2009. "Medieval Europe in world history." In Carol Lansing and Edward D. English, eds., *A companion to the medieval world*. Chichester: Wiley-Blackwell, 563–80.

Moore, Robert I. 2015. "The First Great Divergence?" *Medieval Worlds* 1: 1–24.

Moreland, Jon. 2001. "The Carolingian empire: Rome reborn?" In Alcock et al. 2001, 392–418.

Morgan, Kenneth. 2000. *Slavery, Atlantic trade and the British economy, 1660–1800*. Cambridge: Cambridge University Press.

Morley, Neville. 2010. *The Roman empire: Roots of imperialism*. London: Pluto Press.

Morris, Colin. 1989. *The papal monarchy: The western church from 1050 to 1250*. Oxford: Oxford University Press.

Morris, Ian. 2009. "The greater Athenian state." In Morris and Scheidel 2009, 99–177.

Morris, Ian. 2010. *Why the West rules—for now: The patterns of history, and what they reveal about the future*. New York: Farrar, Straus and Giroux.

Morris, Ian. 2013a. "Greek multicity states." In Bang and Scheidel 2013, 279–303.

Morris, Ian 2013b. *The measure of civilization: How social development decides the fate of nations*. Princeton, NJ: Princeton University Press.

Morris, Ian. 2014. *War! What is it good for? Conflict and the progress of civilization from primates to robots*. New York: Farrar, Straus and Giroux.

Morris, Ian and Scheidel, Walter, eds. 2009. *The dynamics of ancient empires: State power from Assyria to Byzantium*. New York: Oxford University Press.

Moser, Leo J. 1985. *The Chinese mosaic: The peoples and provinces of China*. Boulder, CO: Westview Press.

Mote, Frederick W. 1999. *Imperial China 900–1800*. Cambridge, MA: Harvard University Press.

Motyl, Alexander J. 2001. *Imperial ends: The decay, collapse, and revival of empire*. New York: Columbia University Press.

Mouritsen, Henrik 1998. *Italian unification: A study in ancient and modern historiography*. London: Institute of Classical Studies.

Mouritsen, Henrik 2001. *Plebs and politics in the late Roman republic*. Cambridge: Cambridge University Press.

Mouritsen, Henrik. 2007. "The *civitas sine suffragio*: Ancient concepts and modern ideology." *Historia* 56: 141–58.

Mouritsen, Henrik. 2017. *Politics in the Roman republic*. Cambridge: Cambridge University Press.

Mullen, Alex. 2013. *Southern Gaul and the Mediterranean: Multilingualism and multiple identities in the Iron Age and Roman periods*. Cambridge: Cambridge University Press.

Münkler, Herfried. 2007. *Empires: The logic of world domination from ancient Rome to the United States*. Cambridge: Polity Press.

Munro, John. 2005. "Spanish *merino* wool and the *nouvelles draperies*: An industrial transformation in the late medieval Low Countries." *Economic History Review* 58: 431–84.

Murphey, Rhoads. 1999. *Ottoman warfare, 1500–1700*. New Brunswick, NJ: Rutgers University Press.

Murray, Charles. 2003. *Human accomplishment: The pursuit of excellence in the arts and sciences, 800 B.C. to 1950*. New York: HarperCollins.

Murray, William M. 2012. *The age of titans: The rise and fall of the great Hellenistic navies.* New York: Oxford University Press.

Mutschler, Fritz-Heiner and Scheidel, Walter. 2017. "The benefits of comparison: A call for the comparative study of ancient civilizations." *Journal of Ancient Civilizations* 32: 107–21.

Neal, Larry. 1990. *The rise of financial capitalism: International capital markets in the Age of Reason.* Cambridge: Cambridge University Press.

Needham, Joseph. 1969. *The great titration: Science and society in East and West.* London: Allen and Unwin.

Nelson, Janet L. 1995a. "The Frankish kingdoms, 814–898: The West." In McKitterick 1995, 110–41.

Nelson, Janet L. 1995b. "Kingship and royal government." In McKitterick 1995, 383–430.

Netz, Reviel. Forthcoming. *Scale, space and canon in ancient literary culture.* Cambridge: Cambridge University Press.

Neumann, Günter and Untermann, Jürgen, eds. 1980. *Die Sprachen im römischen Reich der Kaiserzeit.* Cologne: Rheinland.

Neumann, Iver B. and Wigen, Einar. 2018. *The steppe tradition in international relations: Russians, Turks and European state-building 4000 BCE–2018 CE.* Cambridge: Cambridge University Press.

Newfield, Timothy P. 2013. "The contours, frequency and causation of subsistence crises in Carolingian Europe (750–950 CE)." In Pere Benito i Monclús, ed., *Crisis alimentarias en la edad media: Modelos, explicaciones y representaciones.* Lleida: Editorial Milenio, 117–72.

Ni, Shawn and Van, Pham H. 2006. "High corruption income in Ming and Qing China." *Journal of Development Economics* 81: 316–36.

Nicolet, Claude 1980. *The world of the citizen in Republican Rome.* Berkeley: University of California Press.

Norberg, Johan. 2017. *Progress: Ten reasons to look forward to the future.* Updated ed. London: Oneworld.

Noreña, Carlos F. 2015. "Urban systems in the Han and Roman empires: State power and social control." In Scheidel 2015c, 181–229.

Noreña, Carlos F. Forthcoming. "Private associations and urban experience in the Han and Roman empires." In Hans Beck and Griet Vankeerberghen, eds., *Citizens and commoners in ancient Greece, Rome, and China.*

North, Douglass C. 1981. *Structure and change in economic history.* New York: W. W. Norton.

North, Douglass C. and Thomas, Robert P. 1970. "An economic theory of the rise of the Western world." *Economic History Review* 23: 1–17.

North, Douglass C. and Thomas, Robert P. 1973. *The rise of the Western world: A new economic history.* Cambridge: Cambridge University Press.

North, Douglass C., Wallis, John J., and Weingast, Barry R. 2009. *Violence and social orders: A conceptual framework for interpreting recorded human history.* New York: Cambridge University Press.

North, Douglass C. and Weingast, Barry R. 1989. "Constitutions and commitment: The evolution of institutions governing public choice in seventeenth-century England." *Journal of Economic History* 49: 803–32.

North, John A. 1981. "The development of Roman imperialism." *Journal of Roman Studies* 71: 1–9.

Oakley, Stephen. 1993. "The Roman conquest of Italy." In Rich and Shipley 1993, 9–37.

Oakley, Stephen P. 2005. *A commentary on Livy Books VI–X*, vol. 3: *Book IX*. Oxford: Clarendon Press.

Ober, Josiah. 1999. "Conquest denied: The premature death of Alexander the Great." In Cowley 1999, 37–56.

Ober, Josiah. 2015. *The rise and fall of classical Greece.* Princeton, NJ: Princeton University Press.

O'Brien, Patrick. 2011. "The nature and historical evolution of an exceptional fiscal state and its possible significance for the precocious commercialization and industrialization of the British economy from Cromwell to Nelson." *Economic History Review* 64: 408–46.

O'Brien, Patrick K. 2012a. "Afterword: Reflections on fiscal foundations and contexts for the formation of economically effective Eurasian states from the rise of Venice to the Opium War." In Yun-Casalilla and O'Brien 2012, 442–53.

O'Brien, Patrick K. 2012b. "Fiscal and financial preconditions for the formation of developmental states in the West and the East from the conquest of Ceuta (1415) to the Opium War (1839)." *Journal of World History* 23: 513–53.

O'Brien, Patrick 2017. "The contributions of warfare with Revolutionary and Napoleonic France to the consolidation and progress of the British Industrial Revolution." London School of Economics Economic History Working Paper no. 264.

O'Brien, Patrick K. and Prados de la Escosura, Leandro. 1998. "The costs and benefits for Europeans from their empires overseas." *Revista de Historia Económica* 16: 29–89.

Ogilvie, Sheilagh. 2011. *Institutions and European trade: Merchant guilds, 1000–1800.* Cambridge: Cambridge University Press.

Ogilvie, Sheilagh. 2019. *The European guilds: An economic analysis.* Princeton, NJ: Princeton University Press.

Oikonomides, Nicolas. 2002. "The role of the Byzantine state in the economy." In Angeliki E. Laiou, ed., *The economic history of Byzantium from the seventh to the fifteenth century.* Washington, DC: Dumbarton Oaks Research Library and Collection, 973–1058.

Oldland, John. 2014. "Wool and cloth production in late medieval and early Tudor England." *Economic History Review* 67: 25–47.

Oleson, John P., ed. 2008. *The Oxford handbook of engineering and technology in the classical world.* New York: Oxford University Press.

Olmstead, Alan L. and Rhode, Paul W. 2018. "Cotton, slavery, and the new history of capitalism." *Explorations in Economic History* 67: 1–17.

Ormrod, David. 2003. *The rise of commercial empires: England and the Netherlands in the age of mercantilism, 1650–1770.* Cambridge: Cambridge University Press.

Osborne, Anne. 2004. "Property, taxes, and state protection of rights." In Zelin, Ocko, and Gardella 2004, 120–58.

Osterhammel, Jürgen. 1996. "Transkulturell vergleichende Geschichtswissenschaft." In Haupt and Kocka 1996a, 271–314.

Ostrowski, Donald. 1998. *Muscovy and the Mongols: Cross-cultural influences on the steppe frontier, 1304–1589.* Cambridge: Cambridge University Press.

O'Sullivan, Shaun. 2006. "Coptic conversion and the Islamization of Egypt." *Mamluk Studies Review* 10, no. 2: 65–80.

Overton, Mark. 1996. *Agricultural revolution in England: The transformation of the agrarian economy, 1500–1800*. Cambridge: Cambridge University Press.

Padilla Peralta, Dan-el. 2014. "Divine institutions: Religious practice, economic development, and social transformation in mid-Republican Rome." PhD diss., Stanford University.

Pagden, Anthony. 2001. *Peoples and empires: A short history of European migration, exploration, and conquest, from Greece to the present*. New York: Modern Library.

Palma, Nuno. 2016. "Sailing away from Malthus: Intercontinental trade and European economic growth, 1500–1800." *Cliometrica* 10: 129–49.

Pamuk, Şevket. 2007. "The Black Death and the origins of the 'Great Divergence' across Europe, 1300–1600." *European Review of Economic History* 11: 289–317.

Parker, Geoffrey. 1996. *The military revolution: Military innovation and the rise of the West, 1500–1800*. 2nd ed. Cambridge: Cambridge University Press.

Parker, Geoffrey. 1998. *The grand strategy of Philip II*. New Haven, CT: Yale University Press.

Parker, Geoffrey. 1999. "The repulse of the English fire ships: The Spanish armada triumphs, August 8, 1588." In Cowley 1999, 139–54.

Parker, Geoffrey. 2004. *Sovereign city: The city-state through history*. London: Reaktion Books.

Parker, Geoffrey. 2014. *Imprudent king: A new life of Philip II*. New Haven, CT: Yale University Press.

Parker, Geoffrey and Tetlock, Philip E. 2006. "Counterfactual history: Its advocates, its critics, & its uses." In Tetlock, Lebow, and Parker 2006b, 363–92.

Parthasarathi, Prasannan. 2011. *Why Europe grew rich and Asia did not: Global economic divergence, 1600–1850*. Cambridge: Cambridge University Press.

Patterson, John. 1993. "Military organization and social change in the later Roman Republic." In Rich and Shipley 1993, 92–112.

Patzold, Steffen. 2012. *Das Lehnswesen*. Munich: C. H. Beck.

Payne, Richard. 2016. "The making of Turan: The fall and transformation of the Iranian East in late antiquity." *Journal of Late Antiquity* 9: 4–41.

Peacock, Andrew C. S. 2010. *Early Seljuq history: A new interpretation*. New York: Routledge.

Pearce, Scott A. 1987. "The Yü-Wen regime in sixth century China." PhD diss., Princeton University.

Pearce, Scott, Spiro, Audrey, and Ebrey, Patricia, eds. 2001. *Culture and power in the reconstitution of the Chinese realm, 200–600*. Cambridge, MA: Harvard University Press.

Pederson, Neil et al. 2014. "Pluvials, droughts, the Mongol Empire, and modern Mongolia." *Proceedings of the National Academy of Science* 111: 4375–79.

Perdue, Peter C. 2005. *China marches west: The Qing conquest of central Eurasia*. Cambridge, MA: Harvard University Press.

Pestana, Carla G. 2006. "Nineteenth-century British imperialism undone by a single shell fragment: A response to Jack Goldstone's 'Europe's peculiar path.'" In Tetlock, Lebow, and Parker 2006b, 197–202.

Petersen, Jens Ø. 1995. "Which books *did* the first emperor of Ch'in burn? On the meaning of *pai chia* in early Chinese sources." *Monumenta Serica* 43: 1–52.

Petrushevsky, Il'ia. 1968. "The socio-economic condition of Iran under the Il-Khans." In Boyle 1968, 483–537.

Pfeilschifter, Rene. 2007. "The allies in the Republican army and the Romanisation of Italy." In Roman Roth, ed., *Roman by integration: Dimensions of group identity in material culture and text*. Portsmouth, RI: Journal of Roman Archaeology, 27–42.

Picard, Christophe. 2018. *Sea of the caliphs: The Mediterranean in the medieval Islamic world*. Cambridge, MA: Harvard University Press.

Pietschmann, Horst. 2002. "Karl V. und Amerika: der Herrscher, der Hof und die Politik." In Kohler, Haider, and Ottner 2002, 533–48.

Pina Polo, Francisco. 2006. "Deportation, Kolonisation, Migration: Bevölkerungsverschiebungen im republikanischen Italien und Formen der Identitätsbildung." In Martin Jehne and Rene Pfeilschifter, eds., *Herrschaft ohne Integration? Rom und Italien in republikanischer Zeit*. Frankfurt a.M.: Verlag Antike, 171–206.

Pincus, Steven C. A. and Robinson, James A. 2014. "What really happened during the Glorious Revolution?" In Sebastian Galiani and Itai Sened, eds., *Institutions, property rights, and economic growth: The legacy of Douglass North*. Cambridge: Cambridge University Press, 192–222.

Pines, Yuri. 2000. "'The one that pervades the all' in ancient Chinese political thought: The origins of 'the great unity' paradigm." *T'oung Pao* 86: 280–324.

Pines, Yuri. 2009. *Envisioning eternal empire: Chinese political thought of the Warring States era*. Honolulu: University of Hawai'i Press.

Pines, Yuri. 2012. *The everlasting empire: The political culture of ancient China and its imperial legacy*. Princeton, NJ: Princeton University Press.

Pinke, Zsolt et al. 2016. "Climate of doubt: A re-evaluation of Büntgen and Di Cosmo's environmental hypothesis for the Mongol withdrawal from Hungary, 1242 CE." *Scientific Reports* 7, no. 12695. https://www.nature.com/articles/s41598-017-12128-6.

Pinker, Steven. 2018. *Enlightenment now: The case for reason, science, humanism, and progress*. New York: Viking.

Pollock, Sheldon. 2005. *The ends of man at the end of premodernity*. Amsterdam: Royal Netherlands Academy of Arts and Sciences.

Pollock, Sheldon. 2006. *The language of the gods in the world of men: Sanskrit, culture, and power in premodern India*. Berkeley: University of California Press.

Pomeranz, Kenneth. 2000. *The great divergence: China, Europe, and the making of the modern world economy*. Princeton, NJ: Princeton University Press.

Pomeranz, Kenneth. 2006. "Without coal? Colonies? Calculus? Counterfactuals & industrialization in Europe & China." In Tetlock, Lebow and Parker 2006, 241–76.

Porter, Anne. 2012. *Mobile pastoralism and the formation of Near Eastern civilizations: Weaving together society*. Cambridge: Cambridge University Press.

Porter, Bruce D. 1994. *War and the rise of the state: The military foundations of modern politics*. New York: Free Press.

Potts, Daniel T. 2014. *Nomads in Iran: From antiquity to the modern era*. New York: Oxford University Press.

Pow, Lindsey Stephen. 2012. "Deep ditches and well-built walls: A reappraisal of the Mongol withdrawal from Europe in 1242." MA thesis, University of Alberta.

Prados de la Escosura, Leandro, ed. 2004. *Exceptionalism and industrialisation: Britain and its European rivals, 1688–1815*. Cambridge: Cambridge University Press.

Pritchett, Lant and Woolcock, Michael 2002. "Solutions when the solution is the problem: Arraying the disarray in development." Center for Global Development Working Paper no. 10.

Putnam, Aaron E. et al. 2016. "Little Ice Age wetting of interior Asian deserts and the rise of the Mongol empire." *Quaternary Science Reviews* 131A: 33–50.

Qian, Wen-yuan. 1985. *The great inertia: Scientific stagnation in traditional China*. London: Croom Helm.

Raaflaub, Kurt. 1991. "City-state, territory and empire in classical antiquity." In Molho, Raaflaub, and Emlen 1991, 565–88.

Raaflaub, Kurt. 2016. "'Archē', 'Reich' oder 'athenischer Groß-Staat'? Zum Scheitern integrativer Staatsmodelle in der griechischen Poliswelt des 5. und frühen 4. Jahrhunderts v. Chr." In Ernst Baltrusch, Hans Kopp, and Christian Wendt, eds., *Seemacht, Seeherrschaft und die Antike*. Stuttgart: Steiner, 103–32.

Raaflaub, Kurt. 2018. "The "great leap" in early Greek politics and political thought: A comparative perspective." In Danielle Allen, Paul Christesen, and Paul Millett, eds., *How to do things with history: New approaches to ancient Greece*. New York: Oxford University Press, 21–54.

Raccagni, Gianluca. 2010. *The Lombard League, 1164–1225*. Oxford: Oxford University Press.

Ragin, Charles C. 1987. *The comparative method: Beyond qualitative and quantitative strategies*. Berkeley: University of California Press.

Rathbone, Dominic and Temin, Peter. 2008. "Financial intermediation in first-century AD Rome and eighteenth-century England." In Koenraad Verboeven, Katelijn Vandorpe, and Veronique Chankowski, eds., *Pistoi dia ten technen: Bankers, loans, and archives in the ancient world: Studies in honour of Raymond Bogaert*. Leuven: Peeters, 371–419.

Rawski, Evelyn S. 2015. *Early modern China and Northeast Asia: Cross-border perspectives*. Cambridge: Cambridge University Press.

Reinert, Sophus A. 2011. *Translating empire: Emulation and the origins of political economy*. Cambridge, MA: Harvard University Press.

Reinhard, Wolfgang. 2002. "Governi stretti e tirannici: die Städtepolitik Kaiser Karls V. 1515–1556." In Kohler, Haider, and Ottner 2002, 407–34.

Rees, Martin. 2003. *Our final century: Will the human race survive the twenty-first century?* London: Heinemann.

Rees, Martin. 2018. *On the future: Prospects for humanity*. Princeton, NJ: Princeton University Press.

Reuter, Timothy. 2018. "Assembly politics in Western Europe from the eighth century to the twelfth." In Peter Linehan, Janet L. Nelson, and Marios Costambeys, eds., *The medieval world*. 2nd ed. London: Routledge, 511–29.

Reynolds, Susan. 1994. *Fiefs and vassals: The medieval evidence interpreted*. New York: Oxford University Press.

Rezakhani, Khodadad. 2017. *ReOrienting the Sasanians: East Iran in late antiquity*. Edinburgh: Edinburgh University Press.

Rich, John. 1993. "Fear, greed and glory: The causes of Roman war-making in the middle Republic." In Rich and Shipley 1993, 38–68.

Rich, John and Shipley, Graham, eds. 1993. *War and society in the Roman world*. London: Routledge.

Richards, John F. 2012. "Fiscal states in Mughal and British India." In Yun-Casalilla and O'Brien 2012, 410–41.

Richardson, John S. 1986. *Hispaniae: Spain and the development of Roman imperialism, 218–82 B.C.* Cambridge: Cambridge University Press.

Ringmar, Erik. 2007. *Why Europe was first: Social change and economic growth in Europe and East Asia, 1500–2050*. London: Anthem Press.

Roach, Levi. 2013. *Kingship and consent in Anglo-Saxon England, 871–978: Assemblies and the state in the early Middle Ages*. Cambridge: Cambridge University Press.

Roberts, Andrew. 2014. *Napoleon: A life*. New York: Viking.

Roeck, Bernd. 2017. *Der Morgen der Welt: Geschichte der Renaissance*. Munich: C. H. Beck.

Rogers, Greg S. 1996. "An examination of historians' explanations for the Mongol withdrawal from East Central Europe." *East European Quarterly* 30: 3–26.

Rolett, Barry V. 2002. "Voyaging and Interaction in Ancient East Polynesia." *Asian Perspectives* 41(2): 182–194. https://scholarspace.manoa.hawaii.edu/bitstream/10125/17170/1/AP-v41n2-182-194.pdf.

Roller, Duane W. 2006. *Through the Pillars of Herakles: Greco-Roman exploration of the Atlantic*. New York: Routledge.

Rollinger, Robert and Gehler, Michael, eds. 2014. *Imperien und Reiche in der Weltgeschichte: Epochenübergreifende und globalhistorische Vergleiche*. 2 vols. Wiesbaden: Harrassowitz.

Roselaar, Saskia T. 2010. *Public land in the Roman Republic: A social and economic history of ager publicus in Italy, 396–89 B.C.* Oxford: Oxford University Press.

Rosenstein, Nathan. 1990. Imperatores victi: *Military defeat and aristocratic competition in the middle and late Republic*. Berkeley: University of California Press.

Rosenstein, Nathan. 2004. *Rome at war: Farms, families, and death in the Middle Republic*. Chapel Hill: University of North Carolina Press.

Rosenstein, Nathan. 2008. "Aristocrats and agriculture in the Middle and Late Republic." *Journal of Roman Studies* 98: 1–26.

Rosenstein, Nathan. 2009. "War, state formation, and the evolution of military institutions in ancient China and Rome." In Scheidel 2009d, 24–51.

Rosenthal, Jean-Laurent and Wong, R. Bin. 2011. *Before and beyond divergence: The politics of economic change in China and Europe*. Cambridge, MA: Harvard University Press.

Roser, Max. 2018. "The short history of global living conditions and why it matters that we know it." Our World in Data. https://ourworldindata.org/a-history-of-global-living-conditions-in-5-charts.

Roser, Max. 2019. "Life expectancy." Our World in Data. https://ourworldindata.org/life-expectancy.

Rossabi, Morris, ed. 1983. *China among equals: The Middle Kingdom and its neighbors, 10th–14th centuries*. Berkeley: University of California Press.

Roth, Jonathan P. 1999. *The logistics of the Roman army at war (264 B.C.–A.D. 235)*. Leiden: Brill.

Roy, Kaushik. 2015. *Warfare in Pre-British India—1500 BCE to 1740 CE*. London: Routledge.

Roy, Tirthankar. 2008. "Knowledge and divergence from the perspective of early modern India." *Journal of Global History* 3: 361–87.

Rubin, Jared. 2017. *Rulers, religion, and riches: Why the West got rich and the Middle East did not.* New York: Cambridge University Press.

Rueschemeyer, Dietrich. 2003. "Can one or a few cases yield theoretical gains?" In Mahoney and Rueschemeyer 2003, 305–36.

Runciman, Walter. 1990. "Doomed to extinction: The polis as an evolutionary dead-end." In Oswyn Murray and Simon Price, eds., *The Greek city*. Oxford: Oxford University Press, 347–67.

Rüpke, J. 1990. Domi militia: *Die religiöse Konstruktion des Krieges in Rom*. Stuttgart: Steiner.

Russo, Lucio. 2004. *The forgotten revolution: How science was born in 300 B.C. and why it had to be reborn*. Berlin: Springer.

Ruzicka, Stephen. 2012. *Trouble in the West: Egypt and the Persian empire, 525–332 B.C.* New York: Oxford University Press.

Saller, Richard P. 2002. "Framing the debate over growth in the ancient economy." In Scheidel and von Reden 2002, 251–69.

Sarantis, Alexander. 2016. *Justinian's Balkan wars: Campaigning, diplomacy and development in Illyricum, Thrace and the northern world A.D. 527–65*. Prenton, UK: Francis Cairns.

Sarris, Peter. 2011. *Empires of faith: The fall of Rome to the rise of Islam, 500–700*. Oxford: Oxford University Press.

Sartre, Maurice. 1993. *Inscriptions grecques et latines de la Syrie, XXI: Inscriptions de la Jordanie, IV; Pétra et la Nabatène méridionale, du wadi al-Hasa au golfe de 'Aquaba*. Paris: Paul Geuthner.

Satia, Priya. 2018. *Empire of guns: The violent making of the Industrial Revolution*. New York: Penguin.

Savory, Roger M. 1986. "The Safavid administrative system." In Peter Jackson and Laurence Lockhart, eds., *The Cambridge history of Iran*, vol. 6: *The Timurid and Safavid periods*. Cambridge: Cambridge University Press, 351–72.

Scheidel, Walter. 1996. *Measuring sex, age and death in the Roman empire: Explorations in ancient demography*. Ann Arbor, MI: Journal of Roman Archaeology.

Scheidel, Walter 2001. *Death on the Nile: Disease and the demography of Roman Egypt*. Leiden: Brill.

Scheidel, Walter. 2004. "Human mobility in Roman Italy, I: The free population." *Journal of Roman Studies* 94: 1–26.

Scheidel, Walter. 2005. "Human mobility in Roman Italy, II: The slave population." *Journal of Roman Studies* 95: 64–79.

Scheidel, Walter. 2006. "The demography of Roman state formation in Italy." In Martin Jehne and Rene Pfeilschifter, eds., *Herrschaft ohne Integration? Rom und Italien in republikanischer Zeit*. Frankfurt a.M.: Verlag Antike, 207–26.

Scheidel, Walter. 2007a. "Demography." In Scheidel, Morris, and Saller 2007, 38–86.

Scheidel, Walter. 2007b. "A model of real income growth in Roman Italy." *Historia* 56: 322–46.

Scheidel, Walter. 2007c. "Roman funerary commemoration and the age at first marriage." *Classical Philology* 102: 389–402.

Scheidel, Walter. 2008a. "The comparative economics of slavery in the Greco-Roman world." In Enrico Dal Lago and Constantina Katsari, eds., *Slave systems: Ancient and modern*. Cambridge: Cambridge University Press, 105–26.

Scheidel, Walter. 2008b. "Roman population size: The logic of the debate." In Luuk de Ligt and Simon J. Northwood, eds., *People, land, and politics: Demographic developments and the transformation of Roman Italy, 300 BC–AD 14*. Leiden: Brill, 17–70.

Scheidel, Walter. 2009a. "From the 'Great Convergence' to the 'First Great Divergence': Roman and Qin-Han state formation and its aftermath." In Scheidel 2009d, 11–23.

Scheidel, Walter. 2009b. "In search of Roman economic growth." *Journal of Roman Archaeology* 22: 46–70.

Scheidel, Walter. 2009c. "The monetary systems of the Han and Roman empires." In Scheidel 2009d, 137–207.

Scheidel, Walter, ed. 2009d. *Rome and China: Comparative perspectives on ancient world empires*. New York: Oxford University Press.

Scheidel, Walter. 2011a. "A comparative perspective on the determinants of the scale and productivity of maritime trade in the Roman Mediterranean." In William V. Harris and Kristine Iara, eds., *Maritime technology in the ancient economy: Ship-design and navigation*. Portsmouth, RI: Journal of Roman Archaeology, 21–37.

Scheidel, Walter. 2011b. "Fiscal regimes and the 'First Great Divergence' between eastern and western Eurasia." In Peter F. Bang and Chris A. Bayly, eds., *Tributary empires in global history*. Basingstoke: Palgrave Macmillan, 193–204.

Scheidel, Walter. 2011c. "The Roman slave supply." In Keith Bradley and Paul Cartledge, eds., *The Cambridge world history of slavery*, vol. 1: *The ancient Mediterranean world*. Cambridge: Cambridge University Press, 287–310.

Scheidel, Walter. 2012. "Approaching the Roman economy." In Walter Scheidel, ed., *The Cambridge companion to the Roman economy*. Cambridge: Cambridge University Press, 1–21.

Scheidel, Walter. 2013a. "Italian manpower." *Journal of Roman Archaeology* 26: 678–87.

Scheidel, Walter. 2013b. "Studying the state." In Bang and Scheidel 2013, 5–57.

Scheidel, Walter. 2014. "The shape of the Roman world: Modelling imperial connectivity." *Journal of Roman Archaeology* 27: 7–32.

Scheidel, Walter. 2015a. "The early Roman monarchy." In Monson and Scheidel 2015a, 229–57.

Scheidel, Walter. 2015b. "Introduction." In Scheidel 2015c, 3–10.

Scheidel, Walter, ed. 2015c. *State power in ancient China and Rome*. New York: Oxford University Press.

Scheidel, Walter. 2015d. "State revenue and expenditure in the Han and Roman empires." In Scheidel 2015c, 150–80.

Scheidel, Walter. 2016. "Rome, Tenochtitlan, and beyond: Comparing empires across space and time." In John D. Pohl and Claire L. Lyons, eds., *Altera Roma: Art and empire from Mérida to Mexico*. Los Angeles: Cotsen Institute of Archaeology Press, 21–32.

Scheidel, Walter. 2017. *The great leveler: Violence and the history of inequality from the Stone Age to the twenty-first century*. Princeton, NJ: Princeton University Press.

Scheidel, Walter 2018. "Comparing comparisons." In Geoffrey E. Lloyd and Jingyi J. Zhao, eds., *Ancient Greece and China compared: Interdisciplinary and cross-cultural perspectives*. Cambridge: Cambridge University Press, 40–58.

Scheidel, Walter. In press-a. "Ancient Mediterranean city-state empires." In Bang, Bayly, and Scheidel in press.

Scheidel, Walter. In press-b. "The scale of empire." In Bang, Bayly, and Scheidel in press.

Scheidel, Walter and Friesen, Steven J. 2009. "The size of the economy and the distribution of income in the Roman empire." *Journal of Roman Studies* 99: 61–91.

Scheidel, Walter and Meeks, Elijah. 2014. "Orbis: The Stanford geospatial network model of the Roman world." Version 2.0. http://orbis.stanford.edu.

Scheidel, Walter, Morris, Ian, and Saller, Richard, eds. 2007. *The Cambridge economic history of the Greco-Roman world.* Cambridge: Cambridge University Press.

Scheidel, Walter and von Reden, Sitta, eds. 2002. *The ancient economy.* Edinburgh: Edinburgh University Press.

Schiavone, Aldo. 2000. *The end of the past: Ancient Rome and the modern West.* Cambridge, MA: Harvard University Press.

Schneider, Helmuth. 2007. "Technology." In Scheidel, Morris, and Saller 2007, 144–71.

Schumpeter, Joseph A. 1951 [1919]. "The sociology of imperialisms." In Joseph A.Schumpeter, *Imperialism and social classes.* Trans. Heinz Norden. Ed. Paul M. Sweezy. New York: Augustus M. Kelley, 3–130.

Schumpeter, Joseph A. 1954 [1918]. "The crisis of the tax state." Trans. Wolfgang F. Stolper and Richard A. Musgrave. *International Economic Papers* 4: 5–38.

Scopacasa, Rafael. 2015. *Ancient Samnium: Settlement, culture and identity between history and archaeology.* Oxford: Oxford University Press.

Scott, Tom. 2012. *The city-state in Europe, 1000–1600.* Oxford: Oxford University Press.

Sekunda, Nicholas. 2001. *Hellenistic infantry reform in the 160's BC.* Lodz: Oficyna Naukowa MS.

Sekunda, Nicholas. 2007. "Military forces. A. Land forces." In Philip Sabin, Hans van Wees, and Michael Whitby, eds., *The Cambridge history of Greek and Roman warfare,* vol. 1: *Greece, the Hellenistic world and the rise of Rome.* Cambridge: Cambridge University Press, 325–57.

Sharman, Jason C. 2019. *Empires of the weak: The real story of European expansion and the creation of the new world order.* Princeton, NJ: Princeton University Press.

Shatzman, Israel. 1975. *Senatorial wealth and Roman politics.* Brussels: Latomus.

Shaw, Brent D. 1985. "The divine economy: Stoicism as ideology." *Latomus* 64: 16–54.

Shiue, Carol H. and Keller, Wolfgang. 2007. "Markets in China and Europe on the eve of the Industrial Revolution." *American Economic Review* 97: 1189–216.

Silverberg, Robert. 2003. *Roma eterna.* New York: Harper Voyager.

Sinor, Denis. 1972. "Horse and pasture in Inner Asian history." *Oriens Extremus* 19: 171–83.

Sinor, Denis, ed. 1990. *The Cambridge history of Early Inner Asia.* Cambridge: Cambridge University Press.

Sinor, Denis. 1999. "The Mongols in the West." *Journal of Asian History* 33: 1–44.

Sivin, Nathan. 1991. *Science in ancient China: Researches and reflections.* Aldershot, UK: Ashgate.

Skaff, Jonathan K. 2012. *Sui-Tang China and its Turko-Mongol neighbors: Culture, power, and connections, 580–800.* New York: Oxford University Press.

Skocpol, Theda and Somers, Margaret. 1980. "The uses of comparative history in macrosocial inquiry." *Comparative Studies in Society and History* 22: 174–97.

Slack, Paul. 2015. *The invention of improvement: Information and material progress in seventeenth-century England.* Oxford: Oxford University Press.

Smith, Adam. 1776. *An inquiry into the nature and causes of the wealth of nations*, vol. 2. London: Strahan.

Smith, Christopher. 1996. *Early Rome and Latium: Economy and society c. 1000–500 B.C.* Oxford: Oxford University Press.

Smith, Michael E. 2000. "Aztec city-states." In Hansen 2000a, 581–95.

Sng, Tuan-Hwee. 2014. "Size and dynastic decline: The principal-agent problem in late imperial China, 1700–1850." *Explorations in Economic History* 54: 107–27.

So, Billy K. L. 2000. *Prosperity, region, and institutions in maritime China: The South Fukien pattern, 946–1368.* Cambridge, MA: Harvard University Press.

Soucek, Svat. 1994. "Piri Reis and Ottoman discovery of the great discoveries." *Studia Islamica* 79: 121–42.

Spalinger, Anthony J. 2005. *War in ancient Egypt.* Malden, MA: Blackwell.

Speidel, Michael A. 2016. "Wars, trade and treaties: New, revised, and neglected sources for the political, diplomatic, and military aspects of imperial Rome's relations with the Red Sea and India, from Augustus to Diocletian." In Kuzhippalli S. Mathew, ed., *Imperial Rome, Indian Ocean regions and Muziris: New perspectives on maritime trade.* Milton Park, UK: Routledge, 83–128.

Spruyt, Hendrik. 1994. *The sovereign state and its competitors: An analysis of systems change.* Princeton, NJ: Princeton University Press.

Standen, Naomi. 2007. *Unbounded loyalty: Frontier crossing in Liao China.* Honolulu: University of Hawai'i Press.

Standen, Naomi. 2009. "The five dynasties." In Twitchett and Smith 2009, 38–132.

Stanziani, Alessandro. 2012. *Bâtisseurs d'empires: Russie, Chine et Inde à la croisée des mondes, XVe–XIXe siècle.* Paris: Raisons d'Agir.

Starr, S. Frederick. 2013. *Lost enlightenment: Central Asia's golden age from the Arab conquest to Tamerlane.* Princeton, NJ: Princeton University Press.

Stasavage, David. 2003. *Public debt and the birth of the democratic state: France and Great Britain, 1688–1789.* Cambridge: Cambridge University Press.

Stasavage, David 2010. "When distance mattered: Geographic scale and the development of European representative assemblies." *American Political Science Review* 104: 625–43.

Stasavage, David. 2011. *States of credit: Size, power, and the development of European polities.* Princeton, NJ: Princeton University Press.

Stasavage, David. 2014. "Was Weber right? The role of urban autonomy in Europe's rise." *American Political Science Review* 108: 337–54.

Stasavage, David. In press. *The decline and rise of democracy.* Princeton, NJ: Princeton University Press.

Stathakopoulos, Dionysios C. 2004. *Famine and pestilence in the late Roman and early Byzantine empire: A systematic survey of subsistence crises and epidemics.* Aldershot, UK: Ashgate.

Ste. Croix, Geoffrey E. M. de. 1981. *The class struggle in the ancient Greek world from the archaic age to the Arab conquests.* London: Duckworth.

Stein, Burton. 1989. *Vijayanagara.* Cambridge: Cambridge University Press.

Stein, Peter. 1999. *Roman law in European history.* Cambridge: Cambridge University Press.

Strauss, Barry S. 1999. "The Dark Ages made lighter: The consequences of two defeats." In Cowley 1999, 71–92.

Strauss, Barry. 2006. "The resilient West." In Tetlock, Lebow, and Parker 2006b, 90–118.

Strayer, Joseph R. 1970. *On the medieval origins of the modern state*. Princeton, NJ: Princeton University Press.

Studer, Roman. 2015. *The great divergence reconsidered: Europe, India, and the rise to global economic power*. New York: Cambridge University Press.

Subrahmanyam, Sanjay. 2012. *The Portuguese empire in Asia, 1500–1700*. 2nd ed. Malden, MA: Wiley-Blackwell.

Sunderland, Willard. 2004. *Taming the wild field: Colonization and empire on the Russian steppe*. Ithaca, NY: Cornell University Press.

Sverdrup, Carl F. 2010. "Numbers in Mongol warfare." *Journal of Medieval Military History* 8: 109–17.

Sverdrup, Carl F. 2017. *The Mongol conquests: The military operations of Genghis Khan and Sübe'tei*. Solihull: Helios.

Taaffe, Robert N. 1990. "The geographic setting." In Sinor 1990, 19–40.

Taagepera, Rein. 1978a. "Size and duration of empires: Growth-decline curves, 3000 to 600 B.C." *Social Science Research* 7: 180–96.

Taagepera, Rein. 1978b. "Size and duration of empires: Systematics of size." *Social Science Research* 7: 108–27.

Taagepera, Rein. 1979. "Size and duration of empires: Growth-decline curves, 600 B.C. to 600 A.D." *Social Science History* 3: 115–38.

Taagepera, Rein. 1997. "Expansion and contraction patterns of large polities: Context for Russia." *International Studies Quarterly* 41: 475–504.

Tabacco, Giovanni. 1989. *The struggle for power in medieval Italy: Structures of political rule*. Cambridge: Cambridge University Press.

Tackett, Nicolas 2014. *The destruction of the medieval Chinese aristocracy*. Cambridge, MA: Harvard University Press.

Tainter, Joseph A. 1988. *The collapse of complex societies*. Cambridge: Cambridge University Press.

Tan, James. 2017. *Power and public finance at Rome, 264–49 BCE*. New York: Oxford University Press.

Taylor, Michael J. 2015. "Manpower, finance, and the rise of Rome." PhD diss., University of California, Berkeley.

Taylor, Michael J. 2017. "State finance in the Middle Roman Republic: A reevaluation." *American Journal of Philology* 138: 143–80.

Tedesco, Paolo. 2013. Review of Pablo C. Díaz and Iñaki Martín Viso, eds., *Between taxation and rent: Fiscal problems from late antiquity to early Middle Ages* (Bari: Edipuglia, 2011). *Rivista Storica Italiana* 125: 219–29.

Tedesco, Paolo. 2015. "Late Roman Italy: Taxation, settlement, and economy (A.D. 300–700)." PhD diss., University of Vienna.

Temin, Peter. 2012. *The Roman market economy*. Princeton, NJ: Princeton University Press.

Teng, Mingyu. 2014. "From vassal state to empire: An archaeological examination of Qin culture." In Yuri Pines et al., eds., *Birth of an empire: The state of Qin revisited*. Berkeley: University of California Press, 71–112.

Terpstra, Taco T. 2019. *Trade in the ancient Mediterranean: Private order and public institutions*. Princeton, NJ: Princeton University Press.

Terrenato, Nicola. 2019. *The early Roman expansion into Italy: Elite negotiation and family agendas*. Cambridge: Cambridge University Press.

Tetlock, Philip E. and Belkin, Aaron, eds. 1996. "Counterfactual thought experiments in world politics: Logical, methodological, and psychological perspectives." In Philip E. Tetlock and Aaron Belkin, eds., *Counterfactual thought experiments in world politics: Logical, methodological, and psychological perspectives.* Princeton, NJ: Princeton University Press, 1–38.

Tetlock, Philip E., Lebow, Richard N., and Parker, Geoffrey. 2006a. "Unmaking the Middle Kingdom." In Tetlock, Lebow, and Parker 2006b, 1–13.

Tetlock, Philip E., Lebow, Richard N., and Parker, Geoffrey, eds. 2006b. *Unmaking the West: "What-if?" scenarios that rewrite world history.* Ann Arbor: University of Michigan Press.

Tetlock, Philip E. and Parker, Geoffrey. 2006. "Counterfactual thought experiments: Why we can't live without them & how we must learn to live with them." In Tetlock, Lebow, and Parker 2006b, 14–44.

t'Hart, Marjolein. 1994. "Intercity rivalries and the making of the Dutch state." In Tilly and Blockmans 1994, 196–217.

Thomas, Hugh. 2010. *The golden age: The Spanish empire of Charles V.* London: Allen Lane.

Thomas, Hugh. 2014. *World without end: Spain, Philip II, and the first global empire.* New York: Random House.

Thomas, Russell C. 2014. "Does diffusion of horse-related military technologies explain spatio-temporal patterns of social complexity 1500 BCE–AD 1500?" *Proceedings of the National Academy of Science* 111: E41.

Thompson, William R. and Rasler, Karen. 1999. "War, the military revolution(s) controversy, and army expansion: A test of two explanations of influences on European state making." *Comparative Political Studies* 32: 3–31.

Thomsen, Rudi. 1988. *Ambition and Confucianism: A biography of Wang Mang.* Aarhus: Aarhus University Press.

Tilly, Charles. 1984. *Big structures, large processes, huge comparisons.* New York: Russell Sage Foundation.

Tilly, Charles. 1985. "War making and state making as organized crime." In Peter B. Evans, Dietrich Rueschemeyer, and Theda Skocpol, eds., *Bringing the state back in.* Cambridge: Cambridge University Press, 169–91.

Tilly, Charles. 1992. *Coercion, capital, and European states, AD 990–1992.* Cambridge, MA: Blackwell.

Tilly, Charles and Blockmans, Wim P., eds. 1994. *Cities and the rise of states in Europe, A.D. 1000 to 1800.* Boulder, CO: Westview Press.

Torelli, Mario. 2000. "The Etruscan city-state." In Hansen, 2000a, 189–208.

Tougher, Shaun. 1997. *The reign of Leo VI (886–912): Politics and people.* Leiden: Brill.

Toynbee, Arnold J. 1934–1961. *A study of history.* 12 vols. Oxford: Oxford University Press.

Toynbee, Arnold J. 1969. *Some problems of Greek history.* Oxford: Oxford University Press.

Tracy, James D. 1985. *A financial revolution of the Habsburg Netherlands: Renten and renteniers in the county of Holland.* Berkeley: University of California Press.

Tracy, James D., ed. 1990. *The rise of merchant empires: Long-distance trade in the early modern world, 1350–1750.* Cambridge: Cambridge University Press.

Tracy, James D., ed. 1991. *The political economy of merchant empires: State power and world trade, 1350–1750.* Cambridge: Cambridge University Press.

Tracy, James D. 2002a. "Der Preis der Ehre: Die Finanzierung der Feldzüge Kaiser Karls V." In Kohler, Haidner, and Ottner 2002, 153–64.

Tracy, James D. 2002b. *Emperor Charles V, impresario of war: Campaign strategy, international finance, and domestic politics*. Cambridge: Cambridge University Press.

Treadgold, Warren. 1995. *Byzantium and its army, 284–1081*. Stanford, CA: Stanford University Press.

Tridimas, George. 2018. "Why ancient Greece failed to industrialize: Cost of energy, culture and city-state multiplicity." European Social Science History Conference, Belfast, April 4.

Tsai, Shih-shan Henry. 2001. *Perpetual happiness: The Ming emperor Yongle*. Seattle: University of Washington Press.

Turchin, Peter. 2003. *Historical dynamics: Why states rise and fall*. Princeton, NJ: Princeton University Press.

Turchin, Peter. 2006. *War and peace and war: The life cycles of imperial nations*. New York: Pi Press.

Turchin, Peter. 2009. "A theory for formation of large empires." *Journal of Global History* 4: 191–217.

Turchin, Peter, Currie, Thomas, Turner, Edward A. L., and Gavrilets, Sergey. 2014. "Reply to Thomas: Diffusion of military technologies is a plausible explanation for the evolution of social complexity, 1500 BCE–AD 1500." *Proceedings of the National Academy of Sciences* 111: E415.

Turchin, Peter, Currie, Thomas E., Turner, Edward A. L., and Gavrilets, Sergey. 2013. "War, space, and the evolution of Old World complex societies." *Proceedings of the National Academy of Sciences* 110: 16384–89.

Turchin, Peter and Nefedov, Sergey A. 2009. *Secular cycles*. Princeton, NJ: Princeton University Press.

Tvedt, Terje. 2010. "Why England and not China and India? Water systems and the history of the Industrial Revolution." *Journal of Global History* 5: 29–50.

Twitchett, Denis and Smith, Paul J., eds. 2009. *The Cambridge history of China*, vol. 5, part 1: *The Sung dynasty and its precursors, 907–1279*. Cambridge: Cambridge University Press.

Van Bavel, Bas, Buringh, Eltjo, and Dijkman, Jessica. 2018. "Mills, cranes, and the great divergence: The use of immovable capital goods in western Europe and the Middle East, ninth to sixteenth centuries." *Economic History Review* 71: 31–54.

Van Zanden, Jan Luiten. 2009a. *The long road to the Industrial Revolution: The European economy in a global perspective, 1000–1800*. Leiden: Brill.

Van Zanden, Jan Luiten. 2009b. "The skill premium and the 'Great Divergence.'" *European Review of Economic History* 13: 121–53.

Van Zanden, Jan Luiten, Buringh, Eltjo, and Bosker, Maarten. 2012. "The rise and decline of European parliaments, 1188–1789." *Economic History Review* 65: 835–61.

Vervaet, Frederik J. 2014. *The high command in the Roman Republic: The principle of the* summum imperium auspiciumque *from 509 to 19 BCE*. Stuttgart: Franz Steiner Verlag.

Visscher, M. S. 2011. "Landscape of languages: The position of provincial languages in the Roman empire in the first three centuries AD." MA thesis, University of Leiden.

Voigtländer, Nico and Voth, Hans-Joachim. 2006. "Why England? Demographic factors, structural change and physical capital accumulation during the Industrial Revolution." *Journal of Economic Growth* 11: 319–61.

Voigtländer, Nico and Voth, Hans-Joachim. 2009. "Malthusian dynamism and the rise of Europe: Make love, not war." *American Economic Review* 99: 248–54.

Voigtländer, Nico and Voth, Hans-Joachim. 2013a. "Gifts to Mars: Warfare and Europe's early rise to riches." *Journal of Economic Perspectives* 27: 165–86.

Voigtländer, Nico and Voth, Hans-Joachim. 2013b. "The three horsemen of riches: Plague, war, and urbanization in early modern Europe." *Review of Economic Studies* 80: 774–811.

Von Glahn, Richard. 2016. *An economic history of China: From antiquity to the nineteenth century.* Cambridge: Cambridge University Press.

Vries, Peer. 2001. "Are coal and colonies really crucial? Kenneth Pomeranz and the Great Divergence." *Journal of World History* 12: 407–46.

Vries, Peer. 2002. "Governing growth: A comparative analysis of the role of the state in the rise of the West." *Journal of World History* 13: 67–138.

Vries, Peer. 2012. "Challenges, (non-)responses, and politics: A review of Prasannan Parthasarathi, *Why Europe grew rich and Asia did not: Global economic divergence, 1600–1850.*" *Journal of World History* 23: 639–64.

Vries, Peer. 2013. *Escaping poverty: The origins of modern economic growth.* Vienna: Vienna University Press.

Vries, Peer. 2015. *State, economy, and the great divergence: Great Britain and China, 1680s–1850s.* London: Bloomsbury.

Vries, Peer. 2020. *Averting a great divergence: State and economy in Japan, 1868–1937.* London: Bloomsbury.

Wahl, Fabian. 2017. "Does European development have Roman roots? Evidence from the German limes." *Journal of Economic Growth* 22: 313–49.

Waley-Cohen, Joanna. 1993. "China and Western technology in the late eighteenth century." *American Historical Review* 98: 1525–44.

Waley-Cohen, Joanna. 2006. *The culture of war in China: Empire and the military under the Qing dynasty.* London: I. B. Tauris.

Wallerstein, Immanuel. 1974. *The modern world-system I: Capitalist agriculture and the origins of the European world-economy in the sixteenth century.* New York: Academic Press.

Wallerstein, Immanuel. 1980. *The modern world-system II: Mercantilism and the consolidation of the European world-economy, 1600–1750.* New York: Academic Press.

Wallerstein, Immanuel. 1989. *The modern world-system III: The second era of great expansion of the capitalist world-economy, 1730–1840s.* San Diego: Academic Press.

Wallerstein, Immanuel. 2011. *The modern world-system IV: Centrist liberalism triumphant, 1789–1914.* Los Angeles: University of California Press.

Wang, Gungwu. 1990. "Merchants without empire: The Hokkien sojourning communities." In Tracy 1990, 400–421.

Wang, Jingbin. 2014. Review of Pines 2012. *H-Net Reviews.* http://www.h-net.org/reviews/showrev.php?id=41935.

Warde, Paul. 2007. *Energy consumption in England & Wales 1560–2000.* Naples: Consiglio Nazionale delle Ricerche, Istituto di Studi sulle Società del Mediterraneo.

Warde, Paul. 2013. "The first industrial revolution." In Astrid Kander, Paolo Malanima, and Paul Warde, eds., *Power to the people: Energy in Europe over the last five centuries.* Princeton, NJ: Princeton University Press, 129–247.

Watts, John. 2009. *The making of polities: Europe, 1300–1500.* Cambridge: Cambridge University Press.

Weber, Max. 1920–1921. *Gesammelte Aufsätze zur Religionssoziologie*. 3 vols. Tübingen: Mohr.

Weinstein, Stanley. 1987. *Buddhism under the T'ang*. Cambridge: Cambridge University Press.

Wey Gómez, Nicolás. 2008. *The tropics of empire: Why Columbus sailed south to the Indies*. Cambridge, MA: MIT Press.

Wickham, Chris. 1994. *Land and power: Studies in Italian and European social history, 400–1200*. London: British School at Rome.

Wickham, Chris. 2001. "Society." In Rosamund Kitterick, ed., *The early Middle Ages: Europe 400–1000*. Oxford: Oxford University Press, 59–94.

Wickham, Chris. 2005. *Framing the early Middle Ages: Europe and the Mediterranean, 400–800*. Oxford: Oxford University Press.

Wickham, Chris. 2009. *The inheritance of Rome: Illuminating the Dark Ages 400–1000*. New York: Viking.

Wickham, Chris. 2015. *Sleepwalking into a new world: The emergence of Italian city communes in the twelfth century*. Princeton, NJ: Princeton University Press.

Wickham, Chris. 2016. *Medieval Europe*. New Haven, CT: Yale University Press.

Wickham, Chris. 2017. "Consensus and assemblies in the Romano-Germanic kingdoms: A comparative approach." In Verena Epp and Christoph H. F. Meyer, eds., *Recht und Konsens im frühen Mittelalter*. Ostfildern: Jan Thorbecke Verlag, 389–426.

Wilkinson, David. 1987. "Central civilization." *Comparative Civilizations Review* 17: 31–59.

Williams, Ann. 1999. *Kingship and government in pre-conquest England, c.500–1066*. Basingstoke: Macmillan.

Williams, J.H.C. 2001. *Beyond the Rubicon: Romans and Gauls in Republican Italy*. Oxford: Oxford University Press.

Wilson, Andrew. 2009. "Indicators for Roman economic growth: A response to Walter Scheidel." *Journal of Roman Archaeology* 22: 71–82.

Wilson, Andrew. 2011. "City sizes and urbanization in the Roman empire." In Alan Bowman and Andrew Wilson, eds., *Settlement, urbanization, and population*. Oxford: Oxford University Press, 161–95.

Wilson, Andrew. 2014. "Quantifying Roman economic performance by means of proxies: Pitfalls and potential." In Francois de Callataÿ, ed., *Quantifying the Greco-Roman economy and beyond*. Bari: Edipuglia, 147–67.

Wilson, Andrew and Bowman, Alan, eds. 2018. *Trade, commerce, and the state in the Roman world*. Oxford: Oxford University Press.

Wilson, Peter H. 2016. *Heart of Europe: A history of the Holy Roman Empire*. Cambridge, MA: Harvard University Press.

Wittfogel, Karl. 1957. *Oriental despotism: A comparative study of total power*. New York: Random House.

Wong, R. Bin. 1997. *China transformed: Historical change and the limits of European experience*. Ithaca, NY: Cornell University Press.

Wong, R. Bin. 2012. "Taxation and good governance in China, 1500–1914." In Yun-Casalilla and O'Brien 2012, 353–77.

Wood, Ellen M. 2003. *Empire of capital*. London: Verso.

Woolf, Greg. 1994. "Power and the spread of writing in the West." In Alan K. Bowman and Greg Woolf, eds., *Literacy and power in the ancient world*. Cambridge: Cambridge University Press, 84–98.

Woolf, Greg. 2012. *Rome: An empire's story*. New York: Oxford University Press.

Wright, Arthur F. 1978. *The Sui dynasty*. New York: Knopf.

Wright, Roger. 2013. "Periodization." In Maiden, Smith, and Ledgeway 2013, 107–24.

Wright, Roger. 2016. "Latin and Romance in the medieval period: A sociophilological approach." In Adam Ledgeway and Martin Maiden, eds., *The Oxford guide to the Romance languages*. Oxford: Oxford University Press, 14–23.

Wrigley, E. Anthony. 2016. *The path to sustained growth: England's transition from an organic economy to an industrial revolution*. Cambridge: Cambridge University Press.

Wrigley, E. Anthony. 2018. "Reconsidering the Industrial Revolution: England and Wales." *Journal of Interdisciplinary History* 49: 9–42.

Xigui, Qiu. 2000. *Chinese writing*. Berkeley, CA: Society for the Study of Early China.

Xiong, Victor C. 2006. *Emperor Yang of the Sui dynasty: His life, times, and legacy*. Albany: State University of New York Press.

Yang, Lien-sheng. 1961. *Studies in Chinese institutional history*. Cambridge, MA: Harvard University Press.

Yates, Robin D. D. 2006. "The Song empire: The world's first superpower?" In Tetlock, Lebow, and Parker 2006b, 205–40.

Yazdani, Kaveh. 2017. *India, modernity, and the great divergence: Mysore and Gujarat (17th to 19th C.)*. Leiden: Brill.

Yoffee, Norman and Cowgill, George L., eds. 1988. *The collapse of ancient states and civilizations*. Tucson: University of Arizona Press.

Young, Gary K. 2001. *Rome's eastern trade: International commerce and imperial policy, 31 BC–AD 305*. New York: Routledge.

Yun-Casalilla, Bartolomé and O'Brien, Patrick, eds. 2012. *The rise of fiscal states: A global history, 1500–1914*. Cambridge: Cambridge University Press.

Zelin, Madeleine. 2004. "A critique of rights of property in prewar China." In Madeleine Zelin, Jonathan K. Ocko, and Robert Gardella, eds., *Contract and property in early modern China*. Stanford, CA: Stanford University Press, 17–36.

Zelin, Madeleine. 2009. "The firm in early modern China." *Journal of Economic Behavior and Organization* 71: 623–37.

Zhang, David D. et al. 2015. "The pulse of imperial China: A quantitative analysis of long-term geopolitical and climatic cycles." *Global Ecology and Biogeography* 24: 87–96.

Zhang, Taisu. 2017. *The laws and economics of Confucianism: Kinship and property in preindustrial China and England*. Cambridge: Cambridge University Press.

Zhang, Xiangming. 2010. "A preliminary study of the punishment of political speech in the Ming period." *Ming Studies* 62: 56–91.

Zhao, Dingxin. 2015a. *The Confucian-Legalist state: A new theory of Chinese history*. New York: Oxford University Press.

Zhao, Dingxin. 2015b. "The Han bureaucracy: Its origin, nature, and development." In Scheidel, 2015c, 56–89.

Zhou, Youguang. 2003. *The historical evolution of Chinese languages and scripts*. Columbus, OH: National East Asian Languages Resource Center.

INDEX

Note: Page numbers in *italics* refer to figures and tables.

Abbasid caliphate, 38, 43, 144–45, 150, 151, 256, 301, 432, 541n3

Abernathy, David, 450, 453, 591n71

Académie royal des sciences (Paris), 475

Acemoglu, Daron, 496, 525, 602n45

Achaemenid empire: Athenian empire fighting against, 55, 553n6; in counterfactual to Roman empire, *112*, 112–13, 119, 121; duration and scope of, 221, 300, 522; horsemanship of, 299; imperial consolidation under, 38; logistical challenges of, 139; Middle Eastern political-military network, 90; military of, 299–300, 521; population of, 35, *39*, 140, 219; reach of, 552n5

Actium, battle of (31 BCE), 79

Aetolian league, 95

Afghanistan, 285, 298, 435

Afzelius, Adam, 550n19

Aghlabids, 151, 152

Akkadian empire, *112*, 112, 543n7

Alexander the Great (Macedonian king), 11, 91, 95, 114–17, *115*, 119, 121, 221, 553n8, 553n12

Alfred (English king), 239

Allen, Robert, 491–95, 499, 501, 597n59, 597n71

Ambrose, 315, 574n10

Ameling, Walter, 439n4, 439n6

Americas. *See* maritime exploration and expansion; New World; United States

Anastasius I (Roman emperor), 315

Anatolia, 82, 90, 95, 100, 112, 135, 136, 179, 204, 206, 221, 317

Angkorian empire, 47, 272

Antigonus I (Macedonian king), 117, 553n14

Antiochos IV (Seleucid king), 601n36

Antony, 83

Appian, 85

Aquitaine, 148–49, 153, 156, 160

Arab conquests: Christian Spain repelling, 176, 193; in eighth century, 12, 139–52; fragmentation of, 145–47, 246; inability to maintain a large-scale empire in Europe, 147–48, 152, 215, 512; Islamic religious practices and, 317; in Levant, 301; military practices and, 145–46, 256; Samarra crisis (860s) and, 145; in sixth century, 136, 137, 138; tax practices and, 143, 144, 146–47, 255–56. *See also* Abbasid caliphate; Iberian peninsula; Umayyad caliphate

Arabic language and writing, 311, 329

Aramaic language, 311

Archimedes, 524

aristocracy. *See* nobility

Aristophanes, 553n6

Arrighi, Giovanni, 399, 583n141

Arsaces I (Parthian king), 299

Asia: ecology of, 277; economic development in, 2, 3–4; New World bullion transferred to, 421, 425. *See also specific regions and countries* assemblies and decision-making bodies, 355–57

Assyria, 112, 221, 299, 543n7

Athenian empire, 55, 113–14, 115, 553n6. *See also* Greek city-states

Atlas of World Population History (McEvedy and Jones, eds.), 533–34

Augustus (Roman emperor), 83–84, 101, 457

Avars, 135, 137, 139, 154, 182, 246, 293

Ayyubids, 176

Aztec empire, 46, 55, 193, 464, 543n7

Bacon, Francis, 478

Baechler, Jean, 396, 515

Baghdad, 191, 207, 256

Bang, Peter F., 539n21

Bank of England, 382

Barfield, Thomas, 277, 279, 287, 295, 568n40

Batu, 174–81, t186, 188

Bayle, Pierre, 474

Bayly, Chris A., 478–79, 496, 539n21

Beard, Mary, 542n4

Beckwith, Christopher, 278, 568n40, 568n42

Béla IV (Hungarian king), 176–78, 180

Belich, James, 470

Bennett, James, 552n36

Berbers, 136, 142, 144, 148–49, 151–54, 213, 302

Billows, Richard, 553n14

Black Death, 4, 142, 190, 371, 417, 491, 498, 499, 597n60, 598n79

Bodde, Derk, 405, 594n23, 595n27

Bohemia, 83, 176, 185, 268, 347, 376, 474

Bosworth, A. B., 553n9

Brahe, Tycho, 483

Brandt, Loren, 394

Braudel, Fernand, 32

Britain. *See* England/Britain

Bryant, Joseph, 392, 589n18

Buddhism, 224, 317–20, 322, 329

Bulgars, 136, 137, 152, 155, 175, 290

Burgundians, 132, 134, 153, 165, 166, 193

Burma, 182, 303, 306, 457

Byzantine empire (Byzantium), 136, 143, 168, 187, 316, 508–9, 511, 572n80. *See also* Constantinople; East Roman restoration (sixth century)

California school of scholarship, 575n1

Calvin, Jean, 197, 200, 474

Campanella, Tommaso, 474

capitalism, 391–92, 396, 411, 414, 473, 589n20, 596n58

Carolingian empire, 153–64, 155, 157; compared to Roman empire, 162–63, 213, 228; demise of, 240; elites as warriors in, 159–60, 162; expansion of, 160, 163; factional conflict in, 160–61; income from land grants in, 159; post-Charlemagne, 158, 161; taxes in, 159

Carthage: in counterfactual to Roman empire, 113, 116–19, 521, 524; maritime exploration by, 430; population of, 549n6; as rival to Rome, 62, 77–78, 80, 91–100, 103, 109, 222, 439n4, 543n7, 546nn57–59, 549n4, 549nn6–9; troop numbers for, 551n30. *See also* First Punic War; Second Punic War

Casale, Giancarlo, 447–48

Catholic Church: counterfactual scenario for European unity and, 512–13, 601n33; creation of College of Cardinals, 171, 346; excommunication powers, 315–16, 347, 573n10; French education system and, 488; Great Schism (thirteenth century), 348; harmonization of canon law, 346, 514; Latin as lingua franca of, 517–18; Nicaean creed and, 519; papacy and, 171, 224, 346–48, 512; power of, 340, 345–48, 513; Reformation and, 370, 473–74; as victim of its own success, 348. *See also* Christianity; German empire; Holy Roman Empire

cavalry warfare: Abbasids, 256; Carolingian Empire, 162; in China, 242–45, 248, 250,

252, 285, 570n56; Hellenistic kingdoms, 95; Huns, 295; in India, 296–300; Magyars, 293; Mongols, 175, 177, 181–82, 189; in Muscovy, 292; Parthians, 100; in Roman Empire, 77; steppe effect and, 275, 279–80

Celtic language, 311, 312

Celtic society, 522–23, 526

Central America, 10, 46, 466. *See also* New World

Chagatai khanate, 175, 183, 185

Charlemagne (Frankish king), 35, 36, 154–56, 160–63, 171, 231, 240, 244, 267

Charles the Bald (Frankish king), 161

Charles the Fat (Frankish king), 157

Charles Martel, 154, 160

Charles V (Habsburg ruler and Holy Roman emperor), 193–98; abdication by, 198; army size and, 199; compared to Charlemagne, 199–200; counterfactual scenario for, 200–201, 203; credit to finance wars of, 199; fighting against France, 195, 196, 198; fiscal constraints in waging war and, 199–200; New World conquests by, 193, 196–97; Protestant Reformation and, 197–98

Chen Qiang, 409

China: as agrarian empire, 441–48; agrarian paternalism in, 406–7, 442; ancestor worship in, 321; bureaucracy in, 226–27, 248, 393; capture of population (not territory) as goal of, 242; censorship in, 404; Central Plain in, 264–65; civil service system in, 225, 244, 394; clans in, 408, 410–11, 542n4; commerce and trade in, 397, 442–46, 588n226; compared to Europe (post-1500), 392–96, 406, 411–13; compared to post-Roman Europe, 17, 23, 228, 243, 254–58, 320–28, 329–32, 331, 343–44, 562n30; compared to Roman empire, 72, 221–27, 294, 320, 505, 507; corruption in, 408–9, 506; cotton imports from India, 426; defined, 529;

developmental outcomes of empire structure in, 342, 392–96, 400–407, 506, 583n138; ecology in, conducive to empire building, 252, 281–90; energy constraints on economic development in, 494; examination system in, 322, 394, 480, 563n46, 594n24; fiscal administration in, 251, 257, 395, 407–8, 585n190; fragmentation periods, relationship to innovation in, 396–400; *fubing* system in, 248, 251, 255; geography of, 261–64, 266–67, 282; Great Wall and other protective walls in, 285, 289, 437; hegemony and conservatism in, 479–85; Hundred Schools of Thought, 396; ideologies of empire in, 320–28, 329, 331; institutions, logic of, 392–96; land distribution in, 247, 248, 405; language and writing in, 308–9, 310, 312–13, 573n4, 594n23; Legalism in, 320–21, 322, 393; maritime commerce restrictions in, 402–3; migrants from, lack of homeland interest in protecting, 443–45; military mobilization and warfare in, 242–44, 246–51, 257, 397–99; modern China's leadership from south, 569n49; Mongols in, 4, 175, 182–83, 189–90, 230, 285, 286, 398–99, 440, 558n20; monopolistic policymaking in, 400–407; mountains and rivers in, 261–64, 500; north/northwest as origin of unification events, 223, 224, 227, 244–53, 281–82, 289, 566n13; north-south split in, 230–31; overseas exploration not of interest to, 433, 441–46, 591n77; patronage in, 227, 395–96, 476, 481; patterns of empire in, 40–41, 41–42, 43–44, 44, 228, 279; Period of Disunion (fourth through sixth centuries CE), 43, 246–52, 254, 280, 318, 322, 397, 399; population of, 219, 249, 251, 288, 564n50, 587n224; post-Han China compared to post-Roman Europe, 13, 223, 251–52; post-nineteenth-century economic

China (cont.)

development in, 2; property rights in, 395; Qin-Han China compared to Roman Europe, 72, 221–27; rebellions occurring near end of individual dynasties in, 286–87, 406, 412, 570n61, 586n205; religion and belief systems in, 317–22, 328; serial empire reconstructions in, 9, 12, 224, 229, 246–53, 257, 395, 411; Sixteen Kingdoms period (304 to 439 CE), 227, 242, 284; social development (500 BCE–1500 CE) in, 5; stagnation in thinking and lack of alternative discourse in, 479–85; state formation in, compared to Europe, 228, 251–52, 394, 542n18; steppe effect and, 283–84, 286–90, 444, 452, 569n44, 570n62; tax practices in, 225, 245, 246–47, 252, 253, 257, 394–95, 397, 407–10; Three Kingdoms (mid-third century), 243; urbanization in, 394, 397–98, 442; Warring States period (pre-Qin), 72, 81, 222, 224, 230, 248, 283, 308, 320, 323–24, 327, 339, 393, 396, 406, 480, 481, 544n22, 551n29, 560n4, 575n33; waterworks and flood control in, 264, 499–500, 566n10; White Lotus rebellion (1790s), 412. See also Confucianism; East Asia; specific dynasties and empires

Christianity: ascendance in Europe, 224, 314–17, 511, 518–19, 527; colonization and New World interests of, 450; comparison to Islamic and Chinese belief systems, 329; as divisive factor in Europe, 511–12; Eastern Church's division, 316, 574n13; failure of empire-building and, 512–14; modernity and, 511, 516; state formation and, 317; as supraregional organization, 345–48. See also Catholic Church; Protestantism

church. See Catholic Church; Christian Church; religion and beliefs; specific religions

Cicero, 232

cities. See urban development

clans, 408, 410–11, 542n4

Clark, Gregory, 497

Claudius (Roman emperor), 81, 86, 239

Clement VII (pope), 197

coal, 6, 386–87, 425, 492, 494, 500, 537n7, 588n12, 597nn67–68

colonial empires: conflict over, 449; as extensions of competing European polities, 538n17; slavery and, 388, 423–24. See also maritime exploration and expansion; New World; specific countries controlling colonial empires

Columbus, Christopher, 193, 431, 439, 450, 462–64

commercial transactions and credit: Bourgeois Revaluation, 489–90; Charles V using credit to finance wars, 199; in China, 398–99, 588n226; in Europe and England (post-1500), 356–57, 376, 381–82, 580n77, 581n103; low interest rates, effect of, 497; in Roman empire, 504; unifying set of customs and rule for, 516. See also mercantilism

common law tradition, 378, 497, 498

communalism, 14, 352–53, 376, 416, 474

comparative scholarship, 21–22, 26, 502; analytical comparison between equivalent units, 23; premodern rule and, 42–48; variable-oriented parallel demonstration of theory, 23

competition: (Second) Great Divergence and, 18; significance of, 15; stifled by empire, 17, 339–41, 343, 396

Confucianism, 320–23, 393, 394, 395, 406, 442, 480, 482, 490, 583n143, 594n23

Congjian Yan, Shuyu Zhouzilu, 437–38

Conrad I (German ruler), 164

Conrad II (German ruler), 166, 177

Constantine I (Roman emperor), 194, 314, 508, 519, 601n33

Constantinople, 135–36, 139, 140, 142–44, 148, 152, 204, 223; patriarch of, 316
constitutionalism, 361, 375, 380
Coptic language, 311
corruption, 129, 342, 381, 403, 407–9, 506, 508
Cosandey, David, 260
cotton industry and trade, 424–27, 589n20
Council of Chalcedon (451), 133, 346
Council of Clermont (1095), 347
Council of Nicaea (325), 346
councils and synods, 348–51
counterfactual, significance of use of, 23–26, 215, 540n39
counterfactual scenario for France and England (seventeenth century), 208–10
counterfactual scenario for Holy Roman Empire and Habsburgs, 200–201, 215, 512–13, 559n55
counterfactual scenario for Mongol empire, 185–92, 215
counterfactual scenario for Napoleon, 211–12, 215
counterfactual scenario for Ottoman empire, 206–8
counterfactual scenario for overseas exploration, 454–71; changing orientation to New World (East is West), 459–67, 460–61, 463; Chinese economic development, 468–71; shortcuts to access goods, 455–59
counterfactual scenario for Roman empire, 11, 110–23, 521–26, 525, 602n45; eastern hostilities as source of, 111–20; Etruscization of Rome and, 552n2; Hannibal and Carthage as source of, 118–19, 521, 524, 553n16; Italian domestic developments as source of, 110–11, 120–22, 521; Macedonian intervention in Italy as source of, 114–17, 521, 553n17; Persian invasion of southern Italy as source of, 522, 552n5; Social War (91–89 BCE) as source of, 120; warfare between

rival factions of Roman aristocracy as source of, 121, 554nn21–22
counterfactual scenario for sixteenth-century European powers, 200–204
counterfactual scenario for Song empire, 583n157
Counter-Reformation, 484
Crassus, 83
credit. See commercial transactions and credit
Crone, Patricia, 416, 587n219, 598n85
Crusades, 176, 347
culture and cultural unity, 307–34, 331; benefit of simultaneous fragmentation and cultural unity, 514–16; comparisons between Chinese and European systems, 328–30; counterfactual to Roman empire, effect on cultural unity, 522; First Great Divergence and, 307; hegemony and conservatism in China, India, and Middle East, 341, 479–85; Industrial Enlightenment and, 485–88; knowledge and scientific inquiry, 472–73; language and writing, 308–13, 476; polycentrism and Enlightenment, 473–79; (Second) Great Divergence and Industrial Revolution(s) and, 472–73; values of Enlightenment, 488–91. See also literacy rate; religion and beliefs
Cumans, 175, 177, 291
Cyrus II (Achaemenid king), 299

da Gama, Vasco, 431, 439
Daly, Jonathan, 538n13
Daoism, 319, 321
Dareios I (Achaemenid king), 299, 432
Dead Sea Scrolls, 524
De Angelis, Franco, 549n5
decentralization, 145–46, 224, 228, 230, 232, 235, 240, 268, 561n24, 561n30
De Crespigny, Rafe, 566n13, 575n44
Demandt, Alexander, 128, 552n2, 552n5, 553n11, 553n16, 554n6

democracy, 8, 538n11, 587n220

Deng, Kent Gang, 279, 406, 586n205

Denmark. *See* Scandinavian polities

Descartes, René, 474, 478

Diamond, Jared, 260, 263

di Cosmo, Nicola, 287–88, 568n40

Diet of Worms (1521), 197

Dincecco, Mark, 358

Diodorus, 549n5

diversity, role of, 391, 414, 496

Dong Zhonshu, 480

Doyle, Michael, 102, 542n2, 550n10, 551n26

Duchesne, Ricardo, 496

Durand-Guédy, David, 587n219

Dutch United Provinces, 356

Dutschke, Rudi, 576n7

East Asia: coastline compared to Europe, 261; defined, 33; divergence from European state formation, 220, 560n13; ecology of, 272, 281–90; geography of, 260–67, 262; imperial state formation in, 45, 45–47; mountains and rivers in, 261–64, 262; parallel of state formation to Roman empire, 220, 221–24; parallels of state formation in Europe with, 220, 221–24; patterns of empire, 10, 12, 40–42, 41–42, 43, 230; plain regions and natural core in, 264–66; polycentrism not applicable to, 230, 418–19, 560n16; population of, 34, 35; size of, 33, 34. *See also* China

Eastern Europe: failure to export to richer northwest, 427; Mongol incursion into, 174–75, 178; steppe effect and, 290–93; in tenth century, 268. *See also specific countries*

East Francia, 157

East India Company, 386, 451

East Roman restoration (sixth century), 12, 132, 132–38, 134, 212–14

ecology: East Asia, 281–90; Europe, 290–94; imperial state formation and, 47, 274, 276–80, 331, 332, 501; Iran, 298–301; Levant and North Africa, 301–2; Mongol invasion and, 181–82, 183, 192, 245, 278, 556n1, 557–58n18, 557n9; Roman empire's demise and, 137; South Asia, 295–98; Southeast Asia, 303–4; volcanic activity resulting in famine (ninth century), 162. *See also* steppe effect

economic development: East vs. West, 2, 2–5, 4, 7, 411–13, 537n3; gross domestic product (GDP) correlated with happiness and life evaluation, 8; modestly sized polities' ability to flourish compared to quasi-imperial kingdoms, 415, 431, 494, 578n59; in post-1500 Europe, 370–75; post-nineteenth-century, 1, 6; in Roman empire, 505–6. *See also* Industrial Revolution(s); transformative developmental outcomes; *specific countries and empires*

Egypt: Council of Chalcedon (451) and, 133; in counterfactual to Roman empire, 112; domestic turmoil in, 550n14; empire of eighth and seventh centuries BCE, 221, 302; Fatimid capture of (969), 151, 302; fiscal and tax practices in, 255, 565n71; horses and chariot warfare in, 301–2; Hyksos occupation of, 301; international trade with, 427, 457; language and writing in, 311; Middle Eastern political-military network (c. 1500–500 BCE), 90; Persia's persistent problems with (525 to 332 BCE), 552n5; Roman conquest of, 83, 456, 457; Sasanians annexing, 135; Seleucids and, 521, 601n36. *See also* Ptolemies

Eire, Carlos, 200–201, 203, 601n33

Elvin, Mark, 403

empire: adaptiveness of, 15; agrarian empires, 15, 397, 441–48; beneficial effect on social development, 4; capstone governments, 339, 342, 362,

407, 413, 414, 576n4; causes of demise of, 240–41; city-state–based empires, 543n7; defined, 529; factors leading to demise of, 129; failure of Europe to re-create after fall of Roman empire, 9, 10, 11, 16, 127–28, 131, 166, 168, 172–73, 214, 333, 496, 503; ideology of imperial unity, 320–28, 329, 331; imperiogenesis, 17, 461, 484, 501, 513–14; institutions, importance of, 326–27; measuring imperial dominance, 31–34; monopolistic, 15–17, 32, 38, 47, 204, 339, 341, 343; outside of Europe, durability of empire-bearing structures, 131; patterns of, 35–37, 35–48; perpetuation as negative factor for further development, 17, 341–42, 479–85; population as most meaningful measure of, 32, 213; population size of largest empires (700 BCE to 2000 CE), 15, 16; "shadow empire" model, 277–78, 568n40. *See also specific empires and countries*

energy capture and consumption, 6, 537nn7–8. *See also* coal

England/Britain: alliance with Spain against France, 201; Anglo-Saxon period, 239, 312, 349, 363; bourgeoisie's freedom and dignity in, 489–90; church's role in, 346, 478; Civil War in, 376, 379, 578n59; cohesion and collective action in, 379, 581n110; colonization and New World trade of, 421–23, 424–27, 449; common law tradition in, 378; Commons, 350; corruption and rent-seeking in, 381; counterfactual scenario for economic rise of, 498–99; counterfactual scenario for seventeenth century in, 208–10; cultural change in, 390; domestic conflict in, 376; economic conditions (post-1500) in, 371; Enlightenment in, labeled as Industrial Enlightenment, 485; escape from Rome in, 378; fiscal-naval-mercantilist state and economic development in, 385–90;

fragmentation in, 363–64, 390; ghost acreages of, 424–25, 426–27, 589n19; Glorious Revolution (1688), 379, 474; governance and politics in, 349, 350, 364–65, 377–82; immigrants coming to, 378, 486; industrialization and modernity in, 341, 359, 377–82, 389–92, 415, 428, 485, 491–95; innovation in, 388–90, 485–88, 497, 581n99; iron industry and metal products in, 388, 423, 424, 494; literacy rates and public education in, 373, 375, 477, 485–86, 492, 596n42; Luddite riots, 487; Magna Carta, 350; naval supremacy of, 385–90; Navigation Acts, 385; Netherlands and, 377; in ninth century, 155, 228; nobility rising in importance in, 239; North Sea economy of, 370–77; parliament in, 350, 376, 379–81; path to Industrial Revolution, 377–82, 491–95; post-nineteenth-century economic development in, 1, 2; productivity in, 378, 422; protectionism and, 380–81, 384–87; Reformed Church in, 478; religious tolerance in, 484; Roman empire's end in, 363; sixteenth- and seventeenth-century rise of, 201, 203, 208, 381–82; slave trade and, 424, 425, 426, 589n17; standing army in, 239; taxes and military commitments in, 369, 379; in tenth century, 241; textile industry and trade in, 386, 415, 423–25, 491–93, 581n115, 588n10, 597n60; trade as economic engine in, 390, 493–94; urbanization in, 371, 373–74, 581n99, 597n64; war and, 366, 382–84; waterways and water use, importance of, 499–500; Whigs in, 380

English language and writing, 312

Enlightenment: hegemony and conservatism vs., 479–85, 594n23; Industrial Enlightenment, 485–88; polycentrism and, 473–79, 497; values of, 488–91

Ennius, 546n57

environmental effects. *See* ecology

Epirus, 91, 116, 117, 551n30

estates and grand councils, 349–51, 355, 496

Etruscans, 52, 54–58, 77, 115, 116, 522, 543n8, 545n35

Eugippius, 254

Europe: Christianity's ascendance in, 314–17; coastline of, 260–61; corporate organization in, 410; defined, 33, 529–30; demography as factor in developmental transformation of, 497–99; ecology, 290–94; economic conditions (post-1500) in, 371, 372; ethnic loyalty in, 330; expansionism of, 411–13; geography of, 264–66, 270; globalization and, 420–25; imperial state formation in, 9–10, 44–45, 45, 48, 542n18; marriage pattern in, 498–99, 598n81; mountains and rivers in, 261–64, 262; parliamentarianism in, 14, 350–51, 376; patterns of empire in, 12, 35–38; plain regions and natural core not part of geography of, 264–66; population of, 34–38, 35–38; post-Napoleonic (1812), 211; post-nineteenth-century economic development in, 1, 2; precondition of disappearance of empire for later exceptionalism, 14; recurrent empires, negative possible effects of, 9–11, 14; sixteenth-century rise of, 200–201; size of, 33, 34; social development (5000 BCE–2000 CE), 5; social development (500 BCE–1500 CE), 5; social development (1500–1900 CE), 7; states constituting currently, 229; steppe effect and, 290–94; taxes and credit in, 368–70, 376; unity in diversity of, 514–16; urbanization in, 373–74; war in, 367–68. *See also* Black Death; counterfactuals; First Great Divergence (mid-first-millennium Europe); fragmentation of power; Industrial Revolution(s); maritime exploration and expansion; polycentrism; post-Roman Europe; Roman empire; (Second) Great Divergence; transformative developmental outcomes; *specific countries and kingdoms*

Fatimids, 145, 151, 302

feudalism, 14, 181, 243, 327, 340, 346, 351, 361, 416, 496, 514, 555n41

First Great Divergence (mid-first-millennium Europe), 219–21, 227–32; assignment of term, 231, 560n17; Chinese imperial tradition used as counterpoint to medieval and European state formation, 220; comparative scholarship and, 22, 23; culture and religion in, 307, 317; defined, 13, 530; explanation of factors, 330–34, 331; geography and, 259–70, 331, 332; Moore's proposal of different First Great Divergence, 231–32, 561n17; revenue collection as key to power in, 232–34; serial empire reconstruction of China compared to polycentrism of Europe, 9, 12, 224, 229, 246–53, 257, 395, 411

First Industrial Revolution. *See* Industrial Revolution(s)

First Lateran Council (1123), 346

First Punic War, 96, 99, 109, 118, 120, 549n7, 549n9, 550n13

fiscal extraction, 63, 67, 158, 187, 232–33, 255–58, 330–34, 331, 341. *See also* military mobilization

Flanders, 181, 203, 265, 350, 352, 377

Fletcher, Joseph, 569n45

flood control, 264, 499–500, 566n10

Fourth Lateran Council (1215), 346

Fowden, Garth, 21

fragmentation of power: in Arab empire (late tenth century), 145; Bourgeois Revaluation and, 489; in Carolingian period, 161–62, 240, 555n39; in China, 396–400; development and, 337, 343,

359–60, 495–96; in East Roman restoration (sixth century), 138; Enlightenment and, 474–75, 497; exceptions proving the rule, 396–400, 538n14; fifteen centuries of, 212–15; in first-millennium-BCE Europe and East Asia, 221; in Habsburg domains, 198; in High and Late Middle Ages Europe, 228; modernity resulting from, 9, 359–60; Mongol engagement with fragmented opposition in Latin Europe, 179, 187; as overdetermined outcome for Europe, 220–21, 240, 501; overseas exploration and, 449–53, 471; resilience of state system and, 501, 502; significance of, 15, 27, 359–60; in Southeast Asia, 303; trade and, 360. *See also* polycentrism

France: in alliance with Ottoman empire, 195, 196, 206; aristocracy in, 241, 365; church's role in, 346, 347; class differences inhibiting intellectual innovations in, 487; commune movement in, 352; compared to Roman empire, 213; counterfactual scenario for seventeenth century in, 208–10, 513; French Revolution, 376; German Roman Empire and, 168; governance in, 355; integrity of ruling class in early modern period, 214; late seventeenth to early nineteenth century in, 12, 208–12; Magyar raids into (tenth century), 187, 293; military forces of late seventeenth century in, 78–79, 208; military forces of Napoleonic period in, 214; Netherlands and, 377; New World imperialism of, 426, 432; religious war in, 201; representative assemblies in, 350; taxes and military commitments in, 369; university and academy development in, 485, 488; urban development in, 345. *See also* Gaul

Franks and Frankish kingdom, 12, 35, 153–61; Arab conquests and, 148, 149; aristocracy in, 213; demise of, 353; duration and scope of, 132, 134; East Roman Restoration and, 134, 137; land given in exchange for loyalty and military service in, 240–41; repulsion of Arabs and Berbers by, 512; royal governance in, 349; tax collection in, 237, 254, 565n68; weak internal governance in, 163, 214, 228, 238. *See also* Carolingian empire

Frederick I (German ruler), 165–66

Frederick II (German ruler), 166, 171, 174, 176, 178, 197, 347, 512, 541n11

freedom, 8, 538n11

Fronda, Michael P., 553n15

frontier theory, 275. *See also* steppe effect

Fukuyama, Francis, 539n26

Galileo Galilei, 474

Gaul: Arab conquests and, 139, 140; Carolingian empire and, 153; Celtic influence in, 522; East Roman restoration and, 132, 134; Habsburgs and, 198; language and writing in, 311–12, 601n39; Merovingians and, 237; Roman Empire's conquest of, 83, 101, 198, 239; state deformation in, 234; taxation in, 234, 237, 254

Gelasius I (pope), 315

Gellner, Ernest, 86, 87, 553n7

Genghis Khan (Mongol ruler), 174, 186

Genoa, 355, 377, 430, 439, 450, 499, 509

geographic constraints and differences, 259–70, 331, 332, 429, 502, 526, 565n4; coastlines, 260–61; geographic determinism debunked, 270; mountains and rivers, 261–64, 499–500, 566n6, 566n10; plain regions and natural core, 264–66; shape, isolation, and scale, 266–69. *See also* counterfactual scenario for overseas exploration; *specific mega-regions and countries*

German empire, 164–73, *167*; ability to sustain empire of, 12, 35, 172; aristocracy in, 213, 241; castle construction in, 169;

German empire (cont.)
church's role in and relationship with, 171, 346, 347, 512; compared to China, 562n30; compared to Roman empire, 213; ducal elites in, 168–69, 241; failure to expand, 166, 168, 172–73; fragmentation into quasi-polities, 169, 228; governance in, 350; integrity of ruling class in, 214; internal conflicts in (1025 to 1142), 165; land given in exchange for loyalty and military service in, 235, 238, 240–41, 562n30; Magyar raids into (tenth century), 187, 293–94; military controlled by nobles in, 169–70, 237–38, 244, 245; no standing armies in, 238; weak central power coupled with fiscal constraints in, 169–70, 214; zones of armed conflict in, 168

Germanic languages, 311–12

Germany: position in Holy Roman Empire, 195; Protestants in, 196, 197. *See also* Holy Roman Empire; Prussia

"getting to Denmark," 19, 539n26

Ghaznavids, 296, 301

ghost acreages, 424–25, 426–27, 588n12, 589n19, 589n21

Gibbon, Edward, 18, 128, 131, 149

Glahn, Richard von, 401, 412

globalization: criticism of and response to, 425–28; European colonial reach, 420–25, 452. *See also* maritime exploration and expansion; New World

Goethe, Johann Wolfgang von, 18

Goffart, Walter, 236

Golden Horde in Eastern Europe, 183–85, 188–89, 213, 292

Goldscheid, Rudolf, 232

Goldstone, Jack, 208–10, 497, 560n16, 586n216, 595n38, 596n44, 597n68, 598n76

Goths and Gothic language, 311–12

Grainger, John D., 550n14

Great Divergence. *See* First Great Divergence (mid-first-millennium Europe); Second Great Divergence

Great Escape: British leading the way in, 363, 501; escape simile, 537n1, 539n26; Roman legacy and, 510–26; Second Industrial Revolution's effect, 17; significance of, 1, 8, 27, 502; values at center of modernization and, 489

Greek city-states, 52, 56, 58, 91, 93, 95, 100, 103, 109; in counterfactual to Roman empire, 113–14, 121, 522, 553n7; maritime exploration by, 430; troop numbers for, 554n18

Greek language, 311, 522–23, 573nn5–6, 601n39

Greek mathematics, 524, 601n42

Gregory VII (pope), 165, 347

Gregory IX (pope), 176

Greif, Avner, 585n199

guilds, 352–54, 361, 382, 450, 496, 509

Gungwu, Wang, 444

gunpowder, 182, 200, 399, 452, 453, 558n20

Gupta empire, 40, 219, 295, 432

Guyuk (Mongol ruler), 175, 178, 183, 186, 188

Habsburgs (sixteenth century), 192–204; compared to Roman empire, 213; counterfactual scenario for, 12, 200–201, 215, 512–13, 559n55; failure to subdue Europe, 496; geopolitical dynamics in, 212, 421; integrity of ruling class in, 214; Napoleon and, 18. *See also* Holy Roman Empire

Hall, John, 358, 414, 515

Hall, T., 568n40

Han empire: ancestor worship in, 321; bureaucracy in, 226–27; central government control in, 43; compared to Roman empire, 311; Confucianism in, 324; decentralization during, 230; demise of, 241, 243, 250, 397, 405; First Great Divergence and, 229, 229; in heyday of empire, 281, 560n5; merchant class in, 397; mobilization in, 248, 551n29; patronage and simony in, 227; population of, 243, 564n57; steppe effect and, 284, 444; territorial expansion by, 222, 223

Hannibal, 77, 94, 103, 118–19, 553n16

Hansen, Mogens H., 549n5

Harsha empire, 40, 219, 296

Hartmann, Mary S., 598n81

Heather, Peter, 268

Henry I (German ruler), 164

Henry II (German ruler), 165

Henry III (English king), 176

Henry IV (German ruler), 165, 347, 512

Henry V (German ruler), 165, 166

Henry VIII (English king), 197, 200, 370, 378

Hinduism, 329

Hitler, Adolf, 36, 37, 212

Hittites, 90

Hobbes, Thomas, 370, 474

Hoffman, Philip, 260, 327, 452, 567n26, 574n13

Hohenstaufen dynasty, 165, 177

Holland, Cecilia, 190–91

Holy Roman Empire, 192–204, 194; counterfactual scenario for, 200–201, 215, 512–13, 559n55; duration of, 43, 541n11; Germany's position in, 195; northern Low Countries' revolt against Philip II, 202; resistance to concept of empire within, 195–96

Hoppit, Julian, 381

horses and equine warfare. See cavalry warfare; ecology

Hudson Bay Company, 386

Huguenots, 378

Hume, David, 473

Hundred Years' War, 366, 374, 578n59

Hungary: Austria's claim to, 196; Golden Bull, 350; Mongol incursion into, 175–78, 180–82, 185, 187; Ottoman control of, 204; in tenth century, 268. See also Avars; Magyars

Huns, 130–31, 133, 135, 182, 187, 292, 295, 300

Hurrians, 90

Hus, Jan, 474

Iberian peninsula: Arab conquest of, 139–40, 142–43, 148, 150, 153, 302, 317, 512; British exports to, 423; Castile kingdom in, 176, 431; fiscal value to Roman Empire, 130, 234, 255; language and writing in, 311–12; Magyars in, 187; Napoleon in, 209, 211; Ottomans in, 207; parliamentary tradition in, 350; Roman military mobilizations in, 78, 80–81, 94, 103, 106, 239; Visigoths in, 132, 134, 148, 236, 317

ideologies of imperial unity, 320–28, 329, 331

Ilkhanate in Iran and Iraq, 183–85, 189, 213, 563n30

Inca empire, 193

India: cotton exports from, 426, 427, 589n20; foreign conquest of, 415; fragmentation in, 257, 573n8; geography of, 265, 295; Islamic invasion in, 416–17; Mongols in, 182, 185, 192; no Enlightenment period in, 483–84; patterns of empire, 10, 39–40, 40, 415–16; Portuguese expansion into, 431; post-Gupta period regional empires in, 415–16; post-nineteenth-century economic development in, 2; religious beliefs in, 329; rivers and flooding in, 500; steppe effect and, 295–98. See also Mughals

Indonesia, 47, 430, 434

Industrial Revolution(s): China compared to Europe and, 413–14; conditions conducive to, 392; England as cradle of, 377–82; First Industrial Revolution, 17, 425, 426, 428, 486–88, 491–95, 582n121, 598n81; modern Great Divergence and, 13, 337; Second Industrial Revolution, 6–7, 17. See also England/Britain; Second Great Divergence

Indus Valley, 113, 140, 552n5

Inikori, Joseph, 423

Innocent III (pope), 347

Innocent IV (pope), 347

innovation: Chinese stifling of, 396–400, 415, 479–85; Enlightenment and, 473–79; in Europe and England, 391, 393, 415; Industrial Enlightenment of Britain and, 485–88, 497; knowledge and scientific inquiry, 472–73, 478–79; macroinventions and microinventions, 486; in Roman empire, 504–5; technological innovation of Industrial Revolutions, 6, 472, 487; values of modernization and, 488–91

institutions: Chinese imperial institutions, 392–96; European institutionalization of progress, 344–67, 376, 390–92, 582n136; importance of, 326–27

international trade. See specific countries and empires

Iran: competitor to Roman empire in, 84, 223; in counterfactual assuming no Roman empire, 522; ecology of, 298–301; Safavids in, 207–8, 301; steppe effect and, 298–301, 302; trade with, 456. See also Achaemenid empire; Sasanians

Iraq, 143–46, 182–85, 207, 255–56, 565n71. See also Mesopotamia

Islam and Islamization, 142–43, 150, 317, 573n9; decline in learning and scientific research and, 482–84, 595n32; Islamic (conquest) polity, 587n219; Islamic trusts (waqf), 418; language differences among constituencies of, 329

Italy: aristocracy in, 241; coalition of city-states in, 213; coastline of, 260; commune movement in, 352; German campaigns against (tenth and twelfth centuries), 165, 166; kingdom of, 157; language and writing in, 312; Magyar raids into (tenth century), 187, 293; trade with Byzantium, 509

Iuba II (king of Mauretania), 432

Ivan III (Grand Prince of Moscow), 189

James II (English king), 208–9

Japan: claiming parts of China, 41; Mongols and, 192; Qing and, 306; as secondary Chinese state, 230; Tokugawa Shogunate (after 1600), 452; transformative economic development in, 2

Jews, 360, 378, 483

Jin dynasty (China): conflict under, 227, 242, 253; decentralization during, 230; demise of, 242; ecology and, 280, 282; imperial restoration under, 241–42; militarization under, 242–43; religious beliefs under, 318

John Bar Penkaye, 143

Jones, Eric, 265, 344, 359, 388, 393, 495, 514–15, 592n85

Julian (Roman emperor), 320

Julius Caesar, 101, 198, 239, 562n30

Jurchen empire, 41, 174, 230, 285, 288

Kant, Immanuel, 337–38

Karayalcin, Cem, 598n79

Kassites, 90

Kasten, Brigitte, 555n37, 555n40

Kavadh I (Sasanian king), 300

Kennedy, Hugh, 141

Kepler, Johannes, 483

Khorasan, 143, 144, 301, 572n94

Khwarezmian empire, 174, 301

Kievan Rus', 175, 291

knowledge and scientific inquiry, 472–73, 485–88, 497; Greek influences, 523–24, 601n42; Islamic decline in learning and scientific research, 482–84, 595n32; liberty and dignity for ordinary people tied to, 489; "Republic of Letters," 475, 516, 595n38; in Roman empire, 504–5; values of modernization and, 488–91. See also innovation

Ko, Chiu Yu, 306, 573n102, 587n224

Kocka, Jürgen, 22

Korea, 230, 251, 260, 266–67, 275, 435, 565n2

Koyama, Mark, 306, 573n102, 587n224, 595n32, 599n6
Kublai Khan (Mongol ruler), 182–83, 186, 285
Kushan empire, 40, 223, 295, 560n5

laissez-faire tendencies, 313, 407, 505, 507
land distribution: Carolingian empire, income from land grants in, 159; China (fifth through seventh centuries), 247, 248; Franks, 240–41; German empire, 235, 238, 240–41, 562n30; Mongol empire, 563n30; Roman empire, 56–57, 66, 67, 71–72
Landes, David, 6, 17, 359, 599n1
language and writing, 308–13; China, 308–9, 310, 312–13, 573n4, 594n23; English, 312; Greek, 311, 522–23, 573nn5–6, 601n39; Islamic world and, 311, 329, 483; post-Roman Europe, 311–13; Romance languages, 312, 510, 517; Roman empire and spread of Latin language, 66, 67, 309–13, 476, 510, 515–18; Southeast Asia, 329; spread of knowledge and, 476
Latin language, 66, 67, 309–13, 476, 510, 515–18
Lattimore, Owen, 275, 280, 572n89
Leo III (pope), 154
Levant. See Middle East and North Africa
Levine, Ari D., 575n44
Lewis, Mark, 319
Liao Qidan, 285, 288, 571n70
liberty and dignity for ordinary people, 489–90
Lieberman, Victor, 265, 275, 297–98, 303, 330, 573n4
life expectancy, 7, 537–38n9
literacy rate, 8, 373, 375, 375, 477, 485–86, 492, 538n11, 596n42. See also knowledge and scientific inquiry
Lithuania, 193, 292, 571n72
Little Divergence, 231, 370, 373
Liu, William, 399, 584n168
Livy, 100, 116–17

Locke, John, 474
Lombard League, 168
Lombards, 135, 137, 153, 155, 156, 238, 312
Lorge, Peter, 327
Lotharingia, 156, 181, 240, 353
Louis the Pious (Frankish king), 156, 244
Louis XIV (French king), 78–79, 208
Luther, Martin, 197, 200, 474

Ma, Debin, 394
Macedon: as Carthaginian ally, 551n31; in counterfactual to Roman empire, 114–17, 521, 553n11; Roman conquest of, 92, 95–97, 99, 104; troop numbers for, 550n12, 551n30, 553n18. See also Alexander the Great
macro-regions: described, 33–34, 34; imperial state formation in, 43–48, 45. See also East Asia; Europe; Middle East and North Africa; South Asia
Madagascar, 430
Magellan, Ferdinand, 431, 440, 465
Maghreb, 43, 91, 93, 132, 139, 143–46, 150–51, 204, 207, 293, 302, 311, 317, 512. See also Middle East and North Africa
Magyars, 158, 164, 168, 182, 187, 246, 293–94
Mair, Victor, 282, 569n45
Majapahit empire, 47
Malacca, 431, 434, 438, 441, 443–44
Malaya, 47
Mamluks, 184–85, 204, 360, 416, 431
Manchus. See Qing empire
Mandarin dialects, 308–9, 312
Mann, Michael, 360
Mao Zedong, 338
marginal zones or contact zones, 279–80, 298, 572n89
maritime exploration and expansion: China's lack of interest in or need for, 433, 441–46, 591n77; comparison of Chinese and European missions, 439–40; counterfactual scenarios for, 454–71; by European states, 429–32,

maritime exploration and expansion (cont.)
590n51; by Ming China, 433–39;
Ottoman lack of interest in or need for,
447–48; polycentrism's role in, 449–53;
in Roman empire, 505; South Asia's lack
of interest in or need for, 446–47.
See also New World

Marks, Robert, 496

Mary Stuart, 202, 203

Massimiliano, Onorato, 358

mathematics, 479–80, 524, 601n42

Maurya empire, 39, 43, 219, 295, 432

McCloskey, Deirdre, 489–91, 538n13, 596n44

McNeill, John Robert, 263–64

Medes, 299–300

Meeks, Elijah, 106

MENA. *See* Middle East and North Africa
(MENA)

Menzies, Gavin, 468

mercantilism, 268, 344, 353–56, 376–81, 392,
404, 447–51, 497, 581nn109–10, 582n121;
fiscal-naval-mercantilist state in
England, 385–90, 492–93; unifying set of
customs and rule for, 516. *See also*
commercial transactions and credit

Merovingians, 148, 153–54, 161, 163, 237

Mesopotamia, 83–84, 144, 301. *See also* Iraq

Middle Ages. *See* post-Roman Europe;
specific kingdoms

Middle East and North Africa (MENA):
collapse at end of Bronze Age, 221;
commercial growth and trade in, 417;
defined, 33, 541n7, 541n9; ecology of,
293, 301–2; foreign conquest of, 415;
fragmentation of, 207, 415; geography of,
260, 266, 270; imperial state formation
in, 45, 45–47, 333; language and writing
in, 311; Mongols in, 182, 191, 415; patterns
of empire, 10, 13, 38–42, 43, 254–55, 293;
polycentrism not applicable to, 418–19;
population of, 34, 35, 39, 504; Roman
empire controlling, 84, 142; size of, 33;
steppe effect and, 302, 333; tax practices

in, 255–56, 565n70. *See also* Arab
conquests; *specific countries*

military mobilization: in Achaemenid
empire, 299; in Anglo-Saxon England,
239; in Arab conquests, 145–46; in
China, 242–44, 246–51, 257, 397–99;
compared to Roman empire, 213–14;
fiscal-naval-mercantilist state in
England, 385–90; in France (late
seventeenth century), 78–79, 208; in
German empire, 169–70; in Han empire,
248; importance of, 564n64; in modern
times, 368; in Mongol empire, 176, 214,
557n2, 557n5, 557n17; in Napoleonic
France, 214; in Ottoman empire, 204–6,
453, 507; in post-Roman Europe, 239,
243–44, 257, 339; in Qin empire, 224; in
Roman empire, 63–64, 77–81, *81*, 84, 135,
224, 543n16, 546n49, 550n10, 550nn18–
22, 551n24; in Roman empire compared
to in post-Roman Europe, 239

Ming empire: agrarian focus of, 443;
compared to Roman empire, 507;
decentralization during, 230, 407;
duration and scope of, 229, 282, 569n48;
dynastic discord in, 435; economic
policies inhibiting growth in, 400–402,
440; imperial governance in, 407;
maritime commerce restrictions in, 402,
434, 438, 443, 496; Mongols and, 285,
399, 438; naval expeditions during,
433–39; neo-Confucianism in, 480; rise
of, 433, 569n48; taxes and funding in,
233, 237, 409, 421, 433; walls to fend off
attacks in, 285, 289, 437; Yongle emperor,
434, 435, 437, 438, 590n40

Mitterauer, Michael, 496

modernity: California school of scholarship
on, 575n1; conditions inhibiting, 479–85,
487, 490; conditions over long term
leading to, 14, 128, 501, 526–27;
Eurocentrism and, 501–2; fragmentation
of power as source of, 9, 360–63;

polycentrism as essential to development of, 15; price to humanity for, 502; Roman empire's contribution to, 520; values of modernization, 488–91

Mokyr, Joel, 473, 476, 478, 485, 497, 515, 516, 593n5, 594n21, 595n38, 596n44, 597n68, 598n85

Mongke (Mongol ruler), 175, 183, 185, 186

Mongol empire, 12, 168, 174–92, 184; in Asian countries other than China, 192; Baghdad sacked by, 191; in Central Europe, 175–78, 185; Chagatai khanate in Central Asia, 183; in China, 4, 175, 182–83, 189–90, 230, 285, 286, 398–99, 440, 558n20; compared to Roman empire, 213; counterfactual scenario for, 185–92, 215, 560n16; in Eastern Europe, 174–75, 178; fragmentation of Latin Europe and, 179, 187; inability to maintain a large-scale empire in Europe, 214–15; integrity of ruling class in, 214; internal discord and instability of, 183–85; land allotments in, 563n30; in Middle East (Levant), 182, 191, 301; mobilization of forces in, 176, 214, 288, 557n2, 557n5, 557n17; naval expeditions conducted by, 443, 444; population of, 288, 541n3; reasons for retreat from Europe, 178–79; steppe effect and, 181–82, 183, 192, 245, 278, 556n1, 557–58n18, 557n9; stone fortifications and castle construction as barrier to, 180–81, 188, 557n16, 558n20. See also Genghis Khan; Kublai Khan

monopoly: monopolistic policymaking in China, 400–407, 440; non-monopolization as fundamental to rise of the West, 391; polycentrism vs., 338–44, 339. See also empire

Montesquieu, Baron de, 259, 260, 261, 265, 337

Moore, Robert Ian, 231–32

Morris, Ian: on Chinese lack of need to pursue overseas exploration, 441; counterfactual to Roman empire proposed by, 114; on Norse ability to reach America (compared to Chinese ability), 462, 468, 592n99; social development index of, 4, 6, 537nn5–7

Mughals, 39, 179, 219, 257, 298, 343, 416–17, 432, 452, 483–84, 507, 572n86, 587n221, 590n31

Muscovy, 193, 292

Muslims. See Arab conquests; Islam and Islamization

Napoleon Bonaparte: battle size compared to Roman battles, 79; counterfactual scenario for, 211–12, 215; empire duration and scope under, 36, 37, 483; failure to overcome English and European opposition, 18, 210

nature. See ecology; geographic constraints

naval exploration. See maritime exploration

Needham, Joseph, 266, 594n23

Netherlands: bourgeoisie's freedom and dignity in, 489–90; eclipsed by Britain's rise, 492; economic rise of, 371, 391, 415, 580n81; joining England in war against Spain, 202–3; literacy rate in, 373, 477, 596n42; military and war costs of, 369–70, 376–77; New World trade and imperialism of, 203, 422, 426, 444, 449, 451; Protestantism in, 202; taxes in, 369–70, 579n65

Netz, Reviel, 601n42

Newton, Isaac, 478

New World: agrarian empires, 441–48; Atlantic trade, expansion of, 422; bullion imported from, 194, 233, 421–22, 423, 425, 496; China and, 468–71; cotton imports from, 424–25, 427; counterfactual scenario for seventeenth-century colonies in, 209; counterfactual scenario of flipping Old World on its axis so East is West, 459–67, 460–61, 463; European expansionism, 420–25,

New World (cont.)
449–53; globalist perspective, 420–25; incumbents, 431–40; limits of globalism, 425–28; marginals, 429–31; New Spain, establishment of, 193, 196–97; Pre-Columbian imperial state formation in, 46; sugar imports from, 424–25, 589n17; timber imports from, 424–25

Nicaean creed, 519

Nicholas I (Constantinopolitan patriarch), 573–74n10

Nine Years' War, 208

nobility: in France, 241; in German empire, 169–70, 237–38, 241, 244, 245; inhibiting modernization and innovation, 487, 490; rise of aristocracy in England, 239; rise of aristocracy in Europe, 169–70, 237–41; in Roman empire, ruling class of noble houses, 68–71, 79, 88–89, 225; society of estates in Europe, 349–51; in Spain, 241; in Tang China, 411; values of, no effect on lives of ordinary people, 596n54

nomadic societies, 276–79, 283, 287–89, 291–96, 299, 305, 568n40. *See also specific groups*

North, Douglass, 380

North, John, 73

North Africa. *See* Middle East and North Africa

Northern Song. *See* Song empire

Northern Wei, 230, 246–47, 282, 284, 318–19, 399

North Sea region (post-1500), 202, 370–77, 391, 477, 496, 579n71, 582n132. *See also* England/Britain; Netherlands

O'Brien, Patrick K., 589n22

Odoacer, 254, 562n30, 565n68

Ögödei (Mongol ruler), 174, 178, 179, 183, 186

Ophellas, 91

Orestes, 562n30

Orientalism, 392–93, 583n138, 587n221

Ostrogoths, 132, 134, 137, 153, 254, 562n30

Otto I (German ruler), 164, 187

Otto II (German ruler), 164–65, 168

Otto III (German ruler), 165

Ottoman empire, 204–8, *205*; commercial growth and trade in, 417, 578n48; compared to Roman empire, 213, 507; compared to Umayyad caliphate, 205; counterfactual scenario for, 206–8; duration of, 12, 35; European relationships with, 195, 196, 201–2, 206; extent of empire, 12, 193, 204–5, 267, 301, 415, 452; hegemony and conservatism in, 483; imperial consolidation under, 38, 43; inability to maintain a large-scale empire in Europe, 214–15; integrity of ruling class in, 214; military mobilization and naval strength of, 204–6, 453, 507, 565n73; obstruction of intellectual innovation in, 484; overseas exploration not of interest to, 447–48; population of, 219; tax revenues in, 206, 417, 565n73

Ottonian empire. *See* German empire

overseas exploration. *See* maritime exploration and expansion

Oxford Roman Economy Project, 505

Oxford World History of Empire, 16

Pala empire, 40

Palma, Nuno, 597n64

Papal States, 166. *See also* Catholic Church

parliamentarianism, 14, 350–51, 376

Parthasarathi, Prasannan, 585n191, 587n221

Parthians, 100, 223, 299–300, 521, 560n5, 601n36

pastoralists, 255, 274, 281, 283, 287, 295, 299, 301–2, 306, 568n40, 569n45

patent law, 486–87

patriarchal structures, 498, 544n31

patrimonialism, 68, 225–27, 366, 544n31

Paul, gospels of, 518–19, 523

Peace of Augsburg (1555), 370–71

Peace of Westphalia (1648), 371

Pechenegs, 290, 291

Pepin, 154

Pepin the Short, 160

Peroz I (Sasanian king), 300

Philip II (Habsburg ruler), 195, 199, 201–3, 202, 213, 378

Philippi, battle of (42 BCE), 79

Philippines, 444, 445

Phoenicians, 429, 431–32

Phrygian language, 311

Pines, Yuri, 323–26, 328, 574nn27–29, 575n33, 585n185

Poland: Mongol incursion into, 175–77, 180–81, 185, 187; Pact of Koszyce, 350; in tenth century, 268

political economy, 387, 392, 413, 442, 470, 486–88, 581n110

Pollack, Sheldon, 484

Polybius, 546n57

polycentrism: in Central America, 46; church's role as driver of, 348, 519–20; defined, 530; development dynamics of, 339, 419, 497, 510; Enlightenment and, 473–79; essential to (Second) Great Divergence and Industrial Revolution, 15, 337; intermittent in imperial settings, 17; Mongol presence in Europe and, 190; overseas exploration and, 449–53; in post-Roman Europe, 12, 16, 37, 43, 214, 338, 501, 503, 508; significance of, 9, 338–44, 339; tax practices and, 256. See also fragmentation of power

Polynesian explorations of the Pacific, 430–31, 469, 593n103

Pomeranz, Kenneth, 424, 427, 428, 482, 597n67

population: basis for determination of, 533–35; controversy over estimates, 599n3. See also specific empires and countries

Portugal: Eastern expansion and trade of, 431, 438–39, 444; exploration of New World and colonies established by, 421, 426, 430–31, 449; Genoa and, 450; international trade of, 422, 457–58; as threat to Ottoman trade routes, 447–48. See also Iberian peninsula

post-Roman Europe: compared to China, 17, 23, 228, 243, 254–58, 320–28, 329–32, 331, 343–44, 562n30; cultural evolution and, 327; ethnic loyalty in, 330; fiscal decay, effects of, 257; governance in, 349; language and writing in, 311–13; local resistance to tax remissions to central authority, 235, 237; polycentrism in, 12, 16, 37, 43, 214, 338, 501, 503, 508; possible successors to Rome, failure to emerge, 127–28, 214, 333; principal sources of social power in, 339–40; state formation in, 12, 63, 131; tax collection in, 234–39, 254, 257. See also Carolingian empire; East Roman restoration (sixth century); fragmentation of power; polycentrism

poverty reduction, 7, 538n9

Prados de la Escosura, Leandro, 589n22, 598n85

primogeniture, 240, 555n40, 563n33

property rights, protection of, 360, 380–81, 496

Protestantism, 196–98; counterfactual scenario for, 200–201, 203, 512–13; immigration to England, 378; spread of knowledge and, 477; work ethic and, 477, 491

Prussia, 208, 211, 484

Ptolemaic empire, 95–101, 104–5, 117, 521; annual military outlays of, 550n21; navy of, 552n33, 554n18; overseas exploration by, 458; troop numbers for, 551n30, 553n18

Puritanism, 478

Pyrrhus (Epirote king), 91, 118, 546n57

Pytheas, 430

Qing empire: agrarian focus of, 443; bureaucratic structures and, 587n218; clans in, 411; contact with British, 442; duration and scope of, 229, 452, 470; imperial governance in, 407; maritime commerce restrictions in, 402–3, 443; military mobilization and warfare in, 399; neo-Confucianism in, 480; obstruction of intellectual innovation in, 484; rebellion risks in, 443, 586n205; state revenues used to support warfare in, 585n189; steppe effect and, 281–82, 285–86, 399, 584n162; Taiping rebellion (1850s and 1860s), 287, 412, 586n205; taxes and revenue collection in, 233, 237, 407, 409; walls to fend off attacks in, 289

Qin kingdom/empire: ascent of, 281, 283, 560n4; breaking power of aristocrats and setting up civil service system, 225, 244; core China defined by territory of, 229; demise of, 242, 325; ethnic identity in, 282; geography of, 283; language and writing in, 308; Legalism in, 320–21; manpower mobilization in, 224; merchant class in, 397; military mobilization in, 72, 81, 222, 224, 551n29; state formation in, 222; tax structure in, 225

Rawski, Thomas, 394

Reformation, 370–71, 375, 473–74, 477, 478, 489–90, 512

religion and beliefs, 13, 313–20; in China, 317–22, 328; counterfactual of religious unity in Europe, 512–13, 524; English establishment of national religion, 378; European ascendancy of Christianity, 314–17; religious toleration in European countries (seventeenth century), 484, 497. *See also* Reformation; *specific religions and belief systems*

"Republic of Letters," 475, 516, 595n38

Ringmar, Erik, 391, 496

Robinson, James, 496, 525, 602n45

Romance languages, 312, 510, 517

Roman empire: abolition of debt bondage in, 69; adaptations in the core, 68–69; allies and, 59, 60, 67, 73, 79; bureaucracy in fourth century CE, 226–27; capacity for collective action in, 64; capitalized coercion mode of, 63; Christianity during, 314–15; citizenship rights in, 59, 65–66, 73, 75, 79; civilian governance confined to metropolitan core, 68; colonization schemes in, 66–67, 71, 545n42, 548n75; commercial transactions and credit in, 504; compared to Chinese empire, 72, 221–27, 294, 320, 505, 507; compared to Ottoman empire, 213, 507; co-optation and mobilization of citizenry, 10, 59–65, 62, 75, 549n6; cultural assimilation in, 66; demise of, 16, 128, 223, 338, 344, 363, 541n11, 599n1; domestic conflict, 120–22; in early fourth century BCE, 53; economic development in, 505–6; erosion of, thoroughness of, 131, 136–37; explaining creation of, 21, 51–52; extent and expansion of, 34, 75–77, 76, 83, 83–84, 223, 432, 456, 538n15, 543n9, 566n21; factors leading to demise of, 130; failure of similar empire to return after its fall, 9, 10, 11, 16, 127, 131, 503; final phase of expansion and end of conquest, 82–88, 83, 548n72; geography and, 266; growth and triumph, 75–86, 76, 560n5; Huns' takeover of, 130–31, 133; integration and evolution of Roman commonwealth, 65–68; international trade and trade routes of, 455–58, 504, 592n89; land distribution to soldiers of, 56–57, 66, 67, 71–72; language and writing in, 66, 67, 309–13; legacies of, 14–15, 510–26; legal influence on post-Roman Europe, 514, 516; logic of continuous war, 67, 72–73, 544n31; longevity of, 11, 88, 122, 128–29; manpower as critical to military success, 77–81, 81, 84, 224, 225, 546n49, 550n10,

550nn18–22, 551n24; military leadership of, 57, 68, 70, 85, 547n70; military outlays and payments of, 135, 507, 550nn20–21; modern development resulting from, 503; monarchy in, 226, 234; naval supremacy of, 11, 63, 77, 96, 104–9, *107*, 120, 122–23, 432, 456; Oxford Roman Economy Project, 505; parallel of state formation to East Asia, 220, 221–24; patrimonial and clientelistic society in, 68, 225–27, 544n31; patterns of empire and, 35, *35–38, 36*; peace (pax Romana) duration during, 504; plunder as funding of, 61, 64, 72, 80; population of, 34–38, *35–38*, 55, 62, 74, *76*, 76–77, 219, 504, 542n12, 549n6; positive effect on European development, 4; power and leadership concentrated in Rome, 225; public good provision in, 68; religion allied with war-making in, 69; roots of, 11, 52–58, 222; ruling class of noble houses in, 68–71, 79, 88–89, 225; Samnite federation, conflict with, 75–76, 111, 116, 546n55; slave society in, 69, 74, 599n6; Social War (91–89 BCE), 64, 78, 120; starting advantages enjoyed by, 138; stratified layers of classes and roles in, 86, 87; success in and incentives for war in, 57, 70–72; sustainability of continuous war in, 65, 73–74; taxation and revenue in, 61, 64, 72, 80, 81, 234, 235, 506, 600n10; technological innovation in, 504–5; in third century BCE, *60*, 222; uniqueness of, 10–11, 13, 18, 19, 35, 122–24, 212, 215, 521–22; urban development in, 504; Veii conflict (early fourth century BCE) and, 57–58, 75, 521; war machine of, 67, 79–82, 119–20, 547nn66–67. *See also* counterfactual to Roman empire; Roman periphery

Roman periphery, 89–109; benefit of Rome's location, 89, 551–52n33; Carthage conflict with (third century BCE), 62, 77–78, 80, 91–100, 103, 104, 109, 546n57; characteristics of tribal peripheries, 551n26; compared to Qin China, 225; core and periphery as essential to rise of empire, 213, 225; core and periphery compared, 102–4, 548n1; critical preconditions for military success (mid-third- to mid-second-century BCE), 101, *103*, 109, 222, 234; eastern periphery, 95–101, 538n14; failure to form single political-military network in eastern Mediterranean city-states, 91; Gallic conflicts (fourth century BCE to 225 BCE) and, 58, 77, 101, 116; Macedon, conflicts with, 92, 95–97, 99, 104; Mediterranean advantage of Rome, 104–9; Mediterranean divide, 89–92; Mediterranean political-military network (first millennium BCE), 91, *92*; Middle Eastern political-military network (c. 1500–500 BCE), 90, *90*; northern and western periphery, 101; routes of advance in, 106–8, *107*; Sicily conflicts, 93–94; southern periphery, 93–94; stylized typology of peripheries, *102, 103*; Syracuse conflicts, 91, 92, 93, 103; travel time and transportation cost in, 107, *107*; troop deployment by region (200–168 BCE), 97–99, *98*

Rome, sacked by Charles V (1527), 197

Rosenthal, Jean-Laurent, 358, 389, 492–93, 495, 496, 586n215, 597n60, 597n71, 598n85

Rouran clan, 246, 247, 284, 287, 288, 399

Royal Society of London for Improving Natural Knowledge, 475

Rudolf I (Habsburg ruler), 166

Runciman, Walter, 553n7

Russia: Golden Horde incursion into, 188–89; infrastructure development of, 453; khaganate of Rus', 291; Kievan Rus', 175, 291; Mongol's effect on economy of, 189, 558n29; Muscovy, 193, 292; Orthodox Church and, 511; population size of,

Russia (cont.)
37; pre-Napoleonic Wars, 269; size of
Russian empire, 32, 538n14, 571n72;
Tatars in, 189, 292

Safavid Iran, 207–8, 301
Saka empire, 40, 298, 299–300
Salian dynasty, 165, 168–69, 170, 171, 173.
See also German empire
Samanid dynasty, 145, 301
Samarra crisis, 145
Sanskrit language, 329
Sasanians, 38, 133, 135, 137, 139, 141, 215, 256,
295, 300
scaling-up: challenge of city-state environment for, 54; challenge to Rome from
tribal periphery, 130; co-optation of
Rome and, 59, 79; in counterfactual to
Roman empire, 120; of Germanic tribes
to threaten Roman territory, 551n25;
incorporating manpower of conquered
regions into Roman military and, 63–64,
543n16; Middle Ages, failure to scale-up
during, 128; military scaling up as
essential to empire building, 233, 246; of
steppe peoples, 274, 278–79
Scandinavian polities, 156, 187, 197, 209, 228,
260, 268, 269, 294, 349, 430, 483, 484,
578n59. *See also* Vikings
Scheidel, Walter, 539n21
Schiavone, Aldo, 599n6
Schmalkaldic League, 197, 199
Schumpeterian growth, 79–80, 232, 341,
408, 507, 547n63
Scythians, 290, 299
(Second) Great Divergence, 13; causal
conditions for, 337–44, 491, 497, 501;
counterfactual derailing, 467; culture
and, 472–73; defined, 530; European
trade with New World and, 428; First
Great Divergence paving way for,
231–32; First Industrial Revolution and,
425; fragmentation of power in Europe

and, 343, 497; search for origins of,
19–26. *See also* Industrial Revolution(s)
Second Punic War, 78, 121, 546n59, 549n9,
551n29
sedentism, 32, 275, 277–79, 287, 295, 298, 305,
568n35
Seleucid empire, 95–101; annual military
outlays of, 550n21; ascent of, 117, 521;
Cilician pirates as offshoot from failure
of, 552n34; Egypt and, 521, 601n36;
internal strife and fragmentation in,
550n14; military mobilization in, 104,
550n21, 551n30, 553n18, 554n18; navy of,
554n18; population of, 541n3; Roman
provisioning in war against, 552n35;
troop numbers for, 551n30, 553n18
Seljuqs, 38, 278, 301, 317, 483
Septimius Severus (Roman emperor), 86
Shang dynasty, 282, 308, 323
Siam, 47, 303, 435
Sicily: in counterfactual to Roman empire,
113, 118, 553n6; French rule over
(thirteenth century), 166; German
campaigns against (960s), 165; Roman
empire and, 91, 93–94, 103, 105, 549n3,
549n5; saved from Arab conquest (740),
136
Sima Guang, 251
Singhasari empire, 47
Sivin, Nathan, 482
slavery: British trade in, 424, 425, 426,
589n17; colonial trade and use of, 388,
423–24, 427, 466, 470; Genoa's role in
chattel slavery, 499; in Roman empire,
69, 74
Slavic languages, 311–12
Slavs, 135, 137, 139, 165, 175, 268, 294
Smithian growth, 409, 412, 504, 507,
586n207
Sng, Tuan-Hwee, 306, 573n102, 587n224
social science scholarship, 19–20, 21
social welfare, 539n26
sociology scholarship, 20

solar energy, 6

Song empire: centralization of power in, 249; civil service system in, 394; Confucianism in, 322, 394; duration and scope of, 229; ending fragmentation of tenth century, 227, 231, 253, 285; imperial state formation, 41, 44, 249; kinship networks, rise of, 410, 411; military's effect on economy of, 398, 584n168; money inflation in, 507; Mongol advance on, 175, 182–83, 187, 230, 231, 398, 558n20; population in, 564–65n67, 566n13; positive effect on economic development, 4, 285, 343, 398–99, 400, 403, 409, 440, 443, 585n199; steppe effect in, 282

South Asia: conquests of, 417–18; cultural traits linked to state formation in, 330; defined, 33; ecology and, 276, 295–98; foreign conquest of, 415; fragmentation and fiscal structures in (fourth and fifth centuries), 257; fragmentation into regional states (from sixth to twelfth centuries), 297; geography of, 261, 266, 267, 270, 295, 333; imperial state formation in, 45, 45–47, 257; overseas exploration not of interest to, 446–47; patterns of empire, 10, 13, 39–42, 40; polycentrism not applicable to, 418–19; religious beliefs in, 329; size of, 34, 34; steppe effect and, 295–98, 572n89. See also India

Southeast Asia: cultural traits linked to state formation in, 330; ecology of, 303–4; fragmentation in, 303; geography of, 267; imperial state formation in, 46–48; language and writing in, 329; patterns of empire in, 10; religious beliefs in, 328; steppe effect and, 303–4. See also specific countries

Southern Song. See Song empire

Spain: aristocracy in, 241; bullion imported from New World, 194, 233, 421–22;

counterfactual in which Spain prevails over England (sixteenth century), 203–4; domestic conflict in, 376; failed invasion of England (Spanish Armada defeat 1588), 202, 378; New World colonies of, 201–2, 421, 426, 431, 444, 445, 449; obstruction of intellectual innovation in, 484, 487; representative assemblies in, 350; taxes and military commitments in, 369–70; Unions of Aragon and Valencia, 350. See also Iberian peninsula

Sparta, 91

Sri Lanka, 275, 433, 434, 446, 457

Srivijaya empire, 47, 447, 543n7

Stasavage, David, 353

state: defined, 530–31; formal state, focus on, 43; survival of state structures, 539n23

state formation: Christian Church and, 317; city-state culture and, 327; comparison of East and South Asia and Middle East with Europe, 419; in counterfactual scenario of no Roman empire, 524–26, 525; defined, 531; development dynamics of types of, 338, 339, 498; ecology and, 47, 274, 276–80, 331, 332, 501; geography and, 269–70; homogenization and, 268; imperial state formation and split of Christians into Catholics and Protestants, 197–98; imperial state formation in macro-regions, 9–10, 12, 43–48, 45, 268; in post-Roman Europe, 12, 63; Roman, 11, 52–58; test for effects of threat direction and strength on, 306, 567n33; Tilly's capital-intensive mode of, 63, 67. See also culture and cultural unity; empire; monopoly; polycentrism; scaling-up

state system: defined, 531; institutional development and, 391; productive dynamics of, 17, 344, 475; resilience of, 306, 501. See also institutions status quo, 508–10

Staufers, 169–71, 173

Stein, Peter, 516

steppe effect, 245, 270–81, 271, 331; access to horses and, 181–82, 245–48, 252, 274–75, 278, 280–81, 284, 289, 296; China and, 283–84, 286–90, 399, 569n44, 570n62; conquests by steppe invaders, 274, 276–79, 563n30; defined, 531; Europe and, 290–94; India and, 295–98; Iran and, 298–301; Levant and North Africa and, 302, 333; on polity size, 306; proximity as factor in empire formation, 13, 271–72, 273–74, 275; Rome's limited contact with steppe warriors, 571n80; shadow empires and, 277–78; size of steppe empires, 32; South Asia and, 295–98; Southeast Asia and, 303–4. See also Mongol empire

Strabo, 85, 601n39

Strayer, Joseph, 241, 514

Sui empire, 281, 284, 289, 319, 397

Sumerian empire, 543n7

Sunni-Shia rift and competition, 145, 207

Sweden. See Scandinavian polities

Syracuse, 91, 92, 93, 103, 109, 222, 549n3; in counterfactual to Roman empire, 113, 114, 116; troop numbers for, 551n30

Syria: Council of Chalcedon (451) and, 133; Parthians annexing, 601n36; Sasanians annexing, 135

Syrian Wars (274 to 101 BCE), 96, 550n14

Tabellini, Guido, 585n199

Taiwan, 260, 402, 443, 445–46, 468

Tang empire, 229; An Lushan rebellion (750s), 286; commercial development in, 397; conflict during, 289, 411; Confucianism in, 322; decentralization during, 230, 252; duration of, 43; ecology and, 280, 281; Huang Chao uprising (late ninth century), 286; imperial state formation in, 44, 228, 251, 284–85; positive effect on Chinese development, 4; religious beliefs in, 319; steppe effect and, 444

Tatars in Russia, 189, 292

taxes: in Arab conquest regions, 143, 144, 146–47, 148, 255–56; in Carolingian empire, 159; in China, 225, 245, 252, 253, 257, 394–95, 397, 407–10, 417, 433; comparing post-Roman Europe to Chinese Period of Disunion, 254–58; in England (post-1500), 379; in Europe (post-1500), 368–70, 579n65; in Habsburg territories, 202; in Mongol-controlled Russia, 189; in Mughal empire, 417; in Muscovy, 292; in Netherlands, 369–70, 579n65; in Ottoman empire, 206, 417, 565n73; in post-Roman Europe, 234–39, 254, 257; religious exemptions and, 315–16, 319, 320; in Roman empire, 61, 64, 72, 80, 81, 225, 234, 235, 506; in Umayyad caliphate, 143, 146, 148, 255

Teutonic Order, 175, 292

textile industry and trade, 386, 415, 423–25, 491–93, 581n115, 588n10, 597n60. See also cotton industry and trade

Theodosius I (Roman emperor), 315

Thermopylae, 99, 550n10

Thirty Years' War, 200, 269, 417

Thomas, Robert, 380, 569n46

Thracian languages, 311

Tilly, Charles, 63, 67, 232

Timurid empire, 296, 301, 563n30

Toltec empire, 46

Toynbee, Arnold, 116, 117, 553n12

trade. See specific countries and empires

Trajan (Roman emperor), 86

transformative developmental outcomes, 501, 587n219; causes and trends of, 8–11, 495–500; demography as factor in, 497–99; ecology and geography, effects of, 501–2; Western exceptionalism, avoidance of, 502. See also ecology; First Great Divergence; geographic constraints and differences; Great Escape; Second Great Divergence

Treaty of Meersen (870), 353

Tuoba clan, 242, 246–47, 284, 287, 563nn47–48

Turchin, Peter, 271, 275, 279, 280, 295, 569n46, 573n102

Tvedt, Terje, 499

Uighurs, 174, 285, 287

Umayyad caliphate, 139–44, 140; Arab forces of, 142–43; compared to Roman empire, 213; conflict with Central Asian Turks, 301; demise of, 144, 150, 155; imperial consolidation under, 38; inability to maintain a large-scale empire in Europe, 147–48, 153, 267; integrity of ruling class in, 214; interregional rivalries among armies of, 144; naval blockades of Constantinople by, 135; overseas exploration not of interest to, 432; population of, 219; revenue collection in, 233; taxation in, 143, 146, 148, 255; tribal structures as limitation of, 143

United States: American Civil War, 427; American Revolution and independence, 376, 589n20; Bourgeois Revaluation in, 490; cotton exports to Britain from, 425, 427; transformative economic development in, 2

universities, founding of, 475, 485

urban development: autonomy of cities, 345, 353–55, 577n28; in China, 394, 397–98, 442; in England, 371, 373–74, 581n99, 597n64; growth correlated with, 356–59; Protestantism and, 477; in Roman empire, 504; Roman road network and, 576n8; urbanization rates in Europe (post-1500), 371–76, 373–74, 580n82

Vandals, 132, 134, 135, 138, 153

van Zanden, Jan Luiten, 375, 496, 515, 585n185, 589n19, 597–98n73, 598n81

Venice, 55, 58, 189, 206, 355, 369, 377, 430, 439, 450, 509

Vespucci, Amerigo, 440

Vietnam, 185, 192, 230, 267, 303, 306, 437, 457

Vijayanagara empire, 297

Vikings, 157–58, 161, 430, 465

Visigoths, 132, 134, 135, 137, 138, 140, 148, 153, 239, 317, 349

Vladimir the Great (Kievan ruler), 291

Voigtländer, Nico, 499, 598n83

Voltaire, 474

Voth, Hans-Joachim, 499, 598n83

Vries, Peer, 344, 391, 406, 497, 538n13, 539n22, 567n26, 576n7, 579n63, 582n131, 596n42, 596n44, 596n58

Wallerstein, Immanuel, 420, 440

Wang Anshi (Chinese chancellor), 405

Wang Mang (Chinese regent), 405

war and development, 9; England (post-1500), 382–90; European, 357–59, 579nn61–63, 586n207; financial development and, 368–69, 411, 581n102; increase in state capacity allowing for interstate conflict, 391; Roman empire and, 70–74, 79–82; social responses to warfare, 14; war-making capacity, 6–7. See also military mobilization

Warde, Paul, 537n8

War of the Spanish Succession, 208, 209

Weber, Max, 23, 491, 596n58

Weingast, Barry, 380

Western Europe. See Europe

Western Zhou. See Zhou regime

West Francia, 157, 158, 164

Wickham, Chris, 241, 539n23, 578n59

William the Conqueror (English king), 239

William of Orange, 203, 208–9

Wittfogel, Karl, 264, 566n11

Wong, Bin, 358, 389, 396, 413–14, 493, 495, 496, 586n215, 597n60, 597n71, 598n85

World War II, 12, 41

Wrigley, E. Anthony, 598n79

writing. *See* language and writing

Xerxes I (Achaemenid king), 112, 432

Xianbei, 242, 244, 246–48, 255, 280, 284, 289

Xiongnu, 174, 242, 244, 246, 251, 255, 283–88, 570nn53–54

Yates, Robin D. D., 583n157

Yuan empire, 229, 281, 403, 507

Zhao, Dingxin, 393–94, 412, 583n144

Zheng Chenggong, 445

Zheng He (Chinese eunuch), 433, 439, 445, 468

Zhenzong emperor, 241

Zhou regime: demise of, 221, 222, 570n52; in heyday of empire, 281; language and writing in, 308; religious beliefs in, 319; steppe effect in, 282, 285, 286; unity as concept in, 323

Zoroastrians, 207, 317

Zwingli, Ulrich, 474

THE PRINCETON ECONOMIC HISTORY
OF THE WESTERN WORLD

Joel Mokyr, Series Editor

Going the Distance: Eurasian Trade and the Rise of the Business Corporation 1400–1700 by Ron Harris

Dark Matter Credit: The Development of Peer-to-Peer Lending and Banking in France by Philip T. Hoffman, Gilles Postel-Vinay, and Jean-Laurent Rosenthal

The European Guilds: An Economic Analysis by Sheilagh Ogilvie

Trade in the Ancient Mediterranean: Private Order and Public Institutions by Taco Terpstra

The Winding Road to the Welfare State: Economic Insecurity and Social Welfare Policy in Britain by George R. Boyer

The Mystery of the Kibbutz: Egalitarian Principles in a Capitalist World by Ran Abramitzky

Unequal Gains: American Growth and Inequality since 1700 by Peter H. Lindert and Jeffrey G. Williamson

Uneven Centuries: Economic Development of Turkey since 1820 by Şevket Pamuk

The Great Leveler: Violence and the History of Inequality from the Stone Age to the Twenty-First Century by Walter Scheidel

The Rise and Fall of American Growth: The U.S. Standard of Living since the Civil War by Robert J. Gordon

Brazil in Transition: Beliefs, Leadership, and Institutional Change by Lee J. Alston, Marcus André Melo, Bernardo Mueller, and Carlos Pereira

The Vanishing Irish: Households, Migrations, and the Rural Economy in Ireland, 1850–1914 by Timothy W. Guinnane

Fragile by Design: The Political Origins of Banking Crises and Scarce Credit by Charles W. Calomiris and Stephen H. Haber

The Son Also Rises: Surnames and the History of Social Mobility by Gregory Clark

Why Did Europe Conquer the World? by Philip T. Hoffman

Lending to the Borrower from Hell: Debt, Taxes, and Default in the Age of Philip II
by Mauricio Drelichman and Hans-Joachim Voth

Power to the People: Energy in Europe over the Last Five Centuries
by Astrid Kander, Paolo Malanima, and Paul Warde

*Cities of Commerce: The Institutional Foundations of International Trade in the
Low Countries, 1250–1650* by Oscar Gelderblom

Why Australia Prospered: The Shifting Sources of Economic Growth
by Ian W. McLean

The Chosen Few: How Education Shaped Jewish History, 70–1492
by Maristella Botticini and Zvi Eckstein

Creating Wine: The Emergence of a World Industry, 1840–1914 by James Simpson

Distant Tyranny: Markets, Power, and Backwardness in Spain, 1650–1800
by Regina Grafe

The Evolution of a Nation: How Geography and Law Shaped the American States
by Daniel Berkowitz and Karen B. Clay

The Roman Market Economy by Peter Temin

States of Credit: Size, Power, and the Development of European Polities
by David Stasavage

*Power over Peoples: Technology, Environments, and Western Imperialism, 1400 to
the Present* by Daniel R. Headrick

Unsettled Account: The Evolution of Banking in the Industrialized World since 1800
by Richard S. Grossman

A Farewell to Alms: A Brief Economic History of the World by Gregory Clark

Power and Plenty: Trade, War, and the World Economy in the Second Millennium
by Ronald Findlay and Kevin O'Rourke

War, Wine, and Taxes: The Political Economy of Anglo-French Trade, 1689–1900
by John V. C. Nye

Cultures Merging: A Historical and Economic Critique of Culture by Eric L. Jones

The European Economy since 1945: Coordinated Capitalism and Beyond
by Barry Eichengreen

Feeding the World: An Economic History of Agriculture, 1800–2000
by Giovanni Federico

Understanding the Process of Economic Change by Douglass C. North

The Strictures of Inheritance: The Dutch Economy in the Nineteenth Century
by Jan Luiten van Zanden and Arthur van Riel

Farm to Factory: A Reinterpretation of the Soviet Industrial Revolution by Robert C. Allen

Quarter Notes and Bank Notes: The Economics of Music Composition in the Eighteenth and Nineteenth Centuries by F. M. Scherer

The Big Problem of Small Change by Thomas J. Sargent and François R. Velde

The Great Divergence: China, Europe, and the Making of the Modern World Economy by Kenneth Pomeranz

Black '47 and Beyond: The Great Irish Famine in History, Economy, and Memory by Cormac Ó Gráda

Growth in a Traditional Society: The French Countryside, 1450–1815 by Philip T. Hoffman

Also by
WALTER SCHEIDEL

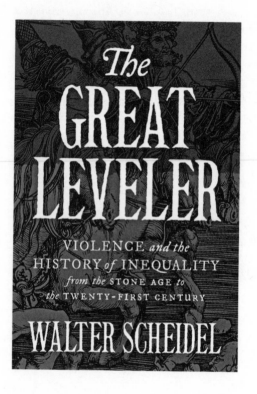

 PRINCETON UNIVERSITY PRESS

Available wherever books are sold.
For more information visit us at www.press.princeton.edu